The

# OXFORD
## Dictionary of
## Abbreviations

Oxford   New York

OXFORD UNIVERSITY PRESS

1993

Oxford University Press, Walton Street, Oxford OX2 6DP

Oxford New York Toronto
Delhi Bombay Calcutta Madras Karachi
Kuala Lumpur Singapore Hong Kong Tokyo
Nairobi Dar es Salaam Cape Town
Melbourne Auckland Madrid
and associated companies in
Berlin Ibadan

Oxford is a trade mark of Oxford University Press

First published 1992
First issued as an Oxford University Press paperback 1993

British Library Cataloguing in Publication Data
Data available

Library of Congress Cataloging in Publication Data
The Oxford dictionary of abbreviations / [compiled by Market House Books].
p. cm. 1. Abbreviations, English—Dictionaries. I. Market House Books Ltd.
423'.1—dc20 PE1693.O94 1993 93–9928
ISBN 0–19–280003–5 (pbk.)

1 3 5 7 9 10 8 6 4 2

Printed in Great Britain by
Biddles Ltd.
Guildford and King's Lynn

# THE OXFORD
# DICTIONARY OF
# ABBREVIATIONS

# Contents

# Editors

# Preface

During the last few decades abbreviations have proliferated to such an extent that they now form a major—and still increasing—part of the language. Most English dictionaries, however, do not fully reflect this important addition to our vocabulary, typically including only a selection of the better known abbreviations. The *Oxford Dictionary of Abbreviations* is designed to fill this gap, providing explanations for the bewildering variety of abbreviations in use today.

This dictionary caters for all levels of usage, from the colloquial, as in **yuppie** and **POETS day**, to the highly specialized abbreviations used in scientific and technical fields. The advances in all aspects of science and technology, notably computing, are reflected in the extensive coverage of abbreviations in these fields in the dictionary. Similar coverage is given to the body of abbreviations generated by the business and financial communities, the medical profession (especially in the fields of immunology and genetics), and the world of sport. Field labels or brief explanations are provided for these and other abbreviations when necessary. As well as abbreviations used in English-speaking countries, the dictionary also includes a selection of abbreviations of foreign terms and organizations, especially those likely to be encountered by businessmen and others with contacts abroad; translations or brief explanations are given for these entries. When the country of origin of an abbreviation is not evident from the definition, a geographical label precedes the definition.

The entries cover all types of shortened forms of words and phrases, including initialisms, such as **BBC** and **FBI**; acronyms (i.e. initialisms that are pronounced as words, rather than as a series of letters), such as **Aids** and **NATO**; shortenings; for example **Gen.** (for General, Geneva, etc.); and symbols for units of measurement, chemical elements, airlines, postal districts, vehicle registration offices, and so on. A selection of symbols that are not formed from letters of the Roman alphabet is given in an Appendix to the dictionary. A pronunciation guide (in brackets preceding the definition), using the International Phonetic Alphabet, is provided for acronyms; an explanation of this guide is given overleaf.

Often there are several possible forms for an abbreviation, with variations in upper and lower case and in the use of points. In deciding the forms of the entry words in this dictionary, the editors have used a number of conventions. Points have been omitted for acronyms (e.g. **Aids**), for all-capital abbreviations (e.g. **NUJ**), for degrees and other qualifications consisting of upper and lower-case letters (e.g. **BSc, FIBiol**), and in other cases when this can be done without flouting convention or causing confusion with a real word (e.g. **plc** rather than p.l.c.). Shortenings are usually followed by a point unless the last letter of the shortened form is the last letter of the word (e.g. **gdn** = garden, guardian). When two or more forms are equally common, variants are included in brackets before the definition.

EAM

*1992*

## Note for the Paperback Edition

In preparing this edition the editors have introduced a number of new abbreviations that have become current since the hardback edition was completed. They have also corrected several errors that appeared in the hardback edition. Many of these were brought to their attention by Mr Adrian Room, to whom they are grateful.

EAM

*1993*

# Pronunciation Guide

The symbols used in indicating pronunciations of acronyms and certain other abbreviations are those of the International Phonetic Alphabet. The following consonants have their usual English sounds: b, d, f, h, k, l, m, n, p, r, s, t, v, w, z. Additional symbols are follows:

| | |
|---|---|
| ɑ: *as in* bar (bɑ:) | j *as in* yet (jɛt) |
| æ *as in* cat (kæt) | dʒ *as in* job (dʒɒb) |
| aɪ *as in* buy (baɪ) | ŋ *as in* bring (brɪŋ) |
| aʊ *as in* gout (gaʊt) | ɒ *as in* got (gɒt) |
| tʃ *as in* cheese (tʃi:z) | əʊ *as in* go (gəʊ) |
| ɛ *as in* get (gɛt) | ɔ: *as in* law (lɔ:) |
| ə *as in* paper ('peɪpə) | ɔɪ *as in* coin (kɔɪn) |
| ᵊ *as in* able (eɪbᵊl) | ʃ *as in* shin (ʃɪn) |
| ɜ: *as in* turn (tɜ:n) | ʒ *as in* measure ('mɛʒə) |
| eɪ *as in* pay (peɪ) | θ *as in* thaw (θɔ:) |
| ɛə *as in* fair (fɛə) | ð *as in* then (ðɛn) |
| ɪ *as in* pin (pɪn) | ʊ *as in* wool (wʊl) |
| i: *as in* be (bi:) | u: *as in* new (nju:) |
| ɪə *as in* hear (hɪə) | ʌ *as in* cup (kʌp) |

For acronyms of two or more syllables the stressed syllables are preceded by the marks ˈor ˌ in the pronunciation. The most strongly stressed syllable is preceded by ˈ, as in ˈpeɪpə (paper); weakly stressed syllables are preceded by ˌ, as in ˈkɒmɪˌkɒm (Comecon). Unstressed syllables are not preceded by stress marks, as in ˈmɛmərɪ (memory).

# A

**a** (ital.) *Physics, symbol for* acceleration • *symbol for* are(s) (metric measure of land) • *symbol for* atto- (prefix indicating $10^{-18}$, as in **am**, attometre) • *symbol for* year (Latin *annus* or French *année*) • *indicating* the first vertical row of squares from the left on a chessboard

**a.** about • accepté (French: accepted; written on a bill of exchange) • accepted • acre(s) • acreage • acting • actual • address • adjective • advance(d) • afternoon • age • akzeptiert (German: accepted; written on a bill of exchange) • *Music* alto • amateur • anno (Latin: in the year) • anonymous • answer • ante (Latin: before) • aqua (Latin: water) • arrive • arriving • *Baseball* assist(s)

**a 2** *Music* a due (Italian: for two (voices or instruments))

**A** *British fishing port registration for* Aberdeen • *Physics, symbol for* absolute (temperature) • (ital.) *Physics, symbol for* absorbance • *Cards, symbol for* ace • *Chem., symbol for* acid-catalysed reaction • (ital.) *Chem., symbol for* activity • *Biochem., symbol for* adenine • *Biochem., symbol for* adenosine • *Films* adult (former certification) • *Education* Advanced (in **A** level) • (ital.) *Chem., symbol for* affinity • *symbol for* ammeter (in circuit diagrams) • *Physics, symbol for* ampere(s) • *Physics, symbol for* ampere-turn • *Botany, symbol for* androecium (in a floral formula) • anode • (ital.) *Maths., symbol for* area • *symbol for* an arterial road (as in **A1**, **A40**, etc.) • assault (in **A-day**) • atom(ic) (as in **A-bomb**) • austral (former monetary unit of Argentina) • *international vehicle registration for* Austria • avancer (French: go faster; on a clock or watch regulator) • (ital.) *Chem., symbol for* Helmholtz function • (bold ital.) *Physics, symbol for* magnetic vector potential • *Physics, symbol for* mass number • (ital.) *Physics, symbol for* nucleon number • (ital.) *Electronics, symbol for* Richardson constant • *symbol for* ten (in hexadecimal notation) • *Med., indicating* a blood group or its associated antigen (*see also under* ABO) • *Education, indicating* the highest mark or grade for work • *indicating* managerial, professional (occupational grade) • *indicating* a musical note or key • *Astronomy, indicating* a spectral type • *indicating* a standard paper size (*see under* A0–A10) • *Logic, indicating* a universal affirmative categorical proposition

**Å** *Physics, symbol for* angstrom unit

**A.** (*or* **A**) academician • academy • acreage • acre(s) • adjutant • admiral • air • Altesse (French: Highness) • *Music* alto • America(n) • *Bible* Amos • *Horticulture* annual • answer • anterior • April • armoured • article • artillery • art(s) • assistant • associate • athletic • August • Australia(n)

**A0** *indicating* a standard paper size, 841 × 1189 mm

**A1** *indicating* a standard paper size, 594 × 841 mm • *indicating* (in Lloyd's Register) ships maintained in good and efficient condition

**A2** *international civil aircraft marking for* Botswana • *indicating* a standard paper size, 420 × 594 mm

**A3** *international civil aircraft marking for* Tonga • *indicating* a standard paper size, 297 × 420 mm

**A4** *indicating* a standard paper size, 210 × 297 mm

**A5** *international civil aircraft marking for* Bhutan • *indicating* a standard paper size, 148 × 210 mm

**A6** *international civil aircraft marking for* United Arab Emirates • *indicating* a standard paper size, 105 × 148 mm

**A7** *international civil aircraft marking for* Qatar • *indicating* a standard paper size, 74 × 105 mm

**A8** *indicating* a standard paper size, 52 × 74 mm

**A9** *indicating* a standard paper size, 37 × 52 mm

**A9C** *international civil aircraft marking for* Bahrain

**A10** *indicating* a standard paper size, 26 × 37 mm

**A40** *international civil aircraft marking for* Oman

**āa** (*or* **ãã**) *Med.* ana (Greek: of each; specifying quantities of ingredients in prescriptions)

**a.a.** absolute alcohol • acting appointment • after arrival • *Shipping* always afloat • approximate absolute • area administrator • arithmetic average • attendance allowance • author's alteration • *Photog., indicating* that one print should be made of each negative

**AA** administrative assistant • advertising agency • Advertising Association • age allowance (for taxation) • Air Attaché • Alcoholics Anonymous • *British fishing port registration for* Alloa • *Chem.* allyl alcohol • *airline flight code for* American Airlines • American Aviation (aircraft) • *Biochem.* amino acid • *Chem.* andesine anorthosite • Anglers' Association • anti-aircraft • *Physics* antiproton accumulator • *Biochem.* arachidonic acid • Architectural Association • *Chem.* aristolochic acid • Army Act • *Biochem.* ascorbic acid • Associate in Accounting • Associate in Agriculture • Associate in (*or* of) Arts • Association of Agriculture • Astronautica Acta (journal of the International Astronautical Federation) • *Physics* atomic absorption • *Physics* atomic adsorption • Augustinians of the Assumption • author's alteration • Automobile Association • *Chem.* azelaic acid • *British vehicle registration for* Bournemouth • *indicating* a certificate issued for a ship stating that all crew matters are in order • (formerly) *indicating* a film not be shown to a child under 14 unless accompanied by an adult • *Electricity, indicating* a size of battery or cell • *Angling, indicating* a size of fine split weights

**AA1** (*or* **AA-one**) *Finance, indicating* a very high quality rating for credit

**AAA** *Med.* abdominal aortic aneurysm • (USA) Agricultural Adjustment Act • (USA) Agricultural Adjustment Administration • Allied Artists of America • Amateur Athletic Association • American Accounting Association • American Automobile Association • *Biochem.* amino acid analogue(s) • (*or* **triple A**) anti-aircraft artillery • (USA) Army Audit Agency • Association of Average Adjusters • Australian Association of Accountants • Australian Automobile Association • Automobile Association of America • *Finance, indicating* the highest quality rating for credit

**AAAA** Amateur Athletic Association of America • American Association of Advertising Agencies • Associated Actors and Artistes of America (trade union) • Australian Association of Advertising Agencies

**AAAC** all-aluminium alloy conductor

**AAAI** American Association for Artificial Intelligence • Associate of the Institute of Administrative Accountants

**AAAL** American Academy of Arts and Letters

**AAAM** American Association of Aircraft Manufacturers

**AA&QMG** Assistant Adjutant and Quartermaster-General

**AAAS** American Academy of Arts and Sciences • American Academy of Asian Studies • American Association for the Advancement of Science • Associate of the American Antiquarian Society

**AAB** Aircraft Accident Board • Association of Applied Biologists

**AABC** American Amateur Baseball Congress

**AABL** Associated Australian Banks in London

**AABM** Australian Association of British Manufacturers

**AABW** Antarctic Bottom Water

**AAC** *US Air Force* Alaskan Air Command • Aeronautical Advisory Council • Agricultural Advisory Council • Amateur Athletic Club • anno ante Christum (Latin: in the year before Christ) • Army Air Corps • *Electronics* automatic amplitude control

**AACB** (USA) Aeronautics and Astronautics Coordinating Board • Association of African Central Banks

**AACC** American Association of Clinical Chemists • *Aeronautics* area-approach control centre

**AACE** American Association of Cost Engineers • Association for Adult and Continuing Education

**AACP** American Association for Child Psychiatry • Anglo-American Council on Productivity

**AACR** *Bibliog.* Anglo-American Cataloguing Rules

**AACS** Aberdeen-Angus Cattle Society • (USA) Airways and Air Communications Service • *Computing* automated-access control system

**AAD** *Med.* atlantoaxial dislocation

**AADC** air aide-de-camp • (USA) Army–Air Defense Command

**AADS** (USA) Army–Air Defense System

**AAE** American Association of Engineers

**AAEC** Australian Atomic Energy Commission

**AAeE** Associate in Aeronautical Engineering

**AAEE** (*or* **A & AEE**) Aircraft and Armament Experimental Establishment • American Association of Electrical Engineers

**AAES** Association of Agricultural Education Staffs • Australian Army Education Service

**AAEW** Atlantic airborne early warning

**AAF** Allied Air Forces • (USA) Army Air Forces

**AAFC** anti-aircraft fire control

**AAFCE** Allied Air Forces in Central Europe

**AAFIS** Army and Air Force Intelligence Staff

**AAFNE** Allied Air Forces in Northern Europe

**AAFSE** Allied Air Forces in Southern Europe

**AAgr** Associate in Agriculture

**AAG** Air Adjutant-General • Assistant Adjutant-General • Association of American Geographers

**AAGS** Association of African Geological Surveys

**AAHPER** American Association for Health, Physical Education, and Recreation

**AAIA** Associate of the Association of International Accountants • Associate of the Australian Institute of Advertising • Association of American Indian Affairs

**AAIB** Associate of the Australian Institute of Bankers

**AAII** Associate of the Australian Insurance Institute

**AAIL** American Academy and Institute of Arts and Letters

**AAL** *Meteorol.* above aerodrome level • Academy of Art and Literature • (USA) Arctic Aeromedical Laboratory • Association of Assistant Librarians

**AALA** American Association for Laboratory Accreditation

**AALD** Australian Army Legal Department

**AALL** American Association of Law Libraries

**AAM** air-to-air missile • American Association of Microbiology • American Association of Museums • Anti-Apartheid Movement • Association of Assistant Mistresses in Secondary Schools • Australian Air Mission

**AAMI** *Med.* age-associated memory impairment

**AAMW** (USA) Association of Advertising Men and Women

**AAMWS** Australian Army Medical Women's Service

**AANA** Australian Association of National Advertisers

**A & A** additions and amendments

**A&AEE** Aeroplane and Armament Experimental Establishment

**A & C** addenda and corrigenda • (ital.) Antony and Cleopatra (Shakespeare)

**A&E** Accident and Emergency (department of a hospital)

**a&h** *Insurance* accident and health

**a&i** *Insurance* accident and indemnity

**A & I** (USA) Agricultural and Industrial (college)

**A & M** (USA) Agricultural and Mechanical (college) • Ancient and Modern (hymn book)

**A & N** Army and Navy (Club *or* Stores)

**A & NI** Andaman and Nicobar Islands

**A & P** advertising and promotion • (New Zealand) Agricultural and Pastoral (Association, Show, etc.)

**A & R** artists and recording • artists and repertoire *or* repertory (as in **A & R man**)

**a&s** *Insurance* accident and sickness

**A & SH** Argyll and Sutherland Highlanders

**AANS** Australian Army Nursing Service

**AAO** American Association of Orthodontists

**AAOC** Australian Army Ordnance Corps

**AAOM** American Academy of Occupational Medicine

**AAOO** American Academy of Ophthalmology and Otolaryngology

**AAP** *Chem.* alumina–aluminum phosphate • Association of American Publishers • Australian Associated Press • *Astronautics* (USA) Apollo Applications Program

**AAPA** Advertising Agency Production Association • American Association of Port Authorities

**AAPB** American Association of Pathologists and Bacteriologists

**AAPC** All African People's Conference

**AAPE** American Academy of Physical Education

**AAPG** American Association of Petroleum Geologists

**AAPHI** Associate of the Association of Public Health Inspectors

**AAPM** American Association of Physicists in Medicine

**AAPS** American Association for the Promotion of Science

**AAPSO** Afro-Asian People's Solidarity Organization

**AAPSS** American Academy of Political and Social Science

**AAPSW** Associate of the Association of Psychiatric Social Workers

**AAPT** American Association of Physics Teachers • Associate of the Association of Photographic Technicians

**a.a.r.** after action report • *Insurance* against all risks • aircraft accident record (*or* report) • average annual rainfall

**AAR** Association of American Railroads

**AARP** American Association of Retired Persons

**AAS** *RC Church* Acta Apostolicae Sedis (Latin: Acts of the Apostolic See; publication) • American Academy of Sciences • American Antiquarian Society • American Astronautical Society • American Astronomical Society • Andersen air sampler • Army Air Service • Associate in Applied Science • Association of Asian Studies • atomic absorption spectrometry (*or* spectroscope *or* spectrophotometry) • Australian Academy of Science • Auxiliary Ambulance Service • Fellow of the American Academy of Arts and Sciences (Latin *Academiae Americanae Socius*)

**AASA** Associate of the Australian Society of Accountants

**AASB** *Aeronautics* aerodynamically airstaged burner • American Association of Small Businesses

**AASC** Allied Air Support Command • Australian Army Service Corps

**AASF** Advanced Air Striking Force

**AASG** Association of American State Geologists

**A'asia** Australasia

**AASM** Associated African States and Madagascar (treaty)

**AASR** Airport and Airways Surveillance Radar (Raytheon)

**AASS** Associate of the American Antiquarian Society (Latin *Americanae Antiquarianae Societatis Socius*)

**AAT** *Psychol.* achievement anxiety test • *Med.* alpha-1-antitrypsin (treatment for cystic fibrosis) • Anglo-Australian Telescope (Siding Spring, NSW) • *Med.* asymptomatic autoimmune thyroiditis

**AATA** (eɪˈɑːtə) Anglo-American Tourist Association

**AATNU** Administration de l'assistance technique des Nations Unies (French: United Nations Technical Assistance Administration)

**AATT** American Association of Textile Technology

**AATTA** Arab Association of Tourism and Travel Agents

**AATUF** All-African Trade Union Federation (replaced by OATUU)

**AAU** (USA) Amateur Athletic Union • Association of American Universities

**AAUN** American Association for United Nations • Australian Association for United Nations

**AAUP** American Association of University Presses • American Association of University Professors (trade union)

**AAUW** American Association of University Women

**AAV** *Microbiol.* adeno-associated virus • assault amphibious vehicle

**AAVC** Australian Army Veterinary Corps

**AAVS** American Anti-Vivisection Society

**AAWC** Australian Advisory War Council

**AAZPA** American Association of Zoological Parks and Aquariums

**ab.** about • abridgment

**a.b.** anchor bolt • *Baseball* (times) at bat

**a/b** airborne

**a.B.** *Commerce* auf Bestellung (German: on order)

**Ab** (formerly) *Chem.*, symbol for astatine (originally called alabamine; *see under* At)

**AB** postcode for Aberdeen • *British fishing port registration for* Aberystwyth • able-bodied seaman • advisory board • air board • airborne • *US Air Force* Airman Basic • Alberta (Canada) • Alliance balkanique (French: Balkan Alliance) • ammonia for bees (applied for stings) • antiballistic (missile) • asthmatic bronchitis • *Baseball* (times) at bat • *Physics* atomic bremsstrahlung • automated bibliography • (USA) Bachelor of Arts (Latin *Artium Baccalaureus*) • *British vehicle registration for* Worcester • *indicating* a human blood group containing A and B antigens (*see also under* ABO)

**A/B** (Sweden) Aktiebolaget (joint-stock company)

**ABA** *Botany* abscisic acid • Amateur Boxing Association • American Badminton Association • American Bankers' Association • American Bar Association • American Basketball Association (now merged with the National Basketball Association) • American Book Award • American Booksellers Association • Antiquarian Booksellers' Association • Associate in Business Administration • Association of British Archaeologists • Australian Bankers' Association

**ABAA** Antiquarian Booksellers' Association of America

**ABAC** Association of British Aero Clubs and Centres

**abb.** abbey • *Commerce* abbuono (Italian: allowance *or* discount)

**Abb.** Abbey • Abbot (*or* Abbess)

**ABBA** ('æbə) American Board of Bio-Analysis

**abbrev.** (*or* **abbr.**) abbreviation

**ABC** Advance Booking Charter (airline ticket) • advanced biomedical capsule • air bridge to Canada • *Med.* airway, breathing, circulation (in first aid) • America–Britain–Canada • American book-prices current • American Broadcasting Company • analysis of benefits and costs • animal birth control • Argentina–Brazil–Chile • Aruba, Bonaire, Curaçao (in **ABC Islands**) • Associated British Cinemas • Atanasoff–Berry computer • atomic, biological, and chemical (weapons or warfare) • Audit Bureau of Circulation • Australian Broadcasting Commission • automatic binary computer • automatic brake control

**ABCA** American Business Communication Association • Army Bureau of Current Affairs

**ABCB** Association of Birmingham Clearing Banks

**ABCC** Association of British Chambers of Commerce • Association of British Correspondence Colleges

**ABCD** American, British, Chinese, Dutch (powers in the Pacific in World War II) • atomic, biological, and chemical protection and damage control

**ABCFM** American Board of Commissioners for Foreign Missions

**ABCM** Associate of Bandsmen's College of Music

**abd.** abdicate(d) • abdomen • abdominal

**ABD** *US Navy* advanced base depot • all but dissertation (of a candidate reading for a higher degree) • (*or* abd) average body dose (of radiation)

**ABDA** ('æbdə) American, British, Dutch, Australian (Command in the Pacific; World War II)

**abdom.** abdomen • abdominal

**ABDP** Association of British Directory Publishers

**ABE** *Chem.* acetone–butanol–ethanol (solvent)

**ABEd** (USA) Bachelor of Arts in Education

**Aber.** Aberdeen • Aberdonian

**ABERCOR** ('æbə,kɔ:) Associated Banks of Europe Corporation

**abf** *Colloquial* absolute bloody final (drink)

**Abf.** Abfahrt (German: departure)

**ABF** Actors' Benevolent Fund • Associated British Foods

**ABFD** Association of British Factors and Discounters

**ABFM** American Board of Foreign Missions

**ABGB** Allgemeines Bürgerliches Gesetzbuch (German; the Austrian Civil Code)

**abgk.** abgekürzt (German: abbreviated)

**ABGWIU** (USA) Aluminum Brick and Glass Workers International Union

**Abh.** Abhandlungen (German: transactions *or* treatises)

**ABI** Associate of the Institute of Bookkeepers • Association of British Insurers

**ABIA** Association of British Introduction Agencies

**ab init.** ab initio (Latin: from the beginning)

**ABINZ** Associate of the Bankers' Institute of New Zealand

**abl.** ablative

**ab$^l$** abril (Spanish: April)

**ABL** atmospheric boundary layer

**ABLA** ('æblə) American Business Law Association

**ABLJ** adjustable buoyancy lifejacket

**ABLS** Association of British Library Schools • (USA) Bachelor of Arts in Library Science

**ABM** antiballistic missile • Associate in Business Management • Australian Board of Missions • automatic batch mix

**ABMA** Army Ballistic Missile Agency

**ABMAC** ('æbmæk) Association of British Manufacturers of Agricultural Chemicals

**ABMEWS** ('æbmjuːz) antiballistic missile early warning system

**ABMPM** Association of British Manufacturers of Printers' Machinery

**ABMT** *Med.* allogeneic bone-marrow transplantation

**abn** airborne

**Abn** Aberdeen

**ABN** *Chem.* acid–base–neutral • Anti-Bolshevik Bloc of Nations

**ABNE** Association for the Benefit of Noncontract Employees

**ABO** American Board of Ophthalmology • American Board of Orthodontics • American Board of Otolaryngology • *Med., indicating* a blood group system based on the presence or absence of antigens A and B (*see also under* A; AB; B; O)

**ABOF** Association of British Organic Fertilizers

**ABOG** American Board of Obstetrics and Gynecology

**A-bomb** atom bomb

**ABOS** American Board of Oral Surgery • American Board of Orthopedic Surgery

**Abp** Archbishop

**ABP** American Board of Pathology • American Board of Pediatrics • American Board of Peridontology • American Board of Prosthodontics • *Biochem.* androgen-binding protein • *Med.* arterial blood pressure • Associated Book Publishers • Associated British Ports

**ABPA** Australian Book Publishers' Association

**ABPC** American Book Publishers' Council • Associated British Picture Corporation

**ABPI** Association of the British Pharmaceutical Industry

**ABPN** American Board of Psychiatry and Neurology • Association of British Paediatric Nurses

**ABPO** Advanced Base Personnel Officer

**ABPS** American Board of Plastic Surgery

**ABPVM** Association of British Plywood and Veneer Manufacturers

**abr.** abridge(d) • abridgment

**ABR** American Board of Radiology • *Med.* auditory brainstem recording

**ABRACADABRA** (ˌæbrəkə'dæbrə) Abbreviations and Related Acronyms Associated with Defense, Astronautics, Business, and Radio-electronics (publication of Raytheon Company, Lexington, USA)

**ABRC** Advisory Board for the Research Councils

**ABRES** advanced ballistic re-entry system

**ABRO** ('æbrəʊ) Animal Breeding Research Organization • Army in Burma Reserve of Officers

**ABRS** Association of British Riding Schools

**ABRSM** Associated Board of the Royal Schools of Music

**ABRV** advanced ballistic re-entry vehicle

**abs.** absence (*or* absent) • absolute • absorbent • abstract

**a.b.s.** aux bons soins (de) (French: care of, c/o; on postal addresses)

**ABS** *Chem.* acrylonitrile–butadiene–styrene (type of plastic) • *Chem.* alkyl benzene sulphonate (usually of sodium) • American Bible Society • American Board of Surgery • American Bureau of Shipping • Antiblockier-system (in **ABS brake**; German: antilocking system) • Architects' Benevolent Society • Australian Bureau of Statistics

**ABSA** Association of Business Sponsorship of the Arts

**abse. re.** *Law* absente reo (Latin: the defendant being absent)

**abs. feb.** *Med.* absente febre (Latin: when there is no fever)

**ABSIE** ('æbsɪ) American Broadcasting Station in Europe (in World War II)

**ABSM** Associate of the Birmingham School of Music

**ABSM(TTD)** Associate of the Birmingham School of Music (Teacher's Training Diploma)

**absol.** absolute

**abs. re.** *Law* absente reo (*see* abse. re.)

**abstr.** abstract(ed)

**abs. visc.** absolute viscosity

**ABSW** Association of British Science Writers

**abt** about

**Abt.** Abteilung (German: division *or* part)

**ABT** Association of Building Technicians

**ABTA** ('æbtə) Allied Brewery Traders' Association • Association of British Travel Agents • Australian British Trade Association

**ABTAC** ('æbtæk) Australian Book Trade Advisory Committee

**ABTUC** All-Burma Trade Union Congress

**ABU** Asian Broadcasting Union • Assembly of the Baptist Union

**A-BU** Anglo-Belgian Union

**abv.** above

**ABWR** *Nuclear physics* advanced boiling water reactor

**ac.** acre • activity

**a.c.** a capo (Italian: new line) • (*or* **à.c.**) à compte (French: on account) • advisory committee • *Physics* alternating current • année courante (French: this year) • anno corrente (Latin: this year) • *Med.* ante cibum (Latin: before meals; in prescriptions) • assegno circolare (Italian: banker's draft *or* cashier's check) • author's correction

**a/c** account • account current • ao cuidado de (Portuguese: care of, c/o; on postal addresses)

**aC** antes de Cristo (Portuguese: before Christ; BC) • avanti Cristo (Italian: before Christ; BC)

**Ac** *Chem., symbol for* acetyl (ethanoyl) group • *Chem., symbol for* actinium • (ital.) *Meteorol.* altocumulus

**AC** *airline flight code for* Air Canada • *Chem.* activated carbon • *Chem.* activated charcoal • *Chem.* active centre • *Med.* acute cholecystitis • *Chem.* acyl-oxygen cleavage • *Biochem.* adenylate cyclase • Aero Club • Air Command • Air Commodore • air conditioning • air control • Air Corps • Air Council • aircraftman • Alcohol Concern (a charity) • Alpine Club • *Physics* alternating current • *Meteorol.* altocumulus • Ambulance Corps • analogue computer • analytical chemist • angular correlation • annual conference • ante Christum (Latin: before Christ) • *Law* Appeal Case(s) • Appeal Court • appellation contrôlée (*see under* AOC) • Army Corps • Army Council • artillery college • Arts Council • Assistant Commissioner • Athletic Club • Atlantic Charter • Auditor Camerae (Latin: Auditor of the Papal Treasury) • Azione Cattolica (Italian: Catholic Action; social organization) • Companion of the Order of Australia • *British vehicle registration for* Coventry

**A/C** account • account current • air conditioning • aircraft • aircraftman

**ACA** *Telecom.* adjacent-channel attenuation • advanced combat aircraft • Agricultural Cooperative Association • American Camping Association • American Canoe Association • *Chem.* ammoniacal copper arsenate • Anglers' Cooperative Association • Arts Council of America • Associate of the Institute of Chartered Accountants • Association of Consulting Actuaries • Australian Consumers' Association • Australian Council for Aeronautics

**7-ACA** *Chem.* 7-aminocephalosporanic acid

**ACAA** Agricultural Conservation and Adjustment Administration • American Coal Ash Association • Associate of the Australasian Institute of Cost Accountants

**ACAB** ('eɪkæb) (USA) Army Contract Adjustment Board

**acac** ('æk,æk) *Chem.* acetylacetonate ion (used in formulae)

**acad.** academic(al) • (*or* **Acad.**) academy

**Acad. fran.** Académie française (French literary academy)

**ACADI** (France) Association des cadres dirigeants de l'industrie (Association of Industrial Executives)

**Acad. med.** Academy of medicine

**Acad. mus.** Academy of music

**Acad. sci.** Academy of science

**ACAE** Advisory Council for Adult and Continuing Education

**ACAL** Advanced Computer Architecture Laboratory

**AC & U** (USA) Association of Colleges and Universities

**ACAO** Assistant County Advisory Officer

**Acap.** Acapulco

**ACAR** *Physics* angular correlation of annihilation radiation

**ACAS** (*or* **Acas**; 'eɪkæs) Advisory Conciliation and Arbitration Service • Assistant Chief of Air Staff

**ACB** Association Canadienne des Bibliothèques (French: Canadian Library Association) • Australian Cricket Board

**ACBG** *Med.* aorto-coronary bypass graft

**ACBI** Associate of the Institute of Book-keepers

**ACBS** Accrediting Commission for Business Schools

**ACBSI** Associate of the Chartered Building Societies Institute

**ACBWS** automatic chemical–biological warning system

**acc.** accelerate • acceleration • accent • *Commerce* acceptance • *Commerce* accepted • *Music* accompanied (by) • *Music* accompaniment • according (to) • *Book-keeping* account • accountant • *Grammar* accusative

**ACC** (New Zealand) Accident Compensation Corporation • *Computing* accumulator • *Chem.* acid copper chromate • *Med.* acute cardiovascular collapse • Administrative Coordination Committee • advanced communications course • Agricultural Credit Corporation Ltd • Anglican Consultative Council • annual capital charge • *Med.* antibody-dependent complement-mediated cytotoxicity • army cadet college • Army Catering Corps • *Scouting* Assistant County Commissioner • Associated Chemical Companies • Association of County Councils

**ACCA** Aeronautical Chamber of Commerce of America • Agricultural Central Cooperative Association • Associate of the Chartered Association of Certified Accountants • Association of Certified and Corporate Accountants

**ACCC** Association of Canadian Community Colleges

**ACCD** American Coalition of Citizens with Disabilities

**acce.** *Commerce* acceptance

**accel.** *Music* accelerando (Italian; with increasing speed)

**access.** accessory

**ACCHAN** Allied Command Channel (in NATO)

**ACCM** Advisory Council for the Church's Ministry

**ACCO** Association of Child Care Officers

**accom.** accommodation

**accomp.** accompanied • accompaniment • accompany

**ACCP** American College of Chest Physicians

**accred.** accredited

**ACCS** Associate of the Corporation of Secretaries (formerly Corporation of Certified Secretaries)

**acct.** accountant • account(ing)

**ACCT** Association of Cinematograph, Television, and Allied Technicians

**accum.** accumulative

**accus.** *Grammar* accusative

**accy** accountancy

**acd.** accord

**ACD** *Med.* acid citrate dextrose (as in **ACD solution**) • *Med.* acquired cystic disease of the kidney • *Chem.* anode–cathode distance

**ACDA** Advisory Committee on Distinction Awards • (USA) Arms Control and Disarmament Agency • Aviation Combat Development Agency

**ACDAS** Automatic Control and Data Acquisition System

**AC/DC** (*or* **AC-DC**) *Physics* alternating current/direct current • *Colloquial, indicating* bisexual

**ACDCM** Archbishop of Canterbury's Diploma in Church Music

**ACdre** Air Commodore

**ACDS** Assistant Chief of Defence Staff

**acdt** accident

**ACE** *Engineering* advanced cooled engine • (eɪs) Advisory Centre for Education • *Med.* alcohol–chloroform–ether (anaesthetic) • (eɪs) Allied Command Europe • American Council on Education • (eɪs) *Biochem., Med.* angiotensin-converting enzyme (as in **ACE inhibitor**) • Association for the Conservation of Energy • (Member of the) Association of Conference Executives • Association of Consulting Engineers • Association of Cultural Exchange • Australian College of Education • (eɪs) *Computing* Automatic Computing Engine

**ACEA** Action Committee for European Aerospace

**ACEd.** Associate in Commercial Education

**ACEEE** American Council for an Energy-Efficient Economy

**ACEF** Australian Council of Employers' Federations

**ACER** Australian Council for Educational Research

**ACERT** Advisory Council for Education of Romanies and other Travellers

**ACES** *Chem.* N-(2-acetamido)-2-aminoethanesulphonic acid

**acet.** acetone

**ACET** Advisory Committee on Electronics and Telecommunications • *Med.* Aids care, education, and treatment

**ACEWEX** Allied Command Europe Weather Exchange

**ACF** (Canada) Académie Canadienne Française (French Canadian Academy) • (South Africa) Active Citizen Force • *Physics* angular correlation function • Army Cadet Force • *Chemical engineering* autogenous-carrier flotation process • Automobile Club de France

**ACFA** Army Cadet Force Association

**ACFAS** (Canada) Association Canadienne-Française pour l'avancement des sciences (French-Canadian Association for the Advancement of Science)

**ACFHE** Association of Colleges of Further and Higher Education

**ACFI** Associate of the Clothing and Footwear Institute

**ACFM** *Physics* alternating-current field measurement

**acft** aircraft

**ACG** An Comunn Gaidhealach (Gaelic: The Gaelic Society; the Highland Association) • Assistant Chaplain-General • automatic control gear

**ACGB** Arts Council of Great Britain

**ACGBI** Automobile Club of Great Britain and Ireland

**ACGI** Associate of the City and Guilds Institute

**ACGS** Assistant Chief of the General Staff

**ACh** *Biochem.* acetylcholine

**ACH** *Building trades* air changes per hour • *Banking* automated clearing house

**AChE** *Biochem.* acetylcholinesterase

**ACHR** American Society of Human Rights

**AChS** Associate of the Society of Chiropodists

**ACI** Alliance coopérative internationale (French: International Cooperative Alliance) • Alloy Castings Institute • American Concrete Institute • army council instruction • Associate of the Institute of Commerce • Automobile Club d'Italia

**ACIA** Associate of the Corporation of Insurance Agents • *Computing* asynchronous communications interface adapter

**ACIAA** Australian Commercial and Industrial Artists' Association

**ACIArb** Associate of the Chartered Institute of Arbitrators

**ACIB** Associate of the Chartered Institute of Bankers • Associate of the Corporation of Insurance Brokers

**ACIC** (USA) Aeronautical Charting and Information Center

**acid.** *Med.* acidulated drop

**ACIGS** Assistant Chief of the Imperial General Staff

**ACII** Associate of the Chartered Insurance Institute

**ACINF** (USA) Advisory Committee on Irradiated and Novel Foods

**ACIOPJF** Association catholique internationale des œuvres de protection de la jeune fille (French; International Catholic Girls' Society)

**ACIS** American Committee for Irish Studies • Associate of the Institute of Chartered Secretaries and Administrators (formerly Chartered Institute of Secretaries)

**ACIT** Associate of the Chartered Institute of Transport

**ACJP** airways corporations joint pensions

**ack.** acknowledge • acknowledgment

**ACK** (*or* **ack**) *Computing, Telecom.* acknowledgment

**ack-ack** ('æk,æk) anti-aircraft (World War I phonetic alphabet for AA)

**ackgt** (*or* **ackt**) acknowledgment

**ACL** *Computing* access control list • action-centred leadership (devised by the Industrial Society) • Analytical Chemistry Laboratory • Atlas Computer Laboratory

**ACLA** Anti-Communist League of America

**ACLANT** (æk'lænt) Allied Command Atlantic

**ACLC** Air Cadet League of Canada

**ACLP** Association of Contact Lens Practitioners

**ACLS** American Council of Learned Societies • automatic carrier landing system

**ACLU** American Civil Liberties Union • American College of Life Underwriters

**ACM** Air Chief Marshal • air combat manoeuvring • American Campaign Medal • asbestos-containing material • (USA) Assistant Chief of Mission • Association for Computing Machinery • authorized controlled material

**ACMA** Agricultural Cooperative Managers' Association • Associate of the Institute of Cost and Management Accountants

**ACMC** Association of Canadian Medical Colleges

**ACME** advanced computer for medical research • (USA) Advisory Council on Medical Education • (USA) Association of Consulting Management Engineers

**ACMET** Advisory Council on Middle East Trade

**ACMF** (USA) Air Corps Medical Forces • Allied Central Mediterranean Forces • Australian Commonwealth Military Forces

**ACMM** Associate of the Conservatorium of Music, Melbourne

**acmp.** accompany

**ACMP** Advisory Committee on Marine Pollution • Assistant Commissioner of the Metropolitan Police

**ACMRR** Advisory Committee on Marine Resources Research (in the FAO)

**ACMT** American College of Medical Technologists

**a.c.n.** all concerned notified

**ACN** *Chem.* alkane carbon number • American College of Neuropsychiatrists • (small caps.) ante Christum natum (Latin: before the birth of Christ)

**ACNA** (USA) Advisory Council on Naval Affairs • Arctic Institute of North America

**ACNS** Assistant Chief of Naval Staff • Associated Correspondents News Service

**ACNY** Advertising Club of New York

**ACO** Admiralty Compass Observatory • Association of Children's Officers

**AC of S** Assistant Chief of Staff

**ac.o.g.** aircraft on ground

**ACom** (*or* **AComm**) Associate in Commerce

**Acops** ('ækɒps) Advisory Commission on Pollution of the Sea

**ACOR** American Center for Oriental Research

**ACORD** (*or* **Acord**) (ə'kɔːd) Advisory Council on Research and Development

**ACORN** ('eɪkɔːn) (ital.) A Classification of Residential Neighbourhoods (directory) • *Computing* associative content retrieval network • *Computing* automatic checkout and recording network

**ACOS** Advisory Committee on Safety • American College of Osteopathic Surgeons • Assistant Chief of Staff

**ACOST** (*or* **Acost**) (ə'kɒst) Advisory Council on Science and Technology

**ACP** *Biochem.* acyl carrier protein • advanced computer program • advanced computer project • African, Caribbean, and Pacific (countries) • American College of Pharmacists • American College of Physicians • Associate of the College of Preceptors • Association of Circus Proprietors of Great Britain • Association of Clinical Pathologists • Automóvel Clube de Portugal (Automobile Club of Portugal)

**ACPA** (USA) Associate of the Institute of Certified Public Accountants

**ACPAR** ('æk,pɑː) *Physics* angular correlation of positron-annihilation radiation

**ACPD** alternating-current plasma detector • alternating-current potential difference

**ACPM** American Congress of Physical Medicine and Rehabilitation

**ACPO** (*or* **Acpo**) ('ækpəʊ) Association of Chief Police Officers

**acpt.** *Commerce* acceptance

**acq.** acquire • acquittal

**ACR** Admiral Commanding Reserves • advanced capabilities radar • aircraft control room • American College in Rome • *Aeronautics* approach control radar • Association of College Registrars • audio cassette recorder

**ACRB** Aero-Club Royal de Belgique (French: Royal Belgian Aero Club)

**acrd** accrued

**ACRE** ('eɪkə) Action with Rural Communities in England • automatic climatological recording equipment

**ACRF** Advanced Computing Research Facility

**acrg.** acreage

**ACRI** (USA) Air-Conditioning and Refrigeration Institute

**ACRL** (USA) Association of College and Research Libraries

**acron.** acronym

**ACRR** American Council on Race Relations

**ACRS** *Taxation* Accelerated Cost Recovery System • Advisory Committee on Reactor Safeguards

**a/cs** aircraft security vessel

**ACS** *Aeronautics* active control system • Additional Curates Society • Admiral Commanding Submarines • Admiralty computing service • advanced communications system • airport catering services • air-conditioning system • *Aeronautics* altitude control system • American Cancer Society • American Ceramic Society • American Chemical Society • American College of Surgeons • assembly control system • Associate in Commercial Science • Australian Computer Society • *Finance* automated confirmation service • *Computing* automated control system

**ACSA** Allied Communications Security Agency

**ACSE** (Australia) Association of Consulting Structural Engineers

**ACSEA** Allied Command South East Asia

**ACSET** Advisory Committee on the Supply and Training of Teachers

**ACSL** *Computing* Advanced Continuous Simulation Language • assistant cub-scout leader

**ACSM** American Congress on Surveying and Mapping • Associate of the Camborne School of Mines

**ACSN** Association of Collegiate Schools of Nursing

**ACSOS** Acoustical Society of America

**ACSPA** Australian Council of Salaried and Professional Associations

**a/cs pay.** accounts payable

**a/cs rec.** accounts receivable

**ACSS** *Printing* automated colour separation system

**act.** acting • *Grammar* active • activities • actor • actual • actuary

**ACT** *Meteorol.* active (*or* activated) • *Aeronautics* active control technology • advance corporation tax • advanced coal technology • Advisory Council on Technology • Agricultural Central Trading Ltd • Air Council for Training •

American College Test • *Computing* analogical circuit technique • Associated Container Transportation • Associate of the College of Technology • Association of Corporate Treasurers • Australian Capital Territory • Australian College of Theology

**a cta.** a cuenta (Spanish: on account)

**ACTC** Art Class Teacher's Certificate

**actg** acting

**ACTH** *Biochem.* adrenocorticotrophic hormone

**ACTO** Advisory Council on the Treatment of Offenders

**ACTP** American College Testing Program

**ACTS** (USA) Acoustic Control and Telemetry System • Associate of the Society of Certified Teachers of Shorthand • Australian Catholic Truth Society

**ACTT** Association of Cinematograph, Television, and Allied Technicians (*see* BECTU)

**ACTU** Australian Council of Trade Unions

**ACTWU** (USA) Amalgamated Clothing and Textile Workers Union

**ACU** Actors' Church Union • American Congregational Union • Asian Clearing Union • Association of Commonwealth Universities • Auto-Cycle Union • *Computing* automatic calling unit

**ACUA** Association of Cambridge University Assistants

**ACUE** American Committee of United Europe

**ACUS** Atlantic Council of the United States

**ACV** (*or* **acv**) actual cash value • air-cushion vehicle • Associated Commercial Vehicles • Associate of the College of Violinists

**ACW** agricultural crop waste • Air Command (*or* Control) and Warning • aircraftwoman • (*or* **a.c.w.**) *Physics* alternating continuous wave • automatic car wash

**ACWS** aircraft control and warning system

**ACWW** Associated Country Women of the World

**ACY** average crop yield

**ad** (æd) advertisement • *Tennis* (North America) advantage

**ad.** adapt(ation) • adapter • *Med.* addatur *or* adde (Latin: let there be added *or* add; in prescriptions) • adverb

**a.d.** (*or* **A/d**) after date • ante diem (Latin: before the day) • autograph document

**a.D.** ausser Dienst (German; retired, on half pay)

**AD** *Insurance* accidental damage • (Venezuela) Acción Democrática (Spanish: Democratic Action Party) • accumulated dose (of radiation) • *Military* active duty • administrative department • *Military* air defence • air dried • Algerian dinar (monetary unit; *see also under* DA) • Alzheimer's disease • (small caps.) anno Domini (Latin: in the year of the Lord) • *British fishing port registration for* Ardrossan • armament depot • Art Director • assembly district • Assistant Director • *Politics* Australian Democrat(s) • autograph document • average deviation • Dame of the Order of Australia • *British vehicle registration for* Gloucester

**A-D** Albrecht Dürer (1471–1528, German painter and engraver)

**A/D** aerodrome • after date • *Computing* analog–digital (conversion)

**ADA** *Chem.* N-(2-acetamido)iminodiacetic acid • *Chem.* acetone dicarboxylic acid • *Biochem., Med.* adenosine deaminase (as in **ADA deficiency**) • Agricultural Development Association • (USA) Air Defense Agency • Aluminium Development Association • American Dental Association • American Diabetes Association • Americans for Democratic Action • *Chem.* ammonium dihydrogen arsenate • Association of Drainage Authorities • Atomic Development Authority • Australian Dental Association • (*or* **Ada**; 'eɪdə) *Computing, indicating* a programming language (after Ada Lovelace (1815–52), British mathematician)

**ADAA** Art Dealers Association of America

**ADAD** ('eɪdæd) (USA) automatic telephone dialing-announcing device

**adag.** (*or* **adago, adgo**) *Music* adagio

**adap.** adapted

**ADAPSO** (ə'dæpsəu) (USA) Association of Data Processing Organizations

**Adapt** (ə'dæpt) Access for Disabled People to Arts Today

**ADAPTS** (ə'dæpts) (USA) Air-Deliverable Antipollution Transfer System (in the Coast Guard)

**ADAS** ('eɪdæs) Agricultural Development and Advisory Service • *Computing* automatic data acquisition system • *Computing* auxiliary data annotation set

**ADAWS** *Military* action data automation and weapons systems • Assistant Director of Army Welfare Services

**A-day** assault day

**ADB** accidental death benefit • African Development Bank • Asian Development Bank • Associate of the Drama Board (Education) • (Canada) Atlantic Development Board • (USA) Bachelor of Domestic Arts

**ADC** advanced developing country (*or* countries) • *Telecom.* advice of duration and charge • aerodrome control • (Jamaica) Agricultural Development Corporation • aide-de-camp • Aid to Dependent Children • (USA) Air Defense Command • *Chem.* allyl diglycol carbonate • Amateur Dramatic Club • *Computing* analogue-to-digital converter • apparent diffusion coefficient • Art Directors' Club • *Scouting* Assistant District Commissioner • Association of District Councils • *Computing* automated distribution control • automatic digital calculator

**ADCC** (USA) Air Defense Control Center • *Med.* antibody-dependent cellular (*or* cell-mediated) cytotoxicity

**ADCCP** *Computing* advanced data communication control procedure

**ADCI** American Die Casting Institute

**ADCM** Archbishop of Canterbury's Diploma in Church Music

**ADCONSEN** ('ædkɒn,sɛn) (USA) (with) advice and consent of the Senate

**ADC(P)** personal aide-de-camp to HM the Queen

**ADCT** Art Directors' Club, Toronto

**add.** *Med.* add *or* let there be added (in prescriptions; Latin *adde* or *addantur*) • addendum (*or* addenda) • addition(al) • address(ed)

**ADD** *Aeronautics* airstream direction detector

**ADDC** (USA) Air Defense Direction Center

**ADDF** Abu Dhabi Defence Force

**addl** (*or* **addnl**) additional

**addn** addition

**addsd** addressed

**ADDS** Association of Directors of Social Services

**ADE** *Immunol.* antibody-dependent enhancement

**ADEF** (France) Agence d'évaluation financière (rating agency)

**ad effect.** *Med.* ad effectum (Latin: until effective; in prescriptions)

**ADEME** Assistant Director, Electrical and Mechanical Engineering

**ad eund.** ad eundem gradum (Latin: to the same degree)

**a.d.f.** after deducting freight

**ADF** *Finance* (Australia) approved deposit fund • Asian Development Fund • Australian Defence Force • *Navigation* automatic direction finder

**ad fin.** ad finem (Latin: at *or* near the end)

**ADFManc** Art and Design Fellow, Manchester

**ADFW** Assistant Director of Fortifications and Works

**ADG** Assistant Director-General

**ADGB** Air Defence of Great Britain

**ADGMS** Assistant Director-General of Medical Services

**ad gr. acid.** *Med.* ad gratam aciditatem (Latin: to an agreeable acidity; in prescriptions)

**ad gr. gust.** *Med.* ad gratum gustum (Latin: to an agreeable taste; in prescriptions)

**ADH** *Biochem.* antidiuretic hormone • Assistant Director of Hygiene • Association of Dental Hospitals

**ADHD** *Med.* attention deficit and hyperactivity disorder

**ad h.l.** ad hunc locum (Latin: at this place)

**ADI** *Med.* acceptable daily intake (of a toxic substance in food) • approved driving instructor

**ad inf.** ad infinitum (Latin: to infinity)

**ad init.** ad initium (Latin: at the beginning)

**ad int.** ad interim (Latin: in the meantime)

**ADIZ** (USA) air defense identification zone

**adj.** adjacent • adjective • adjoining • *Maths.* adjoint • adjourned • adjudged • adjunct • *Insurance, Banking, etc.* adjustment • adjutant

**ADJ** *Meteorol.* adjacent

**Adj.A** (USA) Adjunct in Arts

**ADJAG** Assistant Deputy Judge Advocate-General

**adjt** (*or* **Adjt**) adjutant

**Adjt-Gen** Adjutant-General

**ADK** (Malaysia) Order of Ahli Darjah Kinabalu

**ADL** *Electronics* acoustic delay line • *Med.* activity (*or* activities) of daily living • *Computing* Ada design language • (USA) Anti-Defamation League (of B'nai B'rith) • assistant director of labour

**ad lib.** ad libitum (Latin: according to pleasure, i.e. freely)

**ad loc.** ad locum (Latin: at the place)

**ADLP** Australian Democratic Labor Party

**adm.** administration • administrative • administrator • admission • admitted

**Adm.** Admiral • Admiralty

**ADM** Advanced Diploma in Midwifery • annual delegate meeting • Association of Domestic Management • atomic demolition munitions • average daily membership

**ADMA** American Drug Manufacturers' Association • (USA) Aviation Distributors' and Manufacturers' Association

**Ad. Man.** Advertisement Manager

**admin.** administration • (*or* **Admin.**) administrator

**Admin. Apost.** Administrator Apostolic

**Adml** Admiral

**ADMO(CA)** Assistant Director of the Meteorological Office (Civil Aviation)

**ADMOS** ('ædmɒs) *Computing* automatic device for mechanical order selection

**admov.** *Med.* admoveatur (Latin: let it be applied; in prescriptions)

**Adm. Rev.** Admodum Reverendus (Latin: Very Reverend)

**ADMS** Assistant Director of Medical Services

**ADMT** Association of Dental Manufacturers and Traders of the United Kingdom

**admx** administratrix

**ADN** Allgemeiner Deutscher Nachrichtendienst (German news agency) • *international vehicle registration for* Yemen

**ADNA** Assistant Director of Naval Accounts

**ADNC** Assistant Director of Naval Construction

**ad neut.** *Med.* ad neutralizandum (Latin: until neutral)

**ADNI** Assistant Director of Naval Intelligence

**ADNOC** Abu Dhabi National Oil Company

**ADNS** Assistant Director of Nursing Services

**ADO** (USA) advanced development objective • air defence officer • assistant district officer • Association of Dispensing Opticians • automotive diesel oil

**ADOF** Assistant Director of Ordnance Factories

**ADOS** Assistant Director of Ordnance Services

**ADP** *Biochem.* adenosine diphosphate • air defence position • *Physics* area density of particles • Association of Dental Prosthesis • automatic data processing

**ADPA** Associate Diploma of Public Administration

**ADPLAN** ('æd,plæn) advanced planning

**ADPR** Assistant Director of Public Relations

**ADPSO** Association of Data Processing Service Organizations

**ADR** accident data recorder • *Law* alternative dispute resolution • *Stock exchange* American Depository Receipt

**ADRA** Animal Diseases Research Association (Edinburgh)

**ad s.** *Law* ad sectam (Latin: at the suit of)

**a.d.s.** autograph document signed

**A.d.S.** Académie des Sciences (French: Academy of Sciences)

**ADS** *Computing* accurately defined systems • advanced dressing station • (USA) air defense sector • American Dialect Society • *Engineering* articulated drill string • *Engineering* automatic depressurization system

**ad saec.** ad saeculum (Latin: to the century)

**ADS&T** Assistant Director of Supplies and Transport

**ad sat.** *Med.* ad saturandum (Latin: to saturation)

**ADSOC** ('ædsɒk) (USA) Administrative Support Operations Center

**ADSS** Australian Defence Scientific Service

**ADST** *Finance* approved deferred share trust

**adst. feb.** *Med.* adstante febre (Latin: when fever is present)

**ADT** American District Telegraph • Assistant Director of Transport • average daily traffic

**ADTECH** ('æd,tɛk) advanced decoy technology

**ADTS** Automated Data and Telecommunications Service

**ad us.** ad usum (Latin: according to custom)

**ad us. ext.** *Med.* ad usum externum (Latin: for external use)

**adv.** advance • adverb(ial) • adversus (Latin: against) • advertisement • advertising • advice • advise • adviser • advisory • advocate

**Adv.** Advent • Advocate

**ad val.** ad valorem (Latin: according to value)

**advb** adverb

**adven.** adventure

**adv. pmt.** advance payment

**ADVS** Advanced Diploma in Voice Studies • Assistant Director of Veterinary Services

**advt** advertisement

**advv.** adverbs

**ADW** air defence warning • Assistant Director of Works

**ADWE&M** Assistant Director of Works, Electrical and Mechanical

**ADX** *Computing* automatic data exchange • *Telecom.* automatic digital exchange

**ADXPS** *Chem., Physics* angular dependent X-ray photoelectron spectroscopy

**ae.** *Numismatics* aeneus (Latin: made of copper) • aetatis (Latin: at the age of; aged)

**AE** account executive • *Chem.* acid ester • *Physics* acoustic emission • adult education • aeronautical engineer(ing) • *Taxation* age exemption • agricultural engineer(ing) • Air Efficiency Award • (Sweden) Aktiebolaget Atomenergi (Atomic Energy Corporation) • All England • American English • army education • Associate in Education • Associate in Engineering • atomic energy • *Photog.* autoexposure • *British vehicle registration for* Bristol • *pseudonym of* George Russell, 1867–1935, Irish poet • *Insurance, indicating* (in Lloyd's Register) third-class ships

**AEA** *Physics* acoustic emission analysis • (USA) Actors' Equity Association • *Engineering* air entraining agent • American Economic Association • (USA) Atomic Energy Act • Atomic Energy Authority

**AEAA** Asociación de Escritores y Artistas Americanos (Spanish: Association of Spanish-American Writers and Artists)

**AEAF** Allied Expeditionary Air Force

**AE & MP** Ambassador Extraordinary and Minister Plenipotentiary

**AE & P** Ambassador Extraordinary and Plenipotentiary

**AEAUSA** Adult Education Association of the United States of America

**AEB** Area Electricity Board • Associated Examining Board

**AEBP** atmospheric equivalent boiling point

**AEC** *Insurance* additional extended coverage • Agricultural Executive Council • American Express Company • *Chem.* anion-exchange capacity • Army Electronics Command • Associated Equipment Company • Association of Education Committees • (USA) Atomic Energy Commission • (South Africa) Atomic Energy Corporation • (USA) Atomic Energy Council • *Photog.* automatic exposure control

**AECB** (USA) Atomic Energy Control Board

**AECCG** African Elephant Conservation Coordinating Group

**AECI** African Explosives and Chemical Industries • Associate of the Institute of Employment Consultants

**AECL** Atomic Energy of Canada Limited

**AEd** Associate in Education

**AED** advanced electronics design • *Computing* Algol Extended for Design (programming language) • Association of Engineering Distributors • automated engineering design • Doctor of Fine Arts (Latin *Artium Elegantium Doctor*)

**AEDE** Association européenne des enseignants (French: European Teachers' Association)

**AEDOT** Advanced Energy Design and Operation Technologies

**AEDP** (USA) Alternative Energy Development Program

**AEDS** (USA) Association for Educational Data Systems • Atomic Energy Detection Systems

**AEDU** Admiralty Experimental Diving Unit

**AeE** Aeronautical Engineer

**AEE** airborne evaluation equipment • *Chem.* alkaline-earth element • Atomic Energy Establishment

**AEEC** (USA) Airlines Electronic Engineering Committee • (Canada) Army Equipment Engineering Establishment

**AEEN** Agence européenne pour l'energie nucléaire (French: European Agency for Atomic Energy)

**AEEU** Amalgamated Engineering and Electrical Union (formed from merger of AEU and EETPU)

**AEF** Allied Expeditionary Force • American Expeditionary Force(s) • Australian Expeditionary Force

**A-effect** *Theatre* alienation effect

**AEFM** Association européenne des festivals de musique (French: European Association of Music Festivals)

**a.e.g.** (*or* **aeg**) ad eundem gradum (Latin: to the same degree) • *Bookbinding* all edges gilt

**AEG** (Germany) Allgemeine Elektrizitäts-Gesellschaft (General Electric Company)

**AEGIS** ('i:dʒɪs) Aid for the Elderly in Government Institutions • *Computing* an existing general information system

**AEGM** Anglican Evangelical Group Movement

**AEH** A(lfred) E(dward) Housman (1859–1936, British poet)

**AEI** (USA) Alternative Energy Institute • American Express International • Associated Electrical Industries • Association des écoles internationales (French: International Schools Association)

**AEIOU** Austriae Est Imperare Orbi Universi (Latin: it is given to Austria to rule the whole world) • Austria Erit In Orbe Ultima (Latin: Austria will be the world's last survivor)

**AEJ** Association for Education in Journalism

**AEL** Admiralty Engineering Laboratory • aeronautical (*or* aircraft) engine laboratory • Associated Engineering, Limited • automation engineering laboratory

**AELE** (France) Association européenne de libre-échange (European Free Trade Association; EFTA)

**AELTC** All England Lawn Tennis Club

**AEM** Air Efficiency Medal • analytical electron microscopy

**AEMT** Association of Electrical Machinery Trades

**AEMU** *Astronautics* Advanced Extravehicular Mobility Unit

**aen.** *Numismatics* aeneus (Latin: made of copper)

**Aen.** (ital.) The Aeneid (Virgil's epic)

**AEn** Associate in English

**AENA** All England Netball Association

**AEng** Associate in Engineering

**Aen. Nas.** Aenei Nasi (Brasenose College, Oxford; Latin: of the Brazen Nose)

**AEO** *Chem.* alkaline-earth oxide • Assistant Education Officer • Assistant Experimental Officer • Association of Exhibition Organizers

**AEP** Agence européenne de productivité (French: European Production Agency) • American Electric Power

**AEPI** American Educational Publishers Institute

**aeq.** aequalis (Latin: equal)

**aer.** aeronautics • aeroplane

**AER** Army Emergency Reserve

**aera.** aeration

**AERA** American Educational Research Association • Associate Engraver, Royal Academy • Associate of the British Electrical and Allied Industries Research Association

**AerE** Aeronautical Engineer

**AERE** Atomic Energy Research Establishment (Harwell)

**AERI** Agricultural Economics Research Institute (Oxford University)

**AERNO** aeronautical equipment reference number

**aero.** aeronautic(al)

**AERO** Air Education and Recreation Organization

**aeron.** aeronautical • aeronautics

**aerosp.** aerospace

**Aes.** Aesop (6th century BC, Greek author of fables)

**AES** advanced energy system • (USA) Aerospace Electrical Society • Agricultural Economics Society (Reading University) • (USA) Airways Engineering Society • *Physics* atomic emission spectrum (spectroscopy, spectrometry, *or* spectrography) • Audio Engineering Society • *Physics* Auger electron spectrum (*or* spectroscopy)

**AESE** (USA) Association of Earth Science Editors

**AESL** (USA) Aerospace Energy Systems Laboratory

**aesth.** aesthetics

**aet.** (*or* **aetat.**) aetatis (Latin: at the age of; aged)

**AET** Associate in Electrical (*or* Electronic) Technology

**AETR** advanced engineering test reactor

**AEU** Amalgamated Engineering Union (formerly AUEW; *see* AEEU) • American Ethical Union

**AEU(TASS)** Amalgamated Engineering Union (Technical, Administrative, and Supervisory Section)

**AEV** aerothermodynamic elastic vehicle • air evacuation • *Microbiol.* avian erythroblastosis virus

**AEW** Admiralty Experimental Works • airborne early warning (aircraft)

**AEW & C** airborne early warning and control

**AEWHA** All England Women's Hockey Association

**AEWLA** All England Women's Lacrosse Association

**AEWS** advanced earth satellite weapons system • aircraft early warning system

**a.f.** advanced freight • (*or* **a/f**) *Commerce* a favor (Spanish: in favour) • anno futuro (Latin: next year) • audiofrequency

**Af** *symbol for* afgháni (monetary unit of Afghanistan)

**Af.** Africa(n) • Afrikaans • *symbol for* Aruban florin (monetary unit of Aruba)

**AF** Académie Française (French literary academy) • (*or* **A/F**) *Engineering* across flats (used in denoting sizes of nuts, as in ½**AF**) • (France) Action Française (former journal and political party) • Admiral of the Fleet • air force • (USA) Air Foundation • *airline flight code for* Air France • Anglo-French • Armée Française (French Army) • Associated Fisheries • Associate Fellow • audiofrequency • *Photog.* autofocus • automatic (smoke) filter • *British vehicle registration for* Truro

**A/F** antiflooding • as found (in auction catalogues)

**AFA** *Nuclear engineering* advanced fuel assembly • African Football Association • Air Force Act • (USA) Air Force Association • Amateur Fencing Association • Amateur Football Alliance • American Foundrymen's Association • Associate in Fine Arts • (Scotland) Associate of the Faculty of Actuaries

**AFAC** American Fisheries Advisory Committee

**AFAEP** Association of Fashion Advertising and Editorial Photographers

**AFAFC** (USA) Air Force Accounting and Finance Center

**AFAIAA** Associate Fellow of the American Institute of Aeronautics and Astronautics

**AFAIM** Associate Fellow of the Australian Institute of Management

**AFAITC** (USA) Armed Forces Air Intelligence Training Center

**AFAL** (USA) Air Force Astronautical Laboratory

**AFAM** (*or* **AF & AM**) Ancient Free and Accepted Masons

**AFAS** (France) Association française pour l'avancement des sciences (French Association for the Advancement of the Sciences)

**AFASIC** Association for all Speech-Impaired Children

**AFB** *Microbiol.* acid-fast bacilli • (USA) Air Force Base • American Federation for the Blind

**AFBC** *Chemical engineering* atmospheric fluidized-bed combustor (*or* combustion)

**AFBD** Association of Futures Brokers and Dealers

**AFBF** American Farm Bureau Federation

**AFBMD** (USA) Air Force Ballistic Missile Division

**AFBPsS** Associate Fellow of the British Psychological Society

**AFBS** American and Foreign Bible Society

**AFC** Air Force Cross • Amateur Football Club • *Immunol.* antibody-forming cell • Association Football Club • Australian Flying Corps • (*or* **a.f.c.**) automatic flight control • (*or* **a.f.c.**) automatic frequency control

**AFCAI** Associate Fellow of the Canadian Aeronautical Institute

**AFCE** Associate in Fuel Technology and Chemical Engineering • automatic flight control equipment

**AFCEA** (USA) Armed Forces Communications and Electronics Association

**AFCENT** (*or* **AFCent**) ('æfsɛnt) Allied Forces in Central Europe (of NATO)

**afco** ('æf,kəʊ) *Engineering* automatic fuel cut-off

**AFCO** Admiralty Fleet Confidential Order

**AFCRL** (USA) Air Force Cambridge Research Laboratories

**AFCS** Air Force Communications Service • automatic flight control system

**AFCU** American and Foreign Christian Union

**AFCW** Association of Family Case Workers

**AFD** accelerated freeze dried (*or* drying) • air force depot • (USA) Doctor of Fine Arts

**AFDC** (USA) Aid to Families with Dependent Children

**AFDCS** Association of First Division Civil Servants

**AFDM** *Engineering* advanced fluid-dynamics model

**AFDS** Air Fighting Development Squadron

**AFDW** *Chem.* ash-free dry weight

**AFEA** American Farm Economics Association • American Film Export Association

**AFEE** Airborne Forces Experimental Establishment

**AFEIS** Advanced Further Education Information Service

**AFERO** Asia and the Far East Regional Office (of the FAO)

**AFES** Admiralty Fuel Experimental Station

**AFESC** (USA) Air Force Engineering and Services Center

**AFESD** Arab Fund for Economic and Social Development

**AFEX** (USA) Air Forces Europe Exchange • (USA) Armed Forces Exchange

**aff.** affairs • affectionate • (*or* **affil.**) affiliate(d) • affirmative • affix

**AFF** *Photog.* aberration-free focus

**Aff.IP** Affiliate of the Institute of Plumbing

**AFFL** Agricultural Finance Federation, Ltd

# afft · AFRA

**afft** affidavit

**AFFTC** (USA) Air Force Flight Test Center

**Afg.** Afghanistan

**AFG** *international vehicle registration for* Afghanistan

**AFGE** American Federation of Government Employees

**Afgh.** (*or* **Afghan.**) Afghanistan

**AFGL** (USA) Air Force Geophysics Laboratory

**AFGM** American Federation of Grain Millers

**AFH** American Foundation for Homeopathy

**AFHC** Air Force Headquarters Command

**AFHQ** Allied Force(s) Headquarters • Armed Forces Headquarters

**AFI** American Film Institute

**AFIA** American Foreign Insurance Association • (Australia) Associate of the Federal Institute of Accountants

**AFIAP** Artiste de la Fédération internationale de l'art photographique (French: Artist of the International Federation of Photographic Art)

**AFICD** Associate Fellow of the Institute of Civil Defence

**AFII** American Federation of International Institutes

**AFIIM** Associate Fellow of the Institution of Industrial Managers

**AFIMA** Associate Fellow of the Institute of Mathematics and its Applications

**AFIPS** American Federation of Information Processing Societies, Inc.

**AFL** *Computing* abstract family of languages • Air Force List • American Federation of Labor • American Football League • (Portugal) Associação de Futebol de Lisboa (Lisbon Football Association)

**AFLA** Amateur Fencers' League of America • Asian Federation of Library Associations

**AFLC** (USA) Air Force Logistics Command

**AFL-CIO** American Federation of Labor and Congress of Industrial Organizations

**afit** afloat

**AFM** *Engineering* abrasive flow machining • Air Force Medal • American Federation of Musicians of the United States and Canada • assistant field manager • Associated Feed Manufactur-

ers • *Chem., Physics* atomic force microscope (*or* microscopy) • *Telecom.* audiofrequency modulation

**AFMA** Armed Forces Management Association • Artificial Flower Manufacturers' Association of Great Britain

**AFMDC** (USA) Air Force Missile Development Center

**AFMEC** African Methodist Episcopal Church

**AFMED** (*or* **AFMed**) Allied Forces Mediterranean

**afmo.** afectísimo (Spanish: very affectionately; in correspondence)

**AFMTC** (USA) Air Force Missile Test Center

**AFN** American Forces Network • Armed Forces Network • Association of Free Newspapers

**AFNE** Allied Forces Northern Europe

**AFNIL** ('æfnɪl) (France) Agence francophone pour la numérotation internationale du livre (French Agency for International Standard Book Numbers; ISBN)

**AFNOR** ('æf,nɔ:) Association française de normalisation (the standards organization of France)

**AFNORTH** (*or* **AFNorth**) ('æf,nɔ:θ) Allied Forces Northern Europe

**AFO** Admiralty Fleet Order • army forwarding officer

**AFOAR** (USA) Air Force Office of Aerospace Research

**AFOAS** (USA) Air Force Office of Aerospace Sciences

**AF of M** American Federation of Musicians of the United States and Canada

**AFOM** Associate of the Faculty of Occupational Medicine

**AFOSR** (USA) Air Force Office of Scientific Research

**AFP** Agence France Press (French independent news agency) • (*or* **afp**) *Med.* alpha-fetoprotein

**AFPRB** Armed Forces Pay Review Board

**Afr.** Africa(n)

**AFr.** (*or* **A-Fr.**) Anglo-French

**AFR** accident frequency rate (in industry) • air–fuel ratio • automatic fingerprint recognition

**AFRA** American Farm Research Association • American Federation of Television and Radio Artists

**AFRASEC** ('æfrə,sɛk) Afro-Asian Organization for Economic Cooperation

**AFRC** Agricultural and Food Research Council

**Afrik.** Afrikaans

**AFRO** Africa Regional Office (of the FAO)

**AFRTS** (USA) Armed Forces Radio and Television Service

**AFS** Advanced Flying School · air force station · Alaska Ferry Service · American Field Service · Army Fire Service · Atlantic Ferry Service · *Chem., Physics* atomic fluorescence spectrometry · auxiliary fire service · *Physics* axial field spectrometer

**AFSA** American Foreign Service Association · (USA) Armed Forces Security Agency

**AFSBO** American Federation of Small Business Organizations

**AFSC** Air Force Systems Command · American Friends Service Committee · Armed Forces Staff College

**AFSCME** American Federation of State, County, and Municipal Employees (trade union)

**afsd** aforesaid

**AFSIL** ('æfsɪl) Accommodation for Students in London

**AFSLAET** Associate Fellow of the Society of Licensed Aircraft Engineers and Technologists

**AFSOUTH** (*or* **AFSouth**) ('æf,saʊθ) Allied Forces in Southern Europe

**aft.** after · afternoon

**AFT** American Federation of Teachers · axial-flow turbine

**AFTE** American Federation of Technical Engineers

**AFTM** American Foundation of Tropical Medicine

**aftn** afternoon

**AFTN** Aeronautical Fixed Telecommunications Network

**AFTR** American Federal Tax Reports

**AFTRA** American Federation of Television and Radio Artists (trade union)

**AFU** advanced flying unit

**AFULE** Australian Federated Union of Locomotive Enginemen

**AFV** armoured fighting vehicle · armoured force vehicle

**AFVG** *Aeronautics* Anglo-French variable geometry

**AFVPA** Advertising Film and Videotape Producers' Association

**AFW** army field workshop

**AFWAL** (USA) Air Force Wright Aeronautical Laboratories

**AFWL** (USA) Air Force Weapons Laboratory

**ag.** agent · agreement · agriculture

**a.g.** *Chem., Military* anti-gas

**Ag** *Chem., symbol for* silver (Latin *argentum*)

**Ag.** August

**AG** Accountant-General · (Nigeria) Action Group Party · Adjutant-General · Agent-General (of colonies) · air gunner · (Germany) Aktiengesellschaft (public limited company; plc) · (Italy) Alberghi per la Gioventù (youth hostels) · art gallery · Attorney-General · *British vehicle registration for* Hull

**Aga** ('ɑːgə) Aktiebolaget Gasackumulator (cooker)

**AGA** *Military* air-to-ground-to-air · Amateur Gymnastics Association · American Gas Association · American Genetic Association · *Obstetrics* appropriate for gestational age · Australian Garrison Artillery

**AGAC** American Guild of Authors and Composers

**AGACS** automatic ground-to-air communications system

**AGARD** Advisory Group for Aerospace Research and Development (in NATO)

**a.g.b.** a (*or* any) good brand

**AGBI** Artists' General Benevolent Institution

**AGC** (USA) advanced graduate certificate · American Grassland Council · (*or* **a.g.c.**) *Electronics* automatic gain control

**AGCA** *Aeronautics* automatic ground-controlled approach

**AGCAS** Association of Graduate Careers Advisory Service

**AGCC** Arab Gulf Cooperation Council

**AGCL** *Aeronautics* automatic ground-controlled landing

**AGCM** *Meteorol.* atmospheric general circulation model

**agcy** agency

**agd** agreed

**a.g.d.** *Engineering* axial gear differential

**AGDC** *Freemasonry* Assistant Grand Director of Ceremonies

**AGDL** Attorney-General of the Duchy of Lancaster

**AgE** Agricultural Engineer

**AGE** Admiralty Gunnery Establishment • aerospace ground equipment • Associate in General Education • automatic guidance electronics

**AGES** Association of Agricultural Education Staffs

**AGF** Adjutant-General to the Forces • army ground forces

**ag. feb.** *Med.* aggrediente febre (Latin: when the fever increases)

**agg.** (*or* **aggr.**) aggregate

**AGH** Australian General Hospital

**AGI** (USA) adjusted gross income (in income-tax returns) • American Geographical Institute • American Geological Institute • Année Géophysique Internationale (French: International Geophysical Year, 1 July 1957–31 Dec 1958) • annual general inspection • Artistes graphiques internationaux (French: International Graphic Artists) • Associate of the Institute of Certificated Grocers

**AGIP** Agenzia Generale Italiana Petroli (Italian national oil company)

**agit.** *Med.* agitatum (Latin: shaken)

**agit. ante sum.** *Med.* agita ante sumendum (Latin: shake before taking)

**Agitprop** ('ædʒɪt,prɒp) Agitpropbyuro (Soviet bureau in charge of agitation and propaganda)

**AGL** above ground level

**aglm.** agglomerate

**AGM** advisory group meeting • *Med.* African green monkey • air-to-ground missile • annual general meeting • Award of Garden Merit (awarded by the Royal Horticultural Society)

**AGMA** American Guild of Musical Artists • Athletic Goods Manufacturers' Association

**agn** again • agnomen

**AGN** *Astronomy* active galactic nucleus

**agnos.** agnostic

**ago.** agosto (Italian: August)

**AGOR** Auxiliary-General Oceanographic Research

**AGP** Academy of General Practice • aviation general policy

**AGPA** American Group Psychotherapy Association

**AGPL** Administração-Geral do Pôrto de Lisboa (Portuguese: Port of Lisbon Authority)

**agr.** agreement • agricultural • agriculture • agriculturist

**AGR** *Nuclear physics* advanced gas-cooled reactor • Association of Graduate Recruiters

**AGRA** Army Group Royal Artillery • Association of Genealogists and Record Agents

**AGREE** (ə'griː) Advisory Group on Reliability of Electronic Equipment

**AGRF** American Geriatric Research Foundation

**agric.** agricultural • agriculture • agriculturist

**AGRM** Adjutant-General, Royal Marines

**agron.** agronomy

**AGRS** *Chemical engineering* acid-gas removal system

**AGS** *Astronautics* abort guidance system • aircraft general standard • Air Gunnery School • Alpine Garden Society • American Geographical Society • Associate in General Studies

**AGSM** Associate of the Guildhall School of Music and Drama • Australian Graduate of the School of Management

**AGSRO** Association of Government Supervisors and Radio Officers

**AGSS** American Geographical and Statistical Society

**agst** against

**agt** agent • agreement

**AGT** advanced gas turbine • Art Gallery of Toronto • (USA) Association of Geology Teachers • *Physics* average generation time

**agᵗᵒ** agosto (Italian, Portuguese, and Spanish: August)

**AGU** American Geophysical Union

**AGV** *Pharmacol.* aniline gentian violet • *Electronics* automatic guided vehicle(s)

**AGVA** American Guild of Variety Artists • *Aeronautics* Anglo-German variable geometry

**a.g.w.** (*or* **AGW**) actual gross weight

**AGWAC** Australian Guided Weapons and Analogue Computer

**AGWI** *Marine insurance* Atlantic, Gulf, West Indies

**agy** agency

**a.h.** *Shipping* aft (*or* after) hatch • ampere-hour • armed helicopter

**AH** *airline flight code for* Air Algerie • (small caps.) anno Hebraico (Latin: in the Jewish year) • (small caps.) anno Hegirae (Latin: in the year of the Hegira; in the Muslim calendar) • (*or*

**A/H**) *Marine insurance* Antwerp–Hamburg coastal ports • *British fishing port registration for* Arbroath • *Chem.* aromatic hydrocarbon • *Med.* artificial hyperglycaemia • *British vehicle registration for* Norwich

**AHA** American Heart Association • American Historical Association • American Hospitals Association • (formerly, in the NHS) Area Health Authority • Australian Hotels Association

**AHAM** (USA) Association of Home Appliance Manufacturers

**AH & FITB** Agricultural, Horticultural, and Forestry Industry Training Board

**AHAUS** Amateur Hockey Association of the United States

**AHC** Accepting Houses Committee • American Horticultural Council • Army Hospital Corps

**ahd** ahead

**AHD** (ital.) American Heritage Dictionary

**AHDL** *Med.* alveolar hydatid disease of the liver

**AHE** (USA) Associate in Home Economics

**AHEM** Association of Hydraulic Equipment Manufacturers

**AHF** *Chem.* anhydrous hydrogen fluoride • *Med.* antihaemophilic factor

**AHG** *Med.* antihaemophilic globulin

**AHGMR** Ad Hoc Group on Missile Reliability

**AHH** *Med., Biochem.* aryl hydrocarbon hydroxylase (used in tobacco research)

**AHI** American Health (*or* Hospital) Institute

**AHIL** (USA) Association of Hospital and Institutional Libraries

**a.h.l.** ad hunc locum (Latin: on this passage)

**AHL** American Hockey League

**AHMC** Association of Hospital Management Committees

**AHMPS** Association of Headmistresses of Preparatory Schools

**AHMS** American Home Mission Society

**AHNCV** Area of High Nature Conservation Value

**AHP** *Engineering* absorption heat pump • air horsepower • assistant house physician

**AHPR** Association of Health and Pleasure Resorts

**AHQ** Air Headquarters • Allied Headquarters • Army Headquarters

**a.h.r.** acceptable hazard rate (in risk analysis)

**AHRC** Australian Humanities Research Council

**AHRHS** Associate of Honour of the Royal Horticultural Society

**AHRIH(NZ)** Associate of Honour of the Royal Institute of Horticulture (New Zealand)

**AHS** adult health study • American Helicopter Society • (small caps.) anno humanae salutis (Latin: in the year of human salvation) • annual housing survey • assistant house surgeon

**AHSA** American Horse Shows Association

**AHSB** Authority, Health, and Safety Branch (of the Atomic Energy Authority)

**AHSM** Associate of the Institute of Health Services Management

**AHT** absorption heat transformer • acoustic homing torpedo • Animal Health Trust • Association of Highway Technicians

**a.h.v.** ad hanc vocem (Latin: at this word)

**AHWA** Association of Hospital and Welfare Administrators

**AH-WC** Associate of the Heriot-Watt College

**a.i.** ad interim (Latin: for the meantime)

**AI** Admiralty instruction • Admiralty Islands • *airline flight code for* Air India • air interdiction • Altesse Impériale (French: Imperial Highness) • American Institute • Amnesty International • (small caps.) anno inventionis (Latin: in the year of the discovery) • Anthropological Institute • Army Intelligence • artificial insemination • artificial intelligence • *Physics, Chem.* associative ionization • *Physics* avalanche injection • *Irish vehicle registration for* Meath

**AIA** Abrasive Industries Association • (USA) Aerospace Industries Association • American Institute of Aeronautics • American Institute of Architects • American Insurance Association • *Chem.* aminoimidazoazaarene • Anglo-Indian Association • Archeological Institute of America • Associate of the Institute of Actuaries • Association of International Artists • automated image analysis • (New Zealand) Aviation Industry Association

**AIAA** Aircraft Industries Association of America • American Institute of Aeronautics and Astronautics • Association of International Advertising Agencies

**AIAB** Associate of the International Association of Book-keepers

**AIAC** Air Industries Association of Canada • Association internationale d'archéologie classique (French: International Association for Classical Archaeology)

**AIAE** Associate of the Institution of Automobile Engineers

**AIAgrE** Associate of the Institution of Agricultural Engineers

**AIAL** Associate Member of the International Institute of Arts and Letters

**AIAS** Associate Surveyor Member of the Incorporated Association of Architects and Surveyors • Australian Institute of Agriculture and Science

**AIB** accidents investigation branch (of insurance companies) • American Institute of Banking • Association of Independent Businesses • (Italy) Associazione Italiana Biblioteche (Italian Library Association)

**AIBA** Association internationale de boxe amateur (French: International Amateur Boxing Association)

**AIBC** Architectural Institute of British Columbia

**AIBD** Associate of the Institute of British Decorators

**AIBE** Associate of the Institute of Building Estimators

**AIBM** Associate of the Institute of Baths Management • Association internationale des bibliothèques musicales (French: International Association of Music Libraries)

**AIBP** Associate of the Institute of British Photographers

**AIBS** American Institute of Biological Sciences • (South Africa) Associate of the Institute of Building Societies

**AIBScot** Associate of the Institute of Bankers in Scotland

**AIC** Agricultural Improvement Council • Agricultural Institute of Canada • *Physics* Alfvén ion cyclotron • American Institute of Chemists • artificial insemination centre • Art Institute of Chicago

**AICA** Associate Member of the Commonwealth Institute of Accountants • Association internationale des

critiques d'art (French: International Association of Art Critics)

**AICB** Association internationale contre le bruit (French: International Association Against Noise)

**AICBM** anti-intercontinental ballistic missile

**AICC** All India Congress Committee

**AICE** American Institute of Chemical Engineers • American Institute of Consulting Engineers • Associate of the Institution of Civil Engineers

**AICeram** Associate of the Institute of Ceramics

**AIChE** American Institute of Chemical Engineers

**AICMA** Association internationale des constructeurs de matériel aérospatial (French: International Association of Aerospace Equipment Manufacturers)

**AICPA** American Institute of Certified Public Accountants

**AICRO** Association of Independent Contract Research Organizations

**AICS** Associate of the Institute of Chartered Shipbrokers • Association internationale du cinéma scientifique (French: International Scientific Film Association)

**AICTA** (Trinidad) Associate of the Imperial College of Tropical Agriculture

**AICV** armoured infantry combat vehicle

**AID** acute infectious disease • Aeronautical Inspection Directorate • (USA) Agency for International Development • agricultural industrial development • Aircraft Intelligence Department • American Institute of Decorators • American Institute of Interior Designers • Army Intelligence Department • *Med.* artificial insemination (by) donor • Association internationale pour le développement (French: International Development Association)

**AIDA** Association internationale de droit africain (French: International African Law Association) • Association internationale de la distribution des produits alimentaires (French: International Association of Food Distribution) • *Advertising* attention, interest, desire, action (of the customer)

**AIDAS** Agricultural Industry Development Advisory Service

**AIDB** Association of International Bond Dealers

**AIDD** American Institute for Design and Drafting

**AIDF** African Industrial Development Fund

**AIDIA** Associate of the Industrial Design Institute of Australia

**AIDL** (New Zealand) Auckland Industrial Development Laboratory

**AIDP** Associate of the Institute of Data Processing • Association internationale de droit pénal (French: International Association of Penal Law)

**Aids** (*or* **AIDS**) (eɪdz) acquired immune deficiency syndrome

**AIDS** accident information display system • aircraft integrated data system • air force intelligence data-handling system

**AIE** Associate of the Institute of Education

**AIEA** Agence internationale de l'énergie atomique (French: International Atomic Energy Agency)

**AIED** Association internationale des étudiants dentaires (French: International Association of Dental Students)

**AIEE** Associate of the Institution of Electrical Engineers • Association des instituts d'études européennes (French: Association of Institutes for European Studies)

**AIEP** (USA) Association of Independent Electricity Producers

**AIF** Agenzia Internazionale Fides (Vatican City State news agency) • Alliance internationale des femmes (French: International Alliance of Women) • (USA) Atomic Industrial Forum • (formerly) Australian Imperial Forces

**AIFA** Associate of the International Faculty of Arts

**AIFireE** Associate of the Institution of Fire Engineers

**AIFM** Associate of the Institute of Factory Managers • Association internationale des femmes médecins (French: International Association of Women Doctors)

**AIG** Adjutant (*or* Assistant) Inspector-General • *Chem.* aerosol-ionization gas analyser • Assistant Instructor of Gunnery

**AIGA** American Institute of Graphic Arts

**AIGCM** Associate of the Incorporated Guild of Church Musicians

**AIGS** Agricultural Investment Grant Schemes

**AIH** all in hand • *Med.* artificial insemination (by) husband • Association inter-nationale de l'hôtellerie (French: International Hotel Association)

**AIHA** American Industrial Hygiene Association

**AIHsg** Associate of the Institute of Housing

**AIIA** Associate of the Indian Institute of Architects • Associate of the Insurance Institute of America • Australian Institute of International Affairs

**AIIAL** Associate of the International Institute of Arts and Letters

**AIIE** American Institute of Industrial Engineers

**AIInfSc** Associate of the Institute of Information Scientists

**AIITech** Associate Member of the Institute of Industrial Technicians

**AIJD** Association internationale des juristes démocrates (French: International Association of Democratic Lawyers)

**AIJPF** Association internationale des journalistes de la presse féminine et familiale (French: International Association of Women's Press Journalists)

**AIL** air intelligence liaison • Associate of the Institute of Linguists

**AILAS** *Aeronautics* automatic instrument-landing approach system

**AILO** air intelligence liaison officer

**AILocoE** Associate of the Institution of Locomotive Engineers

**AIM** Africa Inland Mission • (eɪm) American Indian Movement (civil-rights organization) • American Institute of Management • analytical ion microscopy • Association of Industrial Machinery Merchants • *Presbyterianism* Australian Inland Mission • Australian Institute of Management

**a.i.m.a.** as interest may appear

**AIMarE** Associate of the Institute of Marine Engineers

**AIMCO** (USA) Association of Internal Management Consultants

**AIME** American Institute of Mechanical Engineers • American Institute of Mining Engineers

**AIMechE** Associate of the Institution of Mechanical Engineers

**AIMI** Associate of the Institute of the Motor Industry

**AIMinE** Associate of the Institution of Mining Engineers

**AIMM** Australasian Institute of Mining and Metallurgy

**AIMO** Association of Industrial Medical Officers

**AIMPA** Association internationale de météorologie et de physique de l'atmosphère (French: International Association of Meteorology and Atmospheric Physics)

**AIMPE** Australian Institute of Marine and Power Engineers

**AIMS** (eɪmz) Association for Improvement in Maternity Services

**AIMSW** Associate of the Institute of Medical Social Workers

**AIMU** American Institute of Marine Underwriters

**AIN** American Institute of Nutrition

**AINEC** All-India Newspaper Editors' Conference

**AInstBCA** Associate of the Institute of Burial and Cremation Administration

**AInstCE** Associate of the Institution of Civil Engineers

**AInstExE** Associate of the Institute of Executive Engineers and Officers

**AInstFF** Associate of the Institute of Freight Forwarders Ltd

**AInstMO** Associate of the Institute of Market Officers

**AInstP** Associate of the Institute of Physics

**AInstPI** Associate of the Institute of Patentees and Inventors

**AINucE** Associate of the Institution of Nuclear Engineers

**AIP** American Institute of Physics • Associate of the Institute of Plumbing • Association of Independent Producers

**AIPA** Associate Member of the Institute of Practitioners in Advertising • Association internationale de psychologie appliquée (French: International Association of Applied Psychology)

**AIPO** American Institute of Public Opinion

**AIPR** Associate of the Institute of Public Relations

**AIProdE** Associate of the Institution of Production Engineers

**AIPS** Association internationale de la presse sportive (French: International Sports Press Association)

**AIQS** Associate Member of the Institute of Quantity Surveyors

**AIR** All India Radio • American Institute of Refrigeration

**AIRA** (USA) air attaché

**AIRC** Association of Independent Radio Companies

**AIRCENT** ('ɛəsɛnt) Allied Air Forces, Central Europe

**AIRCOM** ('ɛəkɒm) airways communications system

**AIREP** ('ɛərɛp) *Meteorol.* coded air to ground report

**AIRG** Agency for Intellectual Relief in Germany

**AIRH** Association internationale de recherches hydrauliques (French: International Association of Hydraulic Research)

**AIRMET** ('ɛəmɛt) *Meteorol.* regional forecast for civil aviation

**airmiss** ('ɛəmɪs) aircraft miss

**AIRPASS** ('ɛəpɑːs) aircraft interception radar and pilots attack sight system

**AIRS** *Physics, Electronics* acoustic-imaging recognition system

**AIRTE** Associate of the Institute of Road Transport Engineers

**AIRTO** Association of Independent Research and Technology Organizations

**AIS** *Commerce* agreed industry standard • Anglo-Italian Society • Association internationale de sociologie (French: International Sociological Association) • Australian Illawarra Shorthorn (cattle breed)

**AISA** Associate of the Incorporated Secretaries Association

**AISE** Association internationale des sciences économiques (French: International Economics Association)

**AISI** American Iron and Steel Institute • Associate of the Iron and Steel Institute

**AISJ** Association internationale des sciences juridiques (French: International Association of Legal Science)

**AISS** Association internationale de la sécurité sociale (French: International Social Security Association)

**AIST** (USA) Agency of Industrial Science and Technology • Associate of the Institute of Science and Technology

**AIStructE** Associate of the Institution of Structural Engineers

**AIT** Alliance internationale de tourisme (French: International Tourist Alliance) • *Meteorol.* artificial ionospheric turbulence • Asian Institute of Technology • Association of HM Inspectors of Taxes • Association of Investment Trusts

**AITA** Association internationale du théâtre d'amateurs (French: International Amateur Theatre Association)

**AITC** Association internationale des traducteurs de conférence (French: International Association of Conference Translators) • Association of Investment Trust Companies

**AITI** Associate of the Institute of Translators and Interpreters

**AITO** Association of Independent Tour Operators

**AIU** Association internationale des universités (French: International Association of Universities)

**AIV** Association internationale de volcanologie (French: International Association of Volcanology) • *Agriculture, indicating* a method of preserving fodder (initials of its inventor, Artturi Ilmari Virtanen, 1895–1973, Finnish chemist)

**AIW** (International Union of) Allied Industrial Workers of America • Atlantic-Intercoastal Waterway (Cape Cod to Florida Bay)

**AIWC** All-India Women's Conference

**AIWEM** Associate of the Institution of Water and Environmental Management

**AIWM** American Institute of Weights and Measures

**AJ** *Telecom.* anti-jam • (ital.) Archaeological Journal • Associate in Journalism • *British vehicle registration for* Middlesbrough

**AJA** American of Japanese ancestry • Anglo-Jewish Association • Australian Journalists' Association

**AJAG** Assistant Judge Advocate-General

**AJC** Australian Jockey Club

**AJCC** American Joint Committee on Cancer

**AJEX** Association of Jewish Ex-Service Men and Women

**AJPM** ad Jesum per Mariam (Latin: to Jesus through Mary)

**AJR** Association of Jewish Refugees • Australian Jurist Reports (Victoria)

**AJY** Association for Jewish Youth

**AK** *US postcode for* Alaska • automatic Kalashnikov (rifle) • Knight of the Order of Australia • *British vehicle registration for* Sheffield

**a.k.a.** (*or* **AKA**) also known as

**Akad.** Akademie (German: academy)

**AKC** American Kennel Club • Associate of King's College, London

**AKEL** (Cyprus) Anorthotikon Komma Ergazomanou Laou (Greek: Progressive Party of the Working People)

**AKFM** (Madagascar) Ankoton'ny Kongresy ny-Fahaleovantena Malagasy (Congress Party for Malagasy Independence)

**AKOE** (Cyprus) Anti-Killer Organization of Expatriates

**AKR** auroral kilometric radiation (from the earth)

**Aktb** (*or* **Akt, Aktieb**) (Sweden) Aktiebolaget (joint-stock company)

**al.** alcohol(ic) • alia (Latin: other things)

**a.l.** *Finance* allotment letter • *Commerce* après livraison (French: after delivery) • autograph letter

**Al** (ital.) *Physics, symbol for* Alfvén number • *Chem., symbol for* aluminium

**AL** Abraham Lincoln (1809–65, US president 1861–65) • *Med.* activity of living • Admiralty letter • *US postcode for* Alabama • *international vehicle registration for* Albania • *Chem.* alkyl-oxygen cleavage • América Latina (Spanish: Latin America) • *Baseball* American League • American Legion • Anglo-Latin • (small caps.) anno lucis (Latin: in the year of light) • *Physics* antistokes luminescence • army list • *British vehicle registration for* Nottingham • *postcode for* St Albans

**Ala** (*or* **ala**) *Biochem.* alanine

**Ala.** Alabama

**ALA** Air Licensing Authority • (*or* **ala**) all letters answered • American Library Association • Associate in Liberal Arts • Associate of the Library Association • Association of London Authorities • Authors' League of America

**ALAA** Associate of Library Association of Australia • Associate of the London Association of Certified Accountants

**ALAC** Artificial Limb and Appliance Centre

**ALACP** American League to Abolish Capital Punishment

**ALADI** Asociación Latino-Americana de Integración (Spanish: Latin-American Integration Association)

**ALAI** Association littéraire et artistique internationale (French: International Literary and Artistic Association)

**ALA-ISAD** American Library Association—Information Science and Automation Division

**ALAM** Associate of the London Academy of Music and Dramatic Art

**Alap** (*or* **ALAP**) ('ælæp) as low as practicable (describing radiation doses or levels)

**Alara** (*or* **ALARA**) ('ælərə) as low as reasonably achievable (describing radiation doses or levels)

**Alas.** Alaska

**alb.** *Med.* albumin

**Alb.** Albania(n) • (*or* **Alba.**) Alberta • Albion

**Alban.** Albanensis (Latin: (Bishop) of St Albans)

**ALBM** air-launched ballistic missile

**Albq.** Albuquerque

**ALBSU** Adult Literacy and Basic Skills Unit

**alc.** alcohol

**a.l.c.** à la carte

**ALC** Agricultural Land Commission • Associate of Loughborough College of Advanced Technology

**ALCAN** Aluminium Company of Canada

**ALCD** Associate of the London College of Divinity

**alch.** alchemy

**ALCM** air-launched cruise missile • Associate of London College of Music

**ALCS** Authors' Lending and Copyright Society

**Ald.** Alderman

**ALD** *Computing* automatic line drawing

**ALDEV** African Land Development

**Aldm.** Alderman

**ALE** *Insurance* additional living expense • Association for Liberal Education • *Electronics* atomic-layer epitaxy

**A level** *Education* Advanced level

**ALF** Animal Liberation Front • Arab Liberation Front (Iraq) • (*or* **Alf**) automatic letter facer (Post Office sorting machine)

**ALFSEA** Allied Land Forces South-East Asia

**alg.** algebra(ic)

**a.l.g.** advanced landing ground

**Alg.** Algeria(n) • Algiers

**ALG** *Med.* antilymphocyte globulin

**ALGES** Association of Local Government Engineers and Surveyors

**ALGFO** Association of Local Government Financial Officers

**Algol** (*or* **ALGOL**) ('ælgɒl) *Computing* algorithmic language

**ALH** Australian Light Horse

**ALI** American Library Institute • Argyll Light Infantry • Associate of the Landscape Institute

**ALICE** ('ælɪs) Autistic and Language-Impaired Children's Education

**align.** alignment

**ALJ** Administration Law Judge • Australian Law Journal

**ALJR** Australian Law Journal Reports

**alk.** alkali

**ALL** acute lymphatic (lymphoblastic, lymphocytic, *or* lymphoid) leukaemia

**ALLC** Association for Literary and Linguistic Computing

**alleg.** allegory

**All H.** All Hallows

**all'ingr.** all'ingrosso (Italian: wholesale)

**allo.** *Music* allegro

**all'ott.** *Music* all'ottava (Italian; play an octave higher)

**All S.** All Souls

**All SS** All Saints

**ALM** *Med.* alveolar lining material • audiolingual method (in teaching a foreign language) • Master of the Liberal Arts (Latin *Artium Liberalium Magister*)

**ALN** *Med.* axillary lymph nodes

**ALNA** Armée de libération nationale d'Angola (French: Angolan National Liberation Army)

**ALO** air liaison officer • allied liaison officer

**ALOE** A Lady of England (pseudonym of Charlotte M. Tucker, 1821–93, British novelist)

**alp.** alpine

**ALP** American Labor Party • Australian Labor Party • automated learning process • (USA) automated library program

**ALPA** Air Line Pilots' Association

**ALPAL** *Computing* A Livermore Physics Applications Language

**alph.** alphabetical

**ALPO** Association of Land and Property Owners • Association of Lunar and Planetary Observers

**ALPSP** Association of Learned and Professional Society Publishers

**ALPURCOMS** all-purpose communications system

**alr** aliter (Latin: otherwise)

**ALR** American Law Reports

**ALRC** Anti-Locust Research Centre

**ALRI** airborne long-range input

**ALS** accident localization system · Agricultural Land Service · *Med.* amyotrophic lateral sclerosis · *Immunol.* antilymphocytic serum · *Aeronautics* approach lighting systems · Associate of the Linnean Society · (*or* **a.l.s.**) autograph letter signed · automated library system

**Alsat.** Alsatian

**al seg.** *Music* al segno (Italian: to (*or* at) the sign)

**ALSEP** Apollo Lunar Surface Experiment Package

**alt.** alteration · alternate · alternative · alternator · altimeter · altitude · alto

**Alt.** Altesse (French: Highness)

**ALT** Agricultural Land Tribunal · *Biochem., Med.* alanine aminotransferase

**Alta.** Alberta

**alt. dieb.** *Med.* alternis diebus (Latin: every other day)

**alter.** alteration

**alt. hor.** *Med.* alternis horis (Latin: every other hour)

**alt. noct.** *Med.* alternis noctibus (Latin: every other night)

**ALTPR** Association of London Theatre Press Representatives

**ALTU** Association of Liberal Trade Unionists

**ALU** *Computing* arithmetic and logic unit

**alum.** aluminium · alumna(e) · alumnus (*or* alumni)

**ALV** *Microbiol.* avian leucosis virus

**ALWR** *Nuclear physics* advanced light-water reactor

**am** *Physics, symbol for* attometre(s)

**am.** ammeter · ammunition

**a.m.** amplitude modulation · ante meridiem (Latin: before noon)

**a/m** above mentioned

**aM** (*or* **a/M**) am Main (German: on the River Main; after place names)

**Am** *Chem., symbol for* americium

**Am.** America(n) · *Bible* Amos

**AM** Academy of Management · administrative memorandum · air mail · *Astronautics* airlock module · Air Marshal · Air Ministry · Albert Medal · (*or* **A-M**) Alpes-Maritimes (department of France) · *Radio* amplitude modulation · *Physics* angular momentum · (small caps.) anno mundi (Latin: in the year of the world) · annus mirabilis (Latin: year of wonders; 1666) · ante meridiem (*see under* a.m.) · area manager · army manual · assistant

manager · Associate Member · *Insurance* assurance mutuelle (French: mutual insurance) · Ave Maria (Latin: Hail Mary) · Award of Merit (from the Royal Horticultural Society) · (USA) Master of Arts (Latin *Artium Magister*) · Member of the Order of Australia · *British vehicle registration for* Swindon

**AMA** against medical advice · American Management Association · American Marketing Association · American Medical Association · American Missionary Association · American Motorcycle Association · Assistant Masters Association · Associate of the Museums Association · Association of Metropolitan Authorities · Australian Medical Association

**AMAB** Army Medical Advisory Board

**AMAE** American Museum of Atomic Energy

**amal.** amalgamated

**AMAmIEE** Associate Member of the American Institute of Electrical Engineers

**AMARC** Associated Marine and Related Charities

**AMASCE** Associate Member of the American Society of Civil Engineers

**amat.** amateur

**AMAusIMM** Associate Member of the Australasian Institute of Mining and Metallurgy

**Amb.** (*or* **Ambas.**) Ambassador · ambulance

**AMB** Air Ministry bulletin · (USA) Airways Modernization Board

**AMBAC** Associate Member of the British Association of Chemists

**ambig.** ambiguous

**AMC** (USA) Aerospace Manufacturers' Council · Agricultural Mortgage Corporation Ltd · American Motors Corporation · (USA) Army Missile Command · (USA) Army Mobile Command · (USA) Army Munitions Command · Art Master's Certificate · Association of Management Consultants · Association of Municipal Corporations

**AMCA** Architectural Metal Craftsmen's Association

**AMCIB** Associate Member of the Corporation of Insurance Brokers

**AMCIOB** Associate Member of the Chartered Institute of Building

**AMCL** Association of Metropolitan Chief Librarians

**AMCOS** ('æmkɒs) Aldermaston Mechanized Cataloguing and Ordering System (in the Atomic Energy Authority)

**AMCS** airborne missile control system

**AMCT** Associate of the Manchester College of Technology

**am. cur.** *Law* amicus curiae (Latin: a friend of the court)

**amd** amend

**AMD** acid-mine drainage · Admiralty machinery depot · aerospace medical division · air movement data · *Meteorol.* amend · Army Medical Department

**AMDB** Agricultural Machinery Development Board

**AMDEA** Association of Manufacturers of Domestic Electrical Appliances

**AMDEC** Agricultural Marketing Development Executive Committee

**AMDG** ad majorem Dei gloriam (Latin: to the greater glory of God; the Jesuit motto)

**amdt** amendment

**AME** (USA) Advanced Master of Education · African Methodist Episcopal · Association of Municipal Engineers

**AMEC** Australian Minerals and Energy Council

**AMEDS** (*or* **AMedS**) (USA) Army Medical Service

**AMEE** Admiralty Marine Engineering Establishment · Association of Managerial Electrical Executives

**AMEIC** Associate Member of the Engineering Institute of Canada

**AMEM** African Methodist Episcopal Mission

**Am. Emb.** American Embassy

**AMEME** Association of Mining Electrical and Mechanical Engineers

**amend.** (*or* **amendt**) amendment

**Amer. Ind.** American Indian

**Amer. Std.** American Standard

**AMES** Air Ministry Experimental Station · Association of Marine Engineering Schools

**AMet** Associate of Metallurgy

**AMEWA** Associated Manufacturers of Electric Wiring Accessories

**Amex** ('æmɛks) American Express · American Stock Exchange

**AMEZC** African Methodist Episcopal Zion Church

**AMF** Australian Marine Force · Australian Military Forces

**amg** among

**a.m.g.** *Aeronautics* automatic magnetic guidance

**AMG** Allied Military Government

**AMGO** Assistant Master-General of Ordnance

**AMGOT** Allied Military Government of Occupied Territory (in World War II)

**a.m.i.** *Military* advanced manned interceptor · *Aeronautics* air mileage indicator

**AMI** *Med.* acute myocardial infarction · American Meat Institute · American Military Institute · Ancient Monuments Inspectorate · Association Montessori internationale (French: International Montessori Association)

**AMIAE** Associate Member of the Institution of Automobile Engineers

**AMIAP** Associate Member of the Institution of Analysts and Programmers

**AMIBF** Associate Member of the Institute of British Foundrymen

**AMICEI** Associate Member of the Institution of Civil Engineers of Ireland

**AMIChemE** Associate Member of the Institution of Chemical Engineers

**AMICW** Associate Member of the Institute of Clerks of Works of Great Britain

**AMIE** Associate Member of the Institute of Engineers and Technicians

**AMIE(Aust)** Associate Member of the Institution of Engineers, Australia

**AMIED** Associate Member of the Institute of Engineering Designers

**AMIE(Ind)** Associate Member of the Institution of Engineers, India

**AMIElecIE** Associate Member of the Institution of Electrical and Electronic Incorporated Engineers

**AMIERE** Associate Member of the Institute of Electronic and Radio Engineers

**AMIEx** Associate Member of the Institute of Export

**AMIFireE** Associate Member of the Institution of Fire Engineers

**AMIGasE** Associate Member of the Institution of Gas Engineers

**AMIH** Associate Member of the Institute of Housing

**AMIHT** Associate Member of the Institution of Highways and Transportation

**AMII** Association of Musical Instrument Industries

**AMIIM** Associate Member of the Institution of Industrial Managers

**AMILocoE** Associate Member of the Institution of Locomotive Engineers

**AMIMarE** Associate Member of the Institute of Marine Engineers

**AMIMGTechE** Associate Member of the Institution of Mechanical and General Technician Engineers

**AMIMI** Associate Member of the Institute of the Motor Industry

**AMIMinE** Associate Member of the Institution of Mining Engineers

**AMIMM** Associate Member of the Institution of Mining and Metallurgy

**Am. Ind.** American Indian

**AMinIsTech** Associate in Minerals Technology

**AMInstBE** Associate Member of the Institution of British Engineers

**AmInstEE** American Institute of Electrical Engineers

**AMInstR** Associate Member of the Institute of Refrigeration

**AMInstTA** Associate Member of the Institute of Traffic Administration

**AMINucE** Associate Member of the Institution of Nuclear Engineers

**AMIOP** Associate Member of the Institute of Printing

**AMIPA** Associate Member of the Institute of Practitioners in Advertising

**AMIPE** Associate Member of the Institution of Production Engineers

**AMIPM** Associate Member of the Institute of Personnel Management

**AMIPRE** Associate Member of the Incorporated Practitioners in Radio and Electronics

**AMIProdE** Associate Member of the Institution of Production Engineers

**AMIQM** Associate Member of the Institute of Quality Assurance

**AMIRA** Australian Mineral Industries Research Association

**AMIRSE** Associate Member of the Institute of Railway Signalling Engineers

**AMIStructE** Associate Member of the Institution of Structural Engineers

**AMITA** Associate Member of the Industrial Transport Association

**AMITE** (USA) Associate Member of the Institute of Traffic Engineers

**AMIWEM** Associate Member of the Institution of Water and Environmental Management

**AMIWM** Associate Member of the Institution of Works Managers

**AMJ** Assemblée mondiale de la jeunesse (French: World Assembly of Youth)

**AML** abandoned mine land • acute myelocytic (myeloid, or myelogenous) leukaemia • Admiralty materials laboratory • (New Zealand) applied mathematics laboratory

**AMLS** (USA) Master of Arts in Library Science

**amm.** ammunition

**AMM** Physics anomalous magnetic moment • antimissile missile • assistant marketing manager • Association médicale mondiale (French: World Medical Association)

**AMMA** (or **Amma**) ('æmə) Assistant Masters' and Mistresses' Association

**AMMI** American Merchant Marine Institute

**amn** ammunition

**AMNECInst** Associate Member of the North East Coast Institution of Engineers and Shipbuilders

**AMNILP** Associate Member of the National Institute of Licensing Practitioners

**AMNZIE** Associate Member of the New Zealand Institution of Engineers

**AMO** Air Ministry order • Biochem. anaerobic methane oxidation • area medical officer • assistant medical officer

**AMOB** automatic meteorological oceanographic buoy

**AMORC** Ancient Mystical Order Rosae Crucis (Rosicrucians)

**amort.** amortization

**AMOS** automatic meteorological observing station

**amp.** amperage • ampere • amplified • amplitude

**AMP** Biochem. adenosine monophosphate • Air Member for Personnel (in the RAF) • Associated Master Plumbers and Domestic Engineers • Australian Mutual Provident Society

**AMPAS** (USA) Academy of Motion Picture Arts and Sciences

**AMPC** (USA) automatic message processing center • auxiliary military pioneer corps

**amph.** amphibian • amphibious

**AMPHIBEX** ('æmfɪbɛks) amphibious exercise

**ampl.** amplifier

**AMPS** automatic message processing system

**AMPSS** advanced manned precision strike system

**AMQ** American medical qualification

**AMR** Atlantic missile range • automated meter reading • automatic message routing

**Amraam** ('æm,rɑːm) advanced medium-range air-to-air missile

**AMRINA** Associate Member of the Royal Institution of Naval Architects

**Amrit.** Amritsar

**AMRO** Association of Medical Record Officers

**AMRS** Air Ministry radio station

**AMS** *Physics* accelerator mass spectrometry (*or* spectrometer) • accident-monitoring system • (USA) Agricultural Marketing Service • American Mathematical Society • American Meteorological Society • American Microscopical Society • American Musicological Society • Ancient Monuments Society • *Physics* anisotropy of magnetic susceptibility • *Astronautics* Apollo mission simulator • army map service • army medical services (*or* staff) • Assistant Military Secretary • Australian medical services • automatic music search

**AMSA** advanced manned strategic aircraft

**AMSAIEE** Associate Member of the South African Institution of Electrical Engineering

**Am. Sam.** American Samoa

**AMSAM** antimissile surface-to-air missile

**AMSE** Associate Member of the Society of Engineers

**AMSEF** antiminesweeping explosive float

**AMSERT** Associate Member of the Society of Electronic and Radio Technicians

**AMSGA** Association of Manufacturers and Suppliers for the Graphic Arts

**AMSL** above mean sea level

**AMSO** Air Member for Supply and Organization (in the RAF) • Association of Market Survey Organizations

**AMSST** Associate of the Society of Surveying Technicians

**Amst.** Amsterdam

**AMSW** (USA) Master of Arts in Social Work

**amt** amount

**AMT** Academy of Medicine, Toronto • (*or* **a.m.t.**) airmail transfer • Air Member for Training (in the RAF) • (USA) alternative minimum tax • area management team • Associate in Mechanical Technology • Associate in Medical Technology • Association of Marine Traders • (USA) Master of Arts in Teaching

**AMTA** Association of Multiple Travel Agents

**AMTC** Academic Member of the Trinity College of Music • Art Master's Teaching Certificate

**AMTDA** Agricultural Machinery Tractor Dealers' Association

**AMTE** Admiralty Marine Technology Establishment

**AMTI** airborne moving target indicator

**AMTRI** Advanced Manufacturing Technology Research Institute

**AMTS** Associate Member of the Television Society

**amu** (*or* **a.m.u.**) *Physics* atomic mass unit

**AMU** (USA) Associated Midwestern Universities • Association of Master Upholsterers

**AMUA** (Australia) Associate of Music, University of Adelaide

**AMus** Associate in Music

**AMusD** Doctor of Musical Arts

**AMusLCM** Associate in Music, London College of Music

**AMusTCL** Associate in Music, Trinity College of Music, London

**AMV** Association mondiale vétérinaire (French: World Veterinary Association) • *Microbiol.* avian myeloblastosis virus

**AMVAP** Associated Manufacturers of Veterinary and Agricultural Products

**AMVERS** automated merchant vessel report system

**AMVETS** ('æmvɛts) American Veterans (of World War II and subsequent wars)

**AMW** average molecular weight

**an.** anno (Latin: in the year) • anonymous • answer

**a.n.** above named

**An** *Chem.*, *symbol for* actinon

**An.** Annam

**AN** *Chem.* acid number • *Chem.* amino-1-naphthol • *Chem.* ammonium nitrate • Anglo-Norman • *airline flight code for* Ansett Australia • *Med.* antenatal • Associate in Nursing • *Physics* audible noise • *Med.* avascular necrosis • *British vehicle registration for* Reading

**A/N** advice note

**ANA** All Nippon Airways • American Nature Association • American Neurological Association • American Newspaper Association • American Numismatic Association • American Nurses' Association • *Commerce* Article Number Association • (USA) Associate National Academician • Association of Nurse Administrators • Australian Natives' Association

**anac.** (*or* **anacr.**) anacreon

**anaes.** anaesthesia • anaesthetic

**anag.** anagram

**anal.** analogous • analogy • analyse • analysis • analytic

**ANAPO** (Colombia) Alianza Nacional Popular (Spanish: National Popular Alliance)

**ANARE** Australian National Antarctic Research Expedition

**anat.** anatomical • anatomy

**anc.** ancient

**ANC** *Chem.* acid-neutralizing capacity • advanced nuclear computer • African National Congress • Army Nurse Corps • Australian Newspapers Council

**anch.** anchored

**ANCOM** ('ænkɒm) Andean Common Market

**anct.** ancient

**ANCUN** Australian National Committee for the United Nations

**and.** *Music* andante (Italian; at a moderate speed)

**And** *Astronomy* Andromeda

**AND** *international vehicle registration for* Andorra • (ænd) *Computing, Electronics* and (from its sense in logic, as in **AND gate**, **AND operation**)

**ANDB** (USA) Air Navigation Development Board

**ANEC** American Nuclear Energy Council

**ANECInst** Associate of the North-East Coast Institution of Engineers and Shipbuilders

**ANERI** (USA) Advanced Nuclear Equipment Research Institute

**anes.** (USA) anesthetic

**ANF** (USA) Advanced Nuclear Fuels (Corporation) • antinuclear factor • Atlantic Nuclear Force • *Med.* atrial natriuretic factor • Australian National Flag Association

**ang.** angle • angular

**Ang.** Anglesey

**ANG** (USA) Air National Guard • Australian Newspaper Guild

**ANGB** (USA) Air National Guard Base

**Angl.** Angleterre (French: England) • Anglican • Anglicized

**Anglo-Fr.** Anglo-French

**Anglo-Ind.** Anglo-Indian

**Anglo-Ir.** Anglo-Irish

**Anglo-L.** Anglo-Latin

**Anglo-Sax.** Anglo-Saxon

**ANGUS** Air National Guard of the United States

**Anh.** Anhang (German: appendix; of a book, etc.)

**anhyd.** (*or* **anhydr.**) *Chem.* anhydrous

**ANI** (Portugal) Agência de Notícias de Informações (news agency) • (Uruguay) Agencia Nacional de Informaciones (national press agency) • (Portugal) Agência Nacional de Informações (national information agency) • American Nuclear Insurers

**anim.** *Music* animato (Italian: in a lively manner)

**Ank.** Ankunft (German: arrival)

**ANL** (ital.) Archaeological News Letter • (USA) Argonne National Laboratory • *Engineering* automatic noise limiting • National Library of Australia

**Anm.** Anmerkung (German: note)

**ANM** Admiralty Notices to Mariners

**ann.** annals • anni (Latin: years) • anno (Latin: in the year) • annual • annuity

**ANN** *Telecom.* all-figures numbers now

**ANNA** (USA) Army–Navy–NASA–Air Force satellite

**anniv.** anniversary

**annot.** annotate • annotation • annotator

**annuit.** annuitant

**annul.** annulment

**Annunc.** Annunciation

**ANO** (USA) Association of Nuclear Operators

**anon.** anonymous(ly)

**ANOVA** ('ænəʊvə) *Maths.* analysis of variance

**ANP** advanced nursing practice • aircraft nuclear propulsion • (Netherlands) Algemeen Nederlands Persbureau (independent news agency) • ammonium nitrate–phosphate (fertilizer) • Australian National Party

**ANPA** American Newspaper Publishers' Association • Australian National Publicity Association

**anr** another

**anrac** ('ænræk) aids navigation radio control

**ANRC** American National Red Cross • Australian National Research Council

**ANRE** advanced nuclear rocket engine

**ANRPC** Association of Natural Rubber Producing Countries

**ans.** answer

**a.n.s.** autograph note signed

**ANS** *Physics* advanced neutron source • American Nuclear Society • Army News Service • Army Nursing Service • *Computing* artificial neural system • *Anatomy, Zoology* autonomic nervous system

**ANSA** (Italy) Agenzia Nazionale Stampa Associata (national press agency)

**ANSI** ('ænsɪ) American National Standards Institute

**ANSI-SPARC** American National Standards Institute/Systems Planning and Requirements Committee

**ANSL** Australian National Standards Laboratory

**ANSP** Academy of Natural Sciences of Philadelphia • Australian National Socialist Party

**ANSR** advanced neutron source reactor

**ANSTI** African Network of Scientific and Technological Institutions

**ANSTO** Australian Nuclear Science and Technology Organization

**ant.** antenna • anterior • antilog • antiquarian • antique • antiquity • antonym

**Ant** *Astronomy* Antlia

**Ant.** Antarctica • Antigua • Antrim

**ANTA** ('æntə) American National Theatre and Academy • Australian National Travel Association

**Antarc.** Antarctic

**anthol.** anthology

**anthrop.** (*or* **anthropol.**) anthropological • anthropology

**Antig.** Antigua

**antilog** ('æntɪˌlɒg) antilogarithm

**antiq.** antiquarian • antiquity

**Ant. Lat.** antique Latin

**ant. ld.** *Printing* antique laid (paper)

**anton.** antonym

**ANTOR** Association of National Tourist Office Representatives

**Antr.** Antrim

**Ants. J.** (ital.) Antiquaries Journal

**ant. wo.** *Printing* antique wove (paper)

**ANU** Australian National University

**ANWR** Arctic National Wildlife Refuge

**anx** annex

**ANZ** Australia and New Zealand Banking Group

**ANZAAS** ('ænzəs, -zæs) Australian and New Zealand Association for the Advancement of Science

**Anzac** ('ænzæk) Australian and New Zealand Army Corps (in World War I)

**ANZAM** ('ænzæm) Australia, New Zealand, and Malaysia (defence strategy for SE Asia)

**ANZAMRS** Australian and New Zealand Association for Medieval and Renaissance Studies

**ANZCAN** Australia, New Zealand, and Canada

**ANZIA** Associate of the New Zealand Institute of Architects

**ANZIC** Associate of the New Zealand Institute of Chemistry

**ANZLA** Associate of the New Zealand Library Association

**ANZUK** ('ænzək) Australian, New Zealand, and United Kingdom (defence force in Singapore and Malaysia)

**ANZUS** ('ænzəs) Australia, New Zealand, and the United States (referring to the security alliance between them)

**aO** (*or* **a/O**) an der Oder (German: on the River Oder; after place names)

**AO** Accountant Officer • *Chem.* acridine orange (dye) • air ordnance • (small caps.) anno ordinis (Latin: in the year of the order) • *Chem.* anthracene oil • area office • army order • *Physics* atomic orbital • Australian Opera • *British vehicle registration for* Carlisle • Officer of the Order of Australia

**A/O** (*or* **a/o**) *Accounting* account of • and others

**AOA** (USA) Administration on Aging • Aerodrome Owners' Association • Air Officer in charge of Administration • American Ordnance Association • American Orthopedic Association • American Osteopathic Association • American Overseas Association

**a.o.b.** any other business • at or below

**AOB** advanced operational base • Antediluvian Order of Buffaloes • any other business

**AOC** Air Officer Commanding • (small caps.) anno orbis Conditi (Latin: in the year of the Creation) • *Chem.* anodic oxide coating • (*or* **AC**) appellation (d'origine) contrôlée (French: controlled place of origin; wine classification) • Army Ordnance Corps • Artists of Chelsea

**AOCB** any other competent business

**AOC-in-C** Air Officer Commanding-in-Chief

**AOCM** *US Air Force* aircraft out of commission for maintenance

**AOD** acousto-optic device • advanced ordnance depot • Ancient Order of Druids • Army Ordnance Department

**AOER** Army Officers' Emergency Reserve

**AOF** Afrique Occidentale Française (French: French West Africa) • Ancient Order of Foresters • *Chem.* anode oxide film • Australian Olympic Federation

**A of F** Admiral of the Fleet

**AOFP** absolute open-flow potential

**A of S** Academy of Science

**AOG** aircraft on ground

**AOH** Ancient Order of Hibernians

**AoI** aims of industry

**a.o.i.v.** *Engineering* automatically operated inlet valve

**A-OK** (USA) all (systems) OK

**AOL** (USA) absent over leave • Admiralty Oil Laboratory • (USA) Atlantic Oceanographic Laboratories (Environmental Science Services Administration) • (Canada) Atlantic Oceanographic Laboratory (Bedford Institute of Oceanography)

**AOM** amorphous organic matter

**AONB** area of outstanding natural beauty

**AOP** Association of Optical Practitioners

**AOPU** Asian Oceanic Postal Union

**AOQ** average outgoing quality

**AOQL** average outgoing quality limit

**aor.** aorist

**a/or** and/or

**AOR** acetate-oxidizing rod-shaped (bacterium) • *Music* adult-oriented rock • *Law* (USA) advice of rights • *Music* album-oriented rock • *Music* (USA) album-oriented radio

**AOS** *Astronautics* acquisition of signal • American Opera Society • American Ophthalmological Society • Ancient Order of Shepherds • automated office system

**AOSM** (New Zealand) Associate of the Otago School of Mines

**AOSO** advanced orbiting solar observatory

**AOSS** Fellow of the American Oriental Society (Latin *Americanae Orientalis Societatis Socius*)

**AOSTRA** Alberta Oil Sands Technology and Research Authority

**AOSW** Association of Official Shorthand Writers

**AOT** *Engineering* allowed outage (*or* out-of-service) time

**AOU** American Ornithologists' Union

**ap.** apothecary • apparent • apud (Latin: in the works of *or* according to)

**a.p.** above proof • additional premium • advanced post • *Med.* ante prandium (Latin: before a meal; in prescriptions) • *Maths.* arithmetical progression • author's proof

**Ap.** apostle • April

**AP** *Physics* acoustic plasmon • *Physiol.* action potential • (*or* **A/P**) *Insurance* additional premium • *Grammar* adjective phrase • aerosol particle • (USA) airplane • (USA) Air Police • air pollution • air publication (Ministry of Defence) • (Spain) Alianza Popular (Popular Alliance; political party) • *Chem.* alkaline permanganate • *Biochem.* alkaline phosphatase • (USA) American plan (of paying hotel bills) • *Chem.* ammonium perchlorate • *Surveying* Amsterdamsch Peil (German: Amsterdam level; mean level used in the Netherlands, Belgium, and N Germany) • Andhra Pradesh • *Med.* angina pectoris • *Med.* anteroposterior • *Med.* anterior pituitary • antipersonnel • *Commerce* à protester (French: to be protested; on bills of exchange) • armour-piercing • *Computing* array processor • *Med.* arterial (blood) pressure • Associated Presbyterian • Associated Press • atomic power • (*or* **A/p**) authority to pay (*or* purchase) • automotive products • *Insurance* average payable • *British vehicle registration for Brighton* • *international civil aircraft marking for Pakistan*

**APA** *Taxation* additional personal allowance • Alaska Power Authority • (Australia) All Parties Administration • American Philological Association • American Physicists Association • American Pilots Association • American Press Association • American Protestant Association • American Psychiatric Association • American Psychological Association • *Telecom.* annular phased array • Associate in Public Administration • Association for the Prevention of

Addiction • Association of Public Analysts • Australian Physiotherapy Association • Austria Presse Agentur (Austrian Press Agency)

**6-APA** *Biochem.* 6-aminopenicillanic acid

**APACL** Asian People's Anti-Communist League

**APACS** Association for Payment Clearing Services

**APAE** Association of Public Address Engineers

**APANZ** Associate of the Public Accountants of New Zealand

**apart.** apartment

**a-part.** *Physics* alpha particle

**APB** all-points bulletin (police alert)

**APBA** American Power Boat Association

**APBF** Accredited Poultry Breeders' Federation

**APC** *Engineering* advanced process control • *Bacteriol.* aerobic plate count • air-pollution control • (Sierra Leone) All People's Congress • American Philatelic Congress • *Immunol.* antigen-presenting cell • Appalachian Power Company • armoured personnel carrier • Assistant Principal Chaplain • Associated Portland Cement • automatic phase control • *Electronics* automatic power control • automatic public convenience

**APCA** (USA) Air Pollution Control Association • Anglo-Polish Catholic Association

**APCK** Association for Promoting Christian Knowledge (in the Church of Ireland)

**APCN** (small caps.) anno post Christum natum (Latin: in the year after the birth of Christ)

**APCO** Association of Pleasure Craft Operators

**APCOL** All-Pakistan Confederation of Labour

**apd** approved

**APD** Administrative Planning Division • (USA) Air Pollution Division • Army Pay Department

**APDC** Apple and Pear Development Council

**Ap. Deleg.** Apostolic Delegate

**APE** Amalgamated Power Engineering • automatic photomapping equipment • *Physics* available potential energy

**APEC** ('eɪpɛk) Asia-Pacific Economic Cooperation Conference

**APEX** ('eɪpɛks) Advance-Purchase Excursion (reduced airline or rail fare) • Association of Professional, Executive, Clerical, and Computer Staff (now amalgamated with GMB)

**APF** Association for the Propagation of the Faith

**APFC** Asia-Pacific Forestry Commission

**APFIM** *Chem., Physics* atom-probe field-ion microscopy

**APG** *US Air Force* air proving ground

**APGA** American Public Gas Association

**aph.** aphorism

**APH** *Optics* adjusting, principal axis, hyperspherical • A(lan) P(atrick) Herbert (1890–1971, British writer and politician) • *Obstetrics* antepartum haemorrhage • *Biochem.* anterior pituitary hormone

**APHA** American Public Health Association

**aphet.** aphetic

**APHIS** ('eɪfɪs) (USA) Animal and Plant Health Inspection Service

**API** air-pollution index • air-position indicator • American Petroleum Institute (*see also* API scale) • *Computing* application programmer interface • Association phonétique internationale (French: International Phonetic Association) • atmospheric pressure ionization

**APIS** Army Photographic Intelligence Service

**API scale** American Petroleum Institute scale (for measuring the specific gravity of petroleum products)

**ap. J-C** (France) après Jésus-Christ (after Jesus Christ; AD)

**Apl** April

**APL** Alberta Power Limited • alternating polarization laser • (USA) Applied Physics Laboratory (Johns Hopkins University) • *Computing* A Programming Language

**APLA** ('æplə) Azanian People's Liberation Army

**APLE** Association of Public Lighting Engineers

**APM** (USA) Academy of Physical Medicine • airborne particulate matter • Assistant Paymaster • Assistant Provost-Marshal

**APMC** Allied Political and Military Commission

**APMG** Assistant Postmaster-General

**APMI** Associate of the Pensions Management Institute

**apmt** appointment

**APN** (ex-USSR) Agentstvo Pechati Novosti (news press agency)

**APNEC** All-Pakistan Newspaper Employees' Confederation

**apo.** apogee

**APO** acting pilot officer • African People's Organization • Armed Forces (*or* Army) Post Office • Asian Productivity Organization

**Apoc.** Apocalypse • (*or* **Apocr.**) Apocrypha(l)

**apog.** apogee

**apos.** apostrophe

**APOTA** automatic positioning telemetering antenna

**apoth.** apothecary

**app.** apparatus • apparent(ly) • appeal • appended • appendix (of a book) • applied • appointed • apprentice • approved • approximate(ly)

**App.** Apostles

**APP** African People's Party (of Kenya; now part of KANU)

**APPA** African Petroleum Producers Association

**appar.** apparatus • apparent(ly)

**appd** approved

**APPES** American Institute of Chemical Engineers Physical Properties Estimation System

**APPITA** (*or* **Appita**) ('æpɪtə) Australian Pulp and Paper Industries Technical Association

**appl.** appeal • appellant • applicable • applied

**appos.** appositive

**appr.** apprentice

**APPR** (USA) Army Package Power Reactor

**appro** ('æprəʊ) approbation • approval

**approx.** approximate(ly)

**apps** appendices

**appt** appoint • appointment

**apptd** appointed

**APPU** Australian Primary Producers' Union

**appurts** appurtenances

**appx** appendix (of a book)

**Apr.** April

**APR** Accredited Public Relations Practitioner • annual percentage rate (of interest) • annual progress report • annual

purchase rate (in hire-purchase schemes)

**APRA** Air Public Relations Association

**APRC** (small caps.) anno post Romam conditam (Latin: in the year after the foundation of Rome)

**APRI** Associate of the Plastics and Rubber Institute

**A/Prin.** Assistant Principal

**apr. J-C** (France) après Jésus-Christ (*see* ap. J-C)

**APRS** *Navigation* acoustic position reference system • Association for the Protection of Rural Scotland • Association of Professional Recording Studios

**a.p.s.** autograph poem signed

**Aps** *Astronomy* Apus

**APS** (Australia) Aborigines' Protection Society • *Physics* advanced photon source • American Peace Society • American Philatelic Society • American Philosophical Society • American Physics Society • American Physiological Society • American Protestant Society • *Chem., Physics* appearance-potential spectroscopy • Arizona Public Service (Company) • army postal service • Assistant Private Secretary • Associate of the Philosophical Society

**APSA** American Political Science Association • Associate of the Photographic Society of America • Australian Political Studies Association

**APSE** (æps) *Computing* Ada programming support environment

**APSL** Acting Paymaster Sublieutenant

**APsSI** Associate of the Psychological Society of Ireland

**APST** Association of Professional Scientists and Technologists

**APSW** Association of Psychiatric Social Workers

**apt.** apartment

**APT** advanced passenger train • advanced process technology • *Nautical* after peak tank • *Med.* alum-precipitated (diphtheria) toxoid • Association of Polytechnic Teachers • Association of Printing Technologists • Association of Private Traders • automatic picture transmission (from satellites)

**APTC** Army Physical Training Corps

**APTI** Association of Principals of Technical Institutions

**APTIS** all-purpose ticket-issuing systems

**APTS** *Astronautics* Automatic Picture Transmission Subsystem (in NASA)

**APTU** African Postal and Telecommunications Union

**APU** acute psychiatric unit (of a prison, etc.) • Arab Postal Union • *Education* Assessment of Performance Unit (body monitoring pupil performance) • *Aeronautics* auxiliary power unit

**APUC** Association for Promoting Unity of Christendom

**APW** *Optics* approximation of plane waves

**APWA** All Pakistan Women's Association • American Public Welfare (*or* Works) Association

**APWR** advanced pressurized water reactor

**APWU** American Postal Workers Union

**aq.** aqua (Latin: water) • aqueous

**Aq.** *Horticulture* aquatic

**AQ** *Psychol.* accomplishment (*or* achievement) quotient • *Military* Administration and Quartering

**aq. bull.** *Pharmacol.* aqua bulliens (Latin: boiling water)

**AQC** Associate of Queen's College, London

**aq. cal.** *Pharmacol.* aqua calida (Latin: warm water)

**aq. com.** *Pharmacol.* aqua communis (Latin: tap water)

**aq. dest.** *Pharmacol.* aqua destillata (Latin: distilled water)

**aq. ferv.** *Pharmacol.* aqua fervens (Latin: hot water)

**aq. frig.** *Pharmacol.* aqua frigida (Latin: cold water)

**AQI** air-quality index

**Aql** *Astronomy* Aquila

**AQL** acceptable quality level

**AQM** *Physics* additive quark model

**AQMG** Assistant Quartermaster-General

**aq. m.pip.** *Pharmacol.* aqua menthae piperitae (Latin: peppermint water)

**aq. pur.** *Pharmacol.* aqua pura (Latin: pure water)

**Aqr** *Astronomy* Aquarius

**aq. tep.** *Pharmacol.* aqua tepida (Latin: tepid water)

**aque.** aqueduct

**ar.** arrival • arrive(s) *or* arrived

**a.r.** (*or* **a/r, A/r**) *Insurance* all risks • anno regni (Latin: in the year of the reign)

**Ar** *Chem., symbol for* argon • *Chem., symbol for* aryl group

**Ar.** Arabia(n) • Arabic • Aramaic

**AR** *Psychol.* accomplishment (*or* achievement) ratio • (*or* **A/R**) account receivable • acid resisting • acrylic rubber • *Med.* acute rejection • *Physiol.* adrenergic receptor (*or* adrenoceptor) • advice of receipt • (Poland) Agencja Robotnicza (Workers' Press Agency) • (USA) airman recruit • Altesse Royale (French: Royal Highness) • *Chem.* analytical reagent • *Physiol.* androgen receptor • Anna Regina (Latin: Queen Anne) • (ital.) Annual Register of World Events • annual report • *Taxation* annual return • *Med.* aortic regurgitation • *Numismatics* argentum (Latin: silver) • *US postcode for* Arkansas • Army Regulations • Assistant Resident • Associated Rediffusion • *Image technol.* aspect ratio • (ex-USSR) Autonomous Region • *British fishing port registration for* Ayr • *British vehicle registration for* Chelmsford

**ARA** Aircraft Research Association • American Railway Association • Army Rifle Association • Associate of the Royal Academy • (New Zealand) Auckland Regional Authority

**Arab.** Arabia(n) • Arabic

**ARAC** Associate of the Royal Agricultural College

**arach.** arachnology

**ARACI** Associate of the Royal Australian Chemical Institute

**ARAD** Associate of the Royal Academy of Dancing

**ARAeS** Associate of the Royal Aeronautical Society

**ARAIA** Associate of the Royal Australian Institute of Architects

**Aram.** Aramaic

**ARAM** Associate of the Royal Academy of Music

**ARAMCO** Arabian-American Oil Company

**ARAS** Associate of the Royal Astronomical Society • atomic resonance absorption spectroscopy

**arb.** arbiter • arbitrageur • arbitrary • arbitration • arbitrator

**ARB** *Civil aviation* Air Registration Board • Air Research Bureau

**ARBA** Associate of the Royal Society of British Artists

**ARBE** (Belgium) Académie Royale des Beaux-Arts, École Supérieure des Arts Décoratifs et École Supérieure d'Architecture de Bruxelles (Brussels Royal Academy of Fine Arts)

**arbor.** arboriculture

**ARBS** Associate of the Royal Society of British Sculptors

**arc.** *Music* arcato *or* coll'arco (Italian: with the bow)

**ARC** Aeronautical Research Council • Agricultural Research Council (now the AFRC) • *Med.* Aids-related complex • American Red Cross • (USA) Ames Research Center • *Optics* antireflection coating • Archaeological Resource Centre (York) • Architects' Registration Council • Arthritis and Rheumatism Council • Atlantic Research Corporation • *Physics* average resonance capture

**ARCA** (*or* **ARCamA**) Associate of the Royal Cambrian Academy • Associate of the Royal Canadian Academy (of Arts) • Associate of the Royal College of Art

**arccos** ('ɑ:ˌkɒs) *Maths.* arc (inverse) cosine

**arccosec** ('ɑ:kəʊˌsɛk) *Maths.* arc (inverse) cosecant

**arccot** ('ɑ:ˌkɒt) *Maths.* arc (inverse) cotangent

**arch** (ɑ:tʃ) *Maths.* arc (inverse) hyperbolic cosine

**arch.** archaic • archaism • archery • archipelago • architect • architectural • architecture

**Arch.** Archbishop • Archdeacon • Archduke

**archaeol.** archaeology

**Archbp** Archbishop

**Archd.** Archdeacon • Archduke

**archit.** architecture

**archt.** architect

**ARCIC** Anglican/Roman Catholic International Commission

**ARCL** *Chem., Physics* allowable residual contamination level

**ARCM** Associate of the Royal College of Music

**ARCO** Associate of the Royal College of Organists

**ARCO(CHM)** Associate of the Royal College of Organists with Diploma in Choir Training

**arcos** ('ɑ:ˌkɒs) *Maths.* arc (inverse) cosine

**ARCOS** Anglo-Russian Cooperative Society

**arcosech** ('ɑ:kəʊˌsɛtʃ) arc (inverse) hyperbolic secant

**arcosh** ('ɑ:ˌkɒʃ) *Maths.* arc (inverse) hyperbolic cosine

**arcoth** ('ɑ:ˌkɒθ) *Maths.* arc (inverse) hyperbolic cotangent

**ARCPsych** Associate of the Royal College of Psychiatrists

**ARCS** Associate of the Royal College of Science • Associate of the Royal College of Surgeons (of England) • Australian Red Cross Society

**arcsec** ('ɑ:kˌsɛk) *Maths.* arc (inverse) secant • arc second

**arcsin** ('ɑ:kˌsaɪn) *Maths.* arc (inverse) sine

**ARCST** Associate of the Royal College of Science and Technology (Glasgow)

**arctan** ('ɑ:kˌtæn) *Maths.* arc (inverse) tangent

**ARCUK** Architects' Registration Council of the United Kingdom

**ARCVS** Associate of the Royal College of Veterinary Surgeons

**ARD** acute radiation disease

**ARDC** (USA) Air Research and Development Command

**ARDEC** (USA) Army Research Development and Engineering Center

**ARDMS** automated route design and management system

**ARDS** *Med.* adult respiratory distress syndrome

**ARE** activated reactive evaporation • Admiralty Research Establishment • Arab Republic of Egypt • Associate of the Royal Society of Painter-Etchers and Engravers

**AREI** Associate of the Real Estate and Stock Institute of Australia

**ARELS** Association of Recognized English Language Schools

**ARENA** (ə'ri:nə) (Brazil) Aliança Renovadora Nacional (Spanish: National Renewal Alliance)

**ARF** *Med.* acute renal failure • *Med.* acute respiratory failure • Advertising Research Foundation

**Arg** (*or* **arg**) *Biochem.* arginine

**Arg.** *Heraldry* argent • Argentina • Argentine (*or* Argentinian) • Argyll(shire)

**a. Rh.** (*or* **a/Rh**, **a.R.**) am Rhein (German: on the River Rhine; after place names)

**ARHA** Associate of the Royal Hibernian Academy of Painting, Sculpture, and Architecture

**ARHS** Associate of the Royal Horticultural Society

**Ari** *Astronomy* Aries

**ARI** acute respiratory infection

**ARIAS** Associate of the Royal Incorporation of Architects in Scotland

**ARIBA** Associate of the Royal Institute of British Architects (now Member; *see* RIBA)

**ARICS** Professional Associate of the Royal Institution of Chartered Surveyors

**ARIEL** ('ɛərɪəl) Automated Real-time Investments Exchange Limited (former computerized share-dealing system)

**ARIMA** *Computing* autoregressive integrated moving average

**ARINA** Associate of the Royal Institution of Naval Architects

**ARIS** advanced range instrumentation ship

**Arist.** Aristotle (384–322 BC, Greek philosopher)

**Aristoph.** Aristophanes (*c.* 445–*c.* 380 BC, Greek dramatist)

**arith.** arithmetic(al) • arithmetician

**Ariz.** Arizona

**Ark.** Arkansas

**ARL** Admiralty Research Laboratory • Aeronautical Research Laboratory • Arctic Research Laboratory • (USA) Association of Research Libraries • Australian Rugby League

**Arm.** Armagh • Armenia(n) • Armoric(an)

**ArM** Master of Architecture (Latin *Architecturae Magister*)

**ARM** (ɑːm) (USA) adjustable-rate mortgage • Alliance réformée mondiale (French: Worldwide Presbyterian Alliance) • antiradar missile • antiradiation missile • *Obstetrics* artificial rupture of membranes • atomic resolution microscope • Australian Republican Movement

**ARMA** *Computing* autoregressive moving average

**ARMCM** Associate of the Royal Manchester College of Music

**armd** armoured

**ARMET** ('ɑːmɛt) *Meteorol.* area forecast for upper wind and temperature

**ARMIT** Associate of the Royal Melbourne Institute of Technology

**ARMS** (ɑːmz) Action for Research into Multiple Sclerosis • Associate of the Royal Society of Miniature Painters

**ARNA** Arab Revolution News Agency

**ARO** army routine order • Asian Regional Organization • Associate Member of the Register of Osteopaths

**AROD** airborne remote operated device

**AROS** African Regional Organization for Standardization

**arp.** *Music* arpeggio

**ARP** *Finance* (USA) adjustable rate preferred (stock) • air-raid precautions • Associated Reformed Presbyterian

**ARPA** ('ɑːpə) Advanced Research Projects Agency (*see* DARPA)

**ARPANET** (*or* **Arpanet**) ('ɑːpə,nɛt) *Computing* Advanced Research Projects Agency Network

**ARPO** Association of Resort Publicity Officers

**ARPS** Associate of the Royal Photographic Society • Association of Railway Preservation Societies

**arr.** *Music* arrangement • *Music* arranged (by) • arrival • arrive(s) • (*or* **arrd**) arrived

**ARR** accounting rate of return • (small caps.) anno regni Regis *or* Reginae (Latin: in the year of the King's (*or* Queen's) reign) • Association of Radiation Research

**ARRC** Associate of the Royal Red Cross

**arron.** (France) arrondissement (administrative district)

**ARRS** American Roentgen Ray Society

**ARS** *Med.* acute radiation syndrome • (USA) Agricultural Research Service • American Records Society • American Recreation Society • American Rocket Society • (small caps.) anno reparatae salutis (Latin: in the year of our redemption) • *Med.* aortic regurgitation and stenosis • Army Radio School

**ARSA** Associate of the Royal Scottish Academy • Associate of the Royal Society of Arts

**ARSAP** ('ɑːsæp) (USA) Advanced Reactor Severe Accident Program

**ARSCM** Associate of the Royal School of Church Music

**arsech** ('ɑː,sɛtʃ) *Maths.* arc (inverse) hyperbolic secant

**arsh** (ɑːʃ) *Maths.* arc (inverse) hyperbolic sine

**ARSH** Associate of the Royal Society for the Promotion of Health

**arsinh** ('ɑː,saɪn) *Maths.* arc (inverse) hyperbolic sine

**ARSL** Associate of the Royal Society of Literature

**ARSM** Associate of the Royal School of Mines

**ARSR** air route surveillance radar

**ARSW** Associate of the Royal Scottish Society of Painting in Watercolours

**art.** article • artificer • artificial • artillery • artist

**Art.** Artemis (Greek goddess)

**ART** *Computing* algebraic reconstruction technique • *Computing* automated reasoning tool

**artanh** (' $\alpha$ :, tæn) *Maths.* arc (inverse) hyperbolic tangent

**ARTC** air route traffic control

**arth** ( $\alpha$ : $\theta$ ) *Maths.* arc (inverse) hyperbolic tangent

**artif.** artificer

**art. pf.** artist's proof

**arty** artillery

**ARU** American Railway Union • *Computing* audio response unit

**ARV** *Bible* American (Standard) Revised Version

**ARVIA** Associate of the Royal Victoria Institute of Architects

**ARWA** Associate of the Royal West of England Academy

**ARWS** Associate of the Royal Society of Painters in Water-Colours

**ARXPS** *Chem., Physics* angle-resolved X-ray photoelectron spectroscopy

**As** (ital.) *Meteorol.* altostratus • *Chem., symbol for* arsenic • *Chem.* asphaltene

**As.** Asia(n) • Asiatic

**AS** Academy of Science • Admiral Superintendent • admittance spectroscopy • *Education* Advanced Supplementary (in **AS level**) • air speed • air staff • *Insurance* all sections • *Music* al segno (Italian: to (or at) the sign) • *Meteorol.* altostratus • *Geology* aluminium silicate • American Samoa • *Computing* analogue states • (or **A-S**) Anglo-Saxon • (small caps.) anno salutis (Latin: in the year of salvation) • (small caps.) anno Salvatoris (Latin: in the year of the Saviour) • *Chem.* anodic stripping • antisubmarine • Assistant Secretary • assistant surgeon • Associate in Science • *British vehicle registration for* Inverness • *Taxation, symbol for* personal allowance

**A/S** account sales • *Education* Advanced Supplementary (in **A/S level**) • *Banking* after sight • (Denmark) Aktieselskab (joint-stock company) • (Norway) Aktjeselskap (limited company; Ltd) • alongside

**ASA** Acoustic Society of America • (USA) Addiction Services Agency • Advertising Standards Authority • Amateur Swimming Association • American Statistical Association • Army Sailing Association • Associate Member of the Society of Actuaries • (USA) Associate of the Society of Actuaries • Australian Society of Accountants

**ASAA** Associate of the Society of Incorporated Accountants and Auditors

**ASAB** Association for the Study of Animal Behaviour

**ASAI** Associate of the Society of Architectural Illustrators

**ASAM** Associate of the Society of Art Masters

**AS&TS of SA** Associated Scientific and Technical Societies of South Africa

**a.s.a.p.** as soon as possible

**ASAP** automated shipboard aerological programme

**ASAT** (or **Asat**) ('eɪsæt) *Military* anti-satellite (interceptor)

**asb.** asbestos

**a.s.b.** aircraft safety beacon

**ASB** (South Africa) Afrikaans Studentebond (students' union) • *Church of England* Alternative Service Book • American Society of Bacteriologists

**ASBAH** Association for Spina Bifida and Hydrocephalus

**ASBM** air-to-surface ballistic missile

**ASBSBSW** Amalgamated Society of Boilermakers, Shipwrights, Blacksmiths, and Structural Workers

**asc.** ascend (or ascent)

**Asc.** *Astrology* Ascendant

**ASc** Associate in Science

**ASC** Administrative Staff College, Henley • (USA) Air Service Command • altered state of consciousness • American Society of Cinematographers • Anglo-Soviet Committee • Asian Socialist Conference

**ASCA** Associate of the Society of Company and Commercial Accountants

**ASCAB** Armed Services Consultant Approval Board

**ASCAP** ('æskæp) American Society of Composers, Authors, and Publishers

**ASCC** Association of Scottish Climbing Clubs • *Computing* Automatic Sequence Controlled Calculator

**ASCE** American Society of Civil Engineers

**ASCII** ('æski:) *Computing* American Standard Code for Information Interchange

**ASCM** Australian Student Christian Movement

**ASCS** *Engineering* advanced Stirling conversion system

**ASCU** (USA) Association of State Colleges and Universities

**ASD** *Engineering* adjustable speed drive • Admiralty Salvage Department • *Engineering* antislip drive • Armament Supply Department • *Med.* atrial septal defect

**ASDAR** ('æzdɑ:) aircraft-to-satellite data relay

**ASDC** Associate of the Society of Dyers and Colourists

**a/s de** aux soins de (French: care of, c/o; in postal addresses)

**ASDE** Airport Surface Detection Equipment

**Asdic** (*or* **ASDIC**) ('æzdɪk) Allied Submarine Detection Investigation Committee • (USA) Armed Services Documents Intelligence Center

**ASE** Admiralty Signal Department • American Stock Exchange • *Physics* amplified spontaneous emission • Army School of Education • Associate of the Society of Engineers • Association for Science Education • automotive Stirling engine

**ASEA** Association of South East Asia

**ASEAN** ('æsɪ,æn) Association of South East Asian Nations

**ASEC** (USA) Applied Solar Energy Corporation

**ASEE** American Society for Engineering Education • Association of Supervisory and Executive Engineers

**ASF** *Chem.* acid-soluble fraction • Associate of the Institute of Shipping and Forwarding Agents

**ASG** Acting (*or* Assistant) Secretary-General

**ASGB** Aeronautical Society of Great Britain • Anthroposophical Society in Great Britain

**ASGBI** Anatomical Society of Great Britain and Ireland

**asgd** assigned

**asgmt** assignment

**ASH** (æʃ) Action on Smoking and Health

**ashp** airship

**ASHRAE** American Society of Heating, Refrigeration, and Air-Conditioning Engineers

**ASI** airspeed indicator • Association soroptimiste internationale (French: Soroptimist International Association)

**ASIA** Airlines Staff International Association

**ASIAD** Associate of the Society of Industrial Artists and Designers

**ASIA(Ed)** Associate of the Society of Industrial Artists (Education)

**ASIC** ('æsɪk) *Electronics* applications specific integrated circuit

**ASIF** Amateur Swimming International Federation

**ASIO** Australian Security Intelligence Organization

**ASIP** *Astronomy* all-sky imaging photometer

**ASIRC** (USA) Aquatic Sciences Information Retrieval Center (Rhode Island)

**ASIS** *Astronautics* abort sensing and implementation system • American Society for Information Science

**a.s.l.** above sea level

**ASL** Acting Sublieutenant • Advanced Student in Law • American Sign Language • American Soccer League • assistant scout leader

**ASLA** American Society of Landscape Architects

**ASLB** (USA) Atomic Safety and Licensing Board

**ASLE** American Society of Lubrication Engineers

**ASLEF** (*or* **Aslef**) ('æzlɛf) Associated Society of Locomotive Engineers and Firemen

**ASLEP** *Astronautics* Apollo surface lunar experiments package

**A/S level** (*or* **AS level**) *Education* Advanced Supplementary level

**ASLIB** (*or* **Aslib**) ('æzlɪb) Association for Information Management (formerly Association of Special Libraries and Information Bureaux)

**ASLO** American Society of Limnology and Oceanography • Australian Scientific Liaison Office

**ASLP** Amalgamated Society of Lithographic Printers

**ASLW** Amalgamated Society of Leather Workers

**ASM** Acting Sergeant-Major • air-to-surface missile • *Computing* algorithmic state machine • American Society for Metals • assistant sales manager • assistant scoutmaster • assistant stage manager • assistant station master • Association of Senior Members

**ASME** American Society of Mechanical Engineers • Association for the Study of Medical Education

**As. Mem.** Associate Member

**ASMO** Arab Organization for Standardization and Metrology

**ASMP** American Society of Magazine Photographers

**Asn** (*or* **asn**) *Biochem.* asparagine

**ASN** army service number • average sample number

**ASNE** American Society of Newspaper Editors

**ASO** Air Staff Officer • American Symphony Orchestra • area supplies officer

**ASOS** automatic storm observation service

**Asp** (*or* **asp**) *Biochem.* aspartic acid

**ASP** *Commerce* accepté sous protêt (French: accepted under protest) • *US Air Force* aerospace plane • African Special Project (of the IUCN) • (Tanzania) Afro-Shirazi Party • American selling price • (æsp) (USA) Anglo-Saxon Protestant • Astronomical Society of the Pacific

**ASPA** Australian Sugar Producers' Association

**ASPAC** ('æz,pæk) Asian and Pacific Council

**ASPC** *Commerce* accepté sous protêt, pour compte (French: accepted under protest for account) • Association of Swimming Pool Contractors

**ASPCA** American Society for Prevention of Cruelty to Animals

**ASPEP** Association of Scientists and Professional Engineering Personnel

**ASPF** Association of Superannuation and Pension Funds

**ASR** airport surveillance radar • air-sea rescue • *Meteorol.* altimeter setting region

**ASRE** Admiralty Signal and Radar Establishment

**A/SRS** air-sea rescue service

**ass.** assembly • assistant • association • assurance

**ASS** automatic space station

**ASSC** Accounting Standards Steering Committee

**Ass-Com-Gen** Assistant-Commissary-General

**ASSET** ('æsɛt) *US Air Force* aerothermodynamic-elastic structural systems environmental tests

**ASSGB** Association of Ski Schools in Great Britain

**AssIE** Associate of the Institute of Engineers and Technicians

**assigt** assignment

**assim.** assimilate

**assmt** assessment

**assn** association

**assoc.** associate(d) • association

**AssocEng** Associate of Engineering

**AssocIMinE** Associate of the Institution of Mining Engineers

**AssocISI** Associate of the Iron and Steel Institute

**AssocMCT** Associateship of Manchester College of Technology

**AssocMIAeE** Associate Member of the Institution of Aeronautical Engineers

**assocn** association

**AssocSc** Associate in Science

**ASSR** Autonomous Soviet Socialist Republic

**asst** (*or* **ass/t**) assistant

**asstd** assorted

**ASSU** American Sunday School Union

**assy** assembly

**Assyr.** Assyrian

**AST** above-ground storage tank • air service training • *Biochem., Med.* aspartate aminotransferase • assured shorthold tenancy • Atlantic Standard Time • automated screen trading

**ASTA** American Society of Travel Agents • (New Zealand) Auckland Science Teachers' Association

**ASTC** Administrative Service Training Course • Associate of the Sydney Technical College

**ASTIA** (USA) Armed Services Technical Information Agency

**ASTM** American Society for Testing Materials

**ASTMS** ('æztɛmz *or* 'eɪ 'ɛs 'tiː 'ɛm 'ɛs) Association of Scientific, Technical, and Managerial Staffs (now part of the MSF)

**ASTOR** antisubmarine torpedo ordnance rocket

**astr.** astronomer • astronomical • astronomy

**astro.** astronautics • astronomer • astronomy

**ASTRO** (USA) Air Space Travel Research Organization

**astrol.** astrologer • astrological • astrology

**astron.** astronomer • astronomical • astronomy

**astrophys.** astrophysical

**Ast. T.** astronomical time

**ASU** American Students Union • Arab Socialist Union

**ASUA** Amateur Swimming Union of the Americas

**ASV** aircraft-to-surface vessel • *Bible* American Standard Version • *Microbiol.* avian sarcoma virus

**ASVA** Associate of the Incorporated Society of Valuers and Auctioneers

**ASVU** Army Security Vetting Unit

**ASW** Amalgamated Society of Wood Workers • antisubmarine warfare • antisubmarine work • Association of Scientific Workers • Association of Social Workers • *Physics* augmented spherical wave

**ASWDU** Air Sea Warfare Development Unit

**ASWE** Admiralty Surface Weapons Establishment

**at.** atmosphere • atomic • *Navigation* attitude • attorney

**At** *symbol for* ampere-turn (unit) • *Chem., symbol for* astatine • (æt) *Colloquial* (a member of the) Auxiliary Territorial Service

**AT** *Physics* accelerator technology • achievement test • *Immunol.* agglutination test • *Biochem.* alkyl transferase • alternative technology • *Chem.* amino-1,2,4-triazole • (ital.) Angling Times • antitank • apparent time • *Physics* appearance time • (USA) appropriate technology • arrival time • *Med.* ataxia telangiectasia • Atlantic Time • *Education* attainment target • *British vehicle registration for* Hull • *airline flight code for* Royal Air Maroc

**A/T** American terms

**ATA** *Nuclear physics* advanced test accelerator • Air Transport Association • Air Transport Auxiliary • American Translators' Association • Amusement Trades Association • Animal Technicians' Association • Associate Technical Aide • Atlantic Treaty Association

**ATAC** Air Transport Advisory Council

**ATAE** Association of Tutors in Adult Education

**ATAF** Allied Tactical Air Force

**ATAM** Association for Teaching Aids in Mathematics

**AT & T** American Telephone and Telegraph Company

**ATAS** Air Transport Auxiliary Service

**ATB** advanced technology bomber • at the time of the bomb (*or* bombing)

**ATBC** acetyltributyl citrate (a plasticizer)

**ATBM** antitactical ballistic missile

**ATC** acid-treated coal • air-traffic control • Air Training Command • Air Training Corps • Air Transport Command • *Law* Annotated Tax Cases • Art Teacher's Certificate • *Computing* authorization to copy (of software) • automatic temperature control • automatic train control

**ATCC** air traffic control centre

**ATCE** *Astronautics* ablative thrust chamber engine

**atchd** attached

**ATCL** Associate of Trinity College of Music, London

**ATCO** Air Traffic Control Officer

**ATCRBS** Air Traffic Control Radar Beacon System

**ATCSP** Association of Teachers of the Chartered Society of Physiotherapists

**ATD** actual time of departure • advanced technology development • *Physics* alpha-track detector • Art Teacher's Diploma • Australian Tax Decisions

**ATDS** Association of Teachers of Domestic Science

**ATE** Amusement Trades Exhibition • Automatic Telephone and Electric Company • *Electronics* automatic test equipment

**ATEC** Air Transport Electronics Council

**ATEE** *Chem.* N-acetyl-L-tyrosine ethyl ester

**a tem.** *Music* a tempo (Italian: in time)

**ATF** *Nuclear physics* accelerator test facility • *Nuclear physics* advanced toroidal facility

**ATFS** Association of Track and Field Statisticians

**ATG** *Med.* antithymocyte globulin

**ath.** athlete • athletic

**ATHE** Association of Teachers in Higher Education

**Athen.** Athenian

**athl.** athlete • athletic

**ATI** Associate of the Textile Institute • Association of Technical Institutions

**ATII** Associate Member of the Institute of Taxation

**Atl.** Atlantic

**ATL** *Insurance* actual total loss • *Med.* adult T-cell leukaemia • *Computing* automated (*or* automatic) tape library

**ATLAS** ('ætləs) *Astronomy* airborne tunable laser absorption spectrometer • (USA) Argonne tandem-linac accelerator system

**ATLB** Air Transport Licensing Board

**ATLV** adult T-cell leukaemia virus

**atm** *symbol for* atmosphere (unit of pressure)

**atm.** atmospheric

**ATM** air training memorandum • anti-tank missile • approved testing material • Association of Teachers of Management • Association of Teachers of Mathematics • *Banking* automated teller machine

**ATMS** assumption-based truth maintenance system

**ATN** *Med.* acute tubular necrosis • *Maths.* arc tangent • *Telecom.* augmented transition network

**ATNA** Australasian Trained Nurses' Association

**at. no.** atomic number

**ATO** (*or* **ato**) Ammunition Technical Officer (bomb-disposal officer in the RAOC) • *Aeronautics* assisted takeoff

**A to A** air-to-air

**A to J** (New Zealand) Appendices to Journals (of the House of Representatives or Parliament)

**ATOL** ('ætɒl) Air Travel Organizers' Licence

**ATP** *Biochem.* adenosine triphosphate • *Commerce* aid trade provision • Air Technical Publications • Associated Theatre Properties • Association of Tennis Professionals • *Railways* automatic train protection

**ATPAS** Association of Teachers of Printing and Allied Subjects

**ATPG** automatic test-pattern generation

**ATPL(A)** Airline Transport Pilot's Licence (Aeroplanes)

**ATPL(H)** Airline Transport Pilot's Licence (Helicopters)

**ATR** *Nuclear physics* advanced test reactor • *Nuclear physics* advanced thermal reactor • *Aeronautics* air turbo-ram jet engine • *Radar* antitransmit–receive (in **ATR tube**) • Association of Teachers of Russian • *Military* automatic target recognition

**ATRAN** automatic terrain recognition and navigation

**a.t.r.i.m.a.** *Law* as their respective interests may appear

**a.t.s.** *Law* at the suit of

**ATS** (Australia) Amalgamated Television Services • American Temperance Society • American Tract Society • American Transport Service • *Med.* antitetanus serum • (USA) Army Transport Service • Associate of Theological Study • automated trade system • Auxiliary Territorial Service (in World War II)

**ATSC** Associate of the Tonic Sol-Fa College

**ATSDR** (USA) Agency for Toxic Substances and Disease Registry

**ATSIS** *Computing* automated technical-specification information system

**ATSS** Association for the Teaching of Social Sciences

**att.** attached • attention • attorney

**ATT** antitetanus toxoid

**Att-Gen.** Attorney-General

**attn** attention • for the attention of

**attrib.** attribute • attributed (to) • attribution • attributive(ly)

**atty.** (*or* **Atty.**) attorney

**Atty-Gen.** Attorney-General

**ATU** (USA) Amalgamated Transit Union

**ATUC** African Trade Union Confederation

**ATV** all-terrain vehicle • Associated Television

**at. wt.** atomic weight

**Au** *Chem., symbol for* gold (Latin *aurum*)

**AU** (USA) Actors' Union • *Printing* all up (all set in type) • angstrom unit • arithmetic unit • astronomical unit • *British vehicle registration for* Nottingham

**AUA** *Finance* agricultural unit of account (in the EC) • American Unitarian Association • American Urological Association

**AUBC** Association of Universities of the British Commonwealth

**AUBTW** Amalgamated Union of Building Trade Workers

**AUC** ab urbe condita *or* anno urbis conditae (Latin: (in the year) from the founding of the city; indicating years numbered from the founding of Rome) • *Chem.* ammonium uranyl carbonate • *Maths.* area under the curve (on a graph) • Association of Underwater Contractors • Australian Universities Commission

**AUCAS** Association of University Clinical Academic Staff

**auct.** *Botany* auctorum (Latin: of (other) authors; indicating that the specific name of a plant is that given by authorities other than Linnaeus)

**aud.** audit • auditor

**Aud-Gen.** Auditor-General

**AUEW** Amalgamated Union of Engineering Workers (*see under* AEU)

**Aufl.** Auflage (German: edition)

**AUFW** Amalgamated Union of Foundry Workers

**aug.** *Grammar* augmentative • augmented

**Aug.** August

**augm.** *Grammar* augmentative

**AULLA** ('aʊlə) Australasian Universities Language and Literature Association

**AUM** air-to-underwater missile

**AUMLA** Australian Universities Modern Language Association

**a.u.n.** absque ulla nota (Latin: with no identifying mark)

**AUO** African Unity Organization

**AUP** Aberdeen University Press

**Aur** *Astronomy* Auriga

**Aus.** Australia(n) • Austria(n)

**AUS** Army of the United States • Assistant Undersecretary • *international vehicle registration for* Australia

**AUSA** Association of the United States Army

**Ausg.** Ausgabe (German: edition)

**Aust.** Australia(n) • Austria(n)

**Austral.** Australasia • Australia(n)

**aut.** autograph • autumn

**Aut.** Autriche (French: Austria)

**AUT** *Chem.* ammonium uranyl tricarbonate • Association of University Teachers

**AUTEC** *US Navy* Atlantic Underwater Test Evaluation Center

**auth.** authentic • author(ess) • authority • authorize(d)

**Auth. Ver.** Authorized Version (of the Bible)

**auto.** automatic • automobile • automotive

**autobiog.** autobiographical • autobiography

**autog.** autograph

**AUT(S)** Association of University Teachers (Scotland)

**a.u.w.** all-up-weight

**AUWE** Admiralty Underwater Weapons Establishment

**aux.** auxiliary

**AUX** *Linguistics* auxiliary verb

**av.** avenue • average • avoirdupois • avril (French: April)

**a.v.** (*or* **a/v**) *Finance* ad valorem (Latin: according to value) • annos vixit (Latin: (he *or* she) lived (so many) years) • *Finance* asset value

**Av.** Avenue • Avocat (French: lawyer)

**AV** *Chem.* acid value • (*or* **A/V**) *Finance* ad valorem (Latin: according to value) • *Photog.* aperture value • Artillery Volunteers • *Med.* atrioventricular (as in **AV bundle, AV node**) • audiovisual • *Numismatics* aurum (Latin: gold) • Authorized Version (of the Bible) • average value • *airline flight code for* Avianca • *British vehicle registration for* Peterborough

**AVA** (Canada) Alberta Veterinary Association • Amateur Volleyball Association of Great Britain • audiovisual aids • Audiovisual Association • Australian Veterinary Association

**a.v.c.** *Electronics* automatic volume control

**av.C.** (Italy) avanti Cristo (before Christ; BC)

**AVC** additional voluntary contribution (in pension schemes) • American Veterans' Committee • *Electronics* automatic volume control

**Av. Cert.** Aviator's Certificate

**AVCM** Associate of Victoria College of Music

**AVD** Army Veterinary Department

**avdp.** avoirdupois

**ave.** (*or* **Ave.**) avenue • average

**AVF** *Military* (USA) all-volunteer force

**avg.** average

**AVGAS** aviation gasoline (of high octane for piston-type engine)

**avge.** *Cricket* average

**AVI** Association of Veterinary Inspectors

**avia.** aviation

**av. J-C** (France) avant Jésus-Christ (before Jesus Christ; BC)

**AVL** *Computing* Adel'son-Vel'skii–
Landis (as in **AVL tree**) • *Transport*
automatic vehicle location

**AVLA** Audio Visual Language Association

**AVLIS** atomic vapour laser isotope separation

**AVM** Air Vice-Marshal • *Med.* arteriovenous malformation

**AVMA** Action for the Victims of Medical Accidents • Automatic Vending Machine Association

**avn** aviation

**AVO** Administrative Veterinary Officer • *Transport* average vehicle occupancy

**avoir.** avoirdupois

**AVR** Army Volunteer Reserve

**AVRI** Animal Virus Research Institute

**AVRO** ('ævrəʊ) *Aeronautics* A. V. Roe and Co.

**AVRP** audiovisual recording and presentation

**AVS** Anti-Vivisection Society

**AVSL** assistant venture scout leader

**AVTRW** Association of Veterinary Teachers and Research Workers

**a.w.** actual weight • *Shipping* all water • atomic weight

**AW** added water (in foodstuffs, etc.) • Alfred Wainwright (1907–91, British walker and writer) • *Physics* Alfvén wave(s) • Armstrong Whitworth (aircraft) • Articles of War • atomic warfare • *British vehicle registration for* Shrewsbury

**A/W** actual weight • airworthy • artwork

**AWA** Amalgamated Wireless (Australasia) Ltd

**AWACS** (*or* **Awacs**) ('eɪwæks) airborne warning and control system

**AWAM** Association of West African Merchants

**AWAS** Australian Women's Army Service

**AWASM** Associate of the Western Australia School of Mines

**AWB** (South Africa) Afrikaner Weerstandsbeweging (right-wing political party) • Agricultural Wages Board • (USA) air waybill • Australian Wool Board

**AWBA** American World's Boxing Association

**AWC** Allied Works Council • (USA) Army War College • Australian Wool Corporation

**AWE** Atomic Weapons Establishment

**AWEA** American Wind Energy Association

**AWeldI** Associate of the Welding Institute

**AWG** American Wire Gauge • Art Workers' Guild

**AWH** *Physics* Alfvén wave heating

**AWHA** Australian Women's Home Army

**AWJ** *Engineering, Building trades* abrasive water jet

**AWL** (*or* **awl**) absent with leave

**AWMC** Association of Workers for Maladjusted Children

**AWNL** Australian Women's National League

**AWO** American Waterways Operators, Inc • Association of Water Officers

**AWOL** (*or* **awol**) ('eɪwɒl) absent without (official) leave

**AWP** amusements with prizes (forms of minor gaming in British Gaming Acts) • annual wood production

**AWPR** Association of Women in Public Relations

**AWR** Association for the Study of the World Refugee Problem

**AWRA** Australian Wool Realization Agency

**AWRE** Atomic Weapons Research Establishment

**aws** Graduate of Air Warfare Course

**AWS** *Geology* acoustic well sounding • Agricultural Wholesale Society • American Welding Society • automatic warning system

**AWSA** American Water Ski Association

**AWU** Australian Workers' Union

**AWW** (South Africa) Afrikaner Weerstandsbeweging (right-wing political party)

**ax.** axiom

**AX** *British vehicle registration for* Cardiff

**AXAF** Advanced X-ray Astrophysical Facility (at NASA)

**AY** *airline flight code for* Finnair • *British vehicle registration for* Leicester

**AYH** American Youth Hostels

**AYLI** (ital.) As You Like It (Shakespeare)

**AYM** *Freemasonry* Ancient York Mason

**Ayr.** Ayrshire

**az.** azimuth • azure

**AZ** *airline flight code for* Alitalia • *US postcode for* Arizona • *British vehicle registration for* Belfast

**Azapo** (əˈzɑːpəʊ) (South Africa) Azanian People's Organization

**az. ld.** *Printing* azure laid (paper)

**Azo.** Azores

**AZT** azidothymidine (drug used in treating Aids)

**az. wo.** *Printing* azure wove (paper)

• • • • • • • • • • • • • • • • • • • • • • • • • • • • • • • • • • • • • • • • • • • • • • • • • • • • •

# B

**b** *Physics, symbol for* barn • *Physics* bottom (a quark flavour) • *indicating* the second vertical row of squares from the left on a chessboard

**b.** bag • bale • ball • base • *Music* bass (*or* basso) • bath • batsman • bay • beam • bedroom • before • billion • bis (Latin: twice) • bitch • bloody (euphemism) • book • born • bound • *Med.* bowels • *Cricket* bowled by • breadth • brother • bugger (euphemism) • bust • by • *Cricket* bye

**B** *symbol for* baht (Thai monetary unit) • *symbol for* balboa (Panamanian monetary unit) • *Physics, symbol for* baryon number • *Chem., symbol for* base-catalysed reaction • Baumé (temperature scale) • *British fishing port registration for* Belfast • *international vehicle registration for* Belgium • best (quality of wrought iron) • *postcode for* Birmingham • *Chess, symbol for* bishop • black (indicating the degree of softness of lead in a pencil; also in **BB** (*or* **2B**), double black, etc.) • *symbol for* bolívar (Venezuelan monetary unit; *see also under* Bs) • (USA) bomber (as in **B-52**) • *Chem., symbol for* boron • breathalyzer (as in **B-test**) • *Photog.* B-setting • *Immunol.* bursa of Fabricius *or* bone marrow (in **B cell** *or* **lymphocyte**) • *international civil aircraft marking for* China *or* Taiwan • *symbol for* eleven (in hexadecimal notation) • (bold ital.) *Physics, symbol for* magnetic flux density • *symbol for* secondary road (as in **B405**, etc.) • (ital.) *Physics, symbol for* susceptance • *indicating* administrative, professional (occupational grade) • *Med., indicating* a blood group or its associated antigen (*see also under* ABO) • *indicating* a musical note or key • *Astronomy, indicating* a spectral type • *indicating* a standard paper size

(*see under* B0–B10) • *indicating* something of secondary importance or interest (as in **B-film**, **B-road**)

**B.** (*or* **B**) Bachelor (in academic degrees) • Baptist • Baron • *Music* bass (*or* basso) • battle • *Cartography* bay • Beatus (Latin: blessed) • Benediction • Bey • Bible • billion • bishop • Blessed • blue • board • boatswain • book • breadth • British • brotherhood • building

**B0** *indicating* a standard paper size, 1000 × 1414 mm

**B1** *indicating* a standard paper size, 707 × 1000 mm

**B2** *indicating* a standard paper size, 500 × 707 mm

**B3** *indicating* a standard paper size, 353 × 500 mm

**B4** *indicating* a standard paper size, 250 × 353 mm

**B5** *indicating* a standard paper size, 176 × 250 mm

**B6** *indicating* a standard paper size, 125 × 176 mm

**B7** *indicating* a standard paper size, 88 × 125 mm

**B8** *indicating* a standard paper size, 62 × 88 mm

**B9** *indicating* a standard paper size, 44 × 62 mm

**B10** *indicating* a standard paper size, 31 × 44 mm

**b.a.** *Taxation* balancing allowance • blind approach

**Ba** *Chem., symbol for* barium

**BA** able-bodied seaman • Bachelor of Arts • *British fishing port registration for* Ballantrae • *Finance* bank (*or* banker's) acceptance • *postcode for* Bath • *Med.* biliary atresia • (ital.) (USA) Biological Abstracts (publication) • Board of Agriculture • Booksellers' Association (of

Great Britain and Ireland) • *Chem.* boric acid • British Academy • British Airways • British America • British Association (for the Advancement of Science) • British Association (pitch of screw thread, as in **4BA**) • bronchial asthma • Buenos Aires • *Computing* bus automaton • *British vehicle registration for* Manchester

**BAA** Bachelor of Applied Arts • Booking Agents' Association of Great Britain • British Airports Authority • British Archaeological Association • British Astronomical Association

**BAA & A** British Association of Accountants and Auditors

**BAAB** British Amateur Athletic Board

**BA(Admin)** Bachelor of Arts in Administration

**BAAF** British Agencies for Adoption and Fostering

**BAAL** British Association for Applied Linguistics

**BA(Art)** Bachelor of Arts in Art

**BAAS** British Association for the Advancement of Science

**Bab.** Babylonia(n)

**BABIE** ('beɪbɪ) British Association for Betterment of Infertility and Education

**BABS** *Aeronautics* beam (*or* blind) approach beacon system

**Bac.** (France) baccalauréat (school examination) • *Education* Baccalaureus (Latin: bachelor)

**BAc** Bachelor of Acupuncture

**BAC** biologically active compound(s) • blood-alcohol concentration (*or* content) • British Aircraft Corporation • British Association of Chemists • *Med.* bronchoalveolar cell(s) • *Chem.* Brønsted acid centre • Business Archives Council

**BACAH** British Association of Consultants in Agriculture and Horticulture

**BACAT** (bæ'kæt) barge aboard catamaran • barge canal traffic

**BAcc** Bachelor of Accountancy

**bach.** bachelor

**BACIE** British Association for Commercial and Industrial Education

**BACM** British Association of Colliery Management

**BACO** British Aluminium Company Ltd

**BACS** Bankers' Automated Clearing Service

**bact.** bacteria(l) • bacteriology

**bacteriol.** bacteriological • bacteriology

**BAD** base air depot • British Association of Dermatology

**BADA** British Antique Dealers' Association

**BADGE** (bædʒ) base air defence ground environment

**BAdmin** Bachelor of Administration

**BAe** British Aerospace

**BAE** Bachelor of Aeronautical Engineering • Bachelor of Arts in Education • Badminton Association of England • Belfast Association of Engineers • (USA) Bureau of Agricultural Economics

**BAEA** British Actors' Equity Association

**BAEC** Bangladesh Atomic Energy Commission • British Agricultural Export Council

**BA(Econ)** Bachelor of Arts in Economics

**BA(Ed)** Bachelor of Arts in Education

**BAED** Bachelor of Arts in Environmental Design

**BAEF** Belgian-American Educational Foundation

**BAF** biological aerated filter

**BAFM** British Association of Forensic Medicine

**BAFMA** British and Foreign Maritime Agencies

**BAFO** British Air Forces of Occupation • British Army Forces Overseas

**BAFSC** British Association of Field and Sports Contractors

**BAFSV** British Armed Forces Special Vouchers

**BAFTA** ('bæftə) British Academy of Film and Television Arts

**BAGA** ('bɑːgə) British Amateur Gymnastics Association

**BAgEc** Bachelor of Agricultural Economics

**BAgr** Bachelor of Agriculture

**BAgrSc** Bachelor of Agricultural Science

**Bah.** Bahamas

**BAHA** British Association of Hotel Accountants

**BAHOH** British Association for the Hard of Hearing

**BAHS** British Agricultural History Society

**BAI** Bachelor of Engineering (Latin *Baccalaureus Artis Ingeniariae*) • *Military*

battlefield air interdiction • Book Association of Ireland • *Med.* bronchial arterial infusion

**BAIE** British Association of Industrial Editors

**BA(J)** (*or* **BAJour**) Bachelor of Arts in Journalism

**bal.** *Book-keeping* balance

**Bal.** Ballarat • Balliol College (Oxford)

**BAL** blood-alcohol level • British antilewisite (dimercaprol; antidote to war gas and metal poisoning) • *Med.* bronchoalveolar lavage

**BALH** British Association for Local History

**ball.** ballast • ballistics

**Ball.** Balliol College (Oxford)

**BALPA** ('bælpə) British Airline Pilots' Association

**bals.** balsam

**Balt.** Baltic • Baltimore

**balun** ('bælən) *Telecom.* balanced unbalanced (transformer)

**BAM** Bachelor of Applied Mathematics • Bachelor of Arts in Music

**BAMA** British Aerosol Manufacturers' Association • British Amsterdam Maritime Agencies • British Army Motoring Association

**BAMBI** ('bæmbɪ) ballistic missile boost intercept

**BAMTM** British Association of Machine Tool Merchants

**BA(Mus)** Bachelor of Arts in Music

**BAMW** British Association of Meat Wholesalers

**Ban.** Bangor • Bantu

**BAN** British Association of Neurologists

**Banc. Sup.** *Law* Bancus Superior (Latin: higher bench; i.e. Queen's (*or* King's) Bench)

**b. and b.** (*or* **B & B**) bed and breakfast

**B & C** *Insurance* building and contents

**B & D** (*or* **B and D**) bondage and discipline (*or* domination)

**b & e** beginning and ending

**B&FBS** British and Foreign Bible Society

**B and S** (*or* **B & S**) brandy and soda • Brown and Sharpe (wire gauge)

**B&W** (*or* **b&w**) *Photog.* black and white

**B & WE** Bristol and West of England

**BANS** British Association of Numismatic Societies

**BANZARE** British, Australian, New Zealand Antarctic Research Expedition

**BAO** Bachelor of Arts in Obstetrics • Bankruptcy Annulment Order • British American Oil

**BAOD** British Airways Overseas Division

**BA of E** Badminton Association of England

**BAOMS** British Association of Oral and Maxillo-Facial Surgeons

**BAOR** British Army of the Rhine

**b. à p.** billets à payer (French: bills payable)

**bap.** baptized

**Bap.** Baptist

**BAP** *Chem.* 6-benzylaminopurine • *Chem.* bottom agitation process

**BAPA** British Amateur Press Association

**BAPC** British Aircraft Preservation Council

**BAPCO** ('bæp,kəu) Bahrain Petroleum Company

**BA(PE)** Bachelor of Arts in Physical Education

**BAPL** Bettis Atomic Power Laboratory

**BAPLA** British Association of Picture Libraries and Agencies

**BAPM** British Association of Physical Medicine

**BAPNA** *Chem.* Nα-benzoyl-DL-arginine-*p*-nitroaniline

**BAppArts** Bachelor of Applied Arts

**BAppSc** Bachelor of Applied Science

**BAppSc(MT)** Bachelor of Applied Science (Medical Technology)

**BAPS** beacon automated processing system (for lighthouses) • British Association of Paediatric Surgeons • British Association of Plastic Surgeons

**bapt.** baptism • baptized

**Bapt.** Baptist

**BAPT** British Association for Physical Training

**b. à r.** billets à recevoir (French: bills receivable)

**bar.** barleycorn (obsolete unit of length) • barometer • barometric • barrel (container or unit of measure) • barrister

**Bar.** baritone • Barrister • *Bible* Baruch

**BAR** *Computing* base address register • (ital.) Book Auction Records • Browning Automatic Rifle

**Barb.** Barbados

**BARB** (bɑːb) British Association of Rose Breeders • British Audience

Research Bureau • Broadcasters' Audience Research Board

**BARC** British Automobile Racing Club

**BArch** Bachelor of Architecture

**BArchE** Bachelor of Architectural Engineering

**barg.** bargain

**barit.** baritone

**BARP** British Association of Retired Persons

**Barr.** Barrister

**BARR** British Association of Rheumatology and Rehabilitation

**BARS** *Management* behaviourally anchored rating scales • British Association of Residential Settlements

**Bart.** Baronet

**Bart's** St Bartholomew's Hospital, London

**BAS** Bachelor in Agricultural Science • Bachelor of Applied Science • British Antarctic Survey

**BASA** British Architectural Students' Association • British Australian Studies Association

**BASAF** British and South Africa Forum

**BASc** Bachelor of Agricultural Science • Bachelor of Applied Science

**BASC** British Association for Shooting and Conservation

**BASCA** British Academy of Songwriters, Composers, and Authors

**BASF** Badische Anilin und Soda-Fabrik (German chemical and electronics company)

**BASI** British Association of Ski Instructors

**Basic** ('beɪsɪk) (*or* **BASIC**) *Computing* beginners' all-purpose symbolic instruction code (programming language) • (*or* **basic**) British-American scientific international commercial (in **Basic English**)

**BASMA** ('bæsmə) Boot and Shoe Manufacturers' Association and Leather Trades Protection Society

**bass. con.** *Music* basso continuo (Italian: continuous bass)

**BASW** ('bæzwə) British Association of Social Workers

**bat.** battalion • battery • battle

**Bat.** Batavia

**BAT** *Chem.* benzaldehyde–ammonia titration • best available technology • British Aerial Transport (aircraft) • Brit-

ish-American Tobacco Company • *Med.* brown adipose tissue

**BATF** (USA) Bureau of Alcohol, Tobacco, and Firearms

**bath.** bathroom

**BA(Theol)** Bachelor of Arts in Theology

**BATO** balloon-assisted takeoff

**BA(TP)** Bachelor of Arts in Town and Country Planning

**BATS** (bætz) *Ecology* biosphere–atmosphere transfer scheme

**batt.** (*or* **battn**) battalion • *Military* battery

**BAU** *Physics* baryon asymmetry of the universe • British Association Unit • business as usual

**BAUA** Business Aircraft Users' Association

**BAUS** British Association of Urological Surgeons

**b. à v.** *Finance* bon à vue (French: good at sight)

**Bav.** Bavaria(n)

**BAWA** British Amateur Wrestling Association

**BAWLA** British Amateur Weight-Lifters' Association

**BAYS** British Association of Young Scientists

**bb** books

**b.b.** ball bearing • bearer bonds • *Nautical* below bridges

**Bb.** bishops

**BB** bail bond • balloon barrage • bank book • bed and breakfast • best best (quality of wrought iron) • *postcode for* Blackburn • Blue Book (the HMSO publication *UK National Accounts*) • B'nai B'rith (Jewish international society) • Boys' Brigade • Brigitte Bardot (1934– , French film actress) • (*or* **2B**) double black (indicating a very soft lead pencil) • *British vehicle registration for* Newcastle upon Tyne • *Nautical, indicating* a certificate issued to vessels arriving from foreign destinations to the effect that their papers, etc., are in order • *indicating* a standard size of lead shot, 0.18 in. in diameter

**BBA** Bachelor of Business Administration • Big Brothers of America • *Obstetrics* born before arrival • British Bankers' Association • British Beekeepers' Association • British Bloodstock Association • British Board of

Agreement • British Bobsleigh Association

**BBAC** British Balloon and Airship Club

**BBB** bed, breakfast, and bath • (USA) Better Business Bureau • *Physiol.* blood–brain barrier • (*or* **3B**) treble black (indicating a very soft lead pencil)

**BBBC** (*or* **BBB of C**) British Boxing Board of Control

**BBC** British Broadcasting Corporation

**BBCM** Bandmaster of the Bandsmen's College of Music

**BBCMA** British Baby Carriage Manufacturers' Association

**BBEM** bed, breakfast, and evening meal

**BBFC** British Board of Film Censors

**BBI** British Bottlers' Institute

**BBIP** (ital.) British Books in Print (publication)

**BBIRA** British Baking Industries' Research Association

**B. Bisc.** Bay of Biscay

**bbl.** barrel (container or unit of measure for oil, etc.)

**BBM** *Physics* beam-bending magnet • *Histology* brush-border membrane

**BBMA** British Brush Manufacturers' Association • British Button Manufacturers' Association

**9-BBN** *Chem.* 9-borobicyclononane

**BBO** *Chem.* 2,5-bis(4-biphenylyl)-oxazole

**BBOT** *Chem.* 2,5-bis(5-*t*-butyl-2-benzoxazolyl)thiophene

**BBQ** barbecue

**BBS** Bachelor of Business Science (*or* Studies) • *Computing* bulletin board system

**BBSR** Bermuda Biological Station for Research

**BBT** *Med.* basal body temperature

**BBV** Banco Bilbao Vizcaya (Spanish bank)

**b.c.** (*or* **bc**) *Music* basso continuo • blind copy

**BC** Bachelor of Chemistry • Bachelor of Commerce • Bachelor of Surgery (Latin *Baccalaureus Chirurgiae*) • *Military* (formerly) bad character • badminton club • *Taxation* balancing charge • bank clearing • bankruptcy court • *Chemical engineering* barrels of condensate • basketball club • *Music* basso continuo (Italian: continuing bass) • Battery Commander • battle cruiser • bayonet cap (on electric light bulbs) • (small

caps.) before Christ (following a date) • bicycle club • billiards club • (*or* **B/C**) bills for collection • bishop and confessor • *Physics* Bloch curves • *Med.* blood consumption • board of control • boat (*or* boating) club • *Biochem.* body composition • *Astronomy* bolometric correction • Bomber Command • borough council • *Physics* Bose condensation • bowling (*or* bowls) club • boxing club • boys' club • Bristol Channel • British Coal • British Columbia • British Commonwealth • British Council • *Med.* bronchial carcinoma • *airline flight code for* Brymon Airways • *Chem.* bubble combustion • budgeted cost • *Education* Burnham Committee • *Chem.* butyl chloride • *British vehicle registration for* Leicester

**BCA** (New Zealand) Bachelor of Commerce and Administration • *Chem.* bifunctional chelating agent • *Physical chem.* binary collision approximation • Boys' Clubs of America • British-Caribbean Association • *Angling* British Casting Association • British Chiropractic Association

**BCAA** *Biochem.* branched-chain amino acid

**BCAB** Birth Control Advisory Bureau

**BCAC** British Conference on Automation and Computation

**BC&T** (USA) Bakery, Confectionery, and Tobacco Workers International Union

**BCAP** British Code of Advertising Practice

**BCAR** British Civil Airworthiness Requirements • British Council for Aid to Refugees

**BCAS** British Compressed Air Society

**BCBC** British Cattle Breeders' Club

**b.c.c.** (*or* **bcc**) blind carbon copy • *Crystallog.* body-centred cubic

**BCC** *Med.* basal-cell carcinoma • British Coal Corporation • British Colour Council • British Copyright Council • British Council of Churches • British Crown Colony

**BCCA** British Cyclo-Cross Association

**BCCG** British Cooperative Clinical Group

**BCCI** Bank of Credit and Commerce International

**BCD** (USA) bad conduct discharge • *Chem.* betacyclodextrin • *Computing* binary-coded decimal • *Astronomy* blue compact dwarf (type of star)

**BCDP** *Med.* balloon catheter dilation of the prostate

**BCDTA** British Chemical and Dyestuffs Traders' Association

**BCE** Bachelor of Chemical Engineering • Bachelor of Civil Engineering • (small caps.) before common (*or* Christian) era (following a date; the non-Christian equivalent of BC) • Board of Customs and Excise

**BCEAO** Banque centrale des états de l'Afrique de l'Ouest (French: Central Bank of West African States)

**BCECC** British and Central European Chamber of Commerce

**BCF** battle cruiser force • billion cubic feet • British Chess Federation • British Cycling Federation • *Chem.* bromochlorodifluoromethane • *Textiles* bulked continuous filament (indicating yarns in man-made fibres) • (USA) Bureau of Commercial Fisheries

**BCFA** British-China Friendship Association

**BCG** *Med.* bacille Calmette–Guérin (antituberculosis vaccine) • *Med.* ballistocardiography • *Astronomy* blue compact galaxy

**BCGA** British Commercial Gas Association • British Cotton Growing Association

**BCGF** *Biochem.* B-cell growth factor

**bch** (*or* **Bch**) branch • bunch

**b.c.h.** *Crystallog.* body-centred hypercubic

**BCh** (*or* **BChir**) Bachelor of Surgery (Latin *Baccalaureus Chirurgiae*)

**BChD** Bachelor of Dental Surgery (Latin *Baccalaureus Chirurgiae Dentalis*)

**BChE** (*or* **BChemEng**) Bachelor of Chemical Engineering

**BCINA** British Commonwealth International Newsfilm Agency

**BCIRA** British Cast-Iron Research Association

**BCIS** Building Cost Information Service • Bureau central international de séismologie (French: International Central Bureau of Seismology)

**BCK** *British fishing port registration for* Buckie

**BCL** Bachelor of Canon Law • Bachelor of Civil Law • *Chemical engineering* brown-coal liquefaction

**BCM** (USA) Boston Conservatory of Music • British Commercial Monomark • British Consular Mail

**BCMA** British Colour Makers' Association • British Columbia Medical Association

**BCMD** biological and chemical munitions disposal (type of bomb disposal)

**BCMF** British Ceramic Manufacturers' Federation

**BCMG** Birmingham Contemporary Music Group

**BCMS** Bible Churchmen's Missionary Society

**bcn** beacon

**BCNZ** Broadcasting Corporation of New Zealand

**BCO** *Med.* bilateral carotid artery occlusion

**B.Col.P.** British Columbia Pine

**BCom** (*or* **BComm**) Bachelor of Commerce

**BComSc** Bachelor of Commercial Science

**BCP** *Chem.* basic calcium phosphate • Book of Common Prayer • Bulgarian Communist Party (*see under* BSP)

**BCPC** British Crop Protection Council

**BCPIT** British Council for the Promotion of International Trade

**BCPL** Basic Computer Programming Language

**BCPMA** British Chemical Plant Manufacturers' Association

**BCR** *Chem.* base-catalysed rearrangement • battlefield casualty replacement • *Chem.* branched-chain reaction

**BCRA** British Carbonization Research Association • British Ceramic Research Association

**BCRC** British Columbia Research Council

**BCRD** British Council for the Rehabilitation of the Disabled

**BCS** Bachelor of Chemical Science • Bachelor of Commercial Science • *Physics* Bardeen–Cooper–Schrieffer (in **BCS theory** of superconductivity) • battle cruiser squadron • Bengal Civil Service • British Calibration Service • British Cardiac Society • British Ceramic Society • British Computer Society • (USA) Bureau of Criminal Statistics

**BCSA** British Constructional Steelwork Association

**bcst** broadcast

**BCT** Belfast Chamber of Trade • *Med.* body computer tomograph

**BCTA** British Canadian Trade Association • British Children's Theatre Association

**BCTGA** British Christmas Tree Growers Association

**BCTV** *Microbiol.* beet curly top virus

**BCU** *Films* big close-up • British Canoe Union

**BCURA** British Coal Utilization Research Association

**BCVA** British Columbia Veterinary Association

**BCWMA** British Clock and Watch Manufacturers' Association

**BCYC** British Corinthian Yacht Club

**bd** board • bold • *Insurance, Finance* bond • *Bookbinding* bound • broad • bundle

**b.d.** *Med.* bis die (Latin: twice a day; in prescriptions) • *Commerce* bill(s) discounted

**b/d** barrels per day • *Book-keeping* brought down

**Bd** *Computing, symbol for* baud • Band (German: volume) • Board • Boulevard

**BD** Bachelor of Divinity • *symbol for* Bahrain dinar (monetary unit) • *international vehicle registration for* Bangladesh • battle dress • *Physics* beam deflection • *British fishing port registration for* Bideford • *Med.* bile duct • *Commerce* bill(s) discounted • bomb disposal • *Med.* bone density • boom defence • *postcode for* Bradford • *airline flight code for* British Midland • Bundesrepublik Deutschland (Federal Republic of Germany) • *British vehicle registration for* Northampton

**B/D** bank draft • *Commerce* bill(s) discounted • *Book-keeping* brought down

**BDA** Bachelor of Domestic Arts • Bachelor of Dramatic Art • bomb-damage assessment • British Deaf Association • British Dental Association • British Diabetic Association

**b.d.c.** *Engineering* bottom dead centre

**BDC** Book Development Council

**BDCC** British Defence Coordinating Committee

**BDCS** *Chem.* *t*-butyldimethylchlorosilane

**Bde** Bände (German: volumes) • Brigade

**BDE** *Chem.* bond dissociation energy

**BDentSc** Bachelor in Dental Science

**BDes** Bachelor of Design

**BDF** *Computing* backward differentiation formulae (as in **BDF methods**) • Botswana Defence Force

**BDFA** British Dairy Farmers' Association

**bd.ft.** board foot (measure of timber)

**BDG** *Bookbinding* binding

**BDG/ND** *Bookbinding* binding, no date can be given

**BDH** British Drug Houses

**b.d.i.** bearing deviation indicator • both dates (*or* days) included

**BDI** (Germany) Bundesverband der Deutschen Industrie (Federal Association of German Industry)

**bdl.** (*or* **bdle**) bundle

**BDL** British Drama League

**BDM** births, deaths, marriages • bomber defence missile • branch delegates' meeting

**BDMA** British Direct Marketing Association • British Disinfectant Manufacturers' Association

**BDMAA** British Direct Mail Advertising Association

**Bdmr** Bandmaster

**BDNF** *Med.* brain-derived neurotrophic factor

**BDO** Boom Defence Officer

**BDP** breakdown pressure

**BDPA** *Chem.* α,γ-bisdiphenylene-β-phenylallyl

**Bdr** Bombardier • Brigadier

**bdrm** bedroom

**bds** *Bookbinding* boards • bundles

**b.d.s.** *Med.* bis in die sumendus (Latin: to be taken twice a day; in prescriptions)

**BDS** Bachelor of Dental Surgery • *international vehicle registration for* Barbados • bomb disposal squad • British Driving Society

**BDSA** (USA) Business and Defense Services Administration

**BDSc** Bachelor of Dental Science

**BDST** British Double Summer Time

**BDU** *Astronomy* baryon-dominated universe • bomb disposal unit

**b.d.v.** (*or* **BDV**) *Physics* breakdown voltage

**Bdx.** Bordeaux

**be.** bezüglich (German: regarding *or* with reference to)

**b.e.** bill of exchange • binding edge

**Be** *Chem., symbol for* beryllium • *Astronomy, indicating* a spectral type

**Bé** Baumé (temperature scale)

**BE** Bachelor of Economics • Bachelor of
Education • Bachelor of Engineering •
Bank of England • *Physics* Barkhausen
emission • *British fishing port registration
for* Barnstaple • best estimate • bill of
exchange • *Computing* binary encoun-
ter • *Physics* binding energy • (USA)
Board of Education • borough engi-
neer • *Physics* Bose–Einstein • British
Element • British Embassy • British
Empire • *British vehicle registration for*
Lincoln

**B/E** bill of entry • bill of exchange

**BEA** British East Africa • British
Epilepsy Association • British Esperanto
Association • (formerly) British
European Airways

**BEAB** British Electrical Approvals
Board

**BEAC** Banque des états de l'Afrique
centrale (French: Bank of Central African States)

**BEAIRE** British Electrical and Allied
Industries' Research Association

**BEAM** (biːm) *Med.* brain electrical
activity mapping

**BEAMA** (Federation of) British Electrotechnical and Allied Manufacturers'
Associations

**bearb.** bearbeitet (German: compiled
*or* edited)

**BEAS** British Educational Administration Society

**bec.** because

**BEc** Bachelor of Economics

**BEC** Building Employers' Confederation • Bureau européen du café
(French: European Coffee Bureau) •
(USA) Bureau of Employees' Compensation

**BECA** British Exhibition Contractors'
Association

**Bech.** Bechuanaland (now Botswana)

**BECO** booster-engine cut-off

**BEcon** Bachelor of Economics

**BEcon(IA)** Bachelor of Economics in
Industrial Administration

**BEcon(PA)** Bachelor of Economics in
Public Administration

**BECTU** Broadcasting, Entertainment,
and Cinematograph Technicians Union
(formed by amalgamation of BETA
with ACTT)

**BEd** Bachelor of Education

**BED** *Biochem.* bio-emf device

**BEDA** British Electrical Development
Association • Bureau of European
Designers' Associations

**BEd(Com)** Bachelor of Education in
Commerce

**BEd(HEc)** Bachelor of Education in
Home Economics

**BEd(N)** Bachelor of Education in Nursing

**BEd(PE)** Bachelor of Education in
Physical Education

**beds.** bedrooms

**Beds** Bedfordshire

**BEd(Sc)** Bachelor of Education in
Science (*or* Educational Science)

**BEE** Bachelor of Electrical Engineering

**BEEL** biological equivalent exposure
limit (of radiation)

**bef.** before

**b.e.f.** blunt end first

**BEF** British Equestrian Federation •
British Expeditionary Force (in World
Wars I and II)

**BEFA** British Emigrant Families Association

**beg.** beginning

**BEG** (USA) Bureau of Economic Geology

**BEHA** British Export Houses Association

**BEI** Bachelor of Engineering (Dublin) •
*Physics* back-scattered electron imaging • Banque européenne d'investissement (French: European Investments
Bank)

**Beibl.** Beiblatt (German: supplement)

**beigeb.** beigebunden (German: bound,
in with something else)

**beil.** beiliegend (German: enclosed)

**BEIR** biological effects of ionizing radiation

**Bel.** Belgian • Belgium

**BEL** British Electrotechnical Committee

**bel ex.** bel exemplaire (French: fine
copy; of a book or engraving)

**Belf.** Belfast

**Belg.** Belgian • Belgic • Belgium

**BEM** British Empire Medal • bug-eyed
monster

**BEMA** British Essence Manufacturers'
Association • Business Equipment
Manufacturers' Association

**BEMAC** British Exports Marketing
Advisory Committee

**BEMAS** British Education Management and Administration Society

**BEME** ('biː'miː) Brigade Electrical and Mechanical Engineer

**BEMSA** British Eastern Merchant Shippers' Association

**ben.** benedictio (Latin: blessing)

**BEN** *Electronics* broadband electrostatic noise

**Bend.** Bendigo (Australia)

**BenDr** Bachelier en droit (French: Bachelor of Law)

**benef.** benefice

**Benelux** ('benɪ,lʌks) Belgium, Netherlands, Luxembourg (customs union)

**Beng.** Bengal(i)

**BEng** Bachelor of Engineering

**BEngr** Bachelor of Engraving

**BenH** Bachelier en humanités (French: Bachelor of Humanities)

**BEO** Base Engineer Officer

**BEPC** *Physics* Beijing Electron–Positron Collider • British Electrical Power Convention

**beq.** bequeath

**beqt** bequest

**Ber.** (*or* **Berl.**) Berlin

**BERCO** British Electric Resistance Company

**Berks** Berkshire

**Berm.** Bermuda

**Berw.** Berwickshire (former Scottish county)

**BES** Bachelor of Engineering Science • Bachelor of Environmental Studies • Biological Engineering Society • British Ecological Society • Business Expansion Scheme

**BèsA** Bachelier ès arts (French: Bachelor of Arts)

**BESA** British Esperanto Scientific Association

**BESI** bus electronic scanning indicator

**BèsL** Bachelier ès lettres (French: Bachelor of Letters)

**BESO** British Executive Service Overseas

**BèsS** (*or* **BèsSc**) Bachelier ès sciences (French: Bachelor of Science)

**BESS** Bank of England Statistical Summary • *Oceanog.* bottom environmental sensing system

**Best.** *Commerce* Bestellung (German: order)

**BEST** (best) British Expertise in Science and Technology (database)

**bet.** between

**BET** British Electric Traction Company • *Chem.* Brunauer–Emmet–Teller (as in **BET adsorption theory**) • buildings energy technology

**BETA** Broadcasting and Entertainment Trades Alliance (*see* BECTU) • Business Equipment Trades' Association

**BETAA** British Export Trade Advertising Association

**BETRO** British Export Trade Research Organization

**betw.** between

**BEU** *Engineering* batch extraction unit • Benelux Economic Union

**BEUC** ('beɪuːk) Bureau européen des unions de consommateurs (French: European Bureau of Consumers' Unions)

**bev.** bevel

**BeV** (USA) billion electronvolts

**BEVA** British Exhibition Venues' Association

**BEXA** British Exporters Association

**bez.** bezahlt (German: paid) • bezüglich (German: with reference to)

**bezw.** beziehungsweise (German: respectively)

**bf** (*or* **bf.**) brief

**b.f.** bankruptcy fee • base frequency • beer firkin • (*or* **bf**) *Colloquial* bloody fool • (*or* **bf**) *Printing* bold face • bona fide

**b/f** bring forward (date on correspondence) • *Book-keeping* brought forward

**BF** Bachelor of Forestry • *British fishing port registration for* Banff • Banque de France (Bank of France) • *symbol for* Belgian franc • black face (sheep) • blast furnace • *Colloquial* bloody fool • body fat • breathing frequency • British Funds • *British vehicle registration for* Stoke-on-Trent

**B/F** bring forward (date on correspondence) • *Book-keeping* brought forward

**BFA** Bachelor of Fine Arts • British Film Academy

**BFAP** British Forces Arabian Peninsula

**BFASS** *Nuclear physics* BWR fuel assembly sealing system

**BFBPW** British Federation of Business and Professional Women

**BFBS** (*or* **B & FBS**) British and Foreign Bible Society • British Forces Broadcasting Service

**BFCA** British Federation of Commodity Associations

**BFCS** British Friesian Cattle Society

**BFEBS** British Far Eastern Broadcasting Service

**BFET** *Electronics* ballistic field-effect transistor

**BFFA** British Film Fund Agency

**BFFC** British Federation of Folk Clubs

**BFI** British Film Institute

**BFIA** British Flower Industry Association

**BFM** *Physics* boson–fermion coupling model

**BFMA** British Farm Mechanization Association

**BFMF** British Federation of Music Festivals • British Footwear Manufacturers' Federation

**BFMIRA** British Food Manufacturing Industries' Research Association

**BFMP** British Federation of Master Printers

**Bfn** Bloemfontein

**BFN** British Forces Network

**b.f.o.** (*or* **BFO**) *Electronics* beat-frequency oscillator

**BFor** Bachelor of Forestry

**BForSc** Bachelor of Forestry Science

**BFP** Bureau of Freelance Photographers

**BFPA** British Film Producers' Association

**BFPC** British Farm Produce Council

**BFPO** British Forces Post Office

**BFr** Belgian franc

**BFS** *Mining* blast-furnace slag • British Fuchsia Society

**BFSA** British Fire Services' Association

**BFSS** British and Foreign Sailors' Society • British Field Sports Society

**BFT** *Physiol., Psychol.* biofeedback training

**BFTA** British Fur Trade Alliance

**BFUW** British Federation of University Women

**BFV** *Military* Bradley fighting vehicle

**bg** *Commerce* bag

**b.g.** *Horse racing* bay gelding

**b/g** bonded goods

**BG** *airline flight code for* Biman Bangladesh Airlines • Birmingham (wire) gauge • blood group • Brigadier General • British Guiana (now Guyana) • *international vehicle registration for* Bulgaria • *British vehicle registration for* Liverpool

**BGA** (USA) Better Government Association • British Gliding Association • British Graduates Association

**BGB** Booksellers' Association of Great Britain and Ireland • (Germany) Bürgerliches Gesetzbuch (code of civil law)

**BGC** bank giro credit • British Gas Corporation (now British Gas)

**BGCS** Botanic Gardens Conservation Secretariat

**BGEA** Billy Graham Evangelistic Association

**BGenEd** Bachelor of General Education

**bGH** (*or* **BGH**) *Biochem.* bovine growth hormone

**BGIRA** British Glass Industry Research Association

**b.g.l.** below ground level

**BGL** Bachelor of General Laws

**bglr** bugler

**BGM** Bethnal Green Museum

**BGMA** British Gear Manufacturers' Association

**BGMV** *Microbiol.* bean golden mosaic virus

**BGS** Brigadier General Staff • British Geological Survey • British Geriatrics Society • British Goat Society • Brothers of the Good Shepherd

**bgt** bought

**BGV** below-ground vault

**bh** (*or* **b.h.**) barrels per hour • *Colloquial* bloody hell

**BH** base hospital • *international vehicle registration for* Belize (formerly British Honduras) • *Astronomy* black hole • *British fishing port registration for* Blyth • *postcode for* Bournemouth • *Metallurgy* Brinell hardness • British Hovercraft • Burlington House, London (home of the Royal Academy) • *British vehicle registration for* Luton

**B/H** bill of health

**BHA** *Mining* bottom-hole assembly • British Homeopathic Association • British Humanist Association

**B'ham** Birmingham

**BHB** British Hockey Board

**BHC** *Med.* benign hereditary chorea • benzene hexachloride (insecticide) • British High Commissioner

**bhd** beachhead • billhead • bulkhead

**BHDF** British Hospital Doctors' Federation

**BHE** Bachelor of Home Economics

**B'head** Birkenhead

**Bhf** Bahnhof (German: railway station)

**BHF** British Heart Foundation

**BHGA** British Hang Gliding Association

**BHI** British Horological Institute • Bureau hydrographique international (French: International Hydrographic Bureau)

**Bhm** Birmingham

**BHMRA** British Hydromechanics' Research Association

**Bhn** (*or* **BHN**) *Metallurgy* Brinell hardness number

**BHort** Bachelor of Horticulture

**BHortSc** Bachelor of Horticultural Science

**bhp** brake horsepower

**BHP** (Australia) Broken Hill Proprietary

**bhpric** bishopric

**BHQ** Brigade Headquarters

**BHRA** British Hydromechanics' Research Association

**BHRCA** British Hotels, Restaurants, and Caterers' Association

**BHS** boys' high school • British Home Stores • British Horse Society

**BHT** *Electronics* bipolar heterojunction transistor • *Mining* bottom-hole temperature • *Chem.* butylated hydroxytoluene

**BHTA** British Herring Trade Association

**Bhu.** Bhutan

**BHy** Bachelor of Hygiene

**Bi** *Chem.*, *symbol for* bismuth

**BI** background information • Bahama Islands • Balearic Islands • base ignition • *Chem.* benzene-insoluble • Bermuda Islands • *Med.* bone injury • bulk issue • *Irish vehicle registration for* Monaghan • *airline flight code for* Royal Brunei Airlines

**BIA** British Ironfounders' Association • (USA) Bureau of Indian Affairs

**BIAA** British Industrial Advertising Association

**BIAC** Business and Industry Advisory Committee

**BIAE** British Institute of Adult Education

**BIAS** Bristol Industrial Archaeological Society

**BIATA** British Independent Air Transport Association

**bib.** *Med.* bibe (Latin: drink) • bibliothèque (French: library)

**Bib.** Bible • Biblical

**BIB** *Military* baby incendiary bomb • *Electronics* blocked impurity band

**BIBA** British Insurance Brokers' Association (now British Insurance and Investment Brokers' Association, BIIBA)

**BIBC** British Isles Bowling Council

**BIBF** British and Irish Basketball Federation

**bibl.** (*or* **bibliog.**) bibliographer • bibliographical • bibliography

**BIBRA** British Industrial Biological Research Association

**BIC** Bahá'í International Community • *Electronics* biased ion collector • Bureau international du cinéma (French: International Cinema Bureau) • Butter Information Council

**BICC** Berne International Copyright Convention

**BICE** Bureau international catholique de l'enfance (French: International Catholic Child Bureau)

**BICEMA** British Internal Combustion Engine Manufacturers' Association

**BICEP** British Industrial Collaborative Exponential Programme

**BICERI** British Internal Combustion Engine Research Institute

**BICFET** ('bɪk,fɛt) *Electronics* bipolar inversion-channel field-effect transistor

**bi-CMOS** (baɪ'siːmɒs) *Electronics* (merged) bipolar/complementary metal oxide semiconductor

**b.i.d.** *Med.* bis in die (Latin: twice a day; in prescriptions)

**BID** Bachelor of Industrial Design • Bachelor of Interior Design • *Med.* brought in dead

**BIDS** British Institute of Dealers in Securities

**BIE** Bachelor of Industrial Engineering • *Maths.* boundary integral equation • Bureau international d'éducation (French: International Bureau of Education) • Bureau international des expositions (French: International Exhibition Bureau)

**BIEE** British Institute of Energy Economics

**bien.** biennial

**BIET** British Institute of Engineering Technology

**BIF** *Geology* banded iron formation • *Biochem.* B-cell growth inhibitory factor • *Physics* beta-induced fluorescence • British Industries Fair

**BIFFEX** ('bɪfɛks) Baltic International Freight Futures Market (formerly Exchange)

**BIFU** ('bɪfuː) Banking, Insurance, and Finance Union

**BIH** *Med.* benign intracranial hypertension • Bureau international de l'heure (French: International Time Bureau)

**BIHA** British Ice Hockey Association

**BIIBA** British Insurance and Investment Brokers Association

**bim.** bimestrale (Italian: bimonthly) • bimestre (Italian: a two-month period)

**BIM** *Maths.* boundary integral method • British Institute of Management • British Insulin Manufacturers

**BIMCAM** British Industrial Measuring and Control Apparatus Manufacturers' Association

**bin.** *Maths.* binary

**BIN** (ital.) Bulletin of International News

**BINC** Building Industries' National Council

**bind.** binding

**BIO** (Canada) Bedford Institute of Oceanography

**biochem.** biochemistry

**biog.** biographer • biographic(al) • biography

**biogeog.** biogeography

**biol.** biological • biologist • biology

**BIOS** ('baɪɒs) *Computing* basic input-output system • Biological Investigations of Space • (*or* **bios**) *Astronautics* biological satellite • British Intelligence Objectives Subcommittee

**BIOT** British Indian Ocean Territory

**BIP** Botswana Independence Party • British Industrial Plastics • British Institute in Paris

**BIPCA** Bureau international permanent de chimie analytique pour les matières destinées à l'alimentation de l'homme et des animaux (French: Permanent International Bureau of Analytical Chemistry of Human and Animal Food)

**BIPL** Burmah Industrial Products Limited

**BIPM** Bureau international des poids et mesures (French: International Bureau of Weights and Measures)

**BIPP** *Med.* bismuth iodoform paraffin paste (formerly used for treating wounds) • British Institute of Practical Psychology

**BIR** Board of Inland Revenue • British Institute of Radiology

**BIRD** Banque internationale pour la reconstruction et le développement (French: International Bank for Reconstruction and Development; IBRD)

**BIRE** British Institution of Radio Engineers

**BIRF** Brewing Industry Research Foundation

**Birm.** Birmingham

**BIRMO** British Infra-Red Manufacturers' Organization

**BIRS** British Institute of Recorded Sound

**bis.** bissextile

**BIS** Bank for International Settlements • *Physics* beam-induced stripping • British Information Services • British Interplanetary Society • Bureau international du scoutisme (French: Boy Scouts International Bureau)

**BISA** British International Studies Association

**Bisc.** Biscayan

**BISF** British Iron and Steel Federation

**BISFA** British Industrial and Scientific Film Association

**bish.** bishop

**bis in 7d.** *Med.* bis in septem diebus (Latin: twice a week; in prescriptions)

**BISPA** British Independent Steel Producers' Association

**BISRA** British Iron and Steel Research Association

**BISYNC** ('baɪ,sɪŋk) *Computing* binary synchronous communications

**bit** (bɪt) *Computing, Maths.* binary digit

**BIT** Bureau international du travail (French: International Labour Office)

**BITA** British Industrial Truck Association

**bitm.** bituminous

**BITNET** ('bɪt,nɛt) *Computing* Because It's Time Network

**BITO** British Institution of Training Officers

**BITOA** British Incoming Tour Operators' Association

**bitum.** bituminous

**BIU** Bermuda Industrial Union • Bureau international des universités (French: International University Bureau)

**biv.** bivouac

**BIWF** British-Israel World Federation

**BIWS** Bureau of International Whaling Statistics

**BIZ** Bank für Internationalen Zahlungsausgleich (German: Bank for International Settlements)

**BJ** Bachelor of Journalism • *British vehicle registration for* Ipswich
**BJA** British Judo Association
**BJCEB** British Joint Communications Electronics Board
**BJJ** *Electronics* boundary Josephson junction
**BJOS** (ital.) British Journal of Occupational Safety
**BJP** (India) Bharatiya Janata Party
**BJSM** British Joint Services Mission
**BJT** *Electronics* bipolar junction transistor
**BJTRA** British Jute Trade Research Association
**BJur** (*or* **BJuris**) Bachelor of Jurisprudence
**bk** backwardation • bank • bark • barrack • black • block • book • break
**Bk** *Chem.*, *symbol for* berkelium
**BK** *British fishing port registration for* Berwick-on-Tweed • *British vehicle registration for* Portsmouth
**BKA** (Germany) Bundeskriminalamt (criminal investigations office)
**bkble** bookable
**BKC** *Chem.* benzalkonium chloride
**bkcy** bankruptcy
**bkd** blackboard • booked
**BKD** bacterial kidney disease
**bkg** banking • booking • book-keeping
**bkgd** background
**bkkg** book-keeping
**bklt** booklet
**Bklyn** (USA) Brooklyn
**bkm** buckram
**BKN** *Meteorol.* broken (cloud)
**bkpt** (*or* **bkrpt**) bankrupt
**bks** barracks • books
**BKSTS** British Kinematograph, Sound, and Television Society
**bkt** basket • bracket
**bl** barrel (container *or* unit of measure)
**bl.** bale • black • blue
**b.l.** (*or* **b/l**) bill of lading • breech-loading (rifle)
**Bl.** Blat (German: newspaper) • Blessed
**BL** Bachelor of Law • Bachelor of Literature (*or* Letters) • Barrister-at-Law • base line • bill lodged • bill of lading • *Printing* black letter • *Physics* Bloch lines • *Med.* blood lead • boatswain lieutenant • Bodleian Library (Oxford) • *postcode for* Bolton • *British fishing port registration for* Bristol • (formerly) British Leyland • British Library • *Med.*

Burkitt lymphoma • *British vehicle registration for* Reading
**B/L** bill of lading
**BLA** Bachelor of Landscape Architecture • Bachelor of Liberal Arts • British Legal Association • British Liberation Army
**BLACC** British and Latin American Chamber of Commerce
**BLAISE** (bleɪz) British Library Automated Information Service
**BLB** *Horticulture* bacterial leaf blight • Boothby, Lovelace, and Bulbulian (in **BLB nasal oxygen mask**)
**BLC** British Lighting Council
**bld** *Printing* bold(face)
**bldg** building
**BLE** (USA) Brotherhood of Locomotive Engineers (trade union)
**BLESMA** ('blɛsmə) British Limbless Ex-Servicemen's Association
**BLEU** Belgo-Luxembourg Economic Union • *Aeronautics* Blind Landing Experimental Unit
**BLG** (ital.) Burke's Landed Gentry
**BLH** British Legion Headquarters
**BLI** British Lighting Industries
**BLib** (*or* **BLibSc**) Bachelor of Library Science
**BLIC** Bureau de liaison des industries du caoutchouc de la CE (French: Rubber Industries Liaison Bureau of the EC)
**BLIS** (USA) Bibliographic Literature Information System
**Bliss** (blɪs) baby life support systems • *Military* bend, low silhouette, irregular shape, small, secluded (escape technique taught to pilots)
**BLit** Bachelor of Literature
**BLitt** Bachelor of Letters (Latin *Baccalaureus Litterarum*)
**blk** black • blank • block • bulk
**BLL** Bachelor of Laws
**BLM** *Biochem.* bilayer lipid membrane • blind landing machine • (USA) Bureau of Land Management
**BLMA** British Lead Manufacturers' Association
**BLMAS** Bible Lands Missions' Aid Society
**BLMRA** British Leather Manufacturers' Research Association
**BLO** *Meteorol.* below clouds
**BLOF** British Lace Operatives' Federation

**BLOX** (blɒks) *Finance* block order exposure system

**BLP** Barbados Labour Party

**b.l.r.** breech-loading rifle

**BLR** *Spectroscopy* broad-line (emission) region

**BLRA** British Launderers' Research Association

**BLS** Bachelor of Library Science • basic life support • benevolenti lectori salutem (Latin: greeting to the well-wishing reader) • Branch Line Society • *Physics* Brillouin light scattering • (USA) Bureau of Labor Statistics

**BLSN** *Meteorol.* blowing snow

**blt** built

**BLT** bacon, lettuce, and tomato (sandwich)

**BLV** *Microbiol.* bovine leukaemia virus • British Legion Village

**Blvd** Boulevard

**BLWA** British Laboratory Ware Association

**BLWN** *Electronics* band-limited white noise

**b.m.** bene merenti (Latin: to the well-deserving) • *Horse racing* black mare • board measure (measurement of wood) • *Med.* bowel movement • breech mechanism (of a firearm)

**BM** Bachelor of Medicine • Bachelor of Music • bandmaster • *Med.* basal metabolism • base metal • beatae memoriae (Latin: of blessed memory) • Beata Maria (Latin: the Blessed Virgin) • *Surveying* benchmark • Bishop and Martyr • bonae memoriae (Latin: of happy memory) • *Med.* bone marrow • *Computing* Boyer–Moore (in **BM algorithm**) • brigade major • British Monomark • British Museum • *British fishing port registration for* Brixham • Bronze Medallist • (USA) Bureau of Mines • *British vehicle registration for* Luton

**BMA** Bahrain Monetary Agency • British Manufacturers' Association • British Medical Association

**BM algorithm** *Computing* Boyer–Moore algorithm

**BMath** Bachelor of Mathematics

**BMC** *Med.* bone marrow cell(s) • *Med.* bone mineral content (*or* concentration) • Book Marketing Council • British Match Corporation • British Medical Council • British Metal Corporation • (formerly) British Motor Corporation • British Mountaineering

Council • *Bibliog.* British Museum Catalogue (of 15th-century books)

**BMCIS** Building Maintenance Cost Information Service

**BMD** ballistic missile defence • births, marriages, and deaths • *Med.* bone mineral density

**BMDM** *Med.* bone-marrow-derived macrophage(s) • British Museum Department of Manuscripts

**Bmdr** *Military* Bombardier

**BME** Bachelor of Mechanical Engineering • Bachelor of Mining Engineering • Bachelor of Music Education • *Med.* benign myalgic encephalomyelitis

**BMEC** British Marine Equipment Council

**BMed** Bachelor of Medicine

**BMedSci** Bachelor of Medical Science

**BMEF** British Mechanical Engineering Federation

**BMEG** Building Materials Export Group

**BMEO** British Middle East Office

**BMEP** (*or* **bmep**) *Engineering* brake mean effective pressure

**BMet** Bachelor of Metallurgy

**BMetE** Bachelor of Metallurgical Engineering

**BMEWS** (bɪ'mjuːz) ballistic missile early-warning system

**BMFA** Boston Museum of Fine Arts

**BMH** British Military Hospital

**BMI** ballistic missile interceptor • Birmingham and Midland Institute • body-mass index • Broadcast Music Incorporated

**BMJ** (ital.) British Medical Journal

**BML** British Museum Library

**BMM** British Military Mission

**BMMA** Bacon and Meat Marketing Association

**b.m.o.** business machine operator

**B'mouth** Bournemouth

**bmp** (*or* **b.m.p.**) brake mean power

**BMP** biochemical methane potential (*or* production)

**BMPA** British Metalworking Plantmakers' Association

**BMPS** British Musicians' Pension Society

**BMR** *Physiol.* basal metabolic rate

**BMRA** Brigade Major Royal Artillery

**BMRB** British Market Research Bureau

**BMRMC** British Motor Racing Marshals' Club

**BMRR** (USA) Brookhaven Medical Research Reactor

**BMS** Bachelor of Marine Science • Baptist Missionary Society • British Mycological Society • building management system • business modelling system

**BMSE** Baltic Mercantile and Shipping Exchange

**BMT** basic motion time-study • bone-marrow transplant • borehole-mining tool • British Mean Time

**BMTA** British Motor Trade Association

**BMus** Bachelor of Music

**BMusEd** Bachelor of Music Education

**BMV** Blessed Mary the Virgin • *Microbiol.* brome mosaic virus

**BMW** Bayerische Motorenwerke (German: Bavarian Motor Works)

**BMWE** (USA) Brotherhood of Maintenance of Way Employees (trade union)

**BMWS** ballistic missile weapon system

**BMX** bicycle motocross

**bn** bassoon • battalion • beacon • been • billion • born

**Bn** Baron • Battalion

**BN** Bachelor of Nursing • bank note • *Chem.* boron nitride • *British fishing port registration for* Boston • *postcode for* Brighton • Britten-Norman (aircraft) • *British vehicle registration for* Manchester

**BNA** *Chem.* base-neutralized acid • British Naturalists' Association • British North America • *Insurance* British North Atlantic • British Nursing Association

**BNAF** British North Africa Force

**BNB** *Physiol.* blood–nerve barrier • British National Bibliography

**BNBC** British National Book Centre

**BNC** *Chem.* base-neutralizing capacity • Brasenose College, Oxford • *Linguistics* British National Corpus

**BNCC** British National Committee for Chemistry

**BNCI** (Madagascar) Banque nationale pour le commerce et l'industrie (French: National Bank for Commerce and Industry)

**BNCM** (France) Bibliothèque nationale du conservatoire de musique (National Library of Music, Paris)

**BNCS** British National Carnation Society

**BNCSAA** British National Committee on Surface-Active Agents

**BNCSR** British National Committee on Space Research

**BND** (Germany) Bundesnachrichten-dienst (national intelligence service)

**B/ND** *Bookbinding* binding, no date given

**BNDD** (USA) Bureau of Narcotics and Dangerous Drugs

**Bndr** Bandmaster

**BNEC** British National Export Council • British Nuclear Energy Conference

**BNES** British Nuclear Energy Society

**BNF** *Computing* Backus–Naur (*or* Backus normal) form • *Pharmacol.* British National Formulary • (*or* **BNFL**) British Nuclear Fuels (Limited) • British Nutrition Foundation

**BNFC** British National Film Catalogue

**BNFMF** British Non-Ferrous Metals Federation

**BNGA** British Nursery Goods Association

**BNGM** British Naval Gunnery Mission

**BNHQ** battalion headquarters

**bnkg** banking

**BNL** Banca Nazionale del Lavoro (Italian: National Bank of Lavoro) • Brookhaven National Laboratory

**BNM** Bureau national de metrologie (French: National Bureau of Meteorology)

**BNMAU** *international civil aircraft marking for* Mongolia

**BN object** *Astronomy* Becklin–Neugebauer object

**BNOC** British National Oil Corporation • British National Opera Company

**BNP** Banque nationale de Paris (French: National Bank of Paris) • Barbados National Party

**BNS** Bachelor of Natural Science • Bathymetric Navigation System • British Numismatic Society • buyer no seller

**BNSc** Bachelor of Nursing Science

**BNSC** British National Space Centre

**BNTA** British Numismatic Trade Association

**BNurs** Bachelor of Nursing

**BNX** British Nuclear Export Executive

**bnzn** *Chem.* benzoin

**b.o.** back order • blackout • *Med.* bowels open • branch office • broker's order • buyer's option

**b/o** *Book-keeping* brought over

**BO** biological oceanography • *Colloquial* body odour • *British fishing port registration for* Borrowstownness • box office •

*Med.* bowels opened · *British vehicle registration for* Cardiff

**B/O** *Book-keeping* brought over · buyer's option

**BOA** British Olympic Association · British Optical Association · British Orthopaedic Association · broad ocean area

**BOAC** (formerly) British Overseas Airways Corporation

**BOAD** Banque ouest-africaine de développement (French: West African Development Bank)

**BOA(Disp)** British Optical Association, Dispensing Certificate

**BOAI** *Med.* balloon occluded arterial infusion

**BOBA** British Overseas Banks' Association

**BOBMA** British Oil Burner Manufacturers' Association

**BOC** *Computing* beginning of cycle · *Computing* bimodal optical computer · British Oxygen Corporation · Burmah Oil Company

**BOCE** Board of Customs and Excise

**BOC-ON** *Chem.* 2-(*t*-butoxycarbonyl-oxyimino)-2-phenylacetonitrile

**Bod.** (*or* **Bodl.**, **Bodley**) Bodleian Library (Oxford)

**BOD** biochemical oxygen demand

**BOE** Board of Education · *Building trades* brick on edge (in **BOE sill**)

**BOF** *Chemical engineering* basic oxygen furnace · *Computing* beginning of file · British Orienteering Federation · British Overseas Fairs

**B of E** Bank of England

**B of H** Band of Hope Union

**BOGMC** Bangladesh Oil, Gas, and Minerals Corporation

**Boh.** Bohemia(n)

**BOHA** *Med.* balloon occlusion hepatic angiography

**BoJ** (*or* **BOJ**) Bank of Japan

**bol.** *Med.* bolus (Latin: large pill)

**Bol.** Bolívar (1783–1830, South American statesman) · Bolivia(n)

**BOL** beginning of life

**BOLTOP** ('bɒl,tɒp) better on lips than on paper (written on the back of envelopes containing love letters)

**b.o.m.** bill of materials (in manufacturing)

**Bom.** Bombay

**BOM** (USA) Bureau of Mines

**Bomb.** Bombardier · Bombay

**BomCS** Bombay Civil Service

**BomSC** Bombay Staff Corps

**bon.** bataillon (French: battalion)

**BON acid** *Chem.* beta-oxynaphthoic acid

**BONUS** ('bəʊnəs) *Finance* Borrower's Option for Notes and Underwritten Standby

**Boo** *Astronomy* Bootes

**BOP** *Chem.* basic oxygen process · *Mining* blowout preventer · Boy's Own Paper (former magazine)

**BOptom** Bachelor of Optometry

**BOQ** *US military* bachelor officers' quarters · base officers' quarters

**bor.** borough

**BOr** Bachelor of Orientation

**BORAD** British Oxygen Research and Development Association

**boro.** borough

**BOS** *Chemical engineering* basic oxygen steelmaking

**bos'n** boatswain

**Bos Pops** (USA) Boston Pops Orchestra

**BOSS** (bɒs) Bioastronautic Orbiting Space Station · (South Africa) Bureau of State Security

**Boswash** ('bɒs,wɒʃ) (USA) Boston–Washington, DC (indicating the urban area between these cities)

**bot.** botanic(al) · botanist · botany · bottle · bottom · bought

**BOT** *Computing* beginning of tape (in **BOT marker**) · (*or* **BoT**) Board of Trade (now part of DTI)

**BOTB** British Overseas Trade Board

**BOT marker** *Computing* beginning of tape marker

**BOU** British Ornithologists' Union

**boul.** (France) boulevard

**BOV** brown oil of vitriol (commercial sulphuric acid)

**BOWO** Brigade Ordnance Warrant Officer

**bp** (*or* **b.p.**) *Biochem.* base pair(s) (unit of length of nucleic acid) · below proof (of alcohol density) · bills payable · *Chem.* boiling point · bonum publicum (Latin: the public good)

**bp.** baptized · birthplace

**b/p** blueprint · bills payable

**Bp** Bishop

**BP** Bachelor of Pharmacy · Bachelor of Philosophy · back projection · (*or* **B-P**) (Robert) Baden-Powell (1857–1941, founder of the Boy Scout movement · barometric pressure · *Finance* basis point • *Military* beach party • (small caps.) before present (following a number of years) • *Chem.* benzoyl peroxide • be prepared (motto of the Scout movement) • *Shipping* between perpendiculars • *Biochem.* binding protein • *Med.* blood pressure • (Netherlands) Boerenpartij (Farmers' Party) • *Chem.* boiling point • *Physics* bright point • British Patent • British Petroleum • British Pharmacopoeia • British Public • *Chem.* bromopentane • *Chem.* burnable poison • *British vehicle registration for* Portsmouth

**B/P** bills payable

**BPA** Bachelor of Professional Arts • Bahnpostamt (German: railway post office) • (USA) Biological Photographic Association • Bookmakers' Protection Association • British Paediatric Association • British Parachute Association • (USA) Brookhaven (*or* BNL) Plant Analyzer • (USA) Business Publications Audit of Circulation

**BPAA** British Poster Advertising Association

**BPAGB** Bicycle Polo Association of Great Britain

**BPAO** *Biochem.* bovine plasma amine oxidase

**BPAS** British Pregnancy Advisory Service

**b.p.b.** bank post bills

**BPBF** British Paper Box Federation

**BPBIRA** British Paper and Board Industry Research Association

**BPBMA** British Paper and Board Makers' Association

**BPC** Book Prices Current • British Pharmaceutical Codex • British Pharmacopoeia Commission • British Printing Corporation • British Productivity Council • (USA) Business and Professional Code • *Chem.* butyl pyridium chloride

**b.p.c.d.** barrels per calendar day

**BPCF** British Precast Concrete Federation

**BPCR** Brakes on Pedal Cycle Regulations

**BPCRA** British Professional Cycle Racing Association

**b.p.d.** barrels per day

**BPDB** Bangladesh Power Development Board

**BPDMS** *Military* basic point defence missile system

**BPE** (*or* **BPEd**) Bachelor of Physical Education

**BPEA** *Chem.* 9,10-bis(phenylethenyl)-anthracene

**BPEN** *Chem.* 5,10-bis(phenylethenyl)-naphthacene

**b.p.f.** *Commerce* bon pour francs (French: value in francs)

**BPF** bottom pressure fluctuation • British Plastics Federation • British Polio Fellowship

**BPG** Broadcasting Press Guild

**BPh** Bachelor of Philosophy

**BPH** Bachelor of Public Health • *Med.* benign prostatic hyperplasia (*or* hypertrophy)

**BPharm** Bachelor of Pharmacy

**BPhil** Bachelor of Philosophy

**bpi** *Computing* bits per inch

**BPI** Booksellers' Provident Institution • British Pacific Islands

**BPICA** Bureau permanent international des constructeurs d'automobiles (French: International Permanent Bureau of Motor Manufacturers)

**BPIF** British Printing Industries' Federation

**bpl.** birthplace

**Bpl.** Barnstaple

**BPLA** *Physics* Beijing Proton Linear Accelerator

**bpm** (*or* **b.p.m.**) barrels per minute • *Music* beats per minute

**BPMA** British Premium Merchandise Association • British Pump Manufacturers' Association

**BPMF** British Postgraduate Medical Federation • British Pottery Manufacturers' Federation

**BPO** base post office • Berlin Philharmonic Orchestra

**BPOE** (USA) Benevolent and Protective Order of Elks

**BPP** Botswana People's Party

**BPPMA** British Power-Press Manufacturers' Association

**BPRA** Book Publishers' Representatives' Association

**BPRO** Blind Persons Resettlement Officer

**bps** *Computing* bits per second

**BPs** Bachelor of Psychology

**BPS** *Med.* blood-pool scintigraphy • border patrol sector (*or* station) • British Pharmacological Society • (USA) Bureau of Professional Standards (Internal Affairs)

**BPsS** British Psychological Society
**Bp Suff.** Bishop Suffragan
**BPsych** Bachelor of Psychology
**bpt** *Computing* bits per track
**b.pt.** boiling point
**BPT** battle practice target • British Petroleum Tanker
**BPV** *Microbiol.* bovine papilloma virus
**bpy** *Chem.* bipyridine (used in formulae)
**bq.** (*or* **bque**) barque
**Bq** *Physics, symbol for* becquerel
**BQ** bene quiescat (Latin: may he (*or* she) rest well)
**BQA** British Quality Association
**BQMS** battery quartermaster-sergeant
**br.** bearing • branch • bridge • brief • brig • bronze • (*or* **br**) brother • brown
**b.r.** bank rate • (*or* **b/r**) bills receivable
**Br** *symbol for* birr (Ethiopian monetary unit) • Bombardier • *Chem., symbol for* bromine • *RC Church* Brother • Bugler
**Br.** Branch • Brazil • Breton • Britain • British
**BR** *Law* Bancus Reginae *or* Regis (Latin: Queen's (*or* King's) Bench) • bioaccumulation ratio • *Med.* blink reflex • *Education* block release • book of reference • *Physics* branching ratio • *international vehicle registration for* Brazil • breeding ratio • *Physics* bremsstrahlung radiation • *British fishing port registration for* Bridgwater • British Rail • *postcode for* Bromley • (poly)butadiene rubber • butyl rubber • *British vehicle registration for* Newcastle upon Tyne
**B/R** bills receivable • Bordeaux or Rouen (in the grain trade) • *Insurance* builders' risks
**BRA** Bee Research Association • Brigadier Royal Artillery • British Records Association • British Rheumatism and Arthritis Association
**Brad.** Bradford
**BRAD** (bræd) (ital.) British Rates and Data (publications directory)
**Br. Am.** British America
**Bras.** Brasil (Portuguese: Brazil)
**BRAS** ballistic rocket air suppression
**Braz.** Brazil(ian)
**Brazza.** Brazzaville
**BRB** *Med.* blood retinal barrier
**Br. C.** British Columbia
**BRC** (USA) base residence course • Biological Records Centre, Nature Conservancy Council • British Rabbits Council • British Radio Corporation
**brch** (*or* **Brch**) branch

**BRCS** British Red Cross Society
**BRD** *British fishing port registration for* Broadford • (USA) Building Research Division, National Bureau of Standards
**BRDC** British Racing Drivers' Club
**brdcst** broadcast
**BRE** Bachelor of Religious Education • Building Research Establishment
**b. rec.** bills receivable
**BRE(L)** British Rail Engineering (Limited)
**BREMA** British Radio Equipment Manufacturers' Association
**Bret.** Breton
**brev.** brevet • breveté (French: patent) • brevetto (Italian: patent)
**brew.** brewer(y) • brewing
**brf** *Law* brief
**BRF** Bible Reading Fellowship • British Road Federation
**BRFC** *Angling* British Record Fish Committee
**brg** bearing
**br. g.** *Horse racing* brown gelding
**BRG** (formerly) *international vehicle registration for* Guyana (now **GUY**)
**Br. I.** British India • British Isles
**BRI** Banque des règlements internationaux (French: Bank for International Settlement) • (USA) Biological Research Institute • (USA) Brain Research Institute
**Brig.** Brigade • Brigadier
**Brig. Gen.** Brigadier General
**brill.** *Music* brillante (Italian: brilliant)
**BRIMEC** ('brimɛk) British Mechanical Engineering Confederation
**BRINCO** ('briŋkəʊ) British Newfoundland Corporation Limited
**Brisb.** Brisbane
**Brist.** Bristol
**Brit.** Britain • Britannia • British • Briton
**Brit. Mus.** British Museum
**Brit. Pat.** British Patent
**Britt.** *Numismatics* Britanniarum (Latin: of Great Britain)
**brk** brick
**brkt** bracket
**brkwtr** breakwater
**brl** barrel
**BRL** Ballistic Research Laboratory • (USA) Bible Research Library
**BRM** *Computing* binary-rate multiplier • *Med.* biological response modifier • British Racing Motors

**BRMA** Board of Registration of Medical Auxiliaries • British Rubber Manufacturers' Association

**BRMCA** British Ready-Mixed Concrete Association

**BRMF** British Rainwear Manufacturers' Federation

**brn** brown

**BRN** *international vehicle registration for* Bahrain

**BRNC** Britannia Royal Naval College

**brng** *Navigation* bearing • burning

**bro.** (brəʊ) brother

**Bro.** Brotherhood

**BRO** brigade routine order

**brom.** *Chem.* bromide

**bros.** (*or* **Bros.**) (brɒs) brothers

**BRP** biological reclamation process

**BRS** British Record Society • British Road Services • Building Research Station

**BRSA** British Rail Staff Association

**BRSCC** British Racing and Sports Car Club

**brt** bright

**BRT** (Belgium) Belgische Radio en Televisie (Dutch broadcasting company) • *Shipping* Brutto-Register-tonnen (German: gross register tons)

**BRTA** British Racing Toboggan Association • British Regional Television Association • British Road Tar Association

**BRU** *international vehicle registration for* Brunei

**Brum.** (brʌm) Brummagem (colloquial name for Birmingham)

**Brunsw.** Brunswick

**Brux.** Bruxelles (French: Brussels)

**BRW** British Relay Wireless

**bry.** (*or* **bryol.**) bryology

**brz.** bronze

**bs** bags • bales

**b.s.** back stage • balance sheet • bill of sale

**Bs** *symbol for* bolívars (*see under* B) • *symbol for* boliviano (Bolivian monetary unit)

**BS** (USA) Bachelor of Science • Bachelor of Surgery • *international vehicle registration for* Bahamas • battleship • battle squadron • *British fishing port registration for* Beaumaris • below specification • *Chem.* benzene-soluble • Bibliographical Society • bill of sale • *Computing* binary state • Biochemical Society • Blackfriars Settlement • Blessed Sacrament • Boy Scouts • *Angling* breaking strain of line •

*Med.* breath sounds • *postcode for* Bristol • *Aeronautics* Bristol Siddeley • British Standard (indicating the catalogue or publication number of the British Standards Institution) • British Steel plc • Budgerigar Society • building society • *Slang* bullshit • *Computing* bus switch • *British vehicle registration for* Inverness

**B/S** bill of sale • *Commerce* bill of store

**BSA** Bachelor of Science in Agriculture • Bachelor of Scientific Agriculture • Bibliographical Society of America • Birmingham Small Arms Company • *Chem.* bis(trimethylsilyl)-acetamide • *Med.* body surface area • *Med.* bovine serum albumin • Boy Scouts' Association • Boy Scouts of America • British School at Athens • British Speleological Association • Building Societies' Association

**BSAA** Bachelor of Science in Applied Arts • British School of Archaeology at Athens

**BSAC** British Sub-Aqua Club

**BSAdv** Bachelor of Science in Advertising

**BSAE** (*or* **BSAeEng**) Bachelor of Science in Aeronautical Engineering • (*or* **BSAgE**) Bachelor of Science in Agricultural Engineering

**BSAgr** Bachelor of Science in Agriculture

**BS & W** basic (*or* bottom) sediment and water

**BSAP** British Society of Animal Production

**BSArch** Bachelor of Science in Architecture

**BSAS** British Ship Adoption Society

**BSAVA** British Small Animals Veterinary Association

**Bsb.** Brisbane

**BSB** British Satellite Broadcasting (*see* BSkyB) • British Standard brass (type of screw thread)

**BSBA** Bachelor of Science in Business Administration

**BSBC** British Social Biology Council

**BSBI** Botanical Society of the British Isles

**BSBus** Bachelor of Science in Business

**bsc** basic

**BSc** Bachelor of Science

**BSC** Bachelor of Science in Commerce • Bengal Staff Corps • Bibliographical Society of Canada •

*Computing* binary synchronous communications • Biomedical Sciences Corporation • British Safety Council • British Shoe Corporation • British Standard Channel • British Stationery Council • British Steel Corporation • British Sugar Corporation • British Supply Council • Broadcasting Standards Council

**BSCA** British Swimming Coaches' Association • (USA) Bureau of Security and Consular Affairs

**BScA** (*or* **BSc(Ag)**) Bachelor of Science in Agriculture

**BScApp** Bachelor of Applied Science

**BSCC** British Society of Clinical Cytology • British Synchronous Clock Conference

**BSCE** Bachelor of Science in Civil Engineering

**BSChE** Bachelor of Science in Chemical Engineering

**BSCCO** *Physics* Bi-Sr-Ca-Cu-O superconductor

**BScD** Bachelor of Dental Science

**BSc(Dent)** Bachelor of Science in Dentistry

**BSc(Econ)** Bachelor of Science in Economics

**BSc(Ed)** Bachelor of Science in Education

**BSc(Hort)** Bachelor of Science in Horticulture

**BScMed** Bachelor of Medical Science

**BSc(Nutr)** Bachelor of Science in Nutrition

**BSCP** (ital.) British Standard Code of Practice (publication)

**BSCRA** British Steel Castings Research Association

**BScSoc** Bachelor of Social Sciences

**BSD** (*or* **BSDes**) Bachelor of Science in Design • ballistic system division • British Society of Dowsers • British Space Development

**b.s.d.l.** boresight datum line

**BSE** (*or* **BSEd**) Bachelor of Science in Education • (*or* **BSEng**) Bachelor of Science in Engineering • bovine spongiform encephalopathy • *Med.* breast self-examination

**BSEc** Bachelor of Science in Economics

**BSEE** (*or* **BSEEng**) Bachelor of Science in Electrical Engineering • Bachelor of Science in Elementary Education

**BSEIE** Bachelor of Science in Electronic Engineering

**BSEM** Bachelor of Science in Engineering of Mines

**BSES** Bachelor of Science in Engineering Sciences • British Schools Exploring Society

**BSF** Bachelor of Science in Forestry • British Salonica Force • British Slag Federation • British Standard fine (type of screw thread) • British Stone Federation

**BSFA** British Science Fiction Association • British Steel Founders' Association

**BSF(L)** British Shipping Federation (Limited)

**BSFM** Bachelor of Science in Forestry Management

**BSFor** Bachelor of Science in Forestry

**BSFS** Bachelor of Science in Foreign Service • British Soviet Friendship Society

**BSFT** Bachelor of Science in Fuel Technology

**BSG** British Standard Gauge

**b.s.g.d.g.** breveté sans garantie du gouvernement (French: patented without government guarantee)

**BSGE** Bachelor of Science in General Engineering

**bsh.** bushel

**BSH** British Society of Hypnotherapists • British Standard Hardness

**BSHA** Bachelor of Science in Hospital Administration

**BSHE** (*or* **BSHEc**) Bachelor of Science in Home Economics

**BSHS** British Society for the History of Science

**BSHyg** Bachelor of Science in Hygiene

**BSI** British Sailors' Institute • British Standards Institution • Building Societies' Institute

**BSIA** British Security Industry Association

**BSIB** Boy Scouts International Bureau

**BSIC** British Ski Instruction Council

**BSIE** Bachelor of Science in Industrial Engineering

**BSIP** British Solomon Islands Protectorate

**BSIRA** British Scientific Instrument Research Association

**BSIS** Business Sponsorship Incentive Scheme

**BSIU** British Society for International Understanding

**BSJ** Bachelor of Science in Journalism

**BSJA** British Show Jumping Association ·

**bsk.** (or **bskt**) basket

**BSkyB** British Sky Broadcasting (formed by merger of BSB with Sky Television)

**Bs/L** bills of lading

**BSL** Bachelor of Sacred Literature · Bachelor of Science in Linguistics · *Med.* bacterial skin lesion · boatswain sublieutenant · British Sign Language

**BSLS** Bachelor of Science in Library Science

**BSM** Bachelor of Sacred Music · Bachelor of Science in Medicine · battery sergeant-major · *Chem.* benzene-soluble matter · branch sales manager · British School of Motoring · (USA) bronze star medal

**BSMA** British Skate Makers' Association

**BSME** Bachelor of Science in Mechanical Engineering · Bachelor of Science in Mining Engineering

**BSMet** Bachelor of Science in Metallurgy

**BSMetE** Bachelor of Science in Metallurgical Engineering

**BSMGP** British Society of Master Glass-Painters

**bsmt** basement

**BSMT** (or **BSMedTech**) Bachelor of Science in Medical Technology

**BSMV** *Microbiol.* barley stripe mosaic virus

**BSN** Bachelor of Science in Nursing

**BSNE** Bachelor of Science in Nuclear Engineering

**BSNS** Bachelor of Naval Science

**BSO** base supply officer · *Chem.* benzene-soluble organic · Boston Symphony Orchestra · Bournemouth Symphony Orchestra · Business Statistics Office

**BSocSc** Bachelor of Social Science

**BSOT** Bachelor of Science in Occupational Therapy

**BSP** (or **BSPhar**, **BSPharm**) Bachelor of Science in Pharmacy · Bering Sea Patrol · Birmingham School of Printing · *Printing* bleached sulphite pulp · British Standard pipe (type of screw thread) · Bulgarian Socialist (formerly Communist) Party · business systems planning

**BSPA** Bachelor of Science in Public Administration

**BSPE** Bachelor of Science in Physical Education

**BSPH** Bachelor of Science in Public Health

**BSPT** (or **BSPhTh**) Bachelor of Science in Physical Therapy

**BSR** Birmingham Sound Reproducers · *Med.* blood sedimentation rate · *Physics* Bragg scattering region · British School at Rome · *Physics* bulk shielding reactor

**BSRA** British Ship Research Association · British Society for Research on Ageing · British Sound Recording Association

**BSRAE** British Society for Research in Agricultural Engineering

**BSRC** (USA) Biological Serial Record Center

**BSRT** Bachelor of Science in Radiological Technology

**BSS** Bachelor of Secretarial Science · Bachelor of Social Science · *Med.* balanced salt solution · basic safety standards · Bibliothèque Saint-Sulpice (Montreal) · *Geology* borehole seismic system · British Sailors' Society · British Standard size · British Standards Specification

**BSSA** Bachelor of Science in Secretarial Administration

**BSSc** Bachelor of Social Science

**BSSE** Bachelor of Science in Secondary Education

**BSSG** (USA) Biomedical Sciences Support Grant

**BSSO** British Society for the Study of Orthodontics

**BSSS** Bachelor of Science in Secretarial Studies · Bachelor of Science in Social Science · British Society of Soil Science

**BST** Bachelor of Sacred Theology · *Agriculture* bovine somatotrophin · British Standard Time (1968–71) · British Summer Time · bulk supply tariff

**B/St** bill of sight

**BSTA** British Surgical Trades' Association

**BSTC** British Student Travel Centre

**bstd** bastard

**BSTFA** *Chem.* bis(trimethylsilyl)-trifluoroacetamide

**bstr** booster

**bstr rkt** booster rocket
**BSU** *Engineering* bench scale unit
**BSurv** Bachelor of Surveying
**b.s.w.** barrels of salt water
**BSW** Bachelor of Social Work • British Standard Whitworth (type of screw thread)
**BSWB** Boy Scouts World Bureau
**BSWE** British Scouts in Western Europe
**BSWIA** British Steel Wire Industries' Association
**bt** beat • benefit • bent • bought
**Bt** Baronet • *Military* brevet
**BT** Bachelor of Teaching • Bachelor of Theology • basic trainer • *Psychol.* behaviour therapy • *postcode for* Belfast • *Med.* benign tumour • bishop's transcript • British Telecom (*or* Telecommunications) • *British vehicle registration for* Leeds
**BTA** Billiards Trade Association • (USA) Blood Transfusion Association • British Theatre Association • British Tourist Authority (formerly British Travel Association) • British Tuberculosis Association
**BTAC** *Computing* binary tree algebraic computation
**BTASA** Book Trade Association of South Africa
**BTB** *Med.* blood–tumour barrier • *Med.* breakthrough bleeding
**BTBA** British Ten Pin Bowling Association
**BTBS** Book Trade Benevolent Society
**BTC** (USA) Bankers' Trust Company • (USA) basic training center • British Textile Confederation • British Transport Commission
**btca** biblioteca (Spanish: library)
**BTCC** Board of Transportation Commissioners of Canada
**BTCh** Bachelor of Textile Chemistry
**BTCP** Bachelor of Town and Country Planning
**BTCV** British Trust for Conservation Volunteers
**b.t.d.** bomb testing device
**BTDB** Bermuda Trade Development Board
**BTDC** *Engineering* before top dead centre
**bté** breveté (French: patent)
**BTE** Bachelor of Textile Engineering
**BTEC** Business and Technician Education Council

**BTech** Bachelor of Technology
**BTEE** *Chem.* N-benzoyl-L-tyrosine ethyl ester
**BTEF** Book Trade Employers' Federation
**BTEMA** British Tanning Extract Manufacturers' Association
**BTEX** *Chem.* benzene, toluene, ethylbenzene, and xylene (solvents)
**b.t.f.** barrels of total fuel • bomb tail fuse
**BTF** British Tarpaviors' Federation • British Trawlers Federation • British Turkey Federation
**BTG** British Technology Group
**bth** bath(room) • berth
**BTh** Bachelor of Theology
**BTH** British Thomson-Houston Company
**BTHMA** British Toy and Hobby Manufacturers' Association
**BThU** British thermal unit
**BTI** (ital.) British Technology Index (publication)
**BTIA** British Tar Industries' Association
**btk** buttock
**btl.** bottle
**BTL** *Meteorol.* between layers
**btm** bottom
**BTM** *Chem.* bromotrifluoromethane
**BTMA** British Typewriter Manufacturers' Association
**BTMSA** *Chem.* bis(trimethylsilyl)acetylene
**btn** baton • button
**BTN** Brussels Tariff Nomenclature
**BTO** big time operator • British Trust for Ornithology
**BTP** Bachelor of Town Planning
**BTR** *Physics* bimetric theory of relativity • (ital.) British Tax Review • British Telecommunications Research
**BTRA** Bombay Textile Industry's Research Association
**BTRP** Bachelor of Town and Regional Planning
**btry** *Military* battery
**BTS** Blood Transfusion Service • British Telecommunications Systems
**Btss** Baronetess
**BTTA** British Thoracic and Tuberculosis Association
**Btu** British thermal unit
**BTU** Board of Trade unit • (USA) British thermal unit
**BTUC** Bahamas Trade Union Congress
**BTW** by the way (used in electronic mail)

**btwn** between

**BTX** *Chem.* benzene, toluene, and xylene • (Germany) Bildschirmtext (videotext system)

**bty** *Military* battery

**B-type** *Psychol.* Basedow type

**bu.** (*or* **Bu.**) bureau • (*or* **bu**) bushel(s)

**b.u.** base unit • *Finance* break-up

**Bu** *Chem., symbol for* butyl group (in formulae)

**BU** Baptist Union of Great Britain and Ireland • Brown University, Rhode Island • *British fishing port registration for* Burntisland • *British vehicle registration for* Manchester

**BuAer** (USA) Bureau of Aeronautics

**BUAF** British United Air Ferries

**BUA of E** Badminton Umpires' Association of England

**BUAV** British Union for the Abolition of Vivisection

**BUC** Bangor University College

**buck.** buckram

**Bucks** Buckinghamshire

**BUCOP** (ital.) British Union Catalogue of Periodicals

**bud.** budget

**Budd.** (*or* **Bud.**) Buddhism • Buddhist

**BuDocks** *US Navy* Bureau of Yards and Docks

**Budpst** Budapest

**BUF** British Union of Fascists

**BUIC** back-up interceptor control

**BUJ** Bachelor of Canon and Civil Law (Latin *Baccalaureus utriusque juris*)

**bul.** bulletin

**Bulg.** Bulgaria(n)

**bull.** bulla (seal used on a papal bull) • bulletin • *Med.* bulliat (Latin: let it boil)

**buloga** (buˈləugə) business logistics game

**BULVA** Belfast and Ulster Licensed Vintners' Association

**BuMed** *US Navy* Bureau of Medicine and Surgery

**BUN** *Med.* blood urea nitrogen

**Buna** (ˈbuːnə) *Trademark* butadiene + natrium (i.e. sodium) (type of synthetic rubber)

**BUNAC** British Universities North America Club

**BUNCH** (bʌntʃ) Burroughs, Univac, NCR, Control Data, Honeywell (computer manufacturers)

**BuOrd** *US Navy* Bureau of Ordnance

**BUP** British United Press

**BUPA** (ˈbuːpə) British United Provident Association (health-insurance company)

**BuPers** *US Navy* Bureau of Naval Personnel

**Bu. Pub. Aff.** (USA) Bureau of Public Affairs

**bur.** bureau • buried

**Bur.** Burma • Burmese

**BUR** *international vehicle registration for* Burma

**BuRec** (USA) Bureau of Reclamation

**burg.** burgess • burgomaster

**burl.** burlesque

**Burm.** Burma • Burmese

**Burs.** Bursar

**bus.** bushel • business

**BuSandA** *US Navy* Bureau of Supply and Accounts

**BUSF** British Universities' Sports Federation

**bush.** bushel

**BuShips** *US Navy* Bureau of Ships

**bus. mgr** business manager

**but.** butter • button

**buy.** buyer • buying

**bv.** *Taxonomy* biovar

**b.v.** balanced voltage • *Accounting* book value

**BV** Beatitudo Vestra (Latin: Your Holiness) • bene vale (Latin: farewell) • (Netherlands) Besloten Vennootschap (after the name of a private limited company) • Bible Version (of Psalms) • Blessed Virgin (Latin *Beata Virgo*) • *Med.* blood volume • *Shipping* (France) Bureau Veritas (classification society) • *British vehicle registration for* Preston

**BVA** British Veterinary Association

**BVD** *Vet. science* bovine virus diarrhoea

**BVetMed** Bachelor of Veterinary Medicine

**BVetSc** Bachelor of Veterinary Science

**BVF** *Chemical engineering* bulk volume fermenter

**BVI** British Virgin Islands

**BVJ** (ital.) British Veterinary Journal

**BVK** Bundesverdienstkreuz (German: Federal Cross of Merit)

**BVM** Bachelor of Veterinary Medicine • Blessed Virgin Mary (Latin *Beata Virgo Maria*)

**BVMA** British Valve Manufacturers' Association

**BVMS** Bachelor of Veterinary Medicine and Surgery

**BVO** Bundesverdienstorden (German: Federal Order of Merit)

**BVP** British Visitors' Passport • British Volunteer Programme

**BVS** Bachelor of Veterinary Surgery

**BVSc** Bachelor of Veterinary Science

**BVSc & AH** Bachelor of Veterinary Science and Animal Husbandry

**bvt** brevet

**b.w.** bitte wenden (German: please turn over, PTO) • bridleways

**b/w** *Photog., etc.* black and white

**BW** *British fishing port registration for* Barrow • Bath and Wells (episcopal see) • biological warfare • *Photog., etc.* black and white • Black Watch • Board of Works • *Med.* body weight • bonded warehouse • British Waterways • business week • *airline flight code for* BWIA • *British vehicle registration for* Oxford

**B/W** *Photog., etc.* black and white • black to white

**BWA** backward wave amplifier • Baptist World Alliance • British Waterworks Association • (formerly) British West Africa

**B-way** (USA) Broadway

**BWB** British Waterways Board

**BWC** (USA) Board of War Communications • British War Cabinet

**BWCC** British Weed Control Conference

**bwd** backward

**BWD** *Vet. science* bacillary white diarrhoea (pullorum disease)

**BWF** British Whiting Federation • British Wool Federation

**BWG** *Engineering* Birmingham Wire Gauge

**BWI** British West Indies

**BWIA** British West Indian Airways

**BWIR** British West India Regiment

**BWISA** British West Indies Sugar Association

**bwk** brickwork • bulwark

**BWM** British War Medal

**BWMA** British Woodwork Manufacturers' Association

**BWMB** British Wool Marketing Board

**BWO** backward wave oscillator

**BWP** basic war plan

**BWPA** backward wave power amplifier • British Waste Paper Association • British Word Preserving Association

**BWPUC** British Wastepaper Utilization Council

**BWR** *Nuclear physics* boiling-water reactor

**BWS** *Med.* battered woman (*or* wife) syndrome • British Watercolour Society

**BWSF** British Water Ski Federation

**BWTA** British Women's Temperance Association

**BWU** Barbados Workers' Union

**b.w.v.** back water valve

**BWV** *Music* Bach Werke-Verzeichnis (German: Catalogue of Bach's Works; precedes the catalogue number of a work by J. S. Bach)

**BWVA** British War Veterans of America

**BWWA** British Waterworks Association

**bx** box

**BX** *US Air Force* Base Exchange • British Xylonite • *British vehicle registration for* Haverfordwest

**b.y.** billion years

**By.** Barony

**BY** *airline flight code for* Britannia Airways • *British vehicle registration for* NW London

**BYDV** *Microbiol.* barley yellow dwarf virus

**Bye.** Byelorussia(n)

**Byo.** Bulawayo

**BYO** bring your own

**BYOB** bring your own beer (booze, *or* bottle)

**BYOG** bring your own girl

**byr** billion years

**BYT** *Colloquial* bright young things

**BYU** (USA) Brigham Young University

**Byz.** Byzantine

**Bz** (*or* **bz**) *Chem.*, symbol for benzene (in formulae) • *Chem.*, symbol for benzoyl group (in formulae)

**BZ** B'nai Zion • British Zone • *British vehicle registration for* Down

**B-Z** (*or* **BZ**) *Chem.* Belousov–Zhabotinskii (as in **B-Z reaction**)

**BZS** *Chem.* basic zirconium sulphate

**bzw.** beziehungsweise (German: respectively)

# C

**c** *symbol for* centi- (prefix indicating $10^{-2}$, as in **cm**, centimetre) • *Physics* charm (a quark flavour) • *Chem., symbol for* concentration • *Maths., symbol for* constant • cubic (in **cc**, cubic centimetre) • (ital.) *Physics, symbol for* specific heat capacity • (ital.) *Physics, symbol for* speed of light in a vacuum • *indicating* the third vertical row of squares from the left on a chessboard

**c.** canine (tooth) • capacity • caput (Latin: chapter) • carat • carbon (paper) • case • *Baseball* catcher • cathode • *Cricket* caught • cent(s) • *Currency* centavo(s) • centime(s) • centre • century (*or* centuries) • chairman • chairwoman • chapter • child • church • *Med.* cibus (Latin: meal) • (ital.) circa (Latin: about; preceding a date) • circiter (Latin: approximately) • circum (Latin: around) • city • cloudy • cold • colt • compound • consul • contra (Latin: against) • contralto • contrast • convection • copy • copyright • coupon • court • cousin • crowned • *Med.* cum (Latin: with; in prescriptions) • currency • cycle(s)

**c/-** (Australia, New Zealand) care of (in addresses) • case • coupon • currency

**C** *Geology* Cambrian • (ital.) *Physics, symbol for* capacitance • *Chem., symbol for* carbon • *Geology* Carboniferous • (USA) cargo transport (specifying a type of military aircraft, as in **C-5**) • Celsius (in **°C**, degree Celsius; formerly degree centigrade) • *Theatre* centre (of stage) • century • (ital.) *Physics, symbol for* charm quantum number • *Colloquial* cocaine • cold (water) • *Parliamentary procedure* Command Paper (prefix to serial number, 1870–99). *See also under* Cd; Cmd; Cmnd • Companion (in British Orders of Chivalry) • *Immunol., symbol for* complement • *Immunol.* constant region (of an immunoglobulin chain) • (ital.) *Physics, symbol for* compliance • *Pharmacol.* congius (Latin: gallon) • *Irish fishing port registration for* Cork • *Botany, symbol for* corolla (in a floral formula) • *Physics, symbol for* coulomb • crown (a standard paper size; *see under* C4; C8; C16; C32) • *international vehicle registration for* Cuba • *Biochem., symbol for* cytidine • *Biochem., symbol for* cytosine • (ital.) *Physics, symbol for* Euler number • (ital.) *Physics, symbol for* heat capacity • *Roman numeral for* hundred • (ital.) *Chem., symbol for* molecular concentration • *Computing, indicating* a programming language (developed from B) • *indicating* a musical note or key

**C.** (*or* **C**) Caesar • caldo (Italian: hot) • caliente (Spanish: hot) • calle (Spanish: street) • canon • canto • Cape (on maps) • Captain • Cardinal • catechism • Catholic • Celtic • Chancellor • Chancery • chaud (French: hot) • chief • Christ(ian) • circuit • *Cards* clubs • Commander • commended • Commodore • Confessor • Congregation(al) • Congress • Conservative • contract • Corps • council • Count • *Music* counter-tenor • county • coupon • cross • curacy • curate

**C1** *indicating* supervisory, clerical (occupational grade)

**C2** *international civil aircraft marking for* Nauru • *indicating* skilled manual (occupational grade)

**C3** *international civil aircraft marking for* Andorra • *indicating* a low standard of physical fitness; hence inferior (originally a military grade)

**C4** *Television* Channel Four • crown 4to (a standard paper size, $7\frac{1}{2} \times 10$ in)

**C5** *international civil aircraft marking for* Gambia

**C6** *international civil aircraft marking for* Bahamas

**C8** crown 8vo (a standard paper size, $5 \times 7\frac{1}{2}$ in)

**C9** *international civil aircraft marking for* Mozambique

**C16** crown 16mo (a standard paper size, $3\frac{3}{4} \times 5$ in)

**C32** crown 32mo (a standard paper size, $2\frac{1}{2} \times 3\frac{3}{4}$ in)

**ca.** *Med.* carcinoma • *Law* cases • centiare (unit of area) • (ital.) circa (*see under* c.)

**c.a.** *Commerce* capital asset • *Engineering* close annealed • *Music* coll' arco (Italian: with the bow) • *Physics* corriente alterna (Spanish: alternating current) •

*Physics* courant alternatif (French: alternating current)

**Ca** *Chem., symbol for* calcium

**Ca.** Canada • Canadian • compagnia (Italian: company)

**Cᵃ** companhia (Portuguese: company; Co.) • compañia (Spanish: company; Co.)

**CA** *postcode for* California • Canadian army • *Taxation* capital allowances • *Biochem.* carbonic anhydrase • *British fishing port registration for* Cardigan • *postcode for* Carlisle • Caterers' Association • Catholic Association • *Chem.* cellulose acetate • Central America • *Physics* centrifugal atomization • Certificate of Airworthiness • chargé d'affaires • Chartered Accountant • (ital.) Chemical Abstracts • *British vehicle registration for* Chester • Chief Accountant • *Genetics* chromosomal aberration • chronological age • Church Army • Church Assembly • *Chem.* cinnamic aldehyde • citric acid • City Architect • City Attorney • civil affairs • civil aviation • Classical Association • clean air • coast artillery • College of Arms • commercial agent • Community Association • Companies Act • (USA) Confederate Army • Constituent Assembly • Consular Agent • Consumers' Association • *Med.* contrast angiography • controlled atmosphere • Controller of Accounts • Cooperative Agreement • Corps d'Armée (French: Army Corps) • County Alderman • County Architect • Court of Appeal • Croquet Association • Crown Agent • Cruising Association • *Commerce* current assets

**C/A** (*or* **CA**) capital account • credit account • current account

**CAA** Canadian Authors' Association • *Commerce* Capital Allowances Act • Central African Airways Corporation • (USA) Civil Aeronautics Administration (*or* Administrator) • Civil Aviation Authority • Clean Air Act • Commonwealth Association of Architects • (USA) Community Action Agency • Concert Artists' Association • *Med.* coronary artery aneurysm • Cost Accountants' Association • County Agricultural Adviser

**CAAA** Canadian Association of Advertising Agencies

**CAADRP** civil aircraft airworthiness data recording program

**CAAE** Canadian Association of Adult Education

**CAAIS** computer-assisted action information systems

**CAAR** compressed-air accumulator rocket

**CAARC** Commonwealth Advisory Aeronautical Research Council

**CAAT** (Canada) College of Applied Arts and Technology

**CAAtt** Civil Air Attaché

**CAAV** Central Association of Agricultural Valuers

**cab.** cabalistic • cabin • cabinet • cable

**CAB** Canadian Association of Broadcasters • *Chem.* cellulose acetate butyrate • Citizens' Advice Bureau • (USA) Civil Aeronautics Board • Commonwealth Agricultural Bureaux

**CABAS** City and Borough Architects' Society

**CABEI** (*or* **Cabei**) Central American Bank for Economic Integration

**CABG** *Med.* coronary artery bypass graft(ing)

**CABM** Commonwealth of Australia Bureau of Meteorology

**CABMA** Canadian Association of British Manufacturers and Agencies

**CABS** *Med.* coronary artery bypass surgery

**cabtmkr** cabinetmaker

**CAC** Canadian Armoured Corps • Central Advisory Committee • Central Arbitration Committee • (USA) Climate Analysis Center • Colonial Advisory Council • (France) Compagnie des agents de change (French stockbrokers' association) • (USA) Consumer Advisory Council • County Agricultural Committee

**CACA** Canadian Agricultural Chemicals Association

**CAC&W** continental aircraft control and warning

**CACC** Civil Aviation Communications Centre • Council for the Accreditation of Correspondence Colleges

**CACD** computer-aided circuit design

**CACDS** Centre for Advanced Computing and Decision Support

**CACE** Central Advisory Council for Education

**CACGP** Commission on Atmospheric Chemistry and Global Pollution

# CACM · CAIS

**CACM** Central Advisory Council for the Ministry • Central American Common Market

**CACSD** computer-aided control system design

**CACUL** Canadian Association of College and University Libraries

**c-à-d** c'est-à-dire (French: that is to say)

**cad.** *Med.* cadaver • *Music* cadenza • cadet

**Cad.** Cádiz

**CAD** (*or* **c.a.d.**) cash against documents • (USA) civil air defense • comité d'aide au développement (French: development assistance committee) • (kæd) computer-aided design • contract award date • *Med.* coronary artery disease • Crown Agent's Department

**cadav.** *Med.* cadaver

**CADC** central air-data computer • colour analysis display computer

**CADCAM** (*or* **CAD/CAM**) ('kæd,kæm) computer-aided design, computer-aided manufacturing

**CADD** computer-aided drafting and design

**CADE** computer-assisted data evaluation

**CADF** Commutated Antenna Direction Finder

**CADIN** (USA) continental air defense integration north

**CADIS** computer-aided design information system

**CADMAT** ('kæd,mæt) computer-aided design, manufacturing, and testing

**CADO** (USA) central air documents office

**CADPO** communications and data-processing operation

**CADS** computer-aided design system

**Cae** *Astronomy* Caelum

**CAE** Canadian Aviation Electronics • cóbrese al entregar (Spanish: cash on delivery) • (Australia) College of Advanced Education • computer-aided education • computer-aided engineering

**CAEC** County Agricultural Executive Committee

**CAEM** (France) Conseil d'assistance économique mutuelle (Council for Mutual Economic Aid; COMECON)

**CAER** Conservative Action for Electoral Reform

**Caern.** (*or* **Caerns**) Caernarvonshire (former Welsh county)

**Caes.** Caesar

**CAES** compressed-air energy storage

**CAF** *Med.* cardiac assessment factor • Central African Federation • charities aid fund (*or* foundation) • clerical, administrative, and fiscal • (*or* **c.a.f.**) *Commerce* cost and freight • (*or* **c.a.f.**) *Commerce* coût, assurance, fret (French: cost, insurance, freight; c.i.f.)

**CAFBC** *Chemical engineering* circulating atmospheric fluidized bed combustion (process)

**CAFE** (kæ'feɪ) (USA) Corporate Average Fuel Economy (standard for minimum fuel consumption by cars)

**CAFEA-ICC** Commission on Asian and Far Eastern Affairs of the International Chamber of Commerce

**CAFIC** Combined Allied Forces Information Centre

**c.a.f.m.** commercial air freight movement

**CAFS** *Computing* content-addressable file system

**CAFU** civil aviation flying unit

**CAG** Canadian Association of Geographers • *US Navy* carrier air group • (USA) civil air guard • commercial arbitration group • Commercial Artists' Guild • Composers'-Authors' Guild • Concert Artists' Guild

**CAGI** (USA) Compressed Air and Gas Institute

**CAGR** civil (*or* commercial) advanced gas-cooled reactor

**CAGS** (USA) Certificate of Advanced Graduate Study

**CAH** *Med.* chronic active hepatitis • *Med.* congenital adrenal hyperplasia • *Chem.* cyanacetic hydrazide

**Cai.** Caithness (former Scottish county) • Caius College (Cambridge)

**CAI** *Geology* calcium–aluminium-rich inclusion • Canadian Aeronautical Institute • Club Alpino Italiano (Italian Alpine Club) • *Physics* coded-aperture imaging • colour alteration indices • computer-aided (*or* -assisted) instruction • *Chemical engineering* controlled air incineration (*or* incinerator) • *Forestry* current annual increment

**CAIB** Certified Associate of the Institute of Bankers

**CAIRC** (USA) Caribbean Air Command

**CAIS** *Computing* (USA) common APSE interface set (now replaced by **CAIS-A**)

**CAISM** Central Association of Irish Schoolmistresses

**CAISSE** computer-aided information system on solar energy

**Caith.** Caithness (former Scottish county)

**cal** *symbol for* calorie

**cal.** (ital.) *Music* calando (Italian: calming) • calendar • calibre

**Cal** *symbol for* kilocalorie (*or* Calorie)

**Cal.** Calcutta • Caledonia • Calends • California

**CAL** computer-aided (*or* -assisted) learning • *Computing* conversational algebraic language • (USA) Cornell (University) Aeronautical Laboratory

**CALA** Civil Aviation (Licensing) Act

**CALANS** Caribbean and Latin American News Service

**calc.** calculate(d) • calculus

**Calc.** Calcutta

**Calç.** Calçada (Portuguese: street)

**cald** calculated

**CALE** Canadian Army Liaison Executive

**calg** calculating

**Calg.** (Canada) Calgary

**calibr.** calibrate • calibration

**Calif.** California

**caln** calculation

**CALPA** Canadian Air Line Pilots' Association

**CALS** computer-aided (acquisition and) logistics support

**Caltech** ('kæltɛk) California Institute of Technology

**Calv.** Calvin(ism)

**cam.** camber • camouflage

**Cam** *Astronomy* Camelopardalis

**Cam.** Cambodia(n) • Cambrian • Cambridge • Cameroon

**CAM** (kæm) *Biochem.* cellular adhesion (*or* cell adherence) molecule • *Computing* cellular automata machine • commercial air movement • communication, advertising, and marketing (as in **CAM Foundation**) • computer-aided (*or* -assisted) manufacture • *Computing* content-addressable memory • continuous air monitor • *Botany* crassulacean acid metabolism (as in **CAM plant**)

**CAMA** Civil Aerospace Medical Association

**CAMAL** ('kæməl) continuous airborne missile-launched and low-level system

**Camb.** Cambrian • Cambridge

**Cambs** Cambridgeshire

**CAMC** Canadian Army Medical Corps

**CAMD** *Chem.* computer-aided molecular design

**CAMDA** Car and Motorcycle Drivers' Association

**CAMDS** *Military* chemical agent munitions disposal system

**CAMM** computer-aided (*or* -assisted) maintenance management

**cAMP** *Biochem.* cyclic AMP (adenosine 3′-5′-phosphate)

**CAMRA** ('kæmrə) Campaign for Real Ale

**CAMRIC** ('kæmrɪk) Campaign for Real Ice Cream

**CAMS** Certificate of Advanced Musical Study • *Chem.* collision activation mass spectrum • *Engineering* computer-aided manipulation system

**CaMV** *Microbiol.* cauliflower mosaic virus

**CAMW** Central Association for Mental Welfare

**can.** canal • cancel • cannon • *Music* canon • canto • canton

**Can.** Canada • Canadian • Canberra • *Ecclesiast.* Canon(ry) • Cantoris (Latin: the place of the cantor; indicating the side of a choir where the precentor sits, usually the north side)

**CAN** *Chem.* ceric ammonium nitrate • customs-assigned number

**Canad.** Canada • Canadian

**canc.** cancellation • cancelled

**Canc.** Cancellarius (Latin: Chancellor)

**CANCIRCO** (kæn'sɜːkəʊ) Cancer International Research Cooperative

**cand.** candidate

**c & b** *Cricket* caught and bowled (by)

**c & c** carpets and curtains

**c & d** collection and delivery

**C & E** Customs and Excise

**c & f** cost and freight

**C & G** City and Guilds

**c & i** cost and insurance

**C & I** commerce and industry • commercial and industrial

**C & J** *Weightlifting* clean and jerk

**c & m** care and maintenance

**c & p** carriage and packing • *Bookbinding* collated and perfect

**CANDU** ('kændjuː) Canadian Deuterium Uranium Reactor

**C & W** country and western (music)

**C & W Ck** caution and warning (system) check

**CANEL** (USA) Connecticut Advanced Nuclear Engineering Laboratory

**Can. Fr.** Canadian French

**Can. I.** Canary Islands

**CANO** Chief Area Nursing Officer

**Can. Pac.** Canadian Pacific

**CANSG** Civil Aviation Navigational Services Group

**cant.** cantilever

**Cant.** Canterbury • *Bible* Canticles • Cantonese

**Cantab.** (kæn'tæb) Cantabrigiensis (Latin: of Cambridge; used with academic awards)

**canton.** *Military* cantonment

**CANTRAN** ('kæn,træn) cancel in transmission

**Cantuar.** ('kæntjuˌɑː) Cantuariensis (Latin: (Archbishop) of Canterbury)

**CANUS** *Military* Canada–United States

**canv.** canvas

**CAO** Chief Accountant Officer • Chief Administrative Officer • County Advisory Officer • County Agricultural Officer • Crimean Astrophysical Observatory

**CAORB** Civil Aviation Operational Research Branch

**CAORG** Canadian Army Operational Research Group

**CAOT** Canadian Association of Occupational Therapy

**cap.** capacity • *Med.* capiat (Latin: let him (*or* her) take; in prescriptions) • capital • capitalize • capital letter • capitulum *or* caput (Latin: chapter *or* heading) • foolscap

**c.a.p.** (Italy) codice di avviamento postale (postcode number)

**Cap** *Astronomy* Capricornus

**Cap.** Captain

**CAP** Canadian Association of Physicists • *Genetics* catabolite activator protein • (USA) civil air patrol • Code of Advertising Practice • College of American Pathologists • (USA) combat air patrol • Common Agricultural Policy (in the EC) • (USA) Community Action Program • computer-aided planning • computer-aided production

**CAPA** Canadian Association of Purchasing Agents

**CAPAC** Composers', Authors', and Publishers' Association of Canada

**CAPCOM** ('kæp,kɒm) capsule communicator (in NASA)

**CAPD** *Med.* continuous ambulant peritoneal dialysis

**CAPE** Clifton Assessment Procedures for the Elderly

**Capn** Captain

**CAPO** Canadian Army Post Office • Chief Administrative Pharmaceutical Officer

**CAPP** computer-aided process planning

**Capric.** Capricorn

**caps.** capital letters • capsule

**CAPS** (USA) Center for Analysis of Particle Scattering

**capt.** caption

**Capt.** Captain

**car.** carat

**c.a.r.** compounded annual rate (of interest)

**Car** *Astronomy* Carina

**Car.** Carlow

**CAR** Canadian Association of Radiologists • Central African Republic • Civil Air Regulations • *Aeronautics* cloudtop altitude radiometer • *Chemical engineering* coal–alkali reagent • *Nuclear physics* collisionally activated reaction • (ital.) (Australia) Commonwealth Arbitration Reports • *Finance* compound annual return (*or* rate) • computer-assisted retrieval • *Computing* contents of address register

**CARA** combat air rescue aircraft

**CARAC** Civil Aviation Radio Advisory Committee

**carb.** *Chem.* carbon • *Chem.* carbonate

**CARB** California Air Resources Board

**card.** *Maths., Logic* cardinal

**Card.** *RC Church* Cardinal

**CARD** (kɑːd) Campaign Against Racial Discrimination • compact automatic retrieval device • computer-augmented road design

**CARDE** Canadian Armament Research and Development Establishment

**Cards** Cardiganshire (former Welsh county)

**CARE** (kɛə) Christian Action for Research and Education • *Psychiatry* communicated authenticity, regard, empathy • computer-aided risk evaluation • continuous aircraft reliability evaluation • Cooperative for American Relief Everywhere • Cottage and Rural Enterprises

**CAREC** ('kærɛk) Caribbean Epidemiology Centre

**Carib.** Caribbean

**CARIBANK** ('kærɪ,bæŋk) Caribbean Investment Bank

**CARICAD** ('kærɪ,kæd) Caribbean Centre for Administration Development

**CARICOM** ('kærɪ,kɒm) Caribbean Community and Common Market

**CARIFTA** (kæ'rɪftə) Caribbean Free Trade Area

**Carms** Carmarthenshire (former Welsh county)

**carn.** carnival

**Carns** Caernarvonshire (former Welsh county)

**carp.** carpenter • carpentry

**Carp.** Carpathian mountains

**carr. fwd** *Commerce* carriage forward

**CARS** (kɑːz) Canadian Arthritis and Rheumatism Society • *Physics* coherent anti-Stokes Raman spectroscopy

**cart.** cartage

**CART** collision avoidance radar trainer

**Carth.** Carthage

**cartog.** cartographer • cartography

**cas.** castle • casual • casualty

**Cas** *Astronomy* Cassiopeia

**CAS** Cambridge Antiquarian Society • (Guyana) Carib Advertising Services • *Chem.* cationic and ampholytic surfactants • Centre for Administrative Studies • CERN Accelerator School • (USA) Certificate of Advanced Studies • Chemical Abstracts Service • Chief of Air Staff • Children's Aid Society • close air support • *Aeronautics* collision avoidance system • controlled airspace • *Med.* coronary arterial stenosis • *Physics* criticality alarm system • Fellow of the Connecticut Academy of Arts and Sciences (Latin *Connecticutensis Academiae Socius*)

**ca. sa.** (keɪ seɪ) *Law* capias ad satisfaciendum (a writ of execution)

**CA(SA)** Chartered Accountant (South Africa)

**CASA** (USA) Coal Advisory Service Association • Contemporary Art Society of Australia

**CASAC** (USA) Clean Air Scientific Advisory Committee

**CASB** captured anaerobic sludge bed

**CASE** Centre for Advanced Studies in Environment (of the Architecture Association) • (USA) Committee on Academic Science and Engineering • computer-aided (*or* -assisted) software (*or* system) engineering • Confederation for the Advancement of State Education • Cooperative Awards in Science and Engineering

**casevac** ('kæsɪ,væk) *Military* casualty evacuation

**cash.** cashier

**CASI** Canadian Aeronautics and Space Institute

**CASIG** Careers Advisory Service in Industry for Girls

**CASLE** Commonwealth Association of Surveying and Land Economy

**Caspar** (*or* **CASPAR**) ('kæspɑː) *Physics* Cambridge analog simulator for predicting atomic reactions

**Cast.** Castile • Castilian

**CAST** Consolidated African Selection Trust

**CASTE** Civil Aviation Signals Training Establishment

**CASU** Cooperative Association of Suez Canal Users

**CASW** (USA) Council for the Advancement of Scientific Writing

**cat.** catalogue • catamaran • *Med.* cataplasm (a poultice) • catapult • *Christianity* catechism • category • caterpillar tractor • cattle

**Cat.** Catalan • Catholic • Catullus (?84–?54 B.C., Roman poet)

**CAT** Centre for Alternative Technology • *Psychol.* Children's Apperception Test • *Genetics* chloramphenicol acetyl transferase (as in **CAT assay**) • Civil Air Transport • cleanup and treatment • *Aeronautics* clear-air turbulence • College of Advanced Technology • compressed-air tunnel • computer-aided (*or* assisted) teaching • computer-aided (*or* assisted) testing • computer-aided (*or* assisted) trading • computer-aided (*or* assisted) training • computer-aided (*or* assisted) translation • computer-aided (*or* assisted) typesetting • (kæt) *Med.* computerized axial (*or* computer-assisted) tomography

**Cata** ('kætə) Commonwealth Association of Tax Administrators

**catachr.** catachrestic

**Catal.** Catalan

**CATC** Commonwealth Air Transport Commission

**CATCC** Canadian Association of Textile Colorists and Chemists

**cath.** cathode

**Cath.** Cathedral • Catholic • St Catherine's College, Oxford

CATI · CBiol                                          76

**CATI** computer-assisted telephone interviewing

**c.atk** counterattack

**CATOR** Combined Air Transport Operations Room

**CATRA** Cutlery and Allied Trades Research Association

**CATS** *Education* credit accumulation transfer scheme

**CATV** cable television • community antenna television

**caus.** causation • causative

**cav.** cavalier • *Law* caveat

**Cav.** Cavaliere (Italian: Knight) • (*or* **cav.**) cavalry

**CAV** constant air-volume (control system) • *Computing* constant angular velocity • (*or* **c.a.v.**) *Law* curia advisari vult (Latin: the court wishes to consider it; used in law reports when the judgment was given after the hearing) • *Med.* cyclophosphamide, adriamycin, and vincristine (in chemotherapy)

**CAVD** *Psychol.* Completion, Arithmetic Problems, Vocabulary, following Directions (intelligence test)

**CAVI** Centre audio-visuel international (French: International Audio-Visual Centre)

**CAWU** Clerical and Administrative Workers' Union (later amalgamated with APEX, now part of GMB)

**Cay.** Cayenne • Cayman Islands

**c.b.** cash book • cast brass • centre of buoyancy (of a boat, etc.) • circuit breaker • compass bearing • continuous breakdown

**c/b** *Cricket* caught and bowled

**Cb** *Chem., symbol for* columbium • (ital.) *Meteorol.* cumulonimbus

**CB** *postcode for* Cambridge • Cape Breton (Canada) • carbon black • carte blanche • cavalry brigade • (USA) Census Bureau • *Theatre* centre back (of stage) • chemical and biological (weapons *or* warfare) • Chief Baron • *Chem.* chlorobromomethane (used for fire extinction) • *Radio* Citizens' Band • Coal Board • *Law* Common Bench • Companion of the (Order of the) Bath • *Physics* conduction band • *Navy* confidential book • confined to barracks • *Military* construction battalion • cost benefit • county borough • *Chem.* covalent bonding • currency bond • *British vehicle registration for*

Manchester • *airline flight code for* Suckling Airways

**CBA** *Physics* colliding-beam accelerator • Commercial Bank of Australia • Commonwealth Broadcasting Association • (USA) Community Broadcasters' Association • cost benefit analysis • Council for British Archaeology

**CBAA** Canadian Business Aircraft Association

**CB & PGNCS** circuit breaker and primary guidance navigation control system

**CBAT** (USA) College Board Achievement Test

**CBB** Campaign for Better Broadcasting

**CBC** Canadian Broadcasting Corporation • Caribbean Broadcasting Company • (USA) Children's Book Council • (Australia) Christian Brothers' College • (*or* **c.b.c.**) *Med.* complete blood count • County Borough Council

**CBCRL** Cape Breton Coal Research Laboratory

**CBCS** (Australia) Commonwealth Bureau of Census and Statistics

**CBD** cash before delivery • central business district • *Anatomy* common bile duct

**CBDC** Cape Breton Development Corporation

**CBE** chemical, biological, and environmental • Commander of the Order of the British Empire • Council for Basic Education

**CBED** *Physics* convergent-beam electron diffraction

**CBEL** Cambridge Bibliography of English Literature

**CBEVE** Central Bureau for Educational Visits and Exchanges

**CBF** Central Board of Finance • *Med.* cerebral blood flow

**CBG** *Biochem.* corticosteroid-binding (*or* cortisol-binding) globulin

**c.b.i.** complete background investigation

**CBI** Cape Breton Island • (USA) Central Bureau of Identification • computer-based information • computer-based instruction • Confederation of British Industry • (USA) Cumulative Book Index

**CBIM** Companion of the British Institute of Management

**CBiol** Chartered Biologist

**CBIS** computer-based information system

**CBIV** computer-based interactive videodisc

**CBJO** Coordinating Board of Jewish Organizations

**cbk** cheque book

**cbl.** cable

**c.b.l.** commercial bill of lading

**CBL** computer-based learning • *Meteorol.* convective boundary layer

**CBM** Californian Business Machines • *Chem.* carbon-bond mechanism • confidence building measure • conveyor belt monitor (*or* monitoring)

**CBMIS** computer-based management information system

**CBMM** Council of Building Materials Manufacturers

**CBMPE** Council of British Manufacturers of Petroleum Equipment

**CBMS** (USA) Conference Board of Mathematical Sciences

**C-BN** *Chem.* cubic boron nitride

**CBNM** (USA) Central Bureau for Nuclear Measurements

**CBNS** Commander British Navy Staff

**Cbo** Colombo (Sri Lanka)

**CBO** Conference of Baltic Oceanographers • (USA) Congressional Budget Office • Counter-Battery Officer

**CBOE** Chicago Board of Options Exchange

**C-bomb** cobalt bomb

**CBOT** Chicago Board of Trade

**CBPC** Canadian Book Publishers' Council

**CBQ** civilian bachelor quarters

**CBR** (USA) Center for Brain Research • chemical, bacteriological, and radiation (weapons *or* warfare) • *Aeronautics* cloud base recorder • *Immunol.* complement-binding reaction • *Astronomy* cosmic background radiation • crude birth rate

**CBRI** (India) Central Building Research Institute

**CBS** Canadian Biochemical Society • (Netherlands) Centraal Bureau voor de Statistiek (Central Statistical Bureau) • Church Building Society • *Med.* citrate-buffered saline • *Computing* close binary system • *Physics* coherent Bremsstrahlung-radiation spectrum (*or* spectra) • (USA) Columbia Broadcasting System • *Med.* computerized bone scan-

ning • *RC Church* Confraternity of the Blessed Sacrament

**CBSA** Clay Bird Shooting Association

**CBSI** Chartered Building Societies Institute

**CBSM** conveyor-belt service machine

**CBSO** City of Birmingham Symphony Orchestra

**CBT** Chicago Board of Trade • computer-based training • *Physics* conduction-band tail

**c.b.u.** clustered bomb unit • (*or* **CBU**) *Commerce* completely built-up (of goods for immediate use)

**CBV** *Med.* cerebral blood volume

**CBW** chemical and biological warfare

**CBWA** *Physics* counterstreaming electron-beam beta-wave accelerator

**CBX** company branch (telephone) exchange

**CBZ** *Chem.* carbobenzyloxy • coastal boundary zone

**cc** carbon copy (*or* copies) • cubic centimetre(s)

**cc.** centuries • chapters

**c.c.** carbon copy (*or* copies) • cash credit • change course • chronometer correction • close control • colour code • (*or* **c/c**) compte courant (French: current account) • (*or* **c/c**) conto corrente (Italian: current account) • contra credit • *Physics* courant continu (French: direct current) • cubic centimetre(s)

**Cc** (ital.) *Meteorol.* cirrocumulus

**CC** *British vehicle registration for* Bangor • Caius College (Cambridge) • Cape Colony • Caribbean Commission • central committee • Chamber of Commerce • Charity Commission • chess club • Chief Clerk • *international civil aircraft marking for* Chile • circuit court • City Council • City Councillor • civil commotion • civil court • *Physics* close coupling • closed circuit (transmission) • collision course • colour centre • *Photog.* colour correction (*or* conversion; as in **CC filter**) • community council • *Genetics* compact chromosome • Companion of the Order of Canada • company commander • *Electronics* compensating current • computer code • concave • *Military* confined to camp • Consular Clerk • *Commerce* continuation clause • control computer • *Med.* corpus callosum • *Med.* corpus cardiacum • *Physics* correction coil • *Physics* corriente continua

(Spanish: direct current) • *Biology* Coulter counter • Countryside Commission • County Clerk • County Commissioner • County Council • County Councillor • County Court • *Electronics* coupled channel • credit card • cricket club • croquet club • Crown Clerk • cruising club • Curate in Charge • cushion craft • cycling club

**C–C** *Chem.* carbon–carbon (as in **C–C bond**)

**CCA** Canadian Construction Association • *US Navy* carrier-controlled approach • Chief Clerk of the Admiralty • *Chem.* chromated copper arsenate • (USA) Circuit Court of Appeals • *Med.* common carotid artery • Commonwealth Correspondents' Association • (USA) Consumers' Cooperative Association • continental control area • (USA) Council for Colored Affairs • County Councils' Association • (USA) County Court of Appeals • current-cost accounting

**CCAB** Canadian Circulations Audit Board • Consultative Committee of Accountancy Bodies

**CCAFS** (USA) Cape Canaveral Air Force Station

**CCAHC** Central Council for Agricultural and Horticultural Cooperation

**CCAM** Canadian Congress of Applied Mechanics

**CCAMLR** Commission for the Conservation of Antarctic Marine Living Resources

**c.c.b.** cubic capacity of bunkers

**CCB** (South Africa) Civil Cooperation Bureau

**CCBI** Council of Churches for Great Britain and Ireland

**CCBN** Central Council for British Naturism

**CCBW** Committee on Chemical and Biological Warfare

**c.c.c.** cwmni cyfyngedig cyhoeddus (Welsh: public limited company; plc)

**CCC** Canadian Chamber of Commerce • Central Control Commission • Central Criminal Court • (USA) Chemical Control Corporation • Christ's College, Cambridge • (USA) Civilian Conservation Corps • Club Cricket Conference • Commodity Credit Corporation • Conseil de coopération culturelle (French: European Council for Cultural Cooperation) • Corpus Christi College (Oxford or Cambridge) • Council for the Care of Churches • County Cricket Club • cross-country club • *Physics* cryogenic current comparator • Customs Cooperation Council

**CCCA** Cocoa, Chocolate, and Confectionery Alliance • Corps Commander, Coast Artillery

**CCCC** Corpus Christi College, Cambridge

**CCCI** *Military* command, control, communications, and intelligence

**CCCM** Central Committee for Community Medicine

**CCCO** Committee on Climatic Changes and the Ocean

**CCCP** Soyuz Sovietskikh Sotsialisticheskikh Respublik (Russian: Union of Soviet Socialist Republics)

**CCCS** Commonwealth and Continental Church Society

**CCD** Central Council for the Disabled • *Electronics* charged-coupled device • Conseil de coopération douanière (French: Customs Cooperation Council)

**CCDA** (USA) Commercial Chemical Development Association

**CCE** *Chem.* carbon-chloroform extract • Chartered Civil Engineer • compound-cycle engine • Conseil des communes d'Europe (French: Council of European Municipalities) • (USA) Council of Construction Employers • *Electronics* current-carrying element

**c.c.e.i.** composite cost effectiveness index

**CCES** *Physics* cold-cathode discharge induced emission spectroscopy

**CCETSW** Central Council for Education and Training in Social Work

**CCETT** (France) Centre commun d'études de télédiffusion et de télécommunications (national TV and telecommunications research centre)

**CCF** central computing facility • Combined Cadet Force • common-cause failure • Common Cold Foundation • concentrated complete fertilizer • *Med.* congestive cardiac failure • (Canada) Cooperative Commonwealth Federation • *Statistics* cross-correlation function

**CCFA** Combined Cadet Force Association

**CCFD** *Statistics* complementary cumulative frequency distribution

**CCFL** *Electronics* counter-current flow limit

**CCFM** Combined Cadet Forces Medal

**CCFP** Certificate of the College of Family Physicians

**CCG** Control Commission for Germany

**CCGB** Cycling Council of Great Britain

**c.c.h.** commercial clearing house • cubic capacity of holds

**CCHE** Central Council for Health Education

**CChem** Chartered Chemist

**CCHF** Children's Country Holidays Fund

**CCHMS** Central Committee for Hospital Medical Services

**CCI** Calculated Cetane Index • Chambre de commerce internationale (French: International Chamber of Commerce)

**CCIA** Commission of the Churches on International Affairs • (USA) Consumer Credit Insurance Association

**CCIC** Comité consultatif international du coton (French: International Cotton Advisory Committee)

**CCIR** Catholic Council for International Relations • Comité consultatif international des radiocommunications (French: International Radio Consultative Committee)

**CCIS** command control information system

**CCITT** Comité consultatif international télégraphique et téléphonique (French: International Telegraph and Telephone Consultative Committee)

**CCJ** Circuit Court Judge • Council of Christians and Jews • County Court Judge • *Med.* cranio-cervical junction

**CCJO** Consultative Council of Jewish Organizations

**CCK** *Biochem.* cholecystokinin

**CCL** Canadian Congress of Labour • (USA) commodity control list • *Physics* coupled-cavity linac

**C.Cls** (USA) Court of Claims

**CCM** *Med.* caffeine clearance measurement • *Physics* constant current modulation • *Physics* controlled carrier modulation

**CCMA** Canadian Council of Management Association • Commander, Corps Medium Artillery • Contract Cleaning and Maintenance Association

**CCMD** (USA) Carnegie Committee for Music and Drama • *Physics* continuous-current monitoring device

**CCMS** Committee on the Challenge of Modern Society (in NATO)

**CCN** *Meteorol.* cloud condensation nuclei • command control number • contract change notice (*or* notification)

**CCNDT** Canadian Council for Non-Destructive Technology

**CCNR** Consultative Committee for Nuclear Research (in the Council of Europe)

**CCNSC** (USA) Cancer Chemotherapy National Service Center

**CCNY** Carnegie Corporation of New York • City College of the City University of New York

**CCO** Central Coding Office • *Physics* current-controlled oscillator

**CCOA** County Court Officers' Association

**CCOFI** California Cooperative Oceanic Fisheries Investigations

**CCOP** *Chemical engineering* Carnot coefficient of performance • *Chem.* chlorine-catalysed oxidative pyrolysis

**c.c.p.** credit-card purchase • *Crystallog.* cubic close-packed

**CCP** Chinese Communist Party • Code of Civil Procedure • Committee on Commodity Problems (in the FAO) • Court of Common Pleas • *Nuclear physics* critical compression pressure

**CCPE** Canadian Council of Professional Engineers

**CCPF** Comité central de la propriété forestière de la CE (French: Central Committee on Forest Property for the EC)

**CCPI** Cyanamid Canada Pipeline Inc

**CCPIT** China Committee for the Promotion of International Trade

**CCPL** (USA) Computer Center Program Library

**CCPO** Comité central permanent de l'opium (French: Permanent Central Opium Board)

**CCPR** Central Council of Physical Recreation

**CCPS** Consultative Committee for Postal Studies

**CCR** cassette camera recorder • (USA) Commission of Civil Rights • Common Centre of Research • *Chemical engineering* continuous catalyst regeneration •

*Law* contract change request • *Med.* cranial cavity ratio

**CCRA** Commander Corps of Royal Artillery

**CCRE** Commander Corps of Royal Engineers

**CCREME** Commander Corps of Royal Electrical and Mechanical Engineers

**CCRSigs** Commander Corps of Royal Signals

**CCRU** (USA) Common Cold Research Unit

**CCS** *Computing* calculus of communicating systems • Canadian Cancer Society • Canadian Ceramic Society • casualty clearing station • child-care service • collective call sign • (USA) Combined Chiefs of Staff • controlled combustion system • *Chem.* controlled component synthesis

**CCSA** Canadian Committee on Sugar Analysis

**CCSATU** Coordinating Council of South African Trade Unions

**CCSD** *Computing* coupled-cluster single and double

**CCSEM** computer-controlled scanning electron microscopy

**CCSS** centrifugally cast stainless steel

**CCST** (USA) Center for Computer Sciences and Technology

**CCSU** Council of Civil Service Unions

**CCT** *Med.* cerebral circulation time • (USA) clean coal technology • common customs tariff (in the EC) • *Electronics* contact charge-transfer • *Physical chem.* continuous cooling transformation • *Nuclear engineering* continuous-current tokamak • correct corps time • *Med.* cranial computed tomography

**CCTA** Central Computer and Telecommunications Agency • Commission de coopération technique pour l'Afrique (French: Commission for Technical Cooperation in Africa) • Coordinating Committee of Technical Assistance

**CCTG** constant concentration tracer gas (system)

**CCTR** *Nuclear physics* cassette compact toroid reactor

**CCTS** (USA) Canaveral Council of Technical Societies • Combat Crew Training Squadron

**CCTV** closed-circuit television

**CCU** *Med.* coronary care unit

**CCUS** Chamber of Commerce of the United States

**CCV** *Aeronautics* control-configured vehicle

**ccw.** counterclockwise

**CCW** *Nuclear physics* component cooling water • Curriculum Council for Wales

**CCWS** *Nuclear physics* component cooling water system

**cd** *Physics, symbol for* candela • cord • could

**c.d.** (*or* **c/d**) *Book-keeping* carried down • cash discount • *Finance* cum dividend (i.e. with dividend)

**Cd** *Chem., symbol for* cadmium • *Military* Command • *Parliamentary procedure* Command Paper (prefix to serial number, 1900–18). *See also under* C; Cmd; Cmnd • *Military* Commissioned

**CD** *British vehicle registration for* Brighton • Canadian Forces Decoration • *Electronics* carrier density • certificate of deposit • *Law* Chancery Division • *Chem.* chemiluminescence detection • *Physical chem.* circular dichroism • Civil Defence • civil disobedience • closing date • *Immunol.* cluster of differentiation (preceding a number) • coal dust • College Diploma • (Jamaica) Commander of the Order of Distinction • commercial dock • *Electronics* compact disc • Conference on Disarmament (of the UN) • confidential document • (USA) Congressional District • *Med.* contagious disease • *Image technol.* contrast detail • *Physics* convective-dispersive • *Astronomy* Córdoba Durchmusterung (Star Catalogue) • *Nuclear engineering* core damage • Corps Diplomatique (French: Diplomatic Corps) • count down • *Freemasonry* Court of Deliberation • *Electronics* current density

**C/D** consular declaration • customs declaration

**CDA** Canadian Dental Association • (South Africa) Christian Democratic Alliance • Civil Defence Act • College Diploma in Agriculture • Colonial Dames of America • (Canada) Conference of Defence Associations • Copper Development Association

**CDAAA** Committee to Defend America by Aiding the Allies

**Cd Armn** Commissioned Airman

**CDAS** Civil Defence Ambulance Service

**Cd B** Commissioned Boatswain

**CDB** *Computing* comprehensive database

**cdbd** cardboard

**Cd Bndr** Commissioned Bandmaster

**CDC** Canada Development Corporation • canister decontamination cell (*or* chamber) • *Chem.* carbon derived from coal • Caribbean Defence Command • (USA) Center(s) for Disease Control • (USA) Combat Development Command • *Computing* command and datahandling console • Commissioners of the District of Columbia • *Computing* common development cycle • Commonwealth Development Corporation • Control Data Corporation (computer manufacturers) • cost determination committee • *Electronics* critical density of current

**Cd CO** Commissioned Communication Officer

**Cd Con** Commissioned Constructor

**CDD** (USA) certificate of disability for discharge • *Electronics* charge-density distribution • *Chem.* chlorinated dibenzo-*p*-dioxin

**CDE** chemical defence ensemble • (*or* **CD-E**) compact disc erasable • Conference on Confidence- and Security-Building and Disarmament in Europe (as in **CDE treaty**)

**CDEE** Chemical Defence Experimental Establishment

**C de G** Croix de Guerre (French military decoration)

**CDEM** crop disease environment monitor

**Cd Eng** Commissioned Engineer

**c.d.f.** *Statistics* cumulative distribution function

**CDF** *Computing* central database facility • Collider Detector at Fermilab • *Nuclear physics* core-damage frequency

**CDFC** Commonwealth Development Finance Company

**cd fwd** *Book-keeping* carried forward

**Cdg.** Cardigan • Cardiganshire (former Welsh county)

**Cd Gr** Commissioned Gunner

**CDH** College Diploma in Horticulture • *Med.* congenital dislocation of the hip

**CDHS** California Department of Health Services

**CDI** (*or* **CD-I**) compact-disc interactive

**CDIC** (USA) Carbon Dioxide Information Center

**Cd In O** Commissioned Instructor Officer

**CDipAF** Certified Diploma in Accounting and Finance

**c. div.** *Finance* cum dividend (i.e. with dividend)

**Cdl** Cardinal

**CDL** Central Dockyard Laboratory (in the Ministry of Defence) • *Chem.* coal-derived liquid • Council of the Duchy of Lancaster • (Australia) County and Democratic League

**CDLD** chronic diffuse liver disease

**CDM** *Astronomy* cold dark matter (as in **CDM theory**) • *Physics* critical damping mode

**Cd MAA** Commissioned Master-at-Arms

**Cdn** Canadian

**CDN** *international vehicle registration for* Canada • (ital.) Chicago Daily News

**cDNA** *Biochem.* complementary DNA

**Cdo** Commando

**Cd O** Commissioned Officer

**Cd Obs** Commissioned Observer

**Cd OE** Commissioned Ordnance Engineer

**CDOI** Colorado Department of Institutions

**Cd OO** Commissioned Ordnance Officer

**CDP** *Biochem.* collagenase-digestible protein • Committee of Directors of Polytechnics • *Physical chem.* condensed dispersed phase • *Biochem.* cytidine 5′-diphosphate

**CDPE** continental daily parcels express

**Cdr** *Military* Commander • Conductor

**CDR** carbon dioxide research • (Cuba) Committees for the Defence of the Revolution • (*or* **CD-R**) compact-disc recordable • *Computing* contents of decrement register • critical design review • crude death rate

**CDRA** Committee of Directors of Research Associations

**Cd Rad O** Commissioned Radio Officer

**CDRB** Canadian Defence Research Board

**CDRC** Civil Defence Regional Commissioner

**CDRD** (USA) Carbon Dioxide Research Division

**Cdre** *Military* Commodore

**CDRF** Canadian Dental Research Foundation

**CDRH** (USA) Center for Devices and Radiological Health

**CDRI** (India) Central Drug Research Institute

**CD-ROM** (ˌsiː.diːˈrɒm) *Computing* compact disc read-only memory

**CDRS** Civil Defence Rescue Service

**CDS** Chief of the Defence Staff • Civil Defence Services • *Physics* coded Doppler sonography

**CDSE** computer-driver simulation environment

**Cd Sh** Commissioned Shipwright

**Cd SO** Commissioned Stores Officer • Commissioned Supply Officer

**CDSO** Companion of the Distinguished Service Order

**Cdt** Cadet • Commandant

**CDT** Carnegie Dunfermline Trust • (USA and Canada) Central Daylight Time • Craft, Design, and Technology (a subject on the GCSE syllabus)

**CDTA** *Chem.* 1,2-cyclohexylenedinitrotetraacetic acid

**Cdt Mid** Cadet Midshipman

**CDTV** *Computing* Commodore Dynamic Total Vision • compact-disk television

**CDU** Christlich-Demokratische Union (Christian Democratic Union; German political party)

**CDUCE** Christian Democratic Union of Central Europe

**c.d.v.** carte-de-visite (French: visiting card)

**CDV** CD-video (compact-disc player) • Civil Defence Volunteers • current domestic value

**c.d.w.** chilled (*or* cold) drinking water

**CDW** *Physics* charge density wave • (USA) collision damage waiver (in car insurance) • *Physics* continuum distorted wave

**Cd Wdr** Commissioned Wardmaster

**CDWR** California Department of Water Resources

**CDWS** Civil Defence Wardens' Service

**Cdz** Cádiz

**c.e.** *Law* caveat emptor (Latin: let the buyer beware) • compass error • critical examination

**Ce** *Chem.*, *symbol for* cerium

**CE** Canada East • carbon equivalent • *Architect.* centre of effort • *Chem.* centrifugal elutriation • *Med.* cerebral embolism • Chancellor of the Exchequer • Chemical Engineer • Chief Engineer •

*Chem.* cholesteryl ester • Christian Endeavour • (small caps.) Christian Era (following a date) • Church of England • *Computing* circular error • Civil Engineer • *Med.* clinical evaluation • *British fishing port registration for* Coleraine • *Chem.* combustion efficiency • (USA) Combustion Engineering (Inc.) • *Education* Common Entrance • (small caps.) Common Era (following a date) • Communauté européenne (French: European Community, EC; now often used in place of CEE) • compression engine • *Computing* computing efficiency • contrast-enhanced (of picture images) • Corps of Engineers • *Physics* correlation energy • *Chem.* coulomb explosion • Council of Europe • counter-espionage • *Electronics* current efficiency • *British vehicle registration for* Peterborough

**CEA** Canadian Electrical Association • *Med.* carcino-embryonic antigen • Central Electricity Authority • Cinematograph Exhibitors Association • Combustion Engineering Association • Comité européen des assurances (French: European Insurance Committee) • *Commerce* commodity exchange authority • Confédération européenne de l'agriculture (French: European Confederation of Agriculture) • Conference of Educational Associations • control electronics assembly • (USA) Council of Economic Advisers • Council of Educational Advance

**CEAA** (USA) Center for Editions of American Authors • Council of European-American Associations

**CEAC** (USA) Citizens Energy Advisory Committee • Commission européenne de l'aviation civile (French: European Civil Aviation Commission)

**CEB** Central Electricity Board

**CEBAR** (ˈsiːbɑː) chemical, biological, radiological warfare

**CEC** California Energy Commission • Canadian Electrical Code (of standardization) • Catholic Education Council • *Chem.* cation exchange capacity • Church Education Corporation • Civil Engineering Corps • Clothing Export Council • Commission of the European Communities • Commonwealth Economic Committee • Commonwealth Education Conference • Commonwealth Engineering Conference • Council for Exceptional Children

**CECA** Communauté européenne du charbon et de l'acier (French: European Coal and Steel Community)

**CECD** Confédération européenne du commerce de détail (French: European Confederation of Retail Trades)

**CECE** Committee for European Construction Equipment

**CECG** Consumers in the European Community Group

**CECLES** Conseil européen pour la construction de lanceurs d'engins spatiaux (French: European Launching Development Organization)

**CECS** Church of England Children's Society • civil engineering computing system • Communications Electronics Coordination Section

**CED** Committee for Economic Development • computer entry device • (USA) Council for Economic Development

**CEDA** Committee for Economic Development of Australia

**CEDAR** ('si:də) coupling, energetics, and dynamics of atmospheric regions

**CEDI** Centre européen de documentation et d'information (French: European Documentation and Information Centre)

**CEDIC** Church Estates Development and Improvement Company

**CEDO** Centre for Educational Development Overseas

**CEDR** ('si:də) Centre for Dispute Resolution

**CEE** Central Engineering Establishment • Certificate of Extended Education • Commission économique pour l'Europe (French: Economic Commission for Europe) • Commission internationale de réglementation en vue de l'approbation de l'équipement électrique (French: International Commission on Rules for the Approval of Electrical Equipment) • Common Entrance Examination • Communauté économique européenne (French: European Economic Community; *see also under* CE) • Council of Environment Education

**CEEA** Communauté européenne de l'énergie atomique (French: European Atomic Energy Community)

**CEEB** (USA) College Entrance Examination Board

**CEEC** Council for European Economic Cooperation

**CEED** Centre for Economic and Environment Development

**CEEL** (si:l) *Physical chem.* core electron energy loss

**CEEP** Centre européen d'études de population (French: European Centre for Population Studies)

**CEF** Canadian Expeditionary Force • Chinese Expeditionary Force • *Chem.* crystalline electric field

**CEFTRI** (India) Central Food Technological Research Institute

**CEG** (France) collège d'enseignement général (college of general education)

**CEGB** Central Electricity Generating Board

**CEGGS** Church of England Girls' Grammar School

**CEGS** Church of England Grammar School

**CEI** (Switzerland) Centre d'études industrielles (French: Centre for Industrial Studies) • Commission électrotechnique internationale (French: International Electrotechnical Commission) • communications-electronics instructions • cost-effectiveness index • Council of Engineering Institutions

**CEIF** Council of European Industrial Federations

**CEIR** Corporation for Economic and Industrial Research

**cel.** celebrate(d) • celebration • celery • *Music* celesta • celibate

**Cel.** (*or* **Cels.**) Celsius

**CEL** (USA) Constitutional Educational League

**CELA** Council for Exports to Latin America

**CELC** Commonwealth Education Liaison Committee

**CELEX** Communitatis Europeae Lex (Latin: European Community Law; a computerized documentation system for community law)

**CELJ** Conference of Editors of Learned Journals

**CELSS** controlled ecological life-support system

**Celt.** Celtic

**cem.** cement • cemetery

**CEM** Companhia Electricidade de Macáu (Portuguese: Electricity Company of Macao) • *Physics* continuous emission monitoring • cost and effectiveness method • *Chem.* coulomb explosion method · *Astronautics* crew-escape module

**CEMA** Canadian Electrical Manufacturers' Association · Catering Equipment Manufacturers' Association · (USA) Conveyor Equipment Manufacturers' Association · Council for Economic Mutual Assistance · Council for the Encouragement of Music and the Arts

**CEMAC** Committee of European Associations of Manufacturers of Active Electronic Components

**CEMAP** Commission européenne des méthodes d'analyse des pesticides (French: Collaborative Pesticides Analytical Committee)

**CEMF** *Electronics* counter-electromotive force

**CEMLA** Centro de Estudios Monetarios Latino-Americanos (Spanish: Latin-American Centre for Monetary Studies)

**CEMR** Council of European Municipalities and Regions

**CEMS** Church of England Men's Society · *Chem.* conversion electron Mössbauer spectroscopy

**cen.** central · centre · century

**Cen** *Astronomy* Centaurus

**CEN** ('sɛn) Comité européen de normalisation (French: European Standardization Committee)

**CEND** Civil Engineers for Nuclear Disarmament · *Physics* Compton-emission neutron detector

**CENEL** European Electrical Standards Coordinating Committee

**CENELEC** ('sɛnə,lɛk) Comité européen normalisation électrotechnique (French: European Electrotechnical Standardization Committee)

**CEng** Chartered Engineer

**cens.** censor(ship)

**cent.** *Currency* centavo · *Currency* centesimo · centigrade · centime · central · centrifugal · centum (Latin: hundred) · century

**CENTAG** ('sɛntæg) Central (European) Army Group (in NATO)

**centig.** centigrade

**CENTO** (*or* **Cento**) ('sɛntəu) Central Treaty Organization

**CEO** Chief Education Officer · Chief Executive Officer · Confederation of Employee Organizations

**CEOA** Central European Operating Agency (in NATO)

**Cep** *Astronomy* Cepheus

**CEP** *Computing* circular error probability

**CEPCEO** Comité d'études des producteurs de charbon d'Europe occidentale (French: Western European Coal Producers' Association)

**CEPES** Comité européen pour le progrès économique et social (French: European Committee for Economic and Social Progress)

**CEPO** Central European Pipeline Office

**CEPS** Central European Pipeline System · Cornish Engine Preservation Society

**CEPT** Conférence européenne des administrations des postes et des télécommunications (French: European Conference of Postal and Telecommunications Administrations)

**CEQ** (USA) Council on Environmental Quality

**CEQA** (USA) California Environmental Quality Act

**cer.** (*or* **ceram.**) ceramic

**CER** carbon dioxide exchange (*or* evolution) rate · *Physics* ceramic electrochemical reactor · *Electronics* charge-exchange recombination · (Australia and New Zealand) Closer Economic Relations

**CERC** (USA) Center for Energy Research Computation

**CERCA** Commonwealth and Empire Radio for Civil Aviation

**CERCLA** ('sɜːklə) (USA) Comprehensive Environmental Response, Compensation, and Liability Act

**CERES** ('sɪəriːz) (USA) Coalition for Environmentally Responsible Economies

**CERG** *Politics* Conservative European Reform Group

**CERI** Centre for Educational Research and Innovation (of the OECD)

**CERL** (sɜːl) Central Electricity Research Laboratories

**CERN** (sɜːn) Conseil européen pour la recherche nucléaire (French: European Organization for Nuclear Research; now called European Laboratory for Particle Physics)

**CERP** Centre européen des relations publiques (French: European Centre of Public Relations)

**cert.** certificate(d) • certification • certified • certify

**CERT** Charities Effectiveness Review Trust

**CertCAM** Certificate in Communication, Advertising, and Marketing

**Cert Ed** Certificate in Education

**CertHE** Certificate in Higher Education

**certif.** certificate

**cert. inv.** certified invoice

**CertITP** (USA) Certificate of International Teachers' Program

**cerv.** *Med.* cervical

**CES** (USA) Center for Energy Studies • Christian Evidence Society • (France) collège d'enseignement secondaire (college of secondary education) • community energy system • cost-estimating system

**CESAR** (USA) Center for Engineering Systems Advanced Research

**CESE** (USA) Center for Earth Science and Engineering

**CESLS** *Chem.* constant energy synchronous luminescence spectrometry

**CESR** (USA) Cornell electron storage ring

**CESSAC** Church of England Soldiers', Sailors', and Airmen's Clubs

**CESSI** Church of England Sunday School Institution

**CEST** Centre for Exploitation of Science and Technology

**Cestr.** Cestrensis (Latin: (Bishop) of Chester)

**Cet** *Astronomy* Cetus

**CET** Central European Time • (France) collège d'enseignement technique (college of technical education) • Common External Tariff • Council for Educational Technology

**CETA** ('siːtə) (USA) Comprehensive Employment and Training Act

**CETEX** ('siːtɛks) Committee on Extra-Terrestrial Exploration

**CETHV** Council for the Education and Training of Health Visitors

**CETI** communications with extraterrestrial intelligence

**CETO** Centre for Educational Television Overseas

**cet. par.** ceteris paribus (Latin: other things being equal)

**CETS** chemical energy transmission systems • Church of England Temperance Society

**CEU** Christian Endeavour Union

**CEUS** Central and Eastern United States

**CEUSA** Committee for Exports to the United States of America

**CEVS** (USA) controlled environment vitrification system

**CEWMS** Church of England Working Men's Society

**Cey.** Ceylon

**CEYC** Church of England Youth Council

**Ceyl.** Ceylon

**CEZMS** Church of England Zenana Missionary Society

**cf.** *Bookbinding* calfskin • compare (Latin *confer*)

**c.f.** *Music* cantus firmus (Latin: fixed song) • (*or* **c/f**) *Book-keeping* carried forward • *Baseball* center fielder • *Sport* centre field • *Sport* centre forward • chemin de fer (French: railway) • communication factor • context free • (*or* **c/f**) cost and freight • cubic feet

**Cf** *Chem., symbol for* californium

**Cf.** *RC Church* Confessions

**CF** calibration factor • *international civil aircraft marking for* Canada • Canadian Forces • capacity factor • Cardiff (postcode *or* British fishing port registration) • *Commerce* carriage forward • centre of flotation • Chaplain to the Forces • charcoal-filtered • Comédie Française (French national theatre) • Commonwealth Fund • *symbol for* Comorian franc (monetary unit of Comoros) • compensation fee • *Med.* conventional fractionation radiotherapy • Corresponding Fellow • cost and freight • *Chem.* crystal field (as in **CF theory**) • *Med.* cystic fibrosis • *airline flight code for* Faucett Peruvian Airlines • *British vehicle registration for* Reading

**CFA** Canadian Federation of Agriculture • Canadian Field Artillery • Canadian Forestry Association • (USA) Chartered Financial Analyst • Commission of Fine Arts • Commonwealth Forestry Association • Communauté financière africaine (French: African Financial Community, as in **CFA franc**) • *Med.* complete Freund's adjuvant • Cookery and Food Association • Council for Acupuncture • Council of

Foreign Affairs • *Electrical engineering* cross-field amplifier • *Med.* cryptogenic fibrosing alveolitis

**CFAF** CFA (Communauté financière africaine) franc

**CFAL** Current Food Additives Legislation

**CFAM** cogeneration feasibility analysis model

**CFAP** Canadian Foundation for the Advancement of Pharmacy

**CFAR** constant false alarm rate

**CFAT** Carnegie Foundation for the Advancement of Teaching

**CFB** *Chemical engineering* circulating fluid bed • (USA) Consumer Fraud Bureau • Council of Foreign Bondholders

**CFBC** *Chemical engineering* circulating fluid-bed combustion

**CFBS** Canadian Federation of Biological Sciences

**CFC** carbon-fibre composite • *Chem.* chlorofluorocarbon (*or* chlorinated fluorocarbon) • *Chemical engineering* circulating fluidized combustion • *Microbiol.* colony-forming cell • Common Fund for Commodities (in the UN) • Congregatio Fratrum Christianorum (Latin: Congregation of Christian Brothers) • consolidation freight classification

**CFCE** Conseil des fédérations commerciales d'Europe (French: Council of European Commercial Federations)

**c.f.d.** cubic feet per day

**CFD** *Engineering* computational fluid dynamics

**CFDC** Canadian Film Development Corporation

**CFDT** (France) Confederation française démocratique du travail (French Democratic Federation of Labour)

**CFE** Central Fighter Establishment • College of Further Education • *Microbiol.* colony-forming efficiency • *Physics* control fuel element • *Military* Conventional Forces in Europe (as in **CFE treaty**)

**CFF** Chemins de fer fédéraux Suisses (Swiss national railway) • *Physics* critical fusion frequency

**CFFLS** (USA) Consortium for Fossil Fuel Liquefaction Science

**c.f.h.** cubic feet per hour

**CFHT** Canada–France–Hawaii Telescope (Mauna Kea, Hawaii)

**CFI** Chief Flying Instructor • (*or* **c.f.i.**) cost, freight, and insurance

**CFL** Canadian Football League • cease-fire line • Central Film Library

**cfm** confirm(ation)

**c.f.m.** cubic feet per minute

**CFM** Cadet Forces Medal • *Chem.* chlorofluoromethane • Council of Foreign Ministers

**c.f.o.** calling for orders • channel for orders • *Nautical* coast for orders

**CFO** *Meteorol.* Central Forecasting Office • Chief Financial Officer • Chief Fire Officer

**CFOA** Chief Fire Officers' Association

**CFOD** Catholic Fund for Overseas Development

**CFP** Common Fisheries Policy (of the EC) • Communauté financière du Pacifique (French: Pacific Financial Community) • Compagnie Française des Pétroles (French Petroleum Company)

**CFPF** CFP (Communauté financière du Pacifique) franc

**CFPP** coal-fired power plant

**cfr.** chauffeur • confronta (Italian: compare)

**CFR** (USA) Code of Federal Regulations • Commander of the Order of the Federal Republic of Nigeria • *Nuclear engineering* commercial fast reactor • *Engineering* Co-operative Fuel Research (Committee) (as in **CFR engine**) • *Med.* coronary flow reserve • *Metallurgy* corrosion-fatigue resistance • Council on Foreign Relations

**CFRI** (USA) Central Fuel Research Institute

**CFRP** carbon-fibre reinforced plastic

**c.f.s.** cubic feet per second

**CFS** Central Flying School • *Med.* chronic fatigue syndrome • Clergy Friendly Society • *Telecom.* combination frequency signal • *Computing* common file system

**CFSAN** (USA) Center for Food Safety and Applied Nutrition

**CFSE** *Chem.* crystal-field stabilization energy

**CFSTI** (USA) Clearinghouse for Federal Scientific and Technical Information

**cft** craft

**CFT** Compagnie française de télévision (French television company) • *Med.* complement fixation test • *Engineering* cross-flow turbine

**CFTB** Commonwealth Forestry and Timber Bureau

**CFTC** (USA) Commodity Futures Trading Commission • Commonwealth Fund for Technical Cooperation

**CF theory** *Chem.* crystal-field theory

**cftmn** craftsman

**CFU** *Microbiol.* colony-forming unit

**CFV** continuous-flow ventilation

**CFWI** County Federation of Women's Institutes

**CFX** *RC Church* Congregatio Fratrum Xaverianorum (Latin: Congregation of Xaverian Brothers)

**cg** *symbol for* centigram(s) • (*or* **c.g.**) centre of gravity

**CG** *British vehicle registration for* Bournemouth • Captain-General • Captain of the Guard • centre of gravity • *Aviation* cloud-to-ground • coastguard • Coldstream Guards • *US Army* Commanding General • Commissary-General • computer graphics • concentration guide • conjugate gradient • Consul-General • Croix de Guerre (French military decoration)

**C-G** Chaplain-General

**CGA** *Commerce* cargo's proportion of general average • Certified General Accountant • *Chemical engineering* coal-gasification atmosphere • (USA) Coast Guard Academy • (USA) Coast Guard Auxiliary • *Computing* colour graphics adapter • Community of the Glorious Ascension • Country Gentlemen's Association

**CGBR** Central Government Borrowing Requirement

**CGC** *Chem.* capillary gas chromatography • *Chemical engineering* coal-gas condensate • (USA) Coast Guard cutter • (France) Confédération générale des cadres (General Confederation of Executive Staff)

**CGD** *Med.* chronic granulomatous disease

**CGDK** Coalition Government of Democratic Kampuchea

**cge** carriage • charge

**CGE** *Politics* Conservative Group for Europe

**CGG** compensated geothermal gradient

**CGH** Cape of Good Hope

**c.g.i.** corrugated galvanized iron

**CGI** Chief Ground Instructor • Chief Gunnery Instructor • City and Guilds Institute • commercial grade item • computer graphics interface

**CGIA** City and Guilds of London Insignia Award

**CGIAR** Consultative Group on International Agricultural Research

**CGIL** (Italy) Confederazione Generale Italiana del Lavoro (General Italian Confederation of Labour)

**CGL** *Electronics* charge-generation layer • corrected geomagnetic latitude

**CGLI** City and Guilds of London Institute

**cgm** centigram(s)

**CGM** computer graphics metafile • Conspicuous Gallantry Medal

**CGMW** Commission for the Geological Map of the World

**cgo** cargo • *Finance* contango

**CGOU** (USA) Coast Guard Oceanographic Unit

**CGP** College of General Practitioners

**CGPM** Conférence générale des poids et mesures (French: General Conference of Weights and Measures) • Conseil général des pêches pour la Méditerranée (French: General Fisheries Council for the Mediterranean)

**CGPS** Canadian Government Purchasing System

**CGRI** (India) Central Glass and Ceramic Research Institute

**CGRM** Commandant-General of the Royal Marines

**CGRT** *Physics* carbon–glass resistance thermometer

**cgs** (*or* **c.g.s.**) centimetre, gram, second (in **cgs units**)

**CGS** central gunnery school • Chief of General Staff • Coast and Geodetic Survey • *US Army* Commissary General of Subsistence

**CGSB** Canadian Government Specifications Board

**CGSC** (USA) Command and General Staff College

**CGSS** (USA) Command and General Staff School

**CGSUS** Council of Graduate Schools in the United States

**CGT** capital-gains tax • ceramic gas turbine • closed gas turbine • Compagnie générale transatlantique (French shipping company) •

compressed-gas turbomotor • (Argentina) Confederación general del trabajo (Spanish: General Federation of Workers) • (France) Confédération générale du travail (General Confederation of Labour)

**CGTB** Canadian Government Travel Bureau

**CGT-FO** (France) Confédération générale du travail–force ouvrière (General Confederation of Labour–Workers' Force)

**c.g.u.** ceramic glazed units

**ch** *Maths.* cosh

**ch.** chain (unit of measure; crochet stitch) • chaldron • chambre (French: room) • chaplain • chapter • charge(s) • chart • *Horse racing* chase • *Chess* check • chemical • chemistry • *Horse racing* chestnut • cheval-vapeur (French: horsepower) • chief • child(ren) • choir • choke • church

**c.h.** candle hour(s) • central heating • *Sport* centre half • clearing house • compass heading • court house • custom(s) house

**Ch.** Chairman • Chaldean • Chaldee • Chamber • Champion • Chancellor • Chancery • Chapter • Chile(an) • China • Chinese • Chirurgiae (Latin: of surgery; in academic degrees) • Christ • Church

**CH** *Military* Captain of the Horse • *Freemasonry* Captain of the Host • Carnegie Hall • *Med.* cerebral haemorrhage • chapter house • Chester (postcode *or* British fishing port registration) • Christ's Hospital • clearing house • *Physics* collision hypothesis • Companion of Honour • *Med.* contact hypersensitivity • *Astronomy* coronal hole • corporate hospitality • custom(s) house • *British vehicle registration for* Nottingham • *international vehicle registration for* Switzerland (French *Confédération Helvétique*)

**C/H** central heating

**Cha** *Astronomy* Chamaeleon

**CHA** Catholic Hospital Association • Chest and Heart Association • Community Health Association • Country-wide Holidays Association

**chacom** ('tʃeɪkɒm) chain of command

**chal.** chaldron (unit of capacity) • chaleur (French: heat) • challenge

**Chai.** (*or* **Chaid.**) Chaldaic (*or* Chaldee) • Chaldean

**Chamb.** Chamberlain • Chambers

**chan.** channel

**Chan.** (*or* **Chanc.**) Chancellor • Chancery

**CHANCOM** ('tʃæn,kɒm) Channel Committee (in NATO)

**chap.** chapel • (*or* **Chap.**) chaplain • chaplaincy • (*or* **Chap.**) chapter

**CHAPS** (tʃæps) *Chem.* 3-[(3-cholamidopropyl)dimethylammonio]-1-propanesulphonate • Clearing House Automatic Payments System

**char.** character • characteristic • characterize • charity • charter

**CHAR** Campaign for Homeless People (originally Campaign for the Homeless and Rootless)

**charact.** characterize

**charc.** charcoal

**Chauc.** (Geoffrey) Chaucer (?1340–1400, English poet)

**Chb.** Cherbourg

**ChB** Bachelor of Surgery (Latin *Chirugiae Baccalaureus*) • (USA) Chief of the Bureau

**CHB** Companion of Honour of Barbados

**CHC** child health clinic • choke coil • Clerk to the House of Commons • Community Health Council • (USA) Confederate High Command • *Chem.* cyclohexylamine carbonate

**Ch. Ch.** Christ Church (Oxford)

**Ch. Clk** Chief Clerk

**Ch. Coll.** Christ's College (Cambridge)

**ChD** Doctor of Chemistry • Doctor of Surgery (Latin *Chirugiae Doctor*)

**Ch. D.** *Law* Chancery Division

**CHD** congenital heart disease • coronary heart disease

**CHDL** computer hardware description language

**ChE** Chemical Engineer • Chief Engineer

**CHE** Campaign for Homosexual Equality

**CHEAR** Council on Higher Education in the American Republics

**CHEC** Commonwealth Human Ecology Council

**Cheka** ('tʃekə) Chrezvychainaya Comissiya (Russian: Extraordinary Commission (for Fighting Counter-Revolution and Sabotage); forerunner of KGB)

**CHEL** (ital.) Cambridge History of English Literature

**Chelm.** Cheltenham

**chem.** chemical(ly) • chemist(ry)

**CHEM** chemical health effects (assessment) methodology

**ChemE** Chemical Engineer

**Ches.** Cheshire

**CHES** *Chem.* 2-(cyclohexylamino)-ethanesulphonic acid

**CHESS** (tʃes) (USA) Cornell high-energy synchrotron source

**chev.** chevron

**Chev.** Chevalier

**chf** chief

**ChF** Chaplain of the Fleet

**CHF** Carnegie Hero Fund • *Biochem.* combined enzymatic hydrolysis and fermentation • *Med.* congestive heart failure • *Physics* coupled Hartree–Fock (mathematical technique)

**ch. fwd** charges forward

**chg.** change • (*or* **chge**) *Commerce, Finance* charge

**chgd** charged

**chgph.** choreographer • choreographic • choreography

**Ch. hist.** Church history

**Chi.** (*or* **Chic.**) Chicago • China • Chinese

**Chich.** Chichester

**Chin.** China • Chinese

**CHIPS** (tʃɪps) Clearing House Inter-Bank Payments System

**CHIRP** (tʃɜːp) *Civil aviation* Confidential Human Incidence Reporting Programme (pilots' comments on safety trends)

**Chi. Trib.** (ital.) Chicago Tribune

**chiv.** chivalry

**Ch. J.** Chief Justice

**chk** check

**Ch. K.** Christ the King

**chkr** checker

**chl.** chloride • chloroform

**Chl** *Botany, Biochem.* chlorophyll (as in **Chl a**)

**Ch. Lbr.** Chief Librarian

**ChLJ** Chaplain of the Order of St Lazarus of Jerusalem

**chlo.** chloride • chloroform

**CHLW** *Nuclear engineering* commercial high-level waste

**chm.** (*or* **Chm., chmn**) chairman • checkmate • (*or* **Chm.**) choirmaster

**ChM** Master of Surgery (Latin *Chirurgiae Magister*)

**CHM** *Chem.* Cape Horn methanol • *see* ARCO(CHM); FRCO(CHM)

**CHMC** (USA) Children's Hospital Medical Center

**CHMR** (USA) Center for Hazardous Materials Research

**CHNT** Community Health Nurse Tutor

**cho.** choral • chorister • chorus

**CHO** Crop Husbandry Officer

**choc.** chocolate

**Ch. of S.** Chamber of Shipping

**Ch. of the F.** Chaplain of the Fleet

**chor.** choral • chorister • chorus

**CHP** chemical heat pump • combined heat and power (energy use) • (Turkey) Cumhuriyet Halk Partisi (Republican People's Party)

**ch. pd** charges paid

**Ch. ppd.** charges prepaid

**chq.** cheque

**CHQ** Commonwealth Headquarters (central office of the Girl Guides Association for the UK and Commonwealth) • *Military* Corps Headquarters

**Chr.** Christ • Christian(ity) • Christmas • *Bible* Chronicles

**chrm.** (*or* **Chrm.**) chairman

**chron.** chronicle • (*or* **chronol.**) chronological(ly) • (*or* **chronol.**) chronology • chronometry

**Chron.** *Bible* Chronicles

**Chrs** Chambers

**chs** chapters

**CHS** *Physics* calibration heat source • Canadian Hydrographic Service • Church Historical Society

**CHSA** Chest, Heart, and Stroke Association

**CHSC** Central Health Services Council

**ch'ship** championship

**Ch. Skr.** Chief Skipper

**ChStJ** Chaplain of the Order of St John of Jerusalem

**c.h.t.** cylinder-head temperature

**chtg** charting

**ch. v.** check valve

**c.h.w.** constant hot water

**chwdn** churchwarden

**chyd** churchyard

**Chy Div.** *Law* Chancery Division

**c.i.** cast iron

**Ci** (ital.) *Meteorol.* cirrus • *Physics, symbol for* curie

**CI** *Med.* cardiac index • *Physics* cascade ionization • *Med.* cerebral infarction • Channel Islands • *Freemasonry* Chapter of Instruction • chemical inspectorate • chemical ionization • Chief Inspector • Chief Instructor • *airline flight code for* China Airlines • *Chem.* collisional ionization • *Astronomy* Colour Index •

*Med.* combined injury • *Chem.* combustion index • Commonwealth Institute • Communist International • compression-ignition (as in **CI engine**) • *Statistics* confidence interval • *Chem.* configuration interaction • consular invoice • continuous improvement (in management) • *Photog.* contrast index • *Physics* Copenhagen interpretation • *Astronomy* coronal index (of solar activity) • *Engineering* corrosion inhibitor • *international vehicle registration for* Côte d'Ivoire (Ivory Coast) • counter-intelligence • (Imperial Order of the) Crown of India • *Irish vehicle registration for* Laois

**C³I** *Military* command, control, communications, and intelligence

**Cia** compagnia (Italian: company; Co.) • companhia (Portuguese: company; Co.) • compañia (Spanish: company; Co.)

**CIA** cash in advance • (USA) Central Intelligence Agency • Chemical Industries' Association • Chief Inspector of Armaments • Conseil international des archives (French: International Council on Archives) • Corporation of Insurance Agents • Culinary Institute of America

**CIAA** Centre international d'aviation agricole (French: International Agricultural Aviation Centre) • Coordinator of Inter-American Affairs

**CIAB** (USA) Coal Industry Advisory Board • Conseil international des agences bénévoles (French: International Council of Voluntary Agencies)

**CIAgrE** Companion of the Institution of Agricultural Engineers

**CIAI** Commerce and Industry Association Institute

**CIAL** Corresponding Member of the International Institute of Arts and Letters

**CIAPG** Confédération internationale des anciens prisonniers de guerre (French: International Confederation of Former Prisoners of War)

**CIArb** Chartered Institute of Arbitrators

**CIAS** Changi International Airport Services • Conference of Independent African States

**CIB** Central Intelligence Board • Chartered Institute of Bankers • Corporation of Insurance Brokers • (New Zealand) Criminal Investigation Branch

**CIBSE** Chartered Institution of Building Services Engineers (formerly Chartered Institute of Building Services, **CIBS**)

**Cic.** (Marcus Tullius) Cicero (106–43 BC, Roman consul, orator, and writer)

**CIC** Capital Issues Committee • Chemical Institute of Canada • *Immunol.* circulating immune complexes • (USA) Combat Information Center • Commander-in-Chief • (USA) Command Information Center • Commonwealth Information Centre • (USA) Counterintelligence Corps • (USA) Critical Issues Council

**CICA** Canadian Institute of Chartered Accountants

**CICADA** (sɪˈkɑːdə) central instrumentation control and data acquisition

**CICAR** Cooperative Investigations of the Caribbean and Adjacent Regions

**CICB** Criminal Injuries Compensation Board

**CICC** *Electronics* cable-in-conduit conductor • Conférence internationale des charités catholiques (French: International Conference of Catholic Charities)

**Cicestr.** Cicestrensis (Latin: (Bishop) of Chichester)

**CICG** Centre international du commerce de gros (French: International Centre for Wholesale Trade)

**CICHE** Committee for International Cooperation in Higher Education

**CICI** Confederation of Information Communication Industries

**CICP** (USA) Committee to Investigate Copyright Problems

**CICR** Comité international de la Croix-Rouge (French: International Committee of the Red Cross)

**CICRC** Commission internationale contre le régime concentrationnaire (French: International Commission Against Concentration Camp Practices)

**CICRIS** Cooperative Industrial and Commercial Reference and Information Service

**CICT** Conseil international du cinéma et de la télévision (French: International Film and Television Council)

**CID** *Electronics* charge injection device • *Chem.* collision-induced dissociation • Committee for Imperial Defence • computer-assisted imaging device • Council of Industrial Design • Criminal

Investigation Department • *Physics* current-image diffraction

**CIDA** Canadian International Development Agency • Comisión inter-americano de desarrollo agrícola (Spanish: Inter-American Committee for Agricultural Development) • Comité inter-gouvernemental du droit d'auteur (French: Intergovernmental Copyright Committee)

**CIDADEC** Confédération internationale des associations d'experts et de conseils (French: International Confederation of Associations of Experts and Consultants)

**CIDE** (*or* **Cide**) (Uruguay) Comisión de inversion y desarrollo económico (Spanish: Commission for Investment and Economic Development)

**CIDESA** Centre international de documentation économique et sociale africaine (French: International Centre for African Social and Economic Documentation)

**CIDOC** (Mexico) Centre for Intercultural Documentation

**Cie** Compagnie (French: Company; Co.)

**CIE** captain's imperfect entry • Centre international de l'enfance (French: International Children's Centre) • *Chem.* collisional ionization equilibrium • Commission internationale de l'éclairage (French: International Commission on Illumination; ICI) • Companion of the Order of the Indian Empire (former honour) • Confédération internationale des étudiants (French: International Confederation of Students) • (Ireland) Córas Iompair Éireann (Irish Gaelic: Transport Organization of Ireland)

**CIEC** Centre international d'études criminologiques (French: International Centre of Criminological Studies) • Commission internationale de l'état civil (French: International Commission on Civil Status)

**CIEE** Companion of the Institution of Electrical Engineers

**CIEO** Catholic International Education Office

**CIEPS** Conseil international de l'éducation physique et sportive (French: International Council of Sport and Physical Education)

**c.i.f.** (*or* **CIF**) *Commerce* cost, insurance, and freight (as in **c.i.f. contract**)

**CIF** Canadian Institute of Forestry • Clube internacional de futebol (Portuguese: International Football Club) • Conseil international des femmes (French: International Council of Women) • *Physics, Electronics* contrast improvement factor

**c.i.f.c.** *Commerce* cost, insurance, freight, and commission

**c.i.f.c.i.** *Commerce* cost, insurance, freight, commission, and interest

**c.i.f.e.** *Commerce* cost, insurance, freight, and exchange

**CIFE** Colleges and Institutes for Further Education • Conseil des fédérations industrielles d'Europe (French: Council of European Industrial Federations) • Conseil international du film d'enseignement (French: International Council for Educational Films)

**c.i.f.i.** *Commerce* cost, insurance, freight, and interest

**CIFJ** Centre international du film pour la jeunesse (French: International Centre of Films for Children)

**c.i.f.L.t.** *Commerce* cost, insurance, and freight, London terms

**CIG** *Chemical engineering* coal–iron gasification • Comité international de géophysique (French: International Geophysical Committee)

**CIGA** (Italy) Compagnia Italiana dei Grandi Alberghi (hotel group)

**CIGAR** (sɪˈgɑː) *Nuclear physics* channel inspection and gauging apparatus of reactors

**CIGasE** Companion of the Institute of Gas Engineers

**CIGR** Commission internationale du génie rural (French: International Commission of Agricultural Engineering)

**CIGS** Chief of the Imperial General Staff

**CIH** Certificate in Industrial Health • *Med.* chronic inactive hepatitis

**CIHA** Comité international d'histoire de l'art (French: International Committee on the History of Art)

**CII** Centre for Industrial Innovation (of the University of Strathclyde) • Chartered Insurance Institute • Conseil international des infirmières (French: International Council of Nurses)

**CIIA** Canadian Institute of International Affairs • Commission internationale des industries agricoles (French:

International Commission for Agricultural Industries)

**CIIR** Catholic Institute for International Relations

**CIJ** Commission internationale de juristes (French: International Commission of Jurists)

**CIL** Confederation of Irish Labour

**CILB** Commission internationale de lutte biologique contre les ennemis des plantes (French; International Commission for Biological Control)

**CILECT** Central international de liaison des écoles de cinéma et de télévision (French; International Association of National Film Schools)

**CILG** Construction Industry Information Liaison Group

**CIM** Canadian Institute of Mining • China Inland Mission • Commission for Industry and Manpower • computer input on microfilm • computer-integrated manufacturing • Conférence islamique mondial (French: World Muslim Conference) • Conseil international de la musique (French: International Music Council) • Cooperative Investment Management

**CIMA** Chartered Institute of Management Accountants • (USA) Construction Industry Manufacturers' Association

**CIMarE** Companion of the Institute of Marine Engineers

**CIMAS** continuous iron-making and steel-making

**CIME** Comité intergouvernemental pour les migrations européennes (French: Intergovernmental Committee for European Migration) • Council of Industry for Management Education

**CIMechE** Companion of the Institution of Mechanical Engineers

**CIMEMME** Companion of the Institute of Mining Electrical and Mining Mechanical Engineers

**CIMGTechE** Companion of the Institution of Mechanical and General Technician Engineers

**CIMM** Canadian Institute of Mining and Metallurgy

**CIMPM** Comité international de médecine et de pharmacie militaires (French: International Committee of Military Medicine and Pharmacy)

**CIMS** (USA) chemical information management systems • *Physical chem.*

chemical ionization mass spectrometry (*or* spectroscopy)

**CIMTP** Congrès international de médecine tropicale et de paludisme (French: International Congress of Tropical Medicine and Malaria)

**CIN** *Med.* cervical intraepithelial neoplasia (in grading cervical smears) • Commission internationale de numismatique (French: International Numismatic Commission)

**CINAA** *Physics* cyclic instrumental neutron activation analysis

**C-in-C** (*or* **C in C**) Commander-in-Chief

**CINCAFMED** Commander-in-Chief Allied Forces Mediterranean

**CINCEASTLANT** Commander-in-Chief Eastern Atlantic Area

**CINCENT** Commander-in-Chief Allied Forces Central Europe

**CINCEUR** Commander-in-Chief Europe

**CINCHAN** Commander-in-Chief Channel

**CINCLANT** Commander-in-Chief Atlantic

**CINCLANTFLT** *US Navy* Commander-in-Chief, Atlantic Fleet

**CINCMED** Commander-in-Chief British Naval Forces in the Mediterranean

**CINCNELM** Commander-in-Chief US Naval Forces in Europe, the East Atlantic, and the Mediterranean

**CINCNORTH** Commander-in-Chief Allied Forces Northern Europe

**CINCPAC** Commander-in-Chief Pacific

**CINCPACFLT** *US Navy* Commander-in-Chief, Pacific Fleet

**CINCSOUTH** Commander-in-Chief Allied Forces Southern Europe

**CINCWESTLANT** Commander-in-Chief Western Atlantic Area

**CINFO** Chief of Information

**Cinn.** Cincinnati

**CINO** Chief Inspector of Naval Ordnance

**CINR** (USA) Central Institute for Nuclear Research

**CINS** (sɪnz) (USA) Child(ren) In Need of Supervision

**CInstR** Companion of the Institute of Refrigeration

**CInstRE(Aust)** Companion of the Institution of Radio Engineers (Australia)

**CIO** *Physical chem.* catalogue of infrared observations • Church Information Office • Comité international olympique (French: International Olympic Committee) • Commission internationale d'optique (French: International Commission for Optics) • (USA) Congress of Industrial Organizations

**CIOB** Chartered Institute of Building

**CIOMS** Council for International Organizations of Medical Sciences

**CIOS** Combined Intelligence Objectives Subcommittee • Conseil international pour l'organisation scientifique (French: International Committee of Scientific Management)

**CIP** *Mining* carbon-in-pulp • Cataloguing-in-Publication • (Belgium) Centre d'information de la presse (Catholic news agency) • *Engineering* cold isostatic pressing • Common Industrial Policy (of the EC) • *Engineering* constant-injection pressure

**CIPA** Canadian Industrial Preparedness Association • Chartered Institute of Patent Agents

**CIPFA** (*or* **Cipfa**) Chartered Institute of Public Finance and Accountancy

**CIPL** Comité international permanent de linguistes (French: Permanent International Committee of Linguists)

**CIPM** Commission internationale des poids et mesures (French: International Committee on Weights and Measures) • Companion of the Institute of Personnel Management • (USA) Council for International Progress in Management

**CIPO** Comité international pour la préservation des oiseaux (French: International Committee for Bird Preservation)

**CIPP** Conseil indo-pacifique des pêches (French: Indo-Pacific Fisheries Council)

**CIPR** Commission internationale de protection contre les radiations (French: International Commission on Radiological Protection)

**CIPS** Central Illinois Public Service (Company) • Choice in Personal Safety (organization)

**CIPSH** Conseil international de la philosophie et des sciences humaines (French: International Council for Philosophy and the Humanities)

**CIPW** *Geol.* Cross, Iddings, Pirsson, Washington (rock classification; named after its devisers)

**cir.** (ital.) circa (*see under* c.) • circle • circuit • circular • circulation • circumference • circus

**Cir** *Astronomy* Circinus

**CIR** Canada India reactor • Commission (*or* Council) on Industrial Relations • Commissioners of Inland Revenue • cost information report • *Computing* current instruction register

**CIRA** Conference of Industrial Research Associations

**circ.** (ital.) circa (*see under* c.) • circle • circuit • circular • circulation • circumcision • circumference • circus

**CIRCCE** Confédération internationale de la représentation commerciale de la communauté européenne (French: International Confederation of Commercial Representation in the European Community)

**circum.** circumference

**CIRF** Centre international d'information et de recherche sur la formation professionelle (French: International Vocational Training Information and Research Centre) • Corn Industries Research Foundation

**CIRIA** Construction Industry Research and Information Association

**CIRIEC** Centre international de recherches et d'information sur l'économie collective (French: International Centre of Research and Information on Collective Economy)

**CIRP** Collège internationale pour recherche et production (French; International Institution for Production Engineering Research)

**CIRRPC** (USA) Committee on Interagency Radiation Research and Policy Coordination

**CIRT** Community Initiative Research Trust

**cis** *Maths.* cos + i sin

**CIS** (*or* **c.i.s.**) cataloguing in source • (USA) Catholic Information Society • (USA) Center for International Studies • Central Information Service on Occupational Health and Safety (of ROSPA) • Chartered Institute of Secretaries (now Institute of Chartered Secretaries and Administrators) • Coal Industry Society • *Med.* combined-injury syndrome • Commonwealth of

Independent States (former Soviet republics) • Cooperative Insurance Society

**CISA** Canadian Industrial Safety Association

**CISAC** Centre for International Security and Arms Control • Confédération internationale des sociétés d'auteurs et compositeurs (French: International Confederation of Societies of Authors and Composers)

**CISBH** Comité international de standardisation en biologie humaine (French: International Committee for Standardization in Human Biology)

**CISC** complex instruction-set computer

**CISCO** ('sɪskəʊ) Civil Service Catering Organization

**CIS-COBOL** *Computing* compact interactive standard COBOL

**CISF** Confédération internationale des sages-femmes (French: International Confederation of Midwives)

**CISL** Confédération internationale des syndicats libres (French: International Confederation of Free Trade Unions) • (Italy) Confederazione italiana sindacati lavoratori (Italian Confederation of Workers' Trade Unions)

**CISM** Conseil international du sport militaire (French: International Military Sports Council)

**CISPR** Comité international spécial des perturbations radioélectriques (French: International Special Committee on Radio Interference)

**CISS** Conseil international des sciences sociales (French: International Social Science Council)

**Cist.** Cistercian

**CISTI** Canadian Institute for Scientific and Technological Information

**CISV** Children's International Summer Village Association

**cit.** citadel • citation • cited • citizen • citrate

**c.i.t.** compression in transit

**CIT** (USA) California Institute of Technology • (USA) Carnegie Institute of Technology • (New Zealand) Central Institute of Technology • Chartered Institute of Transport • *Astronomy* circumstellar imaging telescope • Comité international des transports par chemins de fer (French: International Railway Transport Committee) • *Nuclear engineering* compact ignition tokamak

**CITB** Construction Industry Training Board

**CITC** Canadian Institute of Timber Construction • Construction Industry Training Centre

**CITCE** Comité international de thermodynamique et de cinétique électrochimiques (French: International Committee of Electrochemical Thermodynamics and Kinetics)

**CITEL** Committee for Inter-American Telecommunications

**CITES** ('saɪtiːz) Convention on International Trade in Endangered Species

**CITI** Confédération internationale des travailleurs intellectuels (French: International Confederation of Professional and Intellectual Workers)

**cito disp.** *Med.* cito dispensetur (Latin: let it be dispensed quickly)

**CIU** Club and Institute Union

**CIUS** Conseil international des unions scientifiques (French: International Council of Scientific Unions)

**CIUSS** Catholic International Union for Social Service

**civ.** civil • civilian • civilization • civilize

**CIV** City Imperial Volunteers • Commission internationale du verre (French: International Glass Commission) • Convention internationale concernant le transport des voyageurs et des bagages par chemin de fer (French: International Convention Concerning the Carriage of Passengers and Baggage by Rail) • *Physics* critical ionization velocity

**CivE** Civil Engineer

**CIW** (USA) Carnegie Institute of Washington

**CIWF** Compassion in World Farming

**CIWO** Companion of the Institute of Welfare Officers

**cj.** conjectural

**CJ** Chief Justice • *British vehicle registration for* Gloucester

**CJA** Commonwealth Journalists' Association

**CJCC** Commonwealth Joint Communications Committee

**CJD** Creutzfeldt–Jakob disease

**CJM** Code de justice militaire (French: Code of Military Justice) • *RC Church* Congregation of Jesus and Mary

**ck** cask • check • cook

**CK** *British fishing port registration for* Colchester • *Biochem.* creatine kinase • *British vehicle registration for* Preston

**CKD** (*or* **c.k.d.**) *Commerce* completely knocked down (i.e. in parts; of goods for sale)

**ckpt** cockpit

**ckw.** clockwise

**cl** *symbol for* centilitre(s)

**cl.** claim • clarinet • (*or* **Cl.**) class • classical • classics • classification • clause • clearance • clergy(man) • clerk • climb • close • closet • closure • cloth • clove • council

**c.l.** carload • centre line • cum laude (Latin: with praise) • cut lengths

**c/l** (*or* **C/L**) cash letter • craft loss

**Cl** *Chem., symbol for* chlorine

**CL** calendar line • *British fishing port registration for* Carlisle • cathode luminescence • *Chem.* chain length • *Electronics* Child–Langmuir • civil law • Civil Lord • (Belgium) Commander of the Order of Leopold • common law • Communication Lieutenant • confidence limits • craft loss • critical list • *Med.* cruciate ligament • *British vehicle registration for* Norwich • *international vehicle registration for* Sri Lanka (formerly Ceylon)

**Cla.** (*or* **Clack.**) Clackmannan

**CLA** Canadian Library Association • Canadian Lumbermen's Association • Copyright Licensing Agency • Country Landowner's Association

**CL(ADO)** Contact Lens Diploma of the Association of Dispensing Opticians

**CLAM** (klæm) chemical ramjet low-altitude missile

**CLAPA** Cleft Lip and Palate Association

**clar.** *Printing* clarendon type • clarinet

**Clar.** *Heraldry* Clarenceux (King of Arms)

**Clasc** (klæsk) Confederación latinoamericana de sindicalistas cristianos (Spanish: Latin-American Central of Workers; originally Latin-American Federation of Christian Trade Unionists, CLAT)

**class.** classic(al) • classification • classified • classify

**CLASS** (klɑːs) Computer-based Laboratory for Automated School Systems

**CLAT** *see* Clasc

**clav.** *Music* clavier

**CLB** (USA) Cape Lookout Bight (North Carolina) • Church Lads' Brigade

**CLC** Canadian Labour Congress • Chartered Life Underwriter of Canada • Commonwealth Liaison Committee

**CLCB** Committee of London Clearing Banks (*or* Bankers)

**CLCert(BOA)** Supplementary Contact Lens Certificate of the British Optical Association

**CLCert(SMC)** Supplementary Contact Lens Certificate of the Worshipful Company of Spectacle Makers

**CLCr** Communication Lieutenant-Commander

**cld** *Stock exchange* called • cancelled • cleared • coloured • cooled • could

**CLD** chronic liver disease • *Biochem.* cross-linked dextran • Doctor of Civil Law

**CLE** Council of Legal Education

**CLEA** Council of Local Education Authorities

**CLEAPSE** Consortium of Local Education Authorities for the Provision of Science Equipment

**CLEM** *Maths.* closed loop eigenvector matrix

**cler.** clerical

**CLFT** *Physics* classical local field theories

**cl.gt.** *Bookbinding* cloth gilt

**CLH** Croix de la Légion d'Honneur (French: Cross of the Legion of Honour)

**CLIBS** ('klɪbz) *Physical chem.* colinear laser ion-beam spectroscopy

**CLIC** Cancer and Leukaemia in Children

**clim.** climate • climatic

**CLIMAP** ('klaɪmæp) Climate: Long-range Interpretation, Mapping, and Prediction (international project)

**clin.** clinic(al)

**CLIP** (klɪp) *Biochem.* corticotrophin-like intermediate lobe peptide

**CLit** (*or* **CLitt**) Companion of Literature

**CLJ** (ital.) Cambridge Law Journal • Commander of the Order of St Lazarus of Jerusalem

**clk** clerk • clock

**clkw.** clockwise

**cl. L.** classical Latin

**CLL** chronic lymphocytic leukaemia

**Cllr** Councillor

**clm** column

**CLM** coal–liquid mixture • conservation and load management

**CLML** (ital.) Current List of Medical Literature

**CLNS** *Computing* connectionless network service

**clo.** closet • clothing

**CLO** chief liaison officer • cod liver oil

**CLP** China Light and Power (Company Limited) • *Chemical engineering* coal liquefaction process • *Computing* concurrent logic programming • Constituency Labour Party

**CLPA** Common Law Procedure Acts

**clr** clear • colour • cooler

**CLR** City of London Rifles • computer-language recorder • (USA) Council on Library Resources

**CLRAE** Conference of Local and Regional Authorities of Europe

**clrm** classroom

**CLRU** Cambridge Language Research Unit

**CLS** Certificate in Library Science • Christian Literature Society • *Statistics* classical least-squares • *Statistics* constrained least-squares • Courts of London Sessions

**CLSES** *Chem.* closed loop solvent extraction system

**CLT** (ital.) Canadian Law Times • computer-language translator

**CLTech(ADO)** Contact Lens Diploma of the Association of Dispensing Opticians

**CLU** Chartered Life Underwriter

**CLV** *Microbiol.* carnation latent virus • *Microbiol.* cassava latent virus • *Computing* constant linear velocity

**clvd** clavichord

**cm** *symbol for* centimetre(s)

**c.m.** carat métrique (French: metric carat) • causa mortis (Latin: by reason of death) • *Music* common metre • court martial

**cM** *Genetics, symbol for* centimorgan

**Cm** *Chem., symbol for* curium

**CM** Canadian Militia • carboxymethyl (in **CM-cellulose**) • Catholic Mission • (USA) Central Maine • central meridian • *Physics* centre of mass • Certificated (*or* Certified) Master • Certificate of Merit • *postcode for* Chelmsford • church mission(ary) • circulation manager • (USA) Cleveland

Museum (of Art) • combustion modification • command module (spacecraft) • Common Market • *Music* common metre • complex mixture • composite material • condition monitoring • *Computing* configuration management • *RC Church* Congregation of the Mission • *Radiology* contrast medium • *Nuclear physics* core meltdown • corporate membership • Corresponding Member • *Microbiol.* culture medium • *Cell biology* cytoplasmic membrane • *British vehicle registration for* Liverpool • Master of Surgery (Latin *Chirurgiae Magister*) • Member of the Order of Canada

**CMa** *Astronomy* Canis Major

**CMA** Cable Makers' Association • *Chem.* calcium magnesium acetate • Canadian Medical Association • Catering Managers' Association • (USA) Certificate of Management Accounting • Church Music Association • civil–military affairs • coal-mineral analysis • (USA) Colorado Mining Association • Commonwealth Medical Association • Communication Managers' Association • (New Zealand) cost and management accountant • Court of Military Appeals • *Optics* cylindrical mirror analyser

**CMAC** Catholic Marriage Advisory Council

**CMACP** Conseil mondial pour l'assemblée constituante des peuples (French: World Council for the People's World Convention)

**CMAS** Clergy Mutual Assurance Society • Confédération mondiale des activités subaquatiques (French: World Underwater Federation)

**CMB** Central Medical Board • Central Midwives Board (superseded by UKCC) • Chase Manhattan Bank • *Chem.* chemical mass balance • coastal motor boat • *Astronomy* cosmic microwave background

**CMBHI** Craft Member of the British Horological Institute

**CMBI** Caribbean Marine Biological Institute

**CMBS** *Chemical engineering* countercurrent moving-bed separator

**cmbt** combat

**CMC** Canadian Marconi Company • Canadian Meteorological Centre • Canadian Music Council • *Chem.* carboxymethyl cellulose • Central

Manpower Committee • ceramic-matrix composite • (USA) certified management consultant • Collective Measures Committee (of the UN) • Commandant of the Marine Corps • *Physical chem.* compact molecular cloud • Conservation Monitoring Centre

**CMChM** Master of Surgery

**CMCW** Calvinistic Methodist Church of Wales

**Cmd** *Parliamentary procedure* Command Paper (prefix to serial number, 1919–56). *See also under* C; Cd; Cmnd

**CMD** *Astronomy* colour-magnitude diagram • *Music* common metre double • conventional munitions disposal (type of bomb disposal) • *Physics* cryogenic magnetic detector

**cmdg** commanding

**Cmdr** *Military* Commander

**Cmdre** Commodore

**Cmdt** Commandant

**CME** *Chem.* chemically modified electrode • Chicago Mercantile Exchange • Conférence mondiale de l'énergie (French: World Power Conference) • *Astronomy* coronal mass ejection • (USA) cost and manufacturability expert

**CMEA** Council for Mutual Economic Assistance (i.e. COMECON)

**CMF** Cement Makers' Federation • Central Mediterranean Force • (Australia) Citizen Military Forces • *Physics* coherent memory filter • Commonwealth Military Forces • *Physics* compressed magnetic field • *RC Church* Cordis Mariae Filii (Latin: Missionary Sons of the Immaculate Heart of Mary)

**CMG** Commission on Marine Geology • Companion of the Order of St Michael and St George • Computer Management Group

**CMH** Campaign for the Mentally Handicapped • combined military hospital • (USA) Congressional Medal of Honor

**CMHA** Canadian Mental Health Association

**CMHC** (Canada) Central Mortgage and Housing Corporation

**CMi** *Astronomy* Canis Minor

**CMI** *Med.* cell-mediated immunity • Comité maritime international (French: International Maritime Committee) • Commission mixte internationale pour la protection des lignes de télécommunication et des canalisations (French: Joint International Committee for the Protection of Telecommunication Lines and Ducts) • Commonwealth Mycological Institute • computer-managed instruction

**CMIA** Coal Mining Institute of America

**CMIR** (USA) Center for Medical Imaging Research

**CMJ** Church's Ministry among the Jews

**cml** commercial • *Computing* current mode logic

**CML** Central Music Library • chronic myelocytic (*or* myelogenous, myeloid) leukaemia

**CMLA** Chief Martial Law Administrator

**CMLJ** Commander of Merit of the Order of St Lazarus of Jerusalem

**CMM** (Canada) Commander of the Order of Military Merit

**CMMA** Concrete Mixer Manufacturers' Association

**CMMC** (USA) Coal Mining Management College

**cmn** commission

**Cmnd** *Parliamentary procedure* Command Paper (prefix to serial number since 1957). *See also under* C; Cd; Cmd

**cmnr** commissioner

**CMO** (Zambia) Central Merchandising Office • Chief Medical Officer • (USA) collateralized mortgage-backed obligation • *Astronomy* compact massive object

**CMOPE** Confédération mondiale des organisations de la profession enseignante (French: World Confederation of Organizations of the Teaching Profession)

**CMOS** (*or* **C/MOS**) ('siːmɒs) *Electronics* complementary metal oxide semiconductor (*or* silicon)

**cmp.** compromise

**CMP** (USA) Central Maine Power Company • *Astronautics* command module pilot • Commissioner of the Metropolitan Police • *Chem.* correlation of molecular pairs • cost of maintaining project • *Biochem.* cytidine monophosphate

**cmpd** compound

**CMPDI** (USA) Central Mine Planning and Design Institute Ltd

**cm. pf.** cumulative preference (*or* preferred) shares

**Cmpn** Companion

**CMR** Cape Mounted Rifles • central meter reading • *Electronics* common mode rejection

**CMRA** Chemical Marketing Research Association

**CMRC** (USA) Coal Mining Research Company

**CMRO** County Milk Regulations Officer

**CMRR** *Electronics* common mode rejection ratio

**CMRS** (USA) Central Mining Research Station

**c.m.s.** *Med.* cras mane sumendus (Latin: to be taken tomorrow morning; in prescriptions)

**CMS** *Chem.* carbon molecular sieve • (USA) Center for Measurement of Science • central materials supply • Certificate in Management Studies • Church Missionary Society • *Computing* conversational monitor system

**CMSER** (USA) Commission on Marine Science, Engineering, and Resources

**CM/SM** command module service module (spacecraft)

**cmt** cement

**CMV** *Med.* cerebral major vessel • *Med.* conventional mechanical ventilation • *Microbiol.* cucumber mosaic virus • *Med., Microbiol.* cytomegalovirus

**CMZS** Corresponding Member of the Zoological Society

**c.n.** *Med.* cras nocte (Latin: tomorrow night)

**Cn.** *Ecclesiast.* Canon

**CN** *British fishing port registration for* Campbeltown • Canadian National (Railway) • *Chem.* cellulose nitrate • Chinese Nationalists • *Chem.* chloracetophenone • Code Napoléon (French: Napoleonic Code) • common network • *Physics* compound nucleus • *Physics* condensation nucleus • Confederate Navy • *Chem.* coordination number • *Biochem.* cyclic nucleotide • *international civil aircraft marking for* Morocco • *British vehicle registration for* Newcastle upon Tyne

**C/N** *Biochem., Ecology* carbon–nitrogen (in **C/N ratio**) • circular note • consignment note • contract note • *Insurance* cover note • *Commerce* credit note

**CNA** Canadian Nuclear Association • *US Navy* Center for Naval Analyses • (Taiwan) Central News Agency •

(USA) Chemical Notation Association • *Astronomy* cosmic noise absorption

**CNAA** Council for National Academic Awards

**CNADS** Conference of National Armaments Directors (in NATO)

**CNAR** *Finance* compound net annual rate

**CNAS** Chief of Naval Air Services

**Cnc** *Astronomy* Cancer

**CNC** computer numerical control

**Cncl** Council

**Cnclr** Councillor

**CNCMH** Canadian National Committee for Mental Hygiene

**cncr.** concurrent

**CND** Campaign for Nuclear Disarmament

**CNDC** China Nuclear Data Centre

**CNE** (Spain) Comisión nacional de energía (National Energy Commission)

**CNEAF** coal, nuclear, electric, and alternate fuels

**CN(Eng)O** Chief Naval Engineering Officer

**CNES** Centre national d'études spatiales (French space agency)

**CNF** Challis National Forest • Commonwealth Nurses' Federation • *Maths.* conjunctive normal form

**CNFD** (USA) Commercial Nuclear Fuel Division

**CNG** compressed (*or* consolidated) natural gas

**CNH** *Chem.* carbon–nitrogen hydrogenolysis

**CNI** Chief of Naval Information • Companion of the Nautical Institute

**CNIPA** Committee of National Institutes of Patent Agents

**cnl** cancel

**CNL** Canadian National Library • (Australia) Commonwealth National Library • (USA) Crocker Nuclear Laboratory

**CNLA** (USA) Council of National Library Associations

**CNLS** *Statistics* complex nonlinear least square

**CNM** (USA) Certified Nurse-Midwife

**CNN** Cable News Network • Certified Nursery Nurse

**CNO** Chief Nursing Officer • Chief of Naval Operations

**CNP** Chief of Naval Personnel

**CNPS** *Physics* compact nuclear power source

**cnr** corner

**CNR** Canadian National Railway • Civil Nursing Reserve • (Burkina Faso) Conseil National de la Révolution (French: National Revolutionary Council) • Council of National Representatives

**CNRE** (USA) cooperative networks on rural energy

**CNRS** (France) Centre national de la recherche scientifique (National Centre for Scientific Research)

**CNS** *Anatomy* central nervous system • (USA) Cherokee Nuclear Station • Chief of the Naval Staff • *Physics* cold-neutron source • Community Nursing Services • Congress of Neurological Surgeons

**CNSI** (USA) Chem-Nuclear Systems, Inc.

**CNSLD** chronic nonspecific lung disease

**CNSSO** Chief Naval Supply and Secretariat Officer

**CNT** Canadian National Telegraphs • celestial navigation trainer • (USA) Center for Neighborhood Technology • (Spain) Confederación nacional del trabajo (National Confederation of Labour)

**cntn** contain

**cntr.** container • contribute • contribution

**cnvt** convict

**c.o.** *Med.* complains of

**c/o** care of • *Book-keeping* carried over • change over

**Co** *Chem., symbol for* cobalt

**Co.** Coalition • Colorado • Company • County

**CO** Cabinet Office • *British fishing port registration for* Caernarvon • *Med.* cardiac output • careers officer • central office • Chief Officer • Clerical Officer • *postcode for* Colchester • *international vehicle registration for* Colombia • *US postcode for* Colorado • *Military* combined operations • Commanding Officer • command order • Commissioner of Oaths • Commonwealth Office (now part of the FCO) • *Finance* compte ouvert (French: open account) • conscientious objector • *airline flight code for* Continental Airlines • criminal offence • Crown Office • *Electronics* current oscillations • *Biochem.* cyclo-oxygenase • *British vehicle registration for* Exeter

**C/O** case oil • cash order • certificate of origin

**CoA** *Biochem.* coenzyme A

**COA** change of address • College of Aeronautics • condition on admission

**coad.** coadjutor

**Coal.** *Politics* Coalition

**COAS** Council of the Organization of American States

**c.o.b.** close of business

**COBCCEE** Comité des organisations de la boucherie et charcuterie de la CE (French: Committee of the Meat Trade Organizations of the EC)

**Cobol** (*or* **COBOL**) ('kəʊ,bɒl) *Computing* common business-oriented language

**c.o.b.q.** cum omnibus bonis quiescat (Latin: may he or she rest with all good souls)

**Cobra** ('kəʊbrə) Cabinet Office Briefing Room

**coc.** cocaine

**COC** Chamber of Commerce • Clerk of the Chapel • *Chem.* colloidal organic carbon • (USA) combat operations center • *Med.* combined oral contraceptive • Corps of Commissionaires

**COCA** (USA) consent order and compliance agreement

**COCAST** Council for Overseas Colleges of Arts, Science, and Technology

**COCEMA** Comité des constructeurs européens de matériel alimentaire (French: Committee of European Machinery Manufacturers for the Food Industries)

**coch.** (*or* **cochl.**) *Med.* cochleare (Latin: spoonful)

**coch. amp.** *Med.* cochleare amplum (Latin: heaped spoonful)

**coch. mag.** *Med.* cochleare magnum (Latin: tablespoonful)

**coch. med.** *Med.* cochleare medium (Latin: dessertspoonful)

**coch. parv.** *Med.* cochleare parvum (Latin: teaspoonful)

**COCI** Consortium on Chemical Information

**COCOM** (*or* **CoCom**) ('kəʊ,kɒm) Coordinating Committee for Multinational Export Controls

**COCOMO** (*or* **CoCoMo**) (kɒ'kəʊməʊ) *Computing* constructive cost model

**cod.** codicil • codification

**c.o.d.** cargo on deck • cash on delivery

**Cod.** (*or* **cod.**) codex

**COD** cash on delivery • Chamber of Deputies • chemical oxygen demand • (USA) collect on delivery • (ital.) Concise Oxford Dictionary

**CODAG** *Engineering* combined diesel and gas turbine

**CODAN** ('kəʊdæn) *Telecom.* carrier-operated device anti-noise

**CODASYL** ('kəʊdəsɪl) *Computing* Conference on Data Systems Languages

**CODATA** Confederation of Design and Technology Associations

**CODC** cuttings-oil discharge content

**codd.** codices

**codec** ('kəʊdɛk) *Computing* coder-decoder

**Codesh** ('kəʊdeʃ) Convention for a Democratic South Africa

**CODIPHASE** *Computing* coherent digital phased array system

**CODOG** *Engineering* combined diesel or gas turbine

**CODOT** Classification of Occupations and Directory of Occupational Titles

**COE** Conseil œcuménique des églises (French: World Council of Churches) • (USA) Corps of Engineers • cost of electricity • cost of energy

**co-ed** (ˌkəʊ'ɛd) coeducational

**COED** computer-operated electronic display • (ital.) Concise Oxford English Dictionary

**coeff.** coefficient

**CoEnCo** Committee for Environmental Conservation

**COESA** (USA) Committee on Extension to the Standard Atmosphere

**COF** Comité olympique française (French Olympic Committee)

**C of A** Certificate of Airworthiness • College of Arms

**COFACE** Compagnie française pour l'assurance du commerce exterieur (French export credit guarantee company)

**C of B** confirmation of balance

**C of C** Chamber of Commerce

**C of E** Church of England • Council of Europe

**C of ECS** Church of England Children's Society

**C of F** Chaplain of the Fleet • chief of finance • *Mechanical engineering* coefficient of friction

**c of g** centre of gravity

**C of GH** Cape of Good Hope

**C of I** Church of Ireland

**COFI** Committee on Fisheries (of the FAO)

**C of L** City of London

**C of M** *Aeronautics* Certificate of Maintenance

**C of S** Chief of Staff • Church of Scotland • conditions of service

**cog.** cognate • cognisant • cognomen

**CoG** (*or* **c.o.g.**) centre of gravity

**COG** Cleansing Officers' Guild • *Chemical engineering* coke oven gas

**COGAG** *Engineering* combined gas and gas turbine

**COGB** certified official government business

**COGECA** Comité général de la coopération agricole des pays de la CE (French: General Committee for Agricultural Cooperation in the EC Countries)

**COGLA** Canada Oil and Gas Lands Administration

**COGS** *Astronautics* continuous orbital guidance system

**coh.** coheir

**c.o.h.** cash on hand

**COHO** ('kəʊˌhəʊ) *Physics* coherent oscillator

**COHSE** (*or* **Cohse**) ('kəʊzɪ) Confederation of Health Service Employees

**COI** Central Office of Information • certificate of origin and interest • Commission océanographique inter-gouvernementale (French: Intergovernmental Oceanographic Commission) • (USA) cost of illness

**COIC** Canadian Oceanographic Identification Centre • Careers and Occupational Information Centre

**CoID** Council of Industrial Design (now Design Council)

**COIL** (kɔɪl) chemical oxygen–iodine laser

**COIN** (kɔɪn) (USA) counter-insurgency

**COINS** (USA) Committee on Improvement of National Statistics

**COJO** Conference of Jewish Organizations

**col.** collect(ed) • collection • collector • college • collegiate • colon • colonial • colony • colour(ed) • column

**Col** *Astronomy* Columba

**Col.** Colombia(n) • Colonel • Colorado • *Bible* Colossians

**COL** computer-oriented language • cost of living

**COLA** ('kəulə) (USA) cost of living adjustment (clause in employment contracts)

**Col Comdt** Colonel Commandant

**coll.** collateral · colleague · collect(ed) · collection · collector · (*or* **Coll.**) college · collegiate · colloquial(ism) · *Med.* collyrium (eyewash)

**collab.** collaborate · (in) collaboration (with) · collaborator

**collat.** collateral(ly)

**collect.** collective(ly)

**Coll of FE** College of Further Education

**colloq.** colloquial(ly) · colloquialism

**coll'ott.** (*or* **col 8ᵛᵃ**) *Music* coll'ottava (Italian: in octaves)

**collr** collector

**colly.** colliery

**Colo.** Colorado

**colog.** cologarithm

**Coloss.** *Bible* Colossians

**Col. P.** *Advertising* colour page

**cols** columns

**COLS** *Computing* communications for online systems

**Col-Sergt** (*or* **Col-Sgt**) Colour-Sergeant

**com.** comedy · comic · comma · commentary · commerce · commercial · commission(er) · committee · common(ly) · commoner · commune · communicate(d) · communication(s) · community

**Com** *Astronomy* Coma Berenices

**Com.** Commander · Commissary · Commissioner · Committee · Commodore · Commonwealth · Communist

**COM** coal–oil mixture · *US Navy* Commander · *Chem.* complex organic mixture · computerized operations management · computer output on microfilm (*or* microfiche)

**COMA** (*or* **Coma**) ('kəumə) Committee on Medical Aspects of Food Policy

**COMACA** Corresponding Member of the Academy of Arts of the USSR

**COMAF** Comité des constructeurs de matériel frigorifique de la CE (French: Committee of Refrigerating Plant Manufacturers of the EC)

**COMAIRCHAN** (,kɒmɛəˈtʃæn) Maritime Air Commander Channel

**COMAIREASTLANT** (,kɒmɛəiːstˈlænt) Air Commander Eastern Atlantic Area

**COMAIRLANT** (,kɒmɛəˈlænt) (USA) Commander Air Force, Atlantic

**COMAL** ('kəumæl) *Computing* common algorithmic language

**COMAR** ('kəumɑː) (USA) Code of Maryland Air Regulations

**COMARE** ('kəumɛə) (USA) Committee on Medical Aspects of Radiation in the Environment

**COMART** ('kæmɑːt) Commander, Marine Air Reserve Training

**comb.** combination · combine(d) · combining · combustible · combustion

**combu.** combustion

**COMCRULANT** (,kɒm,kruːˈlænt) (USA) Commander Cruisers, Atlantic

**comd** command

**Comd.** Commander

**COMDEV** Commonwealth Development Finance Company

**Comdg** *Military* Commanding

**Comdr** *Military* Commander

**Comdt** *Military* Commandant

**COME** Chief Ordnance Mechanical Engineer

**COMECON** ('kɒmɪ,kɒn) Council for Mutual Economic Assistance

**Comet** (*or* **COMET**) ('kɒmɪt) Committee for Middle East Trade · computer-operated management evaluation technique

**COMEX** ('kəu,mɛks) (USA) Commodity Exchange (New York)

**COMEXO** Committee for Exploitation of the Oceans

**Com-Gen** Commissary-General

**COMIBOL** Corporación Minera de Bolivia (Bolivian state mining company)

**Cominform** ('kɒmɪn,fɔːm) Communist Information Bureau

**COMINT** ('kɒmɪnt) communications intelligence

**Comintern** ('kɒmɪn,tɜːn) Communist International

**COMISCO** ('kɒmɪs,kəu) Committee of International Socialist Conference

**coml** commercial

**COMLOGNET** (,kɒm,lɒg'nɛt) *US Air Force* combat logistics network

**comm.** commentary · commerce · commercial(ly) · committee · commonwealth · communication

**Comm.** Commander · Commodore

**Commd** *Military* Commissioned

**commem.** commemoration · commemorative

**Commiss.** Commissary

**Commissr** (*or* **Commr**) Commissioner

**Commn** Commission

**Commnd** *Military* Commissioned

**commun.** communication • community

**Commy** Commissary

**COMNAVNORTH** (ˌkɒm,næv'nɔːθ) Commander Allied Naval Forces Northern Europe

**COMO** Committee of Marketing Organizations

**comp.** companion • comparative • compare • comparison • compass • compensation • compete • competitive • competitor • compilation • compiled • compiler • complete • compose(r) • composite • composition • compositor • compound(ed) • comprehensive • compression • comprising

**Comp** Companion (of an institution; as in **ComplMechE**, Institution of Mechanical Engineers)

**COMPAC** ('kɒmpæk) Commonwealth Trans-Pacific Telephone Cable

**compar.** comparative • comparison

**compd** compound

**Comp-Gen** Comptroller-General

**compl.** complement • complete • compliment • complimentary

**complt** complainant • complaint

**compo.** composition

**compr.** compressive

**compt** compartment

**Compt.** (*or* **Comptr**) Comptroller

**Comr** Commissioner

**Com. Rom.** Common Romance (language)

**comsat** ('kɒmsæt) communications satellite

**ComSec** ('kɒm,sɛk) Commonwealth Secretariat

**COMSER** Commission on Marine Science and Engineering Research (in the UN)

**COMSUBEASTLANT** (ˌkɒm,sʌb-ˌiːst'lænt) Commander Submarine Force Eastern Atlantic

**Com. Teut.** Common Teutonic (language)

**Com. Ver.** Common Version (of the Bible)

**Com. W Ger.** Common West Germanic (language)

**Comy-Gen** Commissary-General

**con.** concentration • concerning • concerto • conclusion • confidence • conics • conjunx (Latin: wife) • connection • consolidate(d) • consols • continue(d) • contra (Latin: against) • convenience • conversation

**Con.** Conformist • Conservative • *Finance* Consols • *Military* Constructor • Consul • *Music* contralto

**Con A** *Immunol.* concanavalin A

**CONAC** ('kɒnæk) *US Air Force* Continental Air Command

**CONAD** ('kɒnæd) (USA) Continental Air Defense Command

**CONARC** ('kɒnɑːk) (USA) Continental Army Command

**conbd** contributed

**conc.** concentrate(d) • concentration • concerning • concerto

**Con. C** Constructor Captain

**concd** concentrated

**concg** concentrating

**conch.** conchology

**concn** concentration

**concr.** concrete

**con. cr.** *Book-keeping* contra credit

**Con. Cr** Constructor Commander

**cond.** condense(r) • condition(al) • conduct(ed) • conductivity • (*or* **condr**) conductor

**con esp.** (*or* **con espr.**) *Music* con espressione (Italian: with expression)

**conf.** *Med.* confection • confectionery • confer (Latin: compare) • conference • confessor

**Confed.** Confederacy • Confederate • Confederation

**cong.** *Pharmacol.* congius (Latin: gallon) • congregation(ist)

**Cong.** Congregational(ist) • Congress • Congressional

**Cong. R.** (*or* **Cong. Rec.**) (USA) Congressional Records

**CONGU** Council of National Golf Unions

**CONI** Comitato olimpico nazionale italiano (Italian National Olympic Committee)

**con. inv.** consular invoice

**conj.** conjugation • conjunction • conjunctive

**Con. L** Constructor Lieutenant

**Con. LCr** Constructor Lieutenant-Commander

**conn.** connect(ed) • connection • connotation

**Conn.** Connecticut

**conq.** conquer(or)

**cons.** consecrate(d) • consecration • consecutive • consequence • conservation • conservative • *Med.* conserve • consigned • consignment • consolidated • consonant • constable • constitution(al) • construction • consul • consult(ing)

**Cons.** Conservative • Conservatoire (*or* Conservatorium, Conservatory) • Constable • Constitution • Consul

**CONS** *Computing* connection-oriented network service

**con. sec.** conic section

**Conserv.** Conservatoire (*or* Conservatorium, Conservatory)

**cons. et prud.** consilio et prudentia (Latin: by counsel and prudence)

**consgt** consignment

**consid.** consideration

**Con. SL** Constructor Sub-Lieutenant

**Consols** ('kɒnsɒlz) consolidated annuities (*or* stock)

**const.** constable • constant • constituency • (*or* **Const.**) constitution • (*or* **constl**) constitutional • construction

**constr.** construct(ion) • construe

**cont.** container • containing • contents • (*or* **Cont.**) continent(al) • continue(d) • (*or* **cont**) *Music* continuo • continuum • contra (Latin: against) • contract • contraction • control(ler)

**contag.** contagious

**contbd** contraband

**contbg** contributing

**cont. bon. mor.** contra bonos mores (Latin: contrary to good manners)

**contd** contained • continued

**contemp.** contemporary

**contg** containing

**contn** continuation

**contr.** contract(s) • contracted • contraction • contralto • contrary • contrast(ed) • control(ler)

**contr. bon. mor.** contra bonos mores (Latin: contrary to good manners)

**cont. rem.** *Med.* continuantur remedia (Latin: let the medicines be continued; in prescriptions)

**contrib.** contributed • contributing • contribution • contributor

**CONUS** continental United States

**conv.** convenient • convent • convention(al) • conversation • converter • convertible

**Conv.** Convocation

**convce** conveyance

**COOC** *Insurance* contact with oil or other cargo

**co-op.** (*or* **coop.**) cooperative

**COORS** communications outage restoral section

**cop.** copper • copulative • copyright(ed)

**Cop.** Copernican • Coptic

**COP** (New Zealand) Certificate of Proficiency (a pass in a university subject) • *Thermodynamics* coefficient of performance • (USA) community-oriented policing • custom of port

**COPA** Comité des organisations professionnelles agricoles de la CE (French: Committee of Agricultural Organizations in the EC)

**COPAL** ('kəʊˌpæl) Cocoa Producers' Alliance

**COPD** chronic obstructive pulmonary disease

**Copec** ('kɒpɛk) Conference on Christian Politics, Economics, and Citizenship

**COPPSO** Conference of Professional and Public Service Organizations

**copr.** copyright

**COPS** Council of Polytechnic Secretaries

**Copt.** Coptic

**coptr** copartner

**COPUS** (*or* **Copus**) ('kəʊpəs) Committee on the Public Understanding of Science

**cor.** corner • cornet • coroner • corpus (Latin: the body) • correct(ed) • correction • correlative • correspondence • correspondent • corresponding • corrupt

**Cor.** *Bible* Corinthians

**Corat** ('kɔːræt) Christian Organizations Research and Advisory Trust

**CORD** chronic obstructive respiratory disease

**CORE** (kɔː) (USA) Congress of Racial Equality

**CORES** *Commerce* (Japan) Computer-Assisted Order Routing and Execution System

**CORGI** ('kɔːgɪ) Confederation for Registration of Gas Installers

**Cor. Mem.** Corresponding Member

**Corn.** Cornish • Cornwall

**Cornh.** (ital.) Cornhill Magazine

**corol.** (*or* **coroll.**) corollary

**Corp.** (*or* **Corpl**) Corporal • (*or* **Corpn**) Corporation • Corpus Christi College, Oxford

**corr.** correct(ed) • correction • corrective • correlative • corrente (Italian: current) • correspond(ent) • correspondence • corresponding • (*or* **Corr.**) corrigenda • corrugated • corrupt(ed) • corruption

**CORRA** Combined Overseas Rehabilitation Relief Appeal

**correl.** correlative

**corresp.** correspondence • corresponding

**Corresp. Mem.** Corresponding Member

**corrupt.** corruption

**Cors.** Corsica(n)

**CORS** (kɔːz) *Chem.* catalytic oxygen removal system • Chief of the Regulating Staff

**Cor. Sec.** Corresponding Secretary

**CORSO** ('kɔːsəʊ) (New Zealand) Council of Organizations for Relief Services Overseas

**cort.** cortex

**cos** (kɒz) *Maths.* cosine

**c.o.s.** *Commerce* cash on shipment

**Cos.** (*or* **cos.**) Companies • Counties

**COS** *Commerce* cash on shipment • Chamber of Shipping • Charity Organization Society • (*or* **CoS**) Chief of Staff

**co. sa.** come sopra (Italian: as above)

**COSA** Colliery Officials and Staffs Association

**COSAG** ('kəʊsæg) combined steam turbine and gas turbine (ship propulsion)

**COSAR** ('kəʊsɑː) compression scanning array radar

**COSATI** (kəʊ'sɑːti) Committee on Scientific and Technical Information

**COSATU** (*or* **Cosatu**) (kəʊ'sɑːtuː) Congress of South African Trade Unions

**COSBA** (kɒsbɑː) Computer Services and Bureaux Association

**cosec** ('kəʊsɛk) *Maths.* cosecant

**COSEC** ('kəʊsɛk) Coordinating Secretariat of the National Union of Students

**cosech** ('kəʊʃɛk) *Maths.* hyperbolic cosecant

**COSFPS** Commons, Open Spaces, Footpaths Preservation Society

**cosh** (kɒʃ) *Maths.* hyperbolic cosine

**COSHH** Control of Substances Hazardous to Health

**CoSIRA** (kəʊ'saɪrə) Council for Small Industries in Rural Areas

**COSLA** (*or* **Cosla**) ('kɒzlə) Convention of Scottish Local Authorities

**COSMD** Combined Operations Signals Maintenance Division

**cosmog.** cosmogony • cosmographical • cosmography

**COSMOS** ('kɒs,mɒs) Coast Survey Marine Observation System

**co. so.** come sopra (Italian: as above)

**COSPAR** ('kəʊ,spɑː) Committee on Space Research

**Coss.** Consules (Latin: Consuls)

**COSSAC** Chief of Staff to Supreme Allied Commander

**COST** (kɒst) Committee for Overseas Science and Technology (of the Royal Society)

**cot** (kɒt) *Maths.* cotangent

**CoT** college of technology

**COT** *Physics* change of temperature

**cotan** ('kəʊ,tæn) *Maths.* cotangent

**COTC** Canadian Officers' Training Corps

**COTE** (*or* **Cote**) Committee for the Accreditation of Teacher Education

**coth** (kɒθ) *Maths.* hyperbolic cotangent

**COTR** (USA) contracting officers' technical representative

**COTT** (South Africa) Central Organization for Technical Training

**couch.** *Heraldry* couchant

**Coun.** Council(lor) • Counsellor

**cour.** courant (French: instant (this month); in correspondence)

**cov.** covenant

**Cov.** Coventry

**COV** *Statistics* coefficient of variation • *Chem.* concentrated oil of vitriol • *Electronics* corona onset voltage • (*or* **Cov**) *Statistics* covariance • *Genetics* crossover value

**covers** ('kəʊvɜːs) *Maths.* coversed sine

**cov. pt.** *Cricket* cover point

**COWAR** Committee on Water Research

**COWPS** (USA) Council on Wages and Price Stability

**Coy.** *Military* company

**COZI** communications zone indicator

**cp** *Chem.* cyclopentadienyl (used in formulae)

**cp.** compare

**c.p.** candlepower • carriage paid • *Aeronautics* centre of pressure • condensation product • constant pressure

**Cp.** *RC Church* compline

**CP** *international civil aircraft marking for* Bolivia • *Med.* Campylobacter pylori (cause of gastric infections) • *airline flight code for* Canadian Airlines International • Canadian Pacific (Railway) • Canadian Press • (South Africa) Cape Province • (Isle of Man) Captain of the Parish • *Navigation* cardinal point • casella postale (Italian: post office box) • *Computing* central processor • centrifugal pump • *Med.* cerebral palsy • *Surveying* change point • *Physics* charge (conjugation)–parity (as in **CP invariance**) • charterparty • chemically pure • Chief of Police • Chief Patriarch • *Chem.* chlorophenol • *Med.* chronic pancreatitis • *Med.* cisplatin (anticancer drug) • civil power • civil procedure • Clarendon Press • Clerk of the Peace • code of procedure • Codice Penale (Italian: penal code) • College of Preceptors • colour printing (as in **CP filter**) • *Military* Command Post • commercial paper • Common Pleas • Common Prayer • Communist Party • community physician • Community Programme (employment scheme) • (Portugal) Companhia dos Caminhos de Ferro Portugueses (railway company) • *Stock exchange* concert party • conference paper • conference proceedings • *RC Church* Congregatio Passionis (Latin: Congregation of the Passion) • (India) Congress Party • convict prison • corporal punishment • (Australia) Country Party (now the National Party) • Court of Probate • *Biochem.* creatine phosphate • *Physics* cross polarization • current paper • *British vehicle registration for* Huddersfield

**C/P** charterparty

**CPA** Canadian Pharmaceutical Association • Canadian Psychological Association • central planning area • (USA) Certified Public Accountant • Chartered Patent Agent • Chick Producers' Association • *Insurance* claims payable abroad • Clyde Port Authority • Commonwealth Parliamentary Association • Communist Party of Australia • Construction Plant Association • Contractors' Plant Association • contract price adjustment • cost planning and appraisal • Council of Provincial Associations • *Computing* critical path analysis

**CPAA** *Physics* charged-particle activation analysis

**CPAC** Collaborative Pesticides Analytical Committee • Consumer Protection Advisory Committee

**CPAG** Child Poverty Action Group • (USA) Collision Prevention Advisory Group

**CPAI** Canvas Products Association International

**C. Pal.** Crystal Palace

**CPAM** Committee of Purchasers of Aircraft Material

**CPAS** Catholic Prisoners' Aid Society • Church Pastoral Aid Society

**CPB** *Book-keeping* casual payments book • Central Planning Bureau • Communist Party of Britain

**CPC** (USA) City Planning Commission • City Police Commissioner • Clerk of the Privy Council • *Med.* clinico-pathological conference • Communist Party of China • Conservative Political Centre

**CPCIZ** Comité permanent des congrès internationaux de zoologie (French: Permanent Committee of International Zoological Congresses)

**CPCU** (USA) Chartered Property and Casualty Underwriter

**cpd** compound

**c.p.d.** *Commerce* charterers pay dues

**CPD** chronic pulmonary disease • *Electronics* contact potential difference • continuing professional development

**CPDL** Canadian Patents and Developments Limited

**CPDM** Centre for Physical Distribution Management

**CPE** Certificate of Physical Education • (USA) Certified Property Exchanger • *Med.* chronic pulmonary emphysema • College of Physical Education • Congrès du peuple européen (French: Congress of European People) • contractor performance evaluation • *Microbiol.* cytopathic effect

**CPEA** Catholic Parents' and Electors' Association • (USA) Cooperative Program for Educational Administration

**c. pén.** code pénal (French: penal code)

**CPEQ** Corporation of Professional Engineers of Quebec

**CPF** contributory pension fund

**CPFF** cost plus fixed fee

**CPFS** Council for the Promotion of Field Studies

**CPGB** Communist Party of Great Britain

**c.p.h.** cycles per hour

**CPH** Certificate in Public Health

**CPHA** Canadian Public Health Association

**CPhys** Chartered Physicist

**cpi** *Printing* characters per inch

**CPI** *Biochem.* carboxypeptidase inhibitor • chief pilot instructor • Communist Party of India • (USA) consumer price index

**CPJI** Cour permanente de justice internationale (French: Permanent Court of International Justice)

**Cpl** *Military* Corporal

**CPL** central public library • Colonial Products Laboratory • Commercial Pilot's Licence

**cpm** cycles per minute

**CPM** (USA) Certified Property Manager • Colonial Police Medal • *Music* common particular metre • Communist Party of Malaya • computer program module • *Computing* critical path method

**CP/M** *Computing, trademark* Control Program Monitor

**CPMEE&W** Council for Postgraduate Medical Education in England and Wales

**cpn** coupon

**Cpn** Copenhagen

**CPN** Communistische Partij van Nederland (Netherlands Communist Party) • Community Psychiatric Nurse

**CPNA** Council of Photographic News Agencies

**Cpnhgn** Copenhagen

**CPNZ** Communist Party of New Zealand

**CPO** cancel previous order • *Chem.* catalytic partial oxidation • Chief Petty Officer • command pay office • Commonwealth Producers' Organization • compulsory purchase order • County Planning Officer

**c.p.p.** controllable pitch propeller

**CPP** chemical processing plant • *Chemical engineering* condensate purification plant • (Ghana) Convention People's Party • *Computing* critical path planning • current purchasing power (in **CPP accounting**)

**CPPA** Canadian Pulp and Paper Association

**CPPCC** Chinese People's Political Consultative Conference

**CPPO** *Chem.* bis(2-carbopentyloxy-3,5,6-trichlorophenyl) oxalate

**CPPS** *Computing* critical path planning and scheduling

**CPR** Canadian Pacific Railway • *Med.* cardiopulmonary resuscitation

**CPRC** Central Price Regulation Committee

**CPRE** Council for the Protection of Rural England

**CPRS** Central Policy Review Staff

**CPRW** Council for the Protection of Rural Wales

**cps** *Computing* characters per second • *Physics* cycles per second

**CPS** Centre for Policy Studies • cents per share • (USA) Certified Professional Secretary • Church Patronage Society • Clerk of Petty Sessions • Commonwealth Public Service • Communist Party of Syria • Congregational Publishing Society • Crown Prosecution Service • Custos Privati Sigilli (Latin: Keeper of the Privy Seal)

**CPSA** Civil and Public Services Association (clerical civil servants' union) • Clay Pigeon Shooting Association

**CPSC** (USA) Consumer Product Safety Commission

**CPSS** Certificate in Public Service Studies

**CPSU** Communist Party of the Soviet Union

**CPsychol** Chartered Psychologist

**cpt** cockpit • counterpoint

**Cpt.** Captain

**CPT** Canadian Pacific Telegraphs • *Physics* charge (conjugation)–parity–time (reversal) (as in **CPT theorem**) • cost per thousand • *Computing* critical path technique

**CPTB** Clay Products Technical Bureau

**CPU** central packaging unit • (*or* **c.p.u.**) *Computing* central processing unit • collective protection unit • Commonwealth Press Union

**CPUSA** Communist Party of the United States of America

**CPVE** Certificate of Pre-vocational Education

**CPWC** (Burma) Central People's Workers' Council

**CQ** *Military* charge of quarters • conditionally qualified

**CQM** Chief Quartermaster • Company Quartermaster

**CQMS** Company Quartermaster-Sergeant

**CQR** (ital.) Church Quarterly Review

**CQS** Court of Quarter Sessions

**CQSW** Certificate of Qualification in Social Work

**cr.** created • creation • (or **Cr.**) credit(or) • creek • *Music* crescendo • crew • crimson • crown • cruise • crux (Latin: cross)

**c.r.** con riserva (Italian: with reservations) • *Finance* cum rights (i.e. with rights)

**c/r** company's risk

**Cr** *Chem., symbol for* chromium • Commander • Councillor • cruiser

**CR** Carolina Regina (Latin: Queen Caroline) • Carolus Rex (Latin: King Charles) • carriage return • carrier's risk • cash receipts • central railway • central registry • Chief Ranger • *Med.* chronic rejection • Civis Romanus (Latin: Roman citizen) • (USA) Commendation Ribbon • *Anglican Church* Community of the Resurrection • company's risk • *Med.* complete regression (or remission) • *Engineering* compression ratio • *Med.* computed radiography • *Chem.* concentration ratio • *Psychol.* conditioned reflex (or response) • conference report • Congo red (dye and chemical indicator) • (USA) consciousness raising • control relay • cosmic rays • Costa Rica (abbrev. or IVR) • credit rating • credit report • *Statistics* critical ratio • *postcode for* Croydon • current rate • Custos Rotulorum (Latin: Keeper of the Rolls) • *British vehicle registration for* Portsmouth

**CrA** *Astronomy* Corona Australis

**CRA** California Redwood Association • Canadian Rheumatism Association • (Northern Ireland) Civil Rights Association • Coal Research Association of New Zealand • Commander of the Royal Artillery • Commercial Rabbit Association • composite research aircraft • corrosion-resistant alloy

**CrAA** Commander-at-Arms

**CRAC** Careers Research and Advisory Centre • Central Religious Advisory Committee • Construction Research Advisory Council

**CRAD** Committee for Research into Apparatus for the Disabled

**CRAeS** Companion of the Royal Aeronautical Society

**CRAF** (USA) Civil Reserve Air Fleet

**CRAMRA** Convention on the Regulation of Antarctic Mineral Resource Activities

**cran.** (or **craniol.**) craniology

**craniom.** craniometry

**CRASC** Commander of the Royal Army Service Corps

**CrB** *Astronomy* Corona Borealis

**CRB** Central Radio Bureau

**CRC** *Printing* camera-ready copy • Cancer Research Campaign • child-resistant closure • Civil Rights Commission • coal rank code (for classifying coals) • Community Relations Council • *Printing* composing room chapel • (USA) Coordinating Research Council • Cycle Racing Club • *Computing* cyclic redundancy check (or code)

**CRCC** Canadian Red Cross Committee

**CRCH** central register and clearing house

**CRCP** Certificant of the Royal College of Physicians

**CRCS** Certificant of the Royal College of Surgeons

**CRD** chronic respiratory disease • Crop Research Division

**CRDEC** (USA) Chemical Research, Development, and Engineering Center

**CRDF** cathode-ray direction-finding

**CRE** (USA) Coal Research Establishment • Commander of the Royal Engineers • Commercial Relations and Exports • Commission for Racial Equality

**CREFAL** Centro Regional de Educación Fundamental para la América Latina (Spanish: Regional Centre of Fundamental Education for Latin America)

**cres.** (or **cresc.**) *Music* crescendo

**Cres.** Crescent (in street names)

**CRF** *Finance* capital recovery factor • chronic renal failure • *Med.* coagulase reacting factor • *Biochem.* corticotrophin-releasing factor

**crg.** carriage

**CRH** corticotrophin-releasing hormone

**CRI** Caribbean Research Institute • *Med.* chronic renal insufficiency • *Photog.* colour reversal intermediate • (USA) Cray Research Incorporated • Croce Rossa Italiana (Italian Red Cross)

**CRIB** Current Research in Britain (publication)

**CRIC** *RC Church* Canons Regular of the Immaculate Conception

**crim.** criminal

**crim. con.** *Law* criminal conversation (i.e. adultery)

**criminol.** criminology

**Crimp.** *Textiles* Crimplene

**CRIS** *Med.* clinical radiology imaging system • *Computing* command retrieval information system • current research information system

**crit.** criterion • critic • critical(ly) • criticism

**Crk** Cork (Ireland)

**CRL** *RC Church* Canons Regular of the Lateran • Certified Record Librarian • Certified Reference Librarian • Chemical Research Laboratory

**CRM** (USA) Central Rocky Mountains • certified reference material • *Physics* chemical remanent magnetization • counter-radar missile • count-rate meter • cruise missile

**CRMA** Cotton and Rayon Merchants' Association

**CRMF** Cancer Relief Macmillan Fund

**CRMP** Corps of Royal Military Police

**crn.** crane • crown

**CRNA** Clinical Research Nurses' Association

**CRNCM** Companion of the Royal Northern College of Music

**CRNSS** Chief of the Royal Naval Scientific Service

**CRO** cathode-ray oscilloscope (*or* oscillograph) • chief recruiting officer • Commonwealth Relations Office (now part of the FCO) • community relations officer • compulsory rights order • Criminal Records Office

**Croat.** Croatia(n)

**CRP** Calendarium Rotulorum Patentium (Latin: Calendar of the Patent Rolls) • *RC Church* Canons Regular of Prémontré • (India) Central Reserve Police • coordinated research programme • *Immunol.* C-reactive protein • *Biochem.* cyclic-AMP receptor protein

**CRPL** (USA) Central Radio Propagation Laboratory

**CRPPH** (USA) Committee on Radiation Protection and Public Health

**CRR** Curia Regis Roll

**CRS** Catholic Record Society • cold-rolled steel • Cooperative Retail Society • cosmic radio source

**CRSA** Cold Rolled Sections Association • Concrete Reinforcement Steel Association

**CRSI** (USA) Concrete Reinforcing Steel Institute

**Crt** Court • *Astronomy* Crater

**CRT** cathode-ray tube • *Maths.* Chinese remainder theorem • combat readiness training • composite rate tax

**CRTC** Canadian Radio-Television Commission

**crtkr** caretaker

**CRTS** Commonwealth Reconstruction Training Scheme

**Cru** *Astronomy* Crux

**CRU** civil resettlement unit • *Computing* control register user

**CRUDESPAC** ('kru:dɛs,pæk) *US Navy* Cruiser-Destroyer Forces, Pacific

**CRULANT** ('kru:lænt) *US Navy* Cruiser Forces, Atlantic

**Crv** *Astronomy* Corvus

**crypto.** cryptographic • cryptography

**cryst.** crystal • crystalline • (*or* **crystallog.**) crystallography

**crystd** crystallized

**crystn** crystallization

**CRZZ** (Poland) Centralna Rada Zwiazkow Zawadowych (Central Council of Trade Unions)

**cs.** case • census • consul

**c.s.** capital stock • come sopra (Italian: as above)

**c/s** cases • cycles per second

**Cs** *Chem., symbol for* caesium • (ital.) *Meteorol.* cirrostratus

**CS** *Chem.* calcium silicate • capital stock • carbon steel • *Biochem.* casein • cast steel • Certificate in Statistics • Chartered Surveyor • Chemical Society • Chief of Staff • Chief Secretary • Christian Science (*or* Scientist) • City Surveyor • civil servant • Civil Service • Clerk of Session • Clerk to the Signet • *Med.* clinical stage • close shot • close support • College of Science • *Mining* colliery screened • Common Serjeant • *Physics* composite superconductor • *Physics* Compton scattering • *Psychol.* conditioned stimulus • (USA) Confederate States • *RC Church* Congregation of Salesians • *Physics* coolant system • Cooperative Society • cotton seed • County Surveyor • Court of Session •

*British fishing port registration for* Cowes • credit sales • cruiser squadron • Custos Sigilli (Latin: keeper of the seal) • *international vehicle registration for* Czech and Slovak Republics • *British vehicle registration for* Glasgow • *international civil aircraft marking for* Portugal • *see* CS gas

**C/S** channel shank (buttons) • cycles per second

**CSA** Canadian Standards Association • Casualty Surgeons' Association • Ceskoslovenské Aerolinie (Czechoslovak Airlines) • Common Services Agency • (USA) Community Services Administration • (Canada) Computer Science Association • Confederate States Army • Confederate States of America

**CSAA** Child Study Association of America

**CSAE** Canadian Society of Agricultural Engineering

**CSAP** Canadian Society of Animal Production

**CSAR** Communication Satellite Advanced Research

**CSB** Bachelor of Christian Science • *Engineering* calcium silicate brick • Central Statistical Board • *Med.* chemical stimulation of the brain

**CSBGM** Committee of Scottish Bank General Managers

**CSBM** *Military* Confidence- and Security-Building Measures

**csc** *Maths.* cosecant

**CSC** Civil Service Commission • Commonwealth Science Council • Comprehensive Schools Committee • (Belgium) Confédération des syndicats chrétiens (French: Federation of Christian Trade Unions) • Congregation of the Holy Cross • Conspicuous Service Cross (replaced by the DSC)

**CSCBS** Commodore Superintendent, Contract-Built Ships

**CSCC** Civil Service Commission of Canada • Council of Scottish Chambers of Commerce

**CSCE** Conference on Security and Cooperation in Europe

**CSD** Chartered Society of Designers • Civil Service Department • Commonwealth Society for the Deaf • *Engineering* constant speed drive • Cooperative Secretaries Diploma • Doctor of Christian Science

**CSDE** *RAF* Central Servicing Development Establishment

**cse** course

**CSE** Central Signals Establishment • Certificate of Secondary Education (replaced by General Certificate of Secondary Education, GCSE) • *Computing* cognitive systems engineering • Council of the Stock Exchange

**CSEA** (USA) Civil Service Employees Association

**CSED** *US Navy* coordinated ship electronics design

**CSEU** Confederation of Shipbuilding and Engineering Unions

**CSF** *Med.* cerebrospinal fluid • Coil Spring Federation • *Med.* colony-stimulating factor (as in **G-CSF**, granulocyte CSF)

**CSFA** Canadian Scientific Film Association

**CSFE** Canadian Society of Forest Engineers

**CSG** Catholic Social Guild • Companion of the Order of the Star of Ghana

**CSGA** Canadian Seed Growers' Association

**CS gas** *indicating* a tear gas (surname initials of its US inventors, Ben Carson and Roger Staughton)

**CSH** *Chem.* calcium silicate hydrate

**CSI** Chartered Surveyors' Institution • *Chem.* chlorosulphonyl isocyanate • Church of South India • *Image technol.* compact source iodide (as in **CSI lamp**) • Commission sportive internationale (French: International Sporting Commission) • Companion of the Order of the Star of India • (USA) Construction Specifications Institute

**CSICC** Canadian Steel Industries Construction Council

**CSIEJB** Certificate of the Sanitary Inspectors Examination Joint Board

**CSIP** Committee for the Scientific Investigation of the Paranormal

**CSIR** Council for Scientific and Industrial Research

**CSIRA** Council for Small Industries in Rural Areas

**CSIRO** Commonwealth Scientific and Industrial Research Organization (Australia)

**CSJ** (ital.) Christian Science Journal

**csk** cask • countersink

**CSL** (Australia) Commonwealth Serum Laboratories • Communication Sub-Lieutenant • computer simulation language • cub scout leader

**CSLATP** Canadian Society of Landscape Architects and Town Planners

**CSLO** Canadian Scientific Liaison Office • Combined Services Liaison Officer

**CSLT** Canadian Society of Laboratory Technologists

**CSM** cerebrospinal meningitis • (ital.) Christian Science Monitor • Christian Socialist Movement • *Astronautics* command service module • Commission for Synoptic Meteorology • Committee on Safety of Medicines • Company Sergeant-Major • (USA) corn, soya, milk (food supplement)

**CSMA** Chemical Specialities Manufacturers' Association • Civil Service Motoring Association

**CSMA/CD** *Computing* carrier sense multiple access, collision detection (network protocol)

**CSMMG** Chartered Society of Massage and Medical Gymnastics

**CSN** Confederate States Navy

**CSNI** (USA) Committee on the Safety of Nuclear Installations

**CSO** Central Selling Organization • Central Statistical Office • Chief Scientific Officer • Chief Signal Officer • Chief Staff Officer • Colonial Secretary's Office • *Image technol.* colour separation overlay • Command Signals Officer • Commonwealth Scientific Office • community service order

**CSP** Chartered Society of Physiotherapists (*or* Physiotherapy) • Civil Service of Pakistan • Congregation of Saint Paul • Council for Scientific Policy

**CSPAA** Conférence de solidarité des pays afro-asiatiques (French: Afro-Asian People's Solidarity Conference)

**CSPCA** Canadian Society for the Prevention of Cruelty to Animals

**CSPR** *Chem.* chlorosulphonated polyethylene rubber

**CSR** (Australia) Colonial Sugar Refining Company • combat-stress reaction • Czechoslovak Socialist Republic

**CSS** Certificate in Social Service • computer systems simulator • (*or* **CSSp**) (member of the) Congregation of the Holy Ghost (Sanctus Spiritus); Holy Ghost Father • Council for Science and Society

**CSSA** Civil Service Supply Association

**CSSB** Civil Service Selection Board

**CSSDA** (USA) Council for Social Science Data Archives

**CSSR** *RC Church* Congregatio Sanctissimi Redemptoris (Latin: Congregation of the Most Holy Redeemer; Redemptorists)

**CSSS** Canadian Soil Science Society

**CST** (USA) Central Standard Time • College of Science and Technology

**CSTA** Canadian Society of Technical Agriculturists • (New Zealand) Canterbury Science Teachers' Association

**CSTI** Council of Science and Technology Institutes

**CStJ** Commander of the Most Venerable Order of the Hospital of St John of Jerusalem

**CSU** *Med.* catheter specimen of urine • Central Statistical Unit • Christlich-Soziale Union (Christian Social Union; German political party) • Civil Service Union • Colorado State University • *Engineering* constant speed unit

**CSV** community service volunteer

**CSW** continuous seismic wave

**CSYS** (Scotland) Certificate of Sixth Year Studies

**ct** carat • caught • cent • circuit • courant (French: instant (this month); in correspondence) • court • crate • credit • current

**ct.** centum (Latin: hundred) • certificate

**Ct.** Canton • Connecticut • Count • (or **Ct**) *Music* countertenor • Court

**CT** cable transfer • Candidate in Theology • *postcode for* Canterbury • Cape Town • *British fishing port registration for* Castletown • *Med.* cell therapy • (USA) Central Time • certificated (*or* certified) teacher • Civic Trust • code telegrams • college of technology • commercial traveller • (Italy) commissario tecnico (sports coach) • *Med.* computerized (*or* computed) tomography (as in **CT scanner**) • *US postcode for* Connecticut • corporation tax • counter trade • *Electrical engineering* current transformer • cycle time • *British vehicle registration for* Lincoln

**C/T** Californian Terms (in the grain trade)

**c.t.a.** *Law* cum testamento annexo (Latin: with the will annexed)

**CTA** Camping Trade Association • Canadian Tuberculosis Association • Caribbean Technical Assistance • Caribbean Tourist Association • Catering Teachers' Association • *Chem.* cellulose triacetate • Channel Tunnel Association • Chaplain Territorial Army • Chicago Transit Authority • Commercial Travellers' Association • (USA) commodities trading adviser • *Med.* computerized (*or* computed) tomographic angiography (*or* arteriography)

**CTAB** *Chem.* cetyltrimethylammonium bromide

**CTAU** Catholic Total Abstinence Union

**CTB** Commonwealth Telecommunications Board • comprehensive test ban

**CTBT** comprehensive test ban treaty

**CTC** Canadian Transport Commission • *Chem.* carbon tetrachloride • centralized traffic control • Central Training Council • (USA) Citizen's Training Corps • city technology college • Civil Technical Corps • Commando Training Centre • Confederación de Trabajadores Cubanos (Spanish: Confederation of Cuban Workers) • Congrès du travail du Canada (French: Canadian Labour Congress) • corn trade clauses • crushing, tearing, and curling (machine) • Cyclists' Touring Club

**ctd** crated

**CTD** central training depot • *Electronics* charge-transfer device • classified telephone directory

**ctDNA** *Biochem.* chloroplast DNA

**Cte** Comte (French: Count)

**CTE** *Physics* coefficient of (linear) thermal expansion

**CTEB** Council of Technical Examining Bodies

**Ctesse** Comtesse (French: Countess)

**CTETOC** Council for Technical Education and Training for Overseas Countries

**CText** Chartered Textile Technologist

**ctf.** certificate • certify

**CTF** Chaplain to the Territorial Forces • coal-tar fuels

**ctge** cartage • cartridge • cottage

**CTH** Corporation of Trinity House

**CTIO** Cerro Tololo Inter-American Observatory (Chile)

**CTK** Ceskoslovenská Tisková Kancelář (Czechoslovak Press Bureau)

**ctl** central

**CTL** constant tensile load • *Insurance* constructive total loss • *Med.* cytotoxic T lymphocyte

**CTM** *Med.* computerized (*or* computed) tomographic myelography

**ctn** carton • *Maths.* cotangent

**CTO** *Philately* cancelled to order (of postage stamps) • Central Telegraph Office • Central Treaty Organization • Chief Technical Officer

**CTOL** ('si:tɒl) conventional takeoff and landing

**CTP** Confederación de Trabajadores del Peru (Spanish: Peruvian Confederation of Labour) • *Biochem.* cytidine 5'-triphosphate

**ctpt** *Music* counterpoint

**ctptal** *Music* contrapuntal

**ctptst** *Music* contrapuntist

**ctr.** centre • contribution • contributor

**CTR** certified test record • controlled thermonuclear reaction • controlled thermonuclear research

**CTRA** Coal Tar Research Association

**CTRP** Confederación de Trabajadores de la République de Panama (Spanish: Confederation of Workers of the Republic of Panama)

**CTRU** Colonial Termite Research Unit

**cts** centimes • cents • certificates • crates

**CTS** *Med.* carpal tunnel syndrome • Catholic Truth Society • characteristic time scale • *Med.* computerized (*or* computed) tomographic scanner • Consolidated Tin Smelters

**CTSA** Crucible and Tool Steel Association

**CTT** capital-transfer tax

**CTTB** Central Trade Test Board (of the RAF)

**Cttee** (*or* **C'ttee**) committee

**CTTSC** Certificate in the Teaching and Training of Subnormal Children

**CTUS** Carnegie Trust for the Universities of Scotland

**CTV** cable television • Canadian Television Network Limited • Confederación de Trabajadores de Venezuela (Spanish: Confederation of Venezuelan Workers)

**CTZ** control traffic zone (around an aerodrome or airport)

**cu.** cubic

**Cu** *Chem.*, *symbol for* copper (Latin *cuprum*) • (ital.) *Meteorol.* cumulus

**CU** Cambridge University • Church Union • *Photog.* close-up • Congregational Union of England and Wales • Cooperative Union • (USA) Cornell University • *international civil aircraft marking for* Cuba • *airline flight code for* Cubana De Aviacion • Customs

Union • *British vehicle registration for* Newcastle upon Tyne

**CUA** Canadian Underwriters' Association • Colour Users' Association

**CUAC** Cambridge University Athletic Club

**CUAFC** Cambridge University Association Football Club

**CUAS** Cambridge University Agricultural Society • Cambridge University Air Squadron

**cub.** cubic

**CUBC** Cambridge University Boat Club • Cambridge University Boxing Club

**CUC** Canberra University College • Coal Utilization Council

**CUCC** Cambridge University Cricket Club

**CUDAT** Community Urban Development Assistance Team

**CUDS** Cambridge University Dramatic Society

**CUEW** Congregational Union of England and Wales

**CUF** Catholicarum Universitatum Foederatio (Latin: Federation of Catholic Universities) • common university fund

**CUGC** Cambridge University Golf Club

**CUHC** Cambridge University Hockey Club

**cuis.** cuisine

**CUKT** Carnegie United Kingdom Trust

**cul.** culinary

**CUL** Cambridge University Library

**CULTC** Cambridge University Lawn Tennis Club

**cum.** *Finance* cumulative

**CUM** Cambridge University Mission

**Cumb.** Cumberland (former county)

**cum div.** *Finance* cum dividend (i.e. with dividend)

**cum. pref.** *Finance* cumulative preference (shares)

**CUMS** Cambridge University Musical Society

**CUNA** Credit Union National Association

**CUNY** City University of New York

**CUOG** Cambridge University Opera Group

**CUP** Cambridge University Press • *symbol for* Cuban peso (monetary unit)

**cur.** currency • current

**CURAC** ('kjʋəræk) (Australia) Coal Utilization Research Advisory Committee

**cur. adv. vult** *Law* curia advisari vult (*see under* CAV)

**CURE** (kjʋə) Care, Understanding, and Research (an organization for the welfare of drug addicts)

**curt.** current (i.e. this month)

**CURUFC** Cambridge University Rugby Union Football Club

**CURV** *US Navy* cable-controlled undersea recovery vehicle

**CUS** Catholic University School

**CUSO** ('kju:səʊ) Canadian University Services Overseas

**CUSRPG** Canada–United States Regional Planning Group (in NATO)

**custod.** custodian

**CUTF** Commonwealth Unit Trust Fund

**CUTS** (kʌts) Computer Users' Tape System

**cv.** *Botany* cultivar

**c.v.** cheval-vapeur (French: horsepower) • chief value • *Med.* cras vespere (Latin: tomorrow evening) • curriculum vitae • cursus vitae (Latin: course of life)

**CV** calorific value • *Crystallog.* carbon vacancy • *Med.* cardiovascular • *Chem.* carrier vehicle (in chromatography) • *Astronomy* cataclysmic variable • cavallo vapore (Italian: horsepower) • cavalos vapor (Portuguese: horsepower) • *Statistics* coefficient of variation • *Maths.* collective vector • common valve • Common Version (of the Bible) • *Med.* contrast ventriculography • *Finance* convertible • *postcode for* Coventry • (Canada) Cross of Valour • *Chem.* crystal violet • curriculum vitae • *British vehicle registration for* Truro

**2CV** 2 cheval-vapeur (deux chevaux; two-horsepower French car)

**CVA** *Med.* cerebrovascular accident • (USA) Columbia Valley Authority

**CVC** current-voltage (*or* capacitance-voltage) characteristics

**CVCP** Committee of Vice-Chancellors and Principals (of the Universities of the United Kingdom)

**c.v.d.** *Commerce* cash versus documents

**CVD** *Physics* Cerenkov viewing device • *Electronics* chemical vapour deposition • common valve development

**CVE** Certificate of Vocational Education • Council for Visual Education

**CVEsc** *symbol for* escudo (monetary unit of Cape Verde)

**CVI** chemical vapour infiltration · *Med.* common variable immunodeficiency

**CVJ** constant velocity joint (in vehicles)

**CVK** centre vertical keel

**CVM** Company of Veteran Motorists

**CVn** *Astronomy* Canes Venatici

**CVN** *Engineering* Charpy V-notch

**CVO** Commander of the Royal Victorian Order

**C.voc.** *Music* colla voce (Italian: with the voice; instruction to accompanist)

**CVP** (Belgium) Christelijk Volkspartif (Flemish Christian Social Party)

**CVS** *Med., Zoology* cardiovascular system · *Med.* chorionic villus sampling · Council of Voluntary Service

**CVSNA** Council of Voluntary Service National Association

**cvt.** *Finance* convertible

**CVT** *Maths.* canonical variational theory · *Chem.* chemical vapour transport · constant variable transmission (in vehicles)

**Cvt Gdn** Covent Garden

**CVWS** combat vehicle weapons system

**cw.** clockwise

**c.w.** *Physics* carrier wave · continuous weld

**c/w** chainwheel (in cycling)

**CW** Canada West · cavity wall · chemical weapons (*or* warfare) · child welfare · clerk of works · Cockcroft–Walton (as in **CW generator**) · cold-worked (of metals) · commercial weight · Commissions and Warrants Department of the Admiralty · complete with · continuous wave(s) (as in **CW radar**; also indicating Morse code, as in **CW speed**) · *postcode for* Crewe · *Physics* Curie–Weiss (in **CW law**) · *British vehicle registration for* Preston

**CWA** Catering Wages Act · chemical warfare agent · (USA) Civil Works Administration · (USA) Clean Water Act · (Australia) Country Women's Association · Crime Writers' Association

**CWB** Canadian Wheat Board · Central Wages Board

**CWBW** chemical warfare–bacteriological warfare

**CWC** Catering Wages Commission · Commonwealth of World Citizens

**CWD** civilian war dead

**CWDE** Centre for World Development Education

**C'wealth** Commonwealth

**CWF** coal–water fuel

**CWGC** Commonwealth War Graves Commission

**CWINC** (India) Central Waterways, Irrigation, and Navigation Commission

**CWL** Catholic Women's League

**Cwlth** Commonwealth

**CWME** Commission on World Mission and Evangelism (of the World Council of Churches)

**CWNA** Canadian Weekly Newspapers Association

**c.w.o.** cash with order

**CWO** Chief Warrant Officer

**CWOIH** Conference of World Organizations Interested in the Handicapped

**CWP** (Malta) Christian Workers' Party · (USA) Communist Workers' Party

**CWR** (*or* **c.w.r.**) continuous welded rail

**CW radar** continuous-wave radar

**CWS** coal–water slurry · *Physics* continuous-wave spectroscopy · Cooperative Wholesale Society · Court Welfare Service

**cwt** *symbol for* hundredweight

**CWT** central war time

**CWU** Chemical Workers' Union

**cx** *Med.* cervix · convex

**CX** *British vehicle registration for* Huddersfield · *international civil aircraft marking for* Uruguay

**CXR** chest X-ray

**CXT** Common External Tariff of the European Community

**cy** capacity · currency · *Chem., symbol for* cyanide (in formulae) · cycle(s)

**CY** calendar year · *British fishing port registration for* Castlebay · *international vehicle registration for* Cyprus · *airline flight code for* Cyprus Airways · *British vehicle registration for* Swansea

**cyath.** *Med.* cyathus (Latin: glassful)

**cyath. vin.** *Med.* cyathus vinarius (Latin: wineglassful)

**cyber.** cybernetics

**cyc.** cycle(s) · cycling · cyclopedia · cyclopedic

**CYCA** Clyde Yacht Clubs Association

**cyclo.** cyclopedia

**CYEE** Central Youth Employment Executive

**Cyg** *Astronomy* Cygnus

**cyl.** cylinder • cylindrical
**Cym.** Cymric
**CYMS** Catholic Young Men's Society
**CYO** (USA) Catholic Youth Organization
**Cyp.** Cyprian • Cyprus

**Cys** (*or* **cys**) *Biochem.* cysteine
**Cz** *Geology* Cenozoic
**CZ** *British vehicle registration for* Belfast • Canal Zone
**CZI** *Cytology* chlor-zinc iodide
**CZMA** (USA) Coastal Zone Management Act

# D

**d** *symbol for* day • *symbol for* deci- (prefix indicating 0.1, as in **dB**, decibel) • *Biochem., symbol for* deoxyribonucleoside (preceding the nucleoside symbol, as in **dT**, thymidine) • *Physics, symbol for* deuteron • (ital.) *Chem.* dextrorotatory (as in **d-tartaric acid**) • (ital.) *symbol for* diameter • *Music* doh (in tonic sol-fa) • *Physics* down (a quark flavour) • (ital.) *symbol for* relative density • (ital.) *symbol for* thickness • *Maths., indicating* a small increment in a given variable or function (as in **d**y/**d**x) • *Physics, Chem., indicating* the electron state $l=2$, where $l$ is the orbital angular momentum quantum number • *indicating* the fourth vertical row of squares from the left on a chessboard

**d.** dam (in animal pedigrees) • damn • date • daughter • day • deacon • dead • deceased • *Dentistry* deciduous • decision • decree • degree • delete • deliver(y) • delta • density • depart(s) • depth • deputy • desert • deserter • destro (Italian: right) • diameter • died • dime • *Currency* dinar(s) (*see also under* D; DA; Din; JD) • discharge • distance • dividend • dollar(s) (symbol **$**) • *Med.* dose • *Currency* drachma(s) (*see also under* Dr) • drama • droite (French: right) • dump • (formerly) penny *or* pennies (Latin *denarius*)

**D** (ital.) *Physics, Med., symbol for* absorbed dose (of radiation) • *symbol for* dalasï (Gambian monetary unit) • *Geology, symbol for* darcy • defence (in **D notice**) • *Government* Department • *Chem., symbol for* deuterium • *Geology* Devonian • (ital.) *symbol for* diameter • (ital.) *Chem., symbol for* diffusion coefficient • dimension *or* dimensional

(preceded by a number) • *symbol for* dinar (Tunisian monetary unit) • *Optics, symbol for* dioptre • (ital.) *Physics, symbol for* dispersion • *Immunol.* diversity region (of an immunoglobulin chain) • *symbol for* dong (Vietnamese monetary unit) • (ital.) *Aeronautics, symbol for* drag • *Irish fishing port registration for* Dublin • (bold ital.) *Physics, symbol for* electric flux density (*or* displacement) • *Roman numeral for* five hundred • *international vehicle registration or civil aircraft marking for* Germany • *Maths., indicating* the first derivative of a function (in **D operator**) • (small cap.) *Chem., indicating* an optically active compound having a configuration related to dextrorotatory glyceraldehyde (as in **D-glucose**) • *indicating* a musical note or key • *Med., indicating* a rhesus antigen (as in **anti-D**) • *indicating* semiskilled *or* unskilled (occupational grade)

**D.** (*or* **D**) Damen (German: ladies) • December • (USA) Democrat(ic) • demy (paper size) • destroyer • Deus (Latin: God) • Deutschland (German: Germany) • *Cards* diamonds • Director • Diretto (Italian: slow train) • distinguished • doctor • dogana (Italian: customs) • Dom (monastic title) • Dominus (Latin: God *or* Christ) • Don (Spanish title) • douane (French: customs) • Dowager • Duchess • Duke • Dutch

**2,4-D** 2,4-dichlorophenoxyacetic acid (herbicide)

**D2** *international civil aircraft marking for* Angola

**D4** *international civil aircraft marking for* Cape Verde Islands

**D6** *international civil aircraft marking for* Comoros Islands

**da** *symbol for* deca- (prefix indicating 10, as in **dam**, decametre)

**d/a** *Commerce* days after acceptance • *Commerce* documents against acceptance

**Da** *Biochem., symbol for* dalton(s)

**Da.** Danish

**D/a** deposit account • discharge afloat

**DA** *British vehicle registration for* Birmingham • *airline flight code for* Dan-Air Services • *postcode for* Dartford • Daughters of America • deed of arrangement • Defence Act • delayed action (bomb) • (USA) Department of Agriculture • Deputy Advocate • deputy assistant • design automation • destructive analysis • *symbol for* dinar (Algerian monetary unit) • Diploma in Anaesthesia (*or* Anaesthetics) • Diploma in Art • direct action • *Chem.* dissolved acetylene • (USA) District Attorney • Doctor of Arts • doesn't answer • *Med.* dopamine • *Irish fishing port registration for* Drogheda • duck's arse (hairstyle)

**D/A** *Commerce* days after acceptance • *Commerce* delivery on acceptance • deposit account • (*or* **D-A**) *Computing, Electronics* digital-to-analogue • *Commerce* documents against acceptance (as in **D/A bill**)

**DAA** défense anti-aérienne (French: anti-aircraft defence) • *Chem.* diacetone acrylamide • *Chem.* diacetone alcohol • Diploma of the Advertising Association

**DAA&QMG** Deputy Assistant Adjutant and Quartermaster-General

**DAAG** Deputy Assistant Adjutant-General

**DA&QMG** Deputy Adjutant and Quartermaster-General

**DAAS** data acquisition and analysis system

**DAB** daily audience barometer • Deutsches Apothekerbuch (German Pharmacopoeia) • (ital.) Dictionary of American Biography • digital audio broadcasting

**DABCO** *Chem.* 1,4-diazobicyclooctane

**DABN** *Med.* diffuse acute bacterial nephritis

**d.a.c.** *Insurance* deductible average clause • direct air cycle

**DAc** Doctor of Acupuncture

**DAC** data analysis and control • Development Assistance Committee (of the OECD) • *Computing* digital-to-analogue converter

**DACC** Dangerous Air Cargoes Committee

**DACG** Deputy Assistant Chaplain-General

**dacr.** dacron (fabric)

**DAD** Deputy Assistant Director (as in **DADMS**, Deputy Assistant Director of Medical Services; **DADOS**, Deputy Assistant Director of Ordnance Services; **DADQ**, Deputy Assistant Director of Quartering; **DADST**, Deputy Assistant Director of Supplies and Transport)

**DADG** Deputy Assistant Director General (as in **DADGMS**, Deputy Assistant Director General of Medical Services)

**DAdmin** Doctor of Administration

**DAE** (USA) Department of Atomic Energy • (ital.) Dictionary of American English • differential algebraic equation • Diploma in Advanced Engineering • Director of Army Education

**DAEP** Division of Atomic Energy Production

**DAER** Department of Aeronautical and Engineering Research

**daf** (dæf) (Netherlands) Doorn Automobielfabriek (Dutch gearless car)

**d.a.f.** described as follows

**DAF** (USA) Department of the Air Force • dissolved air flotation • dry ash-free (coal)

**DAFS** Department of Agriculture and Fisheries for Scotland

**dag** *symbol for* decagram(s)

**DAG** Deputy Adjutant-General • (Germany) Deutsche Angestellten-Gewerkschaft (trade union of salaried staff) • development assistance group

**DAGMAR** ('dægmɑː) *Commerce* defining advertising goals for measured advertising results

**DAgr** Doctor of Agriculture

**DAgrSc** Doctor of Agricultural Science

**DAH** *Med.* disordered action of the heart

**d.a.i.** death from accidental injuries

**DAI** disease activity index • distributed artificial intelligence

**DAJAG** Deputy Assistant Judge Advocate General

**Dak.** Dakota

**dal** *symbol for* decalitre(s)

**DAL** direct acid leaching

**DALR** *Meteorol.* dry adiabatic lapse rate

**dal S.** *Music* dal segno (Italian: (repeat) from the sign)

**dam** *symbol for* decametre(s)

**DAM** Diploma in Ayurvedic Medicine

**DAMN** *Chem.* diaminomaleonitrile

**DAMS** (USA) defense against missiles system(s) • Deputy Assistant Military Secretary

**Dan.** *Bible* Daniel • Danish

**D&AD** Designers and Art Directors Association

**D&B** discipline and bondage

**D & C** dean and chapter • *Med.* dilatation and curettage (of the uterus)

**d and d** drunk and disorderly

**D & D** death and dying

**D & HAA** Dock and Harbour Authorities' Association

**d and p** development and printing

**d & s** demand and supply

**D and V** *Med.* diarrhoea and vomiting

**DAO** district advisory officer

**DAOT** Director of Air Organization and Training

**d.a.p.** do anything possible • documents against payment

**DAP** *Chem.* diammonium phosphate • Director of Administrative Planning • *Computing* distributed array processor • *Electronics* donor–acceptor pair • Draw a Person (psychological test)

**DAP&E** Diploma in Applied Parasitology and Entomology

**DAPM** Deputy Assistant Provost-Marshal

**DAppSc** Doctor of Applied Science

**DAPS** Director of Army Postal Services

**DAQMG** Deputy Assistant Quartermaster-General

**DAR** Daughters of the American Revolution • (USA) Defense Aid Reports • direct absorption receiver (of solar radiation) • (Canada) Directorate of Atomic Research

**DArch** Doctor of Architecture

**DARD** Directorate of Aircraft Research and Development

**DARE** demand and resource evaluation

**DARPA** ('dɑːpə) (USA) Defense Advanced Research Projects Agency (formerly ARPA)

**DArt** Doctor of Art

**d.a.s.** *Commerce* delivered alongside ship

**DAS** *Computing* data-acquisition system • development advisory service • Director of Armament Supply • double algebraic sum • Dramatic Authors' Society

**DASA** (USA) Defense Atomic Support Agency

**DASc** Doctor of Agricultural Science(s)

**DASC** (USA) Direct Air Support Center

**DASD** *Computing* direct-access storage device • Director of Army Staff Duties

**DASH** drone antisubmarine helicopter

**DASM** delayed-action space missile

**DAST** *Chem.* diethylaminosulphur trifluoride

**dat.** dative

**DAT** *Med.* dementia of the Alzheimer type • digital audio tape

**DATEC** ('deɪtɛk) Art and Design Committee, Technician Education Council

**Datel** ('deɪ,tɛl) *Trademark* data telex (data transmission service)

**DATV** digitally assisted television

**dau.** daughter

**DAV** Disabled American Veterans

**DAvMed** Diploma in Aviation Medicine

**DAW** *Nuclear engineering* dry active waste

**DAWS** Director of Army Welfare Services

**DAX** *Stock exchange* Deutsche Aktienindex (German share price index)

**DAyM** Doctor of Ayurvedic Medicine

**d.b.** *Music* double bass • double bed • double-breasted • drawbar (on tractors, etc.)

**dB** *symbol for* decibel(s)

**Db** *symbol for* dobra (monetary unit of São Tomé and Príncipe)

**DB** Bachelor of Divinity (Latin *Divinitatis Baccalaureus*) • *Chem.* dangling bond • database • (*or* **D/B**) *Book-keeping* daybook • deals and battens (timber) • *Radio, Television* delayed broadcast • (Germany) Deutsche Bundesbahn (German Federal Railway) • (Germany) Deutsche Bundesbank (German Federal Bank) • Domesday Book • double-barrelled • *British vehicle registration for* Manchester

**2,4-DB** *Chem.* 4-(2,4-dichloro-phenoxy)butyric acid

**dBA** (*or* **dBa**) *symbol for* decibel A (decibels above reference noise, adjusted: unit for measuring noise)

**DBA** *Computing* database administrator (*or* administration) • dihydrodimethyl-benzopyranbutyric acid (sickle-cell anaemia treatment) • Doctor of Business Administration • (*or* **d.b.a.**) doing business as (*or* at)

**DBB** deals, battens, and boards (timber) • (Germany) Deutscher Beamtenbund (civil servants' trade union)

**DBC** Deaf Broadcasting Council

**DBE** Dame Commander of the Order of the British Empire • design-basis event

**DBEATS** dispatch payable both ends all time saved

**DBELTS** dispatch payable both ends on lay time saved

**Dbh** (*or* **DBH**) *Forestry* diameter at breast height

**DBib** Douay Bible

**DBIU** (Canada) Dominion Board of Insurance Underwriters

**dbk** debark • drawback

**dbl.** (*or* **dble**) double

**DBM** Diploma in Business Management

**DBMS** *Computing* database management system

**DBMT** displacement bone-marrow transplantation

**Dbn** Durban (South Africa)

**DBO** Diploma of the British Orthoptic Board

**dbre** diciembre (Spanish: December)

**DBS** *Physics* diffraction back-scattering • direct broadcast(ing by) satellite

**DBST** double British summer time

**DBT** *Chem.* dual-buffer titration

**d.c.** dead centre • *Physics* direct current • *Printing* double column • *Music* double crochet • *Navigation* drift correction

**d.C.** depois de Cristo (Portuguese: after Christ, i.e. AD) • dopo Cristo (Italian: after Christ, i.e. AD)

**DC** *Music* da capo (Italian: from the head; i.e. repeat from the beginning) • Daughters of Charity of St Vincent de Paul • death certificate • (*or* **DC.**) *Botany* de Candolle (indicating the author of a species, etc.) • decimal currency • (Italy) Democrazia Cristiana (Christian Democratic Party) • (USA) Dental Corps • depth charge • Deputy Chief • Deputy Commissioner • Deputy Consul • Deputy Counsel • Detective Constable • diagnostic centre • diplomatic corps • *Physics* direct current • Disarmament Conference • Disciples of Christ • District Commissioner •

district council • district court • District of Columbia (abbrev. *or* postcode) • Doctor of Chiropractic • *Commerce* documents (against) cash • Douglas Commercial (aircraft, as in **DC10**) • *Theatre* down centre (of stage) • *Physics* drift chamber • *British vehicle registration for* Middlesbrough

**D/C** *Marine insurance* deviation clause

**DCA** (USA) Defense Communications Agency • (Australia) Department of Civil Aviation

**DCAe** Diploma of the College of Aeronautics

**DCAO** Deputy County Advisory Officer

**d.cap.** double foolscap (standard paper size)

**DCAS** Deputy Chief of the Air Staff

**DCB** Dame Commander of the Order of the Bath • double cantilever beam

**DCBE** *Med.* double-contrast barium enema

**DCC** Deputy Chief Constable • digital compact cassette • Diocesan Consistory Court • Diploma of Chelsea College

**DCD** (USA) Department of Community Development • Diploma in Chest Diseases • *Physics* double-crystal (X-ray) diffraction • *Electronics* drain-current drift

**DCE** *Computing* data-communication equipment • design and construction error • *Chem.* dichloroethane • Diploma in Chemical Engineering • Doctor of Civil Engineering • domestic credit expansion

**DCEP** Diploma of Child and Educational Psychology

**DCF** *Accounting* discounted cash flow

**DCG** Deputy Chaplain-General • direct coal gasification

**DCGS** Deputy Chief of the General Staff

**DCh** Doctor of Surgery (Latin *Doctor Chirurgiae*)

**DCH** Diploma in Child Health

**DChD** Doctor of Dental Surgery

**DChE** Doctor of Chemical Engineering

**DCI** desorption chemical ionization • Detective Chief Inspector • (*or* **d.c.i.**) double column inch (in advertisements) • ductile cast iron

**DCJ** (USA) district court judge

**dcl.** declaration

**DCL** Distillers' Company Limited • Doctor of Civil Law

**DCLI** Duke of Cornwall's Light Infantry

**DCLJ** Dame Commander of the Order of St Lazarus of Jerusalem

**DClSc** Doctor of Clinical Science

**DCM** Diploma in Community Medicine • *Military* Distinguished Conduct Medal • district court-martial • Doctor of Comparative Medicine

**DCMG** Dame Commander of the Order of St Michael and St George

**DCMS** Deputy Commissioner Medical Services

**DCnL** Doctor of Canon Law

**DCNS** Deputy Chief of Naval Staff

**DCO** Duke of Cambridge's Own (regiment)

**DC of S** Deputy Chief of Staff

**d.col.** double column (in advertisements)

**DComL** Doctor of Commercial Law

**DComm** Doctor of Commerce

**DCompL** Doctor of Comparative Law

**DCP** Diploma in Conservation of Paintings • Diploma in Clinical Pathology • Diploma of Clinical Psychology • *Physics* direct-current plasma

**DCPA** (USA) Defense Civil Preparedness Agency

**DCPath** Diploma of the College Pathologists

**DCR** Diploma of the College of Radiographers (as in **DCR(MU)**, medical ultrasound; **DCR(NM)**, nuclear medicine; **DCR(R)**, diagnostic radiography; **DCR(T)**, radiotherapy)

**DCrim** Doctor of Criminology

**DCS** Deputy Chief of Staff • Deputy Clerk of Sessions • *Physics* differential cross section • digital camera system • Doctor of Christian Science • Doctor of Commercial Sciences • *Med.* dorsal column stimulator

**DCSO** Deputy Chief Scientific Officer

**DCST** Deputy Chief of Supplies and Transport

**dct** document

**DCT** Doctor of Christian Theology • *Med.* dynamic computerized tomography

**DCU** *Chem.* N,N-dichlorourethane

**DCVO** Dame Commander of the Royal Victorian Order

**DCW** dead carcass weight • domestic cold water

**dd** dated • dedicated • delivered

**d.d.** days after date • delayed delivery • *Commerce* delivered dock • demand draft • dono dedit (Latin: given as a gift) • dry dock • due date (*or* day) • today's date (Latin *de dato*)

**D.d.** Deo dedit (Latin: gave to God)

**D/d** days after date • *Commerce* delivered

**DD** *Insurance* damage done • *Chem.* D dimer • *Banking* demand draft • (USA) Department of Defense • Deputy Director (*or* Directorate) • dichloropropylene and dichloropropane (soil fumigant) • Diploma in Dermatology • *Finance* direct debit • direttissimo (Italian: fast train) • discharged dead • dishonourable discharge • Doctor of Divinity • double demy (standard paper size) • *Med.* Duchenne dystrophy • *postcode for* Dundee • *British vehicle registration for* Gloucester

**D/D** delivered at docks • demand draft • dock dues

**DDA** Dangerous Drugs Act • Disabled Drivers' Association

**D-Day** Day Day (the specified day, i.e. 6 June 1944, for the Allied invasion of Europe)

**DDC** Dewey Decimal Classification (of library books) • *Med.* dideoxycytidine (Aids treatment) • *Computing* direct digital control

**DDD** dat, dicat, dedicat (Latin: gives, devotes, and dedicates) • deadline delivery date • *Chem.* dichlorodiphenyl-dichloroethane • dono dedit dedicavit (Latin: gave and consecrated as a gift)

**DDDA** *Chem.* dodecadien-1-yl acetate

**DDDOL** *Chem.* dodecadien-1-ol

**DDDS** Deputy Director of Dental Services

**DDE** *Computing* direct data entry • Dwight David Eisenhower (1890–1969, US president 1953–61)

**DDG** Deputy Director-General

**DDGAMS** Deputy Director-General, Army Medical Services

**DDH** Diploma in Dental Health

**DDI** (*or* **ddl**) *Med.* dideoxyinosine (Aids treatment) • Divisional Detective Inspector

**d.d. in d.** *Med.* de die in diem (Latin: from day to day)

**DDL** *Computing* data description language(s) • Deputy Director of Labour

**DDM** Diploma in Dermatological Medicine • Doctor of Dental Medicine

**DDME** Deputy Director of Mechanical Engineering

**DDMI** Deputy Director of Military Intelligence

**DDMOI** Deputy Director of Military Operations and Intelligence

**DDMS** Deputy Director of Medical Services

**DDMT** Deputy Director of Military Training

**DDNI** Deputy Director of Naval Intelligence

**DDO** Diploma in Dental Orthopaedics • District Dental Officer

**DDOL** *Chem.* dodecen-1-ol

**DDOS** Deputy Director of Ordnance Services

**DDP** *Chem.* dichlorodiammineplatinum(II) • *Computing* distributed data processing

**DDPH** Diploma in Dental Public Health

**DDPR** Deputy Director of Public Relations

**DDPS** Deputy Director of Personal Services • Deputy Director of Postal Services

**DDR** Deutsche Demokratische Republik (German Democratic Republic *or* East Germany; now part of Germany) • Diploma in Diagnostic Radiology

**DDRA** Deputy Director, Royal Artillery

**DDRD** Deputy Directorate of Research and Development

**dd/s** delivered sound

**DDS** deep diving system • Deputy Directorate of Science • Dewey Decimal System (library-book classification) • *Med.* diaminodiphenyl sulphone (dapsone; leprosy treatment) • Director of Dental Services • (*or* **DDSc**) Doctor of Dental Science • Doctor of Dental Surgery

**DDSD** Deputy Director of Staff Duties

**DDSM** (USA) Defense Distinguished Service Medal

**DDSR** Deputy Director of Scientific Research

**DDST** Deputy Director of Supplies and Transport

**DDT** dichlorodiphenyltrichloroethane (insecticide)

**DDVP** dimethyldichlorovinyl phosphate (dichlorvos; insecticide)

**DDVS** Deputy Director of Veterinary Services

**DDWE&M** Deputy Director of Works, Electrical and Mechanical

**d.e.** deckle edge • diesel-electric • *Fencing* direct elimination • *Book-keeping* double entry

**DE** Dáil Éireann (lower chamber of the Irish parliament) • deflection error • *US postcode for* Delaware • Department of Employment • *postcode for* Derby • *Military* destroyer escort • destruction efficiency • diesel engine • direct electrolysis • Doctor of Engineering • Doctor of Entomology • double elephant (standard paper size) • *British fishing port registration for* Dundee • *British vehicle registration for* Haverfordwest

**Dea.** Deacon • Dean

**DEA** Department of Economic Affairs (former UK government department) • *Chem.* diethanolamine • (USA) Drug Enforcement Administration (*or* Agency)

**DEAD** *Chem.* diethyl azodicarboxylate

**deb.** *Finance* debenture • debit

**deb. stk** *Finance* debenture stock

**dec** *Astronomy* declination

**dec.** deceased • décembre (French: December) • decimal • declaration • declare(d) • *Grammar* declension • decoration • decorative • decrease • *Music* decrescendo (Italian; decrease loudness)

**Dec.** Decani (Latin: of the dean; indicating the dean's side (usually the south side) of a choir) • Decanus (Latin: dean) • (*or* **Dec**) December

**DEc** Doctor of Economics

**DEC** dental examination centre • (USA) Department of Environmental Conservation • (USA) Digital Equipment Corporation • Dollar Export Council

**decd** deceased

**decid.** deciduous

**decl.** *Grammar* declension

**decn** decontamination

**DEcon** Doctor of Economics

**DEconSc** Doctor of Economic Science

**DECR** *Meteorol.* decrease

**decresc.** *Music* decrescendo (Italian; decrease loudness)

**ded.** dedicate(d) • dedication • deduce • deduct(ion)

**DEd** Doctor of Education

**de d. in d.** (ital.) *Med.* de die in diem (Latin: from day to day)

**DEE** Diploma in Electrical Engineering

**DEED** (USA) Department of Energy and Economic Development

**DEEP** Directly Elected European Parliament

**def.** defecate • defecation • defect • defection • defective • defector • defence • defendant • deferred • deficit • define • definite • definition • deflagrate • deflect(ion) • defoliate • defrost • defunct • defunctus (Latin: deceased)

**def. art.** *Grammar* definite article

**DEFCON** ('def,kɒn) *Military* defence readiness condition

**defl.** deflate (*or* deflation) • deflect(ion)

**deft.** defendant

**deg.** degree

**DEG** *Meteorol.* degrees

**DEHA** di-2-ethylhexyl adipate (plasticizer in clingfilm)

**DEI** Dutch East Indies (former name for Indonesia)

**del.** delegate • delegation • delete • delineavit (Latin: he (*or* she) drew it) • deliver(ed)

**Del** *Astronomy* Delphinus

**Del.** Delaware • Delhi

**deld.** delivered

**deleg.** delegate • delegation

**DElo** Doctor of Elocution

**delv.** deliver(ed)

**dely.** delivery

**dem.** demand • demerara • democracy • demurrage

**Dem.** (USA) Democrat(ic)

**DEME** Directorate of Electrical and Mechanical Engineering

**demon.** demonstrate • demonstrative

**DEMS** defensively equipped merchant ships

**DemU** (Northern Ireland) Democratic Unionist

**demur.** demurrage

**den.** denier • denotation • denote(d) • dental • dentist(ry)

**Den.** Denbighshire (former Welsh county) • Denmark • Denver (USA)

**DEn** (*or* **D.En.**) Department of Energy • Doctor of English

**DEN** District Enrolled Nurse

**dend.** (*or* **dendrol.**) dendrology

**DenD** Docteur en droit (French: Doctor of Laws)

**DEng** (*or* **DEngg**) Doctor of Engineering

**DEngS** Doctor of Engineering Science

**DenM** (*or* **DenMed**) Docteur en médecine (French: Doctor of Medicine)

**denom.** *Religion* denomination

**DENR** (USA) Department of Energy and Natural Resources

**dens.** density

**dent.** dental • dentist(ry) • denture

**DEnt** Doctor of Entomology

**DEOVR** Duke of Edinburgh's Own Volunteer Rifles

**dep.** department • depart(s) • departure • dependant • dependency • dependent • deponent • depose(d) • deposit • depositor • depot • (*or* **Dep.**) deputy

**dép.** département (administrative division in France) • député (French: deputy)

**DEP** Department of Employment and Productivity • (USA) Department of Environmental Protection • *Chem.* diethyl pyrocarbonate

**dept** department • deponent

**dept.** deputy

**der.** derecha (Spanish: right) • derivation • derivative • derive(d)

**DER** (USA) Department of Environmental Resources

**Derby.** Derbyshire

**deriv.** derivation • derivative • derive(d)

**DERL** derived emergency reference level (of radiation)

**derm.** dermatitis • (*or* **dermat.**, **dermatol.**) dermatology

**DERR** Duke of Edinburgh's Royal Regiment

**derv** (dɜːv) diesel-engined road vehicle (diesel oil)

**des.** desert • design(er) • designate(d) • designation • desire • dessert

**Des.** Deaconess • Designer

**DES** *Computing* data encryption standard • Department of Education and Science • *Med.* diethylstilboestrol

**desc.** descend • descendant • descent • describe

**desid.** desideratum (Latin: something wanted)

**desig.** designate

**DèsL** Docteur ès lettres (French: Doctor of Letters)

**desp.** despatch(ed)

**DesRCA** Designer of the Royal College of Art

**DèsS** (*or* **DèsSc**) Docteur ès sciences (French: Doctor of Science)

**DèsScPol** Docteur ès science politique (French: Doctor of Political Science)

**dest.** destroyer

**destn** destination

**det.** detach • detachment • detail • determine • *Med.* detur (Latin: let it be given)

**Det** Detective (as in **Det Con**, Detective Constable; **Det Insp**, Detective Inspector; **Det Sgt**, Detective Sergeant; **Det Supt**, Detective Superintendent)

**DET** *Linguistics* determiner • diethyltryptamine (hallucinogenic drug) • direct energy transfer

**detn** determination

**Deut.** *Bible* Deuteronomy

**dev.** develop(ed) • developer • development • deviate • *Navigation* deviation

**Dev.** Devon (*or* Devonshire)

**Devon.** Devonshire

**devp** develop

**devpt** development

**devs.** devotions

**DEW** (dju:) directed-energy weapon • *Military* distant early-warning (as in **DEW line**; network of radar stations)

**dez.** dezembro (Portuguese: December)

**Dez.** Dezember (German: December)

**df.** draft

**d.f.** *Commerce* dead freight

**DF** Dean of Faculty • *Nuclear engineering* decontamination factor • Defender of the Faith • (*or* **D/F**) *Telecom.* direction finder (*or* finding) • *symbol for* Djibouti franc (monetary unit) • Doctor of Forestry • double foolscap (paper) • *British vehicle registration for* Gloucester

**DFA** (USA) Department of Foreign Affairs • Diploma in Foreign Affairs • Doctor of Fine Arts

**DFAA** *Biochem.* dissolved free amino acids

**DFC** Distinguished Flying Cross

**DFD** *Computing* dataflow diagram

**DFDL** dual-frequency dye laser

**DFHom** Diploma of the Faculty of Homeopathy

**DFLS** Day Fighter Leaders' School

**DFM** Diploma in Forensic Medicine • Distinguished Flying Medal

**dfndt** defendant

**DFP** *Chem.* diisopropyl fluorophosphate

**DFR** Dounreay fast reactor

**DFS** disease-free survival

**dft** defendant • draft

**DFT** *Maths.* discrete Fourier transform • dual-flow turbine

**DFW** director of fortifications and works

**dg** *symbol for* decigram(s)

**DG** Dei gratia (Latin: by the grace of God) • Deo gratias (Latin: thanks be to God) • dependence graph • Deutsche Grammophon (German record company) • *Biochem.* D-glucose • differential geometry • *Navigation* directional gyro • Director-General • Dragoon Guards • *postcode for* Dumfries • *British vehicle registration for* Gloucester

**DGA** Director-General, Aircraft • Directors' Guild of America

**DGAA** Distressed Gentlefolks Aid Association

**DGAMS** Director-General, Army Medical Services

**DGB** (Germany) Deutscher Gewerkschaftsbund (German Trade Union Federation)

**DGC** *Biology* density-gradient centrifugation • Diploma in Guidance and Counselling

**DGCA** Director-General of Civil Aviation

**DGCE** Directorate-General of Communications Equipment

**DGCStJ** Dame Grand Cross of the Order of Saint John of Jerusalem

**DGD** Director, Gunnery Division

**DGD&M** Director-General, Dockyards and Maintenance

**DGE** Directorate-General of Equipment

**DGEME** Director-General, Electrical and Mechanical Engineering

**DGI** Director-General of Information • Director-General of Inspection

**DGLP(A)** Director-General, Logistic Policy (Army)

**DGM** Diploma in General Medicine • Director-General of Manpower

**DGMS** Director-General of Medical Services

**DGMT** Director-General of Military Training

**DGMW** Director-General of Military Works

**Dgn** Dragoon

**DGNPS** Director-General of Naval Personal Services

**DGO** Diploma in Gynaecology and Obstetrics

**DGP** *Biochem.* D-glucose 6-phosphate • Director-General of Personnel • Director-General of Production

**DGPS** Director-General of Personal Services

**DGR** Director of Graves Registration

**DGS** Diploma in General Studies • Diploma in General Surgery • Diploma in Graduate Studies • Directorate-General of Signals • Director-General, Ships

**DGSRD** Directorate-General of Scientific Research and Development

**DGT** Director-General of Training

**DGW** Director-General of Weapons • Director-General of Works

**d.h.** das heisst (German: that is; i.e.) • dead heat

**Dh** *symbol for* dirham (monetary unit of United Arab Emirates)

**DH** *British fishing port registration for* Dartmouth • *Sport* dead heat • De Havilland (aircraft) • Department of Health • *Baseball* designated hitter • *symbol for* dirham (Moroccan monetary unit) • district heating • Doctor of Humanities • *Electronics* double heterostructure • *British vehicle registration for* Dudley • *postcode for* Durham

**DHA** District Health Authority

**DHBA** *Chem.* 3,4-dihydroxybenzylamine

**Dhc** Doctor honoris causa (honorary doctorate)

**DHHS** (USA) Department of Health and Human Services

**DHL** Doctor of Hebrew Letters (*or* Literature) • Doctor of Humane Letters

**DHMSA** Diploma in the History of Medicine (Society of Apothecaries)

**DHO** *Electronics* damped harmonic oscillator

**DHQ** district (*or* divisional) headquarters

**DHR** *Nuclear engineering* decay heat removal

**DHS** Diploma in Horticultural Science • Doctor of Health Sciences

**DHSA** Diploma of Health Service Administration

**DHSS** Department of Health and Social Security (former government department, now split into the DoH and DSS)

**DHumLit** Doctor of Humane Letters

**DHW** domestic hot water

**DHyg** Doctor of Hygiene

**di.** diameter

**d.i.** daily inspection • das ist (German: that is; i.e.) • de-ice • diplomatic immunity • document identifier

**Di** *Chem., symbol for* didymium

**DI** Defence Intelligence • Department of the Interior • Detective Inspector • *Aeronautics* direct injection • Director of Infantry • district (*or* divisional) inspector • *Med.* donor insemination • double imperial (standard paper size) • drill

instructor • *Irish vehicle registration for* Roscommon

**dia.** diagram • dialect • diameter

**DIA** (USA) Defense Intelligence Agency • Design and Industries Association • Diploma in International Affairs • Driving Instructors' Association

**DIAD** *Chem.* diisopropyl azodicarboxylate

**diag.** diagnose • diagonal • diagram

**dial.** dialect(al) • dialectic(al) • dialogue

**diam.** diameter

**diamat** ('daɪə,mæt) *Philosophy, Economics* dialectical materialism

**DIANE** (daɪ'æn) Direct Information Access Network for Europe

**diap.** *Music* diapason

**diaph.** diaphragm

**diars** *Chem.* o-phenylenebis(dimethylarsine) (used in formulae)

**DIAS** Dublin Institute of Advanced Sciences

**DIBAL-H** *Chem.* diisobutylaluminium hydride

**dic.** dicembre (Italian: December) • diciembre (Spanish: December)

**DIC** Diploma of Membership of the Imperial College of Science and Technology (London) • *Med.* disseminated intravascular coagulation • *Chem.* dissolved inorganic carbon

**DIChem** Diploma in Industrial Chemistry

**dict.** dictate(d) • dictation • dictator • dictionary

**dicta.** dictaphone

**DICTA** Diploma of Imperial College of Tropical Agriculture

**DIDS** *Electronics* donor-impurity density of states

**DIE** Diploma in Industrial Engineering • Diploma of the Institute of Engineering

**dieb. alt.** *Med.* diebus alternus (Latin: on alternate days)

**DIEME** Directorate of Inspection of Electrical and Mechanical Equipment

**dien** *Chem.* diethylenetriamine (used in formulae)

**diet.** dietary • dieteucs • dietician

**dif.** differ • differential

**DIF** *Meteorol.* diffuse • District Inspector of Fisheries

**diff.** differ • difference • different • differential

**dig.** digest (book or summary) • digestion • digestive • digit(al)

**DIG** Deputy Inspector-General • disablement income group

**digraph** ('daɪgræf) *Computing* directed graph

**DIH** Diploma in Industrial Health

**DIIR** digital image-intensifier radiography

**Dij.** Dijon (France)

**dil.** dilute(d) • dilution

**DIL** *Electronics* dual in-line (as in **DIL switch**)

**diln** dilution

**dim.** dimanche (French: Sunday) • dimension • dimidium (Latin: one-half) • diminish • *Music* diminuendo • diminutive

**DIM** Diploma in Industrial Management

**dimin.** diminutive

**DIMS** *Computing* Data and Information Management System

**din.** dining car (*or* room) • dinner

**Din** *symbol for* dinar (Yugoslavian monetary unit)

**Din.** Dinsdag (Dutch: Tuesday)

**DIN** Deutsches Institut für Normung (German national standards organization; as in **DIN connector**, etc.) • *Computing* digital imaging network

**DIng** Doctor of Engineering (Latin *Doctor Ingeniariae*)

**dinky** (*or* **Dink**, **DINK**) ('dɪŋkɪ *or* dɪŋk) *Colloquial* double (*or* dual) income, no kids (used of couples)

**DInstPA** Diploma of the Institute of Park Administration

**dio.** diocese

**DIO** district intelligence officer

**dioc.** diocesan • diocese

**dioc. syn.** diocesan synod

**DIOP** *Chem.* di-iso-octyl phthalate

**dip.** diploma

**Dip** (dɪp) Diploma (in degrees and qualifications)

**DIP** *Physics* deep inelastic processes • (dɪp) *Electronics* dual in-line package

**DipAD** Diploma in Art and Design

**DipAe** Diploma in Aeronautics

**DipAgr** Diploma in Agriculture

**DipALing** Diploma in Applied Linguistics

**DipAM** Diploma in Applied Mechanics

**DipAppSc** Diploma of Applied Science

**DipArch** Diploma in Architecture

**DipArts** Diploma in Arts

**DipASE** Diploma in Advanced Study of Education, College of Preceptors

**DipAvMed** Diploma of Aviation Medicine, Royal College of Physicians

**DipBA** Diploma in Business Administration

**DipBac** Diploma in Bacteriology

**DipBMS** Diploma in Basic Medical Sciences

**DipBS** Diploma in Fine Art, Byam Shaw School

**DipCAM** Diploma in Communication, Advertising, and Marketing of CAM Foundation

**DipCC** Diploma of the Central College

**DipCD** Diploma in Child Development • Diploma in Civic Design

**DipCE** Diploma in Civil Engineering

**DipChemEng** Diploma in Chemical Engineering

**DipCom** Diploma in Commerce

**DipDHus** Diploma in Dairy Husbandry

**DipDP** Diploma in Drawing and Painting

**DipDS** Diploma in Dental Surgery

**DipEcon** Diploma in Economics

**DipEd** Diploma in Education

**DipEl** Diploma in Electronics

**DipEng** Diploma in Engineering

**DipESL** Diploma in English as a Second Language

**DipEth** Diploma in Ethnology

**DipFA** Diploma in Fine Arts

**DipFD** Diploma in Funeral Directing

**DipFE** Diploma in Further Education

**DipFor** Diploma in Forestry

**DipGSM** Diploma in Music, Guildhall School of Music and Drama

**DipGT** Diploma in Glass Technology

**DipHA** Diploma in Hospital Administration

**DipHE** Diploma in Higher Education • Diploma in Highway Engineering

**DipHum** Diploma in Humanities

**diphos** *Chem.* 1,2-bis(diphenylphosphino)ethane (used in formulae)

**DipHSc** Diploma in Home Science

**diphth.** diphthong

**DipJ** Diploma in Journalism

**dipl.** diploma • diplomacy • diplomat(ic)

**DipL** Diploma in Languages

**DipLA** Diploma in Landscape Architecture

**DipLib** Diploma of Librarianship

**DipLSc** Diploma of Library Science

**DipM** Diploma in Marketing

**DipMechE** Diploma of Mechanical Engineering

**DipMet** Diploma in Metallurgy

**DipMFOS** Diploma in Maxial, Facial, and Oral Surgery

**DipMusEd** Diploma in Musical Education

**DipN** Diploma in Nursing

**DipNEd** Diploma in Nursery School Education

**DipO&G** Diploma in Obstetrics and Gynaecology

**DipOL** Diploma in Oriental Learning

**DipOrth** Diploma in Orthodontics

**DipPA** Diploma in Public Administration

**DipP&OT** Diploma in Physiotherapy and Occupational Therapy

**DipPharmMed** Diploma in Pharmaceutical Medicine

**DipPhysEd** Diploma in Physical Education

**DipQS** Diploma in Quantity Surveying

**DipRADA** Diploma of the Royal Academy of Dramatic Art

**DipREM** Diploma in Rural Estate Management

**DIPS** digital image-processing system

**DipS&PA** Diploma in Social and Public Administration

**DipSMS** Diploma in School Management Studies

**DipSoc** Diploma in Sociology

**DipSpEd** Diploma in Special Education

**DipSS** Diploma in Social Studies

**DipSW** Diploma in Social Work

**DipT** Diploma in Teaching

**DipTA** Diploma in Tropical Agriculture

**DipT&CP** Diploma in Town and Country Planning

**DipTech** Diploma in Technology

**DipTEFL** Diploma in the Teaching of English as a Foreign Language

**DipTh** Diploma in Theology

**DipTP** Diploma in Town Planning

**DipTPT** Diploma in Theory and Practice of Teaching

**dir.** direct(ed) • direction • director • *Currency* dirham (*see also under* Dh; DH)

**DIR** *Photog.* developer inhibitor release

**Dir-Genl** Director-General

**dis.** discharge • disciple • discipline • disconnect • discontinue • discount • dispense • distance • distant • distribute

**DIS** (USA) Defense Intelligence School

**disab.** (*or* **disabl.**) disability

**disb.** disbursement

**disc.** disciple • discipline • discount • discover(ed) • discoverer • discovery

**disch.** discharge

**DISH** *Med.* diffuse idiopathic skeletal hyperostosis

**dishon.** dishonourable • dishonourably

**dismac** ('dɪs,mæk) *Military* digital scene-matching area correlation sensors

**disp.** dispensary • dispensation • dispense • disperse • dispersion

**displ.** displacement

**diss.** dissenter • dissertation • dissolve

**dist.** distance • distant • distilled • distinguish(ed) • district

**Dist. Atty** (USA) District Attorney

**distr.** distribution • distributor

**distrib.** distributive

**DistTP** Distinction in Town Planning

**DIT** *Med.* desferrioxamine infusion test • Detroit Institute of Technology • double income tax (in **DIT relief**)

**div** (dɪv) *Maths.* divergence

**div.** diversion • divide(d) • dividend • divine • division • divisor • divorce(d)

**Div.** Divine • Divinity

**div. in par. aeq.** *Med.* dividatur in partes aequales (Latin: divide into equal parts; in prescriptions)

**divn** division

**divnl** divisional

**DIY** (*or* **d.i.y.**) do-it-yourself

**d.J.** der Jüngere (German: junior) • dieses Jahres (German: of this year)

**DJ** (*or* **d.j.**) dinner jacket • Diploma in Journalism • (*or* **d.j.**) disc jockey • (USA) District Judge • Divorce Judge • Doctor of Law (Latin *Doctor Juris*) • *Finance* Dow Jones • dust jacket (of a book) • *British vehicle registration for* Liverpool

**DJAG** Deputy Judge Advocate-General

**DJI** *Finance* (USA) Dow Jones Index

**DJIA** *Finance* (USA) Dow Jones Industrial Average

**DJS** Doctor of Juridical Science

**DJT** Doctor of Jewish Theology

**DJTA** *Finance* (USA) Dow Jones Transportation Average

**DJUA** *Finance* (USA) Dow Jones Utilities Average

**DJur** Doctor of Law (Latin *Doctor Juris*)

**dk** dark • deck • dock • duck

**DK** *international vehicle registration for* Denmark • *Irish fishing port registration for* Dundalk • *British vehicle registration for* Manchester

**DKB** *Computing* distributed knowledge base

**Dkr** *symbol for* krone (monetary unit of Denmark and Greenland)

**DKS** Deputy Keeper of the Signet

**dkt** docket

**dkyd** dockyard

**dl** (*or* **dL**) *symbol for* decilitre(s)

**DL** *postcode for* Darlington · *British fishing port registration for* Deal · *airline flight code for* Delta Airlines · Deputy Lieutenant · *Physics* detection limit · diesel · *Psychol.* difference limen · *Electronics* distribution line · Doctor of Laws (Latin *Doctor Legum*) · *Physics* dose level · *Physical chem.* double layer · *Book-keeping* double ledger · *Theatre* down left (of stage) · driving licence · *British vehicle registration for* Portsmouth

**D/L** data link · demand loan

**d.l.c.** direct lift control

**DLC** Diploma of Loughborough College · divisional land commissioner · Doctor of Celtic Literature · *Theatre* down left centre (of stage)

**dld.** delivered

**d.l.d.** deadline date

**DLES** Doctor of Letters in Economic Studies

**DLett** Docteur en lettres (French: Doctor of Letters)

**DLG** David Lloyd George (1863–1945, British statesman, prime minister 1916–22)

**DLI** Durham Light Infantry

**D-Lib.** (USA) Liberal Democrat

**DLit** Doctor of Literature

**DLitt** Doctor of Letters (Latin *Doctor Litterarum*)

**DLittS** Doctor of Sacred Letters

**DLJ** Dame of Justice of the Order of St Lazarus of Jerusalem

**DLM** *Genetics* dominant lethal mutation

**DLO** dead letter office (*see under* RLO) · Diploma in Laryngology and Otology (*or* Otorhinolaryngology) · (*or* **d.l.o.**) dispatch (money payable) loading only

**DLOY** Duke of Lancaster's Own Yeomanry

**DLP** (Australia) Democratic Labor Party (former political party) · Democratic Labour Party (of Barbados, Trinidad and Tobago, etc.) · *Chem.* dicalcium lead propionate

**dlr** dealer

**DLR** Docklands Light Railway

**DLS** debt liquidation schedule · (*or* **DLSc**) Doctor of Library Science · Dominion Land Surveyor

**DLTP** dilauryl thiodipropionate (antioxidant for rubber)

**dlvd** delivered

**dlvy** delivery

**DLW** Diploma in Labour Welfare

**dly** daily

**dm** *symbol for* decimetre(s)

**d.M.** dieses Monats (German: this month; inst.)

**DM** *British vehicle registration for* Chester · (ital.) Daily Mail · *Astronomy* dark matter · Deputy Master · design manual · *symbol for* Deutschmark (German monetary unit) · *Physics* dipole moment · direct mail · *Chem.* direct methanation · Director of Music · dispersion measures · *Computing* distributed memory · district manager · Docteur en médecine (French: Doctor of Medicine) · Doctor of Mathematics · Doctor of Medicine · Doctor of Music

**DMA** Diploma in Municipal Administration · *Computing* direct memory access

**DMAC** *Television* duobinary multiplexed analogue component

**DM&CW** Diploma in Maternity and Child Welfare

**DMAP** *Chem.* dimethylaminopyridine

**D-mark** Deutschmark

**DMath** Doctor of Mathematics

**DMC** direct manufacturing costs · district medical committee

**DMD** Doctor of Mathematics and Didactics · Doctor of Medical Dentistry (*or* Dental Medicine) · *Med.* Duchenne muscular dystrophy

**DME** *Chem.* 1,2-dimethoxyethane · Diploma in Mechanical Engineering · *Aeronautics* distance-measuring equipment · *Electronics* dropping mercury electrode

**DMed** Doctor of Medicine

**DMet** Doctor of Metallurgy · Doctor of Meteorology

**DMF** *Chem.* N,N-dimethylformamide · *Electronics* dose-modifying (*or* -modification) factor

**DMFOS** Diploma in Maxillofacial and Oral Surgery

**dmg.** damage

**DMGO** Divisional Machine-Gun Officer

**DMGT** *Genetics* DNA-mediated gene transfer

**DMHS** Director of Medical and Health Services

**DMI** Director of Military Intelligence

**DMin** Doctor of Ministry

**DMJ** Diploma in Medical Jurisprudence

**DMJ(Path)** Diploma in Medical Jurisprudence (Pathology)

**DMK** (India) Dravida Munnetra Kazgham (political party)

**dml.** demolish

**DML** *Computing* data-manipulation language • (formerly, USSR) Defence Medal for Leningrad • Doctor of Modern Languages

**DMLJ** Dame of Merit of the Order of St Lazarus of Jerusalem

**DMLS** Doppler microwave landing system

**DMLT** Diploma in Medical Laboratory Technology

**DMM** (formerly, USSR) Defence Medal for Moscow • *Med.* diffuse malignant mesothelioma

**dmn.** dimension(al)

**DMN** (*or* **DMNA**) *Chem.* dimethylnitrosamine

**DMO** (formerly, USSR) Defence Medal for Odessa • *Astronomy* diffuse massive object • Director of Military Operations • district medical officer

**DMO&I** Director, Military Operations and Intelligence

**DMP** Diploma in Medical Psychology • Director of Manpower Planning

**DMPB** Diploma in Medical Pathology and Bacteriology

**DMPM** *Physics* differential mechanical-properties microprobe

**DMPO** *Chem.* 5,5-dimethyl-l-pyrroline-N-oxide

**DMPP** *Chem.* 1,1-dimethyl-4-phenyl-piperazinium iodide

**DMPS** *Chem.* 2,3-dimercapto-1-propanesulphonic acid

**DMPU** *Chem.* N,N'-dimethylpropylene-urea

**DMR** Diploma in Medical Radiology • Director of Materials Research

**DMRD** Diploma in Medical Radiological Diagnosis • Directorate of Materials Research and Development

**DMRE** (*or* **DMR&E**) Diploma in Medical Radiology and Electrology

**DMRT** Diploma in Medical Radiotherapy

**DMS** *Computing* data-management system • *Mining* dense-medium separation • *Chem.* dimethyl sulphide • Diploma in Management Studies • Directorate of Military Survey • Director of Medical Services • Dis manibus sacrum (Latin: consecrated to the souls of the departed) • Doctor of Medical Science • Doctor of Medicine and Surgery • *Physics* drift magnetic separator

**DMSA** *Med.* dimercaptosuccinic acid (diagnostic aid)

**DMSO** *Med.* dimethylsulphoxide (used in ointments)

**DMSSB** Direct Mail Services Standard Board

**dmstn** (*or* **dmst.**) demonstration

**dmstr.** demonstrator

**DMSV** (formerly, USSR) Defence Medal for Sevastopol

**DMT** *Chem.* dimethyl terephthalate • dimethyltryptamine (hallucinogenic drug) • Director of Military Training

**DMU** *Commerce* decision-making unit (within an organization) • directly managed unit (of NHS hospitals)

**DMus** Doctor of Music

**DMV** (USA) Department of Motor Vehicles • Docteur en médecine vétérinaire (French: Doctor of Veterinary Medicine)

**DMZ** demilitarized zone

**dn** down • dozen

**Dn** Deacon • Dragoon

**D$^n$** Don (Spanish: Mr)

**DN** (*or* **D/N**) debit note • de novo (Latin: from the beginning) • Diploma in Nursing • Diploma in Nutrition • Dominus noster (Latin: our Lord) • *postcode for* Doncaster • *British vehicle registration for* Leeds

**D$^{na}$** Doña (Spanish: Mrs)

**DNA** (USA) Defense Nuclear Agency • *Genetics* deoxyribonucleic acid • Det Norske Arbeiderpartiet (Norwegian Labour Party) • Deutscher Normenausschuss (German Committee of Standards) • *Med.* did not attend • Director of Naval Accounts • District Nursing Association

**DNAD** Director of Naval Air Division

**DNB** (ital.) Dictionary of National Biography

**DNC** *Nuclear engineering* delayed-neutron counting • Director of Naval

Construction • *Computing* distributed numerical control

**DND** Director of Navigation and Direction

**dne.** douane (French: customs)

**DNE** Diploma in Nursing Education • Director of Naval Equipment • Director of Nurse Education • Dounreay Nuclear Establishment

**DNES** Director of Naval Education Service

**DNF** (*or* **dnf**) did not finish (of competitors in a race)

**DNHW** (USA) Department of National Health and Welfare

**DNI** Director of Naval Intelligence

**DNJC** Dominus noster Jesus Christus (Latin: Our Lord Jesus Christ)

**DNMS** Director of Naval Medical Services

**DNO** Director of Naval Ordnance • district naval officer • district nursing officer • divisional nursing officer

**DNOC** dinitro-*o*-cresol (pesticide)

**D notice** defence notice

**DNP** declared national programme • *Immunol.* dinitrophenyl • dynamic nuclear polarization

**DNPDE** Dounreay Nuclear Power Development Establishment

**DNPP** Dominus Noster Papa Pontifex (Latin: Our Lord the Pope)

**DNR** (USA) Department of Natural Resources • Director of Naval Recruiting • *Med.* do not resuscitate

**dns** *Cartography* downs

**DNS** Department for National Savings • *Chem.* 5-dimethylamino-1-naphthalenesulphonic acid

**DNSA** Diploma in Nursing Service Administration

**DNT** Director of Naval Training

**DNWS** Director of Naval Weather Service

**do.** ditto

**d/o** (*or* **DO**) *Commerce* delivery order

**DO** defence order • *Finance* deferred ordinary (shares) • Diploma in Ophthalmology • Diploma in Osteopathy • (*or* **d.o.**) *Grammar* direct object • (*or* **D/O**) *Commerce* direct order • dissolved oxygen • district office (*or* officer) • divisional office (*or* officer) • Doctor of Optometry • Doctor of Oratory • Doctor of Osteopathy • *British fishing port registration for* Douglas • drawing office • *British vehicle registration for* Lincoln

**DOA** date of availability • *Med.* dead on arrival • (USA) Department of the Army • dissolved-oxygen analyser

**DOAE** Defence Operational Analysis Establishment (of the Ministry of Defence)

**d.o.b.** (*or* **DOB**) date of birth

**DObstRCOG** Diploma of the Royal College of Obstetricians and Gynaecologists

**doc.** document(s)

**Doc.** Doctor

**DOC** Denominazione di Origine Controllata (Italian: name of origin controlled; Italian wine classification) • (USA) Department of Commerce • direct operating cost • *Chem.* dissolved organic carbon • District Officer Commanding

**d.o.c.a.** date of current appointment

**d.o.c.e.** date of current enlistment

**DocEng** Doctor of Engineering

**DOCG** Denominazione di Origine Controllata Garantita (Italian: name of origin guaranteed controlled; Italian wine classification)

**docu.** document • documentary • documentation

**d.o.d.** date of death • died of disease

**DOD** (USA) Department of Defense

**DOE** (USA) Department of Energy • (*or* **DoE**) Department of the Environment • (*or* **d.o.e.**) depends on experience (referring to salary in job advertisements) • (*or* **DoE**) Director of Education

**DOF** *Chem., Physics* degrees of freedom

**D. of Corn. LI** Duke of Cornwall's Light Infantry

**D of H** degree of honour

**D of L** Duchy of Lancaster

**D of S** director of stores

**DoH** (*or* **DOH**) Department of Health

**DOHC** double (*or* dual) overhead camshaft

**DOHS** (USA) Department of Health Services

**DOI** (*or* **DoI**) Department of Industry • (USA) Department of the Interior • died of injuries • Director of Information

**DOJ** (USA) Department of Justice

**dol.** *Music* dolce (Italian: sweetly; i.e. gently) • dollar

**DOL** (USA) Department of Labor • Doctor of Oriental Learning

**dolciss.** *Music* dolcissimo (Italian: very sweetly)

**dom.** domain • domenica (Italian: Sunday) • domestic • domicile • dominant • domingo (Spanish, Portuguese: Sunday) • dominion

**Dom.** Dominica • Dominical • *RC Church* Dominican • Dominus (Latin: Lord)

**DOM** Deo Optimo Maximo (Latin: to God, the best, the greatest) • *Colloquial* dirty old man • dissolved (*or* dispersed) organic material • *international vehicle registration for* Dominican Republic • Dominus omnium magister (Latin: God the Lord of all)

**Dom. Proc.** *Law* Domus Procerum (Latin: House of Lords)

**DOMS** Diploma in Ophthalmic Medicine and Surgery

**don.** donec (Latin: until)

**Don.** (*or* **Doneg.**) Donegal

**DON** (USA) Department of the Navy • Diploma in Orthopaedic Nursing • dissolved organic nitrogen

**DOPC** *Biochem.* dioleoylphosphatidylcholine

**DOPS** *Chem.* DL-*threo*-3,4-dihydroxyphenylserine

**DOpt** Diploma in Ophthalmic Optics

**Dor** *Astronomy* Dorado

**Dor.** Dorian • Doric

**DOr** Doctor in Orientation

**DOR** Director of Operational Requirements • *Chem.* direct oxide reduction

**DORA** ('dɔːrə) Defence of the Realm Act (1914)

**Dors.** Dorset

**DOrth** Diploma in Orthodontics • Diploma in Orthoptics

**DOS** day of sale • *Physics* density of states • (USA) Department of State • Diploma in Orthopaedic Surgery • Directorate of Overseas Surveys • Director of Ordnance Services • (dɒs) *Computing* disk operating system • Doctor of Ocular Science

**DOSV** deep ocean survey vehicle

**dot.** *Law* dotation (endowment)

**DoT** Department of Transport

**DOT** Department of Overseas Trade • (USA) Department of Transportation • *Finance* (USA) designated order turnaround (on the New York Stock Exchange) • Diploma in Occupational Therapy • *Physiol.* dissolved oxygen tension

**dott.** dottore (Italian: doctor)

**DOV** double oil of vitriol (commercial sulphuric acid)

**DOVAP** *Physics* Doppler velocity and position

**dow.** (*or* **Dow.**) dowager

**DOW** (*or* **d.o.w.**) died of wounds

**doz.** dozen

**dp** deep • *Baseball* double play

**d.p.** damp-proof(ing) • deep penetration • departure point • *Finance* depreciation percentage • *Med.* directione propria (Latin: with proper direction; in prescriptions) • direct port • double paper • dry powder • dual purpose

**DP** data processing • *Chem.* degree of polymerization • delivery point • Democratic Party • diametral pitch • Diploma in Psychiatry • (by) direction of the president • disabled person • displaced person • Doctor of Philosophy • domestic prelate • *Law* Domus Procerum (Latin: House of Lords) • durable press • duty paid • *Computing* dynamic programming • *British vehicle registration for* Reading

**D/P** delivery on payment • *Commerce* documents against payment (*or* presentation)

**2,4-DP** *Chem.* 2-(2,4-dichlorophenoxy)propionic acid

**d.p.a.** deferred payment account

**DPA** Deutsche-Presse Agentur (German news agency) • Diploma in Public Administration • discharged prisoners' aid • (USA) Doctor of Public Administration

**DPath** Diploma in Pathology

**DPB** *Finance* deposit pass book • *Chem.* 1,4-diphenyl-1,3-butadiene

**DPC** Defence Planning Committee (in NATO) • *Biochem.* DNA–protein cross-links (*or* complex)

**DPCM** *Telecom.* differential pulse code modulation

**DPCP** Department of Prices and Consumer Protection

**DPD** Data Protection Directive • *Botany* diffusion pressure deficit • Diploma in Public Dentistry • *Statistics* discrete probability distributions

**DPE** Diploma in Physical Education

**DPEc** Doctor of Political Economy

**DPed** Doctor of Pedagogy

**DPh** Doctor of Philosophy

**DPH** *Chem.* 1,6-diphenylhexatriene • Diploma in Public Health • Director of Public Health • (USA) Doctor of Public Health

**DPharm** Doctor of Pharmacy

**DPHD** Diploma in Public Health Dentistry

**DPhil** ('di: 'fil) Doctor of Philosophy

**DPHN** Diploma in Public Health Nursing

**DPhysMed** Diploma in Physical Medicine

**dpi** *Computing* dots per inch

**dpl.** diploma • (*or* **DPL**) diplomat • duplex

**DPM** *Chem.* bis(diphenylphosphino)-methane • data-processing manager • Deputy Prime Minister • Deputy Provost-Marshal • Diploma in Psychological Medicine

**DPMI** *Computing* DOS/Protected Mode Interface

**DPN** *Biochem.* diphosphopyridine nucleotide (now called NAD)

**DPO** distributing post office • district pay office

**d.p.o.b.** date and place of birth

**DPolSc** Doctor of Political Science

**DPP** *Insurance* deferred payment plan • Diploma in Plant Pathology • Director of Public Prosecutions

**DPPA** *Chem.* diphenylphosphoryl azide

**DPPH** *Chem.* 2,2-di(4-t-octylphenyl)-1-picrylhydrazyl

**DPR** Data Protection Register • Director of Public Relations

**DPRK** Democratic People's Republic of Korea (North Korea)

**DPS** *Chem.* trans-4,4′-diphenyl-stilbene • Director of Personal Services • Director of Postal Services • dividend per share • Doctor of Public Service

**DPSA** Diploma in Public and Social Administration

**DPsSc** Doctor of Psychological Science

**DPsy** Docteur en psychologie (French: Doctor of Psychology)

**DPsych** Diploma in Psychiatry • Doctor of Psychology

**dpt** department • deponent • deposit • depot

**DPT** diphtheria, pertussis (whooping cough), tetanus (in **DPT vaccine**)

**dpty** deputy

**DPW** Department of Public Works

**dpx** duplex

**d.q.** direct question

**DQ** dispersion quotient • *Sport* disqualify • *international civil aircraft marking for* Fiji

**DQMG** Deputy Quartermaster-General

**DQMS** Deputy Quartermaster-Sergeant

**dr** debtor • *symbol for* dram • *Meteorol.* drizzle and rain

**dr.** debit • door • drachm • drachma (*see also under* Dr) • drama • draw(n) • (*or* **Dr.**) drawer • dresser • driver • drum(mer)

**d.r.** deficiency report • design requirements • development report • document report

**Dr** Director • Doctor • *symbol for* drachma (Greek monetary unit) • Drive (in street names)

**DR** (USA) Daughters of the Revolution • *Navigation* dead reckoning • *Physics* decay ratio • defence regulation • dining room • Diploma in Radiology • discount rate • dispatch rider • dispersion relation • district railway • district registry • double royal (standard paper size) • *British fishing port registration for* Dover • *Theatre* down right (of stage) • dry riser (pipe with attachment for fireman's hose) • dynamic relaxation • *British vehicle registration for* Exeter

**D/R** deposit receipt

**Dra** *Astronomy* Draco

**Drª** Doctora (Spanish: (female) doctor) • Doutora (Portuguese: (female) doctor)

**DRA** de-rating appeals

**DRAC** Director, Royal Armoured Corps

**DrAgr** Doctor of Agriculture

**dram.** drama • dramatic • dramatist

**DRAM** (dræm) *Computing* dynamic random-access memory

**dram. pers.** dramatis personae (Latin: characters in a play)

**Drav.** Dravidian (language)

**DRAW** (drɔː) *Computing* direct read after write

**DrBusAdmin** Doctor of Business Administration

**DRC** Diploma of the Royal College of Science and Technology, Glasgow • *Theatre* down right centre (of stage) • Dutch Reformed Church

**DrChem** Doctor of Chemistry

**DRCOG** Diploma of the Royal College of Obstetricians and Gynaecologists

**DRCPath** Diploma of the Royal College of Pathologists

**DRD** Diploma in Restorative Dentistry

**DRDW** *Computing* direct read during write

**DRE** *Med.* digital rectal examination • Director of Religious Education • (*or* **DRelEd**) Doctor of Religious Education

**DrEng** Doctor of Engineering

**DRG** *Med.* diagnosis-related group

**Dr hc** Doctor honoris causa (Latin: honorary doctor)

**Dr ing** Doctor of Engineering

**Dr jur** Doctor of Laws

**DRK** Deutsches Rotes Kreuz (German Red Cross)

**DRLS** dispatch-rider letter service

**DRM** Diploma in Radiation Medicine • Diploma in Resource Management

**DrMed** Doctor of Medicine

**drn** drawn

**DrNatSci** Doctor of Natural Science

**DRO** daily routine order • disablement resettlement officer • divisional routine order

**DrOecPol** Doctor of Political Economics (Latin *Doctor Œconomiae Politicae*)

**DRP** dividend reinvestment plan

**DrPH** Doctor of Public Health

**DrPhil** Doctor of Philosophy

**DrPolSci** Doctor of Political Science

**Dr rer. nat.** Doctor of Natural Science

**DRS** Diploma in Religious Studies

**DRSAMD** Diploma of the Royal Scottish Academy of Music and Drama

**DRSE** *Med.* drug-related side effects

**DRSN** *Meteorol.* drifting snow

**DRT** *Psychiatry* diagnostic rhyme test

**DrTheol** Doctor of Theology

**Dr. und** (*or* **u**) **Vrl.** Druck und Verlag (German: printed and published (by))

**DRurSc** Doctor of Rural Science

**drx.** drachma

**ds.** destro (Italian: right)

**d.s.** date of service • daylight saving • days after sight • day's sight • document signed

**Ds** Deus (Latin: God) • Dominus (Latin: Lord *or* Master)

**DS** *Music* dal segno (Italian: (repeat) from the sign) • *Finance* debenture stock • defect score • *Physics* defect size • *Chem.* dehydroepiandrosterone sulphate • dental surgeon • Department of State • Deputy Secretary • Detective Sergeant • *Physics* diffractive system • Directing Staff • Doctor of Science • Doctor of Surgery • Down's syndrome • driver seated (in **DS vehicle**) • *British fishing port registration for* Dumfries • *British vehicle registration for* Glasgow

**DSA** *Med.* digital subtraction angiography • Diploma in Social Administration • Docteur en sciences agricoles (French: Doctor of Agriculture)

**DSAC** Defence Scientific Advisory Council

**DSAO** Diplomatic Service Administration Office

**DSASO** Deputy Senior Air Staff Officer

**DSB** (*or* **d.s.b.**) double sideband • Drug Supervisory Body (of the UN)

**DSc** Doctor of Science

**DSC** *Physics* differential scanning calorimetry • *Military* Distinguished Service Cross • *Chem.* N,N'-disuccinimidyl carbonate • Doctor of Surgical Chiropody

**DScA** Docteur en sciences agricoles (French: Doctor of Agricultural Sciences) • Docteur en sciences appliquées (French: Doctor of Applied Sciences)

**DSc(Agr)** Doctor of Science in Agriculture

**DScEng** Doctor of Science in Engineering

**DScFor** Doctor of Science in Forestry

**DSCHE** Diploma of the Scottish Council for Health Education

**DScMil** Doctor of Military Science

**DScTech** Doctor of Technical Science

**DSD** Director of Signals Division • Director of Staff Duties

**dsDNA** *Genetics* double-stranded DNA

**DSDP** Deep-Sea Drilling Project

**DSE** Doctor of Science in Economics

**dsgn.** design(er)

**DSIR** (New Zealand) Department of Scientific and Industrial Research

**DSL** district scout leader • Doctor of Sacred Letters

**DSM** (*or* **d.s.m.**) deputy stage manager • (ital.) Diagnostic and Statistical Manual (of the American Psychiatric Association) • Directorate of Servicing and Maintenance • *Military* Distinguished Service Medal • Doctor of Sacred Music

**dsmd** dismissed

**DSN** *Astronautics* Deep Space Network

**DSO** *Military* (Companion of the) Distinguished Service Order • District Staff Officer

**DSocSc** Doctor of Social Science(s)

**d.s.p.** decessit sine prole (Latin: died without issue)

**DSP** Democratic Socialist Party • *Electronics* digital signal processing • (Canada) Doctor of Political Science (French *Docteur en sciences politiques*)

**dspl** disposal

**d.s.p.l.** decessit sine prole legitima (Latin: died without legitimate issue)

**d.s.p.m.** decessit sine prole mascula (Latin: died without male issue)

**d.s.p.m.s.** decessit sine prole mascula superstite (Latin: died without surviving male issue)

**dspn** disposition

**d.s.p.s.** decessit sine prole superstite (Latin: died without surviving issue)

**d.s.p.v.** decessit sine prole virile (Latin: died without male issue)

**d.s.q.** discharged to sick quarters

**DSR** *Commerce* debt service ratio • *Med.* digital subtraction radiography • Director of Scientific Research • *Med.* dynamic spatial reconstructor

**DSRD** Directorate of Signals Research and Development

**Dss** Deaconess

**DSS** *Computing* decision-support system • Department of Social Security • Director of Social Services • Doctor of Holy (*or* Sacred) Scripture (Latin *Doctor Sacrae Scripturae*) • Doctor of Social Science • duplex stainless steel

**DSSc** Diploma in Sanitary Science • Doctor of Social Science

**DST** Daylight Saving Time • Director of Supplies and Transport • Doctor of Sacred Theology • Double Summer Time • *Mining* drill-stem test

**DStJ** Dame of Justice (*or* of Grace) of the Order of St John of Jerusalem

**dstn** destination

**D. Surg.** Dental Surgeon

**DSW** (New Zealand) Department of Social Welfare • Doctor of Social Welfare (*or* Work)

**d.t.** delirium tremens • double throw

**dT** *Biochem., symbol for* thymidine

**DT** (ital.) Daily Telegraph • damage-tolerant • daylight time • *Med.* dead from tumour • delirium tremens •

dental technician • (USA) Department of Transportation • (USA) Department of Treasury • destructive testing • *Colloquial* (USA) detective • (*or* **D–T**) *Nuclear engineering* deuterium–tritium • Director of Transport • Doctor of Divinity (*or* Theology) (Latin *Doctor Theologiae*) • *postcode for* Dorchester (Dorset) • *British vehicle registration for* Sheffield

**DTA** *Physics* differential thermal analysis • Diploma in Tropical Agriculture • Distributive Trades' Alliance

**d.t.b.a.** *Commerce* date to be advised

**DTC** Diamond Trading Company • *Med.* differentiated thyroid carcinoma • Diploma in Textile Chemistry • Docklands Transportation Consortium

**DTCD** (USA) Department of Technical Cooperation for Development • Diploma in Tuberculosis and Chest Diseases

**dtd** dated

**d.t.d.** *Med.* detur talis dosis (Latin: let such a dose be given)

**DTD** Diploma in Tuberculous Diseases • Director of Technical Development

**DTDP** ditridecyl phthalate (plasticizer for PVC)

**DTE** *Computing* data terminal equipment • *Chem.* dithioerythritol

**DTech** Doctor of Technology

**Dtg** Dienstag (German: Tuesday)

**DTh** (*or* **DTheol**) Doctor of Theology

**DTH** *Immunol.* delayed-type hypersensitivity • Diploma in Tropical Hygiene

**DThPT** Diploma in Theory and Practice of Teaching

**DTI** Department of Trade and Industry

**DTIC** dacarbazine (anticancer drug)

**DTL** *Electronics* diode-transistor logic • down the line (in shooting) • *Physics* drift-tube linac (linear accelerator)

**DTM** Diploma in Tropical Medicine

**DTMH** (*or* **DTM&H**) Diploma in Tropical Medicine and Hygiene

**DTNB** *Chem.* 5,5'-dithiobis-(2-nitrobenzoic acid)

**dtº** direito (Portuguese: right)

**DTOD** Director of Trade and Operations Division

**DTp** Department of Transport

**DTP** desktop publishing

**DTPA** *Med.* diethylenetriaminepentaacetic acid (diagnostic aid)

**DTPH** Diploma in Tropical Public Health

**DTR** *Photog.* diffusion-transfer reversal • Diploma in Therapeutic Radiology • double taxation relief

**DTRP** Diploma in Town and Regional Planning

**DTRT** *Meteorol.* deteriorate (*or* deteriorating)

**DT's** (ˌdiː'tiːz) *Colloquial* delirium tremens

**DTS** deep-sleep therapy • *Med.* dual tracer scintigraphy

**DTT** *Chem.* dithiothreitol

**DTVM** Diploma in Tropical Veterinary Medicine

**Du.** Ducal • Duchy • Duke • Dutch

**DU** *British vehicle registration for* Coventry • *Physics* depleted uranium • died unmarried • Doctor of the University • *Med.* duodenal ulcer

**dub.** dubious • dubitans (Latin: doubting)

**Dub.** (*or* **Dubl.**) Dublin

**DUC** *Meteorol.* dense upper cloud

**Dumf.** Dumfries and Galloway Region

**Dun.** Dundee

**Dunelm.** Dunelmensis (Latin: (Bishop) of Durham)

**DUniv** Doctor of the University

**duo.** duodecimo (standard paper size)

**dup.** duplicate

**DUP** (Northern Ireland) Democratic Unionist Party • Docteur de l'Université de Paris (French: Doctor of the University of Paris)

**Dur.** Durban • Durham

**DUS** Diploma of the University of Southampton

**DUSC** *US Air Force* deep underground support center

**Dut.** Dutch

**DUV** damaging ultraviolet (radiation)

**DV** defective (*or* double) vision • Deo volente (Latin: God willing) • Diploma in Venereology • direct vision • distinguished visitor • district valuer • Douay Version (of the Bible) • *British vehicle registration for* Exeter

**DVA** *Med.* digital video angiography • Diploma of Veterinary Anaesthesia

**DV&D** Diploma in Venereology and Dermatology

**DVC** *Microbiol.* direct viable count

**DVH** Diploma in Veterinary Hygiene

**DVI** *Computing* digital video imaging

**DVLA** Driver and Vehicle Licensing Authority

**DVLC** Driver and Vehicle Licensing Centre (Swansea)

**d.v.m.** decessit vita matris (Latin: died in the lifetime of the mother)

**DVM** digital voltmeter • Doctor of Veterinary Medicine

**DVMS** Doctor of Veterinary Medicine and Surgery

**DVO** District Veterinary Officer

**d.v.p.** decessit vita patris (Latin: died in the lifetime of the father)

**DVPH** Diploma in Veterinary Public Health

**dvr** driver

**DVR** Diploma in Veterinary Radiology • *Computing* discrete-variable representation

**DVS** Doctor of Veterinary Surgery

**DVSc** (*or* **DVSci**) Doctor of Veterinary Science

**DVT** *Med.* deep-vein thrombosis

**d.w.** dead weight • delivered weight

**d/w** dust wrapper

**DW** *British vehicle registration for* Cardiff • *Chem.* deionized water • (*or* **D/W**) *Commerce* dock warrant

**DWA** driving without awareness

**d.w.c.** deadweight capacity

**DWEM** *Colloquial* (USA) dead white European male

**dwg** drawing • (*or* **dwel.**) dwelling

**DWI** (USA) driving while intoxicated • Dutch West Indies (former name for Netherlands Antilles)

**dwr** drawer

**DWR** Duke of Wellington's Regiment

**dwt** pennyweight

**d.w.t.** (*or* **DWT**) deadweight tonnage

**DWU** (USA) Distillery, Wine, and Allied Workers International Union

**DX** *Photog.* daylight exposure (indicating that the speed of a film can be set automatically in a suitably equipped camera) • *British vehicle registration for* Ipswich • *Telecom.* long-distance (*or* -distant)

**DXR** *Med.* deep X-ray

**DXRT** deep X-ray therapy

**DXS** diagnostic X-ray spectrometry

**dy.** delivery • demy (standard paper size)

**Dy** *Chem., symbol for* dysprosium

**DY** *international vehicle registration for* Benin (formerly Dahomey) • *British vehicle registration for* Brighton • dockyard • *postcode for* Dudley

**Dyd.** Dockyard

**dyn** *Physics, symbol for* dyne

**dyn.** dynamics · dynamite · dynamo · dynasty

**DYS** Duke of York's Royal Military School

**dz.** dozen

**DZ** *international vehicle registration for* Algeria · *British vehicle registration for* Antrim · Doctor of Zoology · *Meteorol.* drizzle · *Military* drop zone

**DZool** Doctor of Zoology

**D-Zug** Durchgangszug (German: express train)

# E

**e** *Maths., symbol for* the base of natural (Napierian) logarithms · (ital.) *Maths., symbol for* eccentricity (of an ellipse or other conic) · (*or* **e.**) electromotive · (*or* **e⁻**) *Physics, symbol for* electron · (ital.) *Physics, symbol for* electron (*or* proton) charge · (ital.) *Chem., symbol for* equatorial conformation (of molecules) · *Physics, symbol for* positron (in **e⁺**) · *Maths., symbol for* the transcendental number 2.718 282... · (bold ital.) *Maths., symbol for* unit coordinate vectors (in **e**$_x$, **e**$_y$, **e**$_z$) · *Meteorol., symbol for* wet air · *indicating* the fifth vertical row of squares from the left on a chessboard

**e.** edition · educated · elder · eldest · electric · electricity · engineer(ing) · *Telephony, symbol for* Erlang (unit of traffic intensity) · *Baseball* error · excellence · excellent

**E** earth (indicating the terminal in an electrical circuit) · east(ern) · *postcode for* east London · *Colloquial* Ecstasy (hallucinogenic drug) · (ital.) *Physics, symbol for* electric field strength (light ital. in nonvector equations; bold ital. in vector equations) · (ital.) *Chem., symbol for* electrode potential · *Chem., symbol for* electromeric effect · (ital.) *Physics, symbol for* electromotive force · *Chem., symbol for* elimination reaction · *Astronomy, symbol for* elliptical galaxy (followed by a number) · *symbol for* emalangeni (sing. lilangeni; monetary unit of Swaziland) · (ital.) *Physics, symbol for* energy · *Numismatics* English shilling · E-number (EC-approved code number of a food additive, as in **E200**) · *symbol for* exa- (prefix indicating 10¹⁸, as in **EJ**, exajoule) · *British fishing port registration for* Exeter · (ital.; *or* **E**$_v$) *Physics, symbol for* illuminance · (ital.; *or* **E**$_e$) *Physics, symbol for* irradi-

ance · *symbol for* second-class merchant ship (in Lloyd's Register) · *international vehicle registration for* Spain · (ital.) *Physics, symbol for* Young modulus · *indicating* casual workers (occupational grade) · *indicating* a musical note or key · *Logic, indicating* a universal negative categorical proposition

**E.** (*or* **E**) Earl · earth (planet) · east(ern) · Easter (in the Book of Common Prayer) · Edinburgh · efficiency · Egypt(ian) · elocution · eminence · enemy · engineer(ing) · England · English · envoy · equator · España (Spanish: Spain) · evening · evensong (in the Book of Common Prayer)

**ea.** each

**EA** *British vehicle registration for* Dudley · early antigen · East Anglia · economic adviser · educational age · effective action · effective agent (in **EA content**) · electrical artificer · Ente Autonomo (Italian: Autonomous Corporation) · *Freemasonry* Entered Apprentice · enterprise allowance · environmental assessment · *Chem.* ethylacrylate · Evangelical Alliance · experimental area · exposure age

**E/A** enemy aircraft · experimental aircraft

**EAA** Edinburgh Architectural Association · Electrical Appliance Association · (USA) Engineer in Aeronautics and Astronautics · *Chem.* ethylene (*or* ethene) acrylic acid

**EAAA** European Association of Advertising Agencies

**EAAC** European Agricultural Aviation Centre

**EAAFRO** East African Agriculture and Forestry Research Organization (Kenya)

**EAAP** European Association for Animal Production

**EAB** *Med.* extra-anatomic bypass

**EAC** East African Community • Educational Advisory Committee • Engineering Advisory Council

**EACA** East Africa Court of Appeal Reports • *Med.* epsilon aminocaproic acid

**EACC** East Asia Christian Conference

**EACN** *Chem.* equivalent alkane carbon number

**EACSO** (iː'ɑːksəu) East African Common Services Organization

**EAEG** European Association of Exploration Geophysicists

**EAES** European Atomic Energy Society

**e.a.f.** emergency action file

**EAF** electric-arc furnace

**EAFFRO** (*or* **EAFRO**) East African Freshwater Fisheries Research Organization

**EAG** Economists Advisory Group

**EAGGF** European Agricultural Guidance and Guarantee Fund (in the EC)

**EAK** *international vehicle registration for* (East Africa) Kenya

**EAM** *Physics* embedded-atom method • Ethniko Apelentherotiko Metopo (Greek: National Liberation Front; in World War II)

**EAMF** European Association of Music Festivals

**EAMFRO** East African Marine Fisheries Research Organization

**EAMTC** European Association of Management Training Centres

**EAN** *Chem.* effective atomic number • *Computing* European Academic Network

**e. & e.** each and every

**E & OE** errors and omissions excepted (on invoice forms)

**e.a.o.n.** except as otherwise noted

**EAP** East Africa Protectorate • Edgar Allan Poe (1809–49, US writer) • (USA) employee-assistance program • English for academic purposes

**EAPR** European Association for Potato Research

**EAR** employee attitude research • *Engineering* energy-absorbing resin

**EARCCUS** East African Regional Committee for Conservation and Utilization of Soil

**EARN** (ɜːn) *Computing* European Academic and Research Network

**EAROM** ('ɪərɒm) *Computing* electrically alterable read-only memory

**EAROPH** East Asia Regional Organization for Planning and Housing

**EAS** *Med.* endotoxin-activated serum • *Aeronautics* equivalent air speed • *Physics* extensive air (*or* atmospheric) shower (of cosmic rays)

**EASA** Entertainment Arts Socialist Association

**EASEP** *Astronautics* Early Apollo Scientific Experiments Package

**EASHP** European Association of Senior Hospital Physicians

**east.** eastern

**EASTROPAC** ('iːstrəu,pæk) Eastern Tropical Pacific

**e.a.t.** earliest arrival time

**EAT** *Med.* Ehrlich ascites tumour • Employment Appeal Tribunal • *Med.* experimental autoimmune thyroiditis • *international vehicle registration for* (East Africa) Tanzania (*see also* EAZ)

**EATF** *Physics* externally applied thermal field

**EATRO** East African Trypanosomiasis Research Organization

**EAU** *international vehicle registration for* (East Africa) Uganda

**EAVRO** East African Veterinary Research Organization

**EAW** Electrical Association for Women • equivalent average words

**EAX** *Telecom.* electronic automatic exchange

**EAZ** *international vehicle registration for* (East Africa) Tanzania (Zanzibar; *see also under* EAT)

**EB** electricity board • electron beam • (ital.) Encyclopaedia Britannica • Evans blue (dye) • *British vehicle registration for* Peterborough

**EBA** English Bowling Association

**e.b.a.r.** edited beyond all recognition

**EBC** English Benedictine Congregation • European Billiards Confederation • European Brewery Convention

**EBCDIC** ('ɛpsɪ,dɪk) *Computing* extended binary-coded decimal-interchange code

**e-beam** electron beam

**EBIC** ('ɛbɪk) *Physics* electron-beam induced (*or* induction) current

**EBICON** ('ɛbɪkɒn) *Physics* electron-bombardment-induced conductivity

**EBIS** ('ɛbɪs) *Physics* electron-beam ion source

**EBIT** ('ɛbɪt) *Physics* electron-beam ion trap

**EBL** electron-beam lithography • European Bridge League

**EBM** electron-beam machined (*or* machining) • *Physics* energy-balance model • *Med.* expressed breast milk

**EBMC** English Butter Marketing Company

**EbN** east by north

**EBNF** *Computing* extended BNF (Backus normal form)

**E-boat** Enemy War Motorboat (German torpedo boat in World War II)

**Ebor.** ('iːbɔː) Eboracensis (Latin: (Archbishop) of York)

**EBP** *Physics* electron-beam process • *Physics* electron-beam-pumped

**EBR** electron-beam recording • experimental breeder reactor

**EBRA** (*or* **EB & RA**) Engineer Buyers' and Representatives' Association

**EBRD** European Bank for Reconstruction and Development

**EbS** east by south

**EBS** Emergency Bed Service • emergency broadcast system • engineered barrier system • English Bookplate Society

**EBT** *Med.* electron-beam therapy • *Physics* Elmo Bumpy Torus

**EBU** English Bridge Union • European Badminton Union • European Boxing Union • European Broadcasting Union

**EBV** *Physics* electron-beam vaporization • *Med.* Epstein–Barr virus

**EBW** electron-beam welding

**EBWR** *Nuclear physics* experimental boiling-water reactor

**e.c.** earth closet • enamel-coated (*or* -covered) • error correction • exempli causa (Latin: for example) • extended coverage • extension course

**Ec.** Ecuador

**EC** East Caribbean • *postcode for* East Central London • east coast • Eastern Command • Ecclesiastical Commissioner • *international vehicle registration for* Ecuador • *Physics* eddy current • education (*or* educational) committee • *Chem.* effective concentration • electricity council • electrolytic corrosion • *Physics* electron capture • *Physics* electron cyclotron • electronic computer • emergency commission • *Med.* endothelial cell • Engineering Corps •

*Biochem.* Enzyme Commission (preceding the code number of an enzyme) • Episcopal Church • Established Church • *Chem.* ethylene (*or* ethene) carbonate • (Canada) Etoile du Courage (French: Star of Courage) • European Commission • European Community (now often used in place of EEC) • executive committee • *British vehicle registration for* Preston • *international civil aircraft marking for* Spain

**ECA** Early Closing Association • Economic Commission for Africa (UN agency) • (USA) Economic Cooperation Administration • Educational Centres Association • Electrical Contractors' Association • European Confederation of Agriculture • European Congress of Accountants

**ECAC** Engineering College Administrative Council • European Civil Aviation Conference

**ECAFE** Economic Commission for Asia and the Far East (*see* ESCAP)

**ECAPO** (ɪ'kɑːpəʊ) *Chem.* ethoxy carbonyl amino pyridine N-oxide

**ECAS** Electrical Contractors' Association of Scotland

**ECB** electronic components board

**ecc.** eccetera (Italian: et cetera; etc.)

**Ecc.** Eccellenze (Italian: Excellency)

**ECC** *Electrical engineering* earth continuity conductor • *Chem.* electrochemical concentration cell • *Physics* electron capture to the continuum • *Physics* emergency core cooling (*or* coolant) • energy-conscious construction • European Cultural Centre

**ECCD** electron-cyclotron current drive

**Ecc. Hom.** Ecce Homo (Latin: Behold the Man)

**eccl.** (*or* **eccles.**) ecclesiastic(al)

**Eccles.** (*or* **Eccl.**) *Bible* Ecclesiastes

**ecclesiast.** ecclesiastical

**Ecclus.** *Bible* Ecclesiasticus

**ECCM** *Military* electronic counter-countermeasure(s)

**ECCP** European Committee on Crime Problems

**ECCS** *Physics* emergency core-cooling system

**ECCU** English Cross Country Union

**ECD** early closing day • *Physics* electron-capture detector (*or* detection) • *Electronics* electrostatic charge decay • estimated completion date • *Chem.* ethyl cysteinate dimer

**ECDR** electrostatic corona discharge reactor

**ECE** Economic Commission for Europe (UN agency) • *Physics* electron-cyclotron emission

**ECF** *Med.* (USA) extended-care facility

**ECFA** European Committee for Future Accelerators

**ECFMG** Educational Council for Foreign Medical Graduates

**ECFMS** Educational Council for Foreign Medical Students

**ECG** *Med.* electrocardiogram (*or* electro-cardiograph) • Export Credit Guarantee

**ECGB** East Coast of Great Britain

**ECGC** Empire Cotton Growing Corporation

**ECGD** Export Credits Guarantee Department

**ech.** echelon

**ECH** *Physics* electron-cyclotron heating

**ECHP** (USA) Environmental Compliance and Health Protection

**ECI** East Coast of Ireland • energy-cost indicator

**ECIA** European Committee of Interior Architects

**ECITO** European Central Inland Transport Organization

**ECL** *Physics* emergency cooling limit • *Electronics* emitter-coupled logic

**ECLAC** Economic Commission for Latin America and the Caribbean (UN agency)

**eclec.** eclectic(ism)

**ecli.** eclipse • ecliptic

**ECLO** *Electronics* emitter-coupled logic operator

**ECLOF** Ecumenical Church Loan Fund

**ECLSS** environmental control and life-support systems

**ECM** electric coding machine • electro-chemical machining • *Physics* electron-cyclotron maser • *Military* electronic countermeasure(s) (for jamming enemy signals, destroying guided missiles, etc.) • energy conservation measure • environmental corrosion monitor

**ECMA** ('ɛkmə) *Geology* East Coast Magnetic Anomaly • European Computer Manufacturers' Association (Geneva)

**ECMF** Electric Cable Makers' Federation

**ECMRA** European Chemical Market Research Association

**ECMT** European Conference of Ministers of Transport

**ECMWF** European Centre for Medium-range Weather Forecast

**ECN** epoxy–cresol–novolak (synthetic resin)

**ECNSW** Electricity Commission of New South Wales

**ECO** energy conservation opportunity • English Chamber Orchestra

**ECODU** European Control Data Users

**ecol.** ecological • ecology

**Ecol. Soc. Am.** Ecological Society of America

**econ.** economical • economics • economist • economy

**Econ. J.** (ital.) Economic Journal

**Econ. R.** (ital.) Economic Review

**ECOR** (USA) Engineering Committee on Ocean Resources

**ECOSOC** ('ɛkəʊˌsɒk) Economic and Social Council (of the UN)

**ECOVAST** ('ɛkəʊˌvæst) European Council for the Village and Small Town

**ECOWAS** (ɛ'kəʊəs) Economic Community of West African States

**ECP** *Finance* Euro-commercial paper • European Committee on Crop Protection • Evangelii Christi Praedicator (Latin: Preacher of the Gospel of Christ)

**ECPA** Electric Consumers Protection Act (1986)

**ECPD** (USA) Engineers' Council for Professional Development

**ECPS** European Centre for Population Studies

**ECQAC** Electronic Components Quality Assurance Committee

**ECR** *Physics* electron-cyclotron resonance • electronic cash register

**ECRH** *Physics* electron-cyclotron-resonance heating

**ECS** *Physics* electron-capture spectroscopy • *Physics* electronically collimated system • *Physics* emergency cooling (*or* coolant) system • environmental control system • European Communications Satellite • European Components Service

**ECSC** European Coal and Steel Community

**ECT** *Med.* electroconvulsive therapy • *Med.* emission-computerized (*or* -computed) tomography

**ECTA** Electrical Contractors' Trading Association

**ECTD** (USA) Emission Control Technology Division

**ecu** (*or* **ECU**) ('eɪkjuː *or* 'ɛkjuː) European Currency Unit (in the EC)

**ECU** English Church Union • environmental control unit • European Chiropractic Union • *Photog.* extreme close-up

**Ecua.** Ecuador

**ECUK** East Coast of the United Kingdom

**ECV** *Obstetrics* external cephalic version

**ECWA** Economic Commission for Western Asia (UN agency)

**ECWEC** European Community Wind Energy Conference and Exhibition

**ECY** European Conservation Year

**ECYO** European Community Youth Orchestra

**ed.** edile (*or* edilizia) (Italian: building) • edited • edition • editor • educated • education

**éd.** édition (French: edition)

**e.d.** edge distance • enemy dead • error detecting • excused duty • extra duty

**Ed.** Edinburgh • Editor

**ED** (USA) Department of Education • (USA) Doctor of Engineering • economic dispatch • Education Department • *Pharmacol.* effective dose (as in **ED₅₀**, mean effective dose) • Efficiency Decoration • election district • *Physics* electromagnetic dissociation • *Electronics* electron device • *Physics, Chem.* electron diffraction • *Med.* embryonic day • Employment Department • *Med.* end-diastole (*or* -diastolic) • entertainments duty • equilibrium dialysis • *Physics* equivalent dose (of radiation) • European Democrat • *Finance* ex dividend • existence doubtful • experimental detector • *Med.* extensive disease • *Finance* extra dividend • *British vehicle registration for* Liverpool

**e.d.a.** early departure authorized

**EDA** (USA) Economic Development Administration • Electrical Development Association • electronic design automation • (Greece) Eniea Dimokratiki Aristera (Union of the Democratic Left; political party)

**ED & S** (ital.) English Dance and Song (publication of the English Folk Dance and Song Society)

**EDAS** ('iːdæs) *Computing* enhanced data-acquisition system

**EDAX** ('iːdæks) *Physics* energy-dispersive analysis of X-rays

**EdB** Bachelor of Education

**EDB** ethene dibromide (antiknock agent and soil fumigant)

**EDBS** *Computing* expert database system

**e.d.c.** error detection and correction • extra dark colour

**EDC** Economic Development Committee • *Chem.* effective dielectric constant • *Physics* electron-distribution curve • Engineering Design Centre • European Defence Community • *Obstetrics* expected date of confinement

**edd.** ediderunt (Latin: published by) • editiones (Latin: editions)

**EdD** Doctor of Education

**EDD** exactly delayed detonator • *Obstetrics* expected date of delivery

**EDE** *Physics* effective dose equivalent (of radiation)

**EDF** Electricité de France (French electricity corporation) • (USA) Environmental Defense Fund • European Development Fund

**EDG** emergency diesel generator • European Democratic Group

**EDHE** experimental data handling equipment

**EDI** *Computing* electronic data interchange

**Edin.** Edinburgh

**Ed. in Ch.** Editor in Chief

**EDIP** European Defence Improvement Programme (in NATO)

**EDIS** Engineering Data Information System

**edit.** edited • edition • editor • editore (Italian: publisher) • editorial

**e.d.l.** edition de luxe

**EDL** economic discard limits • *Chem.* electrical double layer • electrodeless discharge lamp

**EdM** Master of Education

**EDM** electrical-discharge machined (*or* machining) • *Chem.* electric dipole moment • *Surveying* electronic distance measurement • *Physics* energy-density model

**EDMA** European Direct Marketing Association

**Edm. and Ipswich** (Bishop of) St Edmundsbury and Ipswich

**Edmn** Edmonton (Canada)

**edn** edition

**Ednbgh** Edinburgh

**EDNS** expected demand not supplied

**e.d.o.c.** effective date of change

**EDP** *Physics* electron-diffraction pattern • (*or* **e.d.p.**) electronic data processing • Emergency Defence Plan • *Med.* end-diastolic pressure

**EDPS** *Computing* electronic data-processing system

**EDR** electronic decoy rocket • (Japanese) Electronic Dictionary Research • European Depository Receipts • except during rain (following a pollen count)

**EDRF** *Med.* endothelium-derived relaxing factor

**EDRP** European Demonstration Reprocessing Plant (for nuclear fuel)

**EdS** Education Specialist

**EDS** Electronic Data Systems Corporation • *Physics* energy-dispersive spectrometry (*or* spectroscopy) • *Physics* energy-dispersive spectrum (*or* spectra) • English Dialect Society • *Computing* exchangeable disk store

**EDSAC** ('ɛdsæk) *Computing* Electronic Delay Storage Automatic Calculator

**EDSAT** ('ɛdsæt) Educational Television Satellite

**EDSS** expert decision-support system

**EDT** (USA, Canada) Eastern Daylight Time • energy design technique

**EDTA** (*or* **edta**) *Chem.* ethylene-diaminetetraacetic acid • European Dialysis and Transplant Association

**EDTN** *Chem.* 1-ethoxy-4-(dichloro-1,3,5-triazinyl)naphthalene

**EDU** European Democratic Union

**educ.** educated • (*or* **educn**) education • educational

**EDV** *Med.* end-diastolic volume

**EDVAC** ('ɛdvæk) *Computing* Electronic Discrete Variable Automatic Computer

**EDX** *Physics* energy-dispersive X-ray

**EDXA** *Physics* energy-dispersive X-ray analysis (*or* analyser)

**EDXD** *Physics, Crystallog.* energy-dispersive X-ray diffraction

**EDXF** *Physics, Chem.* energy-dispersive X-ray fluorescence

**EDXS** *Physics, Chem.* energy-dispersive X-ray spectrometer • *Physics, Chem.* energy-dispersive X-ray spectroscopy

**e.e.** errors excepted • eye and ear

**EE** Early English • Eastern Electricity • edge-to-edge • electrical engineer(ing) • electron emission • electronic engineer(ing) • employment exchange • environmental education • environmental engineering • Envoy Extraordinary • errors excepted • (New Zealand) ewe

equivalent • explosive emission • *British vehicle registration for* Lincoln

**EEA** Electronic Engineering Association • European Economic Area

**EEAIE** Electrical, Electronic, and Allied Industries, Europe

**EE & MP** Envoy Extraordinary and Minister Plenipotentiary

**EEB** European Environmental Bureau

**EEC** *Physics* energy–energy correlation • English Electric Company • European Economic Community (*see also under* EC) • *Electronics* explosive-emission cathode

**EECS** electrical-energy conversion system

**EED** *Physics* effective equivalent dose (of radiation) • electro-explosive device

**EEDC** Economic Development Committee for the Electronics Industry

**EEDQ** *Chem.* 1-ethoxycarbonyl-2-ethoxy-1,2-dihydroquinoline

**EEF** Egyptian Expeditionary Force • Engineering Employers' Federation • equivalent-energy function

**EEG** electroencephalogram (*or* electroencephalograph) • Essence Export Group

**EEI** (USA) Edison Electric Institute • (USA) Environmental Equipment Institute

**EEIBA** Electrical and Electronic Industries Benevolent Association

**EEL** *Physics* electron energy loss (spectroscopy)

**EEMJEB** Electrical and Electronic Manufacturers' Joint Education Board

**EEMS** *Computing* enhanced expanded memory specification

**EEMUA** Engineering Equipment and Materials Users Association

**E Eng.** Early English

**EENT** *Med.* eye, ear, nose, and throat

**EEO** equal employment opportunity

**EEOC** (USA) Equal Employment Opportunities Commission

**EER** energy–efficiency ratio • *Physics* equilibrium equivalent radon

**EERI** (USA) Earthquake Engineering Research Institute

**EEROM** ('ɪərɒm) *Computing* electrically erasable read-only memory

**EES** *Physics* electron-energy spectroscopy (*or* spectrum) • European Exchange System

**EET** Eastern European Time

**EETPU** Electrical, Electronic, Tele-communications, and Plumbing Union (*see* AEEU)

**EETS** Early English Text Society

**EEZ** exclusive economic zone

**EF** edge-to-face • education(al) foundation • elevation finder • *Genetics* elongation factor • emergency fleet • *Physics* enrichment factor • expectant father • expeditionary force • experimental flight • extra fine • *British vehicle registration for* Middlesbrough

**EFA** engine fault analysis • *Biochem.* essential fatty acid • Eton Fives Association • European Fighter Aircraft

**EFB** energy from biomass

**EFC** European Federation of Corrosion • European Forestry Commission

**EFCE** European Federation of Chemical Engineering

**EFCT** European Federation of Conference Towns

**EFD** *Engineering* early fault detection

**EFDSS** English Folk Dance and Song Society

**eff.** effetto (Italian: bill *or* promissory note) • efficiency • effigy

**EFF** European Furniture Federation

**EFG** electric-field gradient

**EFGF** *Electronics* epitaxial ferrite-garnet film

**EFI** electronic fuel injection (of car engines)

**EFIS** *Aeronautics* electronic flight-information system

**EFL** English as a foreign language • external financial limit

**EFM** *Med.* electronic fetal monitor • European Federalist Movement

**EFNS** Educational Foundation for Nuclear Science

**EFP** *Maths.* Einstein–Fokker–Planck (differential equation) • *Photog.* electronic field production • *Commerce* exchange of futures for physicals • explosively formed projectile (*or* penetrator)

**EFPD** effective full-power day

**EFPH** effective full-power hour

**EFPW** European Federation for the Protection of Waters

**EFPY** effective full-power year

**EFR** European Fast Reactor • experimental fast reactor

**EFRC** (USA) Edwards Flight Research Center

**EFSA** European Federation of Sea Anglers

**EFSC** European Federation of Soroptimist Clubs

**EFT** electronic funds-transfer

**EFTA** ('eftə) European Free Trade Association

**EFTC** Electrical Fair Trading Council

**EFTPOS** ('eftpɒs) electronic funds-transfer at point of sale

**EFTS** electronic funds-transfer system • elementary flying training school

**EFU** energetic feed unit • European Football Union

**EFVA** Educational Foundation for Visual Aids

**EFW** energy from waste

**e.g.** ejusdem generis (Latin: of a like kind) • exempli gratia (Latin: for example)

**Eg.** Egypt(ian) • Egyptology

**EG** Engineers' Guild • *Chem.* ethylene glycol • *British vehicle registration for* Peterborough

**EGA** Elizabeth Garrett Anderson (Hospital for Woman) • *Computing* enhanced graphics adapter • European Golf Association

**EGARD** ('egɑːd) environmental gamma-ray and radon detector

**EGAS** Educational Grants Advisory Service

**EGBPS** *Med.* ECG gated blood pool scintigraphy

**EGCI** Export Group for the Construction Industries

**EGCS** English Guernsey Cattle Society

**EGD** epithermal gold deposit

**EGEAS** Electric Generating Expansion Analysis System

**EGF** *Med.* epidermal growth factor

**EGFR** *Med.* epidermal-growth-factor receptor

**EGIFO** Edward Grey Institute of Field Ornithology (Oxford)

**EGL** Engineers' Guild Limited

**EGM** Empire Gallantry Medal (replaced by the George Cross) • European Glass Container Manufacturers' Committee • extraordinary general meeting

**EGmbH** (Germany) Eingetragene Gesellschaft mit beschränkter Haftung (registered limited company)

**EGO** eccentric (orbit) geophysical observatory

**EGR** *Finance* earned growth rate • exhaust gas recirculation (as in **EGR valve**)

**EGSP** electronics glossary and symbol panel

**e.g.t.** exhaust gas temperature

**EGT** *Physics* Einstein-invariant gauge theory (of gravitation)

**EGU** English Golf Union • *Chem.* external gelation of uranium

**Egypt.** Egyptian

**Egyptol.** Egyptologist • Egyptology

**eh.** ehrenhalber (German: honorary)

**EH** *postcode for* Edinburgh • *Music* English horn (cor anglais) • *Med.* essential hypertension • *British vehicle registration for* Stoke-on-Trent

**EHC** effective heat capacity (of a building) • European Hotel Corporation • *Med.* external heart compression

**EHE** *Physics* extraordinary Hall effect

**EHF** *Physics* European Hadron Facility • European Hockey Federation • experimental husbandry farm • *Radio* extremely high frequency

**EHG** electro-hydraulic governor

**EHL** *Physics* effective half-life • *Physics* electron-hole liquid

**EHMO** *Chem.* extended Hückel molecular orbital

**EHO** Environmental Health Officer

**ehp** effective horsepower

**EHP** electric and hybrid propulsion • *Physics* electron-hole plasma

**EHR** Environmental Hazard Ranking

**EHS** (USA) Environmental Health Services • European hybrid spectrometer • extra-high strength

**EHT** (*or* **e.h.t.**) *Electronics* extra-high tension

**EHV** electric and hybrid vehicle • extra-high voltage

**EHWS** extreme high water-level spring tides

**EI** *airline flight code for* Aer Lingus • earth (atmosphere) interface • East Indian • East Indies • electrical insulation • electromagnetic interaction • electron impact • electron ionization • *Finance* endorsement irregular • energy intake • environmentally-induced illness • *Photog.* exposure index • external irradiation • *international civil aircraft marking for* Republic of Ireland • *Irish vehicle registration for* Sligo

**EIA** East Indian Association • economic impact assessment • (USA) Electronic Industries Association • Engineering Industries Association • environmental impact analysis (*or* assessment) • Environmental Investigation Agency • *Med.* enzyme immunoassay • *Med.* exercise-induced asthma

**EIB** European Investment Bank • Export–Import Bank

**EIC** East India Company • Electrical Industries' Club • *Physics* electrostatic ion cyclotron • Engineering Institute of Canada

**EICM** employer's inventory of critical manpower

**EICS** East India Company's Service

**EICW** *Physics* electrostatic ion cyclotron wave

**EID** East India Dock • *Military* Electrical Inspection Directorate (for electrical, electronic, and optical equipment) • *Physics* electron-induced disordering

**EIDCT** Educational Institute of Design, Craft, and Technology

**EIE** *Chem.* equilibrium isotope effect

**EIEE** *Med.* early infantile epileptic encephalopathy

**EIEMA** Electrical Installation Equipment Manufacturers' Association

**EIF** Elderly Invalids Fund

**EIFAC** European Inland Fisheries Advisory Committee (of the FAO)

**E-in-C** Engineer-in-Chief

**E Ind.** East Indies

**einschl.** einschliesslich (German: including *or* inclusive)

**Einw.** Einwohner (German: inhabitant)

**EIO** extended interaction oscillator

**EIPC** European Institute of Printed Circuits

**EIR** *Taxation* earned income relief

**EIRMA** European Industrial Research Management Association

**EIS** economic information system • Educational Institute of Scotland • effluent information system • energy information system • environmental impact statement • epidemic intelligence service

**EISA** *Computing* extended industry standard architecture

**EITB** Engineering Industry Training Board

**EIU** Economist Intelligence Unit

**EIVT** European Institute for Vocational Training

**ej.** ejemplo (Spanish: example)

**EJ** *Physics, symbol for* exajoule(s) • *British vehicle registration for* Haverfordwest

**EJC** (USA) Engineers' Joint Council
**EJMA** English Joinery Manufacturers' Association
**ejusd.** ejusdem (Latin: of the same)
**eK** etter Kristi (Norwegian: after Christ; AD)
**EK** East Kilbride · *airline flight code for* Emirates · (Greece) Enosis Kentron (Centre Union; political party) · *British vehicle registration for* Liverpool
**EKD** Evangelische Kirche in Deutschland (German: Protestant Church in Germany)
**EKE** *Physics* equatorial Kerr effect
**EKG** (USA, Germany) electrocardiogram *or* electrocardiograph (German *Elektrokardiogramm*)
**el.** elect(ed) · electric(ity) · element · elevated · elevated railway · elevation · elongation
**EL** *British vehicle registration for* Bournemouth · electrical laboratory · electronics laboratory · *Physics* electron lattice · Engineer Lieutenant · epitaxial layer · Everyman's Library · explosive limit · *Med.* extracorporeal lithotripsy · *international civil aircraft marking for* Liberia
**ELA** electronic learning aid · (Ethiopia) Eritrean Liberation Army
**elas.** elasticity
**ELAS** Ethnikos Laikos Apeleutherotikos Stratos (Greek: Hellenic People's Army of Liberation; in World War II)
**ELB** Bachelor of English Literature
**ELBS** English Language Book Society
**ELC** *Physics* electron loss to continuum · Environment Liaison Centre (Nairobi)
**eld.** elder · eldest
**ELD** economic load distribution
**ELDC** economic load dispatching centre · equivalent load duration curve
**ELDO** ('ɛldəʊ) *Astronautics* European Launcher Development Organization (now part of ESA)
**elec.** (*or* **elect.**) election · elector(al) · electric(al) · electrically · electrician · electricity · electron · electronic · *Med.* electuary
**ELEC** European League for Economic Cooperation
**electr.** electrical
**Electra** (ɪ'lɛktrə) Electrical, Electronics, and Communications Trades Association

**electron.** electronics
**elem.** element(s) · elementary
**elev.** elevation · elevator
**e.l.f.** early lunar flare
**ELF** (Ethiopia) Eritrean Liberation Front · European Landworkers' Federation · *Radio* extremely low frequency
**ELG** *Astronomy* emission-line galaxy
**ELH** *Biochem.* egg-laying hormone
**Eli** *Sport* electronic line indicator
**Eli.** Elias · Elijah
**Elien.** Eliensis (Latin: (Bishop) of Ely)
**Elint** ('ɛlɪnt) *Military* electronic intelligence
**ELISA** (ɪ'laɪzə) *Med.* enzyme-linked immunosorbent assay
**elix.** *Med.* elixir
**Eliz.** Elizabethan
**ELLA** European Long Lines Agency
**ellipt.** elliptical
**ELM** edge-localized mode
**ELMA** electromechanical aid
**Elmint** ('ɛlmɪnt) *Military* electromagnetic intelligence
**elo.** elocution · eloquence
**ELOISE** (,ɛləʊ'iːz) European Large Orbiting Instrumentation for Solar Experiments
**elong.** elongate(d) · elongation
**E. Long.** east longitude
**ELP** equivalent local potential
**ELR** *Meteorol.* environment lapse rate · exceptional leave to remain (for four years in the UK; granted to asylum-seekers) · export licensing regulations
**ELS** *Physics* energy-loss spectroscopy
**elsewh.** elsewhere
**ELSIE** ('ɛlsɪ) electronic speech information equipment
**ELT** *Physics* effective Lagrangian theory · English language teaching (for foreign students) · European letter telegram
**ELU** English Lacrosse Union
**ELV** expendable launch vehicle · extra-low voltage
**ELWS** extreme low water-level spring tides
**ely.** easterly
**em.** emanation · embargo · eminent
**e.m.** (*or* **em**) electromagnetic · electron microscope · emergency maintenance · expanded metal · external memorandum
**Em.** Eminence
**EM** Earl Marshal · Edward Medal · *Physics* effective mass · Efficiency Medal · electrical and mechanical · elec-

tromagnetic • electromotive • electronic mail • electron microscope (*or* microscopy) • emission measure • engineering model • Engineer of Mines • *Genetics* enhanced mutagenesis • enlisted man • environmental modelling • equipment module • Equitum Magister (Latin: Master of the Horse) • European Movement • evaluation model • expectation maximization • *British vehicle registration for* Liverpool

**EMA** effective medium approximation • *Immunol.* epithelial membrane antigen • European Marketing Association • European Monetary Agreement • Evangelical Missionary Alliance

**EMAD** engine maintenance and disassembly

**email** (*or* **e-mail, E-mail**) ('iːmeɪl) electronic mail

**EMAS** *Computing* Edinburgh multi-access system • Employment Medical Advisory Service

**emb.** embargo • embossed

**Emb.** Embankment (in London) • Embassy

**EMB** (USA) Energy Mobilization Board

**EMBD** *Meteorol.* embedded in cloud

**EMBL** European Molecular Biology Laboratory (Heidelberg)

**EMBO** European Molecular Biology Organization

**embr.** embroider(y)

**embryol.** embryology

**EMC** (USA) Einstein Medical Center • Energy Management Centre (*or* Company) • (USA) Engineering Manpower Commission • environmental monitoring and compliance • *Physics* European muon collaboration

**EMCB** earth-mounded concrete bunker

**EMCC** European Municipal Credit Community

**EMCCC** European Military Communications Coordinating Committee

**EMCOF** ('emkɒf) European Monetary Cooperation Fund

**EMCS** energy monitoring and control system

**EMD** *Chem.* electrolytic manganese dioxide

**EME** East Midlands Electricity

**emer.** emergency

**Emer.** Emeritus

**EMet** Engineer of Metallurgy

**EMEU** East Midlands Educational Union

**emf** (*or* **e.m.f.**) *Physics* electromotive force

**EMF** European Metalworkers' Federation • European Motel Federation

**EMFI** (USA) Energy and Minerals Field Institute

**EMG** *Med.* electromyogram (*or* electromyograph)

**EMI** (USA) Earth Mechanics Institute • Electric and Musical Industries • *Computing* electromagnetic interference • *Physics* external muon identifier

**EMIC** emergency maternity and infant care

**EMK** elektromotorische Kraft (German: electromotive force) • *Chem.* ethyl methyl ketone

**EML** Environmental Measurement(s) Laboratory • Everyman's Library

**Emm.** Emmanuel College, Cambridge

**E. Mn. E.** Early Modern English

**EMNRD** Energy, Minerals, and Natural Resources Department

**e.m.o.s.** earth's mean orbital speed

**emp.** *Med.* emplastrum (Latin: a plaster)

**Emp.** Emperor • Empire • Empress

**EMP** ecological monitoring programme • electromagnetic pulse • electronic materials programme • environmental management (*or* monitoring) plan (*or* programme) • *Physics* exciton-magnetic polaron

**emp. agcy** employment agency

**EMPC** *Chem.* electrostatic molecular potential contour

**empld** employed

**EMR** Eastern Mediterranean Region • (*or* **emr**) electromagnetic radiation

**EMRIC** (USA) Educational Media Research Information Center

**EMRS** East Malling Research Station

**EMS** emergency management system • emergency medical service • energy management system • *Chem.* ethyl methane sulphonate • European Monetary System • *Computing* expanded memory specification

**EMSA** Electron Microscopy Society of America

**EMSC** (USA) Electrical Manufacturers' Standards Council

**EMT** *Physics* effective-mass theory • emergency medical technician • *Physics* energy-momentum tensor

**EMTA** Electro-Medical Trade Association

**emu** (*or* **e.m.u.**) *Physics* electromagnetic unit

**EMU** economic and monetary union (within the EC) • electrical multiple unit • *Astronautics* extravehicular mobility unit

**EMW** energy from municipal waste

**en** *Chem.* ethylenediamine (used in formulae)

**en.** enemy

**En.** Engineer • English

**EN** *Meteorol.* El Niño • (Portugal) Emissora Nacional (national broadcasting station) • *postcode for* Enfield • Enrolled Nurse • (Portugal) Estrada Nacional (national highway) • exceptions noted • extrapolation number • *British vehicle registration for* Manchester

**ENA** Eastern North America • (*or* **Ena**; 'iːnə) (France) École Nationale d'Administration (graduate college for top civil servants) • English Newspaper Association

**ENAA** *Physics* epithermal neutron activation analysis

**ENAB** Evening Newspaper Advertising Bureau

**enam.** enamel(led)

**ENB** English National Ballet • English National Board for Nursing, Midwifery, and Health Visiting

**enc.** enclosed • enclosure

**ENC** equivalent noise charge

**ENCA** European Naval Communications Agency

**Enc. Brit.** (*or* **Ency. Brit.**, **Encyc. Brit.**) Encyclopaedia Britannica

**encl.** enclosed • enclosure

**ency.** (*or* **encyc.**, **encycl.**) encyclopedia • encyclopedic • encyclopedism • encyclopedist

**END** European Nuclear Disarmament

**ENDO** Ethiopian National Democratic Organization

**ENDOR** ('ɛndɔː) *Physics* electron-nuclear double resonance

**endow.** endowment

**endp.** endpaper

**ENDS** Euratom Nuclear Documentation System

**ENE** east-northeast

**ENEA** European Nuclear Energy Agency

**ENF** European Nuclear Force

**eng.** engine • engineer(ing) • engraved • engraver • engraving

**Eng.** England • English

**ENG** electronic news gathering (in TV broadcasting)

**EN(G)** Enrolled Nurse (General) (formerly SEN)

**EngD** Doctor of Engineering

**engg** engineering

**Eng. hn** *Music* English horn

**engin.** engineer(ing)

**Engl.** England • English

**engr** engineer • engraver

**engr.** engrave(d) • engraving

**EngScD** Doctor of Engineering Science

**ENIAC** ('ɛnɪæk) Electronic Numerical Integrator and Calculator (first electronic calculator)

**ENIT** (Italy) Ente Nazionale Industrie Turistiche (state tourist office)

**enl.** enlarge(d) • enlargement • enlisted

**EN(M)** Enrolled Nurse (Mental)

**EN(MH)** Enrolled Nurse (Mental Handicap)

**en°** enero (Spanish: January)

**ENO** English National Opera

**ENR** Energy and Natural Resources

**Ens.** (*or* **ens.**) *Music* ensemble • Ensign

**ENSA** ('ɛnsə) Entertainments National Service Association (in World War II)

**ENSDF** Evaluated Nuclear Structure Data File

**ENSO** *Meteorol.* El Niño southern oscillation

**ent.** entomology • entertainment • entrance

**Ent.** enter (stage direction)

**ENT** *Med.* ear, nose, and throat

**entom.** (*or* **entomol.**) entomological • entomology

**Ent. Sta. Hall** entered (registered) at Stationers' Hall (requirement to secure copyright on books before 1924)

**env.** envelope • environs

**Env.** Envoy

**Env. Ext.** (*or* **Env. Extra.**) Envoy Extraordinary

**e.o.** ex officio

**E.o.** Easter offerings

**EO** *Christianity* Eastern Orthodox • Education Officer • *Physics* electro-optic(al) • emergency operation • employers' organization • Engineer Officer • Entertainments Officer • Equal Opportunities • *Chem.* ethoxylated sulphonates • *Chem.* ethylene oxide •

Executive Officer • executive order • Experimental Officer • *British vehicle registration for* Preston

**EOA** (USA) Essential Oil Association • examination, opinion, and advice

**EOARDC** (USA) European Office of the Air Research and Development Command

**EOB** *Computing* end of block • Executive Office Building

**Eoc** *Geology* Eocene

**EOC** electron-optical camera • (USA) Emergency Operations (*or* Operating) Center • *Physics* end of charge • end of cycle • Equal Opportunities Commission

**e.o.d.** entry on duty • every other day

**EOD** end of data (computing code) • *Military* explosive ordnance disposal (*or* demolition)

**EOE** enemy-occupied Europe • equal opportunity employer • errors and omissions excepted (on invoice forms) • European Options Exchange

**EOF** (USA) Emergency Operations (*or* Operating) Facility • *Maths.* empirical orthogonal function • *Computing* end of file

**e.o.h.p.** except otherwise herein provided

**EOJ** *Computing* end of job

**Eoka** (*or* **EOKA**) (ɪˈəʊkə) Ethniki Organosis Kypriakou Agonos (Greek: National Organization of Cypriot Struggle; for union with Greece)

**EOL** end of life

**EOLM** electro-optical light modulator

**e.o.m.** *Commerce* end of the month • every other month

**EOM** Egyptian Order of Merit • extractable organic material (*or* matter)

**EONR** European Organization for Nuclear Research

**e.o.o.e.** *Commerce* erreur ou omission exceptée (French: errors and omissions excepted; on invoice forms)

**EOP** *Microbiol.* efficiency of plating • emergency operating procedure

**EOPH** Examined Officer of Public Health

**EOQC** European Organization for Quality Control

**EOQL** end of qualified life

**EOR** *Astronautics* earth-orbit rendezvous • *Computing* end of record • enhanced oil recovery

**EORI** (USA) Economic Opportunity Research Institute

**EORTC** European Organization for Research on Treatment of Cancer

**EOS** *Physics* equation of state • *Computing* erasable optical storage • European Orthodontic Society

**e.o.t.** enemy-occupied territory

**EOT** *Computing* end of tape (as in **EOT marker**) • *Computing* end of transmission

**EOTP** European Organization for Trade Promotion

**e.p.** easy projection • editio princeps (Latin: first edition) • electrically polarized • endpaper • engineering personnel • *Chess* en passant • *Navigation* estimated position • extreme pressure

**Ep.** Episcopus (Latin: Bishop) • *Bible* Epistle

**EP** early picture • (USA) educational psychologist • *Electronics* electrically conducting polymer • *Metallurgy* electroplate(d) • electrostatic precipitator • end point • environmental protection • *Navigation* estimated position • *Physics* evoked potentials • expanded polystyrene • extended-play (gramophone record) • extraction procedure • Extraordinary and Plenipotentiary • *international civil aircraft marking for* Iran • *British vehicle registration for* Swansea

**EPA** educational priority area • *Med.* eicosapentaenoic acid (cholesterol-reducing fatty acid) • *Physics* electron–positron annihilation • *Physics* electron probe analyser • Emergency Powers Act • Employment Protection Act • energy-performance assessment • (USA) Environmental Protection Agency • European Productivity Agency

**EPAA** (USA) Emergency Petroleum Allocation Act

**EPACCI** Economic Planning and Advisory Council for the Construction Industries

**EPAQ** electronic parts of assessed quality

**EPB** equivalent pension benefit

**EPC** easy-processing channel (in **EPC black**, filler in rubber compounding) • Economic and Planning Council • Educational Publishers' Council • *Foundry* evaporative pattern-casting

**EPCA** (USA) Energy Policy and Conservation Act • energy production and consumption account • European Petro-Chemical Association

**EPCOT** Experimental Prototype Community of Tomorrow (Florida)

**EPD** earliest practicable date • *Crystallog.* etch-pit density

**EPDA** Emergency Powers Defence Act

**EPDC** (USA) Electric Power Development Company

**EPDM** *Chem.* ethylene–propylene diene monomer

**EPEA** Electrical Power Engineers' Association

**EPF** emulsified petroleum fuel • European Packaging Federation

**EPFM** elastic-plastic fracture mechanics

**EPG** (USA) Electronic Proving Ground • *Med.* electropalatogram (or electropalatology) • Emergency Procedure Guideline(s) • Eminent Persons Group

**EPGS** electric power generating system

**Eph.** (or **Ephes.**) *Bible* Ephesians

**EPI** echo planar imaging • *Physics* effective-pair interaction • electronic position indicator • Eysenck Personality Test

**EPIC** Engineering and Production Information Control • (or **Epic**; 'epɪk) European Prospective Investigation into Cancer

**Epict.** Epictetus (*c.* 55–*c.* 110 AD, Greek Stoic philosopher)

**epid.** epidemic

**epil.** epilogue

**Epiph.** Epiphany

**EPIRB** *Navigation* emergency position indicator radio beacon

**Epis.** (or **Episc.**) Episcopal(ian) • (or **Epist.**) *Bible* Epistle

**epit.** epitaph • epitome

**EPL** exact power law

**EPLD** *Computing* erasable programmable logic device

**EPLF** Eritrean People's Liberation Front

**EPM** (or **EPMA**) electron-probe micro-analysis • extract of particulate matter

**EPMI** Esso Production Malaysia Inc.

**EPN** elemental point number

**EPNdB** effective perceived noise decibels

**EPNG** El Paso Natural Gas Company

**EPNS** electroplated nickel silver • English Place-Name Society

**EPO** *Med.* erythropoietin

**EPOC** Eastern Pacific Oceanic Conference

**EPOS** ('iːpɒs) *Commerce* electronic point of sale (as in **EPOS terminal**, **EPOS system**)

**e.p.p.** (or **EPP**) *Physiol.* endplate potential

**EPP** European People's Party • executive pension plan

**EPPO** European and Mediterranean Plant Protection Organization

**EPPS** *Chem.* 4-(2-hydroxyethyl)-1-piperazinepropanesulphonic acid

**EPPT** *Computing* European printer performance test

**EPPV** electropneumatic proportional valve

**EPR** electron paramagnetic resonance (as in **EPR spectroscopy**) • ethylene–propylene rubber

**EPRDF** Ethiopian People's Revolutionary Democratic Front

**EPRI** (USA) Electric Power Research Institute

**EPROM** ('iːprɒm) *Computing* erasable programmable read-only memory

**e.p.s.** earnings per share

**EPS** electric(al) power system • electrochemical photocapacitance spectroscopy • (USA) Environmental Protection Service

**e.p.s.p.** (or **EPSP**) *Physiol.* excitatory postsynaptic potential

**EPSS** electrical power supervision system

**EPT** *Med.* early pregnancy test • ethylene–propylene terpolymer (synthetic rubber) • excess profits tax

**EPTA** Expanded Programme of Technical Assistance (in the UN)

**Ep. tm.** *Law* Epiphany term

**EPU** European Payments Union

**Epus.** Episcopus (Latin: Bishop)

**EPW** earth-penetrator weapon • enemy prisoner of war

**eq.** equal • equate • equation • equator(ial) • equipment • equitable • equity • equivalent

**Eq.** Equerry

**EQ** educational quotient • equipment qualification • *Electronics* equivalence (as in **EQ gate**)

**EQC** external quality control

**EQD** Electrical Quality Assurance Directorate

**EQDB** equipment qualification data bank

**EQ gate** *Electronics* equivalence gate

**EQI** exhaust quality index

**eqn** equation

**eqpt** equipment

**Equ** *Astronomy* Equuleus

**equil.** equilibrium

**equip.** equipment

**EQUIP** (ɪˈkwɪp) equipment usage information programme

**equiv.** equivalent

**er** elder

**e.r.** echo ranging • effectiveness report • electronic reconnaissance • emergency request • emergency rescue • established reliability • external resistance

**Er** *Chem.*, symbol for erbium

**ER** Eastern Region (British Rail) • (formerly) East Riding (Yorkshire) • Eduardus Rex (Latin: King Edward) • efficiency report • Elizabeth Regina (Latin: Queen Elizabeth) • *Med.* emergency room • *Cytology* endoplasmic reticulum • engine room • *Chem.* enhanced reactivation • *Computing* entity relationship • evaporation residue • *British vehicle registration for* Peterborough

**ERA** *Baseball* earned run average • (USA) Economic Regulatory Administration • Education Reform Act (1988) • Electrical Research Association • electronic reading automation • Electronic Rentals Association • (USA) Emergency Relief Administration • engine-room artificer • *Computing* entity relationship attribute (as in **ERA diagram, ERA model**) • (USA) Equal Rights Amendment • European Ramblers' Association • Evangelical Radio Alliance

**ERAB** Energy Research Advisory Board

**ERAMS** Environmental Radiation Ambients Monitoring System

**Eras.** (Desiderius) Erasmus (1466–1536, Dutch scholar and humanist)

**ERBM** extended-range ballistic missile

**ERBS** Earth Radiation Budget Satellite

**ERC** Economic Research Council • Electronics Research Council • Employment Rehabilitation Centre • *Med.* endoscopic retrograde cholangiography • (USA) Energy Research Corporation

**ERC & I** Economic Reform Club and Institute

**ERCB** (USA) Energy Resources Conservation Board

**ERCH** *Physics* electron-resonance cyclotron heating

**ERCP** *Med.* endoscopic retrograde cholangiopancreatography

**ERCS** emergency response computer system

**ERD** elastic recoil detection • Emergency Reserve Decoration • emergency return device • environmental radiation data • *Physics* equivalent residual dose (of radiation) • extrapolated response dose

**ERDA** (ˈɜːdə) *Electronics* elastic recoil detection analysis • (Australia) Electrical and Radio Development Association • (USA) Energy Research and Development Administration

**ERDAF** (USA) Energy Research and Development in Agriculture and Food

**ERDE** Engineering Research and Development Establishment • Explosives Research and Development Establishment

**ERDF** European Regional Development Fund

**ERDIC** Energy Research, Development, and Information Centre

**ERDL** Engineering Research and Development Laboratory

**ERDS** emergency response data system

**ERE** (Greece) Ethniki Rizospastiki Enosis (National Radical Union; political party) • extent of reaction effect

**erec.** erection

**Erf** (ɜːf) *Chem.* electrorheological fluid

**ERFA** European Radio Frequency Agency

**ERG** electrical resistance gauge • *Med.* electroretinogram

**ERGOM** European Research Group on Management

**ergon.** ergonomics

**Eri** *Astronomy* Eridanus

**ERI** (*or* **ER(I)**, **ER et I**) Edwardus Rex et Imperator (Latin: Edward King and Emperor)

**ERIC** (USA) Educational Resources Information Center • energy rate input controller

**ERIM** Environmental Research Institute of Michigan

**ERIS** Emergency Response Information System • *Astronautics* Exo-atmospheric Re-entry Vehicle Interceptor Subsystem

**ERISA** (ɛˈrɪsə) (USA) Employee Retirement Income Security Act (1974)

**Erit.** Eritrea

**Erl.** Erläuterung (German: explanatory note)

**ERL** Energy Research Laboratory

**erm.** ermine

**ERM** *Finance* Exchange Rate Mechanism

**Ernie** (*or* **ERNIE**) ('ɜːnɪ) electronic random number indicating equipment (premium-bond computer)

**ERO** European Regional Organization of the International Confederation of Free Trade Unions

**EROPA** Eastern Regional Organization for Public Administration

**EROS** ('ɪərɒs) earth resources observation satellite • *Astronautics* experimental reflection orbital shot

**e.r.p.** effective radiated power

**ERP** *Med.* endoscopic retrograde pancreatography • *Biochem.* enzyme-releasing peptide • European Recovery Programme

**ERPF** *Med.* effective renal plasma flow

**ERR** energy release rate

**erron.** erroneous(ly)

**ERS** earnings-related supplement • earth resources satellite • emergency radio service • emergency response system • engine repair section • Ergonomics Research Society • (USA) Experimental Research Society

**ERT** (Greece) Elliniki Radiophonia Tileorasis (Hellenic National Radio and Television Institute) • excess retention tax

**ERTS** Earth Resources Technology Satellite • European Rapid Train System

**ERU** English Rugby Union

**ERV** English Revised Version (of the Bible) • *Med.* exercise radionuclide ventriculography

**erw.** (*or* **erweit.**) erweitert (German: enlarged *or* extended)

**ERW** enhanced radiation weapon

**es.** esempio (Italian: example)

**e.s.** eldest son • electrical sounding • electric starting • *Med.* enema saponis (Latin: soap enema)

**Es** *Chem., symbol for* einsteinium

**ES** *British vehicle registration for* Dundee • Econometric Society • Education Specialist • *Physics* elastic scattering • *Chem.* electronic structure • *Physics* electron synchrotron • electrostatic • *international vehicle registration for* El Salvador • *Med.* endoscopic sphincterotomy • *Med.* end-systole (*or* -systolic) • energy spectrum (*or* spectra) • engine-sized (paper) • Entomological Society • *international civil aircraft marking for* Estonia • *Mining* exploratory shaft

**ESA** Ecological Society of America • electrostatic sector analyser • *Physics* energy sensor array • energy system analysis • Entomological Society of America • environmentally sensitive area • European Space Agency • Euthanasia Society of America • *Physics* excited state absorption

**ESAAB** (USA) Energy System Acquisition Advisory Board

**ESANZ** Economic Society of Australia and New Zealand

**ESAR** electronically steerable array radar

**ESB** electrical stimulation of the brain • (USA) Electricity Supply Board • electric storage battery • Empire State Building • English Speaking Board • environmental specimen bank

**ESBA** English Schools' Badminton Association

**ESBBA** English Schools' Basket Ball Association

**ESBTC** (USA) European Space Battery Test Center

**esc.** escompte (French: discount) • escutcheon

**Esc** *Computing* escape key • *symbol for* escudo (Portuguese monetary unit)

**ESC** Economic and Social Council (of the UN) • electronic structural correlator • (USA) Energy Security Corporation • Energy Study Centre (Netherlands) • English Stage Company • English Steel Corporation • Entomological Society of Canada • European Space Conference • *Computing* extended core storage

**ESCA** *Physical chem.* electron spectroscopy for chemical analysis • English Schools' Cricket Association • English Schools' Cycling Association

**ESCAP** Economic and Social Commission for Asia and the Pacific (UN agency; formerly ECAFE)

**ESCC** *Engineering* external stress corrosion cracking

**ESCCD** electrical short-circuit current decay

**eschat.** eschatology

**ESCO** ('ɛskəʊ) Educational, Scientific, and Cultural Organization (of the UN)

**ESCOM** ('ɛskɒm) Electricity Supply Commission of South Africa

**ESCR** external standard channel ratio

**Esd.** *Bible* Esdras

**ESD** echo-sounding device • electro-magnetic shower detector • (USA) Environmental Sciences Division • Euratom Safeguards Directorate

**Esda** ('ɛzdə) electrostatic deposition (*or* document) analysis (as in **Esda test**)

**ESDAC** ('ɛsdæk) European Space Data Centre

**ESE** east-southeast • *Physics* electron spin echo • engineers stores establishment

**ESECA** (USA) Energy Supply and Environmental Coordination Act

**ESEF** Electrotyping and Stereotyping Employers' Federation

**ESES** environmentally sound energy system

**ESF** European Science Foundation

**ESG** Education Support Grant • *Engineering* English Standard Gauge

**ESH** Environmental Safety and Health • equivalent standard hours • European Society of Haematology

**ESI** Electricity Supply Industry • environment sensitivity index

**ESITB** Electricity Supply Industry Training Board

**Esk.** Eskimo

**e.s.l.** expected significance level

**ESL** English as a second language

**ESLAB** ('ɛslæb) European Space Research Laboratory

**ESMA** Electrical Sign Manufacturers' Association

**esn.** (*or* **esntl**) essential

**ESN** educationally subnormal

**ESNS** educationally subnormal, serious

**ESNZ** Entomological Society of New Zealand

**ESO** Energy Services Operator • European Southern Observatory (Chile)

**ESOC** European Space Operations Centre (Germany)

**ESOL** ('iːsɒl) English for speakers of other languages

**ESOMAR** ('ɛsəʊˌmɑː) European Society for Opinion Surveys and Market Research

**ESOP** ('iːsɒp) employee share-ownership plan

**esp.** especially • *Music* espressivo (Italian: expressively)

**Esp.** Espagne (French: Spain) • España (Spanish: Spain) • Esperanto

**ESP** electric submersible pump (*or* pumping) • *Physics* electron spin polarization • English for specific (*or* special) purposes • extrasensory perception

**espg.** espionage

**espr.** (*or* **espress.**) *Music* espressivo (Italian: expressively)

**ESPRIT** ('ɛsprɪt) European strategic programme for research and development in information technology

**Esq.** esquire (in correspondence)

**ESQA** English Slate Quarries Association

**esq°** esquerdo (Portuguese: left)

**ESR** *Physics* electron-spin resonance • *Med.* erythrocyte sedimentation rate • *Physics* experimental storage ring

**ESRC** Economic and Social Research Council (formerly SSRC) • Electricity Supply Research Council

**ESRD** *Med.* end-stage renal disease

**ESRF** *Med.* end-stage renal failure

**ESRIN** ('ɛzrɪn) European Space Research Institute (Italy)

**ESRO** ('ɛzrəʊ) European Space Research Organization (now part of ESA)

**ESRS** European Society for Rural Sociology

**ess.** essence • *Pharmacol.* essentia (Latin: essence) • essential

**Ess.** Essex

**ESS** energy storage system

**ESSA** English Schools' Swimming Association • (USA) Environmental Science Services Administration (of the Department of Commerce)

**Esso** ('ɛsəʊ) Standard Oil (phonetic spelling of SO)

**est.** establish(ed) • *Law* estate • estimate(d) • estimation • estimator • estuary

**Est.** Established • Estonia(n)

**EST** earliest start time • (USA, Canada) Eastern Standard Time • electroshock therapy (*or* electric-shock treatment) • *Nuclear engineering* ellipsoidal shell tokamak

**estab.** establish(ed) • establishment

**ESTEC** ('ɛztɛk) European Space Technology Centre (Netherlands)

**estg** estimating

**Esth.** *Bible* Esther

**ESTI** European Space Technology Institute

**estn** estimation

**e.s.u.** (*or* **ESU**) *Physics* electrostatic unit

**ESU** English-Speaking Union

**ESV** *Astronautics* earth satellite vehicle • *Engineering* emergency shutdown valve • *Med.* end-systolic (left ventricular) volume

**ESWL** *Med.* extracorporeal shock-wave lithotripsy

**e.t.** educational therapy • electric telegraph • engineering time • English text (*or* translation) • entertainment tax • exchange telegraph

**Et** *Chem., symbol for* ethyl (used in formulae)

**ET** (USA) Eastern Time • *international vehicle registration for* (Arab Republic of) Egypt • *Chem.* electron transfer • *Physics, Chem.* electron transition • *Nuclear engineering* elongated tokamak • *Med.* embryo transfer • emerging technology (in NATO) • Employment Training (for the unemployed) • emptying time • ephemeris time • *Physics* equation of time • *international civil aircraft marking for* Ethiopia • *airline flight code for* Ethiopian Airlines • *Electronics* excitation transport • extraterrestrial • *British vehicle registration for* Sheffield

**ETA** *Physics* emanation thermal analysis • Entertainment Trades' Alliance • estimated time of arrival • European Teachers' Association • (*or* **Eta**; ˈɛtə) Euzkadi ta Askatsuna (Basque: Basque Nation and Liberty; nationalist organization)

**Étab.** Établissement (French: business establishment)

**ETAC** Education and Training Advisory Council

**et al.** et alibi (Latin: and elsewhere) • et alii (Latin: and others)

**ETB** English Tourist Board

**etc.** et cetera (Latin: and other things)

**ETC** Eastern Telegraph Company • European Translation Centre

**ETCTA** Electrical Trades Commercial Travellers' Association

**ETD** estimated time of departure • *Telecom.* extension trunk dialling

**ETE** estimated time en route • evacuation-time estimate • Experimental Tunnelling Establishment

**ETF** *Banking* electronic transfer of funds

**eth.** ether • ethical • ethics

**Eth.** Ethiopia(n) • Ethiopic

**ETH** (Switzerland) Eidgenössische Technische Hochschule (German: Federal Institute of Technology) • *international vehicle registration for* Ethiopia

**ethnog.** ethnography

**ethnol.** ethnological • ethnology

**e.t.i.** elapsed time indicator

**ETI** estimated time of interception • extraterrestrial intelligence

**ETJC** Engineering Trades Joint Council

**e.t.k.m.** every test known to man

**ETMA** English Timber Merchants' Association • European Television Magazine Association

**e.t.o.** estimated time off

**ETO** European Theatre of Operations (in World War II) • European Transport Organization

**e.t.p.** estimated turnaround (*or* turning) point

**Etr.** Etruscan

**ETR** engineering test reactor • estimated time of return • *Nuclear engineering* experimental thermonuclear (*or* test) reactor

**ETS** earth thermal storage • (USA) Educational Testing Service • *Biochem.* electron-transport system • estimated time of sailing • *Military* (USA) estimated time of separation (i.e. discharge from service) • *Med.* exercise thallium scintigraphy • expiration of time of service

**ETSA** Electricity Trust of South Australia • *Chem.* ethyl (trimethylsilyl)-acetate

**et seq.** et sequens (Latin: and the following)

**e.t.s.p.** entitled to severance pay

**et sqq.** et sequentes *or* sequentia (Latin: and the following)

**ETSU** Energy Technology Support Unit (of the Department of Energy)

**ETTA** English Table Tennis Association

**ETTU** European Table Tennis Union

**ETU** experimental test unit

**ETUC** European Trade Union Confederation

**ETUI** European Trade Union Institute

**et ux.** et uxor (Latin: and wife)

**ETV** educational television • engine test vehicle

**ety.** (*or* **etym., etymol.**) etymological • etymologist • etymology

**Eu** (ital.) *Physics, symbol for* Euler number • *Chem., symbol for* europium

**EU** *British vehicle registration for* Bristol • Evangelical Union • *Med.* excretory urography • experimental unit • (France, Spain) United States (French *États-Unis*; Spanish *Estados Unidos*)

**EUA** *Finance* European unit of account • *Med.* examination under anaesthesia • (France, Portugal, Spain) United States of America (French *États-Unis d'Amérique*; Spanish and Portuguese *Estados Unidos da* (Portuguese) or *de* (Spanish) *América*)

**Euc.** (*or* **Eucl.**) Euclid (*c.* 330–*c.* 275 BC, Greek mathematician)

**EUCOM** ('juːkɒm) *Military* (USA) European Command

**EUDISED** ('juːdɪˌsɛd) European Documentation and Information Service for Education

**EUFTT** European Union of Film and Television Technicians

**eugen.** eugenics

**EUI** energy utilization index • energy utilization intensity

**EUL** Everyman's University Library

**EUM** (Mexico, Spain) Mexico (Spanish *Estados Unidos Mexicanos*)

**EUMETSAT** ('juːmɛtˌsæt) European Meteorological Satellite System

**EUP** English Universities Press

**Eur.** Europe(an)

**EUR** Esposizione Universale di Roma (Italian: Roman Universal Exhibition)

**Euratom** (jʊəˈrætəm) European Atomic Energy Community

**Eureca** (jʊəˈriːkə) *Astronautics* European retrievable carrier

**Eur Ing** European Engineer

**Eurip.** Euripides (*c.* 480–406 BC, Greek dramatist)

**EURO** ('jʊərəʊ) European Regional Office (of the FAO)

**EUROCAE** European Organization for Civil Aviation Electronics

**EUROCEAN** European Oceanographic Association

**EUROCHEMIC** European Company for the Chemical Processing of Irradiated Fuels

**EUROCOM** ('jʊərəʊˌkɒm) European Coal Merchants' Union

**EUROFINAS** Association of European Finance Houses

**EuroJazz** ('jʊərəʊˌjæz) European Community Youth Jazz Orchestra

**EUROM** ('jʊərɒm) European Federation for Optics and Precision Mechanics

**EURONET** ('jʊərəʊˌnɛt) European data-transmission network

**EUROP** European Railway Wagon Pool

**EUROSPACE** ('jʊərəʊˌspeɪs) European Industrial Space Study Group

**EUROTOX** ('jʊərəʊˌtɒks) Comité européen permanent de recherches sur la protection de populations contre les risques de toxicité à long terme (French: European Standing Committee for the Protection of Populations against the Risks of Chronic Toxicity)

**Eus.** (*or* **Euseb.**) Eusebius of Caesarea (*fl.* 4th century AD, churchman and historian)

**EUS** Eastern United States

**EUV** *Physics* extreme ultraviolet

**EUW** European Union of Women

**ev.** evangelisch (German: Protestant)

**e.v.** efficient vulcanization

**eV** eingetragener Verein (German: registered society) • *Physics, symbol for* electronvolt

**EV** *British vehicle registration for* Chelmsford • electric vehicle • English Version (of the Bible) • *Astronautics* entry vehicle • *Med.* equilibrium venography • *Med.* erythrocyte volume • *Image technol.* exposure value

**EVA** Electric Vehicle Association of Great Britain • Engineer Vice-Admiral • *Chem.* ethene and vinyl acetate (copolymers) • *Astronautics* extravehicular activity

**evac.** evacuate(d) • evacuation

**eval.** evaluate(d) • evaluation

**evan.** (*or* **evang.**) evangelical • evangelist

**evap.** evaporate(d) • evaporation • evaporator

**EVBA** *Physics* equivalent vector-boson approximation

**evce** evidence

**EVCS** *Astronautics* extravehicular communications system

**EVFU** *Computing* electronic vertical format unit

**evg** evening

**evid.** evidence

**evng** evening

**evol.** evolution(ary) • evolutionist

**EVR** electronics video broadcasting system

**EVT** Educational and Vocational Training

**EVW** European Voluntary Workers

**evy** every

**e.w.** each way (betting)

**EW** early warning • electronic warfare • (USA) enlisted woman • *international vehicle registration for* Estonia • *British vehicle registration for* Peterborough

**EWA** (USA) Education Writers' Association

**EWF** Electrical Wholesalers' Federation

**EWICS** European Workshop for Industrial Computer Systems

**EWL** evaporative water loss

**EWO** Educational Welfare Officer • essential work order • European Women's Orchestra

**EWP** emergency war plan

**EWR** early-warning radar

**EWRC** European Weed Research Association

**EWS** emergency water supply • emergency welfare service

**EWSF** European Work Study Federation

**ex.** examination • examine(d) • examiner • example • excellent • except(ed) • exception • excess • exchange • exclude • excluding • exclusive • excursion • *Literary* excursus • execute(d) • executive • executor • exempt • exercise • export • express • extension • extra

**Ex.** Exeter • Exeter College, Oxford • *Bible* Exodus

**EX** *postcode for* Exeter • *British vehicle registration for* Norwich

**exag.** exaggerate • exaggeration

**exam.** examination • examine(r)

**examd** examined

**examg** examining

**examn** examination

**ex aq.** *Med.* ex aqua (Latin: from water)

**ex b.** *Finance* ex bonus (without bonus)

**exc.** excellent • except(ed) • exception • exchange • excommunication • excudit (Latin: (he *or* she) engraved it; after an engraver's name) • excursion

**Exc.** Excellency

**ex cap.** *Finance* ex capitalization (without capitalization)

**exch.** exchange • (*or* **Exch.**) exchequer

**excl.** (*or* **exclam.**) exclamation • (*or* **exclam.**) exclamatory • exclude • excluding • exclusive

**ex cp.** *Finance* ex coupon (without the interest on the coupon)

**exd** examined

**ex div.** *Finance* ex dividend (without dividend)

**exec.** execute • execution • executive • executor

**execx** executrix

**EXELFS** electron energy-loss fine-structure spectroscopy

**exempl.** exemplaire (French: copy of a printed work)

**exes** expenses

**Exet.** Exeter College, Oxford

**ex. g.** (*or* **ex. gr.**) exempli gratia (Latin: for example)

**exh.** exhaust • exhibition

**exhib.** exhibit • (*or* **exhbn**) exhibition • exhibitioner

**Ex.-Im.** (*or* **Eximbank**) (USA) Export-Import Bank

**ex int.** *Banking* ex interest (without interest)

**ex lib.** ex libris (Latin: from the books (*or* library) of)

**ex n.** *Stock exchange* ex new (of shares)

**EXNOR** ('ɛksnɔ:) *Computing, Electronics* exclusive-NOR (as in **EXNOR gate**)

**Exod.** *Bible* Exodus

**ex off.** ex officio (Latin: by right of office)

**Exon.** Exonia (Latin: Exeter) • Exoniensis (Latin: (Bishop) of Exeter)

**exor** executor

**EXOR** ('ɛksɔ:) *Computing, Electronics* exclusive-OR (as in **EXOR gate**)

**ex p.** *Law* ex parte (Latin: on behalf of one party only)

**exp** *Maths., symbol for* exponential

**exp.** expand • expansion • expedition • expenses • experience • experiment(al) • expiration • expire(d) • export(ed) • exportation • exporter • express • expression • expurgated

**EXP** Exchange of Persons Office (in UNESCO) • *Meteorol.* expect(ed)

**expdn** expedition

**exper.** experimental

**expl.** explain • explanation • explanatory • explosion • explosive

**exploit.** exploitation

**expn** exposition

**exp. o.** experimental order

**expr.** express

**ex-Pres.** ex-President

**expt** experiment

**exptl** experimental

**exptr** exporter

**expurg.** expurgate

**exr** executor
**exrx** executrix
**exs** expenses
**ext.** extend • extension • extent • exterior • external(ly) • extinct • extra • extract • extraction • *Med.* extractum (Latin: extract) • extreme
**EXTD** *Meteorol.* extend
**EXTEL** ('ɛkstɛl) Exchange Telegraph (news agency)
**EXTEND** (ɪk'stɛnd) Exercise Training for the Elderly and/or Disabled
**ext. liq.** extractum liquidum (Latin: liquid extract)

**extn** extension
**extr.** extraordinary
**extrad.** extradition
**exx** examples • executrix
**EY** *British vehicle registration for* Bangor
**EYC** European Youth Campaign
**EYR** East Yorkshire Regiment
**Ez.** *Bible* Ezra
**EZ** *British vehicle registration for* Belfast • easy
**Ezek.** *Bible* Ezekiel
**Ezr.** *Bible* Ezra

# F

**f** *Numismatics* face value • *Music* fah (in tonic sol-fa) • *symbol for* femto- (prefix indicating $10^{-15}$, as in **fm**, femtometre) • (*or* **f/**, **f:**) *Photog.* f-number (ratio of the focal length of a lens to its aperture, as in **f8**) • (ital.) *Physics, symbol for* focal length • (ital.) *Music* forte (Italian: loudly) • (ital.) *Physics, symbol for* frequency • (ital.) *Physical chem., symbol for* fugacity • (ital.) *Maths., symbol for* function (as in $f(x)$) • (ital.) *Biochem., symbol for* furanose • *Chem., Physics, indicating* electron state $l=3$ (where $l$ is orbital angular momentum quantum number) • *indicating* the fifth vertical row of squares from the left on a chessboard

**f.** facing • fair • farthing • father • fathom(s) • feet • female • *Grammar* feminine • *Horse racing* filly • *Metallurgy* fine • flat • fluid • folio • following (page) • foot • for • forecastle • *Botany* form (in plant taxonomy) • formula • *Sport* foul • founded • franc(s) • freehold • from • furlong • furlough • *symbol for* guilder (monetary unit of the Netherlands)

**F** Fahrenheit (in °**F**, degree Fahrenheit) • *Logic, Maths.* false • *symbol for* farad(s) • (ital.) *Physics, symbol for* Faraday constant • fast (on a clock or watch regulator) • *British fishing port registration for* Faversham • (USA) fighter (specifying a type of military aircraft, as in **F-**

**106**) • *Genetics, symbol for* filial generation (as in **F₁**, first generation) • *Chem., symbol for* fluorine • (*or* **F/**, **F:**) *Photog.* f-number (as in **F4**; *see under* f) • Fokker (aircraft) • (ital.) *Physics, symbol for* force • *symbol for* franc (monetary unit of various countries) • *international vehicle registration or international civil aircraft marking for* France • (ital.) *Thermodynamics, symbol for* Helmholtz function • *indicating* a musical note or key • *Astronomy, indicating* a spectral type

**F.** (*or* **F**) family • Father • fathom(s) • February • Federation • Fellow • female • *Grammar* feminine • ferrovia (Italian: railway) • *Med.* fiat (Latin: let it be made) • fiction • *Horse racing* filly • finance • *Metallurgy* fine • fleet • folio • foolscap • *Sport* foul • Frauen (German: women) • freddo (Italian: cold) • French • *Ecclesiast.* Frère (French: Brother) • Friday • frio (Portuguese *or* Spanish: cold)

**fª** factura (Spanish: invoice)

**f.a.** *Slang* fanny adams (*or* fuck all) • fire alarm • first aid • *Commerce* free alongside • *Optics* free aperture • freight agent • friendly aircraft • fuel–air (ratio)

**Fa.** Faeroes • Firma (German: firm *or* business) • Florida

**FA** *Statistics* factor analysis • Factory Act • Faculty of Actuaries • family allowance • *Slang* fanny adams (*or* fuck all) • farm adviser • *Chem.* fatty acid • field activities • field allowance • field ambulance • *Military* field artillery • filtered air • Finance Act • financial adviser • fine art • *Immunol.* fluorescent antibody • *Building trades* fly (*or* fuel) ash • *Biochem.* folic acid • *Biochem.* folinic acid • Football Association • freight agent • *Nuclear engineering* fuel assembly • *Metallurgy* furnace annealing • *British vehicle registration for* Stoke-on-Trent

**F-A** *Chem.* fenitrothion in acetone

**f.a.a.** *Marine insurance* free of all averages

**FAA** (USA) Federal Aviation Administration • Fellow of the Australian Academy (of Science) • Film Artists' Association • Fleet Air Arm • *Chem.* formalin acetic alcohol • *Biochem.* free amino acid

**FAAAS** Fellow of the American Academy of Arts and Sciences • Fellow of the American Association for the Advancement of Science

**FAAC** Food Additives and Contaminants Committee

**FAAO** Fellow of the American Academy of Optometry

**FAAP** Fellow of the American Academy of Pediatrics

**FAARM** Fellow of the American Academy of Reproductive Medicine

**FAAV** Fellow of the Central Association of Agricultural Valuers

**fab.** fabric • fabricate • *Commerce* fabrication (French: make)

**f.a.b.** first aid box

**f. à b.** *Commerce* franco à bord (French: free on board)

**FAB** *Physics, Electronics* fast-atom bombardment (*or* beam) • Flour Advisory Bureau • French–American–British • fuel-air bomb

**fabbr.** fabbrica (Italian: factory)

**FABMDS** (USA) field army ballistic missile defense system

**FABP** *Biochem.* fatty-acid-binding protein

**fabr.** fabricate • fabrication

**Fab. Soc.** Fabian Society

**fabx.** fire alarm box

**fac.** façade • facial • facility • facsimile • factor • factory • (*or* **Fac.**) faculty

**f.a.c.** (as) fast as can (be) • *Marine insurance* franc d'avarie commune (French: free of general average)

**FAC** Federation of Agricultural Cooperatives • *Military* forward air controller

**FACA** Fellow of the American College of Anesthesiologists

**FACC** Fellow of the American College of Cardiology • (USA) Ford Aerospace and Communication Corporation

**FACCA** Fellow of the Association of Certified and Corporate Accountants (now the Chartered Association of Certified Accountants; *see* FCCA)

**FACCP** Fellow of the American College of Chest Physicians

**FACD** Fellow of the American College of Dentistry

**FACE** Fellow of the Australian College of Education • (feɪs) field artillery computer equipments

**FACEM** Federation of the Associations of Colliery Equipment Manufacturers

**FACerS** Fellow of the American Ceramic Society

**facet.** facetious

**FACG** Fellow of the American College of Gastroenterology

**facil.** facility

**FACMTA** (USA) Federal Advisory Council on Medical Training

**FACOG** Fellow of the American College of Obstetricians and Gynecologists

**FACOM** Fellow of the Australian College of Occupational Medicine

**FACP** Fellow of the American College of Physicians

**FACR** Fellow of the American College of Radiology

**FACRM** Fellow of the Australian College of Reproductive Medicine

**facs.** facsimile

**FACS** Fellow of the American College of Surgeons • *Immunol.* fluorescence-activated cell sorter

**facsim.** facsimile

**fact.** (*or* **fact^a**) factura (Spanish: invoice)

**Fact** (*or* **FACT**) (fækt) Federation Against Copyright Theft • fully automatic compiler-translator

**f.a.d.** free air delivered

**FAD** *Biochem.* flavin adenine dinucleotide

**FADO** Fellow of the Association of Dispensing Opticians

**FAE** *Military* fuel-air explosive(s)

**Faer.** Faeroe Islands

**FAeSI** Fellow of the Aeronautical Society of India

**FAGO** Fellowship in Australia in Obstetrics and Gynaecology

**FAGS** Federation of Astronomical and Geophysical Services • Fellow of the American Geographical Society

**Fah.** (*or* **Fahr.**) Fahrenheit

**FAHA** Fellow of the Australian Academy of the Humanities

**FAI** Fédération aéronautique internationale (French: International Aeronautical Federation) • Football Association of Ireland • fresh-air inlet

**FAIA** Fellow of the American Institute of Architects • Fellow of the Association of International Accountants • Fellow of the Australian Institute of Advertising

**FAIAA** Fellow of the American Institute of Aeronautics and Astronautics

**FAIAS** Fellow of the Australian Institute of Agricultural Science

**FAIB** Fellow of the Australian Institute of Builders

**FAIBiol** Fellow of the Australian Institute of Biology

**FAIC** Fellow of the American Institute of Chemists

**FAIE** Fellow of the Australian Institute of Energy

**FAIEx** Fellow of the Australian Institute of Export

**FAIFST** Fellow of the Australian Institute of Food Science and Technology

**FAII** Fellow of the Australian Insurance Institute

**FAIM** Fellow of the Australian Institute of Management

**FAIP** Fellow of the Australian Institute of Physics

**Fak.** Faktura (German: invoice)

**FAK** *Shipping* freights all kinds

**Falk. I.** (*or* **Falk. Is.**) Falkland Islands

**FALN** (Puerto Rico) Fuerzas Armadas de Liberación Nacional (Spanish: Armed Forces of National Liberation)

**fam.** familiar • family

**FAM** Free and Accepted Masons

**FAMA** Fellow of the American Medical Association • Fellow of the Australian Medical Association • Foundation for Mutual Assistance in Africa

**FAME** *Chem.* fatty-acid methyl ester

**FAMEME** Fellow of the Association of Mining Electrical and Mechanical Engineers

**FAMI** Fellow of the Australian Marketing Institute

**FAmNucSoc** Fellow of the American Nuclear Society

**FAMS** Fellow of the Ancient Monuments Society • Fellow of the Indian Academy of Medical Sciences

**f & a** fore and aft

**F & AP** *Insurance* fire and allied perils

**F & C** full and change (tides)

**f & d** fill and drain • (*or* **F & D**) freight and demurrage

**f & f** fixtures and fittings

**F and Gs** (*or* **F&Gs**) *Bookbinding* folded and gathered pages

**F & M** foot and mouth disease

**f & t** (*or* **F & T**) *Insurance* fire and theft

**FANY** (*or* **Fany, Fanny**) ('fænɪ) First Aid Nursing Yeomanry

**f.a.o.** finish all over • for the attention of

**FAO** Fleet Accountant Officer • Food and Agriculture Organization (of the UN)

**FAP** (USA) Family Assistance Program • first aid post • *Ethology* fixed action pattern • Força Aérea Portuguesa (Portuguese Air Force) • (*or* **f.a.p.**) *Marine insurance* franc d'avarie particulière (French: free of particular average)

**FAPA** Fellow of the American Psychiatric Association

**FAPHA** Fellow of the American Public Health Association

**FAPS** Fellow of the American Phytopathological Society

**f.a.q.** *Commerce* fair average quality • *Commerce* free alongside quay

**f.a.q.s.** fair average quality of season

**far.** farriery • farthing

**FAR** (USA) Federal Aviation Regulation(s) • *Insurance* free (of claim) for accident reported

**FArborA** Fellow of the Arboricultural Association

**FARE** Federation of Alcoholic Rehabilitation Establishments

**FARELF** Far East Land Forces

**f.a.s.** firsts and seconds • *Commerce* free alongside ship

**FAS** Federation of American Scientists • Fellow of the Anthropological Society • Fellow of the Antiquarian Society • *Med.* fetal alcohol syndrome • *Commerce* free alongside ship

**FASA** Fellow of the Australian Society of Accountants

**FASB** (USA) Financial Accounting Standards Board

**fasc.** *Anatomy, Printing* fasciculus

**FASc** Fellow of the Indian Academy of Sciences

**FASCE** Fellow of the American Society of Civil Engineers

**FASE** Fellow of the Antiquarian Society, Edinburgh

**FASEB** Federation of American Societies for Experimental Biology

**FASI** Fellow of the Architects' and Surveyors' Institute

**FASS** Federation of the Associations of Specialists and Subcontractors

**FASSA** Fellow of the Academy of Social Sciences in Australia

**FAST** (fɑːst) factor analysis system • fast automatic shuttle transfer • first atomic ship transport • forecasting and assessment in science and technology (in the EC)

**fastnr** fastener

**fath.** fathom

**FATIS** Food and Agriculture Technical Information Service (of the OEEC)

**FAU** Friends' Ambulance Unit

**FAusIMM** Fellow of the Australasian Institute of Mining and Metallurgy

**fav.** favour • favourite

**FAVO** Fleet Aviation Officer

**FAWA** Federation of Asian Women's Associations

**fax** (*or* **FAX**) (fæks) facsimile transmission • fuel-air explosion

**f.b.** flat bar • fog bell • freight bill • *Sport* fullback

**FB** *British vehicle registration for* Bristol • Fenian Brotherhood • *Physics* film badge (for radiation protection) • fire brigade • fisheries (*or* fishery) board • *Railways* flat bottom • *Chemical engineering* fluidized bed • flying boat • *Med.* foreign body • Forth Bridge • Free Baptist

**F-B** full-bore

**FBA** Farm Buildings Association • (USA) Federal Bar Association • Federation of British Artists • Federation of British Astrologers • Fellow of the British Academy • fluorescent brightening agent (used in detergents) • Freshwater Biological Association

**f'ball** football

**f.b.c.** *Insurance* fallen building clause

**FBC** *Chemical engineering* fluidized-bed combustion (*or* combustor)

**FBCM** Federation of British Carpet Manufacturers

**FBCO** Fellow of the British College of Ophthalmic Opticians (*or* Optometrists)

**FBCP** Fellow of the British College of Physiotherapists

**FBCS** Fellow of the British Computer Society

**f.b.c.w.** *Insurance* fallen building clause waiver

**fbd** freeboard

**FBEA** Fellow of the British Esperanto Association

**FBEC(S)** Fellow of the Business Education Council (Scotland)

**FBFM** Federation of British Film Makers

**FBH** fire brigade hydrant

**FBHI** Fellow of the British Horological Institute

**FBHS** Fellow of the British Horse Society

**FBHTM** Federation of British Hand Tool Manufacturers

**FBI** (USA) Federal Bureau of Investigation

**FBIBA** Fellow of the British Insurance Brokers' Association

**FBID** Fellow of the British Institute of Interior Design

**FBIM** Fellow of the British Institute of Management

**FBINZ** Fellow of the Bankers' Institute of New Zealand

**FBIPP** Fellow of the British Institute of Professional Photography

**FBIS** Fellow of the British Interplanetary Society

**FBL** flight-by-light (aircraft control system)

**FBM** fleet ballistic missile

**FBMA** Food and Beverage Managers' Association

**FBO** (*or* **f.b.o.**) for the benefit of

**FBOA** Fellow of the British Optical Association

**FBOU** Fellow of the British Ornithologists' Union

**FBP** *Chem.* final boiling point • *Biochem.* folate-binding protein

**FBPS** Fellow of the British Phrenological Society

**FBPsS** Fellow of the British Psychological Society

**fbr.** fibre

**FBR** *Nuclear engineering* fast breeder reactor • *Chemical engineering* fluidized-bed reactor

**FBRAM** Federation of British Rubber and Allied Manufacturers

**fbro.** febrero (Spanish: February)

**FBS** *Med.* fetal bovine serum • *Military* forward-based system

**FBSC** Fellow of the British Society of Commerce

**FBSE** Fellow of the Botanical Society, Edinburgh

**FBSM** Fellow of the Birmingham School of Music

**FBSS** *Med.* failed back-surgery syndrome

**FBT** (France) Fédération des bourses du travail (Federation of Labour Exchanges; trade union) • fringe benefit tax

**FBu** *symbol for* Burundi franc (monetary unit)

**FBU** Fire Brigades Union

**FBW** *Aeronautics* fly-by-wire

**f.b.y.** future budget year

**f.c.** *Baseball* fielder's choice • fin courant (French: at the end of this month) • *Printing* follow copy • for cash

**Fc** *Immunol.* crystallizable fragment (of an immunoglobulin)

**FC** (Australia) Federal Cabinet • *Freemasonry* fellow craft • Fencing Club • ferrocarril (Spanish: railway) • fidei commissum (Latin: bequeathed in trust) • fieri curavit (Latin: the donor directed this to be done; on gravestones and other monuments) • fifth column • Fighter Command • fire cock • Fishmongers' Company • Football Club • Forestry Commission • *Med.* free cholesterol • Free Church • fuel cell • *Med.* full course (of therapy) • *Meteorol.* funnel cloud • *British vehicle registration for* Oxford

**FCA** (USA) Farm Credit Administration • Federation of Canadian Artists • Fellow of the Institute of Chartered Accountants

**FCAATSI** (Australia) Federal Council for the Advancement of Aborigines and Torres Strait Islanders

**FCA(Aust)** Fellow of the Institute of Chartered Accountants in Australia

**FCAI** Fellow of the New Zealand Institute of Cost Accountants

**FCAnaes** Fellow of the College of Anaesthetists

**fcap** (*or* **f/cap, f'cap**) foolscap

**FCAR** *Insurance* free of claim for accident reported

**FCASI** Fellow of the Canadian Aeronautics and Space Institute

**FCAST** *Meteorol.* forecast

**FCB** *Computing* file control block

**FCBA** Federal Communications Bar Association • Fellow of the Canadian Bankers' Association

**FCBSI** Fellow of the Chartered Building Societies Institute

**FCC** (*or* **f.c.c.**) *Crystallog.* face-centred cubic • (USA) Federal Communications Commission • Federal Council of Churches • first-class certificate • *Chemical engineering* fluid catalytic cracking

**FCCA** Fellow of the Chartered Association of Certified Accountants

**FCCEA** Fellow of the Commonwealth Council for Educational Administration

**FCCEd** Fellow of the College of Craft Education

**FCCS** Fellow of the Corporation of Secretaries (formerly Certified Secretaries)

**FCCSET** (USA) Federal Coordinating Council on Science, Engineering, and Technology

**FCCT** Fellow of the Canadian College of Teachers

**FCD** First Chief Directorate (of the KGB)

**FCDA** (USA) Federal Civil Defense Administration

**FCEC** Federation of Civil Engineering Contractors

**FCFC** Free Church Federal Council

**FCFI** Fellow of the Clothing and Footwear Institute

**fcg** facing

**FCGB** Forestry Committee of Great Britain

**FCGI** Fellow of the City and Guilds London Institute

**FChS** Fellow of the Society of Chiropodists

**FCI** Fédération cynologique internationale (French: International Federation of Kennel Clubs) • Fellow of the Institute of Commerce

**FCIA** Fellow of the Canadian Institute of Actuaries • Fellow of the Corporation of Insurance Agents • Foreign Credit Insurance Association

**FCIArb** Fellow of the Chartered Institute of Arbitrators

**FCIB** Fellow of the Chartered Institute of Bankers • Fellow of the Corporation of Insurance Brokers

**FCIBSE** Fellow of the Chartered Institution of Building Services Engineers

**FCIC** (USA) Federal Crop Insurance Corporation • Fellow of the Chemical Institute of Canada

**FCII** Fellow of the Chartered Insurance Institute

**FCILA** Fellow of the Chartered Institute of Loss Adjusters

**FCIM** Fellow of the Chartered Institute of Marketing

**FCIOB** Fellow of the Chartered Institute of Building

**FCIPA** Fellow of the Chartered Institute of Patent Agents (now CPA, Chartered Patent Agent)

**FCIS** Fellow of the Institute of Chartered Secretaries and Administrators (formerly Chartered Institute of Secretaries)

**FCISA** Fellow of the Chartered Institute of Secretaries and Administrators (Australia)

**FCIT** Fellow of the Chartered Institute of Transport • *Basketball* Four Countries International Tournament

**FCMA** Fellow of the Institute of Cost and Management Accountants

**FCMS** Fellow of the College of Medicine and Surgery

**FCMSA** Fellow of the College of Medicine of South Africa

**FCNA** Fellow of the College of Nursing, Australia

**fco** *Commerce* franco (French: free of charge)

**f. co.** *Printing* fair copy

**FCO** Farmers' Central Organization • fire-control officer • Foreign and Commonwealth Office

**FCOG(SA)** Fellow of the South African College of Obstetrics and Gynaecology

**FCollP** Fellow of the College of Preceptors

**FCOphth** Fellow of the College of Ophthalmologists

**FCOT** Fellow of the College of Occupational Therapists

**fcp.** foolscap

**FCP** *Engineering* fatigue-crack propagation • Fellow of the College of Clinical Pharmacology • Fellow of the College of Preceptors • *Physics* Franck–Condon pumping (*or* principle)

**FCPA** Fellow of the Canadian Psychological Association

**FCPO** Fleet Chief Petty Officer

**FCPS** Fellow of the College of Physicians and Surgeons

**FCP(SoAf)** Fellow of the College of Physicians, South Africa

**FCPSO(SoAf)** Fellow of the College of Physicians and Surgeons and Obstetricians, South Africa

**fcs** (*or* **Fcs**) francs

**f.c.s.** (*or* **f.c. & s.**) *Insurance* warranted free of capture, seizure, arrest, detainment, and the consequences thereof

**FCS** Federation of Conservative Students • Fellow of the Chemical Society (now part of the Royal Society of Chemistry; *see under* FRSC) • *Med.* fetal calf serum

**FCSD** Fellow of the Chartered Society of Designers

**FCSP** Fellow of the Chartered Society of Physiotherapy

**f.c.s.r.c.c.** *Insurance* warranted free of capture, seizure, arrest, detainment, and the consequences thereof, and damage caused by riots and civil commotions

**FCSSA** Fellow of the College of Surgeons, South Africa

**FCST** (USA) Federal Council for Science and Technology • Fellow of the College of Speech Therapists

**FCT** Fellow of the Association of Corporate Treasurers

**FCTB** Fellow of the College of Teachers of the Blind

**FCTU** Federation of Associations of Catholic Trade Unionists

**fcty** factory

**FCU** fighter control unit

**fd** field • fiord • ford • forward • found(ed) • fund

**f.d.** flight deck • focal distance • (*or* **f/d**) free delivery • free discharge • free dispatch

**FD** *British vehicle registration for* Dudley • *Physics* Fermi–Dirac (as in **FD statistics**) • Fidei Defensor (Latin: Defender of the Faith (Henry VIII); e.g. on British coins) • *Computing* finite difference • fire department • fleet duties • *British fishing port registration for* Fleetwood • *Med.* folate deficiency • (*or* **f/d**) free-delivered (at docks) • free delivery • Free Democrat

**FDA** First Division Association (senior civil servants' union) • (USA) Food and Drug Administration

**FD&C** (USA) Food, Drug, and Color Regulations (as in **FD&C colour**)

**FDC** (USA) Fire Detection Center • *Philately* first-day cover • (*or* **f.d.c.**) *Numismatics* fleur de coin (French: mint condition)

**FDDI** *Computing* fibre distributed data interface (high-speed local area network system)

**FDF** Food and Drink Federation

**fdg** funding

**FDG** *Biochem.* fluoro-2-deoxy-D-glucose

**FDHO** Factory Department, Home Office

**FDI** Fédération dentaire internationale (French: International Dental Federation)

**FDIC** (USA) Federal Deposit Insurance Corporation • Food and Drink Industries Council

**FDIF** Fédération démocratique internationale des femmes (French: Women's International Democratic Federation)

**FDM** *Computing* finite-difference method • *Telecom.* frequency-division multiplexing

**FDO** Fleet Dental Officer • *Taxation* for declaration (purposes) only

**FDP** (Germany) Freie Demokratische Partei (Free Democratic Party)

**fdr** founder

**FDR** Franklin Delano Roosevelt (1882–1945, US president 1933–45)

**fdry** foundry

**FDS** Fellow in Dental Surgery • *Physics* Fermi–Dirac–Sommerfeld (in **FDS law**) • *Aeronautics* flight-director system

**FDSRCPSGlas** Fellow in Dental Surgery of the Royal College of Physicians and Surgeons of Glasgow

**FDSRCS** Fellow in Dental Surgery of the Royal College of Surgeons of England

**FDSRCSE** Fellow in Dental Surgery of the Royal College of Surgeons of Edinburgh

**f.e.** first edition • for example

**Fe** *Chem.*, symbol for iron (Latin *ferrum*)

**FE** Far East • *British fishing port registration for* Folkestone • foreign editor • further education • *British vehicle registration for* Lincoln

**FEA** (USA) Federal Energy Administration • (USA) Federal Executive Association • Fédération internationale pour l'éducation artistique (French: International Federation for Art Education) • *Maths.* finite-element analysis

**FEAF** Far East Air Force

**FEANI** Fédération européenne d'associations nationales d'ingenieurs (French: European Federation of National Associations of Engineers)

**feb.** (*or* **febb.**) febbraio (Italian: February)

**Feb** February

**FEB** (USA) Fair Employment Board • functional electronic block

**FEBS** Federation of European Biochemical Societies

**Feby** February

**fec.** fecit (Latin: (he or she) made it; on works of art next to the artist's name)

**FEC** (USA) Federal Election Commission • First Edition Club • Fondation européenne de la culture (French: European Cultural Foundation) • Foreign Exchange Certificate (tourist currency used in China; *compare* RMB)

**FECB** Foreign Exchange Control Board

**FECI** Fellow of the Institute of Employment Consultants

**Fed.** (*or* **fed.**) Federal(ist) • Federated • Federation

**FED** Federal Reserve System

**FEDC** Federation of Engineering Design Consultants

**FEER** *Banking* fundamental equilibrium exchange rate

**FEF** Far East Fleet

**FEI** Fédération équestre internationale (French: International Equestrian Federation) • (USA) Financial Executive Institute

**FEIDCT** Fellow of the Educational Institute of Design Craft and Technology

**FEIS** Fellow of the Educational Institute of Scotland

**FEL** free-electron laser

**FELF** Far East Land Forces

**Fell.** Fellow

**FeLV** *Microbiol.* feline leukaemia virus

**fem.** female • feminine

**f.é.m.** force électromotrice (French: electromotive force; emf)

**FEM** *Physics* field-emission microscope (*or* microscopy) • *Maths.* finite-element method

**FEMA** (USA) Federal Emergency Management Agency

**FEMO** *Chem.*, *Physics* free-electron molecular orbital (in **FEMO theory**)

**fenc.** fencing

**FEng** Fellow of the Fellowship of Engineering

**FENSA** ('fɛnsə) Film Entertainments National Service Association

**FEO** Fleet Engineer Officer

**FEOGA** Fonds européen d'orientation et de garantie agriculturel (French: European Agricultural Guidance and Guarantee Fund; in the EC)

**FEP** fluorinated ethene propene (a plastic)

**FEPA** (USA) Fair Employment Practices Act

**FEPC** (USA) Fair Employment Practices Committee

**FEPEM** Federation of European Petroleum Equipment Manufacturers

**Fer.** Fermanagh

**FERA** (USA) Federal Emergency Relief Administration

**FERC** (USA) Federal Energy Regulatory Commission

**FERDU** Further Education Review and Development Unit

**Ferm.** Fermanagh

**ferr.** ferrovia (Italian: railway)

**ferv.** *Pharmacol.* fervens (Latin: boiling)

**FES** Federation of Engineering Societies • Fellow of the Entomological Society • Fellow of the Ethnological Society • *Fencing* foil, épée, and sabre • F(rederick) E(dwin) Smith, Earl of Birkenhead (1872–1930, British statesman and lawyer)

**Fest.** Festival

**FET** ('ɛf 'iː 'tiː *or* fɛt) (USA) federal estate tax • (USA) federal excise tax • field-effect transistor • fossil-energy technology

**FEU** Further Education Unit

**feud.** feudal(ism)

**fev.** fevereiro (Portuguese: February)

**fév.** février (French: February)

**FEV** *Med.* forced expiratory volume

**FEX** *US Navy* fleet exercise

**ff** (*or* **ff.**) fecerunt (Latin: (they) made it; on works of art next to the artists' names) • folios • following (pages, lines, etc.) • forms • (ital.) *Music* fortissimo (Italian; very loudly) • *Nautical* thick fog

**f.f.** fixed focus

**FF** *British vehicle registration for* Bangor • Felicissimi Fratres (Latin: Most Fortunate Brothers) • Fellows • Fianna Fáil (Irish Gaelic: warriors of Ireland; Irish political party) • *Military* field force •

(USA) Ford Foundation • *Military* frontier force

**f.f.a.** free foreign agency • *Commerce* free from alongside (ship)

**FFA** (Scotland) Fellow of the Faculty of Actuaries • Fellow of the Institute of Financial Accountants • *Biochem.* free fatty acid • Future Farmers of America

**FFARACS** Fellow of the Faculty of Anaesthetists of the Royal Australasian College of Surgeons

**FFARCS** Fellow of the Faculty of Anaesthetists of the Royal College of Surgeons of England

**FFARCSI** Fellow of the Faculty of Anaesthetists of the Royal College of Surgeons in Ireland

**FFA(SA)** Fellow of the Faculty of Anaesthetics (South Africa)

**FFB** Fellow of the Faculty of Building

**FFC** Foreign Funds Control

**FFCMI** Fellow of the Faculty of Community Medicine of Ireland

**FFD** Fellow of the Faculty of Dental Surgeons.

**FFDRCSI** Fellow of the Faculty of Dentistry of the Royal College of Surgeons in Ireland

**fff** (ital.) *Music* fortississimo (Italian; as loudly as possible)

**FFF** Free French Forces

**FFHC** Freedom from Hunger Campaign

**FFHom** Fellow of the Faculty of Homoeopathy

**FFI** Finance for Industry • (*or* **f.f.i.**) free from infection • French Forces of the Interior

**FFJ** Franciscan Familiar of Saint Joseph

**FFL** Forces françaises libres (Free French Forces)

**ffly** faithfully

**FFOM** Fellow of the Faculty of Occupational Medicine

**FFOMI** Fellow of the Faculty of Occupational Medicine of Ireland

**FFPath, RCPI** Fellow of the Faculty of Pathologists of the Royal College of Physicians of Ireland

**FFPHM** Fellow of the Faculty of Public Health Medicine

**FFPM** Fellow of the Faculty of Pharmaceutical Medicine

**FFPS** Fauna and Flora Preservation Society

**FFr** (*or* **Ffr**) French franc

**FFRR** full-frequency range recording

**FFS** (Algeria) Front des Forces Socialistes (French: Front of Socialist Forces)

**f.f.s.s.** full-frequency stereophonic sound

**FFT** *Computing* fast Fourier transform

**FFV** (USA) First Families of Virginia

**FFWM** free-floating wave meter

**ffy** faithfully

**FFY** Fife and Forfar Yeomanry

**fg** fog

**f.g.** *Sport* field goal • fine grain • *Commerce* fully good

**FG** *British vehicle registration for* Brighton • Federal Government • Fine Gael (Irish Gaelic: tribe of the Gaels; Irish political party) • fire guard • *Engineering* flue gas (as in **FGD**, flue-gas desulphurization) • *Meteorol.* fog • foot guards • frais généraux (French: overheads) • full gilt

**FGA** Fellow of the Gemmological Association • (*or* **f.g.a.**) foreign general average

**FGCM** Fellow of the Guild of Church Musicians • field general court martial

**FGDS** (France) Fédération de la gauche démocrate et socialiste (Federation of the Democratic and Socialist Left)

**f.g.f.** *Commerce* fully good, fair

**FGI** Fédération graphique internationale (French: International Graphical Federation) • Fellow of the Institute of Certified Grocers

**Fgn** Foreign

**FGO** Fleet Gunnery Officer

**FGS** Fellow of the Geological Society

**FGSM** Fellow of the Guildhall School of Music and Drama

**fgt** freight

**FGT** (USA) federal gift tax

**FGTB** Fédération générale du travail de Belgique (French: Belgian General Federation of Labour)

**f.h.** *Med.* fiat haustus (Latin: make a draught) • fog horn • fore (*or* forward) hatch

**FH** *Med.* fetal heart • *British fishing port registration for* Falmouth • *Med.* family history • *Med.* Ficoll-Hypaque (used in radiography and gradient separation) • field hospital • fire hydrant • *Rugby* fly-half • *British vehicle registration for* Gloucester

**F/H** freehold

**FHA** (USA) Farmers' Home Administration • (USA) Federal Housing Administration • Finance Houses Association

**FHAS** Fellow of the Highland and Agricultural Society of Scotland

**FHB** (*or* **f.h.b.**) *Colloquial* family hold back

**FHCIMA** Fellow of the Hotel Catering and Institutional Management Association

**FHH** *Med.* fetal heart heard

**FHI** Fédération haltérophile internationale (French: International Weightlifting Federation)

**FHLB** (USA) Federal Home Loan Bank

**FHLBA** (USA) Federal Home Loan Bank Administration

**FHLBB** (USA) Federal Home Loan Bank Board

**fhld** (*or* **f'hold**) freehold

**FHLMC** (USA) Federal Home Loan Mortgage Corporation

**FHNH** *Med.* fetal heart not heard

**fhp** friction horsepower

**FHR** (Australia) Federal House of Representatives • *Med.* fetal heart rate

**FHS** Fellow of the Heraldry Society

**FHSA** Family Health Services Authority

**FHSM** Fellow of the Institute of Health Services Management

**FHWA** (USA) Federal Highway Administration

**f.i.** for instance • *Commerce* free in

**FI** Faeroe Islands • Falkland Islands • Fiji Islands • fire insurance • *Engineering* flow injection • *Irish vehicle registration for* Tipperary (N Riding)

**FIA** (USA) Federal Insurance Administration • Fédération internationale de l'automobile (French: International Automobile Federation) • Fellow of the Institute of Actuaries • *Chem.* flame ionization analyser • (*or* **f.i.a.**) *Commerce* full interest admitted

**FIAA** Fédération internationale athlétique d'amateur (French: International Amateur Athletic Federation) • Fellow of the Institute of Actuaries of Australia

**FIAA&S** Fellow of the Incorporated Association of Architects and Surveyors

**FIAAS** Fellow of the Institute of Australian Agricultural Science

**FIAB** Fédération internationale des associations de bibliothécaires (French: International Federation of Library

Associations and Institutions) • Fellow of the International Association of Bookkeepers

**FIAF** Fédération internationale des archives du film (French: International Federation of Film Archives)

**FIAgrE** Fellow of the Institution of Agricultural Engineers

**FIAI** Fédération internationale des associations d'instituteurs (French: International Federation of Teachers' Associations) • Fellow of the Institute of Industrial and Commercial Accountants

**FIAJ** Fédération internationale des auberges de la jeunesse (French: International Youth Hostel Federation)

**FIAL** Fellow of the International Institute of Arts and Letters

**FIAM** Fellow of the Institute of Administrative Management • Fellow of the International Academy of Management

**FIAP** Fédération internationale de l'art photographique (French: International Federation of Photographic Art) • Fellow of the Institution of Analysts and Programmers

**FIAPF** Fédération internationale des associations de producteurs de films (French: International Federation of Film Producers' Associations)

**FIArbA** Fellow of the Institute of Arbitrators of Australia

**FIASc** Fellow of the Indian Academy of Sciences

**Fiat** (or **FIAT**) ('fi:ət, -æt) Fabbrica Italiana Automobili Torino (Italian Motor Works in Turin)

**fib.** *Med.* fibula

**f.i.b.** free into barge • free into bond • free into bunker

**FIBA** Fédération internationale de basketball amateur (French: International Amateur Basketball Federation) • Fellow of the Institute of Business Administration (Australia)

**FIBD** Fellow of the Institute of British Decorators

**FIBiol** Fellow of the Institute of Biology

**FIBOR** Frankfurt Inter-Bank Offered Rate

**FIBOT** Fair Isle Bird Observatory Trust

**FIBP** Fellow of the Institute of British Photographers

**FIBScot** Fellow of the Institute of Bankers in Scotland

**FIBST** Fellow of the Institute of British Surgical Technicians

**FIBT** Fédération internationale de bobsleigh et de tobogganing (French: International Bobsleighing and Tobogganing Federation)

**fic.** fiction(al) • fictitious

**FIC** Fellow of Imperial College, London • frequency interference control

**FICA** ('fi:kə) (USA) Federal Insurance Contributions Act • Fellow of the Commonwealth Institute of Accountants • Food Industries Credit Association

**FICAI** Fellow of the Institute of Chartered Accountants in Ireland

**FICC** Fédération internationale de camping et de caravanning (French: International Federation of Camping and Caravanning) • Fédération internationale des ciné-clubs (French: International Federation of Film Societies)

**FICCI** Federation of Indian Chambers of Commerce and Industry

**FICD** Fellow of the Indian College of Dentists • Fellow of the Institute of Civil Defence

**FICE** Fellow of the Institution of Civil Engineers

**FICeram** Fellow of the Institute of Ceramics

**FICFor** Fellow of the Institute of Chartered Foresters

**FIChemE** Fellow of the Institution of Chemical Engineers

**FICI** Fellow of the Institute of Chemistry of Ireland

**FICM** Fellow of the Institute of Credit Management

**FICMA** Fellow of the Institute of Cost and Management Accountants

**FICS** Fellow of the Institute of Chartered Shipbrokers • Fellow of the International College of Surgeons

**FICSA** Federation of International Civil Servants' Associations

**fict.** fictilis (Latin: made of pottery) • fiction(al) • fictitious

**FICT** Fellow of the Institute of Concrete Technologists

**FICW** Fellow of the Institute of Clerks of Works of Great Britain

**fid.** fidelity • fiduciary

**FID** Falkland Island Dependencies • Fédération internationale de documentation (French: International Federation for Documentation) • Fédération internationale du diabète (French: International Diabetes Federation) • field intelligence department

**FIDA** Fellow of the Institute of Directors, Australia

**Fid. Def.** (*or* **FID DEF**) Fidei Defensor (*see under* FD)

**FIDE** Fédération internationale des échecs (French: International Chess Federation) • Fellow of the Institute of Design Engineers

**FIDO** ('faɪdəʊ) Film Industry Defence Organization • (*or* **Fido**) *Astronautics* (USA) Flight Dynamics Officer • Fog Investigation Dispersal Operation (in the RAF during World War II)

**FIDP** Fellow of the Institute of Data Processing

**FIE** Fédération internationale d'escrime (French: International Fencing Federation) • Fellow of the Institute of Engineers and Technicians

**FIE(Aust)** Fellow of the Institution of Engineers, Australia

**FIED** Fellow of the Institution of Engineering Designers

**FIEE** Fellow of the Institution of Electrical Engineers

**FIEEE** (USA) Fellow of the Institute of Electrical and Electronics Engineers

**FIEI** Fellow of the Institution of Engineers in Ireland

**FIEJ** Fédération internationale des éditeurs de journaux et publications (French: International Federation of Newspaper Publishers)

**FIElecIE** Fellow of the Institution of Electronic Incorporated Engineers

**FIET** Fédération internationale des employés, techniciens et cadres (French: International Federation of Commercial, Clerical, and Technical Employees)

**FIEx** Fellow of the Institute of Export

**fi. fa.** *Law* fieri facias (writ of execution; Latin: have it done)

**FIFA** ('fiːfə) Fédération internationale de football association (French: International Federation of Association Football) • Fédération internationale du film d'art (French: International Federation of Art Films) • Fellow of the International Faculty of Arts

**FIFCLC** Fédération internationale des femmes de carrières libérales et commerciales (French: International Federation of Business and Professional Women)

**FIFDU** Fédération internationale des femmes diplômées des universités (French: International Federation of University Women)

**FIFF** Fellow of the Institute of Freight Forwarders

**FIFireE** Fellow of the Institution of Fire Engineers

**FIFO** (*or* **fifo**) ('faɪfəʊ) *Computing, Accounting* first in first out

**FIFSP** Fédération internationale des fonctionnaires supérieurs de police (French: International Federation of Senior Police Officers)

**FIFST** Fellow of the Institute of Food Science and Technology

**fig.** figurative(ly) • (*or* **Fig.**) figure(s)

**FIG** Fédération internationale de gymnastique (French: International Gymnastic Federation)

**FIGasE** Fellow of the Institution of Gas Engineers

**FIGC** Federazione Italiana Gioco Calcio (Italian Football Association)

**FIGCM** Fellow of the Incorporated Guild of Church Musicians

**FIGED** Fédération internationale des grandes entreprises de distribution (French: International Federation of Distributors)

**FIGO** Fédération internationale de gynécologie et d'obstétrique (French: International Federation of Gynaecology and Obstetrics)

**FIGRS** Fellow of the Irish Genealogical Research Society

**FIH** Fédération internationale de hockey (French: International Hockey Federation) • Fédération internationale des hôpitaux (French: International Hospital Federation) • Fellow of the Institute of Housing • *Image technol.* focused-image holography

**FIHE** Fellow of the Institution of Health Education

**FIHort** Fellow of the Institute of Horticulture

**FIHospE** Fellow of the Institute of Hospital Engineering

**FIHsg** Fellow of the Institute of Housing

**FIHT** Fellow of the Institution of Highways and Transportation

**FIIA** Fellow of the Institute of Internal Auditors

**FIIC** Fellow of the International Institute for Conservation of Historic and Artistic Works

**FIIM** Fellow of the Institution of Industrial Managers

**FIInfSc** Fellow of the Institute of Information Scientists

**FIInst** Fellow of the Imperial Institute

**FIITech** Fellow of the Institute of Industrial Technicians

**FIJ** Fédération internationale de judo (French: International Judo Federation) • Fédération internationale des journalistes (French: International Federation of Journalists)

**fil.** filament • fillet • filter • filtrate

**FIL** Fédération internationale de laiterie (French: International Dairy Federation) • Fellow of the Institute of Linguists

**FILA** Fédération internationale de lutte amateur (French: International Amateur Wrestling Federation)

**FILDM** Fellow of the Institute of Logistics and Distribution Management

**FILO** first in last out

**FILT** Fédération internationale de lawn tennis (French: International Lawn Tennis Federation)

**FIM** Fédération internationale des musiciens (French: International Federation of Musicians) • Fédération internationale motocycliste (French: International Motorcycle Federation) • Fellow of the Institute of Metals • field-ion microscope (*or* microscopy)

**FIMA** Fellow of the Institute of Mathematics and its Applications

**FIMarE** Fellow of the Institute of Marine Engineers

**FIMBRA** ('fimbrə) Financial Intermediaries, Managers, and Brokers Regulatory Association

**FIMC** Fellow of the Institute of Management Consultants

**FIMechE** Fellow of the Institution of Mechanical Engineers

**FIMGTechE** Fellow of the Institution of Mechanical and General Technician Engineers

**FIMH** Fellow of the Institute of Military History

**FIMI** Fellow of the Institute of the Motor Industry

**FIMinE** Fellow of the Institution of Mining Engineers

**FIMIT** Fellow of the Institute of Musical Instrument Technology

**FIMLS** Fellow of the Institute of Medical Laboratory Sciences (formerly Technology, FIMLT)

**FIMM** Fellow of the Institution of Mining and Metallurgy

**FIMP** Fédération internationale de médecine physique (French: International Federation of Physical Medicine)

**FIMS** Fellow of the Institute of Mathematical Statistics • *Chem.* field-ion mass spectrometer (*or* spectrometry)

**fin.** ad finem (Latin: at (*or* near) the end) • final • finance • financial • financier • finis (Latin: the end) • finish

**Fin.** Finland • Finnish

**FIN** *international vehicle registration for* Finland

**f.i.n.a.** following items not available

**FINA** Fédération internationale de natation amateur (French: International Amateur Swimming Federation)

**Fin. Sec.** Financial Secretary

**FInstAM** Fellow of the Institute of Administrative Management

**FInstB** Fellow of the Institution of Buyers

**FInstCh** Fellow of the Institute of Chiropodists

**FInstD** Fellow of the Institute of Directors

**FInstE** Fellow of the Institute of Energy

**FInstFF** Fellow of the Institute of Freight Forwarders

**FInstLEx** Fellow of the Institute of Legal Executives

**FInstMC** Fellow of the Institute of Measurement and Control

**FInstO** Fellow of the Institute of Ophthalmology

**FInstP** Fellow of the Institute of Physics

**FInstPet** Fellow of the Institute of Petroleum

**FInstPI** Fellow of the Institute of Patentees and Inventors

**FInstPS** Fellow of the Institute of Purchasing and Supply

**FInstSMM** Fellow of the Institute of Sales and Marketing Management

**FINucE** Fellow of the Institution of Nuclear Engineers

**f.i.o.** for information only • *Commerce* free in and out

**FIOA** Fellow of the Institute of Acoustics

**FIOP** Fellow of the Institute of Plumbing • Fellow of the Institute of Printing

**FIP** Fédération internationale de philatélie (French: International Philatelic Federation) • Fédération internationale pharmaceutique (French: International Pharmaceutical Federation)

**FIPA** Fédération internationale des producteurs agricoles (French: International Federation of Agricultural Producers) • Fellow of the Institute of Practitioners in Advertising

**FIPENZ** Fellow of the Institution of Professional Engineers, New Zealand

**FIPG** Fellow of the Institute of Professional Goldsmiths

**FIPM** Fellow of the Institute of Personnel Management

**FIPR** Fellow of the Institute of Public Relations

**FIProdE** Fellow of the Institution of Production Engineers

**FIQ** Fédération internationale de quilleurs (French: International Bowling Federation) • Fellow of the Institute of Quarrying

**FIQA** Fellow of the Institute of Quality Assurance

**FIQS** Fellow of the Institute of Quantity Surveyors

**fir.** firkin

**f.i.r.** flight information region • floating-in rate • fuel-indicator reading

**FIR** far-infrared radiation

**FIRA** Fédération internationale de rugby amateur (French: International Amateur Rugby Federation) • Furniture Industry Research Association

**FIREE(Aust)** Fellow of the Institute of Radio and Electronics Engineers (Australia)

**FIRS** Fédération internationale de patinage à roulettes (French: International Roller Skating Federation)

**FIRTE** Fellow of the Institute of Road Transport Engineers

**FIRSE** Fellow of the Institute of Railway Signalling Engineers

**FIS** Family Income Supplement • farm improvement scheme • Fédération internationale de sauvetage (French: International Life Saving Federation) • Fédération internationale de ski (French: International Ski Federation) •

Fellow of the Institute of Statisticians • flight information service • (or **f.i.s.**) free into store • (fiːs) (Algeria) Front Islamique du Salut (French: Islamic Salvation Front)

**FISA** Fédération internationale des sociétés d'aviron (French; International Rowing Federation) • Fédération internationale du sport automobiles (French; International Motoring Federation) • Fellow of the Incorporated Secretaries Association

**FISE** Fédération internationale syndicale de l'enseignement (French; World Federation of Teachers' Unions) • Fellow of the Institution of Sales Engineers • Fellow of the Institution of Sanitary Engineers • Fonds international de secours à l'enfance (French; United Nations Children's Fund)

**fish.** fishery • fishes • fishing

**FISITA** Fédération internationale des sociétés d'ingénieurs des techniques de l'automobile (French: International Federation of Automobile Engineers' and Technicians' Associations)

**FIST** Fellow of the Institute of Science Technology

**FISTC** Fellow of the Institute of Scientific and Technical Communicators

**FIStructE** Fellow of the Institution of Structural Engineers

**FISU** Fédération internationale du sport universitaire (French: International University Sports Federation)

**FISVA** Fellow of the Incorporated Society of Valuers and Auctioneers

**FISW** Fellow of the Institute of Social Work

**f.i.t.** *Commerce* free in truck • free of income tax

**FIT** (USA) Federal Income Tax • Fédération internationale des traducteurs (French: International Federation of Translators)

**FITA** Fédération internationale de tir á l'arc (French: International Archery Federation)

**FITC** *Immunol.* fluorescein isothiocyanate

**FITCE** Fédération des ingénieurs des télécommunications de la communauté européenne (French: Federation of Telecommunications Engineers in the European Community)

**FITD** Fellow of the Institute of Training and Development

**FITE** Fellow of the Institution of Electrical and Electronics Technician Engineers

**FITT** Fédération internationale de tennis de table (French: International Table Tennis Federation)

**f.i.t.w.** (USA) federal income tax withholding

**FIVB** Fédération internationale de volley-ball (French: International Volleyball Federation)

**f.i.w.** *Commerce* free in (*or* into) wagon(s)

**FIWC** Fiji Industrial Workers' Congress

**FIWEM** Fellow of the Institution of Water and Environmental Management

**FIWSc** Fellow of the Institute of Wood Science

**fix.** fixture

**Fj.** Fjord

**FJ** *British vehicle registration for* Exeter

**FJA** Future Journalists of America

**Fjd** Fjord

**FJI** Fellow of the Institute of Journalists • *international vehicle registration for* Fiji

**fk** fork

**f.k.** flat keel

**FK** *British vehicle registration for* Dudley • *postcode for* Falkirk • *Astronomy* Fundamental Katalog (German: Fundamental Catalogue, as in **FK5**)

**FKC** Fellow of King's College (London)

**FKCHMS** Fellow of King's College Hospital Medical School

**Fkr** *symbol for* Faroese krone (monetary unit)

**fl.** fleuve (French: river) • floor • *Med.* flores (Latin: flowers; powdered form of a drug) • florin • floruit (Latin: flourished; indicates the period of greatest activity of a person whose birth and death dates are not known) • flourish • fluid • *Music* flute • (Netherlands) guilder (from its former name *florin*)

**f.l.** falsa lectio (Latin: false reading; in a text)

**Fl.** Flanders • Flemish

**FL** Flag Lieutenant • Flight Lieutenant • *US postcode for* Florida • football league • *international vehicle registration for* Liechtenstein • *British vehicle registration for* Peterborough

**Fla.** Florida

**FLA** Fellow of the Library Association • fiat lege artis (Latin: let it be done by rules of the art) • Film Laboratory Association

**flag.** *Music* flageolet

**FLAI** Fellow of the Library Association of Ireland

**FLCM** Fellow of the London College of Music

**FLCO** Fellow of the London College of Osteopathy

**fld** field

**FLD** *Metallurgy* forming limit diagram

**fldg** folding

**fl. dr.** fluid dram

**Flem.** Flemish

**flex.** flexible

**flg** flagging • flooring • flying • following

**FLHS** Fellow of the London Historical Society

**FLI** Fellow of the Landscape Institute

**FLIA** Fellow of the Life Insurance Association

**Flint.** Flintshire (former Welsh county)

**FLIP** (flɪp) *US Navy* floating instrument platform

**FLIR** *Military* forward-looking infrared

**Flli** Fratelli (Italian: Brothers)

**FLN** (Algeria) Front de Libération Nationale (French: National Liberation Front)

**FLOOD** (flʌd) (USA) fleet observation of oceanographic data

**flops** (*or* **FLOPS**) (flops) *Computing* floating-point operations per second (a measure of computer power, as in **Mflops**, megaflops)

**flor.** floruit (*see under* fl.)

**Flor.** Florence • Florentine • Florida

**fl oz** *symbol for* fluid ounce

**f.l.p.** *Aeronautics* fault location panel

**fl. pl.** *Botany* flore pleno (Latin: with double flowers)

**FLQ** (Canada) Front de Liberation du Québec (French: Quebec Liberation Front)

**flr.** florin

**FLRA** (USA) Federal Labor Relations Authority

**flrg** flooring

**fl. rt.** flow rate

**FLS** Fellow of the Linnean Society

**FLSA** (USA) Fair Labor Standards Act

**flst.** flautist

**Flt** *Air force* Flight

**F/Lt** (*or* **F.Lt**) Flight Lieutenant

**Flt Cmdr** Flight Commander

**fltg** floating

**Flt Lt** Flight Lieutenant
**Flt Off.** Flight Officer
**Flt Sgt** Flight Sergeant
**fluc.** fluctuant • fluctuate(d) • fluctuation
**FLUC** *Meteorol.* fluctuating
**fluor.** fluorescent • fluoridation • fluoride • fluorspar
**fly.** *Boxing* flyweight
**fm** farm(er) • fathom(s) • *Physics, symbol for* femtometre(s) • from
**f.m.** face (*or* facial) measurement • femmes mariées (French: married women) • *Med.* fiat mistura (Latin: let a mixture be made) • fine measure-(ment) • *Radio* frequency modulation
**Fm** *Chem., symbol for* fermium
**F.m.** facing matter (in advertisement placing)
**FM** *British vehicle registration for* Chester • *Computing* facilities management • *Metallurgy* ferritic and martensitic (describing iron) • *Electrical engineering* field magnet • Field Marshal • *Aeronautics* figure of merit • Flight Mechanic • foreign mission • Fraternitas Medicorum (Latin: Fraternity of Physicians) • fraternité mondiale (French: world brotherhood) • freemason • *Radio* frequency modulation • Friars Minor
**FMA** Farm Management Association • Fellow of the Museums Association • Food Machinery Association
**fman** foreman
**FMANZ** Fellow of the Medical Association of New Zealand
**FMAO** Farm Machinery Advisory Officer
**FMAS** Foreign Marriage Advisory Service
**FMB** (Malawi) Farmers' Marketing Board • (USA) Federal Maritime Board • Federation of Master Builders
**FMC** (USA) Federal Maritime Commission • Fellow of the Medical Council • Forces Motoring Club • Ford Motor Company
**FMCE** Federation of Manufacturers of Construction Equipment
**FMCG** fast-moving consumer goods
**FMCP** Federation of Manufacturers of Contractors' Plant
**FMCS** (USA) Federal Mediation and Conciliation Service
**FMCW** *Electronics* frequency modulated continuous wave
**fmd** formed

**FMD** foot and mouth disease
**FMES** Fellow of the Minerals Engineering Society
**FMF** *Med.* fetal movements felt • Fiji Military Forces • Fleet Marine Force • Food Manufacturers' Federation
**FMFPAC** (USA) Fleet Marine Forces, Pacific
**FMG** (Nigeria) Federal Military Government • *symbol for* franc (monetary unit of Madagascar)
**FMI** Fellow of the Motor Industry • Filii Mariae Immaculatae (Latin: Sons of Mary Immaculate)
**FMIG** Food Manufacturers' Industrial Group
**Fmk** (*or* **FMk**) *symbol for* markka (Finnish monetary unit) • Finnmark
**fml** formal
**FMLN** (El Salvador) Farabundo Martí National Liberation Front (left-wing guerrilla movement)
**fmn** formation
**FMN** *Biochem.* flavin mononucleotide
**FMO** Fleet Medical Officer • Flight Medical Officer
**fmr** former
**fmrly** formerly
**FMRS** Foreign Member of the Royal Society
**FMS** Federated Malay States (now part of the Union of Malaya) • Fédération mondiale des sourds (French: World Federation of the Deaf) • Fellow of the Institute of Management Studies • Fellow of the Medical Society • *Computing* flexible manufacturing system • *Aeronautics* flight-management systems
**FMSA** Fellow of the Mineralogical Society of America
**FMTS** field maintenance test station
**FMVSS** (USA) Federal Motor Vehicle Safety Standards
**f.n.** footnote
**FN** *British vehicle registration for* Maidstone
**f.n.a.** for necessary action
**FNA** Fellow of the Indian National Science Academy • French North Africa
**FNAEA** Fellow of the National Association of Estate Agents
**FNAL** Fermi National Accelerator Laboratory
**FNCB** (USA) First National City Bank
**FNCO** Fleet Naval Constructor Officer
**fnd** found • foundered
**fndd** founded

**fndr** founder
**fndry** foundry
**fne** fine
**FNECInst** Fellow of the North East Coast Institution of Engineers and Shipbuilders
**FNI** Fédération naturiste internationale (French: International Naturist Federation) • Fellow of the Nautical Institute
**FNIF** Florence Nightingale International Foundation
**FNILP** Fellow of the National Institute of Licensing Practitioners
**FNL** Friends of the National Libraries
**FNLA** Frente Nacional de Libertação de Angola (Portuguese: National Front for the Liberation of Angola)
**FNMA** (USA) Federal National Mortgage Association
**FNO** Fleet Navigation Officer
**FNU** Forces des Nations Unies (French: United Nations Forces)
**FNWC** (USA) Fleet Numerical Weather Center
**FNZEI** Fellow of the New Zealand Educational Institute
**FNZIA** Fellow of the New Zealand Institute of Architects
**FNZIAS** Fellow of the New Zealand Institute of Agricultural Science
**FNZIC** Fellow of the New Zealand Institute of Chemistry
**FNZIE** Fellow of the New Zealand Institution of Engineers
**FNZIM** Fellow of the New Zealand Institute of Management
**FNZPsS** Fellow of the New Zealand Psychological Society
**fo.** folio
**f.o.** fast operating • *Commerce* free overside • fuel oil
**f/o** *Commerce* for orders • full out
**Fo** (ital.) *Physics,* symbol for Fourier number
**FO** federal official • *Army* Field Officer • *Commerce* firm offer • First Officer • *Navy* Flag Officer • *Air force* Flying Officer • Foreign Office (now part of the FCO) • formal offer (to shareholders in business mergers) • *Military* forward observer • *Music* full organ • *British vehicle registration for* Gloucester
**FOB** (*or* **f.o.b.**) *Commerce* free on board
**FOBFO** Federation of British Fire Organizations
**FOBS** *Military* fractional orbital bombardment system

**FOBTSU** forward observer target survey unit
**FoC** father of the (trade-union) chapel
**FOC** (*or* **f.o.c.**) *Commerce* free of charge • free of claims
**FOCL** fibre-optic communications line
**FOCOL** Federation of Coin-Operated Launderettes
**FOCT** flag officer carrier training
**FOD** (*or* **f.o.d.**) free of damage
**FODA** Fellow of the Overseas Doctors' Association
**FOE** (USA) Fraternal Order of Eagles • (*or* **FoE**) Friends of the Earth
**FOFA** follow-on forces attack
**FOFATUSA** Federation of Free African Trade Unions of South Africa
**F of F** Firth of Forth
**FOH** *Theatre* front of house
**FOI** (USA) freedom of information
**FOIA** (USA) Freedom of Information Act
**FOIC** Flag Officer in charge
**f.o.k.** *Stock exchange* fill or kill (carry out instruction or cancel)
**fol.** folio • follow(ed) • following
**FOL** (New Zealand) Federation of Labour
**folg.** following
**foll.** followed • following
**FOM** *Statistics* figure of merit
**FOMC** (USA) Federal Open Market Committee
**FONA** Flag Officer, Naval Aviation
**FONAC** Flag Officer, Naval Air Command
**FOP** forward observation post
**FOQ** (*or* **f.o.q.**) *Commerce* free on quay
**for.** foreign(er) • forensic • forest(er) • forestry • *Music* forte
**For** *Astronomy* Fornax
**FOR** Fellowship of Operational Research • flying objects research • (*or* **f.o.r.**) free on rail
**FORATOM** Forum atomique européen (French: European Atomic Forum)
**Ford** (fɔːd) (Kenya) Forum for the Restoration of Democracy
**FOREST** ('fɒrɪst) Freedom Organization for the Right to Enjoy Smoking Tobacco
**formn** foreman • formation
**form. wt** *Chem.* formula weight
**for. rts** foreign rights
**fort.** fortification • fortified • fortify
**f.o.r.t.** *Commerce* full out rye terms

**Fortran** (*or* **FORTRAN**) ('fɔːtræn) *Computing* formula translation (a programming language)

**Forts.** Fortsetzung (German: continuation)

**forz.** *Music* forzando (Italian: with force)

**f.o.s.** *Finance* free of stamp • *Commerce* free on ship (*or* steamer) • *Commerce* free on station

**FOS** Fisheries Organization Society

**FOSDIC** *Computing* film optical sensing device

**f.o.t.** (*or* **FOT**) *Commerce* free of tax • *Commerce* free on truck(s)

**Found.** Foundation • Foundry

**FOV** field of view

**f.o.w.** *Commerce* first open water • *Commerce* free on wagon

**FOX** (fɒks) *Commerce* Futures and Options Exchange (in **London FOX**)

**fp** (ital.) *Music* forte-piano (Italian; loud (then) soft) • freezing point

**fp.** fireplace • foolscap

**f.p.** *Med.* fiat pilula (Latin: let a pill be made) • fine paper • *Cricket* fine point • fixed price • flameproof • *Chem.* flash point • footpath • foot pound • *Sport* forward pass • freezing point • full point • fully paid (of shares)

**Fp.** frontispiece

**FP** Federal Parliament • field punishment • filter paper • *Insurance* fire policy • *Nuclear engineering* fission product • *Insurance* floating policy • *Optics* focal plane • former pupil • fowl pest • Free Presbyterian • freezing point • fresh paragraph • fully paid (of shares) • *Computing* functional programming • *British vehicle registration for* Leicester

**FPA** Family Planning Association • Film Production Association of Great Britain • Fire Protection Association • *Astronomy* first point of Aries • *Computing* floating-point accelerator • Foreign Press Association • *Marine insurance* free of particular average

**f.p.b.** fast patrol boat

**f.p.b.g.** fast patrol boat with guided missiles

**f.p.c.** for private circulation

**FPC** (formerly) Family Practitioner Committee • Federation of Painting Contractors • fish protein concentrate • Flowers Publicity Council

**FPEA** Fellow of the Physical Education Association

**FPF** Federação Portuguesa de Futebol (Portuguese Football Federation)

**FPHA** (USA) Federal Public Housing Authority

**FPhS** Fellow of the Philosophical Society of England

**FPhyS** Fellow of the Physical Society

**FPI** *Physics* Fabry–Perot interferometer • (USA) Federal Prison Industries

**FPIA** Fellow of the Plastics Institute of Australia

**FPLA** *Electronics, Computing* field-programmable logic array

**fpm** (*or* **FPM**) feet per minute

**FPMI** Fellow of the Pensions Management Institute

**FPMR** (USA) Federal Property Management Regulation

**FPO** field post office • fire prevention officer • *US Navy* fleet post office

**FPRC** Flying Personnel Research Committee

**FPRI** Fellow of the Plastics and Rubber Institute

**fps** (*or* **f.p.s.**) feet per second • *Physics* foot-pound-second (as in **fps units**) • *Photog.* frames per second

**FPS** Fellow of the Philharmonic Society • Fellow of the Philological Society • Fellow of the Philosophical Society • (USA) Fluid Power Society

**fpsps** feet per second per second

**FPT** *Commerce* fixed price tenders • *Nautical* forepeak tank

**f.q.** *Finance* fiscal quarter

**FQS** (USA) Federal Quarantine Service

**fr.** fragment • frame • franc(s) • free • frequent • from • front • (ital.) *Physics, symbol for* Froude number • fruit • *Botany* fruiting

**f.r.** folio recto (Latin: on the right-hand page)

**Fr** *RC Church* Brother (Latin *Frater*) • *Christianity* Father • *Chem., symbol for* francium

**Fr.** France • Fratelli (Italian: Brothers) • Frau (German: Mrs) • French • Friar • Friday

**FR** *international vehicle registration for* Faroe Islands • Federal Republic • Federal Reserve (System) • *Chem.* fluorine rubber • Forum Romanum (Latin: Roman Forum) • *British fishing port registration for* Fraserburgh • freight release • frequency rate • *Nuclear engineering* fusion reactor • *British vehicle registration for* Preston • *airline flight code for* Ryanair

**F/R** folio reference

**f.r.a.** flame retardant additive

**Fra** (frɑː) *RC Church* Brother (Italian *frate*)

**FRA** *Finance* forward rate agreement

**FRACDS** Fellow of the Royal Australian College of Dental Surgeons

**FRACGP** Fellow of the Royal Australian College of General Practitioners

**FRACI** Fellow of the Royal Australian Chemical Institute

**FRACMA** Fellow of the Royal Australian College of Medical Administrators

**FRACO** Fellow of the Royal Australian College of Ophthalmologists

**FRACOG** Fellow of the Royal Australian College of Obstetricians and Gynaecologists

**FRACP** Fellow of the Royal Australasian College of Physicians

**FRACR** Fellow of the Royal Australasian College of Radiologists

**FRACS** Fellow of the Royal Australasian College of Surgeons

**FRAD** Fellow of the Royal Academy of Dancing

**FRAeS** Fellow of the Royal Aeronautical Society

**FRAgSs** Fellow of the Royal Agricultural Societies

**FRAHS** Fellow of the Royal Australian Historical Society

**FRAI** Fellow of the Royal Anthropological Institute

**FRAIA** Fellow of the Royal Australian Institute of Architects

**FRAIC** Fellow of the Royal Architectural Institute of Canada

**FRAIPA** Fellow of the Royal Australian Institute of Public Administration

**FRAM** Fellow of the Royal Academy of Music

**FRAME** (freɪm) Fund for the Replacement of Animals in Medical Experiments

**Franc.** Franciscan

**f.r. & c.c.** *Insurance* free of riot and civil commotions

**Frank.** Frankish

**FRANZCP** Fellow of the Royal Australian and New Zealand College of Psychiatrists

**FRAP** (Chile) Frente de Acción Popular (Spanish: Popular Action Front)

**FRAPI** Fellow of the Royal Australian Planning Institute

**FRAS** Fellow of the Royal Asiatic Society • Fellow of the Royal Astronomical Society

**FRASE** Fellow of the Royal Agricultural Society of England

**FRATE** (freɪt) *Railways* formulae for routes and technical equipment

**fraud.** fraudulent

**FRB** (USA) Federal Reserve Bank • (USA) Federal Reserve Board • Fisheries Research Board of Canada • Frente de la Revolución Boliviana (Spanish: Bolivian Revolutionary Front)

**FRBS** Fellow of the Royal Botanic Society • Fellow of the Royal Society of British Sculptors

**FRC** (USA) Federal Radiation Council • (USA) Federal Radio Commission • Flight Research Center (at NASA)

**FRCA** Fellow of the Royal College of Art

**Fr-Can.** French-Canadian

**FRCCO** Fellow of the Royal Canadian College of Organists

**FRCD** *Banking* floating-rate certificate of deposit • Fellow of the Royal College of Dentists of Canada

**FRCGP** Fellow of the Royal College of General Practitioners

**FRCM** Fellow of the Royal College of Music

**FRcn** Fellow of the Royal College of Nursing

**FRCO** Fellow of the Royal College of Organists

**FRCO(CHM)** Fellow of the Royal College of Organists with Diploma in Choir Training

**FRCOG** Fellow of the Royal College of Obstetricians and Gynaecologists

**FRCP** Fellow of the Royal College of Physicians

**FRCPA** Fellow of the Royal College of Pathologists of Australasia

**FRCP&S(Canada)** Fellow of the Royal College of Physicians and Surgeons of Canada

**FRCPath** Fellow of the Royal College of Pathologists

**FRCP(C)** Fellow of the Royal College of Physicians of Canada

**FRCPE** (*or* **FRCPEd**) Fellow of the Royal College of Physicians of Edinburgh

**FRCPGlas** Fellow of the Royal College of Physicians and Surgeons of Glasgow

**FRCPI** Fellow of the Royal College of Physicians of Ireland

**FRCPsych** Fellow of the Royal College of Psychiatrists

**FRCR** Fellow of the Royal College of Radiologists

**FRCS** Fellow of the Royal College of Surgeons

**FRCSCan** Fellow of the Royal College of Surgeons of Canada

**FRCScI** Fellow of the Royal College of Science, Ireland

**FRCSE** (*or* **FRCSEd**) Fellow of the Royal College of Surgeons of Edinburgh

**FRCSGlas** Fellow of the Royal College of Physicians and Surgeons of Glasgow

**FRCSI** Fellow of the Royal College of Surgeons of Ireland

**FRCSoc** Fellow of the Royal Commonwealth Society

**FRCVS** Fellow of the Royal College of Veterinary Surgeons

**frd** friend

**FR Dist.** (USA) Federal Reserve District

**fre** fracture (French: invoice)

**Fre.** Freitag (German: Friday) • French

**FREconS** Fellow of the Royal Economic Society

**FRED** (frɛd) Fast Reactor Experiment, Dounreay • figure reading electronic device

**Free.** (USA) freeway

**FREGG** (frɛg) Free Range Egg Association

**FREI** Fellow of the Real Estate Institute (Australia)

**Frelimo** (freɪ'liːməu) Frente de Libertação de Moçambique (Portuguese: Mozambique Liberation Front)

**freq.** frequency • frequent(ly) • *Grammar* frequentative

**FRES** Federation of Recruitment and Employment Services • Fellow of the Royal Entomological Society

**FRESH** (frɛʃ) foil research hydrofoil

**Fr.G.** French Guiana

**FRG** Federal Republic of Germany

**FRGS** Fellow of the Royal Geographical Society

**FRGSA** Fellow of the Royal Geographical Society of Australasia

**frgt** freight

**FRHB** Federation of Registered House Builders

**FRHistS** Fellow of the Royal Historical Society

**Frhr** Freiherr (German: Baron)

**FRHS** Fellow of the Royal Horticultural Society

**Fri.** Fribourg • Friday

**FRI** Fellow of the Royal Institution • Food Research Institute

**FRIA** Fellow of the Royal Irish Academy

**FRIAI** Fellow of the Royal Institute of Architects of Ireland

**FRIAS** Fellow of the Royal Incorporation of Architects in Scotland • Fellow of the Royal Institute for the Advancement of Science

**FRIBA** Fellow of the Royal Institute of British Architects

**fric.** (*or* **frict.**) friction(al)

**FRIC** Fellow of the Royal Institute of Chemistry (now part of the Royal Society of Chemistry; *see under* FRSC)

**FRICS** Fellow of the Royal Institution of Chartered Surveyors

**FRIH** (New Zealand) Fellow of the Royal Institute of Horticulture

**FRIIA** Fellow of the Royal Institute of International Affairs

**FRIN** Fellow of the Royal Institute of Navigation

**FRINA** Fellow of the Royal Institution of Naval Architects

**FRIPA** Fellow of the Royal Institute of Public Administration

**FRIPHH** Fellow of the Royal Institute of Public Health and Hygiene

**Fris.** Friesland • Frisian

**Frk.** Frøken (Danish *or* Norwegian: Miss) • Fröken (Swedish: Miss)

**Frl.** Fräulein (German: Miss)

**FRL** full repairing lease

**frld** foreland • freehold

**frm** from

**FRMCM** Fellow of the Royal Manchester College of Music

**FRMCS** Fellow of the Royal Medical and Chirurgical Society

**FRMedSoc** Fellow of the Royal Medical Society

**FRMetS** Fellow of the Royal Meteorological Society

**FRMS** Fellow of the Royal Microscopical Society

**FRN** *Finance* floating-rate note

**FRNCM** Fellow of the Royal Northern College of Music

**FRNS** Fellow of the Royal Numismatic Society

**FRNSA** Fellow of the Royal Navy School of Architects

**FRO** Fellow of the Register of Osteopaths • Fire Research Organization • *Insurance* fire risk only

**f.r.o.f.** *Insurance* fire risk on freight

**Frolinat** Front de Libération Nationale Tchadienne (French: Chad National Liberation Front)

**front.** (*or* **frontis.**) frontispiece

**FRP** fibre- (*or* fibreglass-)reinforced plastic • fuel-reprocessing plant

**frpf** fireproof

**FRPharmS** Fellow of the Royal Pharmaceutical Society

**FRPS** Fellow of the Royal Photographic Society

**FRPSL** Fellow of the Royal Philatelic Society, London

**FRQ** *Meteorol.* frequent

**Frs.** Frisian

**FRS** (USA) Federal Reserve System • Fellow of the Royal Society • Festiniog Railway Society • fuel research station

**FRSA** Fellow of the Royal Society of Arts

**FRSAI** Fellow of the Royal Society of Antiquaries of Ireland

**FRSAMD** Fellow of the Royal Scottish Academy of Music and Drama

**FRSC** (*or* **FRSCan**) Fellow of the Royal Society of Canada • Fellow of the Royal Society of Chemistry (formerly FCS; FRIC)

**FRSCM** Fellow of the Royal School of Church Music

**FRSE** Fellow of the Royal Society of Edinburgh

**FRSGS** Fellow of the Royal Scottish Geographical Society

**FRSH** Fellow of the Royal Society for the Promotion of Health

**FRSL** Fellow of the Royal Society of Literature

**FRSM** Fellow of the Royal Society of Medicine

**FRSNA** Fellow of the Royal School of Naval Architecture

**FRSNZ** Fellow of the Royal Society of New Zealand

**FRSSA** Fellow of the Royal Scottish Society of Arts • (*or* **FRSSAF**) Fellow of the Royal Society of South Africa

**FRSSI** Fellow of the Royal Statistical Society of Ireland

**FRSSS** Fellow of the Royal Statistical Society of Scotland

**FRST** Fellow of the Royal Society of Teachers

**FRSTM&H** Fellow of the Royal Society of Tropical Medicine and Hygiene

**frt** (*or* **Frt**) freight

**Frt fwd** freight forward

**FRTPI** Fellow of the Royal Town Planning Institute

**Frt ppd** freight prepaid

**FRTS** Fellow of the Royal Television Society

**Fru** *Biochem.* fructose

**frum** fratrum (Latin: of the brothers)

**frust.** *Med.* frustillatim (Latin: in small portions)

**FRVC** Fellow of the Royal Veterinary College

**FRVIA** Fellow of the Royal Victorian Institute of Architects

**frwk** framework

**frwy** (*or* **fry.**) freeway

**FRZSScot** Fellow of the Royal Zoological Society of Scotland

**fs.** facsimile

**f.s.** factor of safety • faire suivre (French: please forward) • far side • film strip • fire station • flight service • flying saucer • flying status

**FS** *British vehicle registration for* Edinburgh • Fabian Society • Faraday Society • feasibility study • (Italy) Ferrovie dello Stato Italia (State Railways) • field security • financial secretary • financial statement • Fleet Surgeon • Flight Sergeant • Foreign Service • (USA) Forest Service • Friendly Society

**f.s.a.** fuel storage area

**FSA** (USA) Farm Security Agency • (USA) Federal Security Agency • (USA) Fellow of the Society of Actuaries • Fellow of the Society of Antiquaries • Field Survey Association • Financial Services Act (1986) • *Computing* finite-state automaton • foreign service allowance • Friendly Societies Act

**FSAA** Fellow of the Society of Incorporated Accountants and Auditors

**FSAE** Fellow of the Society of Art Education • Fellow of the Society of Automotive Engineers

**FSAI** Fellow of the Society of Architectural Illustrators

**FSAIEE** Fellow of the South African Institute of Electrical Engineers

**FSAM** Fellow of the Society of Art Masters

**FSAScot** (*or* **FSAS**) Fellow of the Society of Antiquaries of Scotland • Fellow of the Society of Arts of Scotland

**FSASM** Fellow of the South Australian School of Mines

**FSBI** Fellow of the Savings Bank Institute

**FSC** (USA) Federal Supreme Court • Fellow of the Society of Chiropodists • Field Studies Council • *RC Church* Fratres Scholarum Christianorum (Latin: Brothers of the Christian Schools *or* Christian Brothers) • Friends Service Council

**FSCA** Fellow of the Society of Company and Commercial Accountants

**FSD** full-scale deflection (of a measuring instrument)

**FSDC** Fellow of the Society of Dyers and Colourists

**FSE** Fellow of the Society of Engineers • field support equipment

**FSF** Fellow of the Institute of Shipping and Forwarding Agents

**FSG** Fellow of the Society of Genealogists

**FSgt** Flight Sergeant

**FSGT** Fellow of the Society of Glass Technology

**FSH** *Biochem.* follicle-stimulating hormone

**FSHM** Fellow of the Society of Housing Managers

**FSI** Fédération spirite internationale (French: International Spiritualist Federation) • Free Sons of Israel

**FSK** *Telecom.* frequency shift keying

**FSL** First Sea Lord

**FSLAET** Fellow of the Society of Licensed Aircraft Engineers and Technologists

**FSLIC** (USA) Federal Savings and Loan Insurance Corporation

**FSLN** (Nicaragua) Frente Sandinista de Liberación Nacional (Spanish: Sandinista National Liberation Front)

**FSLTC** Fellow of the Society of Leather Technologists and Chemists

**FSM** Fédération syndicale mondiale (French: World Federation of Trade Unions) • *Electronics* flying-spot microscope • (USA) Free Speech Movement

**FSMC** Freeman of the Spectacle-Makers' Company

**FSME** Fellow of the Society of Manufacturing Engineers

**FSN** federal stock number

**FSNA** Fellow of the Society of Naval Architects

**FSO** field security officer • Fleet Signals Officer • Foreign Service Officer

**FSP** field security police • foreign service pay

**FSR** Field Service Regulations • (ital.) Fleet Street Patent Law Reports

**FSRP** Fellow of the Society for Radiological Protection

**FSS** Fellow of the Royal Statistical Society • (Algeria) Front des forces socialistes (French: Socialist Forces Front)

**FSSI** Fellow of the Statistical Society of Ireland

**FSSU** Federated Superannuation Scheme for Universities

**FSTD** Fellow of the Society of Typographic Designers

**FSU** family service unit

**FSUC** Federal Statistics Unit Conference

**FSVA** Fellow of the Incorporated Society of Valuers and Auctioneers

**ft** feint • *Med.* fiat (Latin: let there be made) • *symbol for* foot (*or* feet) • fort

**ft.** fortification • fortify

**f.t.** formal training • full terms

**Ft** *symbol for* forint (Hungarian monetary unit) • Fort

**FT** *Meteorol.* feet (unit) • Financial Times • (*or* **F-T**) *Chem.* Fischer–Tropsch (in **FT process**) • *Physics, Maths.* Fourier transform • *British vehicle registration for* Newcastle upon Tyne

**FTA** *Med.* fluorescent treponemal antibody • Free Trade Agreement • Freight Transport Association • Future Teachers of America

**FTA (Index)** Financial Times Actuaries Share Index

**FTAM** *Computing* file transfer, access, and management

**FTASI** Financial Times Actuaries All-Share Index

**FTAT** Furniture, Timber, and Allied Trades Union

**FTB** fleet torpedo bomber

**ftbrg.** footbridge

**FTC** (USA) Federal Trade Commission • (USA) flight test center • flying training command • Full Technological Certificate (of City and Guilds Institute)

**FTCD** Fellow of Trinity College, Dublin

**FTCL** Fellow of Trinity College of Music, London

**FTD** foreign technology division

**FTDA** Fellow of the Theatrical Designers and Craftsmen's Association

**f.t.e.** full-time equivalent

**FTESA** Foundry Trades Equipment and Supplies Association

**ftg** fitting

**FTG** Fuji Texaco Gas

**fth.** (*or* **fthm**) fathom

**FTI** Fellow of the Textile Institute

**FTII** Fellow of the Institute of Taxation

**FT (Index)** Financial Times Ordinary Share Index

**FT-IR** *Chem.* Fourier-transform infra-red (in **FT-IR spectroscopy**)

**ft-lb** foot-pound

**Ft Lieut** Flight Lieutenant

**FTM** flying training manual • *Med.* fractional test meal

**ft. mist.** *Med.* fiat mistura (Latin: let a mixture be made)

**FT-NMR** *Chem.* Fourier-transform nuclear magnetic resonance (in **FT-NMR spectroscopy**)

**FTO** Fleet Torpedo Officer

**FT Ord** Financial Times (Industrial) Ordinary Share Index

**FTP** Fellow of Thames Polytechnic • *Computing* file-transfer protocol

**FTPA** Fellow of the Town and Country Planning Association

**ft. pulv.** *Med.* fiat pulvis (Latin: let a powder be made)

**ft/s** feet (*or* foot) per second

**ft/s²** feet (*or* foot) per second squared

**FTS** Fellow of the Australian Academy of Technological Sciences and Engineering • Fellow of the Tourism Society • flying training school • *Chem.* Fourier-transform spectroscopy

**FTSC** Fellow of the Tonic Sol-Fa College

**FTSE 100** (*or* **FT-SE 100**) Financial Times Stock Exchange 100 Index (*or* Footsie)

**fttr** fitter

**FTU** (Hong Kong) Federation of Trade Unions • *Photog.* Freeman time-unit

**FTW** *Commerce* free-trade wharf

**FTZ** free-trade zone

**FU** Farmers' Union • feed unit • *Photog.* Freeman time-unit • (Germany) Freie Universität (Free University of Berlin) • *British vehicle registration for* Lincoln

**FUACE** Fédération universelle des associations chrétiennes d'étudiants (French: World Student Christian Federation)

**FUEN** Federal Union of European Nationalities

**FUMIST** Fellow of the University of Manchester Institute of Science and Technology

**fund.** fundamental

**fur.** furlong(s) • further

**furn.** furnace • furnish(ed) • furniture

**fus.** fuselage • fusilier

**fut.** future • *Finance* futures

**FUW** Farmers' Union of Wales

**f.v.** fire vent • fishing vessel • flush valve • (*or* **fv**) folio verso (Latin: on the reverse (i.e. left-hand) page)

**FV** *British vehicle registration for* Preston

**FVC** *Med.* forced vital capacity (in respiratory function tests)

**FVRDE** Fighting Vehicle Research and Development Establishment

**FW** *Chem.* formula weight • fresh water • *British vehicle registration for* Lincoln

**FWA** Factories and Workshops Act • Family Welfare Association • (USA) Federal Works Agency • Fellow of the World Academy of Arts and Sciences • Free Wales Army

**FWAG** Farming and Wildlife Advisory Group

**f.w.b.** four wheel brake (*or* braking)

**FWB** Free Will Baptists

**FWCC** Friends' World Committee for Consultation

**fwd** forward

**f.w.d.** four-wheel drive • front-wheel drive

**fwdg** forwarding

**FWeldI** Fellow of the Welding Institute

**FWFM** Federation of Wholesale Fish Merchants

**f.w.h.** flexible working hours

**FWHM** *Physics* full width at half maximum (in spectroscopy)

**FWI** Federation of West Indies • French West Indies

**FWL** Foundation of World Literacy

**FWO** Federation of Wholesale Organizations • Fleet Wireless Officer

**FWPCA** (USA) Federal Water Pollution Control Administration

**FWS** fighter weapons school • fleet work study

**FWSG** farm water supply grant

**fwt** *Boxing* featherweight

**f.w.t.** (*or* **FWT**) fair wear and tear

**FX** *British vehicle registration for* Bournemouth • (*or* **f.x.**) foreign exchange • Francis Xavier (1506–52, Spanish Jesuit missionary) • *Films, Theatre* special effects (from phonetic spelling of *effects*)

**fxd** fixed • foxed

**fxg** fixing

**fxle** *Nautical* forecastle

**FY** *postcode for* Blackpool • (*or* **f.y.**) (USA, Canada) fiscal year • *British fishing port registration for* Fowey • *British vehicle registration for* Liverpool

**FYC** Family and Youth Concern

**FYI** (*or* **f.y.i.**) for your information

**FYM** farmyard manure

**FYP** *Economics* Five-Year Plan

**fz.** *Music* forzando *or* forzato (Italian; to be strongly accentuated)

**FZ** *British vehicle registration for* Belfast • *Meteorol.* freezing • Free Zone • French Zone

**FZA** (USA) Fellow of the Zoological Academy

**FZDZ** *Meteorol.* freezing drizzle

**FZFG** *Meteorol.* freezing fog

**FZGB** Federation of Zoological Gardens of Great Britain and Ireland

**FZRA** *Meteorol.* freezing rain

**FZS** Fellow of the Zoological Society

**F-Zug** Fernschnellzug (German: long-distance express train)

# G

**g** *Physics, symbol for* acceleration of free fall • (ital.) *Physics, symbol for* degeneracy • *Meteorol., symbol for* gale • gallon(s) • *Chem.* gaseous (as in $H_2O(g)$) • *Physics* gerade (German: even; in spectroscopy) • *Physics, symbol for* gluon • (superscript) *Maths., symbol for* grade (as in **20ᵍ**) • *symbol for* gram(s) • *Physics, symbol for* grav • *indicating* the seventh row of vertical squares from the left on a chessboard

**g.** garage • gauche (French: left) • gauge • gelding • gender • general • genitive • geographical (as in **g. mile**) • gilt • goal(keeper) • gold • government • grand • great • green • grey • gros *or* grosse (French: large) • guardian • guide • guilder(s) • guinea(s) • *Navy* gunnery

**G** (ital.) *Physics, symbol for* conductance • *Irish fishing port registration for* Galway • *Magnetism, symbol for* gauss • *Films* (Australia, USA) general exhibition (certification) • (ital.) *Thermodynamics, symbol for* Gibbs function • *symbol for* giga- (prefix indicating 10⁹, as in **GHz** (gigahertz), *or* (in computing) 2³⁰) • *postcode for* Glasgow • *Biochem., symbol for* glycine • *symbol for* gourde (Haitian monetary unit) • *Slang* grand (1000

pounds or dollars) • (ital.) *Physics, symbol for* gravitational constant • *Biochem., symbol for* guanine • *Biochem., symbol for* guanosine • *symbol for* guarani (Paraguayan monetary unit) • *Botany* gynoecium (in a floral formula) • (ital.) *Physics, symbol for* shear modulus • *Meteorol., symbol for* storm • *international civil aircraft marking for* UK • *indicating* a musical note or key • *Astronomy, indicating* a spectral type

**G.** (*or* **G**) German(y) • good • green • Guernsey • Gulf (on maps, etc.)

**G³** *Electronics* gadolinium gallium garnet

**G3** Group of Three (most powerful western economies)

**G5** *Finance* Group of Five (nations that agreed to exchange-rate stabilization)

**G7** (*or* **G-7**) Group of Seven (leading industrial nations)

**G10** *Finance* Group of Ten (nations lending money to the IMF)

**G24** Group of Twenty Four (industrialized nations)

**G77** Group of Seventy Seven (developing countries)

**g.a.** *Marine insurance* general average

**Ga** *Chem., symbol for* gallium

**Ga.** Gallic • Georgia

**GA** Gaelic Athletic (Club) • Gamblers Anonymous • garrison artillery • *airline flight code for* Garuda Indonesia • general agent • *Linguistics* General American • general anaesthetic • General Assembly (of the UN) • general assignment • *Marine insurance* general average • Geographical Association • Geologists' Association • *US postcode for* Georgia • *Botany, symbol for* gibberellin (as in **GA₃**) • *British vehicle registration for* Glasgow • *Sport* goal attack • government actuary • graphic arts

**G/A** *Marine insurance* general average • (*or* **g/a**) ground to air

**GAA** (Ireland) Gaelic Athletic Association

**Gab.** Gabon

**GAB** general arrangements to borrow (in the IMF)

**GABA** ('gæbə) *Biochem.* gamma-aminobutyric acid (a neurotransmitter)

**GAC** *Chem.* granular activated carbon

**GAD** *Biochem.* glutamic acid decarboxylase

**Gael.** (*or* **Gae.**) Gaelic

**GAFTA** ('gæftə) Grain and Free Trade Association

**GAG** *Biochem.* glycosaminoglycan

**GAI** (USA) guaranteed annual income • Guild of Architectural Ironmongers

**gal** (*or* **gal.**) gallon(s)

**Gal** *Geophysics, symbol for* gal • *Biochem.* galactose

**Gal.** *Bible* Galatians • Galicia • Galway

**gall.** gallery • gallon

**GALT** *Med.* gut-associated lymphoid tissue

**galv.** galvanic • galvanize(d) • galvanometer

**Gam.** Gambia

**GAM** (gæm) guided aircraft missile

**G&AE** *Accounting* general and administrative expense

**G and O** *Med.* gas and oxygen (in anaesthetic)

**G & S** Gilbert and Sullivan

**G & T** (*or* **g and t**) gin and tonic

**GAO** (USA) General Accounting Office

**GAP** (gæp) general assembly programme • Great American Public

**GAPAN** (*or* **Gapan**) ('gæpæn) Guild of Air Pilots and Air Navigators

**GAPCE** General Assembly of the Presbyterian Church of England

**gar.** garage • garrison

**GAR** Grand Army of the Republic (in the American Civil War) • guided aircraft rocket

**gard.** garden

**GARIOA** government aid and relief in occupied areas

**GARP** (gɑ:p) Global Atmospheric Research Programme

**GASC** German-American Securities Corporation

**GASP** (gɑ:sp) (USA) Group Against Smokers' Pollution

**gastroent.** gastroenterological • gastroenterology

**GATCO** ('gæt,kəʊ) Guild of Air Traffic Control Officers

**GATT** (*or* **Gatt**) (gæt) General Agreement on Tariffs and Trade

**GAUFCC** General Assembly of Unitarian and Free Christian Churches

**GAV** *Accounting* gross annual value

**GAW** guaranteed annual wage

**GAWF** Greek Animal Welfare Fund

**gaz.** gazette • gazetteer

**Gb** *Magnetism, symbol for* gilbert

**GB** *Med.* gall bladder • Gas Board • Girls' Brigade • *British vehicle registration for* Glasgow • government and binding • *Crystallog.* grain boundary • Great Britain (abbrev. *or* IVR) • guide book • gunboat

**GBA** *international vehicle registration for* Alderney • Governing Bodies Association

**GB and I** Great Britain and Ireland

**GBCW** Governing Body of the Church in Wales

**GBDO** Guild of British Dispensing Opticians

**GBE** (Knight *or* Dame) Grand Cross of the Order of the British Empire

**GBG** *international vehicle registration for* Guernsey

**GBGSA** Governing Bodies of Girls' Schools Association

**GBH** grievous bodily harm

**GBJ** *international vehicle registration for* Jersey

**GBM** *international vehicle registration for* Isle of Man

**GBN** *Chem.* graphite boron nitride

**g.b.o.** goods in bad order

**GBP** *Biochem.* glutamate-binding protein • great British public

**GBRE** General Board of Religious Education

**GBS** George Bernard Shaw (1856–1950, Irish-born dramatist and critic)

**GBSM** Graduate of Birmingham and Midland Institute School of Music

**GBTA** Guild of Business Travel Agents

**GBZ** *international vehicle registration for* Gibraltar

**GC** *Astronomy* galactic centre • gas chromatograph(ic) • gas chromatography • Gas Council • *Chem.* gel chromatography • George Cross • gliding club • Goldsmiths' College • golf club • good conduct • government chemist • Grand Chancellor • Grand Chaplain • Grand Chapter • Grand Conductor • Grand Cross • *British vehicle registration for* SW London

**GCA** Girls' Clubs of America • *Aeronautics* ground-controlled approach • *international vehicle registration for* Guatemala

**G Capt** Group Captain

**GCB** (Knight *or* Dame) Grand Cross of the Order of the Bath

**GCBS** General Council of British Shipping

**GCC** Gas Consumers Council • Girton College, Cambridge • Gonville and Caius College, Cambridge • Gulf Cooperation Council

**GCD** general and complete disarmament • (*or* **g.c.d.**) *Maths.* greatest common divisor

**GCE** General Certificate of Education • (USA) General College Entrance

**GCF** (*or* **g.c.f.**) *Maths.* greatest common factor

**GCH** (Knight) Grand Cross of the Hanoverian Order • Guild Certificate of Hairdressing

**GCHQ** Government Communications Headquarters

**GCI** *Aeronautics* ground-controlled interception

**GCIE** (Knight) Grand Commander of the Order of the Indian Empire

**GCIU** (USA) Graphic Communications International Union

**GCL** Guild of Cleaners and Launderers

**GCLJ** Grand Cross of St Lazarus of Jerusalem

**GCLH** Grand Cross of the Legion of Honour

**GCM** *Meteorol.* general circulation model • general court martial • Good Conduct Medal • (*or* **g.c.m.**) *Statistics*

greatest common measure • (*or* **g.c.m.**) *Maths.* greatest common multiple

**GCMG** (Knight *or* Dame) Grand Cross of the Order of St Michael and St George

**GCMS** gas-chromatography mass spectroscopy

**GCO** *Navy* Gun Control Officer

**GCON** Grand Cross of the Order of the Niger

**GCR** ground-controlled radar

**GCRO** General Council and Register of Osteopaths

**GCSE** General Certificate of Secondary Education

**GCSG** (Knight) Grand Cross of the Order of St Gregory the Great

**GCSI** (Knight) Grand Commander of the Order of the Star of India

**GCSJ** (Knight) Grand Cross of Justice of the Order of St John of Jerusalem

**GCStJ** (Bailiff *or* Dame) Grand Cross of the Most Venerable Order of the Hospital of St John of Jerusalem

**GCVO** (Knight *or* Dame) Grand Cross of the Royal Victorian Order

**gd** good • grand-daughter • ground

**g.d.** general duties • grand-daughter • gravimetric density

**Gd** *Chem., symbol for* gadolinium

**GD** *Obstet.* gestational day • *British vehicle registration for* Glasgow • *Electronics* glow discharge • *Netball* goal defence • Graduate in Divinity • Grand Duke (*or* Duchess *or* Duchy) • Gunnery Division

**GDBA** Guide Dogs for the Blind Association

**GDC** General Dental Council • General Dynamics Corporation

**Gdk** Gdansk

**gdn** garden • guardian

**Gdns** Gardens

**GDP** (*or* **gdp**) gross domestic product • *Biochem.* guanosine diphosphate

**GDR** German Democratic Republic (East Germany; now part of Germany)

**gds** goods

**Gds** Guards

**Gdsm.** Guardsman

**g.e.** *Bookbinding* gilt edges

**Ge** *Chem., symbol for* germanium

**GE** garrison engineer • general election • (USA) General Electric (Company) • *British vehicle registration for* Glasgow • *British fishing port registration for* Goole • gross energy • *airline flight code for* Guernsey Airlines

**GEA** Garage Equipment Association

**geb.** geboren (German: born) • gebunden (German: bound)

**GEBCO** ('gɛbkəʊ) general bathymetric chart of the oceans

**Gebr.** Gebrüder (German: brothers)

**GEC** (UK) General Electric Company

**GED** general educational development

**gegr.** gegründet (German: founded)

**gel.** gelatin

**Gem** *Astronomy* Gemini

**GEM** genetically engineered microorganism • (dʒɛm) ground effect machine (air-cushion vehicle) • guidance evaluation missile • Guild of Experienced Motorists

**GEMS** (dʒɛmz) Global Environmental Monitoring System (in the UN)

**gen.** gender • genealogy • general(ly) • generator • generic • genetic(s) • genital • genitive • genuine • *Biology* genus

**Gen.** General • *Bible* Genesis • Geneva • Genoa

**gen. av.** *Marine insurance* general average

**gend.** gendarme (French: policeman)

**geneal.** genealogy

**genit.** genitive

**Genl** General

**genn.** gennaio (Italian: January)

**GEO** geostationary (*or* geosynchronous) earth orbit

**geod.** geodesy • geodetic

**geog.** geographer • geographic(al) • geography

**geol.** geologic(al) • geologist • geology

**geom.** geometric(al) • geometry

**geon** (*or* **GEON**) ('dʒɪɒn) gyro-erected optical navigation

**geophys.** geophysics

**geopol.** geopolitics

**GEOREF** ('dʒɪəʊˌrɛf) World Geographic Reference System

**ger.** gerund(ive)

**Ger.** German(y)

**GER** gross energy requirement

**Gerbil** ('dʒɜːbɪl) Great Education Reform Bill (1988)

**Ges.** Gesellschaft (German: company *or* society)

**gest.** gestorben (German: deceased)

**Gestapo** (gɛ'stɑːpəʊ) Geheime Staatspolizei (German: secret state police; in Nazi Germany)

**GETT** (USA) Grants Equal To Tax

**GeV** *Physics, symbol for* gigaelectron-volt(s)

**gez.** gezeichnet (German: signed)

**GF** General Foods Ltd • glass fibre • government form • gradient freezing • *Maths.* Green function • Guggenheim Foundation • *symbol for* Guinean franc • airline flight code for Gulf Air • *British vehicle registration for* SW London

**g.f.a.** *Commerce* good fair average • *Commerce* good freight agent

**GFCM** General Fisheries Council for the Mediterranean (in the FAO)

**GFD** geophysical fluid dynamics

**GFG** (ital.) Good Food Guide

**GFH** George Frederick Handel (1685–1759, German composer)

**GFOFs** *Stock exchange* geared futures and options funds

**GFR** German Federal Republic • *Med.* glomerular filtration rate

**GFS** Girls' Friendly Society

**GFTU** (USA) General Federation of Trade Unions

**GFWC** General Federation of Women's Clubs

**g.g.** gas generator

**GG** *Med.* gamma globulin • Girl Guides • *British vehicle registration for* Glasgow • Governor General • great gross • Grenadier Guards

**GGC** generalized genetic code

**ggd** (*or* **g.gd.**) great grand-daughter

**gge** garage

**GGG** *Electronics* gadolinium gallium garnet

**g.gr.** great gross (144 dozen)

**ggs** (*or* **g.gs.**) great grandson

**GGSM** Graduate (in Music) of the Guildhall School of Music and Drama

**GH** general hospital • *international vehicle registration for* Ghana • airline flight code for Ghana Airways • *British fishing port registration for* Grangemouth • *Military* Green Howards • Greenwich Hospital • *Biochem.* growth hormone • *British vehicle registration for* SW London

**GHA** *Astronomy* Greenwich hour angle

**GHCIMA** Graduate of the Hotel Catering and Institutional Management Association

**g.h.e.** ground handling equipment

**GHI** Good Housekeeping Institute

**GHM** *Physics* generalized Hall model

**GHMS** Graduate in Homeopathic Medicine and Surgery

**GHOST** (gəʊst) global horizontal sounding technique (for collecting atmospheric data)

**GHQ** *Military* General Headquarters

**GHRH** *Biochem.* growth-hormone-releasing hormone

**GHS** Girls' High School

**GHz** *symbol for* gigahertz

**gi.** gill (unit of measure)

**Gi** *Magnetism, symbol for* gilbert

**GI** (*or* **g.i.**) galvanized iron • (*or* **g.i.**) gastrointestinal • generic issue • (Royal) Glasgow Institute (of the Fine Arts) • (USA) government (*or* general) issue (hence, a US serviceman) • Government of India • *Biochem.* growth inhibitor • *Irish vehicle registration for* Tipperary

**GIA** Garuda Indonesian Airways

**Gib.** Gibraltar

**GIB** Gulf International Bank

**GIC** *Chem.* graphite intercalation compound • Guilde internationale des coopératrices (French: International Cooperative Women's Guild)

**GIE** Graduate of the Institute of Engineers and Technicians

**GIEE** Graduate of the Institution of Electrical Engineers

**GIFT** (gɪft) *Med.* gamete intrafallopian transfer (for assisting conception)

**GIGO** (*or* **gigo**) ('gaɪgəʊ) *Computing* garbage in, garbage out

**GIMechE** Graduate of the Institution of Mechanical Engineers

**GINO** ('dʒiːnəʊ) graphical input output (for computer graphics)

**GInstAEA** Graduate of the Institute of Automotive Engineer Assessors

**GInstT** Graduate of the Institute of Transport

**GINucE** Graduate of the Institution of Nuclear Engineers

**gio.** (*or* **giov.**) giovedì (Italian: Thursday)

**GIP** (*or* **g.i.p.**) glazed imitation parchment (a type of paper)

**GIS** *Computing* geographical (*or* geological) information system

**GISS** Goddard Institute for Space Studies

**giu.** giugno (Italian: June)

**GIUK** Greenland, Iceland, United Kingdom

**GIXS** *Physics* grazing-incidence X-ray scattering

**GJ** *British vehicle registration for* SW London

**GJD** *Freemasonry* Grand Junior Deacon

**Gk** Greek

**GK** goalkeeper • *British fishing port registration for* Greenock • *British vehicle registration for* SW London

**GKA** Garter King of Arms

**GKC** G(ilbert) K(eith) Chesterton (1874–1936, British journalist and author)

**GKS** graphics kernel system (for computer graphics)

**gl.** gill (unit of measure) • glass • gloss

**g/l** grams per litre

**Gl.** Gloria (Latin: glory; in the liturgy)

**GL** *Shipping* (Germany) Germanischer Lloyd (classification society) • *postcode for* Gloucester • *Printing* gothic letter • government laboratory • *Freemasonry* Grand Lodge • Grand Luxe (of a car) • ground level • gun licence • *British vehicle registration for* Truro

**4GL** *Computing* fourth-generation language

**glab.** *Botany* glabrous

**GLAB** Greater London Arts Board

**glam** (glæm) *Colloquial* greying, leisured, affluent, married

**Glam.** Glamorgan

**Glas.** Glasgow

**glau.** *Botany* glaucous

**GLB** Girls' Life Brigade

**GLC** *Chem.* gas–liquid chromatography • Greater London Council (abolished 1986) • ground-level concentration (of radioactive material) • Guild of Lettering Craftsmen

**GLCM** Graduate of the London College of Music • ground-launched cruise missile

**gld.** guilder

**GLDP** Greater London Development Plan

**GLM** *Skiing* graduated length method

**Gln** (*or* **gln**) *Biochem.* glutamine

**GLOBECOM** ('gləʊbkɒm) *US Air Force* Global Communications System

**GLOMEX** ('gləʊmeks) Global Oceanographic and Meteorological Experiment (1975–80)

**GLORIA** ('glɔːrɪə) Geological Long Range Asdic

**Glos** Gloucestershire

**gloss.** glossary

**GLS** *Freemasonry* Grand Lodge of Scotland

**glt** *Bookbinding* gilt

**GLT** greetings letter telegram

**Glu** (*or* **glu**) *Biochem.* glutamic acid

**Gly** (*or* **gly**) *Biochem.* glycine

**gm** gram

**g m** *symbol for* gram metre

**gm²** grams per square metre (used in measuring weight of paper)

**GM** *Physics* Geiger–Müller (as in **GM counter**) • general manager • general merchandise • general mortgage • General Motors Corporation • Geological Museum • geometric mean • George Medal • gold medal(list) • Grand Marshall • *Freemasonry* Grand Master • *Education* grant maintained • guided missile • *British vehicle registration for* Reading

**GMAG** Genetic Manipulation Advisory Group

**G-man** (USA) Government man (an FBI agent)

**g.m.b.** good merchantable brand

**GMB** General, Municipal, Boilermakers (trade union; formerly GMBATU; GMWU) • Grand Master (of the Order) of the Bath • *Archery* Grand Master Bowman

**GMBATU** (formerly) General, Municipal, Boilermakers' and Allied Trades Union (*see under* GMB)

**GMBE** Grand Master of the Order of the British Empire

**GmbH** (Germany) Gesellschaft mit beschränkter Haftung (private limited company; Ltd)

**Gmc** Germanic

**GMC** general management committee • General Medical Council • *Astronomy* giant molecular cloud • Guild of Memorial Craftsmen

**GMF** Glass Manufacturers' Federation

**GMIE** Grand Master of the Order of the Indian Empire

**GMKP** Grand Master of the Knights of St Patrick

**GMMG** Grand Master of the Order of St Michael and St George

**GMO** genetically modified organism

**GMP** (USA) Glass, Molders, Pottery, Plastics, and Allied Workers International Union • Grand Master of the Order of St Patrick • gross material product • *Biochem.* guanosine monophosphate • Gurkha Military Police

**g.m.q.** good merchantable quality

**GMR** ground-mapping radar

**GMS** *Education* grant-maintained status

**GMSC** General Medical Services Committee

**GMSI** Grand Master of the Order of the Star of India

**GMST** *Astronomy* Greenwich Mean Sidereal Time

**GMT** Greenwich Mean Time

**GMV** *Microbiol.* golden mosaic virus

**GMW** gram-molecular weight

**GMWU** (formerly) General and Municipal Workers' Union (*see under* GMB)

**gn.** guinea

**g.n.** grandnephew • grandniece

**GN** (USA) Graduate Nurse • *British fishing port registration for* Granton • *British vehicle registration for* SW London

**GNAS** Grand National Archery Society

**GNC** General Nursing Council (replaced by UKCC)

**gnd** ground

**GND** *Meteorol.* ground

**GNMA** (USA) Government National Mortgage Association

**GNP** gross national product

**Gnr** *Military* Gunner

**GNR** (Portugal) Guarda Nacional Republicana (National Republican Guard)

**GnRH** *Biochem.* gonadotrophin-releasing hormone

**gns** guineas

**GNTC** Girls' Nautical Training Corps

**GNVQ** General National Vocational Qualification

**GO** gas operated • General Office(r) • *Military* general order • *Music* great organ • Group Officer • *British vehicle registration for* SW London

**g.o.b.** good ordinary brand

**GOC** General Officer Commanding • General Optical Council • Greek Orthodox Church

**GOC-in-C** General Officer Commanding-in-Chief

**GOCO** government-owned, contractor-operated

**GOE** General Ordination Examination

**GOES** (USA) Geostationary Operational Environmental Satellite

**GOM** Grand Old Man

**GOP** (USA) Grand Old Party (the Republican Party)

**Gopa** ('gəupə) Government Oil and Pipeline Agency

**Gosplan** ('gɒs,plæn) (USSR) State Planning Commission (Russian *Gos(udarstvennaya) Plan(ovaya) Comissiya)*)

**Gosud.** Gosudarstvo (Russian: state)

**GOT** *Biochem., Med.* glutamatic oxaloacetatic transaminase (renamed aspartate aminotransferase, AST)

**Goth.** Gothic

**gou.** gourde (Haitian monetary unit)

**Gov.** (*or* **gov.**) government · governor

**Gov-Gen** Governor-General

**Govt** (*or* **govt**) government

**gox** (*or* **GOX**) (gɒks) *Chem.* gaseous oxygen

**gp** (*or* **Gp**) group

**g.p.** *Printing* galley proofs · *Maths.* geometrical progression · *Printing* great primer

**GP** Gallup Poll · gas-permeable (of contact lenses) · general paralysis · *Music* general pause · general practitioner · general purpose · Gloria Patri (Latin: glory be to the Father) · graduated pension · Graduate in Pharmacy · grand(e) passion · Grand Prix · *British vehicle registration for* SW London

**GPA** General Practitioners' Association · *Education* (USA) grade point average

**GPALS** Global Protection Against Limited Strikes (reduced SDI programme)

**GPC** *Chem.* gel permeation chromatography · general purposes committee

**Gp Capt** Group Captain

**Gp Comdr** Group Commander

**gpd** gallons per day

**GPDST** Girls' Public Day School Trust

**gph** (*or* **GPH**) gallons per hour

**GPh** Graduate in Pharmacy

**GPHI** Guild of Public Health Inspectors

**GPI** *Med.* general paralysis of the insane

**GPIB** *Computing* general-purpose interface bus

**GPKT** Grand Priory of the Knights of the Temple

**GPM** (*or* **gpm**) gallons per minute · (USA) graduated payment mortgage · *Freemasonry* Grand Past Master

**GPMU** Graphical, Paper, and Media Union (formed by merger of NGA and SOGAT)

**GPO** General Post Office · (USA) Government Printing Office

**GPR** genio populi Romani (Latin: to the genius of the Roman people) · ground-penetrating radar

**GPS** (*or* **gps**) gallons per second · Global Positioning System (US defence satellite) · Graduated Pension Scheme · (Australia) Great Public Schools (indicating a group of mainly nonstate schools, and of sporting competitions between them)

**GPT** *Biochem., Med.* glutamic pyruvic transaminase (renamed alanine aminotransferase, ALT) · Guild of Professional Toastmasters

**GPU** General Postal Union (*see* UPU) · (USA) General Public Utilities Corporation · Gosudarstvennoye Politicheskoye Upravlenie (Russian: State Political Administration; Soviet state security system, 1922–23)

**GQ** *Military* general quarters

**GQG** Grand Quartier Général (French: General Headquarters)

**gr.** grade · (*or* **gr**) grain (the unit) · gram · grammar · grand · great(er) · grey · gross · ground · group

**Gr** (ital.) *Physics, symbol for* Grashof number · Gunner

**Gr.** Grecian · Greece · Greek

**GR** *Science* gamma ray · general reconnaissance · *Physics* general relativity · general reserve · Georgius Rex (Latin: King George) · *British fishing port registration for* Gloucester · grand recorder · *international vehicle registration for* Greece · ground rent · Gulielmus Rex (Latin: King William) · Gurkha Rifles · *British vehicle registration for* Newcastle upon Tyne

**GRA** Game Research Association · Greyhound Racing Association

**grad** (græd) *Maths.* gradient

**grad.** grading · gradual · graduate(d)

**GradIAE** Graduate of the Institution of Automobile Engineers

**GradIM** Graduate of the Institute of Metals

**GradInstBE** Graduate Member of the Institution of British Engineers

**GradInstP** Graduate of the Institute of Physics

**GradInstR** Graduate of the Institute of Refrigeration

**GradIPM** Graduate of the Institute of Personnel Management

**GradPRI** Graduate of the Plastics and Rubber Institute

**GradSE** Graduate of the Society of Engineers

**gram.** grammar(ian) · grammatical

**GRAS** (USA) generally regarded as safe

**GRB** *Astronomy* gamma-ray burst

**GRBI** Gardeners' Royal Benevolent Institution

**Gr. Br.** (*or* **Gr. Brit.**) Great Britain

**GRBS** Gardeners' Royal Benevolent Society

**GRC** General Research Corporation

**Gr. Capt.** Group Captain

**GRCM** Graduate of the Royal College of Music

**GRDF** Gulf Rapid Deployment Force

**GRE** (USA) Graduate Record Examination • grant-related expenditure • Guardian Royal Exchange Assurance plc

**gr.f.** *Horse racing* grey filly

**GRF** *Biochem.* growth-hormone releasing factor

**GRI** (New Zealand) guaranteed retirement income

**Gr-L** Graeco-Latin

**grn** green

**GRN** goods received note

**gro.** gross (unit of quantity)

**GRO** Gamma Ray Observatory • General Register Office • Greenwich Royal Observatory

**GROBDM** General Register Office for Births, Deaths, and Marriages

**gro. t.** gross tons (*or* tonnage)

**grp** group

**GRP** *Biochem.* gastrin-releasing peptide • glass- (*or* glassfibre-)reinforced plastic (*or* polyester)

**grs** grains • gross

**GRS** *Astronomy* Great Red Spot (Jupiter)

**GRSC** Graduate of the Royal Society of Chemistry

**GRSE** Guild of Radio Service Engineers

**GRSM** Graduate of the Royal Schools of Music

**gr. t.** gross ton

**GRT** (*or* **g.r.t.**) gross registered tonnage

**Gru** *Astronomy* Grus

**GRU** (ex-USSR) Glavnoye Razvedyvatelnoye Upravleniye (Central Intelligence Office)

**gr. wt.** gross weight

**g.r.y.** *Finance* gross redemption yield

**gs.** guineas

**g.s.** (*or* **gs**) grandson • *Aeronautics* groundspeed

**Gs** *Magnetism, symbol for* gauss

**GS** (USA) General Schedule (civil service job-classification scheme) • General Secretary • general service • *Military* General Staff • geographical survey • geological survey • *Netball* goal shooter • gold standard • grammar school • *British vehicle registration for* Luton

**GSA** (USA) General Services Administration • Girl Scouts of America • Girls' Schools Association • Glasgow School of Art

**GS&WR** (Ireland) Great Southern and Western Railway

**GSB** Government Savings Bank

**GSC** *Chem.* gas–solid chromatography • General Service Corps • (USA) General Staff Corps

**GSD** general supply depot

**GSE** ground service (*or* support) equipment

**GSEE** Geniki Synomospondia Ergaton Hellados (Greek General Confederation of Labour)

**GSL** Geological Society of London • group scout leader • (USA) guaranteed student loan

**gsm** gram per square metre (unit indicating paper thickness)

**g.s.m.** *Commerce* good sound merchantable (quality)

**GSM** Garrison Sergeant-Major • general sales manager • General Service Medal • (*or* **GSMD**) (Member of the) Guildhall School of Music and Drama

**GSO** General Staff Officer

**GSP** *Chem.* glassfibre-strengthened polyester • Good Service Pension • *Economics* gross social product

**GSR** galvanic skin reflex (*or* response)

**GSS** geostationary satellite • global surveillance system • Government Statistical Service

**GST** (New Zealand, Canada) goods and services tax • *Astronomy* Greenwich Sidereal Time • *Meteorol.* gust

**g-st** *Knitting* garter-stitch

**GSW** gunshot wound

**gt** *Bookbinding* gilt • great

**gt.** *Med.* gutta (Latin: a drop)

**g.t.** gas tight • gross tonnage

**GT** gas turbine • *Physics* gauge theory • *airline flight code for* GB Airways • Good Templar • *Freemasonry* Grand Tiler • Gran Turismo (Italian: grand touring; sports car) • greetings telegram • *British vehicle registration for* SW London

**GTA** gas–tungsten arc

**Gt Brit.** (*or* **Gt Br.**) Great Britain

**GTC** (Scotland) General Teaching Council • Girls' Training Corps • (*or* **g.t.c.**) *Commerce* good till cancelled (*or* countermanded) • Government Training Centre

**GTCL** Graduate of Trinity College of Music, London

**gtd** guaranteed

**gtee** guarantee

**GTI** Gran Turismo Injection (sports car)

**g.t.m.** good this month

**GTO** Gran Turismo Omologata (Italian: certified for grand touring; of sports cars)

**GTP** *Biochem.* guanosine triphosphate

**gtr** greater

**GTR** general theory of relativity

**GTS** gas turbine ship • (USA) General Theological Seminary

**gtt.** *Med.* guttae (Latin: drops) • *Med.* guttatim (Latin: drop by drop)

**GTT** *Med.* glucose tolerance test

**g.t.w.** good this week

**gu.** guinea • *Heraldry* gules (red)

**Gu.** Guinea

**GU** gastric ulcer • (*or* **g.u.**) genito-urinary • *US postcode for* Guam • *British fishing port registration for* Guernsey • *postcode for* Guildford • *British vehicle registration for* SE London

**guar.** guarantee(d)

**Guat.** Guatemala

**gui.** *Music* guitar

**GUI** Golfing Union of Ireland • ('guːɪ) *Computing* graphic user interface

**GUIDO** (*or* **Guido**) ('gaɪdəu) *Astronautics* (USA) Guidance Officer

**guil.** guilder

**Guin.** Guinea

**Gulag** ('guːlæg) Glavnoye Upravleniye Lagerei (Soviet prison and labour camp system)

**GUM** genito-urinary medicine • (gʊm) (Russia) Gosudarstvenni Universalni Magazin (Universal State Store)

**gun.** gunnery

**GUR** *Med.* glucose utilization rate

**GUS** Great Universal Stores

**GUT** (gʌt) *Physics* grand unified theory

**guttat.** *Med.* guttatim (Latin: drop by drop)

**g.u.v.** gerecht und vollkommen (German: correct and complete)

**GUY** *international vehicle registration for* Guyana

**g.v.** gravimetric volume • gross valuation

**GV** (France) grande vitesse (fast goods train) • *British vehicle registration for* Ipswich

**GVH** *Med.* graft-versus-host

**GVHD** *Med.* graft-versus-host disease

**gvt** (*or* **Gvt**) government

**GVW** gross vehicle weight

**GW** George Washington (1732–99, US president 1789–97) • *symbol for* gigawatt(s) • *British fishing port registration for* Glasgow • guided weapons (as in **GW cruiser**) • *British vehicle registration for* SE London

**GWP** Government White Paper • gross world product

**GWR** Great Western Railway

**GWS** *Physics* Glashow–Weinberg–Salam (in **GWS theory**)

**GX** *British vehicle registration for* SE London

**Gy** *Physics, symbol for* gray

**GY** *British fishing port registration for* Grimsby • *British vehicle registration for* SE London

**gyn.** (*or* **GYN, gynaecol.**) gynaecological • gynaecology

**GZ** *British vehicle registration for* Belfast

**G-Z** *Astronomy* Giacobini–Zinner (a comet)

# H

**h** (ital.) *Physics, symbol for* heat transfer coefficient • *symbol for* hecto- (prefix indicating 100, as in **hm**, hectometre) • (ital.) *symbol for* height • *symbol for* hour • (ital.) *Physics, symbol for* Planck constant • (ital.) *Thermodynamics, symbol for* specific enthalpy • (ital.) *Maths., indicating* a small increment •

*indicating* the eighth vertical row of squares from the left on a chessboard

**h.** harbour • hard(ness) • heat • height • high • hip • *Sport* hit • horizontal • *Music* horn • horse • hot • hour • house • hundred • husband

**H** (bold ital.) *Mechanics, symbol for* angular impulse • (ital.) *Physics, Med., symbol for* dose equivalent • (ital.) *Thermodynamics, symbol for* enthalpy • (ital.) *Physics, symbol for* Hamiltonian • hard (indicating the degree of hardness of lead in a pencil; also in **HB**, hard black; **HH** (*or* **2H**), double hard; etc.) • *Immunol.* heavy (in **H-chain** of an immunoglobulin molecule) • *Physics, symbol for* henry(s) • *Slang* heroin • *Med., Pharmacol.* histamine receptor (in **H₁, H₂**; used in specifying types of antihistamines) • *Biochem.* histidine • *British fishing port registration for* Hull • *international vehicle registration for* Hungary • *Chem., symbol for* hydrogen • (ital.) *Physics, Photog., symbol for* light exposure • (bold ital.) *Physics, symbol for* magnetic field strength

**H.** (*or* **H**) *Advertising* halfpage • Harbour • hardness • *Cards* hearts • herbaceous • Holy • *Music* horn • hospital • hour • hydrant

**H4** *international civil aircraft marking for* Solomon Islands

**ha** *symbol for* hectare

**h.a.** heir apparent • *Gunnery* high angle • hoc anno (Latin: in this year)

**Ha** *Chem., symbol for* hahnium (element 105)

**Ha.** Haiti(an) • Hawaii(an)

**HA** *British vehicle registration for* Dudley • *Horticulture* hardy annual • *postcode for* Harrow • Hautes-Alpes (department of France) • *airline flight code for* Hawaiian Air • Health Authority • heavy artillery • high altitude • Highway(s) Act • *Biochem.* histamine • *Historical Association* • Hockey Association • *Astronomy* hour angle • *Geology* humic acid • *international civil aircraft marking for* Hungary • *Biochem.* hyaluronic acid • Hydraulic Association of Great Britain

**HAA** heavy anti-aircraft • *Immunol.* hepatitis-associated antigen

**HAAC** (USA) Harper Adams Agricultural College

**HA & M** (ital.) Hymns Ancient and Modern

**hab.** habitat • habitation

**Hab.** *Bible* Habakkuk

**HAB** high-altitude bombing

**HABA** *Chem.* 2-(4-hydroxyphenylazo)benzoic acid

**hab. corp.** *Law* habeas corpus (writ)

**habt.** habeat (Latin: let him have)

**HAC** high-alumina cement • Honourable Artillery Company • *Chem.* hydrogenated amorphous carbon

**h.a.d.** hereinafter described

**haem.** haemoglobin • haemorrhage

**HAF** Hellenic Air Force

**Hag.** *Bible* Haggai

**hagiol.** hagiology

**HAI** hospital-acquired infection

**hal.** halogen

**Hal. Orch.** Hallé Orchestra

**Ham.** Hamburg

**Han.** Hanover(ian)

**H. & B.** *Botany* Humboldt and Bonpland (indicating the authors of a species, etc.)

**h & c** (*or* **H & C**) hot and cold (water)

**h & t** hardened and tempered

**H & W** Harland and Wolff (shipbuilders)

**Hants** Hampshire

**HAO** hydrogenated anthracene oil

**HAP** hazardous air pollutant

**h. app.** heir apparent

**HaPV** *Microbiol.* hamster polyomavirus

**har.** harbour

**HARCVS** Honorary Associate of the Royal College of Veterinary Surgeons

**harm.** harmonic • harmony

**HARM** (hɑːm) *Military* high-speed anti-radiation missile

**harp.** harpsichord

**HART** (hɑːt) (New Zealand) Halt All Racist Tours (antiracist sports organization)

**Harv.** (USA) Harvard University

**HAS** Headmasters' Association of Scotland • Health Advisory Service • Helicopter Air Service • Hospital Advisory Service

**HASAWA** Health and Safety at Work Act

**HAT** housing action (*or* association) trust

**haust.** *Med.* haustus (Latin: draught)

**HAV** hepatitis A virus

**HAWT** horizontal-axis wind turbine

**haz.** hazard(ous)

**h.b.** *Sport* halfback • handbook • hardback (of books) • homing beacon • human being

**Hb** *Biochem.* haemoglobin

**HB** *British vehicle registration for* Cardiff • hard-black (on pencils; indicating medium-hard lead) • *Horticulture* hardy biennial • (Spain) Herri Batasuna (Basque independentist party) • *Electronics* horizontal Bridgman • House of Bishops • *international civil aircraft marking for* Switzerland and Liechtenstein

**H.B. & K.** *Botany* Humboldt, Bonpland, and Kunth (indicating the authors of a species, etc.)

**HBC** *Electrical engineering* high breaking capacity • Historic Buildings Council • Hudson's Bay Company

**HBCU** (USA) Historically Black Colleges and Universities

**HBD** had (*or* has) been drinking

**Hbf.** Hauptbahnhof (German: central (*or* main) station)

**HBIG** hepatitis B immunoglobulin

**HBLV** *Med.* human B-lymphotropic virus

**HBM** Her (*or* His) Britannic Majesty (*or* Majesty's)

**H-bomb** hydrogen bomb

**HBP** high blood pressure

**hbr** harbour

**HBS** Harvard Business School

**Hbt** Hobart (Australia)

**HBT** *Electronics* heterojunction bipolar transistor

**HBV** hepatitis B virus

**hby** hereby

**h.c.** habitual criminal • hand control • heating cabinet • high capacity • (*or* **hc**) honoris causa (Latin: for the sake of honour; honorary) • hot and cold (water)

**h/c** *Insurance* held covered

**HC** *British vehicle registration for* Brighton • *international civil aircraft marking for* Ecuador • Hague Convention • Headmasters' (*or* Headteachers') Conference • health certificate • Heralds' College • High Church • High Commission(er) • High Court • higher certificate • highly commended • Highway Code • hockey club • Holy Communion • home counties • hors concours (French: not competing) • House of Clergy • House of Commons • house of correction • housing centre • housing corporation

**H/C** *Insurance* held covered

**HCA** Hospital Caterers' Association

**HCAAS** Homeless Children's Aid and Adoption Society

**hcap** (*or* **h'cap**) handicap

**HCB** House of Commons Bill

**HCBA** Hotel and Catering Benevolent Association

**h.c.c.** hydraulic cement concrete

**h.c.d.** high current density

**h.c.e.** human-caused error

**h.c.f.** *Maths.* highest common factor • hundred cubic feet

**HCF** high-calorific fuel • high carbohydrate and fibre • *Maths.* highest common factor • Honorary Chaplain to the Forces

**HCFC** hydrochlorofluorocarbon

**hCG** (*or* **HCG**) *Biochem., Med.* human chorionic gonadotrophin

**HCH** Herbert Clark Hoover (1874–1964, US president 1929–33) • hexachlorocyclohexane (an insecticide)

**HCI** Hotel and Catering Institute • human–computer interface (*or* interaction)

**HCIL** Hague Conference on International Law

**HCIMA** Hotel Catering and Institutional Management Association

**HCJ** High Court of Justice • Holy Child Jesus

**h.c.l.** high cost of living

**HCM** High Court Master • His (*or* Her) Catholic Majesty

**HCO** Harvard College Observatory • Higher Clerical Officer

**hcp** handicap

**h.c.p.** *Crystallog.* hexagonal close-packed

**HCP** House of Commons Paper

**HCPT** Historic Churches Preservation Trust

**hcptr** helicopter

**HCR** High Chief Ranger • (USA) highway contract route

**h.c.s.** high-carbon steel

**HCS** Home Civil Service

**HCSA** Hospital Consultants and Specialists Association

**hd** hand • head

**h.d.** heavy duty • high density • *Med.* hora decubitus (Latin: at bedtime)

**HD** *Chemical engineering* heavy distillate • *Med.* herniated disc • high density • *Physics* high dose (of radiation) • (51st) Highland Division • Hodgkin's disease • home defence • honourable discharge • Hoover Dam • Huddersfield (postcode *or* British vehicle registration) • *Chem.* hydrogen-deuterium

**H-D** *Photog.* Hurter–Driffield (in **H-D curve**)

**H/D** *Shipping* Havre–Dunkirk

**HDA** (Australia) Hawkesbury Diploma in Agriculture • high-duty alloy

**HDAL** *Chem.* hexadecenal

**h.d.a.t.z.** high-density air-traffic zone

**hdbk** handbook

**HDC** *Med.* high-dose chemotherapy • *Law* holder in due course

**HDCR** Higher Diploma of the College of Radiographers

**HDD** *Aeronautics, Computing* head-down display • heavy-duty diesel • Higher Dental Diploma

**hdg** heading

**HDipEd** Higher Diploma in Education

**hdkf** handkerchief

**hdl.** handle

**HDL** *Biochem., Med.* high-density lipoprotein

**HDLC** *Computing* high-level data link control (a communications protocol)

**hdle** *Horse racing* hurdle

**hdlg** handling

**HDM** high-duty metal

**hdn** harden

**HDODA** *Chem.* 1,6-hexanediol diacrylate

**HDP** heavy-duty petrol • (*or* **HDPE**) *Chem.* high-density polyethylene (*or* polyethene)

**hdqrs** headquarters

**HDR** *Physics* high dose rate (of radiation) • hot dry rock (in **HDR energy**)

**HDTV** high-definition television

**HDV** heavy-duty vehicle • *Med.* hepatitis delta virus

**hdw.** *Computing* hardware

**hdwd** hardwood • headword

**h.e.** heat engine • hic est (Latin: this is) • hub end

**He** *Chem., symbol for* helium

**He.** Hebrew

**HE** *Med.* hepatic encephalopathy • high-energy • higher education • high explosive • His Eminence • His (*or* Her) Excellency • home establishment • horizontal equivalent • hydraulic engineer • *Crystallog.* hydrogen embrittlement • *British vehicle registration for* Sheffield

**HEA** Health Education Authority • Horticultural Education Association

**HEAO** High Energy Astronomy (*or* Astrophysical) Observatory

**Heb.** Hebrew (language) • *Bible* Hebrews

**Hebr.** Hebrew (language) • Hebrides

**HEC** (école des) hautes études commerciales (French: (college of) higher commercial studies) • Health Education Council • Higher Education Corporation • *Chem.* hydroxyethyl cellulose

**HEDCOM** ('hɛd,kɒm) *US Air Force* headquarters command

**HEDTA** *Chem.* hydroxyethylethylene-diaminotriacetate

**HEED** (hiːd) *Physics* high-energy electron diffraction

**HEF** high-energy fuel

**HEH** His (*or* Her) Exalted Highness

**h.e.i.** high-explosive incendiary

**HEIC** Honourable East India Company

**HEICS** Honourable East India Company's Service

**heir app.** heir apparent

**heir pres.** heir presumptive

**hel.** (*or* **heli.**) helicopter

**HEL** high-energy laser

**Hellen.** Hellenic • Hellenism • Hellenistic

**helo.** heliport

**HELP** (hɛlp) helicopter electronic landing path • Help Establish Lasting Peace

**HEM** *Physics* hybrid electromagnetic wave

**HEMM** heavy earth-moving machinery

**HEMT** *Electronics* high-electron-mobility transistor

**HEO** Higher Executive Officer • highly elliptic-inclined orbit (as in **HEO satellite**)

**HEOS** high-elliptic-inclined-orbit satellite

**HEP** *Statistics* human error probability

**HEPC** (USA) hydroelectric power commission

**HEPCAT** ('hɛp,kæt) helicopter pilot control and training

**her.** heraldic • heraldry • *Law* heres (Latin: heir)

**Her** *Astronomy* Hercules

**hera** high-explosive rocket-assisted

**herb.** herbaceous • herbalist • herbarium

**hered.** heredity

**Herod.** Herodotus (*c.* 484–*c.* 424 BC, Greek historian)

**herp.** (*or* **herpet., herpetol.**) herpetologist • herpetology

**Hert** Hertford College, Oxford

**Herts** Hertfordshire

**HERU** Higher Education Research Unit

**HET** heavy-equipment transporter

**HETP** *Chem.* height equivalent per theoretical plate

**HEU** highly enriched uranium

**HEW** (USA) Department of Health, Education, and Welfare (former government department; replaced by HHS)

**hex** (hεks) *Computing* hexadecimal (notation)

**hex.** hexachord • hexagonal

**hexa.** hexamethylene tetramine (type of synthetic rubber)

**hf** half

**h.f.** hold fire • *Military* horse and foot

**Hf** *Chem., symbol for* hafnium

**HF** hard firm (on pencils; indicating hard lead) • *Physics* Hartree–Fock (approximation) • *Radio, etc.* high frequency • Holy Father • home fleet • home forces • *British vehicle registration for* Liverpool

**Hfa** Haifa (Israel)

**HFA** hydrofluoroalkane

**HFARA** Honorary Foreign Associate of the Royal Academy

**hf. bd.** *Bookbinding* half binding (*or* bound)

**HFC** *Electricity* high-frequency current • *Chem.* hydrofluorocarbon

**HFDF** high-frequency direction finder

**HFO** heavy fuel oil • high-frequency oscillation

**HFR** *Nuclear engineering* high-flux reactor

**HFRA** Honorary Foreign Member of the Royal Academy

**hg** *symbol for* hectogram(s)

**Hg** *Chem., symbol for* mercury (Latin *hydrargyrum*)

**HG** *postcode for* Harrogate • Haute-Garonne (department of France) • High German • high grade • His (*or* Her) Grace • Holy Ghost • Home Guard • Horse Guards • *British vehicle registration for* Preston

**HGCA** Home Grown Cereals Authority

**hgd** hogshead

**HGDH** His (*or* Her) Grand Ducal Highness

**HGG** *Med.* hypogammaglobulinaemia

**hGH** (*or* **HGH**) *Biochem.* human growth hormone

**HGMM** Hereditary Grand Master Mason

**h.g.pt.** hard gloss paint

**hgr** hangar • hanger

**hgt** height

**HGTAC** Home Grown Timber Advisory Committee

**HGV** heavy goods vehicle

**HGW** heat-generating waste • H(erbert) G(eorge) Wells (1866–1946, British writer)

**hgy** (*or* **hgwy**) highway

**hh** hands (height measurement for horses)

**HH** *British vehicle registration for* Carlisle • (*or* **2H**) double hard (on pencils; indicating very hard lead) • *international civil aircraft marking for* Haiti • *British fishing port registration for* Harwich • *Chem., Physics* heavy hydrogen • *Astronomy* Herbig–Haro (in **HH object**) • (Member of the) Hesketh Hubbard Art Society • His (*or* Her) Highness • His Holiness (title of the Pope) • His (*or* Her) Honour

**HHA** *Horticulture* half-hardy annual • Historic Houses Association

**HHB** *Horticulture* half-hardy biennial

**hhd** hogshead

**HHD** (USA) Doctor of Humanities (Latin *Humanitatum Doctor*) • hypertensive heart disease

**HHDWS** heavy handy deadweight scrap

**HHFA** (USA) Housing and Home Finance Agency

**HHH** (*or* **3H**) treble hard (on pencils; indicating very hard lead)

**HHI** Highland Home Industries

**HHNK** *Med.* hyperglycaemic hyperosmolar nonketoacidotic coma (in diabetes)

**H-Hour** Hour Hour (i.e. the specified time at which an operation is to begin)

**HHP** *Horticulture* half-hardy perennial

**HHS** (USA) Department of Health and Human Services (replaced HEW)

**HHV** human herpesvirus

**Hi.** Hindi

**HI** *international civil aircraft marking for* Dominican Republic • *US postcode for* Hawaii • Hawaiian Islands • hearing impaired • *Surveying* height of instrument • hic iacet (Latin: here lies; on gravestones) • high intensity • *Irish vehicle registration for* Tipperary

**HIA** Housing Improvement Association

**hi. ac.** (*or* **hiac**) high accuracy

**HIAS** (USA) Hebrew Immigrant Aid Society

**Hib.** Hibernia(n)

**HIB** *Physics* heavy-ion beam

**hicat** ('haɪˌkæt) high-altitude clear air turbulence

**Hi. Com.** High Command • High Commission(er)

**HIDB** Highlands and Islands Development Board

**hier.** hieroglyphics

**hi-fi** ('haɪˈfaɪ) high fidelity

**hifor** ('haɪfɔː) high-level forecast

**HIH** His (*or* Her) Imperial Highness

**HIL** *Chem.* hazardous immiscible liquid

**hilac** (*or* **HILAC**) ('haɪlæk) *Nuclear physics* heavy-ion linear accelerator

**HILAT** ('haɪlæt) high-latitude (in **HILAT satellite**)

**HIM** His (*or* Her) Imperial Majesty

**Hind.** Hindi • Hindu • Hindustan(i)

**HIP** ('eɪtʃ 'aɪ 'piː *or* hɪp) (USA) health-insurance plan

**HIPAR** high-power acquisition radar

**HIPDA** *Chem.* hydroxyisophthalyl dihydroxamic acid

**hipot** ('haɪˌpɒt) high potential

**Hipp.** Hippocrates (*c.* 460–*c.* 375 BC, Greek physician)

**HIPS** (hɪpz) high-impact polystyrene (type of synthetic plastic)

**hirel** ('haɪˌrɛl) high reliability

**hi-res** ('haɪˈrɛz) *Physics* high resolution

**His** (*or* **his**) *Biochem.* histidine

**HIS** hic iacet sepultus *or* sepulta (Latin: here lies buried; on gravestones)

**hist.** (*or* **histol.**) histology • (*or* **histn**) historian • historic(al) • history

**Hitt.** Hittite

**HIUS** Hispanic Institute of the United States

**HIV** human immunodeficiency virus (the cause of AIDS)

**HJ** *British vehicle registration for* Chelmsford • hic jacet (Latin: here lies; on gravestones) • high jump • Hilal-e-Jurat (Pakistani honour) • Hitler Jugend (German: Hitler Youth)

**HJBT** *Electronics* heterojunction bipolar transistor

**HJS** hic jacet sepultus *or* sepulta (Latin: here lies buried; on gravestones)

**HK** *British vehicle registration for* Chelmsford • *international civil aircraft marking for* Colombia • Hong Kong (abbrev. *or* IVR) • *Taxation* housekeeper allowance • House of Keys (Manx Parliament)

**hkf** handkerchief

**HKJ** *international vehicle registration for* (Hashemite Kingdom of) Jordan

**hl** (*or* **hL**) *symbol for* hectolitre(s)

**h.l.** hoc loco (Latin: in this place)

**Hl.** Heilige(r) (German: Saint)

**HL** hard labour • *British fishing port registration for* Hartlepool • Haute-Loire (department of France) • honours list • House of Laity • House of Lords • *British vehicle registration for* Sheffield • *international civil aircraft marking for* South Korea

**HLA** *Immunol.* human lymphocyte antigen (as in **HLA system**)

**HLB** *Chem.* hydrophilic-lipophilic balance

**HLBB** (USA) Home Loan Bank Board

**HLD** Doctor of Humane Letters

**HLE** *Physics* high-level exposure (to radiation)

**HLI** Highland Light Infantry

**HLL** *Computing* high-level language

**HLNW** high-level nuclear waste

**hlpr** helper

**HLPR** Howard League for Penal Reform

**HLRW** high-level radioactive waste

**HLS** Harvard Law School

**HLW** high-level (radioactive) waste

**HLWN** highest low water of neap (tides)

**hm** *symbol for* hectometre(s)

**h.m.** hallmark • hoc mense (Latin: in this month)

**HM** *airline flight code for* Air Seychelles • harbour master • *Music* harmonic mean • Haute-Marne (department of France) • *Chem.* hazardous material • headmaster (*or* headmistress) • heavy metal • Her (*or* His) Majesty • home mission • *British vehicle registration for* London (central)

**HMA** Head Masters' Association • *Computing* high-memory area

**HMAC** Her (*or* His) Majesty's Aircraft Carrier

**HMAS** Her (*or* His) Majesty's Australian Ship

**HMBDV** Her (*or* His) Majesty's Boom Defence Vessel

**HMC** Headmasters' Conference • Her (*or* His) Majesty's Customs • Historical Manuscripts Commission • Horticultural Marketing Council • Hospital Management Committee • Household Mortgage Corporation

**HMCA** Hospital and Medical Care Association

**HMCIC** Her (*or* His) Majesty's Chief Inspector of Constabulary

**HMCIF** Her (*or* His) Majesty's Chief Inspector of Factories

**HMCN** Her (*or* His) Majesty's Canadian Navy

**HMCS** Her (*or* His) Majesty's Canadian Ship

**HMCSC** Her (*or* His) Majesty's Civil Service Commissioners

**hmd** humid

**HMD** Her (*or* His) Majesty's Destroyer

**HMF** *Chem.* heavy-metal fluoride • Her (*or* His) Majesty's Forces

**HMFI** Her (*or* His) Majesty's Factory Inspectorate

**HMG** heavy machine gun • Her (*or* His) Majesty's Government • *Med.* human menopausal gonadotrophin

**HMHS** Her (*or* His) Majesty's Hospital Ship

**HMI** Her (*or* His) Majesty's Inspector (of schools) • Her (*or* His) Majesty's Lieutenant • *Computing* human–machine interface

**HMIED** Honorary Member of the Institute of Engineering Designers

**HMIP** Her (*or* His) Majesty's Inspectorate of Pollution

**HMIT** Her (*or* His) Majesty's Inspector of Taxes

**HMLR** Her (*or* His) Majesty's Land Registry

**HMML** Her (*or* His) Majesty's Motor Launch

**HMMS** Her (*or* His) Majesty's Mine Sweeper

**HMNZS** Her (*or* His) Majesty's New Zealand Ship

**HMO** (USA) health maintenance organization

**HMOCS** Her (*or* His) Majesty's Overseas Civil Service

**h.m.p.** handmade paper

**HMP** Her (*or* His) Majesty's Prison • hoc monumentum posuit (Latin: (he *or* she) erected this monument)

**HMPA** *Chem.* hexamethylphosphoramide

**HMPT** *Chem.* hexamethylphosphorous triamide

**HMRT** Her (*or* His) Majesty's Rescue Tug

**h.m.s.** hours, minutes, seconds

**HMS** *Mining* heavy media separation • Her (*or* His) Majesty's Service • Her (*or* His) Majesty's Ship • *Biochem.* hexose monophosphate shunt

**HMSO** Her (*or* His) Majesty's Stationery Office

**hmstd** homestead

**HMT** Her (*or* His) Majesty's Trawler • Her (*or* His) Majesty's Treasury • Her (*or* His) Majesty's Tug

**HMV** His Master's Voice (gramophone-record company)

**HMW** *Biochem.* high molecular weight

**HMWA** Hairdressing Manufacturers' and Wholesalers' Association

**hn** *Music* horn

**h.n.** *Med.* hac nocte (Latin: tonight)

**HN** *British vehicle registration for* Middlesbrough

**HNC** *Education* Higher National Certificate

**HND** *Education* Higher National Diploma

**hndbk** handbook

**HNL** *Physics* helium–neon laser

**hnRNA** *Biochem.* heterogeneous nuclear RNA

**hnRNP** *Biochem.* heterogeneous nuclear ribonucleoprotein

**Hnrs** Honours

**ho.** house

**h.o.** hold over

**Ho** *Chem.*, *symbol for* holmium

**HO** *British vehicle registration for* Bournemouth • *Law* habitual offender • head office • Home Office • Hydrographic Office

**h.o.c.** held on charge

**HOC** *Chem.* halogenated organic compound • heavy organic chemical

**HoC** House of Commons

**HoD** head of department

**H of C** House of Commons

**H of K** House of Keys

**H of L** House of Lords

**H of R** (USA) House of Representatives

**Hol** *Geology* Holocene

**Hol.** (*or* **Holl.**) Holland

**HOLC** (USA) Home Owners' Loan Corporation

**HOLLAND** hope our love lasts (*or* lives) and never dies

**Holmes** (həʊmz) Home Office Large Major Enquiry System (computer used in crime investigation)

**Hom.** Homer (8th century BC, Greek poet)

**homeo.** (or **homo.**) homeopath(ic) · homeopathy

**HOMO** *Chem.* highest occupied molecular orbital

**hon.** honorary · honour · honourable

**Hon** (or **Hon.**) Honorary (in titles, as in **HonFInstP**, Honorary Fellow of the Institute of Physics) · Honorary Member (in titles, as in **HonRCM**, Honorary Member of the Royal College of Music) · Honourable (title)

**Hond.** Honduras

**Hono.** Honolulu

**hons** honours

**Hon. Sec.** Honorary Secretary

**HOOD** (hʊd) *Computing* hierarchical object-oriented design

**Hook.** *Botany* (Sir William) Hooker (indicating the author of a species, etc.)

**Hook. fil.** *Botany* Hooker fils (Sir Joseph Hooker, son of Sir William Hooker; indicating the author of a species, etc.)

**hor.** horizon · horizontal · horology

**Hor** *Astronomy* Horologium

**Hor.** Horace (65–8 BC, Roman poet)

**hor. decub.** *Med.* hora decubitus (Latin: at bedtime)

**HoReCa** (International Union of National Associations of) Hotel, Restaurant, and Café Keepers

**horol.** horological · horology

**hort.** horticultural · horticulture

**HORU** Home Office Research Unit

**Hos.** *Bible* Hosea

**hosp.** hospital

**Hotol** ('həʊ,tɒl) *Astronautics* horizontal takeoff and landing (launch vehicle)

**HOV** *Transport* high-occupancy vehicle

**how.** howitzer

**hp** *symbol for* horsepower

**h.p.** half pay · heir presumptive · *Electricity* high power · hire purchase · horizontally polarized

**HP** *British vehicle registration for* Coventry · Handley Page (aircraft) · *Horticulture* hardy perennial · Hautes-Pyrénées (department of France) · *postcode for* Hemel Hempstead · (USA) Hewlett-Packard (electronics and computing manufacturer) · high performance · *Electricity* high power · high pressure · high priest · Himachal Pradesh (India) · hire purchase · hot-pressed (paper) · house physician · Houses of Parliament · *Horticulture* hybrid perpetual (rose) · *international civil aircraft marking for* Panama

**HPA** Hospital Physicists' Association

**HPC** *Med.* history of present complaint

**hpch.** (or **hpd**) harpsichord

**HPk** Hilal-e-Pakistan (Pakistani honour)

**HPLC** *Chem.* high-performance liquid chromatography · *Chem.* high-pressure liquid chromatography

**HPP** *Chem.* high-pressure polyethylene (or polyethene)

**HPS** high-pressure steam · high-protein supplement

**HPT** high-pressure turbine

**HPTA** Hire Purchase Trade Association

**HPTLC** *Chem.* high-performance thin-layer chromatography

**HPV** *Med.* human papilloma virus

**h.q.** headquarters · hoc quaere (Latin: look for this)

**HQ** headquarters

**HQA** Hilal-i-Quaid-i-Azam (Pakistani honour)

**HQBA** Headquarters Base Area

**HQMC** (USA) Headquarters, Marine Corps

**hr** *Meteorol.* hail and rain · hour

**h.r.** *Baseball* home run

**Hr** Herr (German: Mr, Sir) · Hussar

**HR** *Med.* heart rate · *postcode for* Hereford · Highland Regiment · *Optics* high resolution · Home Rule(r) · *Baseball* home run · *international civil aircraft marking for* Honduras · (USA) House of Representatives · *British vehicle registration for* Swindon

**H-R** *Astronomy* Hertzsprung–Russell (in **H-R diagram**)

**HRA** (USA) Health Resources Administration

**HRC** *Chem.* high-resolution chromatography · Holy Roman Church

**HRCA** Honorary Royal Cambrian Academician

**HRCT** *Med.* high-resolution computerized (or computed) tomography

**HRE** Holy Roman Emperor (or Empire)

**HREM** high-resolution electron microscopy

**HRGC** *Chem.* high-resolution gas chromatography

**HRGI** Honorary Member of the Royal Glasgow Institute of the Fine Arts

**HRH** His (or Her) Royal Highness

**HRHA** Honorary Member of the Royal Hibernian Academy

**HRI** Honorary Member of the Royal Institute of Painters in Water Colours

**HRIP** hic requiescit in pace (Latin: here rests in peace; on gravestones)

**HRMS** *Chem.* high-resolution mass spectrometry

**Hrn** Herr(e)n (German: Messrs, Sirs)

**HROI** Honorary Member of the Royal Institute of Oil Painters

**HRP** *Military* human remains pouch

**HRR** *Taxation* higher reduced rate

**hrs** hours

**HRSA** Honorary Member of the Royal Scottish Academy

**hrsg.** herausgegeben (German: edited *or* published)

**HRSW** Honorary Member of the Royal Scottish Water Colour Society

**HRT** *Med.* hormone replacement therapy

**HRTEM** high-resolution transmission electron microscopy

**hs** *Meteorol.* hail and snow

**h.s.** highest score • hoc sensu (Latin: in this sense) • *Med.* hora somni (Latin: at bedtime)

**Hs.** Handschrift (German: manuscript)

**HS** *British vehicle registration for* Glasgow • Haute-Saône (department of France) • Hawker Siddeley (aircraft) • hic sepultus *or* sepulta (Latin: here is buried; on gravestones) • high school • Home Secretary • hospital ship • house surgeon • *Numismatics, symbol for* sesterce (Roman coin) • *international civil aircraft marking for* Thailand

**HSA** (USA) Health Systems Agency • *Med.* human serum albumin

**HSAB** *Chem.* hard and soft acids and bases

**HSC** *Med.* haemopoietic stem cell • Health and Safety Commission • Higher School Certificate (replaced by GCE A level)

**HSD** heat-storage device • high-speed diesel

**HSDU** hospital sterilization and disinfection unit

**hse** (*or* **Hse**) house

**HSE** Health and Safety Executive • hic sepultus (*or* sepulta) est (Latin: here lies buried; on gravestones)

**hsekpr** housekeeper

**hsg** housing

**HSH** His (*or* Her) Serene Highness

**HSI** *Computing* human–system interface (*or* interaction)

**HSL** Huguenot Society of London

**HSLA** high-strength, low-alloy (steel)

**HSM** His (*or* Her) Serene Majesty

**HSO** Hamburg Symphony Orchestra

**HSP** *Med.* heat-shock protein

**HSR** *Genetics* homogeneously staining region

**Hss.** Handschriften (German: manuscripts)

**HSS** Fellow of the Historical Society (Latin *Historicae Societatis Socius*) • high-speed steel

**HSSU** hospital sterile supply unit

**HST** Harry S Truman (1884–1972, US president 1945–53) • Hawaii Standard Time • highest spring tide • high-speed train • Hubble Space Telescope • hypersonic transport

**HSV** herpes simplex virus

**HSWA** (USA) Hazardous and Solid Waste Act (*or* Amendments)

**ht** heat • height

**h.t.** *Sport* half time • halftone • heavy tank • hoc tempore (Latin: at this time) • hoc titulo (Latin: in (*or* under) this title)

**HT** *British vehicle registration for* Bristol • *Sport* half time • Hawaii Time • heat treatment • high temperature • *Electrical engineering* high tension • high tide • high treason • *Horticulture* hybrid tea (rose)

**5-HT** *Biochem.* 5-hydroxytryptamine

**HTA** Horticultural Traders' Association • Household Textile Association

**h.t.b.** high-tension battery

**HTB** *Metallurgy* hexagonal tungsten bronze

**HTC** *Physics* heat-transfer coefficient

**htd** heated

**Hte** (*pl.* **Htes**) Haute (French: High; used in place names)

**HTGR** *Nuclear engineering* high-temperature gas-cooled reactor

**HTLV** *Med.* human T-cell lymphotropic virus

**HTM** heat-transfer medium

**HTO** *Chem.* hydrous titanium oxide (catalyst)

**HTOL** *Astronautics* horizontal takeoff and landing

**htr** heater

**HTR** *Nuclear engineering* high-temperature (gas-cooled) reactor

**H. Trin.** Holy Trinity

**h.t.s.** half-time survey • high-tensile steel

**Hts** Heights (in place names)

**HTS** high-temperature superconductor (*or* superconductivity)

**HTT** heavy tactical transport

**HTTR** *Nuclear engineering* high-temperature test reactor

**HTU** *Chemical engineering* height of a transfer unit

**HTV** Harlech Television

**ht wkt** *Cricket* hit wicket

**HU** *British vehicle registration for* Bristol • Harvard University • *postcode for* Hull

**HUAC** ('hjuːæk) House (of Representatives) Un-American Activities Committee

**HUD** *Aeronautics, Computing* head-up display • (USA) (Department of) Housing and Urban Development

**Hugo** ('hjuːɡəʊ) Human Genome Organization

**HUJ** Hebrew University of Jerusalem

**HUKFORLANT** *US Navy* hunter-killer forces, Atlantic

**HUKS** *US Navy* hunter-killer submarine

**hum.** human • humane • (*or* **Hum.**) humanities (classics) • humanity • humble • humorous

**HUMINT** (*or* **humint**) ('hjuːmɪnt) *Military* human intelligence (espionage activities)

**HUMRRO** Human Resources Research Office

**HUMV** ('hʌm,viː) *Military* human light vehicle

**hund.** hundred

**Hung.** Hungarian • Hungary

**Hunts** Huntingdonshire (former county)

**HUP** Harvard University Press • *Chem.* hydrogenuranylphosphate tetrahydrate

**hur.** (*or* **hurr.**) hurricane

**HURCN** *Meteorol.* hurricane

**Husat** ('hjuːsæt) Human Science and Advanced Technology Research Institute

**husb.** husbandry

**h.v.** high vacuum • high velocity

**HV** health visitor • *Anatomy* hepatic vein • high velocity • high voltage • hoc verbum (Latin: this word) • *British vehicle registration for* London (central) • *airline flight code for* Transavia • *international civil aircraft marking for* the Vatican

**HVA** Health Visitors' Association (trade union; now a section of the MFS) • *Chem.* homovanillic acid

**HVAC** heating, ventilation, air conditioning • high-voltage alternating current

**HVAR** high-velocity aircraft rocket

**HVCA** Heating and Ventilating Contractors' Association

**HVCert** Health Visitor's Certificate

**HVDC** high-voltage direct current

**HVEM** high-voltage electron microscope

**HVO** Hrvatsko vijeće odbrane (Croatian Defence Council)

**HVP** hydrolysed vegetable protein

**HVT** *Physics* half-value thickness • health visitor teacher

**hvy** heavy

**h.w.** *Cricket* hit wicket

**h/w** herewith • husband and wife

**HW** *British vehicle registration for* Bristol • hazardous waste • high water • hot water

**HWL** Henry Wadsworth Longfellow (1807–82, US poet) • (*or* **h.w.l.**) high-water line

**HWM** high-water mark

**HWONT** high water, ordinary neap tides

**HWOST** high water, ordinary spring tides

**HWR** *Nuclear physics* heavy-water reactor

**HWS** hurricane warning system

**HWW** *Engineering* hot-and-warm worked

**hwy** highway

**HX** *postcode for* Halifax • *British vehicle registration for* London (central)

**HXR** hard X-ray

**hy** heavy • highway

**HY** *British vehicle registration for* Bristol

**Hya** *Astronomy* Hydra

**hyb.** hybrid

**hyd.** hydrate • hydraulic • (*or* **hydrog.**) hydrographic

**hydt** hydrant

**hyg.** hygiene

**Hyi** *Astronomy* Hydrus

**hyp.** hypodermic • *Maths.* hypotenuse • (*or* **hypoth.**) hypothesis • (*or* **hypoth.**) hypothetical

**Hz** *Physics, symbol for* hertz

**HZ** *Meteorol.* dust haze • *international civil aircraft marking for* Saudi Arabia • *British vehicle registration for* Tyrone

**HZD** *Chem.* hydrated zirconium dioxide

**HZO** *Chem.* hydrated zirconium oxide

**hzy** *Meteorol.* hazy

# I

**i** *symbol for* the imaginary number $\sqrt{-1}$ • (ital.) *Physics, symbol for* instantaneous current • (bold ital.) *Maths., symbol for* unit coordinate vector • (ital.) *Chem., symbol for* a van't Hoff factor

**i.** id (Latin: that) • incisor (tooth) • indicate • *Banking* interest • *Grammar* intransitive

**I** (ital.) *Physics, symbol for* electric current • *Chem., symbol for* inductive (*or* inductomeric) effect • *Biochem.* inosine • *symbol for* inti (Peruvian monetary unit) • *Chem., symbol for* iodine • (ital.) *Chem., symbol for* ionic strength • (ital.) *Chem., Physics, symbol for* ionization potential • *Biochem.* isoleucine • (ital.) *Physics, symbol for* isospin quantum number • *international vehicle registration or international civil aircraft marking for* Italy • (ital.; *or* $I_v$) *Physics, symbol for* luminous intensity • (ital.) *Mechanics, symbol for* moment of inertia • *Roman numeral for* one • (ital.; *or* $I_e$) *Physics, symbol for* radiant intensity • (ital.) *Maths., symbol for* unit matrix • *Logic, indicating* a particular affirmative categorial statement

**I.** (*or* **I**) Iesus (Latin: Jesus) • Imperator (Latin: Emperor) • Imperatrix (Latin: Empress) • Imperial • Imperium (Latin: Empire) • (single column) inch (of advertisements) • incumbent • Independence • Independent • India(n) • Infidelis (Latin: unbeliever, infidel) • Inspector • Institute • Instructor • intelligence • interceptor • International • interpreter • Ireland • Irish • Island (*or* Isle) • issue • Italian

**i.a.** immediately available • in absentia (Latin: while absent) • *Aeronautics* indicated altitude • initial appearance

**i.A.** im Auftrage (German: by order of)

**Ia.** Iowa

**IA** *British vehicle registration for* Antrim • Incorporated Accountant • Indian Army • infected area • information anxiety • *Taxation* initial allowance • Institute of Actuaries • Inter-American • *Med.* intra-arterial • *US postcode for* Iowa • *airline flight code for* Iraqi Airways

**I/A** Isle of Anglesey

**IA5** *Computing* International Alphabet, Number 5

**IAA** indoleacetic acid (plant hormone) • Institute of Industrial Administration • International Academy of Astronautics • International Actuarial Association • International Advertising Association

**IAAA** Irish Amateur Athletic Association • Irish Association of Advertising Agencies

**IAAE** (USA) Institution of Automotive and Aeronautical Engineers

**IAAF** International Amateur Athletic Federation

**IAAP** International Association of Applied Psychology

**IAAS** Incorporated Association of Architects and Surveyors

**IAB** Industrial Advisory Board • Industrial Arbitration Board • Inter-American Bank

**IABA** International Association of Aircraft Brokers and Agents

**IABO** International Association of Biological Oceanography

**i.a.c.** integration, assembly, and checkout

**IAC** (USA) Industrial Advisory Council • Institute of Amateur Cinematographers

**IACA** Independent Air Carriers' Association

**IACB** International Advisory Committee on Bibliography (in UNESCO)

**IACCP** Inter-American Council of Commerce and Production

**IACOMS** International Advisory Committee on Marine Sciences (in the FAO)

**IACP** International Association for Child Psychiatry and Allied Professions • International Association of Chiefs of Police • (USA) International Association of Computer Programmers

**IACS** International Annealed Copper Standard

**IADB** Inter-American Defense Board • Inter-American Development Bank

**IADR** International Association for Dental Research

**IAE** (USA) Institute of Atomic Energy • Institute of Automobile (*or* Automotive) Engineers

**IAEA** International Atomic Energy Agency

**IAEC** Israel Atomic Energy Commission

**IAECOSOC** Inter-American Economic and Social Council

**IAEE** International Association of Energy Economists

**i.a.f.** *Aviation* interview after flight

**IAF** Indian Air Force • Indian Auxiliary Force • International Astronautical Federation

**IAFD** International Association on Food Distribution

**IAG** International Association of Geodesy • International Association of Geology • International Association of Gerontology

**IAGB & I** Ileostomy Association of Great Britain and Ireland

**IAgrE** Institution of Agricultural Engineers

**IAH** International Association of Hydrogeologists • International Association of Hydrology

**IAHA** Inter-American Hotel Association

**IAHM** Incorporated Association of Headmasters

**IAHP** International Association of Horticultural Producers

**IAHR** International Association for Hydraulic Research • International Association for the History of Religions

**IAI** International African Institute

**IAL** Imperial Arts League • Irish Academy of Letters

**IALA** International African Law Association • International Association of Lighthouse Authorities

**IALL** International Association of Law Libraries

**IALS** International Association of Legal Science

**IAM** Institute of Administrative Management • Institute of Advanced Motorists • Institute of Aviation Medicine • *Anatomy* internal auditory meatus • (USA) International Association of Machinists and Aerospace Workers (trade union) • International Association of Meteorology • International Association of Microbiologists

**IAMA** Incorporated Advertising Managers' Association

**IAMAP** International Association of Meteorology and Atmospheric Physics

**IAMC** Indian Army Medical Corps

**IAML** International Association of Music Libraries

**IAMS** International Association of Microbiological Societies (*or* Studies)

**IANC** International Airline Navigators' Council

**IANE** Institute of Advanced Nursing Education (of the Rcn)

**IANEC** Inter-American Nuclear Energy Commission

**IAO** *Meteorol.* in and out of cloud • Incorporated Association of Organists

**IAOC** Indian Army Ordnance Corps

**IAOS** Irish Agricultural Organization Society

**IAP** *Physics* imaging atom probe • International Academy of Pathology

**IAPA** Inter-American Press Association

**IAPB** International Association for the Prevention of Blindness

**IAPG** International Association of Physical Geography

**IAPH** International Association of Ports and Harbours

**IAPO** International Association of Physical Oceanography

**IAPS** Incorporated Association of Preparatory Schools

**IAPSO** International Association for the Physical Sciences of the Oceans

**IAPT** International Association for Plant Taxonomy

**IARA** Inter-Allied Reparations Agency

**IARC** Indian Agricultural Research Council • International Agency for Research on Cancer

**IARD** International Association for Rural Development

**IARF** International Association for Religious Freedom

**IARI** Indian Agricultural Research Institute

**IARO** Indian Army Reserve of Officers

**IARU** International Amateur Radio Union

**IAS** *Computing* immediate access store • Indian Administrative (formerly Civil) Service • (*or* **i.a.s.**) *Aeronautics* indicated air speed • *Chem.* infrared absorbed spectroscopy • (USA) Institute for Advanced Studies (as in **IAS computer**) • (USA) Institute of the Aerospace Sciences • (*or* **i.a.s.**) *Aeronautics* instrument approach system

**IASA** International Air Safety Association

**IASC** Indian Army Service Corps

**IASH** International Association of Scientific Hydrology

**IASI** Inter-American Statistical Institute

**i.a.s.o.r.** ice and snow on runway

**IASS** International Association for Scandinavian Studies • International Association of Soil Science

**i.a.t.** inside air temperature

**IAT** International Atomic Time

**IATA** (aɪˈɑːtə, ɪˈɑːtə) International Air Transport Association • International Amateur Theatre Association

**IATUL** International Association of Technological University Libraries

**IAU** International Association of Universities • International Astronomical Union

**IAUPL** International Association of University Professors and Lecturers

**IAV** International Association of Vulcanology

**IAVG** International Association for Vocational Guidance

**i.a.w.** in accordance with

**IAW** International Alliance of Women

**IAWPRC** International Association on Water Pollution Research and Control

**ib.** ibidem (*see* ibid.)

**IB** *British vehicle registration for* Armagh • *airline flight code for* Iberia International Airlines of Spain • in bond • incendiary bomb • industrial business • information bureau • instruction book • intelligence branch • *Physics* internal bremsstrahlung • International Bank (for Reconstruction and Development) • invoice book

**IBA** Independent Bankers' Association • Independent Broadcasting Authority • *Horticulture* indole 3-butyric acid (rooting compound) • Industrial Bankers' Association • *Taxation* industrial buildings allowances • International Bar Association • International Bowling Association • Investment Bankers' Association • *Chem.* ion-beam analysis

**IBAA** Investment Bankers' Association of America

**IBAE** Institution of British Agricultural Engineers

**IBB** Institute of British Bakers • International Bowling Board • Invest in Britain Bureau

**IBBISB/BF&H** (USA) International Brotherhood of Boilermakers, Iron Shipbuilders, Blacksmiths, Forgers, and Helpers

**IBBR** *Finance* interbank bid rate

**IBC** International Broadcasting Corporation

**IBD** Incorporated Institute of British Decorators and Interior Designers • *Med.* inflammatory bowel disease • *Electronics* ion-beam deposition

**IBE** Institute of British Engineers • International Bureau of Education (now part of UNESCO)

**IBEL** *Finance* interest-bearing eligible liability

**IBEW** (USA) International Brotherhood of Electrical Workers

**IBF** Institute of British Foundrymen • International Badminton Federation • International Boxing Federation

**IBFM** *Physics* interacting boson-fermion model

**IBG** Incorporated Brewers Guild • Institute of British Geographers • *Computing* interblock gap

**IBI** (*or* **i.b.i.**) *Book-keeping* invoice book inwards

**ibid.** ibidem (Latin: in the same place; indicating a previously cited reference to a book, etc.)

**IBID** (ˈɪbɪd) international bibliographical description

**IBiol** Institute of Biology

**IBK** Institute of Book-Keepers

**IBM** *Physics* interacting boson model • intercontinental ballistic missile • International Business Machines (Corporation; computer manufacturer)

**IBMBR** *Finance* interbank market bid rate

**IBO** (*or* **i.b.o.**) *Book-keeping* invoice book outwards

**i.b.p.** initial boiling point

**IBP** Institute of British Photographers • International Biological Programme (for conservation of natural communities)

**IBPAT** (USA) International Brotherhood of Painters and Allied Trades

**IBRD** International Bank for Reconstruction and Development (the World Bank)

**IBRO** International Bank Research Organization • International Brain Research Organization

**IBS** (*or* **IB(Scot)**) Institute of Bankers in Scotland • *Physics* ion-beam sputtering • *Chem.* ion-beam synthesis

**IBST** Institute of British Surgical Technicians

**IBT** International Brotherhood of Teamsters, Chauffeurs, Warehousemen, and Helpers of America

**IBTE** Institution of British Telecommunications Engineers

**IBWM** International Bureau of Weights and Measures

**i.c.** index correction • instrument correction • internal communication

**i/c** in charge (of) • in command

**IC** *Irish vehicle registration for* Carlow • identity card • Iesus Christus (Latin: Jesus Christ) • *Grammar* immediate constituent • *Immunol.* immune complex • Imperial College (of Science and Technology, London) • *Astrology* Imum Coeli (the lowest point on the ecliptic below the horizon) • *Astronomy* Index Catalogue • industrial court • information centre • *Electronics* integrated circuit • Intelligence Corps • *Chem.* intermetallic compound • *Engineering* internal-combustion (engine) • *Physics* internal conversion • *Chem.* ion chromatography • *Physics* ionization chamber

**I-C** Indo-China

**ICA** ignition control additive (for motor vehicles) • Industrial Caterers' Association • Institute of Chartered Accountants in England and Wales • Institute of Contemporary Arts • *Med.* internal carotid artery • International Cartographic Association • International Chefs' Association • International Coffee Agreement • International Colour Authority • International Commercial Arbitration • International Commission on Acoustics • International Commodity Agreement • International Cooperation Administration • International Cooperative Alliance • International Council on Archives • International Court of Arbitration • International Cyclist Association • invalid care allowance

**ICAA** Invalid Children's Aid Association

**ICAE** International Commission on Agricultural Engineering

**ICAEW** Institute of Chartered Accountants in England and Wales

**ICAI** Institute of Chartered Accountants in Ireland • International Commission for Agricultural Industries

**ICAM** Institute of Corn and Agricultural Merchants

**ICAN** International Commission for Air Navigation

**IC & CY** Inns of Court and City Yeomanry

**ICAO** International Civil Aviation Organization

**ICAP** Institute of Certified Ambulance Personnel • International Congress of Applied Psychology

**ICAR** Indian Council of Agricultural Research

**ICAS** Institute of Chartered Accountants of Scotland • International Council of Aeronautical Sciences • International Council of Aerospace Sciences

**ICB** Institute of Comparative Biology

**ICBA** International Community of Booksellers' Associations

**ICBD** International Council of Ballroom Dancing

**ICBHI** Industrial Craft (Member) of the British Horological Institute

**ICBM** intercontinental ballistic missile

**ICBN** International Code of Botanical Nomenclature

**ICBP** International Council for Bird Preservation

**ICC** (USA) Indian Claims Commission • intercounty championship • International Chamber of Commerce • International Children's Centre • International Congregational Council • International Convention Centre (Birmingham) • International Correspondence Colleges • International (formerly Imperial) Cricket Conference • (USA) Interstate Commerce Commission

**ICCA** International Cocoa Agreement

**ICCB** Intergovernmental Consultation and Coordination Board

**ICCE** International Council of Commerce Employers

**ICCF** International Correspondence Chess Federation

**ICCH** International Commodities Clearing House

**ICCPR** International Covenant on Civil and Political Rights (of the UN)

**ICCROM** International Centre for Conservation at Rome

**ICCS** International Centre of Criminological Studies

**ICD** Institute of Cooperative Directors • International Classification of Diseases (WHO publication)

**ICDO** International Civil Defence Organization

**Ice.** Iceland(ic)

**ICE** *Med.* ice, compress, elevation (treatment for limb bruises) • *Meteorol.* icing • Institution of Civil Engineers • internal-combustion engine • International Cultural Exchange

**ICED** International Council for Educational Development

**ICEF** International Federation of Chemical, Energy, and General Workers' Unions

**ICEI** Institution of Civil Engineers of Ireland

**Icel.** Iceland(ic)

**IC engine** internal-combustion engine

**ICES** *Physical chem.* internal-conversion electron spectroscopy • International Council for the Exploration of the Sea

**ICETT** Industrial Council for Educational and Training Technology

**ICF** Industrial and Commercial Finance Corporation (now part of Investors in Industry) • *Nuclear engineering* inertial-confinement fusion • International Canoe Federation

**ICFTU** International Confederation of Free Trade Unions

**ICGS** interactive computer-graphics system • International Catholic Girls' Society

**ich.** ichthyology

**ICH** *Nuclear engineering* ion cyclotron heating

**ICHCA** International Cargo Handling Co-ordination Association

**IChemE** Institution of Chemical Engineers

**ICHEO** Inter-University Council for Higher Education Overseas

**ICHPER** International Council for Health, Physical Education, and Recreation

**ichth.** (*or* **ichthyol.**) ichthyology

**ICI** Imperial Chemical Industries • International Commission on Illumination • (USA) Investment Casting Institute

**ICIA** International Credit Insurance Association

**ICIANZ** Imperial Chemical Industries, Australia and New Zealand

**ICID** International Commission on Irrigation and Drainage

**ICIDH** International Classification of Impairments, Disabilities, and Handicaps (WHO publication)

**ICJ** International Commission of Jurists • International Court of Justice

**ICJW** International Council of Jewish Women

**ICL** International Computers Ltd • International Confederation of Labour

**ICLA** International Committee on Laboratory Animals

**IcInd** Iceland

**ICM** Institute for Complementary Medicine • Institute of Credit Management • Intergovernmental Committee for Migrations (of the UN) • International Confederation of Midwives • Irish Church Missions

**ICMMP** International Committee of Military Medicine and Pharmacy

**ICMS** International Centre for Mathematical Sciences (Edinburgh)

**ICN** in Christi nomine (Latin: in Christ's name) • Infection Control Nurse • International Council of Nurses

**ICNA** Infection Control Nurses' Association

**ICNB** International Code of Nomenclature of Bacteria

**ICNCP** International Code of Nomenclature of Cultivated Plants

**ICNV** International Code of Nomenclature of Viruses

**ICO** Institute of Careers Officers • International Coffee Organization • Islamic Conference Organization

**ICOM** International Council of Museums

**ICOMOS** International Council of Monuments and Sites

**icon.** iconography

**ICOR** Intergovernmental Conference on Oceanic Research (in UNESCO)

**ICorrST** Institution of Corrosion Science and Technology

**ICP** *Physics* inductively coupled plasma • *Med.* intracranial pressure

**ICPA** International Commission for the Prevention of Alcoholism • International Cooperative Petroleum Association

**ICPHS** International Council for Philosophy and Humanistic Studies

**ICPO** International Criminal Police Organization (Interpol)

**ICPU** International Catholic Press Union

**ICR** *Computing* intelligent character recognition • *Physics* ion cyclotron resonance

**ICRC** International Committee of the Red Cross

**ICRF** Imperial Cancer Research Fund

**ICRH** *Nuclear engineering* ion cyclotron resonance heating

**ICRP** International Commission on Radiological Protection

**ICRU** International Commission on Radiation Units (and Measurements)

**ICS** Imperial College of Science and Technology (London) • Indian Civil Service (*see under* IAS) • instalment credit selling • Institute of Chartered Shipbrokers • International Chamber of Shipping • international consultancy service • *Finance* investors' compensation scheme

**ICSA** Institute of Chartered Secretaries and Administrators

**ICSH** *Biochem.* interstitial-cell-stimulating hormone

**ICSID** International Council of Societies of Industrial Design

**ICSLS** International Convention for Safety of Life at Sea

**ICSPE** International Council of Sport and Physical Education

**ICST** Imperial College of Science and Technology (London)

**ICSU** International Council of Scientific Unions (in UNESCO)

**ICTA** International Council of Travel Agents

**ICTP** International Centre for Theoretical Physics

**ICTU** Irish Congress of Trade Unions

**ICTV** International Committee on Taxonomy of Viruses

**ICU** *Med.* intensive care unit • international code use (of signals)

**ICVA** International Council of Voluntary Agencies

**i.c.w.** in connection with

**ICW** Institute of Clerks of Works of Great Britain • International Congress of Women • *Telecom.* interrupted continuous waves • *Physics* ion-cyclotron waves

**ICWA** Indian Council of World Affairs • Institute of Cost and Works Accountants

**ICWG** International Cooperative Women's Guild

**ICWU** (USA) International Chemical Workers Union

**ICYF** International Catholic Youth Federation

**ICZN** International Code of Zoological Nomenclature

**id.** idem (Latin: the same)

**Id.** Idaho

**ID** *Irish vehicle registration for* Cavan • *US postcode for* Idaho • identification • infectious disease(s) • information department • (*or* **i.d.**) inside diameter • Institute of Directors • Intelligence Department • (*or* **i.d.**) *Med.* intradermal • *symbol for* Iraqi dinar (monetary unit)

**IDA** Industrial Diamond Association • International Development Association • Irish Dental Association • Islamic Democratic Association • *Chem.* isotope dilution analysis

**IDB** illicit diamond buying (*or* buyer) • Industrial Development Bank • Inter-American Development Bank • Internal Drainage Board

**IDC** industrial development certificate

**ID card** identification card

**IDD** insulin-dependent diabetes • international direct dialling

**IDDD** *Telecom.* international direct distance dial(ling)

**IDDM** insulin-dependent diabetes mellitus

**iden.** (*or* **ident.**) identification • identify

**IDF** International Dairy Federation • International Democratic Fellowship • International Dental Federation • International Diabetes Federation

**IDGS** *Physics* isotope-dilution gamma spectrometry

**IDIB** Industrial Diamond Information Bureau

**IDL** *Biochem., Med.* intermediate-density lipoprotein • international date line

**IDLH** immediately dangerous to life and health

**IDMS** *Computing* integrated data-management system • *Chem.* isotope-dilution mass spectrometry

**IDN** in Dei nomine (Latin: in God's name) • *Computing* integrated data network

**IDOE** International Decade of Ocean Exploration (1970–80)

**IDP** *Biochem.* inosine diphosphate • Institute of Data Processing • *Comput-*

*ing* integrated data processing • International Driving Permit • *Astronomy* interplanetary dust particle(s)

**IDPM** Institute of Data Processing Management

**IDRC** International Development Research Centre

**IDS** Income Data Services • Industry Department for Scotland • Institute of Development Studies

**IDSM** Indian Distinguished Service Medal

**IDT** industrial design technology

**IDV** International Distillers and Vintners

**i.e.** id est (Latin: that is) • inside edge

**IE** *Irish vehicle registration for* Clare • *Med.* immunoelectrophoresis • index error • Indian Empire • Indo-European (languages) • *Chem.* ion exchange • *Chem.* ionization energy • *British fishing port registration for* Irvine

**IEA** Institute of Economic Affairs • (*or* **IE(Aust)**) Institution of Engineers, Australia • International Economic Association • International Energy Agency • International Ergonomics Association

**IEC** industrial energy conservation • integrated environmental control • International Electrotechnical Commission • *Chem.* ion-exchange chromatography

**IED** improvised explosive device • Information Engineering Directorate • Institution of Engineering Designers

**IEDD** improvised explosive device disposal (type of bomb disposal)

**IEE** (USA) Institute of Energy Economics • Institution of Electrical Engineers

**IEEE** (USA) Institute of Electrical and Electronics Engineers

**IEEIE** Institution of Electrical and Electronics Incorporated Engineers

**IEF** Indian Expeditionary Force

**IEHO** Institution of Environmental Health Officers

**IEI** Industrial Engineering Institute • Institution of Engineers of Ireland

**IEME** Inspectorate of Electrical and Mechanical Engineering

**IEng** Incorporated Engineer

**IER** Institute of Environmental Research

**IERE** Institution of Electronic and Radio Engineers

**IES** Indian Educational Service • Institution of Engineers and Shipbuilders in Scotland

**IET** interest equalization tax

**IEW** intelligence and electronic warfare

**IExpE** Institute of Explosives Engineers

**i.f.** information feedback • ipse fecit (Latin: he did it himself)

**IF** *Irish vehicle registration for* Cork • *Nuclear engineering* inertial fusion • *Baseball* infield • *Biochem.* inhibitory factor • *Genetics* initiation factor • *Sport* inside forward • *Med.* interferon • *Electronics* intermediate frequency

**IFA** *Med.* immunofluorescence assay • Incorporated Faculty of Arts • independent financial adviser • instrumented fuel assembly • International Federation of Actors • International Fertility Association • International Fiscal Association • Irish Football Association

**IFAC** International Federation of Automatic Control

**IFAD** International Fund for Agricultural Development (of the UN)

**IFALPA** International Federation of Air Line Pilots' Associations

**IFAP** International Federation of Agricultural Producers

**IFATCA** International Federation of Air Traffic Controllers' Associations

**IFAW** International Fund for Animal Welfare

**IFB** *Finance* invitation for bid

**IFBPW** International Federation of Business and Professional Women

**IFC** International Finance Corporation • (USA and Canada) International Fisheries Commission

**IFCC** International Federation of Camping and Caravanning

**IFCCPTE** International Federation of Commercial, Clerical, Professional, and Technical Employees

**IFCO** International Fisheries Cooperative Organization

**IFCTU** International Federation of Christian Trade Unions (now called World Confederation of Labour, WCL)

**IFDM** *Maths.* integrated finite-difference method

**IFE** (USA) Institute for Energy Technology • *Computing* intelligent front end

**IFEL** *Physics* induction free-electron laser

**iff** *Logic, Maths.* if and only if

**IFF** Identification, Friend or Foe (radar identification system) • Institute of Freight Forwarders

**IFFA** International Federation of Film Archives

**IFFPA** International Federation of Film Producers' Associations

**IFFS** International Federation of Film Societies

**IFFTU** International Federation of Free Teachers' Unions

**IFGA** International Federation of Grocers' Associations

**IFGO** International Federation of Gynaecology and Obstetrics

**IFIP** International Federation for Information Processing

**IFJ** International Federation of Journalists

**IFK** *Maths.* integral equation of the first kind

**IFL** International Friendship League

**IFLA** International Federation of Landscape Architects • International Federation of Library Associations

**IFMC** International Folk Music Council

**IFMSA** International Federation of Medical Students' Associations

**IFOR** International Fellowship of Reconciliation

**IFORS** International Federation of Operational Research Societies

**IFP** (South Africa) Inkatha Freedom Party

**IFPA** Industrial Film Producers' Association

**IFPAAW** International Federation of Plantation, Agricultural, and Allied Workers

**IFPCS** International Federation of Unions of Employees in Public and Civil Services

**IFPI** International Federation of the Phonographic Industry

**IFPM** International Federation of Physical Medicine

**IFPW** International Federation of Petroleum (and Chemical) Workers

**IFR** *Aeronautics* instrument flying regulations • *Nuclear engineering* integral fast reactor

**IFRB** International Frequency Registration Board

**IFS** Indian Forest Service • International Federation of Surveyors • Irish Free State

**IFSPO** International Federation of Senior Police Officers

**IFST** Institute of Food Science and Technology

**IFSW** International Federation of Social Workers

**IFTA** International Federation of Teachers' Associations • International Federation of Travel Agencies

**IFTC** International Film and Television Council

**IFTU** International Federation of Trade Unions (forerunner of WFTU)

**IFUW** International Federation of University Women

**IFWEA** International Federation of Workers' Educational Associations

**IFWL** International Federation of Women Lawyers

**ig.** ignition

**Ig** *Immunol.* immunoglobulin (as in **IgA**, **IgE**, **IgG**)

**IG** *postcode for* Ilford • Indo-Germanic (languages) • industrial group • *Astronautics* inertial guidance • Inspector General • Instructor in Gunnery • Irish Guards

**IGA** International Geographical Association • International Golf Association

**IGasE** Institution of Gas Engineers

**IGD** illicit gold dealer

**IGF** Inspector-General of Fortifications • *Med.* insulin-like growth factor • International Gymnastic Federation

**IGFA** International Game Fish Association

**IGFET** ('ɪgfɛt) *Electronics* insulated-gate field-effect transistor

**IGH** Incorporated Guild of Hairdressers

**IGM** *Chess* International Grandmaster

**ign.** ignite(s) • ignition • ignotus (Latin: unknown)

**IGO** intergovernmental organization

**IGPP** Institute of Geophysics and Planetary Physics

**IGS** Imperial General Staff • independent grammar school

**IGSCC** *Engineering* intergranular stress corrosion cracking

**IGU** International Gas Union • International Geographical Union

**IGY** International Geophysical Year (1.7.57 to 31.12.58)

**IH** *Irish vehicle registration for* Donegal • iacet hic (Latin: here lies; on gravestones) • industrial hygiene • *Computing* interrupt handler • *British fishing port registration for* Ipswich

**IHA** International Hotel Association

**IHAB** International Horticultural Advisory Bureau

**IHB** International Hydrographic Bureau

**IHC** (New Zealand) intellectually handicapped child

**IHCA** International Hebrew Christian Alliance

**IHD** International Hydrological Decade (1965–74) • ischaemic heart disease

**IHE** *Metallurgy* internal hydrogen embrittlement

**IHEU** International Humanist and Ethical Union

**IHF** Industrial Hygiene Foundation • International Hockey Federation • International Hospitals Federation

**IHM** Jesus Mundi Salvator (Latin: Jesus, Saviour of the World)

**IHospE** Institute of Hospital Engineering

**ihp** indicated horsepower

**IHR** Institute of Historical Research

**IHS** Iesus Hominum Salvator (Latin: Jesus, Saviour of Mankind) • in hoc signo (Latin: in this sign) • Jesus (Greek ΙΗΣΟΥΣ)

**IHSM** Institute of Health Services Management

**IHT** Institution of Highways and Transportation

**IHU** Irish Hockey Union

**II** *Electronics* image intensifier • *Electronics* ion implantation

**IIA** International Institute of Agriculture

**IIAC** Industrial Injuries Advisory Council

**IIAL** International Institute of Arts and Letters

**IIAS** International Institute of Administrative Sciences

**IIB** Institut international des brevets (French: International Patent Institute)

**IIBD&ID** Incorporated Institute of British Decorators and Interior Designers

**iid** *Statistics* independent identically distributed (of random variables)

**IID** insulin-independent diabetes • *Electronics* ion-implantation doping

**IIE** Institute for International Education • International Institute of Embryology

**IIEE** *Physical chem.* ion-induced electron emission

**IIEP** International Institute of Educational Planning

**IIHF** International Ice Hockey Federation

**3i** Investors in Industry

**III** International Institute of Interpreters

**IIL** (*or* I²L) *Electronics* integrated injection logic

**IIM** Institution of Industrial Managers

**IInfSc** Institute of Information Scientists

**IIP** Institut international de la presse (French: International Press Institute) • International Ice Patrol • International Institute of Philosophy

**IIR** *Chem.* isobutylene-isoprene rubber

**IIRS** (Irish Republic) Institute for Industrial Research and Standards

**IIS** Institute of Information Scientists • International Institute of Sociology

**IISO** Institution of Industrial Safety Officers

**IISS** International Institute of Strategic Studies

**IIT** Indian Institute of Technology

**i.J.** im Jahre (German: in the year)

**IJ** *British vehicle registration for* Down

**IK** *Irish vehicle registration for* Dublin

**IKBS** *Computing* intelligent knowledge-based system

**i.l.** inside leg

**IL** *British vehicle registration for* Fermanagh • *US postcode for* Illinois • Ilyushin (aircraft) • *Sport* inside left • Institute of Linguists • *Aeronautics* instrument landing • *Immunol.* interleukin (as in **IL-1**, **IL-2**) • *Physical chem.* ionization (energy) loss (spectroscopy) • *international vehicle registration for* Israel

**I/L** import licence

**I²L** *Electronics* integrated injection logic

**ILA** *Physics* induction linear accelerator • Institute of Landscape Architects • *Aeronautics* instrument landing approach • International Law Association • International Longshoremen's Association

**ILAA** International Legal Aid Association

**ILAB** International League of Antiquarian Booksellers

**ILC** International Law Commission (of the UN)

**ILD** *Med.* interstitial lung disease

**Ile** (*or* **ile**) isoleucine

**ILEA** ('ɪliə) Inner London Education Authority

**ILEC** Inner London Education Committee

**ILF** International Landworkers' Federation

**ILGA** Institute of Local Government Administration

**ILGWU** (USA) International Ladies' Garment Workers' Union

**ill.** illustrate(d) • illustration • illustrissimus (Latin: most distinguished)

**Ill.** Illinois

**illegit.** illegitimate

**illit.** illiterate

**illum.** illuminate(d)

**illus.** (*or* **illust.**) illustrate(d) • illustration • illustrator

**ILN** (ital.) Illustrated London News

**i.l.o.** in lieu of

**ILO** industrial liaison officer • International Labour Organization (of the UN)

**ILP** Independent Labour Party

**ILR** Independent Law Reports • independent local radio

**ILRM** International League for the Rights of Man

**ILS** Incorporated Law Society • *Aeronautics* instrument landing system • *Statistics* inverse least-squares • *Chem.* ionization-loss spectroscopy

**ILTF** International Lawn Tennis Federation

**ILU** Institute of London Underwriters

**ILW** *Nuclear engineering* intermediate-level waste

**Im.** Imperial

**IM** *Irish vehicle registration for* Galway • Indian Marines • Institute of Metals • interceptor missile • *Chess* International Master • (*or* **i.m.**) *Med.* intramuscular

**IMA** Indian Military Academy • Institute of Mathematics and its Applications • International Music Association • Irish Medical Association

**imag.** imaginary • imagination • imagine

**IM & AWU** (USA) International Molders' and Allied Workers' Union

**IMarE** Institute of Marine Engineers

**IMARSAT** (*or* **Imarsat**) ('ɪmɑːˌsæt) International Maritime Satellite Organization

**IMAS** International Marine and Shipping Conference

**IMB** Institute of Marine Biology

**IMC** *Photog.* image motion compensation • Institute of Management Consultants • Institute of Measurement and Control • *Aeronautics* instrument meteorological conditions • International Maritime Committee • International Missionary Council • International Music Council

**IMCO** Intergovernmental Maritime Consultative Organization (of the UN)

**IMEA** Incorporated Municipal Electrical Association

**IMechE** Institution of Mechanical Engineers

**IMINT** (*or* **Imint**) ('ɪmɪnt) *Military* image intelligence (gained from aerial photography)

**IMet** Institute of Metals

**I. Meth.** Independent Methodist

**IMF** International Monetary Fund • *Astrophysics* interplanetary magnetic field

**IMGTechE** Institution of Mechanical and General Technician Engineers

**IMinE** Institution of Mining Engineers

**IMINT** (*or* **Imint**) ('ɪmɪnt) *Military* image intelligence (gained from aerial photography)

**imit.** imitate • imitation • imitative

**IMM** Institution of Mining and Metallurgy • International Mercantile Marine • International Monetary Market

**immed.** immediate

**IMMTS** Indian Mercantile Marine Training Ship

**immun.** immunity • immunization • immunology

**IMO** International Maritime Organization • International Meteorological Organization • International Miners' Organization

**imp.** imperative • imperfect • imperial • impersonal • implement • import(ed) • important • importer • impression • imprimatur • imprimé (French: printed) • imprimeur (French: printer) • imprint

**Imp.** Imperator (Latin: Emperor) • Imperatrix (Latin: Empress) • Imperial

**IMP** (ɪmp) *Physics* indeterminate mass particle • *Biochem.* inosine monophosphate • (ɪmp) *Computing* interface message processor (in a network) • (ɪmp) *Bridge* International Match Point • interplanetary measurement probe

**IMPA** International Master Printers' Association

**IMPACT** ('ɪmpækt) implementation, planning, and control technique

**IMPATT** ('ɪmpæt) *Electronics* impact ionization avalanche transit time

**impce** importance

**imper.** imperative

**imperf.** imperfect • imperforate (of stamps)

**impers.** impersonal

**impf.** (*or* **impft**) imperfect

**imposs.** impossible
**IMPR** *Meteorol.* improving
**impreg.** impregnate(d)
**improp.** improper(ly)
**impt** important
**imptr** importer
**impv.** imperative
**IMR** individual medical report • infant mortality rate • Institute of Medical Research
**IMRA** Industrial Marketing Research Association
**IMRAN** ('ɪmræn) international marine radio aids to navigation
**IMRO** ('ɪmrəʊ) Investment Management Regulatory Organization
**IMS** Indian Medical Service • industrial methylated spirit • *Computing, trademark* Information Management System • Institute of Management Services • International Musicological Society
**IMSM** Institute of Marketing and Sales Management
**IMT** *Meteorol.* immediate(ly) • International Military Tribunal
**IMU** International Mathematical Union
**IMunE** Institution of Municipal Engineers (now part of the Institution of Civil Engineers)
**IMVS** (Australia) Institute of Medical and Veterinary Science
**IMW** Institute of Masters of Wine • *Biochem.* intermediate molecular weight
**in** *symbol for* inch(es)
**in.** inch(es)
**In** *Chem., symbol for* indium
**In.** India(n) • *Military* Instructor
**IN** *US postcode for* Indiana • Indian Navy • *Irish vehicle registration for* Kerry
**INA** Indian National Army • Institution of Naval Architects • International Newsreel Association
**INAO** (France) Institut national des appellations d'origine des vins et eaux-de-vie (body controlling wine production)
**inaug.** inaugurate(d)
**inbd** inboard (on an aircraft, boat, etc.)
**Inbucon** ('ɪnbjuːˌkɒn) International Business Consultants
**inc.** include(d) • including • inclusive • income • incomplete • incorporate(d) • increase • incumbent
**Inc.** Incorporated (after names of business organizations; US equivalent of Ltd)

**INC** *Meteorol.* in cloud • Indian National Congress • in nomine Christi (Latin: in the name of Christ)
**INCA** International Newspaper Colour Association
**incalz.** *Music* incalzando (Italian; increasing speed and tone)
**INCB** International Narcotics Control Board (of the UN)
**incho.** *Law* inchoate
**incid.** incidental
**incl.** incline • include(s) • included • including • inclusive
**incog.** incognito
**incorp.** (*or* **incor.**) incorporated • incorporation
**incorr.** incorrect
**INCPEN** ('ɪŋkˌpɛn) Industry Committee for Packaging and the Environment
**incr.** increase(d) • increasing • increment
**INCR** *Meteorol.* increase
**incun.** incunabula
**in d.** *Med.* in dies (Latin: daily)
**ind.** independence • independent • index • indicate • indication • indicative • indigo • indirect(ly) • industrial • industry
**Ind** *Astronomy* Indus
**Ind.** *Politics* Independent • India(n) • Indiana • Indies
**IND** *international vehicle registration for* India • in nomine Dei (Latin: in God's name) • *Pharmacol.* (USA) investigational (*or* investigative) new drug
**indecl.** *Grammar* indeclinable
**indef.** indefinite
**indic.** indicating • indicative • indicator
**Ind. Imp.** Indiae Imperator (Latin: Emperor of India)
**indiv.** (*or* **individ.**) individual
**Ind. Meth.** Independent Methodist
**Indo-Eur.** Indo-European
**Indo-Ger.** Indo-German(ic)
**indre.** indenture
**induc.** induction
**indust.** industrial • industrious • industry
**ined.** ineditus (Latin: unpublished)
**INER** Institute of Nuclear Energy Research
**INET** Institute of Nuclear Energy Technology
**in ex.** in extenso (Latin: in full)
**inf** *Maths.* infinum
**inf.** (*or* **Inf.**) infantry • inferior • infinitive • influence • information • infra

(Latin: below) • *Med.* infusum (Latin: infusion)

**INF** intermediate-range nuclear forces (as in **INF treaty**) • International Naturist Federation

**infin.** infinitive

**infirm.** infirmary

**infl.** inflammable • inflated • inflect • *Botany* inflorescence • influence(d)

**infm.** information

**Ing.** Ingenieur (German: engineer)

**Ingl.** Inghilterra (Italian: England)

**INGO** international nongovernmental organization

**Inh.** Inhaber (German: proprietor) • Inhalt (German: contents)

**INH** *Med.* isonicotinic acid hydrazide (isoniazid; antituberculosis drug)

**inhab.** inhabitant

**INI** in nomine Iesu (Latin: in the name of Jesus)

**init.** initial(ly) • initio (Latin: in the beginning)

**inj.** injection • injury

**INJ** in nomine Jesu (Latin: in the name of Jesus)

**INLA** International Nuclear Law Association • Irish National Liberation Army

**in lim.** in limine (Latin: at the outset)

**in loc.** in loco (Latin: in place of)

**in loc. cit.** in loco citato (Latin: in the place cited (in text))

**INMARSAT** (*or* **Inmarsat**) ('ɪnmɑ:-ˌsæt) International Maritime Satellite Organization

**in mem.** in memoriam (Latin: to the memory (of))

**inn.** *Cricket* innings

**INO** inspectorate of naval ordnance

**inorg.** inorganic

**INP** Institute of Nuclear Physics

**in pr.** in principio (Latin: in the beginning)

**in pro.** in proportion

**inq.** inquiry • inquisition

**INR** independent national radio (as in **INR licence**) • Index of Nursing Research

**INRI** Iesus Nazarenus Rex Iudaeorum (Latin: Jesus of Nazareth, King of the Jews)

**in s.** in situ

**ins.** inches • inscribe • inscription • inspector • insular • insulate(d) • insulation • insurance

**INS** Indian Naval Ship • *Physics* inelastic neutron scattering • inertial naviga-

tion system • International News Service • *British fishing port registration for* Inverness

**INSA** Indian National Science Academy

**INSAG** International Nuclear Safety Advisory Group

**insce** insurance

**inscr.** inscribe • inscription

**INSEA** International Society for Education through Art

**INSEAD** (*or* **Insead**) Institut européen d'administration des affaires (French: European Institute of Administrative Affairs)

**insep.** inseparable

**INSET** (*or* **Inset**) ('ɪnsɛt) *Education* in-service training

**insol.** insoluble

**insolv.** insolvent

**insp.** inspect(ed) • inspection • (*or* **Insp.**) inspector

**Insp. Gen.** Inspector General

**inst.** instance • instant (this month) • instantaneous • (*or* **Inst.**) institute • (*or* **Inst.**) institution • instruct(ion) • instructor • instrument(al)

**INST** in nomine Sanctae Trinitatis (Latin: in the name of the Holy Trinity)

**INSTAB** ('ɪnstæb) Information Service on Toxicity and Biodegradability (water pollution)

**InstAct** Institute of Actuaries

**InstBE** Institution of British Engineers

**InstCE** Institution of Civil Engineers

**InstD** Institute of Directors

**InstE** Institute of Energy

**InstEE** Institution of Electrical Engineers

**instl.** installation

**InstMet** Institute of Metals

**InstMM** Institution of Mining and Metallurgy

**instn** (*or* **Instn**) institution

**InstP** Institute of Physics

**InstPet** Institute of Petroleum

**InstPI** Institute of Patentees and Inventors

**instr.** instruction • instructor • instrument(al)

**InstR** Institute of Refrigeration

**InstSMM** Institute of Sales and Marketing Management

**InstT** Institute of Transport

**int.** (military) intelligence • intercept • interest • interim • interior • interjection • intermediate • internal • (*or* **Int.**) international • interpret(er) • interpretation • interval • intransitive • *Music* introit

**INT** Isaac Newton Telescope (La Palma)

**int. al.** inter alia (Latin: among other things)

**INTAL** ('ıntæl) Institute for Latin American Integration (Buenos Aires)

**Intelsat** (*or* **INTELSAT**) ('ıntɛl,sæt) International Telecommunications Satellite Consortium

**intens.** intensifier • intensify • intensive

**inter.** intermediate • interrogation mark

**INTER** *Meteorol.* intermittent

**interj.** interjection

**internat.** international

**interp.** interpreter

**Interpol** ('ıntə,pɒl) International Criminal Police Organization

**interrog.** interrogate • interrogation • interrogative

**intl** international

**INTO** Irish National (Primary) Teachers' Organization

**intr.** (*or* **intrans.**) intransitive

**in trans.** in transit

**intro.** (*or* **introd.**) introduce • introduction • introductory

**INTSF** *Meteorol.* intensify

**INTST** *Meteorol.* intensity

**INTUC** ('ıntʌk) Indian National Trade Union Congress

**INucE** Institution of Nuclear Engineers

**inv.** invenit (Latin: (he *or* she) designed this) • invent(ed) • invention • inventor • inversion • invert • investment • invoice

**Inv.** Inverness

**inv. et del.** invenit et delineavit (Latin: (he *or* she) designed and drew this)

**invt.** (*or* **invty**) inventory

**IO** India Office • inspecting officer • integrated optics • intelligence officer • *Irish vehicle registration for* Kildare

**I/O** *Computing* input/output • inspecting order

**IOB** (*or* **IoB**) Institute of Bankers (renamed Chartered Institute of Bankers, CIB) • Institute of Biology • Institute of Bookkeepers • Institute of Brewing • Institute of Building (renamed Chartered Institute of Building, CIOB)

**IOC** Intergovernmental Oceanographic Commission • International Olympic Committee

**IOCU** International Organization of Consumers' Unions

**IoD** Institute of Directors

**IODE** (Canada) Imperial Order of Daughters of the Empire

**IOE** International Organization of Employers

**IOF** Independent Order of Foresters • International Oceanographic Foundation • International Orienteering Federation

**I of E** Institute of Export

**I of M** Isle of Man

**IOGT** International Order of Good Templars

**IoJ** Institute of Journalists

**IOJ** International Organization of Journalists

**IOM** Indian Order of Merit • Institute of Metals • Isle of Man

**IOMTR** International Office for Motor Trades and Repairs

**Ion.** Ionic

**IOO** Inspecting Ordnance Officer

**IOOF** Independent Order of Oddfellows

**IOP** *Computing* input/output processor • Institute of Painters in Oil Colours • Institute of Petroleum • Institute of Physics • Institute of Plumbing • Institute of Printing

**IOPAB** International Organization for Pure and Applied Biophysics

**IoS** (ital.) The Independent on Sunday

**IOS** *Computing* integrated office system

**IOSCO** (*or* **Iosco**) (aɪ'ɒskəʊ) International Organization of Securities Commissions

**IOSM** Independent Order of the Sons of Malta

**IoT** Institute of Transport

**IOU** Industrial Operations Unit • I owe you

**IOW** Institute of Welding • (*or* **IoW**) Isle of Wight

**i.p.** identification point • incentive pay • indexed and paged • initial phase • *Electrical engineering* input primary

**IP** *Electronics* image processing • Imperial Preference • India Paper • *Baseball* innings pitched • *Biochem.* inositol phosphate • *Med.* in-patient • *Electrical engineering* input primary • instalment plan • Institute of Petroleum • Institute of Plumbing • *Chem.* ionization potential • *postcode for* Ipswich • *Irish vehicle registration for* Kilkenny

**IP₃** *Biochem.* inositol triphosphate

**IPA** India Pale Ale • Insolvency Practitioners' Association • Institute of Park Administration • Institute of Practitioners in Advertising • International Phonetic Alphabet • International Phonetic Association • International Poetry Archives (Manchester) • International Police Academy • International Police Association • International Publishers' Association • *Biochem.* isopentenyl adenosine • *Chem.* isopropanol (*or* isopropyl alcohol)

**IPAA** International Petroleum Association of America • International Prisoners' Aid Association

**IPARS** International Programmed Airline Reservation System

**IPC** International Petroleum Company (Peru) • International Polar Commission • International Publishing Corporation • Iraq Petroleum Company

**IPCC** Intergovernmental Panel on Climatic Change (of the UN)

**IPCS** *Astronomy, Physics* image photon counting system • Institution of Professional Civil Servants • *Computing* intelligent process-control system

**IPD** individual package delivery • *Law* (Scotland) in praesentia dominorum (Latin: in the presence of the Lords (of Session)) • *Med.* intermittent peritoneal dialysis

**IPE** Institution of Plant Engineers • Institution of Production Engineers • International Petroleum Exchange

**IPF** *Med.* interstitial pulmonary fibrosis • Irish Printing Federation

**IPFA** (Member or Associate of the Chartered) Institute of Public Finance and Accountancy

**IPFC** Indo-Pacific Fisheries Council (of the FAO)

**IPG** Independent Publishers' Guild • Industrial Painters' Group

**IPH** *Med.* idiopathic portal hypertension • industrial process heat(ing)

**IPHE** Institution of Public Health Engineers (*see* IWEM)

**i.p.i.** in partibus infidelium (Latin: in the regions of unbelievers)

**IPI** Institute of Patentees and Inventors • Institute of Professional Investigators • International Press Institute

**IPL** *Computing* initial program load

**IPlantE** Institution of Plant Engineers

**IPM** *Freemasonry* immediate past master • (*or* **ipm**) inches per minute • Institute of Personnel Management

**IPO** *Computing* input-process-output • Israel Philharmonic Orchestra • *Stock exchange* (USA) initial public offering (a flotation)

**IPP** Institute for Plasma Physics • *Med.* intermittent positive pressure (ventilation)

**IPPA** Independent Programme Producers' Association

**IPPF** International Planned Parenthood Federation

**IPPR** Institute for Public Policy Research

**IPPS** Institute of Physics and the Physical Society

**IPPV** *Med.* intermittent positive-pressure ventilation

**IPR** Institute of Public Relations

**IPRA** International Public Relations Association

**IPRE** Incorporated Practitioners in Radio and Electronics

**IProdE** Institution of Production Engineers

**ips** inches per second • *Computing* instructions per second

**Ips.** Ipswich

**IPS** inches per second • Indian Police Service • Indian Political Service • Institute of Purchasing and Supply • International Confederation for Plastic Surgery • *Computing* interpretative programming system

**IPSA** International Political Science Association

**IPSE** ('IPSI) *Computing* integrated project support environment

**i.p.s.p.** (*or* **IPSP**) *Physiol.* inhibitory postsynaptic potential

**IPT** Institute of Petroleum Technologists

**IPTO** (*or* **i.p.t.o.**) *Astronautics* independent power takeoff

**IPTPA** International Professional Tennis Players' Association

**IPTS** *Physics* International Practical Temperature Scale

**IPU** Inter-Parliamentary Union

**i.q.** idem quod (Latin: the same as)

**IQ** Institute of Quarrying • intelligence quotient • international quota

**IQA** Institute of Quality Assurance

**IQS** Institute of Quantity Surveyors

**i.r.** inside radius

**i.R.** im Ruhestand (German: retired *or* emeritus)

**Ir** *Chem., symbol for* iridium

**Ir.** Ireland • Irish

**IR** *Meteorol.* ice on runway • incidence rate • index register • informal report • information retrieval • infrared (radiation) • Inland Revenue • *Sport* inside right • inspector's report • Institute of Refrigeration • instrument reading • international registration • *international vehicle registration for* Iran • *airline flight code for* Iran Air • Iranian rial (monetary unit) • *Chem.* isoprene rubber • *Irish vehicle registration for* Offaly

**IRA** (USA) individual retirement account • Institute of Registered Architects • Irish Republican Army

**IRAD** Institute for Research on Animal Diseases

**Iran.** Iranian

**IRAS** ('aıræs) Infrared Astronomical Satellite

**IRB** Irish Republican Brotherhood

**IRBM** intermediate-range ballistic missile

**IRC** Industrial Reorganization Corporation • Infantry Reserve Corps • International Red Cross • International Research Council

**IRCert** Industrial Relations Certificate

**IRD** International Research and Development Company

**IRDA** Industrial Research and Development Authority

**Ire.** Ireland

**IRE** (USA) Institute of Radio Engineers

**IREE(Aust)** Institution of Radio and Electronics Engineers (Australia)

**IRF** International Road Federation • International Rowing Federation

**IRFB** International Rugby Football Board

**IRFU** Irish Rugby Football Union

**IRI** Institution of the Rubber Industry (now part of the Plastics and Rubber Institute) • (Italy) Istituto per la Ricostruzione Industriale (Industrial Reconstruction Institute)

**irid.** iridescent

**Iris** ('aɪrɪs) infrared intruder system

**IRIS** International Research and Information Service

**IRL** *international vehicle registration for* Republic of Ireland

**IRLS** *Navigation* interrogation recording location system

**IRM** *Ethology* innate releasing mechanism • Islamic Republic of Mauritania •

*Geology* isothermal remanent magnetization

**IRN** Independent Radio News

**IRO** industrial relations officer • Inland Revenue Office • International Refugee Organization • International Relief Organization

**IRPA** International Radiation Protection Association

**IRQ** *Computing* interrupt request • *international vehicle registration for* Iraq

**irr.** *Finance* irredeemable • irregular

**IRR** infrared radiation • Institute of Race Relations • *Finance* internal rate of return

**irreg.** irregular(ly)

**IRRI** International Rice Research Institute

**IRRV** Institute of Revenues, Rating, and Valuation

**IRS** *Computing* information retrieval system • (USA) Internal Revenue Service

**IRTE** Institute of Road Transport Engineers

**IRTF** Infrared Telescope Facility (Mauna Kea, Hawaii)

**IRU** industrial rehabilitation unit • International Relief Union • International Road Transport Union

**IRWC** International Registry of World Citizens

**Is.** *Bible* Isaiah • Islam(ic) • Island(s) • Isle(s) • Israel(i)

**IS** *international vehicle registration for* Iceland • Industrial Society • information science • information service • information system • (*or* **i.s.**) *Electrical engineering* input secondary • *Genetics* insertion sequence • International Society of Sculptors, Painters, and Gravers • Irish Society • *Physical chem.* isomer shift • *Irish vehicle registration for* Mayo

**Isa.** *Bible* Isaiah

**ISA** Independent Schools' Association • International Sociological Association • *Aeronautics* International Standard Atmosphere (formerly Interim Standard Atmosphere)

**ISAB** Institute for the Study of Animal Behaviour

**ISAC** Industrial Safety Advisory Council

**ISAM** *Computing* indexed sequential access method

**ISAS** (Japan) Institute of Space and Astronautical Science

**ISBA** Incorporated Society of British Advertisers

**ISBN** International Standard Book Number

**ISC** Imperial Service College (Haileybury) • Imperial Staff College • Indian Staff Corps • *Med.* intermittent self-catheterization • International Seismological Centre • International Student Conference • International Sugar Council • *Freemasonry* International Supreme Council

**ISCE** International Society of Christian Endeavour

**ISCh** Incorporated Society of Chiropodists

**ISCM** International Society for Contemporary Music

**ISCO** Independent Schools Careers Organization • International Standard Classification of Occupations

**ISD** international standard depth • international subscriber dialling

**ISDN** *Computing, Telecom.* Integrated Services Digital Network

**ISE** Indian Service of Engineers • Institution of Structural Engineers • International Stock Exchange of the UK and the Republic of Ireland Ltd

**ISF** International Shipping Federation • International Spiritualist Federation

**ISGE** International Society of Gastroenterology

**ISH** International Society of Haematology

**ISHS** International Society for Horticultural Science

**ISI** Indian Standards Institution • International Statistical Institute • Iron and Steel Institute

**ISIS** ('aɪsɪs) (*or* **Isis**) Independent Schools Information Service • International Shipping Information Services

**ISJC** Independent Schools Joint Council

**ISK** *symbol for* króna (Icelandic monetary unit)

**isl.** (*or* **Isl.**) island • isle

**ISM** Iesus Salvator Mundi (Latin: Jesus, Saviour of the World) • Imperial Service Medal • Incorporated Society of Musicians • *Astronomy* interstellar medium

**ISME** International Society for Musical Education

**ISMRC** Inter-Services Metallurgical Research Council

**ISO** Imperial Service Order • International Standards Organization (International Organization for Standardization) • International Sugar Organization

**isol.** isolate(d) • isolation

**ISOL** *Meteorol.* isolated

**ISP** Institute of Sales Promotion • International Study Programme

**ISPA** International Society for the Protection of Animals • International Sporting Press Association

**ISPEMA** Industrial Safety (Personal Equipment) Manufacturers' Association

**ISQ** *Med.* in statu quo (Latin: in the same state; unchanged)

**ISR** information storage and retrieval • Institute of Social Research • International Society for Radiology • *Physics* intersecting storage ring

**ISRB** Inter-Services Research Bureau

**ISRD** International Society for Rehabilitation of the Disabled

**ISRO** International Securities Regulatory Organization

**iss.** issue

**ISS** Institute of Space Sciences (*or* Studies) • International Social Service • *Physical chem.* ion-scattering spectrometry • *Physics* isotope separation system

**ISSA** International Social Security Association

**ISSC** International Social Science Council

**ISSN** International Standard Serial Number

**ISSS** International Society of Soil Science

**IST** Indian Standard Time • information sciences technology • Institute of Science Technology

**ISTC** Institute of Scientific and Technical Communicators • Iron and Steel Trades' Confederation

**ISTD** Imperial Society of Teachers of Dancing

**ISTEA** Iron and Steel Trades Employers' Association

**isth.** (*or* **Isth.**) isthmus

**IStructE** Institution of Structural Engineers

**ISU** International Seamen's Union • International Shooting Union • International Skating Union

**ISV** independent software vendor • International Scientific Vocabulary

**ISVA** Incorporated Society of Valuers and Auctioneers

**ISWG** *Engineering* Imperial Standard Wire Gauge

**it.** italic

**i.t.** inspection tag • *Tools* internal thread • in transit

**It.** Italian • Italy

**IT** ignition temperature • income tax • (USA) Indian Territory • industrial tribunal • infantry training • information technology • *Law* Inner Temple • *Physics* International Table (in **IT calorie**) • *Irish vehicle registration for* Leitrim

**i t a** (*or* **ITA**) initial teaching alphabet

**ITA** Independent Television Authority (superseded by the IBA) • industrial and technical assistance • Industrial Transport Association

**ITAI** Institution of Technical Authors and Illustrators

**ital.** italic

**Ital.** Italian • Italy

**ITALY** I trust and love you

**ITB** Industry Training Board • International Time Bureau • Irish Tourist Board

**i.t.c.** installation time and cost

**ITC** Imperial Tobacco Company • Independent Television Commission • Industrial Training Council • International Tin Council • International Trade Centre • *Meteorol.* intertropical confluence • (USA) investment tax credit

**ITCZ** *Meteorol.* intertropical convergence zone

**ITDA** *Military* indirect target damage assessment

**ITE** Institute of Terrestrial Ecology

**ITEME** Institution of Technician Engineers in Mechanical Engineering

**ITER** international thermonuclear engineering reactor • international tokamak engineering reactor

**ITF** International Tennis Federation • International Trade Federations • International Transport Workers' Federation

**itin.** itinerary

**Itl.** Italian

**ITMA** Institute of Trade Mark Agents • ('ɪtmə) It's That Man Again (BBC radio series)

**ITN** Independent Television News

**ITO** *Electronics* indium–tin oxide • International Trade Organization

**ITP** *Biochem.* inosine triphosphate

**ITS** Industrial Training Service • (USA) Intermarket Trading System • International Trade Secretariat

**ITT** *Med.* insulin tolerance test • International Telephone and Telegraph Corporation

**ITTF** International Table Tennis Federation

**ITU** *Med.* intensive therapy unit • International Telecommunication Union (of the UN) • International Temperance Union • International Typographical Union

**ITV** Independent Television • (USA) instructional television

**ITVA** International Television Association

**ITWF** International Transport Workers' Federation

**IU** immunizing unit • *Pharmacol.* international unit(s) • (Spain) Izquierda Unida (United Left; political party) • *Irish vehicle registration for* Limerick

**IUA** International Union Against Alcoholism • International Union of Architects

**IUAA** International Union of Advertisers' Associations

**IUAES** International Union of Anthropological and Ethnological Sciences

**IUAI** International Union of Aviation Insurers

**IUAO** International Union for Applied Ornithology

**IUAPPA** International Union of Air Pollution Prevention Associations

**IUB** International Union of Biochemistry • International Universities Bureau

**IUBS** International Union of Biological Sciences

**IUCD** *Med.* intrauterine contraceptive device

**IUCN** International Union for the Conservation of Nature and Natural Resources

**IUCr** International Union of Crystallography

**IUCW** International Union for Child Welfare

**IUD** *Med.* intrauterine death • *Med.* intrauterine (contraceptive) device

**IUE** *Astronomy* International Ultraviolet Explorer • (USA) International Union of Electronic, Electrical, Salaried,

Machine, and Furniture Workers (trade union)

**IUF** International Union of Food and Allied Workers' Associations

**IUFO** International Union of Family Organizations

**IUFRO** International Union of Forest Research Organizations

**IUGG** International Union of Geodesy and Geophysics

**IUGR** *Med.* intrauterine growth retardation

**IUGS** International Union of Geological Sciences

**IUHPS** International Union of the History and Philosophy of Science

**IULA** International Union of Local Authorities

**IUMF** (France) institut d'universitaires de formation des maîtres (advanced teacher-education institute)

**IUMI** International Union of Marine Insurance

**IUMSWA** Industrial Union of Marine and Shipbuilding Workers of America

**IUNS** International Union of Nutritional Sciences

**IUOE** (USA) International Union of Operating Engineers

**IUPAB** International Union of Pure and Applied Biophysics

**IUPAC** ('juːpæk) International Union of Pure and Applied Chemistry

**IUPAP** ('juːpæp) International Union of Pure and Applied Physics

**IUPS** International Union of Physiological Sciences

**IUS** *Astronautics* inertial upper stage • International Union of Students

**IUSP** International Union of Scientific Psychology

**IUSY** International Union of Socialist Youth

**IUT** *Med.* intra-uterine transfusion

**IUTAM** International Union of Theoretical and Applied Mechanics

**i.v.** increased value • *Med.* intravenous(ly) • invoice value

**i.V.** in Vertretung (German: by proxy)

**IV** *airline flight code for* Air Gambia • *Chem.* intermediate valency • *Med.* intravenous(ly) • *postcode for* Inverness • invoice value

**IVA** individual voluntary arrangement (in bankruptcy proceedings) • invalidity allowance

**IVB** *Physics* intermediate vector boson • invalidity benefit

**IVBF** International Volley-Ball Federation

**IVC** *Med.* inferior vena cava

**IVF** *Med.* in vitro fertilization

**IVP** *Med.* intravenous pyelogram

**IVR** international vehicle registration

**IVS** International Voluntary Service

**IVT** *Astronautics* intravehicular transfer

**IVU** International Vegetarian Union

**i.w.** indirect waste • inside width

**IW** Inspector of Works • Isle of Wight • *British vehicle registration for* Londonderry

**IWA** Inland Waterways Association • Institute of World Affairs

**IWC** International Whaling Commission • International Wheat Council

**IWD** (*or* **IW&D**) Inland Waterways and Docks

**IWEM** Institution of Water and Environmental Management (formerly IPHE; IWPC)

**IWGC** Imperial War Graves Commission (now Commonwealth War Graves Commission)

**IWM** Imperial War Museum

**IWO** Institute of Welfare Officers

**IWPC** Institute of Water Pollution Control (*see* IWEM)

**IWS** International Wool Secretariat

**IWW** Industrial Workers of the World • International Workers of the World

**IX** Iesus Christus (Latin: Jesus Christ) • *Chem.* ion exchange • *Irish vehicle registration for* Longford

**IY** Imperial Yeomanry • *Irish vehicle registration for* Louth • *airline flight code for* Yemen Airways

**IYHF** International Youth Hostels Federation

**IYRU** International Yacht Racing Union

**iyswim** ('ɪz,wɪm) if you see what I mean

**IZ** I Zingari (cricket club) • *Irish vehicle registration for* Mayo

**IZS** *Med.* insulin zinc suspension (diabetes treatment)

# J

**j** (ital.) *Physics, symbol for* current density • *Electrical engineering, symbol for* the imaginary number √–1 • (bold ital.) *Maths., symbol for* a unit coordinate vector

**j.** juris (Latin: of law) • jus (Latin: law)

**J** *Engineering, symbol for* advance ratio • (bold ital.) *Physics, symbol for* angular momentum • (ital.) *Physics, symbol for* coupling constant • (ital.) *Physics, symbol for* current density • *British vehicle registration for* Durham • *Cards* jack • *Maths., symbol for* Jacobian determinant • *international vehicle registration for* Japan • *British fishing port registration for* Jersey • *Immunol.* joining region (of an immunoglobulin chain) • *Science, symbol for* joule(s) • *Geology* Jurassic • (bold ital.) *Physics, symbol for* magnetic polarization • (ital.) *Physics, obsolete symbol for* mechanical equivalent of heat • (ital.) *Physics, symbol for* nuclear spin quantum number • (ital.) *Chem., symbol for* rotational quantum number • (ital.) *Physics, symbol for* sound intensity • (ital.) *Physics, symbol for* total angular momentum quantum number

**J.** (*or* **J**) Jacobean • Jahr (German: year) • January • Jesus • jet • Jew(ish) • Journal • Judaic • Judaism • Judge • July • June • Justice

**J2** *international civil aircraft marking for* Djibouti

**J3** *international civil aircraft marking for* Grenada

**J5** *international civil aircraft marking for* Guinea Bissau

**J6** *international civil aircraft marking for* St Lucia

**J7** *international civil aircraft marking for* Dominica

**J8** *international civil aircraft marking for* St Vincent

**Ja.** January

**JA** *international vehicle registration for* Jamaica • *international civil aircraft marking for* Japan • (*or* **J/A**) *Banking* joint account • Judge Advocate • Justice of Appeal • *British vehicle registration for* Manchester

**JAA** Japan Aeronautic Association • Jewish Athletic Association

**Jaat** *Military* joint air attack team

**Jac.** Jacobean

**JAC** (USA) Joint Apprenticeship Committee • (USA) Junior Association of Commerce

**Jacq.** *Botany* J. F. Jacquin (1766–1839) *or* N. J. Jacquin (1727–1817) (indicating the author of a species, etc.)

**JACT** Joint Association of Classical Teachers

**JAD** Julian Astronomical Day

**JADB** (USA) Joint Air Defense Board

**JAEC** Japan Atomic Energy Commission • Joint Atomic Energy Committee (of US Congress)

**JAF** Judge Advocate of the Fleet

**JAFC** Japan Atomic Fuel Corporation

**Jafo** (dʒæfəʊ) *Military slang* just another fucking observer

**JAG** Judge Advocate General

**JAIEG** Joint Atomic Information Exchange Group

**JAL** Japan Airlines • jet approach and landing chart

**Jam.** Jamaica • *Bible* James

**JAMA** ('dʒɑːmə) (ital.) Journal of the American Medical Association

**jan.** janitor

**Jan** (*or* **Jan.**) January

**J. & K.** Jammu and Kashmir (Indian state)

**j. & w.o.** *Insurance* jettisoning and washing overboard

**JANET** ('dʒænɪt) *Computing* Joint Academic Network

**janv.** janvier (French: January)

**jap.** japanned

**Jap.** Japan(ese)

**JAP** (dʒæp) *Colloquial* (USA) Jewish American Princess

**jar.** jargon

**JARE** Japanese Antarctic Research Expedition

**Jas.** *Bible* James

**JAS** Jamaica Agricultural Society • Junior Astronomical Society

**jastop** ('dʒæstɒp) *Aeronautics* jet-assisted stop

**JAT** Jugoslovenski Aero-Transport (Yugoslav Airlines)

**JATCC** Joint Aviation Telecommunications Coordination Committee

**JATCRU** joint air traffic control radar unit

**JATO** (*or* **jato**) ('dʒeɪtəʊ) *Aeronautics* jet-assisted takeoff

**JATS** joint air transportation service

**jaund.** jaundice

**Jav.** Java(nese) • (*or* **jav.**) *Athletics* javelin

**j.b.** jet bomb • joint board • junction box

**Jb.** Jahrbuch (German: annual *or* yearbook)

**JB** Bachelor of Laws (Latin *Juris Baccalaureus*) • junior beadle • *British vehicle registration for* Reading

**JBAA** (ital.) Journal of the British Archaeological Association

**JBC** Jamaica Broadcasting Corporation • Japan Broadcasting Corporation

**JBCNS** Joint Board of Clinical Nursing Studies

**Jber.** Jahresbericht (German: annual report)

**JBES** Jodrell Bank Experimental Station

**JBL** (ital.) Journal of Business Law

**JBS** (USA) John Birch Society

**j.c.** joint compound

**JC** *British vehicle registration for* Bangor • (*or* **J.C.**) Jesus Christ • (ital.) Jewish Chronicle • Jockey Club • (*or* **J.C.**) Julius Caesar • (USA) (member of a) Junior Chamber (of Commerce) • (USA) junior college • *Law* jurisconsult (legal adviser; jurist) • Justice Clerk • justiciary case • juvenile court

**J-C** Jésus-Christ (French: Jesus Christ)

**JCAC** (USA) Joint Civil Affairs Committee

**JCAR** Joint Commission on Applied Radioactivity

**JCB** Bachelor of Canon Law (Latin *Juris Canonici Baccalaureus*) • Bachelor of Civil Law (Latin *Juris Civilis Baccalaureus*) • Joseph Cyril Bamford (excavating machine; named after its manufacturer)

**JCC** Jesus College, Cambridge • Joint Consultative Committee • Junior Chamber of Commerce

**JCD** Doctor of Canon Law (Latin *Juris Canonici Doctor*) • Doctor of Civil Law (Latin *Juris Civilis Doctor*)

**JCI** Junior Chamber International

**JCL** *Computing* job-control language • Licentiate in Canon Law (Latin *Juris Canonici Licentiatus*) • Licentiate in Civil Law (Latin *Juris Civilis Licentiatus*)

**JCNAAF** Joint Canadian Navy-Army-Air Force

**JC of C** Junior Chamber of Commerce

**JCP** Japan Communist Party

**JCR** junior common room (in certain universities)

**JCS** Joint Chiefs of Staff • Joint Commonwealth Societies • (ital.) Journal of the Chemical Society

**jct.** (*or* **jctn**) junction

**JCWI** Joint Council for the Welfare of Immigrants

**jd** joined

**JD** Diploma in Journalism • Doctor of Laws *or* Jurisprudence (Latin *Jurum Doctor*) • *symbol for* Jordan dinar (monetary unit) • *Astronomy* Julian date • junior deacon • junior dean • jury duty • (USA) Justice Department • juvenile delinquent • *British vehicle registration for* (central) London

**JDA** Japan Defence Agency

**JDB** Japan Development Bank

**JDipMA** Joint Diploma in Management Accounting Services

**JDL** (USA) Jewish Defense League

**j.d.s.** job data sheet

**JE** *airline flight code for* Manx Airlines • *British vehicle registration for* Peterborough

**j.e.a.** joint export agent

**JEA** Jesuit Educational Association • Joint Engineering Association

**JEC** Joint Economic Committee (of US Congress)

**JECI** Jeunesse étudiante catholique internationale (French: International Young Catholic Students)

**J. Ed.** (ital.) Journal of Education

**Jer.** *Bible* Jeremiah • Jersey • Jerusalem

**JERC** Joint Electronic Research Committee

**JERI** Japan Economic Research Institute

**jerob.** jeroboam

**Jes.** Jesus

**JESA** Japanese Engineering Standards Association

**JESSI** Joint European Submicron Silicon Initiative

**jet.** jetsam • jettison

**JET** (dʒet) *Nuclear engineering* Joint European Torus (Culham, Oxfordshire) • Joint European Transport

**JETCO** ('dʒɛt,kəʊ) Jamaican Export Trading Company • Japan Export Trading Company

**JETP** (ital.) Journal of Experimental and Theoretical Physics

**JETRO** ('dʒɛtrəʊ) Japan External Trade Organization

**jett.** jettison

**jeu.** jeudi (French: Thursday)

**JF** *British vehicle registration for* Leicester

**J/F** *Book-keeping* journal folio

**JFET** ('dʒɛɪfɛt) *Electronics* junction field-effect transistor

**JFK** John Fitzgerald Kennedy (US president (1961–63) *or* airport)

**JFM** Jeunesses fédéralistes mondiales (French: Young World Federalists)

**JFTC** Joint Fur Trade Committee

**JFU** Jersey Farmers' Union

**j.g.** junior grade

**JG** *British vehicle registration for* Maidstone

**JGTC** Junior Girls' Training Corps

**JGW** *Freemasonry* Junior Grand Warden

**Jh.** Jahrehundert (German: century)

**JH** *Numismatics* Jubilee head-Victoria • *Biochem.* juvenile hormone • *British vehicle registration for* Reading

**j.h.a.** job hazard analysis

**JHDA** Junior Hospital Doctors' Association

**JHMO** junior hospital medical officer

**JHS** Jesus Hominum Salvator (Latin: Jesus Saviour of Men) • (USA) junior high school

**JHU** (USA) Johns Hopkins University

**JHVH** Jehovah

**JI** *British vehicle registration for* Tyrone

**JIB** joint intelligence bureau

**jic** just in case

**JIC** joint industrial council • (USA) joint intelligence center

**JICRAR** ('dʒɪkrɑː) Joint Industry Committee for Radio Audience Research

**JICTAR** ('dʒɪktɑː) Joint Industry Committee for Television Advertising Research

**JIM** Japan Institute of Metals

**JINS** (dʒɪnz) (USA) Juvenile(s) In Need of Supervision

**JINucE** Junior Member of the Institution of Nuclear Engineers

**JIS** Jamaica Information Service • Japan Industrial Standard • Jewish Information Society • joint intelligence staff

**JIT** (*or* **jit**) just-in-time (manufacturing method)

**JJ** *Electronics* Josephson junction • (*or* **JJ.**) Judges • (*or* **JJ.**) Justices • *British vehicle registration for* Maidstone

**JK** *British vehicle registration for* Brighton

**jkt** jacket

**j.k.t.** job knowledge test

**Jl.** (*or* **jl.**) journal • July

**JL** *airline flight code for* Japan Airlines • *British vehicle registration for* Lincoln

**JLA** Jewish Librarians' Association

**JLB** Jewish Lads' Brigade

**JLC** (USA) Jewish Labor Committee

**JLP** Jamaica Labour Party

**JM** *airline flight code for* Air Jamaica • *British vehicle registration for* Reading

**JMA** Japanese Meteorological Agency

**JMB** James Matthew Barrie (1860–1937, Scottish dramatist and novelist) • Joint Matriculation Board

**JMBA** (ital.) Journal of the Marine Biological Association

**JMCS** Junior Mountaineering Club of Scotland

**JMJ** *RC Church* Jesus, Mary, and Joseph

**JMSAC** Joint Meteorological Satellite Advisory Committee

**jn** join • (*or* **Jn**) junction • (*or* **Jn**) junior

**JN** *British vehicle registration for* Chelmsford

**JNA** Jordan News Agency

**jnc.** (*or* **Jnc.**) junction

**JNC** joint negotiating committee

**j.n.d.** just noticeable difference

**JNEC** Jamaican National Export Corporation

**JNF** Jewish National Fund

**jnl** (*or* **Jnl**) journal

**jnlst** journalist

**jnr** (*or* **Jnr**) junior

**JNR** Japanese National Railways

**j.n.s.** just noticeable shift

**jnt** joint

**JNTO** Japan National Tourist Organization

**jnt stk** joint stock

**JO** job order • (ital.) Journal Officiel (French: Official Gazette) • junior officer • *British vehicle registration for* Oxford

**joc.** jocose • jocular

**JOC** Jeunesse ouvrière chrétienne (French: Young Christian Workers) • (USA) joint operations center

**j.o.d.** joint occupancy date

**J. of E.** (ital.) Journal of Education
**JOG** *Yachting* junior offshore group
**Johan.** Johannesburg
**join.** joinery
**Jon.** *Bible* Jonah
**Josh.** *Bible* Joshua
**JOT** joint observer team
**jour.** journal(ist) · journey · journeyman
**JOVIAL** ('dʒəʊvɪəl) *Computing* Jules' own version of international algorithmic language (named after Jules Schwarz, computer scientist)
**JP** *airline flight code for* Adria Airways · (*or* **j.p.**) jet propulsion (*or* jet-propelled) · Justice of the Peace · *British vehicle registration for* Liverpool
**JPA** Jamaica Press Association
**JPC** joint planning council · joint production council · Judge of the Prize Court
**JPCAC** Joint Production, Consultative, and Advisory Committee
**JPL** Jet Propulsion Laboratory (California) · (ital.) Journal of Planning Law
**Jpn** Japan
**JPRS** (USA) Joint Publications Research Service
**JPS** jet-propulsion system(s) · (USA) Jewish Publications Society · Joint Parliamentary Secretary · joint planning staff · Junior Philatelic Society
**JPTO** *Astronautics* jet-propelled takeoff
**jr.** jour (French: day)
**Jr** (*or* **jr**) Junior
**Jr.** (*or* **jr.**) journal · juror
**JR** Jacobus Rex (Latin: King James) · joint resolution · Judges' Rules · Jurist Reports · *British vehicle registration for* Newcastle upon Tyne
**JRA** juvenile rheumatoid arthritis
**JRAI** (ital.) Journal of the Royal Anthropological Institute
**JRC** Junior Red Cross
**JS** *British vehicle registration for* Inverness · (USA) Japan Society · *Law* judgment summons · *Law* judicial separation
**JSAWC** Joint Services Amphibious Warfare Centre
**JSB** joint-stock bank
**JSC** Johnson Space Center (Texas)
**JSD** Doctor of Juristic Science
**JSDC** Joint Service Defence College
**Jsey** Jersey
**JSLS** Joint Services Liaison Staff
**JSP** *Computing, tradename* Jackson structured programming (named after

Michael Jackson, computer scientist) · Japan Socialist Party
**JSPS** Japan Society for the Promotion of Science
**JSS** joint services standard
**JSSC** Joint Services Staff College · joint shop stewards' committee
**J-stars** ('dʒeɪˌstɑːz) joint surveillance and targeting acquisition radar system
**jt** joint
**j.t.** *Law* joint tenancy
**JT** *British vehicle registration for* Bournemouth
**JTC** Junior Training Corps
**Jt Ed.** Joint Editor
**JTIDS** Joint Tactical Information Distribution Systems
**jtly** jointly
**JTO** jump takeoff (of an aircraft)
**JTS** job training standards
**JTST** *Meteorol.* jet stream
**JTUAC** Joint Trade Union Advisory Committee
**j.u.** joint use
**Ju.** June
**JU** *airline flight code for* JAT Yugoslav Airlines · *British vehicle registration for* Leicester
**jud.** judgment · judicial · judo
**Jud.** *Bible* Judah · Judaism · Judea · Judge · (*or* **Judg.**) *Bible* Judges · *Bible* Judith
**JUD** Doctor of Canon and Civil Law (Latin *Juris Utriusque Doctor*)
**judgt** judgment
**juev.** jueves (Spanish: Thursday)
**JUGFET** ('dʒʌgfɛt) *Electronics* junction-gate field-effect transistor
**juil.** juillet (French: July)
**jul.** julho (Portuguese: July) · julio (Spanish: July)
**Jul.** July
**Jun.** June · (*or* **jun.**) junior
**junc.** (*or* **Junc.**) junction
**jun. part.** junior partner
**Junr** (*or* **junr**) junior
**JurD** Doctor of Law (Latin *Juris Doctor*)
**jurisd.** jurisdiction
**jurisp.** jurisprudence
**jus.** (*or* **just.**) justice
**JUSMAG** Joint United States Military Advisory Group
**juss.** *Grammar* jussive
**Juss.** *Botany* Jussieu (indicating the author of a species, etc.)
**juv.** juvenile

**Juv.** Juvenal (Decimus Junius Juvenalis, ?60–?140 A.D., Roman poet)

**JUWTFA** Joint Unconventional Warfare Task Force, Atlantic

**jux.** juxtaposition

**Jv.** Java(nese)

**JV** *Commerce* joint venture · (USA) junior varsity · *British vehicle registration for* Lincoln

**JW** *British vehicle registration for* Birmingham · Jehovah's Witness · junior warden

**JWB** Jewish Welfare Board · joint wages board

**JWEF** Joinery and Woodwork Employers' Federation

**jwlr** jeweller

**j.w.o.** *Insurance* jettisoning and washing overboard

**JWS** (*or* **jws**) Joint Warfare Staff

**JWV** Jewish War Veterans

**JX** *British vehicle registration for* Huddersfield · Jesus Christ

**Jy** *Astronomy, symbol for* jansky · July · (*or* **jy**) jury

**JY** *British vehicle registration for* Exeter · *airline flight code for* Jersey European Airways · *international civil aircraft marking for* Jordan

**JZ** *British vehicle registration for* Down

# K

**k** (ital.) *Physics, symbol for* Boltzmann constant · *Maths., symbol for* a constant · *Maths., symbol for* curvature · *symbol for* kilo- (prefix indicating 1000, as in **km**, kilometre; *or* (in computing) 1024, as in **kbyte**, kilobyte) · (ital.) *Mechanics, symbol for* radius of gyration · (ital.) *Chem., symbol for* rate coefficient (*or* constant) · (ital.) *Physics, symbol for* thermal conductivity · (bold ital.) *Maths., symbol for* a unit coordinate vector

**k.** (USA) karat · keel · killed · king · knight · knot

**K** (ital.) *Physics, symbol for* bulk modulus · *Botany, symbol for* calyx (in a floral formula) · *international vehicle registration for* Cambodia · (ital.) *Ecology, symbol for* carrying capacity (as in **K-strategist**) · *Geology, symbol for* Cretaceous · (ital.) *Chem., symbol for* equilibrium constant · *Physics, symbol for* kaon · *Science, symbol for* kelvin(s) · (ital.) *Physics, symbol for* kerma (kinetic energy released) · *Immunol.* killer (in **K cell**) · *Computing, symbol for* kilo- (*see under* k) · *symbol for* kina (monetary unit of Papua New Guinea) · (ital.) *Physics, symbol for* kinetic energy · *Chess, symbol for* king · kip (Laotian monetary unit; *see also under* KN) · *Music* Kirkpatrick (preceding a number in Ralph Kirkpatrick's catalogue of Domenico Scarlatti's works) · *British fishing port registration for* Kirkwall · *Music* Köchel (preceding a number in Ludwig von Köchel's catalogue of Mozart's works) · *symbol for* (Zambian) kwacha (monetary unit; *see also under* MK) · *symbol for* kyat (Burmese monetary unit) · *British vehicle registration for* Liverpool · (ital.) *Physics, symbol for* luminous efficacy · *Biochem., symbol for* lysine · *Chem., symbol for* potassium (Latin *kalium*) · *Astronomy, symbol for* solar constant · *Baseball, symbol for* strikeout · *Astronomy, indicating* a spectral type · *indicating* one thousand

**K.** (*or* **K**) Kalt (German: cold) · King (*or* King's) · knit

**K9** *Military* canine (K9 dogs; army dogs)

**KA** *postcode for* Kilmarnock · King of Arms · Knight of St Andrew, Order of Barbados · *British vehicle registration for* Liverpool

**KADU** ('kɑːduː) Kenya African Democratic Union (now absorbed by KANU)

**KAK** (Sweden) Kungl Automobil Klubben (Royal Automobile Club)

**Kal.** Kalendae (Latin: calends; first day of each month)

**Kan.** (*or* **Kans.**) Kansas

**k & b** kitchen and bathroom

**KANTAFU** Kenya African National Traders' and Farmers' Union

**KANU** ('kɑːnuː) Kenya African National Union

**KANUPP** ('kænʌp) (Pakistan) Karachi Nuclear Power Plant

**KAO** Kuiper Airborne Observatory

**Kap.** *Finance* Kapital (German: capital) • Kapitel (German: chapter)

**Kar.** Karachi

**KAR** King's African Rifles

**Karel.** Karelia(n)

**Kash.** Kashmir

**KASSR** (formerly) Karelian Autonomous Soviet Socialist Republic

**kb** *Physics, symbol for* kilobar(s) • *Genetics, symbol for* kilobase(s)

**KB** *Computing* kilobyte • King's Bench • *Chess* king's bishop • Knight Bachelor • *Knitting* knit into back of stitch • *Computing* knowledge base • Koninkrijk België (Flemish: Kingdom of Belgium) • *British vehicle registration for* Liverpool

**KBASSR** (formerly) Kabardino-Balkar Autonomous Soviet Socialist Republic

**KBC** *Law* King's Bench Court

**kbd** keyboard

**KBD** *Law* King's Bench Division

**KBE** Knight Commander of the Order of the British Empire

**KBES** *Computing* knowledge-based expert system

**Kbhvn** København (Danish: Copenhagen)

**kbp** *Genetics, symbol for* kilobase pair

**KBP** *Chess* king's bishop's pawn

**KBS** Knight of the Blessed Sacrament • *Computing* knowledge-based system

**KBW** King's Bench Walk (Temple, London)

**kbyte** *Computing* kilobyte

**kc** *Physics* kilocycle

**KC** Kansas City • Kennel Club • King's College • King's Counsel • King's Cross (London) • Knight Commander • *RC Church* Knights of Columbus • *British vehicle registration for* Liverpool

**KCA** Keesing's Contemporary Archives

**kcal** *symbol for* kilocalorie(s)

**KCB** Knight Commander of the Order of the Bath

**KCC** King's College, Cambridge • (Knight) Commander of the Order of the Crown, Belgium and the Congo Free State

**K cell** *Immunol.* killer cell

**KCH** King's College Hospital (London) • Knight Commander of the Hanoverian Order

**KCHS** Knight Commander of the Order of the Holy Sepulchre

**KCIE** Knight Commander of the Order of the Indian Empire

**KCL** King's College, London

**KCLJ** Knight Commander of the Order of St Lazarus of Jerusalem

**KCMG** Knight Commander of the Order of St Michael and St George

**kcs** (*or* **kc/s**) kilocycles per second

**Kčs** *symbol for* koruna (Czech and Slovak monetary unit)

**KCSA** Knight Commander of the Military Order of the Collar of St Agatha of Paterna

**KCSG** Knight Commander of the Order of St Gregory the Great

**KCSI** Knight Commander of the Order of the Star of India

**KCSJ** Knight Commander of the Order of St John of Jerusalem (Knights Hospitaller)

**KCSS** Knight Commander of the Order of St Silvester

**KCVO** Knight Commander of the Royal Victorian Order

**kd** killed

**KD** kiln dried • (*or* **k.d.**) knock down (at an auction sale) • (*or* **k.d.**) *Commerce* knocked down (of goods for sale) • Kongeriget Danmark (Danish: Kingdom of Denmark) • *symbol for* Kuwaiti dinar (monetary unit) • *British vehicle registration for* Liverpool

**KDC** (*or* **k.d.c.**) *Commerce* knocked-down condition (of goods)

**KDF** (*or* **KdF**) Kraft durch Freude (German: Strength through Joy; Nazi holiday scheme)

**KDG** King's Dragoon Guards

**KDM** Kongelige Danske Marine (Royal Danish Navy)

**KE** kinetic energy • kinetic equation • *airline flight code for* Korean Air • *British vehicle registration for* Maidstone

**KEAS** (*or* **k.e.a.s.**) *Aeronautics* knots equivalent airspeed

**Keb** Keble College, Oxford

**KEH** King Edward's Horse

**Ken.** Kensington • Kentucky • Kenya

**KEO** King Edward's Own

**keV** *Physics, symbol for* kiloelectronvolt(s)

**KEY** (kiː) keep extending yourself

**KF** *British vehicle registration for* Liverpool

# KFA · KNA

216

**KFA** Kenya Farmers' Association

**KFAED** Kuwait Fund for Arab Economic Development

**KFL** Kenya Federation of Labour

**kfm.** kaufmännisch (German: commercial)

**Kfm.** Kaufmann (German: merchant)

**Kfz.** Kraftfahrzeug (German: motor vehicle)

**kg** keg • *symbol for* kilogram(s)

**KG** *British vehicle registration for* Cardiff • *Physics* Klein–Gordon (as in **KG equation**) • Knight of the Order of the Garter • Kommanditgesellschaft (German: limited partnership)

**KGB** Komitet Gosudarstvennoi Bezopasnosti (Russian: Committee of State Security)

**KGCB** Knight Grand Cross of the Bath

**kgf** *Physics, symbol for* kilogram-force

**KGFR** *Med.* kidney glomerular filtration rate

**Kgl.** Königlich (German: Royal)

**Kgs** *Bible* Kings

**KGS** known geological structure

**KH** *British vehicle registration for* Hull • *Physics* Kelvin–Helmholtz (as in **KH formula**) • kennel huntsman • *Astronautics* keyhole (as in **KH-11, KH-12**; imaging NASA satellites) • King's Hussars • Knight of the Hanoverian Order

**KHC** Honorary Chaplain to the King

**KHDS** Honorary Dental Surgeon to the King

**KHNS** Honorary Nursing Sister to the King

**KHP** Honorary Physician to the King

**KHS** Honorary Surgeon to the King • Knight of the Order of the Holy Sepulchre

**kHz** *symbol for* kilohertz

**KI** *Irish vehicle registration for* Waterford

**KIA** killed in action

**KIAS** (*or* **k.i.a.s.**) *Aeronautics* knots indicated airspeed

**K-i-H** Kaisar-i-Hind (Emperor of India; medal)

**kil.** (*or* **kild.**) *Brewing* kilderkin (size of cask)

**Kild.** Kildare

**Kilk.** Kilkenny

**KIM** (kɪm) *Chem.* kinetic isotope method

**Kinc.** Kincardine (former Scottish county)

**kind.** kindergarten

**kingd.** kingdom

**Kinr.** Kinross (former Scottish county)

**KIO** Kuwait Investment Office

**Kirk.** Kirkcudbright (former Scottish county)

**KISS** (kɪs) *Colloquial* (USA) keep it simple, stupid • *Stock exchange* (Germany) Kurs Information Service System

**kJ** *symbol for* kilojoule(s)

**KJ** *Med.* knee jerk • Knight of St Joachim • *British vehicle registration for* Maidstone

**KJV** King James Version (of the Bible)

**KK** Kabushiki Kaisha (Japanese: joint-stock company) • *Physics* Kaluza–Klein (as in **KK theory**) • *British vehicle registration for* Maidstone

**KKASSR** (formerly) Kara-Kalpak Autonomous Soviet Socialist Republic

**KKK** Ku Klux Klan

**KKt** *Chess* king's knight

**KKtP** *Chess* king's knight's pawn

**KL** *Astronomy* Kleinmann–Low (as in **KL nebula**) • *airline flight code for* KLM – Royal Dutch Airlines • Kuala Lumpur • *British vehicle registration for* Maidstone

**KLH** *Immunol.* keyhole-limpet haemocyanin • Knight of the Legion of Honour

**KLJ** Knight of the Order of St Lazarus of Jerusalem

**KLM** Koninklijke Luchtvaart Maatschappij (Royal Dutch Airlines)

**KLSE** Kuala Lumpur Stock Exchange

**km** *symbol for* kilometre(s)

**KM** King's Medal • Knight of Malta • *British vehicle registration for* Maidstone

**KMO** Kobe Marine Observatory (Japan)

**KMT** Kuomintang (Chinese Nationalist Party)

**KMUL** (Germany) Karl Marx Universität Leipzig

**kn** *Nautical, symbol for* knot • krona (Swedish monetary unit; *see also* SKr) • krone (Danish or Norwegian monetary unit; *see also* Dkr; NKr)

**KN** *Chess* king's knight • *Numismatics* King's Norton (mint-mark, Birmingham) • *symbol for* kip (Laotian monetary unit) • Kongeriket Norge (Norwegian: Kingdom of Norway) • *British vehicle registration for* Maidstone

**KNA** Kongelig Norsk Automobil-klubb (Royal Norwegian Automobile Club)

**KNM** Kongelige Norske Marine (Royal Norwegian Navy)

**KNP** *Chess* king's knight's pawn • Kruger National Park (South Africa)

**KNPC** Kuwait National Petroleum Company

**Knt** Knight

**k.o.** keep off • keep out • *Football* kick off • *Colloquial* knock out (*or* knockout)

**KO** *Colloquial* knock out (*or* knockout) • *British vehicle registration for* Maidstone

**KOC** Kuwait Oil Company

**KOD** *Navigation* kick-off drift

**K of C** *RC Church* Knights of Columbus

**K of K** (Lord) Kitchener of Khartoum

**K of P** (USA) Knights of Pythias

**Komintern** ('kɒmɪn,tɜːn) Communist International (Russian *Kom(munisti-cheskiĭ) Intern(atsionál)*)

**Komp.** Kompanie (German: company)

**Kor.** Koran • Korea(n)

**KORR** King's Own Royal Regiment

**KOSB** King's Own Scottish Borderers

**KOYLI** King's Own Yorkshire Light Infantry

**k.p.** key personnel

**KP** King's Parade • *Chess* king's pawn • *Military* (USA) kitchen police • Knight of the Order of St Patrick • *British vehicle registration for* Maidstone

**KPD** Kommunistische Partei Deutschlands (German Communist Party)

**KPFSM** King's Police and Fire Service Medal

**kph** kilometres per hour

**KPM** King's Police Medal

**Kpmtr** *Music* Kapellmeister (German: conductor)

**KPNLF** Khmer People's National Liberation Front

**KPNO** Kitt Peak National Observatory (Arizona)

**KPP** Keeper of the Privy Purse

**kpr** keeper

**KPU** Kenya People's Union

**KQ** *airline flight code for* Kenya Airways

**kr.** krona (Swedish monetary unit; *see also* SKr) • króna (Icelandic monetary unit; *see also* ISK) • krone (Danish or Norwegian monetary unit; *see also* Dkr; NKr)

**Kr** *Chem., symbol for* krypton

**KR** King's Regiment • *Military* King's Regulations • *Chess* king's rook • *British vehicle registration for* Maidstone

**KRL** *Computing* knowledge representation language (in artificial intelligence)

**KRP** *Chess* king's rook's pawn

**KRR** King's Royal Rifles

**KRRC** *British vehicle registration for* Edinburgh • King's Royal Rifle Corps

**KS** *US postcode for* Kansas • *Med.* Kaposi's sarcoma • King's Scholar • King's School • Kipling Society • Kitchener Scholar • Konungariket Sverige (Swedish: Kingdom of Sweden)

**KSC** Kennedy Space Center (Florida) • King's School, Canterbury • Knight of St Columba • (formerly) Komunistická Strana Československá (Communist Party of Czechoslovakia)

**KSG** Knight of the Order of St Gregory the Great

**KSh** *symbol for* Kenya shilling (monetary unit)

**KSI** Knight of the Order of the Star of India

**KSIE** *Chem.* kinetic solvent isotope effect

**KSJ** Knight of the Order of St John of Jerusalem (Knights Hospitaller)

**KSLI** King's Shropshire Light Infantry

**KSM** Korean Service Medal • Kungliga Svenska Marinen (Royal Swedish Navy)

**KSS** Knight of the Order of St Silvester

**KSSR** Kazakh Soviet Socialist Republic (now Kazakhstan)

**KSSU** KLM, SAS, Swissair, UTA (international airline organization)

**KStJ** Knight of the Order of St John of Jerusalem (Knights Hospitaller)

**KSU** Kansas State University

**kt** (USA) karat • *symbol for* kilotonne(s) • *Nautical* knot

**Kt** knight

**KT** *postcode for* Kingston-upon-Thames • Knight Templar • Knight (of the Order) of the Thistle • *Meteorol.* knot • *British vehicle registration for* Maidstone

**Kt Bach.** Knight Bachelor

**Kto** *Banking* Konto (German: account)

**Ku** *Chem., symbol for* kurchatovium (element 104)

**KU** *airline flight code for* Kuwait Airways • *British vehicle registration for* Sheffield

**Kuw.** Kuwait

**kV** *symbol for* kilovolt(s)

**KV** *British vehicle registration for* Coventry • *Music* Köchel Verzeichnis (German: Köchel catalogue; *see under* K)

**kVAr** *Electrical engineering, symbol for* kilovar(s)

**kVp** kilovolts, peak (applied across an X-ray tube)

**kW** *symbol for* kilowatt(s)

**KW** *postcode for* Kirkwall, Orkney · *British vehicle registration for* Sheffield

**kWh** (*or* **kW h**) *symbol for* kilowatt hour(s)

**KWIC** (kwɪk) key word in context (as in **KWIC index**)

**KWOC** (kwɒk) key word out of context (as in **KWOC index**)

**KWP** Korean Workers' Party

**KWT** *international vehicle registration for* Kuwait

**KX** *airline flight code for* Cayman Airways · *British vehicle registration for* Luton

**ky.** kyat (Burmese monetary unit; *see also under* K)

**Ky.** Kentucky

**KY** *US postcode for* Kentucky · Kirkcaldy (postcode *or* British fishing port registration) · Kol Yisrael (Israeli broadcasting station) · *British vehicle registration for* Sheffield

**kybd** keyboard

**Kyr.** *Ecclesiast.* Kyrie eleison

**kz** *Meteorol., symbol for* duststorm *or* sandstorm

**KZ** *British vehicle registration for* Antrim · *Military* killing zone

# L

**l** (*ital.*) *Chem.* laevorotatory (as in **l-tartaric acid**) · *Music* lah (in tonic sol-fa) · (*ital.*) *symbol for* length · (*ital.*) *Physics, symbol for* lepton number · *Meteorol.* lightning · *Chem.* liquid (as in $H_2O(l)$) · *symbol for* litre(s) · (*ital.*) *Physics, symbol for* orbital angular momentum quantum number

**l.** lake · lambda · land · late · lateral · law · leaf · league · leasehold · left · legitimate · length · light · line (of written matter) · link · literate · little · loch · long · lost · lough · low · *Currency* pound (Latin *libra*; symbol: £)

**L** (bold ital.) *Physics, symbol for* angular momentum · (*ital.*) *Chem., symbol for* Avogadro constant · *Roman numeral for* fifty · *Electrical engineering, symbol for* inductor · (*ital.*) *Physics, symbol for* Lagrangian function · *Physics, symbol for* lambert (obsolete unit of luminance) · *Linguistics* language (as in $L_1$, first language; $L_2$, second language) · (*ital.*) *Physics, symbol for* latent heat · learner (driver; on British motor vehicles) · *symbol for* lempira (Honduran monetary unit) · (*ital.*) *symbol for* length · *Biochem., symbol for* leucine · *Aeronautics* lift · *Immunol.* light (in **L-chain** of an immunoglobulin molecule) · linear · (*ital.*) *Biochem., symbol for* linking number · *symbol for* litre(s) · live (on electric plugs) · *postcode for* Liverpool · (*ital.*) *Geography, symbol for* longitude · (*ital.; or* $L_v$) *Physics, symbol for* luminance · (*ital.*) *Astronomy, symbol for* luminosity · *international vehicle registration for* Luxembourg · (*ital.*) *Physics, symbol for* orbital angular momentum quantum number · (*ital., or* $L_e$) *Physics, symbol for* radiance · (*ital.*) *Electrical engineering, symbol for* self-inductance · (*ital.*) *Physics, symbol for* sound intensity · (small cap.) *Chem., indicating* an optically active compound having a configuration related to laevorotatory glyceraldehyde (as in **L-lactic acid**)

**L.** (*or* **L**) Lady · Lake · *Military* Lancers · large · Latin · law · League · left *or* (in the theatre) stage left · lethal · liber (Latin: book) · *Politics* Liberal · Licentiate (in degrees, etc.) · Lieutenant · line (of written matter) · link · *Biology* Linnaeus (indicating the author of a species, etc.) · lira *or* (pl.) lire (Italian monetary unit; *see also* Lit) · Loch · locus (Latin: place) · Lodge (fraternal) · London · Lord · *Sport* lost · Lough · low · *Currency* pound (Latin *libra*; symbol: £)

**l.a.** landing account · leading article · *Med.* lege artis (Latin: as directed; in prescriptions) · lighter than air

**La** *Chem., symbol for* lanthanum

**La.** Lancastrian • Lane • Louisiana

**LA** *postcode for* Lancaster • *airline flight code for* Lan Chile • *Photog.* large aperture • Latin America(n) • law agent • leave allowance • *Med.* left atrium (*or* atrial) • legal adviser • Legislative Assembly • letter of authority • Library Association • Licensing Act • licensing authority • Lieutenant-at-Arms • *Physics* linear accelerator • Literate in Arts • Liverpool Academy • *British fishing port registration for* Llanelly • Lloyd's agent • local agent • local anaesthetic • local association • local authority • *British vehicle registration for* London NW • long acting • Los Angeles • *US postcode for* Louisiana • low altitude

**LAA** (USA) League of Advertising Agencies • Library Association of Australia • Libyan Arab Airlines • Lieutenant-at-Arms • (USA) Life Assurance Advertisers • light anti-aircraft

**LAADS** (USA) Los Angeles Air Defense Sector

**LAAOH** Ladies' Auxiliary, Ancient Order of Hibernians

**LAAR** liquid-air accumulator rocket

**lab.** label • laboratory • labourer

**Lab.** (USA) Laborite • *Politics* Labour • Labrador

**LAB** *Chem.* linear alkyl benzene • load aboard barge • low-altitude bombing

**LABA** (USA) Laboratory Animal Breeders' Association

**lac.** lacquer • lactation

**Lac** *Astronomy* Lacerta

**LAC** Laboratory Animals Centre • leading aircraftman • Licentiate of the Apothecaries' Company • London Athletic Club

**LACES** London Airport cargo electronic processing scheme • (USA) Los Angeles Council of Engineering Societies

**LACONIQ** *Computing* laboratory computer online inquiry

**LACSA** Lineas Aéreas Costarricenses (Costa Rican Airlines)

**LACSAB** Local Authorities' Conditions of Service Advisory Board

**LACW** leading aircraftwoman

**LAD** *Linguistics* language acquisition device • light aid detachment

**ladar** ('leɪdɑː) laser detection and ranging

**Ladp** Ladyship

**L. Adv.** Lord Advocate

**LAE** *Maths.* linear algebraic equation

**laev.** *Med.* laevus (Latin: left)

**LaF** Louisiana French

**LAF** L'Académie Française (French Academy)

**LAFC** Latin-American Forestry Commission

**La Font.** (Jean de) La Fontaine (1621–95, French poet)

**LAFTA** ('læftə) Latin American Free Trade Association (*see* LAIA)

**lag.** lagoon

**Lah.** Lahore

**LAH** Licentiate of the Apothecaries' Hall (Dublin)

**LAHS** low altitude, high speed

**LAI** *Botany* leaf area index • Library Association of Ireland

**LAIA** Latin American Integration Association (formerly LAFTA)

**LAK** (læk) *Med.* lymphokine-activated killer (in **LAK cell**; used in cancer treatment)

**LAL** (France) Laboratóire de l'accélérateur linéaire (Linear Accelerator Laboratory)

**lam.** laminate(d)

**Lam.** *Botany* Lamarck (indicating the author of a species, etc.) • *Bible* Lamentations

**LAM** London Academy of Music • Master of the Liberal Arts (Latin *Liberalium Artium Magister*)

**LAMA** Locomotive and Allied Manufacturers' Association of Great Britain

**LAMC** Livestock Auctioneers' Market Committee of England and Wales

**LAMCO** Liberian-American-Swedish Mineral Corporation

**LAMDA** ('læmdə) London Academy of Music and Dramatic Art

**LAMIDA** Lancashire and Merseyside Industrial Development Association

**LAMP** (læmp) low-altitude manned penetration • (USA) Lunar Analysis and Mapping Program

**LAMS** launch acoustic measuring system

**LAMSAC** Local Authorities' Management Services and Computer Committee

**LAN** *Meteorol.* inland • (*or* **Lan**; læn) Linea Aérea Nacional (de Chile) (Chilean national airlines; Lan Chile) • local apparent noon • (læn) *Computing* local-area network

**LANBY** ('lænbɪ) large automatic navigation buoy

**Lanc.** Lancaster • *Military* Lancers

**Lancs** Lancashire

**L & D** loans and discounts • loss and damage

**L&ID** London and India Docks

**L&NRR** (USA) Louisville and Nashville Railroad

**L & NWR** London and North-Western Railway

**L & SWR** London and South-Western Railway

**L & YR** Lancashire and Yorkshire Railway

**Lan. Fus.** Lancashire Fusiliers

**lang.** language

**Lang.** Languedoc

**LANICA** Lineas Aéreas de Nicaragua (Nicaraguan national airlines)

**LANL** (USA) Los Alamos National Laboratory

**LANRAC** (*or* **Lanrac**) ('lænræk) Land Army Reunion Association Committee

**LanR(PWV)** Lancashire Regiment (Prince of Wales' Volunteers)

**Lantirn** ('læntən) *Military* low-altitude navigation and targeting infrared system

**LAO** *international vehicle registration for* Laos • Licentiate in the Art of Obstetrics

**LAOAR** *US Air Force* Latin American Office of Aerospace Research

**Lap.** Lapland • Lappish

**LAP** (USA) Laboratory of Aviation Psychology • Lineas Aéreas Paraguayas (Paraguayan national airlines)

**LAPD** Los Angeles Police Department

**LAPES** low-altitude parachute extraction system

**LAPO** Los Angeles Philharmonic Orchestra

**LAPT** London Association for the Protection of Trade

**LAR** *Botany* leaf area ratio • *international vehicle registration for* Libya • *Taxation* life assurance relief • *Computing* limit address register

**LARA** light armed reconnaissance aircraft

**larg.** *Music* largamente (Italian; broadly) • largeur (French: width) • *Music* largo (Italian; very slowly)

**LARO** Latin American Regional Office (in the FAO)

**LARSP** Language Assessment, Remediation, and Screening Procedure

**laryngol.** laryngologist • laryngology

**LAS** Land Agents' Society • large astronomical satellite • League of Arab States • Legal Aid Society • London Archaeological Service • Lord Advocate of Scotland • low-altitude satellite • *Physics* low-angle scattering • lower airspace

**laser** ('leɪzə) light amplification by stimulated emission of radiation

**LASER** London and South Eastern Library Region

**LASH** (læʃ) *Commerce* lighter aboard ship

**LASL** (USA) Los Alamos Scientific Laboratory

**LASMO** London and Scottish Marine Oil

**LASP** low-altitude space platform

**LASS** lighter-than-air submarine simulator

**lat.** lateral • (*or* **lat**) *Geography* latitude • latus (Latin: wide)

**Lat.** Latin • Latvia(n)

**LAT** local apparent time • (ital.) Los Angeles Times

**LATCC** London air traffic control centre

**LATCRS** London air traffic control radar station

**lat. ht** latent heat

**LATS** (læts) *Med.* long-acting thyroid stimulator

**Latv.** Latvia

**Latvn** Latvian

**LAUK** Library Association of United Kingdom

**laun.** launched

**LAUTRO** (*or* **Lautro**) ('lɔːtrəʊ) Life Assurance and Unit Trust Regulatory Organization

**LAV** light armoured vehicle • Lineas Aéreas Venezolanas (Venezuelan Airlines) • lymphadenopathy-associated virus (original name for the Aids virus, HIV)

**law.** lawyer

**LAW** League of American Writers • light anti-tank weapon

**Law Rept.** (*or* **Law Rpts**) Law Reports

**LAWRS** limited airport weather reporting system

**LAWS** *Meteorol.* low-altitude wind shear

**lax.** laxative

**LAX** Los Angeles international airport

**lb** *symbol for* binary logarithm • (*or* **lb.**) pound(s) (weight; Latin *libra*)

**l.b.** landing barge • *Sport* left back • *Cricket* leg bye • letter box • link belt

**L.b.** Lectori benevolo (Latin: to the kind reader)

**LB** Bachelor of Letters (*or* Literature) (Latin *Litterarum Baccalaureus*) • *international vehicle registration for* Liberia • light bomber • *airline flight code for* Lloyd Aereo Boliviano • local board • *British vehicle registration for* London NW

**LBA** late booking agent (euphemism for ticket tout)

**LB & SCR** London, Brighton, and South Coast Railway

**LBB** *Engineering* leak before break

**LBBB** *Med.* left bundle-branch block

**Lbc.** Lübeck

**LBC** Land Bank Commission • London Broadcasting Company

**LBCH** London Bankers' Clearing House

**LBCM** Licentiate of the Bandsmen's College of Music • London Board of Congregational Ministers

**LBD** League of British Dramatists

**L/Bdr** (*or* **LBdr**) Lance-Bombardier

**lbf** *Physics, symbol for* pound-force

**lb-ft** pound-foot

**LBH** length, breadth, height

**LBJ** Lyndon Baines Johnson (1908–73, US president 1963–69)

**LBO** *Commerce* leveraged buyout

**LBP** length between perpendiculars

**lbr** labour • lumber

**L.b.s.** Lectori benevolo salutem (Latin: to the kind reader, greeting)

**LBS** Libyan Broadcasting Service • lifeboat station • London Business School

**LBV** landing barge vehicle • Late Bottled Vintage (of port wine)

**lbw** *Cricket* leg before wicket

**LBW** live body weight

**l.c.** label clause • law courts • lead covered • leading cases • left centre • legal currency • letter card • (*or* **lc**, **l/c**) letter of credit • loco citato (Latin: in the place cited; textual annotation) • low-calorie • low-carbon • (*or* **lc**) *Printing* lower case

**LC** Cross of Leo • landing craft • *Med.* Langerhans cells • Leander Club • Legislative Council • (*or* **L/C**) letter of credit • level crossing • (USA) Library of Congress • Lieutenant-Commander • *Chem.* linear chain • *Electronics* linear

contact • *Military slang* line crosser (a defector) • *Chem.* liquid chromatography • livestock commissioner • *airline flight code for* Loganair • *British vehicle registration for* London NW • Lord Chamberlain • Lord Chancellor • Lower Canada • *Electronics* lumped constant

**LCA** Library Club of America • Licensed Company Auditor • low-cost automation

**LCAD** London Certificate in Art and Design

**LCAO** *Chem.* linear combination of atomic orbitals

**LCAP** *Computing* loosely coupled array of processors

**l.c.b.** longitudinal centre of buoyancy

**LCB** *Theatre* left centre back (of stage) • (USA) Liquor Control Board • London Convention Bureau • Lord Chief Baron

**LCC** *Electronics* leadless chip carrier • *Accounting, Computing* life-cycle cost(ing) • *Electrical engineering* load-carrying capability • London Chamber of Commerce • London County Council (superseded by the Greater London Council, GLC)

**LCCC** (USA) Library of Congress Catalog Card

**LCD** *Electronics* liquid-crystal display • Lord Chamberlain's Department • Lord Chancellor's Department • lower court decisions • (*or* **l.c.d.**) *Maths.* lowest common denominator

**LCDT** London Contemporary Dance Theatre

**LCE** Licentiate in Civil Engineering • London Commodity Exchange

**l.c.f.** longitudinal centre of flotation • (*or* **LCF**) *Maths.* lowest common factor

**LCFA** *Chem.* long-chain fatty acid

**l.c.g.** longitudinal centre of gravity

**LCG** *Chem.* lamellar compound of graphite

**LCGB** Locomotive Club of Great Britain

**LCh** Licentiate in Surgery (Latin *Licentiatus Chirurgiae*) • Lord Chancellor

**LCIGB** Locomotive and Carriage Institution of Great Britain and Ireland

**LCJ** Lord Chief Justice

**l.c.l.** lower control limit

**LCL** *Commerce* (USA) less-than-carload lot • *Commerce* less-than-container load • Licentiate in Canon Law

**LCLS** Livestock Commission Levy Scheme

**LCM** landing craft mechanized • *Computing* life-cycle management • London College of Music • (*or* **l.c.m.**) *Maths.* lowest (*or* least) common multiple

**LC-MS** *Chem.* liquid chromatography-mass spectrometry

**Lcn** Lincoln

**LCN** *Aeronautics* load classification number • local civil noon

**LCO** landing craft officer • launch control officer

**L-Col** Lieutenant-Colonel

**L-Corp.** Lance-Corporal

**LCP** last complete programme • least-cost planning • Licentiate of the College of Preceptors • *Chem.* liquid-crystal polymer • London College of Printing • low-cost production

**LCP&SA** Licentiate of the College of Physicians and Surgeons of America

**LCP&SO** Licentiate of the College of Physicians and Surgeons of Ontario

**L/Cpl** Lance-Corporal

**LCPS** Licentiate of the College of Physicians and Surgeons

**l/cr.** lettre de crédit (French: letter of credit)

**LCS** London Cooperative Society

**LCSP** London and Counties Society of Physiologists

**LCST** Licentiate of the College of Speech Therapists

**LCT** landing craft tank • local civil time

**LCU** *Photog.* large close-up

**LCV** Licentiate of the College of Violinists

**ld** land • *Printing* lead • load

**l.d.** legal dose • light difference • line of departure • line of duty

**Ld** Limited (company) • Lord (title)

**LD** Doctor of Letters *or* Literature (Latin *Litterarum Doctor*) • Lady Day • Laus Deo (Latin: Praise be to God) • *Education, Psychol.* learning-disabled • lepide dictum (Latin: wittily said) • *Pharmacol.* lethal dose (as in **LD₅₀**, median lethal dose) • Liberal and Democratic • *symbol for* Libyan dinar (monetary unit) • Licentiate in Divinity • Light Dragoons • Litera Dominicalis (Latin: Dominical letter) • *postcode for* Llandrindod Wells • London Docks • *British vehicle registration for* London NW • low density • Low Dutch

**L/D** letter of deposit

**Lda** (*or* **Ldª**) (Portugal) Sociedade de responsabilidade limitada (limited company; Ltd)

**LDA** Lead Development Association

**l.d.b.** light distribution box

**l.d.c.** long-distance call • lower dead centre

**LDC** less-developed country • local distribution company

**LDDC** London Docklands' Development Corporation

**LDEG** laus Deo et gloria (Latin: praise and glory be to God)

**LDentSc** Licentiate in Dental Science

**Lderry** Londonderry

**ldg** landing • leading • loading • lodging

**Ldg** *Navy* Leading (rank)

**Ldge** Lodge

**L.d'H.** Légion d'Honneur

**LDiv** Licentiate in Divinity

**ldk** lower deck

**LDL** *Biochem.* low-density lipoprotein

**LDM** *Physics* liquid-drop model (of the nucleus)

**ldmk** landmark

**Ldn** London

**LDN** less-developed nation

**LDOS** *Physics* local density of occupied states • Lord's Day Observance Society

**Ldp** Ladyship • Lordship

**LDP** (Japan) Liberal-Democratic Party • *Finance* London daily price • long-distance path

**LDPE** *Chem.* low-density polyethylene (used in packaging materials)

**ldr** leader • ledger • lodger

**LDR** low dose rate

**ldry** laundry

**lds** loads

**LDS** Latter-day Saints • laus Deo semper (Latin: praise be to God for ever) • Licentiate in Dental Surgery

**LDSc** Licentiate in Dental Science

**LDV** *Physics* laser Doppler velocity (*or* velocimetry) • Local Defence Volunteers (Home Guard)

**LDX** long-distance xerography

**LDY** Leicestershire and Derbyshire Yeomanry

**l.e.** leading edge • left eye • library edition • light equipment • limited edition • low explosive

**Le** *symbol for* leone (monetary unit of Sierra Leone) • (*ital.*) *Physics, symbol for* Lewis number

**Le.** Lebanese • Lebanon

**LE** (*or* **£E**) *symbol for* Egyptian pound (monetary unit) • *postcode for* Leicester • London Electricity • *British vehicle registration for* London NW • low energy • *Med.* lupus erythamatosus

**lea.** league • leather • leave

**LEA** Local Education Authority

**LEAJ** (USA) Law Enforcement and Administration of Justice

**LEAP** (li:p) Life Education for the Autistic Person • lift-off elevation and azimuth programmer • Loan and Educational Aid Programme

**LEAR** (lɪə) *Physics* low-energy antiproton ring

**Leb.** Lebanese • Lebanon

**LEB** London Electricity Board • *Astronautics* low-energy booster

**LEC** *Chem.* ligand-exchange chromatography • *Electronics* liquid-encapsulated Czochralski • Local Enterprise Company

**lect.** lectio (Latin: lesson) • lecture(r)

**lectr** lecturer

**led.** ledger

**LED** *Electronics* light-emitting diode

**LEDC** Lighting Equipment Development Council

**LEED** (li:d) *Physics, Chem.* low-energy electron diffraction

**LEFM** linear elastic fracture mechanics

**leg.** legal • legate • (*or* **Leg.**) legation • *Music* legato (Italian: bound; i.e. smoothly) • (*or* **legis.**) legislation • (*or* **legis.**) legislative • (*or* **legis.**) legislature

**legg.** *Music* leggero (Italian: light *or* rapid)

**Leics** Leicestershire

**Leip.** Leipzig

**Leit.** Leitrim

**LEL** Laureate in English Literature • *Physics* linear energy loss

**LEM** (lɛm) *Astronautics* lunar excursion module

**LEMA** Lifting Equipment Manufacturers' Association

**LEO** ('li:əu) *Astronautics* low earth orbit • Lyons Electronic Office (early computer built by J. Lyons & Co.)

**Lep** *Astronomy* Lepus

**LEP** (lɛp) *Physics* Large Electron-Positron (collider; at CERN)

**LEPMA** (USA) Lithographic Engravers' and Plate Makers' Association

**LEPORE** (USA) long-term and expanded program of oceanic research and exploration

**LEPRA** ('lɛprə) Leprosy Relief Association

**LEPT** long-endurance patrolling torpedo

**LES** launch escape system • Liverpool Engineering Society

**LèsL** Licencié ès lettres (French: Bachelor of Arts)

**LèsS** Licencié ès sciences (French: Bachelor of Science)

**LESS** least-cost estimating and scheduling

**LET** *Physics* linear energy transfer

**LETS** Local Employment and Trade System

**Leu** (*or* **leu**) *Biochem.* leucine

**LEU** *Physics* low-enriched uranium

**lev** (*or* **LEV**) lunar excursion vehicle

**Lev.** Levant • (*or* **Levit.**) *Bible* Leviticus

**lex.** lexicon

**LEX** (lɛks) land exercise

**lexicog.** lexicographer • lexicographical • lexicography

**LEY** Liberal European Youth

**lf** leaf • *Printing* light face

**l.f.** ledger folio • life float

**Lf** limit of flocculation (in toxicology)

**LF** Lancashire Fusiliers • *British vehicle registration for* London NW • *Radio* low frequency • *Astronomy* luminosity function

**l.f.a.** local freight agent

**LFB** London Fire Brigade

**LFBC** London Federation of Boys' Clubs

**l.f.c.** low-frequency current

**LFC** Lutheran Free Church

**LFCDA** London Fire and Civil Defence Authority

**LFD** least fatal dose • low-fat diet

**LFE** laboratory for electronics

**Lfg** Lieferung (German: delivery)

**LFO** low-frequency oscillator

**LFRD** lot fraction reliability deviation

**LFS** laser (*or* laser-induced) fluorescent spectroscopy

**lft** leaflet

**LFTU** landing force training unit

**lg** *symbol for* common logarithm • long

**lg.** lagoon • large

**LG** *British vehicle registration for* Chester • Lady Companion of the Order of the Garter • landing ground • Lewis gun • Lieutenant-General • Life

Guards • (David) Lloyd George (1863–1945, British statesman) • London Gazette • Low German • *airline flight code for* Luxair

**LGAR** (USA) Ladies of the Grand Army of the Republic

**LGB** Local Government Board

**LGC** lunar (module) guidance computer

**lge** large • league

**LGEB** Local Government Examination Board

**L-Gen** Lieutenant-General

**LGer** Low German

**LGIO** Local Government Information Office

**LGk** Late Greek

**LGM** Little Green Men • Lloyd's Gold Medal

**LGO** (USA) Lamont Geological Observatory

**LGPRA** Local Government Public Relations Association

**LGr** Late Greek

**LGR** leasehold ground rent • local government reports

**LGSM** Licentiate of the Guildhall School of Music

**LGTB** Local Government Training Board

**lgth** length

**lg tn** long ton

**LGU** Ladies' Golf Union

**l.h.** left half • left hand(ed)

**LH** left hand(ed) • *British fishing port registration for* Leith • licensing hours • Licentiate in Hygiene • *Military* Light Horse • *British vehicle registration for* London NW • *airline flight code for* Lufthansa • *Biochem.* luteinizing hormone

**LHA** landing helicopter assault • local health authority • local hour angle • Lord High Admiral • lower hour angle

**lhb** *Sport* left halfback

**LHC** *Physics* Large Hadron Collider (at CERN) • Lord High Chancellor

**LHCIMA** Licentiate of the Hotel Catering and Institutional Management Association

**l.h.d.** left-hand drive

**LHD** Doctor of Humanities *or* of Literature (Latin *Litterarum Humaniorum Doctor*)

**LHDC** lateral homing depth charge

**LHeb** Late Hebrew

**LHMC** London Hospital Medical College

**LHO** livestock husbandry officer

**lhr** *Physics* lumen-hour

**LHRC** Light and Health Research Council

**LH-RH** *Biochem., Med.* luteinizing-hormone-releasing hormone

**LHS** left hand side

**LHSM** Licentiate of the Institute of Health Services Management

**LHT** Lord High Treasurer

**LHWN** lowest high water neap (tides)

**li.** link

**l.i.** letter of introduction • longitudinal interval

**Li** *Chem., symbol for* lithium

**LI** Leeward Islands • Liberal International • (USA) Licentiate in Instruction • Light Infantry • *Law* Lincoln's Inn • *British fishing port registration for* Littlehampton • Long Island (New York) • *Irish vehicle registration for* Westmeath

**LIA** (USA) Laser Industry Association • (USA) Lead Industries Association • Leather Industries of America • *Physics* linear-induction accelerator

**LIAB** Licentiate of the International Association of Book-Keepers

**LIAT** London International Arbitration Trust

**lib.** liber (Latin: book) • liberty • librarian • library • libretto

**Lib** *Astronomy* Libra

**Lib.** (*or* **Lib**) *Politics* Liberal • Liberia

**LIB** *Physical chem.* light-ion beam

**LIBA** Lloyd's Insurance Brokers' Association

**lib. cat.** library catalogue

**Lib. Cong.** (USA) Library of Congress

**Lib Dem** Liberal Democrat

**LIBER** Ligue des bibliothèques européennes de recherche (French: League of European Research Libraries)

**LIBID** ('li:bɪd) London Inter-Bank Bid Rate

**LIBOR** ('li:bɔ:) *Finance* London Inter-Bank Offered Rate

**libst** librettist

**Lic.** Licenciado (Spanish: Bachelor; in academic degrees) • (*or* **Lic**) Licentiate (in degrees, etc.)

**LIC** Lands Improvement Company • *Electronics* linear integrated circuit

**LicAc** Licentiate of Acupuncture

**LICeram** Licentiate of the Institute of Ceramics

**LicMed** Licentiate in Medicine

**LicTheol** Licentiate in Theology

**LICW** Licentiate of the Institute of Clerks of Works

**lidar** ('li:dɑ:) light detection and ranging

**LIDC** Lead Industries Development Council

**Lieut** Lieutenant

**Lieut-Cdr** Lieutenant-Commander

**Lieut-Col** Lieutenant-Colonel

**Lieut-Com** Lieutenant-Commander

**Lieut-Gen** Lieutenant-General

**Lieut-Gov** Lieutenant-Governor

**LIF** *Chem.* laser-induced fluorescence • *Med.* left iliac fossa

**LIFFE** (laɪf) London International Financial Futures and Options Exchange

**LIFireE** Licentiate of the Institution of Fire Engineers

**LIFO** ('laɪfəʊ) *Accounting, Computing* last in, first out

**LIFS** *Physics* laser-induced fluorescence spectroscopy

**Lig.** Liguria • Limoges

**LILO** last in, last out

**lim.** limit

**Lim.** Limerick

**LIM** Licentiate of the Institute of Metals • linear-induction motor

**LIMEAN** London Inter-Bank Mean Rate

**lin.** lineal • linear • liniment

**linac** ('lɪnæk) *Physics* linear accelerator

**Linc** Lincoln College, Oxford

**Lincs** Lincolnshire

**ling.** linguistics

**lin-log** *Physics, Maths.* linear-logarithmic

**Linn.** (Carolus) Linnaeus (1707–78, Swedish botanist)

**LInstP** Licentiate of the Institute of Physics

**LIOB** Licentiate of the Institute of Building

**LIP** life insurance policy • *Med.* lymphocytic (*or* lymphoid) interstitial pneumonitis

**LIPM** Lister Institute of Preventive Medicine

**LIPS** (*or* **lips**) (lɪps) *Computing* logical inferences per second

**liq.** liquid • liquor

**LIRA** Linen Industry Research Association

**Lis.** Lisbon

**LIS** laser isotope separation

**LISA** (ital.) Library and Information Science Abstracts

**LISM** Licentiate of the Incorporated Society of Musicians

**LISP** (lɪsp) *Computing* list processing (a programming language)

**lit.** literal(ly) • literary • literature • litre(s) • litter • little

**Lit** *symbol for* lira (Italian monetary unit)

**LitB** Bachelor of Letters *or* Literature (Latin *Litterarum Baccalaureus*)

**lit. crit.** (lɪt krɪt) *Colloquial* literary criticism

**LitD** Doctor of Letters *or* Literature (Latin *Litterarum Doctor*)

**lith.** lithograph(y)

**Lith.** Lithuania(n)

**litho.** (*or* **lithog.**) lithograph(ic) • lithography

**lithol.** lithology

**Lit. Hum.** Literae Humaniores (Latin: the humanities; classics course at Oxford University)

**LitM** Master of Letters *or* Literature (Latin *Litterarum Magister*)

**Lit. Sup.** (ital.) Times Literary Supplement

**LittB** Bachelor of Letters *or* Literature (Latin *Litterarum Baccalaureus*)

**LittD** Doctor of Letters *or* Literature (Latin *Litterarum Doctor*)

**LittM** Master of Letters *or* Literature (Latin *Litterarum Magister*)

**liturg.** liturgical • liturgy

**LIUNA** Laborers' International Union of North America

**liv.** *Commerce* livraison (French: delivery)

**Liv.** Liverpool • Livy (59 BC–17 AD, Roman historian)

**liv. st.** livre sterling (French: pound sterling)

**l.j.** life jacket

**LJ** *British vehicle registration for* Bournemouth • *Chem.* Lennard-Jones (as in **LJ potential**) • Library Journal • *Athletics* long jump • Lord Justice

**LJC** London Juvenile Courts

**LJJ** *Electronics* long Josephson junction • Lords Justices

**LK** *British fishing port registration for* Lerwick • *British vehicle registration for* London NW

**lkd** locked

**lkg** locking

**lkge** *Commerce* leakage

**lkr** locker

**ll.** leaves • leges (Latin: laws) • lines (of written matter)

**l.l.** live load • loco laudato (Latin: in the place quoted) • lower left • lower limit

**LL** *Physics* Landau–Lifshitz (as in **LL splitting factor**) • Late Latin • Law Latin • (ital.) Law List • (*or* **£L, £Leb.**) *symbol for* Lebanese pound (monetary unit) • lending library • limited liability • *Physics, Maths.* linear-linear • *British fishing port registration for* Liverpool • *postcode for* Llandudno • London Library • *British vehicle registration for* London NW • Lord-Lieutenant • *Med.* lower limb • Low Latin

**LL.** laws • lines (of written matter) • Lords

**L/L** (Norway) Lutlang (limited company; Ltd)

**LLA** Lady Literate in Arts

**LL.AA.II.** Leurs Altesses Impériales (French: Their Imperial Highnesses)

**LL.AA.RR.** Leurs Altesses Royales (French: Their Royal Highnesses)

**LLB** (*or* **LIB**) Bachelor of Laws (Latin *Legum Baccalaureus*)

**l.l.c.** lower left centre

**LLCM** Licentiate of London College of Music

**LLCO** Licentiate of the London College of Osteopathy

**LLD** (*or* **LID**) Doctor of Laws (Latin *Legum Doctor*)

**Llds** *Insurance* Lloyd's

**LLE** *Chemical engineering* liquid-liquid extraction • low-level exposure (to radiation)

**LL.EE.** Leurs Éminences (French: Their Eminences) • Leurs Excellences (French: Their Excellencies)

**LLett** Licentiate of Letters

**l.l.i.** latitude and longitude indicator

**LLI** Lord-Lieutenant of Ireland

**LLL** Licentiate in Laws • loose leaf ledger • *Computing* low-level logic

**LLLW** liquid low-level (radioactive) waste

**LLM** Master of Laws (Latin *Legum Magister*)

**LLMCom** Master of Laws in Commercial Law

**LL.MM.** Leurs Majestés (French: Their Majesties)

**LLN** (USA) League for Less Noise

**LLNL** (USA) Lawrence Livermore National Laboratory

**LLNW** low-level nuclear waste

**LLRW** low-level radioactive waste

**LLS** *Astronautics* lunar logistics system

**LLSV** *Astronautics* lunar logistics system vehicle

**LLU** lending library unit

**LLV** *Astronautics* lunar logistics vehicle

**LLW** low-level (radioactive) waste

**lm** *Physics, symbol for* lumen

**l.m.** land mine • light metal • locus monumenti (Latin: place of the monument)

**l.M.** laufenden Monats (German: of the current month)

**Lm** *symbol for* Maltese lira (monetary unit)

**LM** Legion of Merit • Licentiate in Medicine • Licentiate in Midwifery • Licentiate in Music • light microscopy • liquid metal • *Electrical engineering* load management • London Museum • *British vehicle registration for* London NW • *Music, Prosody* long metre • (Scotland) Lord Marquis • Lord Mayor • *Aeronautics* lunar module

**LMA** *Physics* laser microprobe analyser • Linoleum Manufacturers' Association • low moisture avidity

**LMBC** Lady Margaret Boat Club (St John's College, Cambridge) • Liverpool Marine Biological Committee

**LMC** *Astronomy* Large Magellanic Cloud • *Nuclear engineering* liquid-metal coolant • Lloyd's Machinery Certificate • Local Medical Committee

**LMCC** Licentiate of the Medical Council of Canada

**lmd** leafmould

**LMD** local medical doctor • *Music, Prosody* long metre double

**LME** London Metal Exchange

**LMed** Licentiate in Medicine

**LMFBR** *Nuclear engineering* liquid-metal-cooled fast breeder reactor

**LMG** light machine gun

**LMH** Lady Margaret Hall (Oxford University)

**LMi** *Astronomy* Leo Minor

**LMI** (USA) Logistics Management Institute

**LMMS** *Chem.* laser microprobe mass spectrometry

**LMO** lens-modulated oscillator • light machine oil

**LMP** *Med.* last menstrual period • lunar module pilot

**LMR** *Nuclear engineering* liquid-metal reactor • *Railways* London Midland Region

**LMRCP** Licentiate in Midwifery of the Royal College of Physicians

**LMRSH** Licentiate Member of the Royal Society for the Promotion of Health

**LMRTPI** Legal Member of the Royal Town Planning Institute

**LMS** *Chem.* laser mass spectrometry • Licentiate in Medicine and Surgery • *Education* local management of schools • London Mathematical Society • London Medical Schools • (*or* **LMS(R)**) London, Midland and Scottish Railway • London Missionary Society • *Med.* loss of memory syndrome

**LMSSA** Licentiate in Medicine and Surgery of the Society of Apothecaries

**LMT** *Physics* length, mass, time • *Astronomy* local mean time

**LMus** Licentiate in Music

**LMVD** (New Zealand) Licensed Motor Vehicle Dealer

**LMW** *Biochem.* low molecular weight (as in **LMW protein**)

**LMX** London Market Excess of Loss (at Lloyd's)

**ln** *symbol for* natural logarithm

**Ln** Lane (in place names)

**LN** *British fishing port registration for* King's Lynn • *airline flight code for* Libyan Arab Airlines • *postcode for* Lincoln • liquid nitrogen • *British vehicle registration for* London NW • *Med.* lymph node • *international civil aircraft marking for* Norway

**LNat** Liberal National

**LNC** League of Nations Covenant

**LNER** London and North Eastern Railway

**LNG** liquefied natural gas

**Lnrk** Lanark

**LNS** land navigation system

**LNT** liquid-nitrogen temperature

**LNU** League of Nations Union

**LNWR** London and North-Western Railway

**l.o.** lubricating oil

**l/o** *Commerce* leur ordre (French: their order)

**Lo.** Lord

**LO** Landsorganisationen i Sverige (General Federation of Swedish Trade Unions) • launch operator • liaison officer • *British fishing port registration for* London • *British vehicle registration for* London NW • London office • *airline flight code for* Lot Polish Airlines

**l.o.a.** length over all (in technical drawing)

**LOA** leave of absence • light observation aircraft

**LOB** *Baseball* left on base • line of balance • Location of Offices Bureau

**LOBAL** ('ləʊbæl) long-base-line buoy

**LOBAR** ('ləʊbɑː) long-base-line radar

**loc.** local • location • *Grammar* locative

**l.o.c.** lines of communication

**LOC** launch operations centre • (USA) Library of Congress • *Meteorol.* locally

**LOCA** *Nuclear engineering* loss-of-coolant accident

**loc. cit.** loco citato (*see under* l.c.)

**loc. laud.** loco laudato (Latin: in the place cited with approval)

**locn** location

**loco.** locomotion • locomotive

**loc. primo cit.** loco primo citato (Latin: in the place first cited)

**LOD** limit(s) of detection

**LOF** loss of flow (*or* fluid) • loss of function

**L of C** (USA) Library of Congress • lines of communication

**L of N** League of Nations

**LOFT** (lɒft) low-frequency radio telescope

**log** (lɒg) logarithm

**log.** logic(al) • logistic

**LOH** light observation helicopter

**LOI** lunar orbit insertion

**LOLA** ('ləʊlə) library on-line acquisition • lunar orbit landing approach

**LOM** (USA) Loyal Order of Moose

**LOMA** (USA) Life Office Management Association

**Lomb.** Lombard(y)

**Lond.** London • Londonderry

**Londin.** Londiniensis (Latin: (Bishop) of London)

**long.** (*or* **long**) longitude

**Long.** Longford

**longl** longitudinal

**Lonrho** ('lɒnrəʊ) *Finance* London Rhodesian

**LOOM** (USA) Loyal Order of Moose

**l.o.p.** (*or* **LOP**) *Navigation* line of position

**LOPAR** ('ləʊpɑː) low-power acquisition radar

**loq.** loquitur (Latin: he (*or* she) speaks)

**LOR** light output ratio • lunar orbit rendezvous

**LORAC** ('lɒræk) long-range accuracy

**LORAD** ('lɒræd) long-range active detection

**LORAN** ('lɒræn) long-range navigation

**LORAPH** ('lɒræf) long-range passive homing system

**LORCS** League of Red Cross and Red Crescent Societies

**LORV** (lɔːv) low observable re-entry vehicle

**LOS** Latin Old Style • Law of the Seas • line of sight • loss of signal

**LOSS** large-object salvage system

**lot.** lotion

**Lot** (lɒt) Polskie Linie Lotnicze (Polish Air Lines)

**LOT** large orbital telescope

**LOTC** *Finance* London over-the-counter market

**Lou.** Louisiana

**LOX** (*or* **lox**) (lɒks) liquid oxygen

**loy.** loyal(ty)

**LOYA** League of Young Adventurers

**l.p.** last paid • latent period • launch platform • long primer (a size of printer's type) • low pressure

**Lp** Ladyship • Lordship

**LP** Labour Party • large paper (edition of a book) • large post (a standard paper size) • last post • legal procurator • Liberal Party • life policy • Limited Partnership • *Computing* linear programming • liquid petroleum • liquid propellant • *British vehicle registration for* London NW • long-playing (of a gramophone record) • Lord Provost • low pressure • *Med.* lumbar puncture

**L/P** letterpress • life policy

**LPA** Leather Producers' Association for England • Local Productivity Association

**l.p.c.** low pressure chamber

**LPC** leaf protein concentrate (in nutrition) • Lord President of the Council

**LPE** *Electronics* liquid-phase epitaxy

**LPEA** Licentiate of the Physical Education Association

**LPed** Licentiate in Pedagogy

**LPG** liquefied petroleum gas

**LPh** (*or* **LPH**) Licentiate in Philosophy

**lpi** lines per inch

**LPLC** low-pressure liquid chromatography

**lpm** lines per millimetre • lines per minute

**LPN** (USA) Licensed Practical Nurse

**LPNA** (USA) Lithographers' and Printers' National Association

**LPO** local purchasing officer • London Philharmonic Orchestra

**L'pool** Liverpool

**LPRP** Laotian People's Revolutionary Party

**LPS** *Biochem.* lipopolysaccharide • *Engineering* liquid-phase sintering • London Philharmonic Society • Lord Privy Seal

**LPSO** Lloyd's Policy Signing Office

**LPU** low pay unit

**l.p.w.** *Optics* lumens per watt

**Lpz.** Leipzig

**l.q.** lege quaeso (Latin: please read)

**LQ** *Computing* letter quality (of printed output) • *Maths.* linear-quadratic

**lqdr** liquidator

**LQR** (ital.) Law Quarterly Review

**LQT** *Commerce* Liverpool quay terms

**lr** lower

**l.r.** landing report • log run • long range • long run

**l.R.** laufen de Rechnung (German: current account)

**Lr** Lancer • *Chem.*, *symbol for* lawrencium • ledger

**LR** *British fishing port registration for* Lancaster • Land Registry • Law Report • left-right (*or* left-to-right) • liquor/liquor-to-goods ratio (in dyeing) • Lloyd's Register (of Shipping) • *British vehicle registration for* London NW • Lowland Regiment • Loyal Regiment

**LRA** Local Radio Association

**LRAC** Law Reports, Appeal Cases

**LRAD** Licentiate of the Royal Academy of Dancing

**LRAM** Licentiate of the Royal Academy of Music

**LRB** London Residuary Body (in local government) • London Rifle Brigade

**LRC** Labour Representation Committee • Langley Research Center (in NASA) • Leander Rowing Club • London Rowing Club

**LRCh** Law Reports, Chancery Division

**LRCM** Licentiate of the Royal College of Music

**LRCP** Licentiate of the Royal College of Physicians

**LRCPE** (*or* **LRCPEd**) Licentiate of the Royal College of Physicians of Edinburgh

**LRCPI** Licentiate of the Royal College of Physicians of Ireland

**LRCPSGlas** Licentiate of the Royal College of Physicians and Surgeons of Glasgow

**LRCS** League of Red Cross Societies • Licentiate of the Royal College of Surgeons of England

**LRCSE** Licentiate of the Royal College of Surgeons of Edinburgh

**LRCSI** Licentiate of the Royal College of Surgeons in Ireland

**LRCVS** Licentiate of the Royal College of Veterinary Surgeons

**LREC** *Med.* Local Research Ethics Committee

**LRHL** Law Reports, House of Lords

**LRIBA** Licentiate of the Royal Institute of British Architects (now Member; *see* RIBA)

**LRKB** Law Reports, King's Bench

**LRP** Law Reports, Probate Division

**LRPS** Licentiate of the Royal Photographic Society

**LRQB** Law Reports, Queen's Bench

**Lrs** Lancers

**LRS** Land Registry Stamp • *Physical chem.* laser Raman spectroscopy • (ital.) Lloyd's Register of Shipping

**LRSC** Licentiate of the Royal Society of Chemistry

**LRSM** Licentiate of the Royal Schools of Music

**LRT** light rail transit • London Regional Transport • long-range transport

**LRTI** *Med.* lower respiratory tract infection

**LRU** least recently used • line replaceable unit

**LRV** light rail vehicle • lunar roving vehicle

**LRWES** long-range weapons experimental station

**l.s.** landing ship • left side • (*or* **L.s.**) letter signed • local sunset • *Law* locus sigilli (Latin: the place of the seal) • long sight • low speed • lump sum

**LS** *British vehicle registration for* Edinburgh • Law Society • Leading Seaman • *postcode for* Leeds • legal seal • *international vehicle registration for* Lesotho • letter service • Licensed Surveyor • Licentiate in Surgery • *Psychol.* liminal sensitivity • Linnean Society • locus sigilli (*see under* l.s.) • London Scottish • London Sinfonietta • *Films* long shot • loudspeaker • (*or* **£S, £Syr.**) *symbol for* Syrian pound (monetary unit)

**LSA** Land Settlement Association • leading supply assistant • Licence in Agricultural Sciences • Licentiate of the Society of Apothecaries

**LSAA** Linen Supply Association of America

**LS&GCM** Long Service and Good Conduct Medal

**LSB** *Computing* least significant bit • London School Board

**l.s.c.** loco supra citato (Latin: in the place before cited)

**LSC** Licentiate in Sciences • liquid scintillation counting (*or* counter) • *Chem.* liquid–solid chromatography • London Salvage Corps

**LScAct** Licentiate in Actuarial Science

**LSCF** *Statistics* least squares curve fitting

**LSCS** *Obstetrics* lower segment Caesarean section

**LSd** (*or* **£Sd**) *symbol for* Sudanese pound (monetary unit)

**LSD** League of Safe Drivers • *Computing* least significant digit • Lightermen, Stevedores, and Dockers • lysergic acid diethylamide (hallucinogenic drug)

**L.S.D.** (*or* **£.s.d., l.s.d.**) librae, solidi, denarii (Latin: pounds, shillings, pence)

**l.s.e.** limited signed edition

**LSE** *Chem.* liquid–solid extraction • *Chem.* liquid-solvent extraction • London School of Economics and Political Science • London Stock Exchange

**L-Sgt** Lance-Sergeant

**LSHTM** London School of Hygiene and Tropical Medicine

**LSI** Labour and Socialist International • *Electronics* large-scale integration (*or* integrated)

**LSJ** London School of Journalism

**LSJM** laus sit Jesu et Mariae (Latin: praise be to Jesus and Mary)

**LSL** landing ship logistic • low-speed logic

**l.s.m.** litera scripta manet (Latin: the written word remains)

**LSM** laser scanning microscope • *Maths., Physics* least-squares method • *Electrical engineering* linear synchronous motor

**LSO** London Symphony Orchestra

**LSQ** *Meteorol.* line squall

**LSR** *Astronomy* local standard of rest

**LSS** large-scale structure (*or* system) • Licentiate in Sacred Scripture • (USA)

Lifesaving Service • life-saving station • life-support system

**LSSc** Licentiate in Sanitary Science

**l.s.t.** local standard time

**LST** landing ship (for) tank(s) *or* transport • Licentiate in Sacred Theology • *Astronomy* local sidereal time • local standard time

**LSU** Louisiana State University

**LSZ** (New Zealand) limited speed zone

**lt** light

**l.t.** landed terms • landing team • large tug • local time • locum tenens • long ton • loop test

**Lt** Lieutenant • *Military* Light

**LT** Licentiate in Teaching • *international vehicle registration for* Lithuania • *British vehicle registration for* London NW • London Transport • *Physics* Lorentz transformation • *British fishing port registration for* Lowestoft • low temperature • *Electrical engineering* low tension • *symbol for* Turkish lira (monetary unit)

**LTA** Lawn Tennis Association • *Chem.* lead tetraacetate • lighter than air (of an aircraft) • London Teachers' Association

**LTAA** Lawn Tennis Association of Australia

**LT & SR** London, Tilbury, and Southend Railway

**l.t.b.** low-tension battery

**LTB** London Tourist Board

**LTBT** Limited Test Ban Treaty

**LTC** Lawn Tennis Club • *Chemical engineering* low-temperature carbonization

**Lt-Cdr** Lieutenant-Commander

**LTCL** Licentiate of Trinity College of Music, London

**Lt-Col** Lieutenant-Colonel

**Lt-Com** Lieutenant-Commander

**Ltd** Limited (after the name of a private limited company)

**LTDP** long-term defence programme

**LTF** Lithographic Technical Foundation

**ltg** lettering • lighting

**ltge** *Commerce* lighterage

**Lt-Gen** Lieutenant-General

**Lt-Gov** Lieutenant-Governor

**LTh** Licentiate in Theology

**LTH** light training helicopter • *Biochem.* luteotrophic hormone

**LTI** Licentiate of the Textile Institute

**LTIB** Lead Technical Information Bureau

**Lt Inf.** Light Infantry

**LTL** *Commerce* (USA) less-than-truckload lot

**LTM** Licentiate in Tropical Medicine • London Terminal Market

**LTO** leading torpedo operator

**LTOM** London Traded Options Market

**LTOS** Law Times, Old Series

**LTP** *Biochem.* lipid-transfer protein • *Science* long-term potentiation

**ltr** letter • lighter

**LTR** *Genetics* long terminal repeat

**LTRA** Lands Tribunal Rating Appeals

**LtRN** Lieutenant, Royal Navy

**LTRS** Low Temperature Research Station

**LTSC** Licentiate of Tonic Sol-Fa College

**LTTE** (Sri Lanka) Liberation Tigers of Tamil Eelam

**lu.** luglio (Italian: July)

**l/u** *Shipping* laid (*or* lying) up

**Lu** *Chem.*, *symbol for* lutetium

**Lu.** Lucerne

**LU** Liberal Unionist • *British vehicle registration for* London NW • loudness unit • *postcode for* Luton

**LUA** Liverpool Underwriters' Association

**lub.** (*or* **lubr.**) lubricant • lubricate • lubrication

**LUC** London Underwriters Centre

**LUCOM** ('luːkɒm) lunar communication system

**lug.** luggage • lugger

**LUG** light utility glider • *Computing* local users group

**LUHF** *Electronics* lowest useful high frequency

**LULOP** (ital.) London Union List of Periodicals

**lum.** lumbago • lumber • luminous

**LUM** lunar excursion module

**LUMAS** ('luːmæs) lunar mapping system

**LUMO** ('luːməʊ) *Chem.* lowest unoccupied molecular orbital

**lun.** lundì (French: Monday) • lunedì (Italian: Monday) • lunes (Spanish: Monday)

**LUNCO** Lloyd's Underwriters Non-Marine Claims Office

**LUOTC** London University Officers' Training Corps

**Lup** *Astronomy* Lupus

**LUS** Land Utilization Survey

**LUSCS** *Obstetrics* lower uterine segment Caesarean section

**LUSI** lunar surface inspection

**lusing.** *Music* lusingando (Italian: coaxing *or* caressing)

**LUT** *Astronautics* launch umbilical tower · *Computing* look-up table

**Luth.** Lutheran

**lux.** luxurious

**Lux.** Luxembourg

**LuxF** *symbol for* Luxembourg franc (monetary unit)

**lv.** leave (of absence, as from military duty) · livre (French: book)

**l.v.** low voltage

**Lv** lev (Bulgarian monetary unit)

**LV** *international civil aircraft marking for* Argentina · *international vehicle registration for* Latvia · *Med.* left ventricle (*or* ventricular) · licensed victualler · *Meteorol.* light and variable · *British vehicle registration for* Liverpool · luncheon voucher

**LVA** Licensed Victuallers' Association

**LVF** *Med.* left ventricular function

**LVI** laus Verbo Incarnato (Latin: praise to the Incarnate Word) · low viscosity index

**LVLO** Local Vehicle Licensing Office

**LVN** (USA) licensed vocational nurse

**LVO** Lieutenant of the Royal Victorian Order

**lvs** leaves

**LVS** Licentiate in Veterinary Science

**LVT** landing vehicle, tracked

**Lw** (formerly) *Chem., symbol for* lawrencium (*see under* Lr)

**LW** left wing · light weight · *British vehicle registration for* London NW · *Radio, etc.* long-wave (*or* long waves) · low water

**LWA** London Welsh Association

**l.w.b.** long wheelbase

**LWEST** low water equinoctial spring tide

**LWF** Lutheran World Federation

**LWL** (*or* **lwl**) length (at) waterline (of a ship) · *Shipping* load waterline

**LWM** (*or* **lwm**) low water mark

**LWONT** low water, ordinary neap tides

**LWOST** low water, ordinary spring tides

**LWR** *Nuclear engineering* light-water reactor

**LWRA** London Waste Regulation Authority

**LWT** London Weekend Television

**LWV** (USA) League of Women Voters

**lx** *Physics, symbol for* lux

**LX** *British vehicle registration for* London NW · *international civil aircraft marking for* Luxembourg

**Lxmbrg** Luxembourg

**LXX** *Bible, symbol for* Septuagint (from its 70 translators)

**l.y.** *Astronomy* light year

**LY** *airline flight code for* El Al Israel Airlines · *international civil aircraft marking for* Lithuania · *British fishing port registration for* Londonderry · *British vehicle registration for* London NW

**Lyn** *Astronomy* Lynx

**lyr.** lyric(al)

**Lyr** *Astronomy* Lyra

**LYR** *Meteorol.* layer(ed)

**Lys** (*or* **lys**) *Biochem.* lysine

**LZ** *British vehicle registration for* Armagh · *international civil aircraft marking for* Bulgaria

**LZT** *Chem.* lead zirconate–titanate

# M

**m** (ital.) *Astronomy, symbol for* apparent magnitude · (bold ital.) *Physics, symbol for* magnetic moment · (ital.) *Physics, symbol for* magnetic quantum number · (ital.) *Chem., symbol for* mass · *Music* me (in tonic sol-fa) · (ital.) *Chem.* meta (as in **m-dichlorobenzene**) · *symbol for* metre(s) · *symbol for* milli- (prefix indicating 1/1000 (i.e. $10^{-3}$), as in **mm**, millimetre) · million · (ital.) *Chem., symbol for* molality

**m.** *Cricket* maiden (over) · male · manipulus (Latin: handful) · mare · *Currency* mark(s) · married · masculine · medical · medicine · medium · memorandum · meridian · meridies (Latin: noon) · meridional · midday · middle · mile(s) · (USA, Canada) mill(s) (monetary unit) • mille (French: thousand) • minim (liquid measure) • minor • minute(s) • *Med.* misce (Latin: mix) • *Meteorol.* mist • mixture • moderate • mois (French: month) • molar (tooth) • month • moon • morning • mort *or* morte (French: dead) • morto (Italian: dead) • mountain

**M** (ital.) *Astronomy, symbol for* absolute magnitude • *Printing, symbol for* em • *symbol for* loti (monetary unit of Lesotho; pl. maloti) • (ital.; *or* **M**ᵥ) *Physics, symbol for* luminous exitance • *Aeronautics* Mach (followed by a number) • (ital.) *Physics, symbol for* magnetic quantum number • (bold ital.) *Physics, symbol for* magnetization • *international vehicle registration for* Malta • *postcode for* Manchester • (ital.) *symbol for* mass, especially molar mass • *Films* (Australia) mature audience (certification) • medium (size) • *symbol for* mega- (prefix indicating one million, as in **MW**, megawatt; *or* in computing) 2²⁰, as in **Mbyte**, megabyte) • *Chem., symbol for* mesomeric effect • *Astronomy* Messier Catalogue (followed by a number) • *Chem., symbol for* metal (in a chemical formula, as in **MOH**) • *Biochem., symbol for* methionine • *British fishing port registration for* Milford • million • minim (liquid measure) • (bold ital.) *Physics, symbol for* moment of a force • *Economics* monetary aggregate (as in **M0**, **M1**, etc.; measures of the money supply) • motorway (as in **M1**, **M4**, etc.) • mud (on charts) • (ital.) *Electrical engineering, symbol for* mutual inductance • (ital.; *or* **M**ₑ) *Physics, symbol for* radiant exitance • *Navigation, symbol for* sea mile • *Roman numeral for* thousand • *Astronomy, indicating* a spectral type • *Logic, indicating* the middle term of a syllogism

**M.** (*or* **M**) Magister (Latin: Master) • magistrate • Majesty • Manitoba • March • Marquess • Marquis • martyr • Master (in titles) • May • medal • Medieval • Member (in titles) • Methodist • *Music* metronome • metropolitan • mezzo *or* mezza (Italian: half) • Middle • militia • minesweeper • Monday • Monsieur (French: Mr *or* Sir) • Monte (Italian: mount) • mother • Mountain

**m.a.** manufacturing assembly • map analysis • menstrual age

**m/a** *Book-keeping* my account

**mA** *symbol for* milliampere(s)

**Ma** (ital.) *Aeronautics, symbol for* Mach number

**Ma.** Mater (Latin: Mother)

**MA** *British vehicle registration for* Chester • Magistrates' Association • *airline flight code for* Malev Hungarian Airlines • (USA) Manpower Administration • (USA) Maritime Administration • *US postcode for* Massachusetts • Master of Arts • Mathematical Association • medieval archaeology • *Psychol.* mental age • Middle Ages • Military Academy • military assistant • military attaché • Missionarius Apostolicus (Latin: Apostolic Missionary) • mobility allowance • *international vehicle registration for* Morocco • Mountaineering Association

**MAA** Manufacturers' Agents Association of Great Britain • master-at-arms • Mathematical Association of America • Member of the Architectural Association • *Chem.* methacrylic acid • Motor Agents' Association

**MAAF** Mediterranean Allied Air Forces

**MAAT** Member of the Association of Accounting Technicians

**MABS** (USA) marine air base squadron

**Mac.** Macao • (*or* **Macc.**) Maccabees (books of the Apocrypha)

**MAc** Master of Accountancy

**MAC** (*or* **m.a.c.**) maximum allowable concentration • (mæk) *Television* multiplexed analogue components • (USA) Municipal Assistance Corporation

**MACA** ('mækə) Mental After Care Association

**MACC** military aid to the civilian community

**MACE** Member of the Association of Conference Executives • Member of the Australian College of Education

**Maced.** Macedonia(n)

**mach.** machine(ry) • machinist

**MACM** Member of the Association of Computing Machines

**macroecon.** macroeconomics

**MACS** Member of the American Chemical Society

**Mad.** Madeira

**MAD** (mæd) magnetic anomaly detection • maintenance, assembly, and disassembly • *Psychiatry* major affective disorder • *Military* mutual assured destruction

**Madag.** Madagascar

**MADD** (mæd) (USA) Mothers Against Drunk Driving

**MADO** Member of the Association of Dispensing Opticians

**Madr.** Madras · Madrid

**MaE** Master in Engineering

**MAE** Master of Aeronautical Engineering · Master of Art Education · Master of Arts in Education

**MA(Econ)** Master of Arts in Economics

**MA(Ed)** Master of Arts in Education

**MAEE** Marine Aircraft Experimental Establishment

**maesto.** *Music* maestoso (Italian: majestic, stately)

**MAFA** Manchester Academy of Fine Arts

**MAFF** (mæf) Ministry of Agriculture, Fisheries, and Food

**mag.** magazine · maggio (Italian: May) · magnesium · magnet(ic) · magnetism · magneto · magnitude · magnum

**Mag.** Magyar

**MAg** Master of Agriculture

**Magd** Magdalen College, Oxford · Magdalene College, Cambridge

**MAgEc** Master of Agricultural Economics

**magg.** maggio (Italian: May) · *Music* maggiore (Italian: major)

**maglev** ('mæg,lɛv) magnetic levitation

**MAGPI** ('mægpaɪ) *Surgery* meatal advancement and glanuloplasty (operation)

**MAgr** Master of Agriculture

**MAgrSc** Master of Agricultural Science

**mah.** (*or* mahog.) mahogany

**MAI** Master of Engineering (Latin *Magister in Arte Ingeniaria*) · *Forestry* mean annual increment · Member of the Anthropological Institute

**MAIAA** Member of the American Institute of Aeronautics and Astronautics

**MAIB** Marine Accident Investigation Branch

**MAICE** Member of the American Institute of Consulting Engineers

**MAIChE** Member of the American Institute of Chemical Engineers

**maint.** maintenance

**MAISE** Member of the Association of Iron and Steel Engineers

**maj.** major · majority

**Maj** *Military* Major

**Maj-Gen** Major-General

**Mal.** *Bible* Malachi · Malay(an) · Malaysia(n) · Malta · Maréchal (French: Field Marshal)

**MAL** *international vehicle registration for* Malaysia

**MALD** Master of Arts in Law and Diplomacy

**mall.** malleable

**MAM** *Computing* multiple allocation memory

**MAMBO** ('mæmbəʊ) Mediterranean Association for Marine Biology and Oceanography

**MAMEME** Member of the Association of Mining Electrical and Mechanical Engineers

**man.** management · manager · manual(ly) · manufacture(r)

**Man.** Manchester · Manila · Manitoba

**MAnaes** Master of Anaesthesiology

**Manch.** Manchester · Manchuria

**mand.** *Law* mandamus (an order from the High Court) · *Music* mandolin

**M & B** May and Baker (pharmaceutical company) · mild and bitter (beer) · Mills and Boon (publisher of romantic fiction)

**M & E** music and effects

**Man. Dir.** Managing Director

**m & r** maintenance and repairs

**m & s** maintenance and supply

**M&S** Marks & Spencer plc

**Man. Ed.** Managing Editor

**manf.** manufacturer

**MANF** May, August, November, February (months for quarterly payments)

**mang. B** manganese bronze

**Manit.** Manitoba

**man. op.** manually operated

**man. pr.** *Med.* mane primo (Latin: early in the morning)

**Mans.** Mansion(s)

**Mansf** Mansfield College, Oxford

**manuf.** (*or* manufac.) manufacture(d) · manufacturer · manufacturing

**MANWEB** ('mænwɛb) Merseyside and North Wales Electricity Board

**MAO** Master of Obstetric Art · *Biochem., Pharmacol.* monoamine oxidase

**MAOI** monoamine oxidase inhibitor (antidepressant)

**MAOT** Member of the Association of Occupational Therapists

**MAOU** Member of the American Ornithologists' Union

**MAP** major air pollutant • *Computing* Manufacturing Automation Protocol • maximum average price • *Med.* mean arterial (blood) pressure • medical aid post • Ministry of Aircraft Production • modified American plan (payment system in US hotels)

**MAppSc** Master of Applied Science

**MAPsS** Member of the Australian Psychological Society

**mar.** *Music* marimba • marine • maritime • marriage • married • martedì (Italian: Tuesday) • marzo (Italian: March)

**Mar.** March

**MAR** *Taxation* marginal age relief • Master of Arts in Religion • *Computing* memory address register

**MARAC** Member of the Australasian Register of Agricultural Consultants

**marc.** *Music* marcato (Italian: marked; i.e. each note emphasized)

**MARC** (mɑːk) *Bibliog.* machine-readable cataloguing

**March.** Marchioness

**MArch** Master of Architecture

**marg.** margin(al)

**mar. insce.** marine insurance

**marit.** maritime

**mar. lic.** marriage licence

**MARMAP** ('mɑːˌmæp) (USA) Marine Resources Monitoring Assessment and Prediction

**Marq.** Marquess • Marquis

**MARS** meteorological automatic reporting station (*or* system)

**mart.** martyr

**MARV** (mɑːv) *Military* manoeuvrable re-entry vehicle

**mas.** masculine

**MAS** Master of Applied Science • Military Agency for Standardization

**MASAE** Member of the American Society of Agricultural Engineers

**masc.** masculine

**MASc** Master of Applied Science

**MASC** Member of the Australian Society of Calligraphers

**MASCAM** ('mæskæm) *Electronics* masking-pattern adaptive sub-band coding and multiplexing

**MASCE** Member of the American Society of Civil Engineers

**mascon** ('mæskon) *Astronomy* mass concentration

**maser** ('meizə) microwave amplification by stimulated emission of radiation

**MASH** (mæʃ) (USA) mobile army surgical hospital

**MASME** Member of the American Society of Mechanical Engineers

**Mass.** Massachusetts

**MA(SS)** Master of Arts in Social Science

**mat.** maternity • matinée • matins • *Printing* matrix • *Finance* maturity

**MAT** *Insurance* marine, aviation, and transport • Master of Arts in Teaching

**MATA** ('mætə) multiple answering teaching aid

**math.** mathematical(ly) • mathematician • (USA, Canada) mathematics

**MATh** Master of Arts in Theology

**maths.** mathematics

**MATIF** marché à terme des instruments financiers (French: financial futures market)

**matr.** matrimonium (Latin: marriage)

**MATS** *US Air Force* Military Air Transport Service

**MATSA** Managerial Administrative Technical Staff Association

**Matt.** *Bible* Matthew

**MATTS** ('mætz) *Military* multiple airborne target trajectory system

**MATV** master antenna television

**Maur.** Mauritius

**Mau Re** (pl. **Mau Rs**) *symbol for* Mauritian rupee (monetary unit)

**MAusIMM** Member of the Australasian Institute of Mining and Metallurgy

**MAW** *Military* medium assault weapon

**max.** maxim • (*or* **max, MAX**) maximum

**mb** *Meteorol., symbol for* millibar(s)

**m.b.** magnetic bearing • main battery • medium bomber • *Med.* misce bene (Latin: mix well) • (*or* **m/b**) motor boat (*or* barge)

**MB** Bachelor of Medicine (Latin *Medicinae Baccalaureus*) • Bachelor of Music (Latin *Musicae Baccalaureus*) • *British vehicle registration for* Chester • maritime board • mark of the Beast • marketing board • maternity benefit • (Canada) Medal of Bravery • medical board • *Electronics* megabit • *Computing* megabyte • metropolitan borough • *Meteorol.* millibar(s) • motor boat (*or* barge) • municipal borough

**Mba.** Mombasa

**MBA** Master of Business Administration

**MBAC** Member of the British Association of Chemists

**MBAcA** Member of the British Acupuncture Association

**mbar** *Meteorol., symbol for* millibar(s)

**MBASW** Member of the British Association of Social Workers

**MBBA** *Chem.* N-(4-methoxybenzylidene)-4-butylaniline

**m.b.c.** *Med.* maximum breathing capacity

**MBC** *Chem.* methyl benzimidazole carbamate • metropolitan borough council • municipal borough council

**MBCO** Member of the British College of Ophthalmic Opticians (*or* Optometrists)

**MBCPE** Member of the British College of Physical Education

**MBCS** Member of the British Computer Society

**MBD** *Med.* minimal brain dysfunction

**MBdgSc** Master of Building Science

**MBE** Member of the Order of the British Empire • *Electronics* molecular-beam epitaxy

**MBF** Musicians Benevolent Fund

**MBFR** *Military* mutual and balanced force reduction

**MBG** microemulsion-based gel

**mbH** mit beschränkter Haftung (German: with limited liability)

**MBH** *Astronomy* massive black hole

**MBHI** Member of the British Horological Institute

**MBIFD** Member of the British Institute of Funeral Directors

**MBK** *Military* missing, believed killed

**MBKSTS** Member of the British Kinematograph, Sound, and Television Society

**MBM** Master of Business Management

**MBMS** *Chem.* molecular-beam mass spectrometry

**MBNOA** Member of the British Naturopathic and Osteopathic Association

**MBO** *Finance* management buyout • management by objectives

**MBOU** Member of the British Ornithologists' Union

**MBP** *Med.* mean blood pressure

**MBPICS** Member of the British Production and Inventory Control Society

**MBPsS** Member of the British Psychological Society

**MBPT** *Physics, Astronomy* many-body perturbation theory

**mbr** member

**MBR** *Astronomy* microwave background radiation

**MBS** Manchester Business School

**MBSc** Master of Business Science

**MBT** *Military* main battle tank • (*or* **m.b.t.**) *Med.* mean body temperature

**MBuild** Master of Building

**Mbyte** *Computing* megabyte

**m.c.** mois courant (French: current month) • motor cycle

**m/c** machine • motor cycle

**MC** *British vehicle registration for* London NE • machinery certificate • Magistrates' Court • *Navigation* magnetic course • marginal cost • (USA) Marine Corps • (USA) Maritime Commission • marriage certificate • Master of Ceremonies • Master of Surgery (Latin *Magister Chirurgiae*) • medical certificate • medical college • (USA) Medical Corps • *Astrology* Medium Coeli (Latin: Midheaven) • (USA) Member of Congress • Member of Council • mess committee • Methodist Church • military college • Military Cross • Missionaries of Charity • *Astronomy* molecular cloud • *Chem.* molecular cluster • *international vehicle registration for* Monaco • *Politics* Monday Club • Monte Carlo • morse code • motor contact

**M/C** Manchester • *Finance* marginal credit

**MCA** Management Consultants' Association • Manufacturing Chemists' Association • Master of Commerce and Administration • Matrimonial Causes Act (1937) • *Computing, trademark* micro channel architecture • monetary compensatory amount(s) • *Electronics* multichannel (*or* multiple channel) analyser • multicriteria analysis • multiple classification analysis

**MCAB** (USA) Marine Corps air base

**MCAM** Member of the CAM Foundation

**MC&G** mapping, charting, and geodesy

**MCB** (USA) Marine Corps Base • Master in Clinical Biochemistry • *Computing* memory control block • miniature circuit breaker • *Military* multiple-cratering bomblets

**MCBSI** Member of the Chartered Building Societies Institute

**MCC** Manchester Computer Centre • Marylebone Cricket Club • Maxwell

Communication Corporation • Melbourne Cricket Club • member of the county council • metropolitan county council • *Navigation* mid-course correction

**MCCA** Minor Counties Cricket Association

**MCCC** Middlesex County Cricket Club

**MCCD RCS** Member in Clinical Community Dentistry of the Royal College of Surgeons

**MCD** *Chem.* magnetic circular dichroism • Master of Civic Design • *Med.* mean cell (*or* corpuscular) diameter • Movement for Christian Democracy • *Physical chem.* multiconcentration diffusion

**MCE** Master of Civil Engineering • *Chem.* methylene chloride extraction

**MCF** *Nuclear engineering* magnetic confinement fusion

**MCFP** (Canada) Member of the College of Family Physicians

**MCG** Melbourne Cricket Ground

**MCGA** *Computing* multicolour graphics array

**MCGB** Master Chef of Great Britain

**McGU** McGill University (Canada)

**MCh** (*or* **MChir**) Master of (*or* in) Surgery (Latin *Magister Chirurgiae*)

**MCH** *Med.* mean cell (*or* corpuscular) haemoglobin • *Biochem.* melanin-concentrating hormone

**MCHC** *Med.* mean cell (*or* corpuscular) haemoglobin concentration

**MChD** Master of Dental Surgery (Latin *Magister Chirurgiae Dentalis*)

**MChE** Master of Chemical Engineering

**MChemA** Master in Chemical Analysis

**MChOrth** Master of Orthopaedic Surgery (Latin *Magister Chirurgiae Orthopaedicae*)

**MChS** Member of the Society of Chiropodists

**mcht** merchant

**mchy** machinery

**m.c.i.** malleable cast iron

**MCIBSE** Member of the Chartered Institution of Building Services Engineers

**MCIM** Member of the Chartered Institute of Marketing

**MCIOB** Member of the Chartered Institute of Building

**M.CIRP** Member of the International Institution for Production Engineering

Research (French *Collège internationale pour recherche et production*)

**MCIS** Member of the Institute of Chartered Secretaries and Administrators (formerly Chartered Institute of Secretaries)

**MCIT** Member of the Chartered Institute of Transport

**MCL** Master of (*or* in) Civil Law • maximum contamination (*or* contaminant) levels

**MClinPsychol** Master of Clinical Psychology

**MClSc** Master of Clinical Science

**MCM** *Maths.* Monte Carlo method • multistage conventional munitions

**MCMES** Member of the Civil and Mechanical Engineers' Society

**Mco** Morocco

**mcol.** musicological • (*or* **mcolst**) musicologist • musicology

**MCollH** Member of the College of Handicrafts

**MCom** Master of Commerce

**MCommH** Master of Community Health

**MConsE** Member of the Association of Consulting Engineers

**MCOphth** Member of the College of Ophthalmologists

**MCP** (*or* **m.c.p.**) male chauvinist pig • (USA) Master of City Planning • Member of Colonial Parliament • Member of the College of Preceptors • *Astronomy* microchannel plate (as in **MCP detector**)

**MCPA** 2-methyl-4-chlorophenoxyacetic acid (used in herbicides)

**MCPB** *Chem.* 4-(2-methyl-4-chlorophenoxy)butanoic acid (weedkiller)

**MCPBA** *Chem.* m-chloroperoxybenzoic acid

**MCPP** Member of the College of Pharmacy Practice

**MCPS** Mechanical Copyright Protection Society • Member of the College of Physicians and Surgeons

**MCR** *Engineering* maximum continuous rating • *Med.* metabolic clearance rate • middle common room (in certain universities) • mobile control room

**MCS** Madras Civil Service • Malayan Civil Service • Master of Commercial Science • Military College of Science • monitoring and control system • *Electronics* multichannel scaler

**MCSEE** Member of the Canadian Society of Electrical Engineers

**MCSP** Member of the Chartered Society of Physiotherapy

**MCST** Member of the College of Speech Therapists

**MCT** mainstream corporation tax • Member of the Association of Corporate Treasurers

**MCU** main control unit • *Photog.* medium close-up

**MCV** *Med.* mean cell (*or* corpuscular) volume

**MCW** *Telecom.* modulated continuous wave

**Md** *Chem., symbol for* mendelevium

**Md.** Maryland

**M/d** *Commerce* months after date

**MD** Doctor of Medicine (Latin *Medicinae Doctor*) • *British vehicle registration for* London NE • *Music* main droite (French: right hand) • malicious damage • managing director • *Music* mano destra (Italian: right hand) • map distance • market day • *US postcode for* Maryland • medical department • (*or* **M/D**) *Banking* memorandum of deposit • mentally deficient • mess deck • Middle Dutch • military district • mini-disc (in sound recording) • molecular dynamics • Monroe Doctrine • musical director

**MDA** methylenedioxyamphetamine (hallucinogenic drug; ice) • minimum detectable amount (*or* activity) • *Computing* monochrome display adaptor • Muscular Dystrophy Association

**MDAM** *Computing* multidimensional access memory

**MDAP** (USA) Mutual Defense Assistance Program

**M-day** (USA) mobilization day

**MdB** Mitglied des Bundestages (German: Member of the Bundestag)

**MDB** Movimento Democrático Brasileiro (Spanish: Brazilian Democratic Movement)

**MDC** metropolitan district council • minimum detectable concentration • modification and design control • more developed country

**MDD** minimal detectable dose

**Mddx** Middlesex

**MDEA** *Chem.* N-methyldiethanolamine

**MDentSc** Master in Dental Science

**MDes** Master of Design

**MDG** Medical Director-General

**MDHB** Mersey Docks and Harbour Board

**MDI** *Chem.* methylene diisocyanate

**m. dict.** *Med.* more dicto (Latin: in the manner directed; in prescriptions)

**MDip** Master of Diplomacy

**mdise** merchandise

**MDiv** Master of Divinity

**mdl** model

**MDL** minimum detectable level (of radioactivity)

**Mdlle** Mademoiselle (French: Miss)

**Mdm** Madam

**MDMA** methylenedioxymethamphetamine (hallucinogenic drug; Ecstasy)

**Mdme** Madame (French: Mrs)

**mdn** median

**mdnt** midnight

**MDP** Mongolian Democratic Party

**MDQ** minimum detectable quantity

**MDR** *Computing* memory data register • (*or* **m.d.r.**) minimum daily requirement

**MDS** Master of Dental Surgery

**MDSc** Master of Dental Science

**mdse** merchandise

**MDT** *Computing* mean downtime • (USA) Mountain Daylight Time

**MDu** Middle Dutch

**MDU** Medical Defence Union

**MDV** Doctor of Veterinary Medicine

**MDW** Military Defence Works

**m.e.** maximum effort • mobility equipment

**Me** Maine (USA) • (*or* **Me**) Maître (French lawyer's title) • Messerschmitt (German aircraft) • *Chem., symbol for* methyl (used in formulae)

**ME** *British vehicle registration for* London NE • *US postcode for* Maine • managing editor • marine engineer(ing) • (USA) marriage encounter • Master of Education • Master of Engineering • mechanical engineer(ing) • (USA) Medical Examiner • *postcode for* Medway • *Med.* metabolizable energy • Methodist Episcopal • Middle East(ern) • *airline flight code for* Middle East Airlines • Middle English • military engineer • mining engineer(ing) • *British fishing port registration for* Montrose • *Physics* Mössbauer effect • Most Excellent (in titles) • mottled edges (of book pages) • *Med.* myalgic encephalomyelitis

**MEA** Member of the European Assembly • Middle East Airlines

**MEAF** Middle East Air Force

**meas.** measurable • measure • measurement

**MEB** Midlands Electricity Board

**MEBA/NMU** (USA) Marine Engineer Beneficial Association/National Maritime Union

**MEc** Master of Economics

**MEC** Master of Engineering Chemistry • Member of the Executive Council • Methodist Episcopal Church • Middle East Command

**MECAS** Middle East Centre for Arab Studies

**mech.** mechanic • mechanical(ly) • mechanics • mechanism

**MechE** Mechanical Engineer

**ME(Chem)** Master of Chemical Engineering

**MECI** Member of the Institute of Employment Consultants

**MECO** ('miːkəʊ) *Astronautics* main engine cut off

**MEcon** Master of Economics

**med.** medallist • median • medical • medicine • medieval • medium

**Med.** Mediterranean

**MEd** Master of Education

**MED** maximum equivalent dose • minimum effective dose • *Chem.* molecular electronic device • (New Zealand) Municipal Electricity Department

**Medico** ('mɛdɪkəʊ) Medical International Corporation (*or* Cooperation Organization) (US medical agency)

**Medit.** Mediterranean

**med. jur.** medical jurisprudence

**MEDLARS** ('mɛd,lɑːz) (USA) Medical Literature Analysis and Retrieval System

**MedRC** Medical Reserve Corps

**MedScD** Doctor of Medical Science

**med. tech.** medical technician • medical technology

**MEE** (*or* **ME(Elec)**) Master of Electrical Engineering

**MEF** Middle East Force

**meg** (mɛg) *Computing* megabyte

**MEIC** Member of the Engineering Institute of Canada

**Mej.** Mejuffrouw (Dutch: Miss)

**MEK** *Chem.* methyl ethyl ketone

**Melan.** Melanesia(n)

**Melb.** Melbourne

**MELF** Middle East Land Forces

**mem.** member • memento (Latin: remember) • memoir(s) • memorandum • memorial

**ME(Mech)** Master of Mechanical Engineering

**Men** *Astronomy* Mensa

**MEN** *Med.* multiple endocrine neoplasia

**MENCAP** (*or* **Mencap**) ('mɛnkæp) Royal Society for Mentally Handicapped Children and Adults

**MEng** Master of Engineering

**mensur.** mensuration

**mentd** mentioned

**MEO** Marine Engineering Officer

**MEP** (Sri Lanka) Mahajana Eksath Peramuna (People's United Front) • Master of Engineering Physics • (*or* **m.e.p.**) mean effective pressure • Member of the European Parliament

**MEPA** Master of Engineering and Public Administration

**mer.** mercantile • merchandise • mercoledì (Italian: Wednesday) • mercredi (French: Wednesday) • mercury • meridian • meridional

**Mer.** Merionethshire (former Welsh county)

**merc.** mercantile • mercoledì (Italian: Wednesday) • mercury

**MERLIN** ('mɜːlɪn) *Astronomy* Multi-Element Radio-linked Interferometer Network (UK)

**Mert** Merton College, Oxford

**MES** *Chem.* molecular emission spectrometry • *Chem.* Mössbauer emission spectroscopy

**MèsA** Maître ès arts (French: Master of Arts)

**MESc** Master of Engineering Science

**MESFET** ('mɛsfɛt) *Electronics* metal-semiconductor field-effect transistor

**Messrs** ('mɛsəz) Messieurs (French: gentlemen *or* sirs; used in English as pl. of Mr; *see also under* MM)

**met.** metallurgical • metallurgist • metallurgy • metaphor • metaphysics • (*or* **met**; **mɛt**) meteorological (as in **met. office**) • meteorology • metronome • metropolitan

**Met** (*or* **met**) *Biochem.* methionine • (mɛt) Metropolitan Opera House (New York) • (mɛt) Metropolitan Police

**metal.** (*or* **metall.**) metallurgical • metallurgy

**metaph.** metaphor(ical) • metaphysical • metaphysics

**METAR** Meteorological Airfield Report

**met. bor.** metropolitan borough

**MetE** Metallurgical Engineer

**meteorol.** (*or* **meteor.**) meteorological · meteorology
**Meth.** Methodist
**M-et-L** Maine-et-Loire (department of France)
**M-et-M** Meurthe-et-Moselle (department of France)
**m. et n.** *Med.* mane et nocte (Latin: morning and night; in prescriptions)
**MetR** Metropolitan Railway (London)
**metrol.** metrological · metrology
**metrop.** (*or* **metropol.**) metropolis · metropolitan
**metsat** ('mɛtsæt) meteorological satellite
**Mev.** Mevrouw (Dutch: Mrs)
**MeV** *symbol for* megaelectronvolt(s)
**MEW** *Military* microwave early warning (system)
**Mex.** Mexican · Mexico
**MEX** *international vehicle registration for* Mexico
**MEXE** Military Engineering Experimental Establishment
**Mex.Sp.** Mexican Spanish
**mez.** *Music* mezzo *or* mezza (Italian: half *or* medium)
**Mez** mezzo-soprano
**MEZ** Mitteleuropäische Zeit (German: Central European Time)
**mezzo.** mezzotint
**mf** (ital.) *Music* mezzo forte (Italian; moderately loudly) · *Slang* (USA) motherfucker
**mF** *symbol for* millifarad(s)
**MF** *British vehicle registration for* London NE · machine finish(ed) (of paper) · magnetic field · Master of Forestry · *Telecom.* medium frequency · melamine–formaldehyde (as in **MF resin**) · *Chem.* methyl formate · Middle French · mill finish · *Slang* (USA) motherfucker · *Telecom.* multifrequency
**M/F** (*or* **m/f**) male or female (in advertisements)
**MFA** Master of Fine Arts
**MFAMus** Master of Fine Arts in Music
**MFARCS** Member of the Faculty of Anaesthetists of the Royal College of Surgeons
**MFB** Metropolitan Fire Brigade
**MFC** Mastership in Food Control · motor-fuel consumption
**MFCM** Member of the Faculty of Community Medicine
**mfd** manufactured
**MFD** minimum fatal dose

**mfg** manufacturing
**MFH** Master of Foxhounds · mobile field hospital
**MFHom** Member of the Faculty of Homeopathy
**MFlem** Middle Flemish
**MFLOPS** ('ɛm,flɒps) *Computing* million floating-point operations per second
**MFM** *Computing* modified frequency modulation
**MFN** most favoured nation (in trade agreements)
**MFOM** Member of the Faculty of Occupational Medicine
**MFP** *Physics* mean free path
**MFPA** Mouth and Foot Painting Artists
**mfr.** (*or* **mfre**) manufacture · manufacturer
**MFr** Middle French
**MFS** Master of Food Science · Master of Foreign Study
**m. ft.** *Med.* mistura fiat (Latin: let a mixture be made; in prescriptions)
**m.f.t.** motor freight tariff
**MFV** motor fleet vessel
**mg** *symbol for* milligram(s)
**Mg** *Chem., symbol for* magnesium
**MG** *British vehicle registration for* London NE · machine glazed (of paper) · machine gun · *Music* main gauche (French: left hand) · Major-General · *Building trades* make good · Morris Garages (sports car; named after its original manufacturer) · motor generator · *Med.* myasthenia gravis
**MGA** Major-General in charge of Administration
**m.g.a.w.d.** make good all works disturbed (in commercial contracts)
**MGB** metropolitan green belt · Ministerstvo Gosudarstvennoi Bezopasnosti (Russian: Ministry of State Security; Soviet secret police, 1946–54) · motor gunboat
**MGC** Machine Gun Corps · (formerly) Marriage Guidance Council (renamed Relate)
**MGDS RCS** Member in General Dental Surgery of the Royal College of Surgeons
**mge** message
**MGGS** Major-General, General Staff
**MGI** Member of the Institute of Certificated Grocers
**MGk** Medieval Greek
**M. Glam** Mid Glamorgan

**MGM** Metro-Goldwyn-Mayer (film studio) • mobile guided missile

**MGO** Master General of the Ordnance • Master of Gynaecology and Obstetrics

**MGP** manufactured-gas plant

**Mgr** Manager • Monseigneur (French: my lord) • *RC Church* Monsignor

**MGr** Medieval Greek

**MGR** *Nuclear engineering* modular gas-cooled reactor

**Mgrs** Managers • Monseigneurs (French: my lords) • *RC Church* Monsignors

**mgt** management

**mH** *Physics, symbol for* millihenry(s)

**MH** *British vehicle registration for* London NE • *Navigation* magnetic heading • *Nautical* main hatch • *airline flight code for* Malaysia Airlines • marital history • Master of Horse • Master of Horticulture • Master of Hounds • Master of Hygiene • (USA) Medal of Honor • mental health • *British fishing port registration for* Middlesbrough • military hospital • Ministry of Health

**MHA** (USA) Master of (*or* in) Hospital Administration • (Australia, Canada) Member of the House of Assembly • Methodist Homes for the Aged • *Chem.* methyl-3-hydroxyanthranilic acid

**MHC** *Immunol.* major histocompatibility complex

**MHCIMA** Member of the Hotel Catering and Institutional Management Association

**MHD** *Physics* magnetohydrodynamics

**MHE** Master of Home Economics

**MHeb** Middle Hebrew

**MHF** massive hydraulic fracture (*or* fracturing)

**MHG** Middle High German

**MHK** (Isle of Man) Member of the House of Keys

**MHLG** Ministry of Housing and Local Government

**M.Hon.** Most Honourable

**MHortSc** Master of Horticultural Science

**MHR** (USA, Australia) Member of the House of Representatives

**MHRA** Modern Humanities Research Association

**MHRF** Mental Health Research Fund

**MHS** medical history sheet • Member of the Historical Society • *Computing* message-handling system

**MHTGR** *Nuclear engineering* modular high-temperature gas-cooled reactor

**MHum** Master of Humanities

**MHW** mean high water (of tides)

**MHWN** mean high water neaps (tides)

**MHWS** mean high water springs (tides)

**MHy** Master of Hygiene

**MHz** *symbol for* megahertz

**mi.** mile • (USA, Canada) mill(s) (monetary unit)

**Mi.** minor (in names)

**MI** malleable iron • *international civil aircraft marking for* Marshall Islands • *US postcode for* Michigan • Military Intelligence (*see* MI5; MI6) • Ministry of Information • *Biology* mitotic index • moment of inertia • mounted infantry • *Med.* myocardial infarction • *Irish vehicle registration for* Wexford

**MI5** Military Intelligence, section five (British counterintelligence agency)

**MI6** Military Intelligence, section six (British intelligence and espionage agency)

**MIA** Master of International Affairs • *Military* missing in action • (Australia) Murrumbidgee Irrigation Area

**MIAA&S** Member of the Incorporated Association of Architects and Surveyors

**MIAeE** Member of the Institute of Aeronautical Engineers

**MIAgrE** Member of the Institution of Agricultural Engineers

**MIAM** Member of the Institute of Administrative Management

**MIAP** Member of the Institution of Analysts and Programmers

**MIAS** Member of the Institute of Accounting Staff

**MIBF** Member of the Institute of British Foundrymen

**MIBiol** Member of the Institute of Biology

**MIBK** *Chem.* methyl isobutyl ketone

**MIBritE** Member of the Institution of British Engineers

**MIB(Scot)** Member of the Institute of Bankers in Scotland

**Mic** *Astronomy* Microscopium

**Mic.** *Bible* Micah

**MICE** Member of the Institution of Civil Engineers

**MICEI** Member of the Institution of Civil Engineers of Ireland

**MICFor** Member of the Institute of Chartered Foresters

**Mich.** Michaelmas • Michigan

**MIChemE** Member of the Institution of Chemical Engineers

**MICorrST** Member of the Institution of Corrosion Science and Technology

**MICR** *Computing* magnetic-ink character recognition

**micRNA** *Biochem.* messenger-RNA-interfering complementary RNA

**Micro.** Micronesia

**microbiol.** microbiology

**micros.** (*or* **micro.**) microscope • microscopist • microscopy

**MICS** Member of the Institute of Chartered Shipbrokers

**MICV** *Military* mechanized infantry combat vehicle

**mid.** middle • midnight

**Mid.** Midlands • Midshipman

**MIDAS** ('maɪdəs) *Computing* measurement information and data analysis system • missile defence alarm system

**Middx** Middlesex

**MIDELEC** ('mɪdɪlɛk) Midlands Electricity Board

**MIDI** (*or* **Midi**) ('mɪdɪ) musical instrument digital interface

**Midl.** Midlands • Midlothian (Scotland)

**Mid. Lat.** Middle Latin

**MIDPM** Member of the Institute of Data Processing Management

**MIE(Aust)** Member of the Institution of Engineers, Australia

**MIED** Member of the Institution of Engineering Designers

**MIEE** Member of the Institution of Electrical Engineers

**MIEEE** (USA) Member of the Institute of Electrical and Electronics Engineers

**MIEI** Member of the Institution of Engineering Inspection

**MIE(Ind)** Member of the Institution of Engineers, India

**MIES** Member of the Institution of Engineers and Shipbuilders, Scotland

**MIEx** Member of the Institute of Export

**MIExpE** Member of the Institute of Explosives Engineers

**MIF** *Immunol.* migration inhibition factor

**MIFA** Member of the Institute of Field Archaeologists

**MIFF** Member of the Institute of Freight Forwarders

**MIFG** *Meteorol.* shallow fog

**MIFireE** Member of the Institute of Fire Engineers

**MiG** (mɪg) Mi(koyan and) G(urevich) (Soviet jet fighter; named after its designers)

**MIG** (mɪg) metal-inert gas (as in **MIG welding**)

**MIGasE** Member of the Institution of Gas Engineers

**MIGeol** Member of the Institution of Geologists

**MIH** Master of Industrial Health • Member of the Institute of Housing

**MIHort** Member of the Institute of Horticulture

**MIHT** Member of the Institution of Highways and Transportation

**MIIE** Member of the Institution of Industrial Engineers

**MIIM** Member of the Institute of Industrial Managers

**MIInfSc** Member of the Institute of Information Sciences

**mil.** mileage • military • militia

**Mil.** Milan

**MIL** Member of the Institute of Linguists • (USA) one million

**Mil. Att.** Military Attaché

**MILGA** Member of the Institute of Local Government Administrators

**milit.** military

**mill.** million

**MILocoE** Member of the Institution of Locomotive Engineers

**Milw.** Milwaukee

**MIM** Member of the Institute of Metals

**MIMarE** Member of the Institute of Marine Engineers

**MIMC** Member of the Institute of Management Consultants

**MIMD** *Computing* multiple instruction (stream), multiple data (stream)

**MIMechE** Member of the Institution of Mechanical Engineers

**MIMGTechE** Member of the Institution of Mechanical and General Technician Engineers

**MIMI** Member of the Institute of the Motor Industry

**MIMinE** Member of the Institution of Mining Engineers

**MIMM** Member of the Institution of Mining and Metallurgy

**MIMS** (mɪmz) Monthly Index of Medical Specialities

**MIMunE** Member of the Institution of Municipal Engineers (now amalgamated with the Institution of Civil Engineers)

**min** minimum • *symbol for* minute(s)

**min.** mineralogical • mineralogy • minim (liquid measure) • minimum • mining • ministerial • minor • minute(s)

**Min.** Minister • Ministry

**MIND** *indicating* National Association for Mental Health

**mineral.** mineralogical • mineralogy

**Minn.** Minnesota

**Min. Plen.** Minister Plenipotentiary

**Min. Res.** Minister Resident (*or* Residentiary)

**MINS** (mɪnz) (USA) minor(s) in need of supervision

**MInstAM** Member of the Institute of Administrative Management

**MInstBE** Member of the Institution of British Engineers

**MInstD** Member of the Institute of Directors

**MInstE** Member of the Institute of Energy

**MInstEnvSci** Member of the Institute of Environmental Sciences

**MInstMC** Member of the Institute of Measurement and Control

**MInstME** Member of the Institution of Mining Engineers

**MInstMM** Member of the Institution of Mining and Metallurgy

**MInstP** Member of the Institute of Physics

**MInstPet** Member of the Institute of Petroleum

**MInstPI** Member of the Institute of Patentees and Inventors

**MInstPkg** Member of the Institute of Packaging

**MInstPS** Member of the Institute of Purchasing and Supply

**MInstR** Member of the Institute of Refrigeration

**MInstRA** Member of the Institute of Registered Architects

**MInstT** Member of the Institute of Transport

**MInstTM** Member of the Institute of Travel Managers in Industry and Commerce

**MInstWM** Member of the Institute of Wastes Management

**MINucE** Member of the Institution of Nuclear Engineers

**Mio** *Geology* Miocene

**MIOSH** Member of the Institution of Occupational Safety and Health

**m.i.p.** mean indicated pressure

**MIP** marine insurance policy • maximum investment plan • Member of the Institute of Plumbing • monthly investment plan

**MIPA** Member of the Institute of Practitioners in Advertising

**MIPM** Member of the Institute of Personnel Management

**MIPR** Member of the Institute of Public Relations

**MIProdE** Member of the Institution of Production Engineers

**MIPS** (*or* **mips**) (mɪps) *Computing* million instructions per second

**MIQ** Member of the Institute of Quarrying

**MIRA** Member of the Institute of Registered Architects • Motor Industry's Research Association

**MIRAS** ('maɪˌræs) mortgage interest relief at source

**MIRD** medical internal radiation dose

**MIREE(Aust)** Member of the Institution of Radio and Electronics Engineers (Australia)

**MIRT** Member of the Institute of Reprographic Technicians

**MIRTE** Member of the Institute of Road Transport Engineers

**MIRV** (mɜːv) *Military* multiple independently targeted re-entry vehicle

**Mis** *Geology* Mississippian

**MIS** management information system • manufacturing information system • Member of the Institute of Statisticians • meteorological information system • Mining Institute of Scotland

**misc.** miscellaneous • miscellany

**MISD** *Computing* multiple instruction (stream), single data (stream)

**MISFET** ('mɪsfɛt) *Electronics* metal-insulator-semiconductor field-effect transistor

**MIS(India)** Member of the Institution of Surveyors (India)

**Miss.** Mission • Missionary • Mississippi

**mist.** *Med.* mistura (Latin: mixture)

**mistrans.** mistranslation

**MIStructE** Member of the Institution of Structural Engineers

**Mit.** Mittwoch (German: Wednesday)

**MIT** Massachusetts Institute of Technology

**MITA** Member of the Industrial Transport Association

**MITD** Member of the Institute of Training and Development

**MITE** Member of the Institution of Electrical and Electronics Technician Engineers

**MITI** (Japan) Ministry of International Trade and Industry

**MITL** magnetically insulated transmission line

**MITT** Member of the Institute of Travel and Tourism

**Mitts** (mɪts) minutes of telecommunications traffic

**MIWEM** Member of the Institution of Water and Environmental Management

**MIX** *Chem.* 1-methyl-3-isobutylxanthine

**mixt.** mixture

**MJ** *British vehicle registration for* Luton • *symbol for* megajoule(s) • Ministry of Justice

**MJA** Medical Journalists' Association

**MJD** management job description

**MJI** Member of the Institute of Journalists

**MJQ** Modern Jazz Quartet

**MJS** Member of the Japan Society

**MJSD** March, June, September, December (months for quarterly payments)

**MJur** Magister Juris (Latin: Master of Law)

**mk** *Currency* mark

**Mk** mark (type of car)

**MK** *airline flight code for* Air Mauritius • *British vehicle registration for* London NE • *symbol for* Malawi kwacha (monetary unit) • *postcode for* Milton Keynes

**mkd** marked

**MKO** Mauna Kea Observatory (Hawaii)

**mks** *Currency* marks • (*or* **m.k.s.**, **MKS**) metre kilogram second (as in **mks units**)

**mksA** (*or* **MKSA**) metre kilogram second ampere (as in **mksA system**)

**mkt** market

**ml** (*or* **mL**) *symbol for* millilitre(s)

**ml.** mail

**ML** Licentiate in Medicine (Latin *Medicinae Licentiatus*) • Licentiate in Midwifery • *British vehicle registration for* London NE • Master of Law(s) • *Statistics* maximum likelihood • Medieval Latin • *British fishing port registration for* Methil (Scotland) • *postcode for* Motherwell • motor launch • muzzle-loading (of firearms)

**MLA** (*or* **MLArch**) Master of (*or* in) Landscape Architecture • Master of the Liberal Arts • Member of the Legisla-

tive Assembly • (USA) Modern Language Association

**MLC** Meat and Livestock Commission • (India, Australia) Member of the Legislative Council • *Chem.* micellar liquid chromatography • *Med.* mixed lymphocyte culture (test for donor–recipient compatibility)

**MLCOM** Member of the London College of Osteopathic Medicine

**MLCT** *Chem.* metal-to-ligand charge transfer

**mld.** mould(ed)

**MLD** Master of Landscape Design • *Pharmacol.* minimal lethal dose

**mldg** moulding

**MLF** Mouvement de libération des femmes (French: Women's Liberation Movement) • *Military* multilateral (nuclear) force

**MLG** Middle Low German

**MLib** (*or* **MLibSc**) Master of Library Science

**MLitt** Master of Letters (Latin *Magister Litterarum*)

**Mlle** Mademoiselle (French: Miss)

**MLNS** *Med.* mucocutaneous lymph node syndrome

**MLO** military liaison officer • *Microbiol.* mycoplasma-like organism(s)

**MLR** *Banking* minimum lending rate • *Med.* mixed lymphocyte reaction (test for donor–recipient compatibility) • (ital.) Modern Language Review • *Statistics* multiple linear regression

**MLRS** multiple-launch rocket system

**MLS** Master of Library Science • *Aeronautics* microwave landing system • mixed language system • multilanguage system

**MLSO** Medical Laboratory Scientific Officer

**MLW** mean low water (of tides)

**MLWN** mean low water neaps (tides)

**MLWS** mean low water springs (tides)

**mm** *symbol for* millimetre(s)

**m.m.** (*or* **M/m**) made merchantable • mutatis mutandis (Latin: with the necessary changes)

**MM** *British vehicle registration for* London NE • *Music* Maelzel's metronome (indicating the tempo of a piece) • maintenance manual • Majesties • *Med.* malignant melanoma • Martyrs • *Freemasonry* Master Mason • Master Mechanic • Master of Music • Medal of Merit • mercantile marine •

Messieurs (French: gentlemen *or* sirs; used in French as pl. of M (Monsieur); *compare* Messrs) • Military Medal

**MMA** Metropolitan Museum of Art

**MMath** Master of Mathematics

**MMB** Milk Marketing Board

**MMC** *Chem.* magnesium methyl carbonate • metal-matrix composite • Monopolies and Mergers Commission

**MMD** (Zambia) Movement for Multiparty Democracy

**MMDA** (USA) money market deposit account

**MMDS** *Radio* multipoint microwave distribution system

**Mme** Madame (French: Mrs)

**MME** Master of Mechanical Engineering • Master of Mining Engineering • Master of Music Education

**MMechE** Master of Mechanical Engineering

**MMed** Master of Medicine

**MMedSci** Master of Medical Science

**Mmes** Mesdames (French: pl. of Mme)

**MMet** Master of Metallurgy

**MMetE** Master of Metallurgical Engineering

**mmf** *Physics* magnetomotive force

**MMG** *Military* medium machine gun

**MMGI** Member of the Mining, Geological, and Metallurgical Institute of India

**mmHg** millimetre(s) of mercury (unit of pressure)

**MMin** Master of Ministry

**MMI** *Computing* man–machine interface • Municipal Mutual Insurance

**MMM** (Canada) Member of the Order of Military Merit

**3M** Minnesota Mining and Manufacturing Company

**m.m.p.** *Chem.* mixture melting point

**MMP** matrix metalloproteinase (enzyme) • Military Mounted Police

**MMPI** *Psychol.* Minnesota Multiphasic Personality Inventory

**MMQ** minimum manufacturing quantity

**MMR** *Med.* mass miniature radiography • measles, mumps, rubella (in **MMR vaccine**)

**MMRBM** *Military* mobile medium-range ballistic missile

**MMS** Marine Meteorological Services • Member of the Institute of Management Services • *Chem.* methyl methanesulphonate • multimission modular spacecraft

**MMSA** Master of Midwifery of the Society of Apothecaries

**MMSc** Master of Medical Science

**MMT** methylcyclopentadienyl manganese tricarbonyl (antiknock petrol additive) • Multiple Mirror Telescope (Arizona)

**MMTS** *Chem.* methyl methylthiomethyl sulphoxide

**MMU** *Computing* memory management unit • *Finance* million monetary units

**MMus** Master of Music

**MMusEd** Master of Musical Education

**mn.** midnight

**m.n.** mutato nomine (Latin: with the name changed)

**Mn** *Chem.*, *symbol for* manganese • Modern (of languages)

**MN** magnetic north • *British fishing port registration for* Maldon • Merchant Navy • *US postcode for* Minnesota

**MNA** Master of Nursing Administration • Member of the National Assembly (of Quebec) • *Chem.* molybdenum–nickel–alumina (catalyst)

**MNAD** Multinational Airmobile Division (of NATO)

**MNAEA** Member of the National Association of Estate Agents

**MNAS** (USA) Member of the National Academy of Sciences

**MNC** multinational company

**MnE** Modern English

**MNE** multinational enterprise

**MNECInst** Member of the North East Coast Institution of Engineers and Shipbuilders

**mng** managing

**mngmt** management

**mngr** manager

**MnGr** (*or* **MnGk**) Modern Greek

**MNI** Member of the Nautical Institute

**MNIMH** Member of the National Institute of Medical Herbalists

**Mnl.** Manila

**MNM** *Meteorol.* minimum

**MNOS** *Electronics* metal-nitride-oxide semiconductor

**Mnr** Mjnheer (Dutch: Mr *or* Sir)

**MNR** marine nature reserve • mean neap rise (of tides) • Mozambique National Resistance

**MNT** mean neap tide

**MNurs** Master of Nursing

**mo.** moment • month • mouth

**m.o.** mail order • modus operandi • money order

**m-o** months old

**Mo** *Chem.*, *symbol for* molybdenum

**Mo.** Missouri • Monday

**MO** mail order • manually operated • mass observation • Master of Obstetrics • Medical Officer • Meteorological Office • military operations • *US postcode for* Missouri • modus operandi • *Chem.* molecular orbital • money order • motor-operated • municipal officer • *British vehicle registration for* Reading

**MoA** Ministry of Aviation

**MOA** memorandum of agreement

**MO&G** Master of Obstetrics and Gynaecology

**mob.** mobile • (*or* **mobizn**) mobilization • mobilize

**MOBS** (mɒbz) multiple-orbit bombardment system (nuclear-weapon system)

**MoC** mother of the (trade-union) chapel

**MOC** management and operating contractor

**MOCVD** *Electronics* metal-organic chemical vapour deposition

**mod** (mɒd) *Maths.*, *Computing* modulo

**mod.** moderate • *Music* moderato (Italian; at a moderate tempo) • modern • modification • modified • *Maths.* modulus

**MoD** Ministry of Defence

**MOD** mail-order department • *Meteorol.* moderate (icing, etc.)

**mod. dict.** *Med.* modo dicto (Latin: as prescribed)

**modem** ('məʊdɛm) *Computing* modulator demodulator

**MODFET** ('mɒd,fɛt) *Electronics* modulation-doped field-effect transistor

**modif.** modification

**mod. praes.** *Med.* modo praescripto (Latin: in the manner directed)

**Mods** Honour Moderations (at Oxford University)

**mod^to** *Music* moderato (*see under* mod.)

**MODU** mobile offshore drilling unit

**MOEH** Medical Officer for Environmental Health

**MoH** Ministry of Housing and Local Government

**MOH** Master of Otter Hounds • Medical Officer of Health

**MOHLG** Ministry of Housing and Local Government

**Moho** ('məʊhəʊ) *Geology* Mohorovičić discontinuity

**MOI** military operations and intelligence • Ministry of Information • Ministry of the Interior

**mol** *Chem.*, *symbol for* mole(s)

**mol.** molecular • molecule

**MOL** *Astronautics* manned orbital laboratory • Ministry of Labour

**Mold.** (*or* **Moldv.**) Moldavia(n)

**mol. wt.** molecular weight

**m.o.m.** middle of month

**MOM** milk of magnesia

**MOMA** Museum of Modern Art (New York)

**MOMI** Museum of the Moving Image

**mon.** monastery • monastic • monetary • monitor • monsoon

**Mon** *Astronomy* Monoceros

**Mon.** Monaco • Monaghan • Monday • Monmouthshire (former Welsh county) • Montag (German: Monday)

**MON** *Meteorol.* above mountains

**MONEP** Marché des options négotiables de Paris (French traded option market)

**Mong.** (*or* **Mongol.**) Mongolia(n)

**monog.** monograph

**Mont.** Montana • (*or* **Montgom.**) Montgomeryshire (former Welsh county)

**Montr.** Montreal

**MOPA** *Electronics* master oscillator power amplifier

**MOPH** (USA) Military Order of the Purple Heart

**mor.** *Music* morendo (Italian; dying away) • *Bookbinding* morocco

**Mor.** Moroccan • Morocco

**MOR** middle-of-the-road • *Engineering* modulus of rupture

**MORB** *Geology* mid-oceanic ridge basalts

**MORC** Medical Officers Reserve Corps

**mor. dict.** *Med.* more dicto (Latin: in the manner directed)

**MORI** (*or* **Mori**) ('mɔːrɪ) Market and Opinion Research Institute (as in **MORI poll**)

**morn.** morning

**morph.** (*or* **morphol.**) morphological • morphology

**MORS** *Geology* mid-oceanic ridge system

**mor. sol.** *Med.* more solito (Latin: in the usual manner; in prescriptions)

**mort.** mortal • mortality • mortar • mortgage • mortuary

**mos.** months

**Mos.** Moscow • Moselle

**MOS** magneto-optical system • (mɒs) *Electronics* metal–oxide–silicon (*or* –semiconductor)

**MOSFET** ('mɒsfɛt) *Electronics* metal–oxide–silicon (*or* –semiconductor) field-effect transistor

**MOST** (mɒst) *Electronics* metal–oxide–silicon (*or* –semiconductor) transistor • Molonglo Observatory Synthesis Telescope

**mot.** motor(ized)

**MOT** (*or* **MoT**) Ministry of Transport (usually referring to the road-vehicle test, as in **MOT certificate**)

**MOTNE** meteorological operational telecommunications network

**MOUSE** (*or* **mouse**) (maʊs) *Military* minimum orbital unmanned satellite of the earth (for gathering data)

**mov.** *Music* movimento (Italian: movement *or* speed)

**MOV** *Engineering* motor-operated valve • *Meteorol.* move (*or* moving)

**MOVE** (muːv) Men Over Violence (association for wife batterers)

**movt** movement

**MOW** (New Zealand) Ministry of Works • Movement for the Ordination of Women

**MOX** mixed oxide (as in **MOX fuel**)

**Moz.** Mozambique

**mp** melting point • (ital.) *Music* mezzo piano (Italian; moderately softly)

**m.p.** meeting point • melting point • *Cartography* mile post • months after payment • mooring post

**MP** *British vehicle registration for* London NE • Madhya Pradesh (Indian state) • *Metallurgy* martensitic phase • medium pressure • Member of Parliament • *Physiol.* membrane potential • *Cartography* Mercator's projection • metal pollutant • *Chem.* methyl-2-pyrrolidone • Metropolitan Police • *Cartography* mile post • Military Police(man) • mille passuum (Latin: 1000 paces; i.e. Roman mile) • Minister Plenipotentiary • miscellaneous papers (*or* publications) • Mounted Police(man)

**M/P** memorandum of partnership

**MPA** Master of Professional Accounting • Master of Public Administration • Master Printers Association • Member of the Parliamentary Assembly of Northern Ireland • Music Publishers' Association

**MPAA** Motion Picture Association of America

**MPAGB** Modern Pentathlon Association of Great Britain

**MPB** (USA) Missing Persons Bureau

**MPBW** Ministry of Public Building and Works

**MPC** (*or* **m.p.c.**) mathematics, physics, chemistry • maximum permissible concentration • Metropolitan Police College • Metropolitan Police Commissioner

**MPD** maximum permissible dose

**MPE** Master of Physical Education • maximum permissible exposure (to radiation)

**MPEA** Member of the Physical Education Association

**mpg** miles per gallon

**MPG** *Education* main professional grade (teacher's basic salary) • (Germany) Max-Planck-Gesellschaft zur Förderung der Wissenschaften (Max Planck Society for the Advancement of Science)

**mph** miles per hour

**MPh** Master of Philosophy

**MPH** Master of Public Health

**MPhil** Master of Philosophy

**MPI** Max Planck Institute

**MPIA** Master of Public and International Affairs

**MPL** maximum permissible level

**MPLA** Movimento Popular de Libertação de Angola (Portuguese: Popular Movement for the Liberation of Angola)

**mpm** metres per minute

**MPO** management and personnel office • Metropolitan Police Office • military post office • mobile printing (*or* publishing) office

**m.p.p.** most probable position

**MPP** Member of the Provincial Parliament (of Ontario)

**MPPH** *Chem.* 5-(4-methylphenyl)-5-phenylhydantoin

**MPR** (Indonesia) Majelis Permusyawaratan Rakyat (People's Consultative Assembly) • Mongolian People's Republic

**MPRISA** Member of the Public Relations Institute of South Africa

**MPRP** Mongolian People's Revolutionary Party (communists)

**mps** metres per second

**MPs** Master of Psychology

**MPS** manufacturer's part specification • Medical Protection Society • Member of the Philological Society • Member of the Physical Society • *Meteorol.* metres per second • *Med.* mucopolysaccharide (as in **MPS disease**)

**MPsSc** Master of Psychological Science

**MPsych** Master of Psychology

**MPsyMed** Master of Psychological Medicine

**m. pt.** melting point

**MPU** *Computing* microprocessor unit

**Mpy** (Netherlands) Maatschappij (Company; Co.)

**mq.** mosque

**MQ** metol-quinol (photographic developer)

**Mqe** Martinique

**MQS** *Electronics* modified Q-switching

**m.r.** memorandum receipt

**Mr** Mister

**MR** magnetic resonance (as in **MR scanner**) • *British fishing port registration for* Manchester • map reference • *Law* Master of the Rolls • match rifle • (*or* **M/R**) *Commerce* mate's receipt • mental retardation • metabolic rate • Middlesex Regiment • Minister Residentiary • motivation(al) research • motorways (traffic) regulations • municipal reform • *British vehicle registration for* Swindon

**MRA** Maritime Royal Artillery • Moral Rearmament

**MRAC** Member of the Royal Agricultural College

**MRACP** Member of the Royal Australasian College of Physicians

**MRACS** Member of the Royal Australasian College of Surgeons

**MRadA** Member of the Radionic Association

**MRAeS** Member of the Royal Aeronautical Society

**MRAF** Marshal of the Royal Air Force

**MRAIC** Member of the Royal Architectural Institute of Canada

**MRAS** Member of the Royal Academy of Science • Member of the Royal Asiatic Society • Member of the Royal Astronomical Society

**MRB** Mersey River Board

**MRBM** *Military* medium-range ballistic missile

**MRBS** Member of the Royal Botanic Society

**MRC** Medical Registration Council • Medical Research Council • Medical Reserve Corps • Model Railway Club

**MRCA** multirole combat aircraft

**MRCGP** Member of the Royal College of General Practioners

**MRC-LMB** Medical Research Council Laboratory of Molecular Biology

**MRCO** Member of the Royal College of Organists

**MRCOG** Member of the Royal College of Obstetricians and Gynaecologists

**MRCP** Member of the Royal College of Physicians

**MRCPA** Member of the Royal College of Pathologists of Australia

**MRCPath** Member of the Royal College of Pathologists

**MRCPE** Member of the Royal College of Physicians of Edinburgh

**MRCPGlas** Member of the Royal College of Physicians and Surgeons of Glasgow

**MRCPI** Member of the Royal College of Physicians of Ireland

**MRCPsych** Member of the Royal College of Psychiatrists

**MRCS** Member of the Royal College of Surgeons

**MRCSE** Member of the Royal College of Surgeons of Edinburgh

**MRCSI** Member of the Royal College of Surgeons of Ireland

**MRCVS** Member of the Royal College of Veterinary Surgeons

**MRD** machine-readable dictionary

**MRe** Mauritian rupee (monetary unit)

**MRE** Master of Religious Education • *Military* meal, ready to eat • Microbiological Research Establishment • Mining Research Establishment

**MRG** Minority Rights Group

**MRGS** Member of the Royal Geographical Society

**MRH** Member of the Royal Household

**MRHS** Member of the Royal Horticultural Society

**MRI** *Med.* magnetic resonance imaging (*or* image) • Member of the Royal Institution

**MRIA** Member of the Royal Irish Academy

**MRIAI** Member of the Royal Institute of the Architects of Ireland

**MRIC** Member of the Royal Institute of Chemistry (*see* MRSC)

**MRIN** Member of the Royal Institute of Navigation

**MRINA** Member of the Royal Institution of Naval Architects

**MRIPHH** Member of the Royal Institute of Public Health and Hygiene

**mrkr** marker

**MRM** mechanically recovered meat (in food processing)

**MRMetS** Member of the Royal Meteorological Society

**mRNA** *Biochem.* messenger RNA

**mrng** morning

**MRO** Member of the Register of Osteopaths

**MRP** manufacturers' recommended price • Master in (*or* of) Regional Planning

**MRPharmS** Member of the Royal Pharmaceutical Society

**Mrs** ('mɪsɪz) Mistress (title of a married woman)

**MRS** *Physics* magnetic resonance spectroscopy • Market Research Society • *Computing* monitored retrievable storage

**MRSA** *Med.* methicillin-resistant *Staphylococcus aureus*

**MRSC** Member of the Royal Society of Chemistry (formerly MRIC)

**MRSH** Member of the Royal Society for the Promotion of Health

**MRSL** Member of the Royal Society of Literature

**MRSM** Member of the Royal Society of Medicine • Member of the Royal Society of Musicians of Great Britain

**MRSPE** Member of the Royal Society of Painter-Etchers and Engravers

**MRSPP** Member of the Royal Society of Portrait Painters

**MRST** Member of the Royal Society of Teachers

**MRT** *Med.* magnetic resonance tomography • mass rapid transit

**MRTPI** Member of the Royal Town Planning Institute

**MRU** manpower research unit • mobile repair unit

**MRUSI** Member of the Royal United Service Institution

**MRV** *Military* multiple re-entry vehicle

**MRVA** Member of the Rating and Valuation Association

**ms** manuscript • *symbol for* millisecond(s)

**m.s.** mail steamer • margin of safety • maximum stress • mild steel

**m/s** metre(s) per second • (*or* **M/s**) *Finance* months after sight

**m/s²** metre(s) per second squared

**Ms** (mɪz *or* məz) Miss *or* Mrs (unspecified)

**MS** *British vehicle registration for* Edinburgh • *airline flight code for* Egyptair • *Physics* magnetic susceptibility • (*or* **M/S**) mail steamer • *Astronomy* main sequence • *Music* mano sinistra (Italian: left hand) • manuscript • *Chem., Physics* mass spectrometer (*or* spectrometry) • (USA) Master of Science • Master of Surgery • *international vehicle registration for* Mauritius • medical staff • *Photog.* medium shot (*or* mid-shot) • memoriae sacrum (Latin: sacred to the memory of; on gravestones) • mess sergeant • *Cartography* milestone • minesweeper • *Meteorol.* minus • *US postcode for* Mississippi • *Med.* mitral stenosis • *Physics* Mössbauer spectroscopy • (*or* **M/S**) (USA) motor ship • multiple sclerosis • municipal surveyor

**MSA** Malaysia-Singapore Airways • Master of Science and Arts • Master of Science in Agriculture • Media Studies Association • Member of the Society of Apothecaries • Merchant Shipping Act • *Chem.* methane sulphonic acid • Mineralogical Society of America • Motor Schools' Association of Great Britain • (USA) Mutual Security Agency

**MSAE** (USA) Master of Science in Aeronautical Engineering • (USA) Member of the Society of Automotive Engineers

**MSAgr** Master of Science in Agriculture

**MSAICE** Member of the South African Institution of Civil Engineers

**MSAInstMM** Member of the South African Institute of Mining and Metallurgy

**MS&R** Merchant Shipbuilding and Repairs

**MSArch** Master of Science in Architecture

**MSAutE** Member of the Society of Automobile Engineers

**MSB** Maritime Safety Board • Metropolitan Society for the Blind • *Computing* most significant bit

**MSBA** Master of Science in Business Administration

**MSBus** Master of Science in Business

**msc.** miscellaneous

**m.s.c.** moved, seconded, and carried

**MSc** Master of Science

**MSC** Manchester Ship Canal • Manpower Services Commission • medical staff corps • Metropolitan Special Constabulary

**MScA** (*or* **MSc(Ag)**) Master of Science in Agriculture

**MScApp** Master of Applied Science

**MSc(Arch)** Master of Science in Architecture

**MScD** (USA) Doctor of Medical Science • Master of Dental Science

**MSCE** Master of Science in Civil Engineering

**MSc(Econ)** Master of Science in Economics

**MSc(Ed)** Master of Science in Education

**MSChE** Master of Science in Chemical Engineering

**MSc(Hort)** Master of Science in Horticulture

**MSCI Index** *Finance* Morgan Stanley Capital International World Index

**MScMed** Master of Medical Science

**MSc(Nutr)** Master of Science in Nutrition

**MSCP** Master of Science in Community Planning

**MSD** Doctor of Medical Science • Master of Science in Dentistry • Master Surgeon Dentist • *Computing* most significant digit

**MSDent** Master of Science in Dentistry

**MS-DOS** (ˌɛmˌɛsˈdɒs) *Computing, trademark* MicroSoft Disk Operating System

**MSE** Master of Science in Education • Master of Science in Engineering • Member of the Society of Engineers

**MSEd** Master of Science in Education

**MSEE** Master of Science in Electrical Engineering

**MSEM** Master of Science in Engineering Mechanics • Master of Science in Engineering of Mines

**MSF** Manufacturing, Science, and Finance (Union) • Master of Science in Forestry • Médecins sans frontières (French: Doctors Without Frontiers; charitable organization) • mine-sweeping flotilla

**MSFC** (USA) Marshall Space Flight Center

**msg.** message

**MSG** monosodium glutamate (food additive)

**msgr** messenger

**Msgr** Monseigneur (French: my lord) • *RC Church* Monsignor

**MSgt** *US military* Master Sergeant

**MSH** Master of Staghounds • *Biochem.* melanocyte-stimulating hormone

**MSHE** (*or* **MSHEc**) Master of Science in Home Economics

**Mshl** Marshal

**MSHyg** Master of Science in Hygiene

**MSI** *Electronics* medium-scale integration • (Italy) Movimento Sociale Italiano (Italian Social Movement)

**MSIAD** Member of the Society of Industrial Artists and Designers

**MSIE** Master of Science in Industrial Engineering

**MSINZ** Member of the Surveyors' Institute of New Zealand

**MSJ** Master of Science in Journalism

**MSL** Master of Science in Linguistics • (*or* **msl**) mean sea level

**MSLS** Master of Science in Library Science

**MSM** Master of Sacred Music • Master of Science in Music • Meritorious Service Medal

**MSME** Master of Science in Mechanical Engineering

**MSMed** Master of Medical Science

**MSMetE** Master of Science in Metallurgical Engineering

**MSMus** Master of Science in Music

**MSN** Master of Science in Nursing

**MSO** Member of the Society of Osteopaths

**MSocIS** Membre de la société des ingénieurs et scientifiques de France (French: Member of the Society of Engineers and Scientists of France)

**MSocSc** Master of Social Science(s)

**MSPE** Master of Science in Physical Education

**MSPH** Master of Science in Public Health

**MSPhar** (*or* **MSPharm**) Master of Science in Pharmacy

**MSPHE** Master of Science in Public Health Engineering

**MSQ** managing service quality

**MSR** (*or* **m.s.r.**) main supply route • mean spring rise (of tides) • Member of the Society of Radiographers • *Military* missile-site radar

**MSS** (*or* **MS(S)**, **mss**) manuscripts • *Computing* mass storage system • (*or* **MSSc**) Master of Social Science • Master of Social Service • Member of the Royal Statistical Society • *Med.* midstream specimen (of urine) • *Physics* multichannel spectrum (*or* multispectral) scanner

**MSSE** (USA) Master of Science in Sanitary Engineering

**MST** Master of Sacred Theology • Master of Science in Teaching • mean spring tide • mean survival time • (USA) Mountain Standard Time

**MStat** Master of Statistics

**MSTD** Member of the Society of Typographic Designers

**Mstr** Master

**MSTS** *US Navy* Military Sea Transportation Service

**MSU** *Med.* midstream (specimen of) urine

**MSUL** Medical Schools of the University of London

**MSurv** Master of Surveying

**MSurvSc** Master of Surveying Science

**MSw** Middle Swedish

**MSW** magnetic surface wave(s) • Master in (*or* of) Social Work • Master of Social Welfare • medical social worker • municipal solid waste

**MSY** maximum sustainable yield (of a natural resource)

**mt.** *Military* megaton

**m.t.** metric ton(s) • missile test • (USA) Mountain Time

**Mt** *symbol for* metical (monetary unit of Mozambique) • Mount • Mountain

**MT** *British vehicle registration for* London NE • magnetic tape • mail transfer • *Med.* malignant tumour • mandated territory • *British fishing port registration for* Maryport • mass transport • mean time • mechanical transport • *Military* megaton • *Law* Middle Temple • *US postcode for* Montana • motor tanker • motor transport • (USA) Mountain Time

**M/T** empty (used on gas cylinders) • mail transfer

**MTA** minimum terms agreement • Music Teachers' Association • Music Trades' Association

**MTAI** Member of the Institute of Travel Agents

**MTB** motor torpedo boat

**MTBE** methyl *t*-butyl ether (lead-free antiknock petrol additive)

**MTBF** *Computing* mean time between failures

**MTC** Mechanized Transport Corps • Music Teacher's Certificate

**MTCA** Ministry of Transport and Civil Aviation

**mtd** mounted

**MTD** maximum tolerated dose • mean temperature difference • Midwife Teacher's Diploma

**mtDNA** *Biochem.* mitochondrial DNA

**MTech** Master of Technology

**MTEFL** Master in the Teaching of English as a Foreign (*or* Second) Language

**MTF** *Image technol.* modulation transfer function

**mtg** meeting • (*or* **mtge**) mortgage • mounting

**MTG** (USA) methanol to gasoline

**mtgee** mortgagee

**mtgor** mortgagor

**mth** month

**MTh** Master of Theology

**MTI** *Radar* moving-target indicator (*or* indication)

**mtl.** material • monatlich (German: monthly)

**MTL** mean tide level

**MTM** methods-time measurement

**mtn** motion • mountain

**MTN** multilateral trade negotiations

**MTNA** Music Teachers' National Association

**MTO** made to order • Mechanical Transport Officer

**MTP** Master of Town Planning

**mtr.** meter

**MTR** *US Air Force* mean time to restore • minimum time rate

**Mt Rev** Most Reverend (title of archbishop)

**Mts** Mountains • Mounts

**MTS** Master of Theological Studies • Merchant Taylors' School • motor transport service • (USA) multichannel television sound

**MTT** *Electronics* mean transit time

**MTTR** mean time to repair (*or* restore)

**MTU** *Computing* magnetic tape unit • *US Air Force* missile training unit

**MTV** motor torpedo vessel • (USA) music television

**MTW** *Meteorol.* mountain waves

**m/u** make up

**MU** *British vehicle registration for* London NE • maintenance unit • monetary unit • Mothers' Union • Musicians' Union

**MUC** Missionary Union of the Clergy

**MU car** *Railways* (USA) multiple-unit car

**MUF** *Telecom.* maximum usable frequency

**MUFTI** ('mʌftɪ) *Military* minimum use of force tactical intervention

**MUGA** ('mʌgə) *Med.* multiple-gated arteriography (as in **MUGA scan**)

**mun.** (*or* **munic.**) municipal(ity)

**MUniv** Master of the University

**mus.** museum • music(al) • musician

**Mus** *Astronomy* Musca

**musa** ('mjuːzə) multiple unit steerable aerial (*or* antenna)

**MusB** Bachelor of Music (Latin *Musicae Baccalaureus*)

**MusD** Doctor of Music (Latin *Musicae Doctor*)

**MusM** Master of Music (Latin *Musicae Magister*)

**musn** musician

**mut.** mutilated • mutual

**MUX** (*or* **mux**) (mʌks) multiplexer

**mv** (ital.) *Music* mezza voce (Italian: half voice; i.e. softly)

**m.v.** market value • mean variation • motor vessel

**mV** *symbol for* millivolt(s)

**MV** *British vehicle registration for* London SE • *symbol for* megavolt(s) • merchant vessel • *Chem.* mixed valence • (*or* **M/V**) motor vessel • muzzle velocity (of firearms)

**MVB** Bachelor of Veterinary Medicine

**MVD** Doctor of Veterinary Medicine • Ministerstvo Vnutrennikh Del (Russian: Ministry of Internal Affairs; Soviet police organization, 1946–60) • *Med.* mitral valve disease

**MVEE** Military Vehicles and Engineering Establishment

**MVetMed** Master of Veterinary Medicine

**MVetSc** Master of Veterinary Science

**MVL** motor-vehicle licence

**MVO** Member of the Royal Victorian Order

**MVP** *Baseball* Most Valued Player (award)

**MVSc** (*or* **MVS**) Master of Veterinary Science

**mvt** movement

**mW** *symbol for* milliwatt(s)

**MW** *international vehicle registration for* Malawi • Master of Wine • *Radio* medium wave • *symbol for* megawatt(s) • Middle Welsh • *Nuclear engineering* mixed waste • *Chem.* molecular weight • Most Worshipful • Most Worthy • *British vehicle registration for* Swindon

**MWA** Mystery Writers of America

**MWC** municipal-waste combustion

**MWeldI** Member of the Welding Institute

**MWF** Medical Women's Federation

**m.w.g.** music wire gauge

**MWGM** *Freemasonry* Most Worshipful (*or* Worthy) Grand Master

**MWh** (*or* **MW h**) *symbol for* megawatt hour

**MWI** municipal-waste incineration (*or* incinerator)

**MWIA** Medical Women's International Association

**MWO** Meteorological Watch Office

**MWP** mechanical wood pulp

**MWPA** Married Women's Property Act

**Mx** *Magnetism, symbol for* maxwell • Middlesex

**MX** *British vehicle registration for* London SE • *airline flight code for* Mexicana • missile, experimental • *Meteorol.* mixed (types of icing)

**mxd** mixed

**my** million years (following a number)

**my.** myopia

**MY** *British vehicle registration for* London SE • motor yacht

**myc.** (*or* **mycol.**) mycological • mycology

**MYOB** *Colloquial* mind your own business

**MYRA** *Finance* multiyear rescheduling agreement

**myst.** mystery (*or* mysteries)

**myth.** (*or* **mythol.**) mythological • mythology

**Mz** *Geology* Mesozoic

**MZ** *British vehicle registration for* Belfast

# N

**n** (ital.) *Chem.*, *symbol for* amount of substance • *Printing*, *symbol for* en • (ital.) *Genetics*, *symbol for* haploid chromosome number (also in **2n** (diploid), **3n** (triploid), etc.) • (ital.) *Maths*, *symbol for* indefinite number • *symbol for* nano- (prefix denoting $10^{-9}$, as in **nm**, nanometre) • *Physics*, *symbol for* neutron • (ital.) *Chem.* normal (i.e. unbranched, as in **n-butane**) • *Electronics* n-type (semiconductor) • (ital.) *Physics*, *Chem.*, *symbol for* number density (of atoms, particles, etc.) • (ital.) *Physics*, *symbol for* principal quantum number • (ital.) *Optics*, *symbol for* refractive index • (ital.) *Physics*, *symbol for* rotational frequency

**n.** nail (obsolete unit; 2¼ inches) • name • natus (Latin: born) • near • negative • nephew • *Commerce* net • neuter • new • night • nominative • noon • nostro (Italian: our) • note • notre (French: our) • noun • nous (French: us *or* we) • number

**N** *Biochem.*, *symbol for* asparagine • *Printing*, *symbol for* en • *Chess*, *symbol for* knight • naira (Nigerian monetary unit) • *Electrical engineering* neutral • (ital.) *Physics*, *symbol for* neutron number • *British fishing port registration for* Newry • *Physics*, *symbol for* newton(s) • ngultrum (monetary unit of Bhutan; *see also under* Nu) • *Chem.*, *symbol for* nitrogen • north(ern) • *postcode for* north London • *international vehicle registration for* Norway • nuclear (as in **N-weapon**) • *Physics*, *symbol for* nucleon • (ital.) *Chem.*, *Physics*, *symbol for* number of molecules, particles, etc • *international civil aircraft marking for* USA • (ital.) *Chem.*, *indicating* substitution on a nitrogen atom (as in **N-phenylhydroxylamine**)

**N.** (*or* **N**) National(ist) • navigation • Navy • New • Norse • north(ern) • November • *Law* nullity • nurse (*or* nursing)

**n/a** not applicable • not available

**Na** *Chem.*, *symbol for* sodium (Latin *natrium*)

**NA** *British vehicle registration for* Manchester • (USA) Narcotics Anonymous • (USA) National Academician • National Archives • Nautical Almanac • naval architect • naval attaché • naval auxiliary • *international vehicle registration for* Netherlands Antilles • *Engineering* neutral axis • *Banking* new account • *Biochem.* nicotinic acid • *Med.* Nomina Anatomica (Latin: Anatomical Names; official anatomical terminology) • *Biochem.* noradrenaline • North America(n) • *Optics* numerical aperture • nursing auxiliary

**N/A** (*or* **N/a**) *Banking* new account • (*or* **N/a**) *Banking* no account • (*or* **N/a**) *Banking* no advice • *Banking*, *Commerce* nonacceptance • not available

**n.a.a.** *Shipping* not always afloat

**NAA** *Chem.* naphthalene acetic acid • (USA) National Aeronautic Association • (USA) National Automobile Association • *Physics* neutron activation analysis

**NAAA** National Alliance of Athletic Associations

**NAACP** (USA) National Association for the Advancement of Colored People

**NAAFA** National Association to Aid Fat Americans

**NAAFI** (*or* **Naafi**) ('næfi) Navy, Army, and Air Force Institutes

**NAAQS** (USA) National Ambient Air Quality Standard

**NAAS** National Agricultural Advisory Service

**NAB** National Advisory Body for Public Sector Higher Education • National Alliance of Businessmen • National Assistance Board (former government department) • (USA) National Association of Broadcasters • National Australia Bank • naval air (*or* amphibious) base • New American Bible

**NABC** National Association of Boys' Clubs

**NABS** National Advertising Benevolent Society

**NAC** National Advisory Council • National Agriculture Centre • National Association for the Childless • *Geology* North American craton

**NACA** (USA) National Advisory Committee for Aeronautics

**NACAB** National Association of Citizens Advice Bureaux

**NACCAM** National Coordinating Committee for Aviation Meteorology

**NACCB** National Accreditation Council for Certification Bodies

**NACEIC** National Advisory Council on Education for Industry and Commerce

**NACM** National Association of Colliery Managers

**NACNE** National Advisory Committee on Nutrition Education

**NACODS** ('neɪkɒdz) National Association of Colliery Overmen, Deputies, and Shotfirers

**NACOSS** National Approved Council for Security Systems

**NACRO** (or **Nacro**) ('nækrəʊ) National Association for the Care and Resettlement of Offenders

**NACTST** National Advisory Council on the Training and Supply of Teachers

**NAD** (USA) National Academy of Design • *Biochem.* nicotinamide adenine dinucleotide • *Med.* no abnormality detected • (or **n.a.d.**) no appreciable difference • not on active duty

**NADC** naval aide-de-camp

**NADEC** National Association of Development Education Centres

**NADFAS** National Association of Decorative and Fine Arts Societies

**NADGE** NATO Air Defence Ground Environment

**NADH** *Biochem., indicating* a reduced form of NAD (H is the symbol for hydrogen)

**NADOP** (USA) North American Defense Operational Plan

**NADP** *Biochem.* nicotinamide adenine dinucleotide phosphate

**NADW** North Atlantic deep water

**NADWARN** ('næd,wɔːn) (USA) Natural Disaster Warning System

**NAE** (USA) National Academy of Engineering

**NAEA** National Association of Estate Agents

**NAEP** (USA) National Assessment of Educational Progress

**NAEW** NATO Airborne Early Warning

**NA f.** *symbol for* Netherlands Antillean guilder (monetary unit)

**NAFD** National Association of Funeral Directors

**NAFO** ('næfəʊ) National Association of Fire Officers • Northwest Atlantic Fisheries Organization

**NAFTA** ('næftə) New Zealand and Australia Free Trade Agreement • North American Free Trade Agreement

**n.a.g.** net annual gain

**Nag.** Nagasaki (Japan)

**NAG** *Biochem.* N-acetyl D-glucosamine • National Association of Goldsmiths

**NAGC** National Association for Gifted Children

**NAGS** National Allotments and Gardens Society

**Nah.** *Bible* Nahum

**Nahal** (nəˈhɑːl) (Israel) No'ar Halutzi Lohem (Hebrew: Pioneer and Military Youth)

**NAHAT** National Association of Health Authorities and Trusts

**NAHB** (USA) National Association of Home Builders

**NAHT** National Association of Head Teachers

**NAI** nonaccidental injury

**NAIR** (USA) national arrangements for incidents involving radioactivity

**NAIRU** ('neɪruː) *Economics* nonaccelerating inflation rate of unemployment

**NAITA** ('neɪtə) National Association of Independent Travel Agents

**NAK** (or **nak**) (næk) *Telecom.* negative acknowledgment

**NAL** (USA) National Aerospace Laboratory

**NALC** (USA) National Association of Letter Carriers (trade union)

**NALGO** ('nælgəʊ) National and Local Government Officers' Association

**N. Am.** North America(n)

**NAM** (USA) National Association of Manufacturers

**NAMAS** National Measurement and Accreditation Service

**NAMB** National Association of Master Bakers

**NAMCW** National Association of Maternal and Child Welfare

**NAMH** National Association for Mental Health (now called MIND)

**NAMMA** NATO MRCA Management Agency

**NAMS** (USA) national air-monitoring sites

**NAND** (nænd) *Computing, Electronics* not AND (as in **NAND gate, NAND operation**)

**N and Q** notes and queries
**NAO** National Audit Office
**Nap.** Naples • Napoleonic
**NAP** (næp) National Association for the Paralysed
**NAPA** (USA) National Association of Performing Artists
**NAPE** National Association of Port Employers
**NAPF** National Association of Pension Funds
**naph.** *Chem.* naphtha
**NAPO** ('næpəu) National Association of Probation Officers (trade union)
**NAPT** National Association for the Prevention of Tuberculosis
**nar.** narrow
**NAR** *Botany* net assimilation rate
**narc.** narcotic(s)
**NARM** (nɑːm) natural and accelerator-produced radioactive material
**NAS** (USA) National Academy of Sciences • National Adoption Society • National Association of Schoolmasters (now part of NAS/UWT) • naval air station • Noise Abatement Society • nursing auxiliary service
**NASA** (*or* **Nasa**) ('næsə) (USA) National Aeronautics and Space Administration
**NASCAR** ('næskɑː) (USA) National Association for Stock Car Auto Racing
**NASD** National Amalgamated Stevedores and Dockers • (USA) National Association of Securities Dealers
**NASDA** ('næsdə) (Japan) National Space Development Agency
**NASDAQ** ('næs,dæk) (USA) National Association of Securities Dealers Automated Quotations (system)
**Nash.** Nashville (USA)
**Nass.** Nassau (Bahamas)
**NAS/UWT** National Association of Schoolmasters/Union of Women Teachers
**nat.** national(ist) • native • natural • naturalize • naturist • natus (Latin: born)
**n.a.t.** normal allowed time
**Nat.** Natal
**N. At.** North Atlantic
**NAT** National Arbitration Tribunal
**NATE** National Association for the Teaching of English

**NATFHE** National Association of Teachers in Further and Higher Education
**natl** national
**NATLAS** ('nætlæs) National Testing Laboratory Accreditation Scheme
**NATO** (*or* **Nato**) ('neitəu) North Atlantic Treaty Organization
**NATS** (næts) National Air Traffic Services • (USA) Naval Air Transport Service
**nat. sc.** (*or* **nat. sci.**) natural science(s)
**NatScD** Doctor of Natural Science
**NATSOPA** (næt'səupə) National Society of Operative Printers, Graphical and Media Personnel (formerly National Society of Operative Printers and Assistants; now merged with the GPMU)
**N.Att.** Naval Attaché
**NATTS** National Association of Trade and Technical Schools
**natur.** naturalist
**naut.** nautical
**nav.** naval • navigable • navigation • navigator
**NAV** *Finance* net asset value (of an organization)
**NAVAIR** ('næveə) (USA) Naval Air Systems Command
**Nav.E.** Naval Engineer
**navig.** navigation • navigator
**NAVS** National Anti-Vivisection Society
**NAVSAT** ('næv,sæt) navigational satellite
**NAWB** National Association of Workshops for the Blind
**NAWC** National Association of Women's Clubs
**NAWO** National Alliance of Women's Organizations
**NAYC** Youth Clubs UK (formerly National Association of Youth Clubs)
**NAYT** National Association of Youth Theatres
**Nazi** ('nɑːtsɪ) Nationalsozialisten (German: National Socialist)
**nb** (*or* **n.b.**) *Cricket* no ball • nota bene (Latin: note well)
**Nb** *Chem., symbol for* niobium
**NB** *British vehicle registration for* Manchester • narrow-bore • naval base • *Med.* needle biopsy • *Physics* neutral beam • New Brunswick (Canada) • North Britain (i.e. Scotland) • nota bene (Latin: note well)

**NBA** (USA) National Basketball Association • (USA) National Book Award • (USA) National Boxing Association • National Building Agency • Net Book Agreement • North British Academy

**NBC** (USA) National Basketball Committee • National Book Council (*see under* NBL) • National Boys' Club • (USA) National Broadcasting Company • National Bus Company • nuclear, biological, and chemical (of weapons or warfare)

**NBCD** *Computing* natural binary-coded decimal

**NBD** *Statistics* negative binomial distribution

**NbE** north by east

**NBER** (USA) National Bureau of Economic Research

**NBG** (*or* **nbg**) *Colloquial* no bloody good

**NBI** National Benevolent Institution • *Physics* neutral-beam injection • *Med.* no bone injury

**NBK** National Bank of Kuwait

**NBL** National Book League (formerly Council) • (*or* **nbl**) *Colloquial* not bloody likely

**NBP** *Chem.* normal boiling point

**NBPI** National Board for Prices and Incomes

**NBR** National Buildings Record • *Chem.* nitrile-butadiene rubber

**nbre.** noviembre (Spanish: November)

**NBRI** National Building Research Institute

**NBS** *Chem.* N-bromosuccinimide • (USA) National Bureau of Standards • Newcastle Business School

**NBTS** National Blood Transfusion Service

**NBV** *Accounting* net book value (of an asset)

**NbW** north by west

**NC** *British vehicle registration for* Manchester • National Certificate • National Congress (*or* Council) • *Education* National Curriculum • Nature Conservancy • New Caledonia • New Church • *Physics* nickel–cadmium (of electric cells) • nitrocellulose • *Chem.* nitrogen compound • *Meteorol.* no change (*or* not changing) • no charge • normally closed • North Carolina (abbrev. *or* postcode) • Northern Command • numerical control *or* numerically controlled (as in **NC machine**) • (USA) Nurse Corps

**N/C** (*or* **n/c**) new charter • nitrocellulose • no charge

**NCA** National Certificate of Agriculture • National Childminding Association • National Cricket Association • no copies available

**NCAA** (USA) National Collegiate Athletic Association • Northern Counties Athletic Association

**NCACC** National Civil Aviation Consultative Committee

**NCAR** National Center for Atmospheric Research (Colorado)

**NCARB** (USA) National Council of Architectural Registration Boards

**NCB** National Children's Bureau • National Coal Board (now British Coal Corporation, BCC) • *Insurance* no claim bonus

**NCBA** National Cattle Breeders' Association

**NCBAE** *Insurance* no claim bonus as earned

**NCBW** nuclear, chemical, and biological warfare

**NCC** (USA) National Climatic Center • National Computing Centre • National Consumer Council • (USA) National Council of Churches • *Education* National Curriculum Council • Nature Conservancy Council

**NCCI** National Committee for Commonwealth Immigrants

**NCCJ** National Conference of Christians and Jews

**NCCL** National Council for Civil Liberties (now called Liberty)

**NCCS** national command and control system • National Council for Civic Responsibility

**n.c.d.** *Colloquial* no can do

**NCDAD** National Council for Diplomas in Art and Design

**NCDL** National Canine Defence League

**NCERT** National Council for Educational Research and Training

**NCET** National Council for Educational Technology

**NCFT** National College of Food Technology

**NCH** National Children's Home • National Clearing House

**n.Chr.** nach Christus (German: after Christ; AD)

**n.c.i.** no common interest

**NCI** (USA) National Cancer Institute • *Finance* New Community Instrument

**NCIC** National Cancer Institute of Canada • (USA) National Crime Information Center

**NCL** National Central Library • National Chemical Laboratory • National Church League

**NCLC** National Council of Labour Colleges

**NCNA** New China News Agency

**NCNC** National Convention of Nigeria and the Cameroons • National Convention of Nigerian Citizens (political party)

**NCO** noncommissioned officer

**n.c.p.** *Engineering* normal circular pitch

**NCP** National Car Parks Ltd • (Australia) National Country Party (now called National Party) • national cycling proficiency

**NCPL** National Centre for Programmed Learning

**NCPS** noncontributory pension scheme

**NCPT** (USA) National Congress of Parents and Teachers

**NCR** National Cash Register (Company Ltd) • no carbon required (of paper)

**NCRE** Naval Construction Research Establishment

**NCRL** National Chemical Research Laboratory

**NCRP** (USA) National Council on Radiation Protection and Measurements

**NCS** (USA) National Communications System

**NCSC** (Australia) National Companies and Securities Commission • (USA) National Computer Security Center

**NCSE** National Council for Special Education

**NCSS** National Council of Social Service

**NCT** National Chamber of Trade • National Childbirth Trust • *Med.* neutron-capture therapy • *Med.* neutron computed tomography

**NCTA** (USA) National Community Television Association

**NCTE** (USA) National Council of Teachers of English

**NCU** National Communications Union • National Cyclists' Union

**n.c.u.p.** no commission until paid

**NCV** (*or* **n.c.v.**) no commercial value

**NCVCCO** National Council of Voluntary Child Care Organizations

**NCVO** National Council for Voluntary Organizations

**NCVQ** National Council for Vocational Qualifications

**NCW** National Council of Women (of Great Britain)

**n.d.** *Photog.* neutral density • *Stock exchange* (USA) next day (delivery) • no date (*or* not dated) • no decision • no deed (*or* not deeded) • no delay • no demand • nondelivery • *Banking* not drawn • nothing doing

**Nd** *Chem., symbol for* neodymium

**ND** *British vehicle registration for* Manchester • national debt • National Diploma • Naturopathic Diploma • *Photog.* neutral density • *Physics* neutron diffraction • no date • nondelivery • North Dakota (abbrev. *or* postcode)

**N-D** Notre-Dame (French: Our Lady; in church names, etc.)

**NDA** National Diploma in Agriculture • *Engineering* nondestructive analysis (*or* assay)

**NDAC** (USA) National Defense Advisory Commission

**N. Dak.** North Dakota

**NDB** *Aeronautics* nondirectional beacon

**ndc** National Defence College

**NDC** National Dairy Council • NATO Defence College

**NDCS** National Deaf Children's Society

**NDD** National Diploma in Dairying • National Diploma in Design

**NDE** near-death experience • *Engineering* nondestructive evaluation (*or* examination)

**NDF** National Diploma in Forestry

**NDH** National Diploma in Horticulture

**NDIC** National Defence Industries Council

**NDN** National District Nurse Certificate

**n.d.p.** *Engineering* normal diametric pitch

**NDP** National Democratic Party (of various countries) • *Economics* net domestic product • (Canada) New Democratic Party • *Biochem.* nucleoside diphosphate

**NDPS** National Data Processing Service

**NDR** *Electronics* negative differential resistance (*or* resistivity)

**NDRC** National Defence Research Committee

**NDSB** Narcotic Drugs Supervisory Body (of the UN)

**NDT** *Engineering* nondestructive testing • *Commerce* nondistributive trade

**NDTA** (USA) National Defense Transportation Association

**NDU** Nursing Development Unit

**NDV** *Vet. science* Newcastle disease virus

**n.e.** not essential • not exceeding

**n/e** new edition • *Banking* no effects (i.e. no funds)

**Ne** *Chem., symbol for* neon

**Ne.** Nepal(ese) • Netherlands

**NE** *British vehicle registration for* Manchester • national emergency • National Executive • Naval Engineer • *US postcode for* Nebraska • Newcastle (postcode *or* British fishing port registration) • new edition • New England • news editor • *Banking* no effects (i.e. no funds) • northeast(ern) • nuclear energy • nuclear explosion

**N/E** new edition • *Banking* no effects (i.e. no funds) • *Accounting* not entered

**NEA** (USA) National Education Association • (USA) National Endowment for the Arts

**NEAC** New English Art Club

**NEACP** ('ni:,kæp) (USA) National Emergency Airborne Command Post (aircraft in readiness for nuclear war)

**NEAF** Near East Air Force

**NEAFC** North-East Atlantic Fisheries Commission

**NEARELF** Near East Land Forces

**Neb.** (*or* **Nebr.**) Nebraska

**NEB** (USA) National Electricity Board • (USA) National Energy Board • National Enterprise Board • New English Bible

**NEBSS** National Examinations Board for Supervisory Studies

**n.e.c.** not elsewhere classified

**NEC** (USA) National Electric Code • National Electronics Council • National Equestrian Centre • National Executive Committee • National Exhibition Centre (Birmingham) • National Extension College (Cambridge) • *Med.* necrotizing enterocolitis • (Japan) Nippon Electric Company

**NECCTA** National Educational Closed Circuit Television Association

**NECInst** North East Coast Institution of Engineers and Shipbuilders

**necr.** necrosis

**necrol.** necrology

**NED** *Med.* no evidence of disease

**NEDC** National Economic Development Council (*or* Neddy) • North East Development Council

**NEDO** National Economic Development Office

**NEEB** North Eastern Electricity Board

**NEF** *Acoustics* noise exposure forecast (value)

**NEFA** *Chem.* nonesterified fatty acid

**neg.** negation • negative(ly) • negligence • negotiate

**NEG** negative (in transformational grammar)

**Neh.** *Bible* Nehemiah

**NEH** National Endowment for the Humanities

**n.e.i.** non est inventus (*or* inventa, inventum) (Latin: he (*or* she, it) has not been found) • not elsewhere indicated

**NEL** (USA) National Electronics Laboratory • National Engineering Laboratory

**NEM** *Chem.* N-ethylmaleimide

**nem. con.** (*or* **dis.**) nemine contradicente (*or* dissentiente) (Latin: no-one opposing; unanimously)

**NE/n.d.** new edition, no date given

**N. Eng.** New England • northern England

**neol.** neologism

**n.e.p.** new edition pending

**Nep.** Nepal(ese) • Neptune (planet)

**NEP** New Economic Policy (in the USSR, 1921–28)

**NEPA** (USA) National Environmental Policy Act (1969)

**NEPP** (USA) National Energy Policy Plan

**NEQ** *Electronics* nonequivalence (as in **NEQ gate**)

**NERA** (USA) National Emergency Relief Administration

**NERC** Natural Environment Research Council

**n.e.s.** not elsewhere specified

**NES** *Physics* nuclear elastic scattering

**NESC** (USA) National Electric Safety Code

**n.e.t.** not earlier than

**NET** (USA) National Educational Television • *Nuclear engineering* Next European Torus

**Neth.** Netherlands

**Neth. Ant.** Netherlands Antilles

**n. et m.** *Med.* nocte et mane (Latin: night and morning; in prescriptions)

**neurol.** neurological • neurology
**neut.** neuter • neutral • neutralize(d)
**Nev.** Nevada
**NEW** *Economics* (USA) net economic welfare
**Newf.** Newfoundland
**New M** New Mexico
**New Test.** New Testament
**n.f.** *Engineering* near face • no fool • noun feminine
**NF** *British vehicle registration for* Manchester • National Front • *Med.* neurofibromatosis • New Forest • Newfoundland • New French • (*or* **N/F**) *Banking* no funds • *Telecom.* noise factor (*or* figure) • Norman French (language) • *Pharmacol.* (USA) National Formulary
**n.f.a.** no further action
**NFA** National Farmers' Association • National Federation of Anglers • (USA) National Food Administration
**NFAL** National Foundation of Arts and Letters
**NFB** National Film Board (of Canada)
**NFBPM** National Federation of Builders' and Plumbers' Merchants
**NFBTE** National Federation of Building Trades Employers
**n.f.c.** not favourably considered
**NFC** (USA) National Football Conference • National Freight Consortium
**NFCO** National Federation of Community Organization
**Nfd** Newfoundland
**NFD** Newfoundland • no fixed date
**NFDM** nonfat dry milk
**NFER** National Foundation for Educational Research
**NFFC** National Film Finance Corporation
**NFFE** (USA) National Federation of Federal Employees
**NFFO** nonfossil-fuel obligation (for electricity companies)
**NFFPT** National Federation of Fruit and Potato Trades
**NFHA** National Federation of Housing Associations
**NFI** National Federation of Ironmongers
**NFL** (USA, Canada) National Football League
**Nfld** Newfoundland
**NFMPS** National Federation of Master Printers in Scotland
**NFMS** National Federation of Music Societies

**NFO** National Freight Organization
**NFPW** National Federation of Professional Workers
**n.f.r.** no further requirements
**NFRN** National Federation of Retail Newsagents
**NFS** National Fire Service • National Flying Services • National Forest Service • *Computing* network file service (*or* system) • not for sale
**NFSE** National Federation of Self-Employed (and Small Businesses)
**NFT** National Film Theatre
**NFU** National Farmers' Union
**NFUW** National Farmers' Union of Wales
**NFWI** National Federation of Women's Institutes
**n.g.** no good • not given
**Ng** *Geology* Neogene
**Ng.** Norwegian
**NG** *Railways* narrow gauge • National Gallery • (USA) National Guard (*or* Guardsman) • New Granada • *Med.* new growth • New Guinea • nitroglycerine • *Freemasonry* Noble Grand (*or* Guard) • no good • *British vehicle registration for* Norwich • *postcode for* Nottingham
**NGA** National Glider Association • National Graphical Association (*see* GPMU)
**NGC** (USA) National Grid Company • *Astronomy* New General Catalogue (prefixed to a number to designate a Catalogue object)
**NGF** *Biochem.* nerve growth factor
**NGk** New Greek
**NGL** *Chem.* natural-gas liquid(s)
**NGNP** nominal gross national product
**NGO** (India) nongazetted officer • nongovernmental organization
**NGr** New Greek
**NGRC** National Greyhound Racing Club
**NGRS** Narrow Gauge Railway Society
**NGS** National Geographic Society • nuclear generating station
**NGT** National Guild of Telephonists
**NGTE** National Gas Turbine Establishment
**NGU** *Med.* nongonococcal urethritis
**NGV** natural-gas vehicle
**NH** *airline flight code for* All Nippon Airways • National Hunt • naval hospital • New Hampshire (abbrev. *or* postcode) • *British vehicle*

*registration for* Northampton • northern hemisphere • Northumberland Hussars

**NHA** National Horse Association of Great Britain • (USA) National Housing Agency

**NHBC** National House-Building Council

**NHBRC** National House-Builders' Registration Certificate

**NHC** National Hunt Committee

**NHD** Doctor of Natural History

**N.Heb.** (*or* **NHeb**) New Hebrew • New Hebrides

**NHF** National Hairdressers' Federation

**NHG** New High German

**NHI** National Health Insurance

**NHK** Nippon Hōsō Kyōkai (Japan Broadcasting Corporation)

**NHL** (USA) National Hockey League • *Med.* non-Hodgkin lymphoma

**NHLBI** (USA) National Heart, Lung, and Blood Institute

**NHMRCA** National Health and Medical Research Council of Australia

**NHO** Navy Hydrographic Office

**NHR** National Housewives Register • National Hunt Rules

**NHS** National Health Service

**NHSTA** National Health Service Training Authority

**NHTPC** National Housing and Town Planning Council

**Ni** *Chem., symbol for* nickel

**NI** National Insurance • Native Infantry • Naval Instructor • Naval Intelligence • new impression • Northern Ireland • North Island (New Zealand) • *Irish vehicle registration for* Wicklow

**NIA** (USA) National Intelligence Authority • Newspaper Institute of America

**NIAAA** Northern Ireland Amateur Athletic Association

**NIAB** National Institute of Agricultural Botany

**NIACRO** Northern Ireland Association for the Care and Resettlement of Offenders

**NIAE** National Institute of Agricultural Engineering

**NIAID** National Institute of Allergy and Infectious Diseases

**Nibmar** (*or* **NIBMAR**) ('nɪb,mɑː) no independence before majority African rule

**NIBSC** National Institute for Biological Standards Control

**n.i.c.** not in contact

**Nic.** Nicaragua(n)

**NIC** National Incomes Commission • (*or* **nic**) National Insurance contribution • newly industrialized country • *international vehicle registration for* Nicaragua

**Nica.** (*or* **Nicar.**) Nicaragua(n)

**NiCad** (*or* **NiCd, Ni/Cd**) nickel–cadmium (battery)

**NICAM** ('naɪkæm) *Electronics* near-instantaneous companded audio multiplex (for digital coding of audio signals)

**NICEC** National Institute for Careers Education and Counselling

**NICEIC** National Inspection Council for Electrical Installation Contracting

**NICF** Northern Ireland Cycling Federation

**NICG** Nationalized Industries Chairmen's Group

**NICRA** Northern Ireland Civil Rights Association

**NICS** Northern Ireland Civil Service

**NICU** *Med.* neonatal intensive care unit

**NID** National Institute for the Deaf • (India) National Institute of Design • Naval Intelligence Division • Northern Ireland District

**NIDC** Northern Ireland Development Council

**NIDD** non-insulin-dependent diabetes

**NIES** Northern Ireland Electricity Service

**NIESR** National Institute of Economic and Social Research

**NIF** *Finance* note issuance facility

**NIFES** National Industrial Fuel Efficiency Service

**Nig.** Nigeria(n)

**NIH** (USA) National Institutes of Health • North Irish Horse (former regiment)

**NIHCA** Northern Ireland Hotels and Caterers Association

**NIHE** (Ireland) National Institute for Higher Education

**NII** Nuclear Installations Inspectorate

**NIIP** National Institute of Industrial Psychology

**NILP** Northern Ireland Labour Party

**nimby** ('nɪmbɪ) *Colloquial* not in my back yard (indicating liberals, reformers, etc., in principle but not in practice)

**NIMH** National Institute of Medical Herbalists • (USA) National Institute of Mental Health

**n.imp.** new impression

**NIMR** National Institute for Medical Research

**NIN** national information network

**NINO** ('niːnəʊ) no inspector, no operator (system)

**NIO** National Institute of Oceanography

**NIOSH** (USA) National Institute for Occupational Safety and Health

**nip.** *Engineering* nipple

**Nip.** Nippon(ese)

**ni. pri.** nisi prius (Latin: unless previously)

**N. Ir.** Northern Ireland

**NIR** Nauchno-Issledovatel'skaya Rabota (Russian colour-television system) • nonionizing radiation

**NIRA** (USA) National Industrial Recovery Act (1933)

**NIRC** National Industrial Relations Court

**N. Ire.** Northern Ireland

**NIREX** ('naɪrɛks) Nuclear Industry Radioactive Waste Executive

**NIRS** (USA) National Institute of Radiological Sciences

**n.i.s.** not in stock

**NIS** *symbol for* new Israeli shekel (monetary unit)

**NISA** National Independent Supermarkets' Association

**NISC** National Industrial Safety Committee

**NIST** (USA) National Institute of Standards and Technology

**NISTRO** Northern Ireland Science and Technology Regional Organization

**NISW** National Institute for Social Workers

**NIT** negative income tax

**NIV** New International Version (of the Bible)

**NIWAAA** Northern Ireland Women's Amateur Athletic Association

**n.J.** nächsten Jahres (German: next year)

**NJ** *British vehicle registration for* Brighton • New Jersey (abbrev. *or* postcode)

**NJA** National Jewellers' Association

**NJAC** National Joint Advisory Council

**NJC** National Joint Council

**NJCC** National Joint Consultative Committee

**NJNC** National Joint Negotiating Committee

**NK** *British vehicle registration for* Luton • *Immunol.* natural killer (as in **NK cell**) • not known

**NKC** *Immunol.* natural killer cell

**NKGB** Narodny Komissariat Gosudarstvennoi Bezopasnosti (Russian: People's Commissariat of State Security; Soviet agency, 1943–46)

**NKr** *symbol for* Norwegian krone (monetary unit)

**NKVD** Narodny Komissariat Vnutrennikh Del (Russian: People's Commissariat of Internal Affairs; Soviet agency, 1934–46)

**NKz** *symbol for* new kwanza (Angolan monetary unit)

**n.l.** (*or* **nl**) *Printing* new line • non licet (Latin: it is not permitted) • non liquet (Latin: it is not clear)

**Nl** National

**NL** National Labour • (USA) National League (baseball league) • National Liberal • Navy League • Navy List • *international vehicle registration for* Netherlands • *British vehicle registration for* Newcastle-upon-Tyne • New Latin • (Australia) no liability (after the name of a public limited company; equivalent to plc) • (*or* **N.Lat.**) north latitude

**NLB** National Library for the Blind

**NLC** National Liberal Club • National Library of Canada

**NLCS** North London Collegiate School

**NLD** (Burma) National League for Democracy

**n.l.f.** nearest landing field

**NLF** National Labour Federation • National Liberal Federation • National Liberation Front • National Loans Fund

**NLI** National Library of Ireland

**NLLST** National Lending Library for Science and Technology

**NLM** National Library of Medicine

**NLMC** National Labour Management Council

**NLN** National League for Nursing

**NLO** naval liaison officer

**NLP** *Computing* natural language processing • (USA) neighborhood loan program • *Computing* neurolinguistic programming

**NLQ** *Computing* near letter quality

**NLRB** (USA) National Labor Relations Board

**NLS** National Library of Scotland

**n.l.t.** not later than • not less than

**NLW** National Library of Wales

**nly** northerly

**NLYL** National League of Young Liberals

**nm** *symbol for* nanometre(s)

**nm.** nutmeg

**n.m.** nautical mile(s) • new moon • *Med.* nocte et mane (Latin: night and morning; in prescriptions) • nonmetallic • noun masculine

**n.M.** nächsten Monats (German: next month)

**Nm.** Nachmittag (German: afternoon)

**N.m.** next matter (in advertisement placing)

**N/m** no mark(s) (on a bill of lading)

**NM** *British vehicle registration for* Luton • national marketing • *Meteorol.* nautical mile(s) • New Mexico (abbrev. *or* postcode) • nuclear medicine

**NMA** National Management Association • National Medical Association

**NMB** National Maritime Board

**n.m.c.** no more credit

**NMC** National Marketing Council • (USA) National Meteorological Center

**NMDA** *Biochem.* N-methyl-D-aspartate (as in **NMDA receptor**)

**N. Mex.** New Mexico

**NMFS** (USA) National Marine Fisheries Service

**n mile** nautical mile

**NMP** *Economics* net material product

**NMR** *Physical chem.* nuclear magnetic resonance

**NMRI** *Med.* nuclear magnetic resonance imaging

**NMS** (USA) National Market System

**NMSQT** (USA) National Merit Scholarship Qualifying Test

**NMSS** (USA) National Multiple Sclerosis Society

**n.m.t.** not more than

**NMTF** National Market Traders' Federation

**NMU** National Maritime Union

**NMW** national minimum wage (as in **NMW policy**)

**nn.** names • notes • nouns

**NN** *Chem.* neutralization number • *British fishing port registration for* Newhaven • no name • *postcode for* Northampton • *British vehicle registration for* Nottingham

**N/N** not to be noted

**NNE** north-northeast

**NNEB** National Nursery Examination Board

**NNF** Northern Nurses' Federation

**NNHT** Nuffield Nursing Homes Trust

**NNI** noise and number index (to evaluate aircraft noise) • noise nuisance index

**NNMA** Nigerian National Merit Award

**NNOM** Nigerian National Order of Merit

**NNP** *Economics* net national product

**NNR** National Nature Reserve

**NNSA** (USA) National Nuclear Safety Administration

**NNT** nuclear nonproliferation treaty

**NNW** north-northwest

**n°** numéro (French: number)

**no.** north(ern) • number (from Italian *numero*)

**n.o.** normally open • *Cricket* not out

**No** *Chem., symbol for* nobelium

**No.** north(ern) • Norway • Norwegian • number (from Italian *numero*)

**NO** *British vehicle registration for* Chelmsford • naval officer • naval operations • Navigation Officer • New Orleans • Nuffield Observatory (Jodrell Bank, Cheshire) • Nursing Officer

**N/O** (*or* **N/o**) *Banking* no orders

**NOA** National Opera Association • National Orchestral Association • not otherwise authorized

**NOAA** (USA) National Oceanic and Atmospheric Administration

**NOAO** (USA) National Optical Astronomy Observatories

**nob.** nobis (Latin: for (*or* on) our part) • noble

**NOB** naval operating base

**n.o.c.** notation of content • not otherwise classified

**NOC** National Olympic Committee • not otherwise classified

**NOCD** *Colloquial* not our class, dear

**No. Co.** northern counties

**noct.** *Med.* nocte (Latin: at night)

**NOD** Naval Ordnance Department • night observation device

**NODA** National Operatic and Dramatic Association

**NODC** non-OPEC developing country

**n.o.e.** notice of exception • not otherwise enumerated

**NOERC** North of England Regional Consortium

**n.o.h.p.** not otherwise herein provided

**n.o.i.b.n.** not otherwise indexed by name

**NOIC** Naval Officer in Charge

**NOISEP** ('nɔɪsɛp) (USA) National Organization to Insure a Sound-controlled Environment

**n.o.k.** next of kin

**NOL** (USA) Naval Ordnance Laboratory

**nol. con.** *Law* nolo contendere (Latin: I do not wish to contend)

**nol. pros.** *Law* nolle prosequi (Latin: do not prosecute; procedure for ending criminal proceedings)

**nom.** nomenclature • nominal • nomination • nominative

**nom. cap.** *Finance* nominal capital

**nomen.** nomenclature

**nomin.** nominative

**nomm.** nomination

**nom. nov.** nomen novum (Latin: new name)

**NOMSS** (USA) National Operational Meteorological Satellite System

**noncom.** noncommissioned

**Noncon.** Nonconformist

**non cul.** non culpabilis (Latin: not guilty)

**non obst.** non obstante (Latin: notwithstanding)

**non pros.** *Law* non prosequitur (Latin: he does not prosecute; former judgment in favour of defendant)

**non repetat.** (*or* **non rep.**) *Med.* non repetatur (Latin: do not repeat; in prescriptions)

**non seq.** non sequitur (Latin: (a statement that) does not follow logically)

**nonstand.** (*or* **nonstd**) nonstandard

**n.o.p.** not otherwise provided (for)

**NOP** National Opinion Poll • not our publication

**nor.** normal

**Nor** *Astronomy* Norma

**Nor.** Norman • (*or* **nor.**) north • Norway • Norwegian • Norwich

**NOR** (nɔː) *Computing, Electronics* not OR (as in **NOR gate**, **NOR operation**) • *Biology* nucleolar-organizing region

**NORAD** ('nɔːræd) North American Air Defense Command

**Norf.** Norfolk

**norm.** normal • normalized

**Norm.** Norman

**NORM** not operationally ready maintenance

**NORML** (USA) National Organization for the Reform of Marijuana Laws

**NORS** not operationally ready supplies (*or* supply)

**Northants** Northamptonshire

**Northd** (*or* **Northumb.**) Northumberland

**Norvic.** Norvicensis (Latin: (Bishop) of Norwich)

**Norw.** Norway • Norwegian

**NORWEB** ('nɔːwɛb) North Western Electricity Board

**n$^{os}$** numéros (French: numbers)

**n.o.s.** not otherwise specified

**Nos.** (*or* **nos.**) numbers (from Italian *numeros*)

**NOS** Nederlandse Omroep Stichting (Netherlands Broadcasting Corporation)

**NOSC** *US Navy* Naval Ordnance Systems Command

**NOSIG** *Meteorol.* no significant change

**not.** notice

**Not.** Notary

**NOT** (nɒt) *Computing, Electronics* not (from its sense in logic, as in **NOT gate**, **NOT operation**)

**NOTAR** (*or* **Notar**) ('nəʊtɑː) no-tail rotor (of an aircraft)

**NOTB** National Ophthalmic Treatment Board

**Nottm** Nottingham

**Notts** Nottinghamshire

**notwg** notwithstanding

**nov.** novel(ist) • novembre (French *or* Italian: November) • novice • novitiate

**Nov.** (*or* **Nov**) November

**NOW** (USA) National Organization for Women • *Banking* (USA) negotiable order of withdrawal (as in **NOW account**) • New Opportunities for Women

**NOX** (nɒks) nitrogen oxide(s)

**n.o.y.** not out yet

**noz.** nozzle

**np** neap (tides) • *Printing* new paragraph • new pence

**n.p.** near point • *Law* net personalty • net proceeds • *Printing* new paragraph • new pattern • nickel-plated • nisi prius (Latin: unless previously) • nonparticipating • *Bibliog.* no place of publication given • no printer • no publisher • normal pitch • not paginated • nursing procedure

**n/p** net proceeds

**Np** napalm • neap (tides) • *Telecom.*, symbol for neper • *Chem.*, symbol for neptunium

**NP** national park • National (*or* Nationalist) Party • National Power plc • neuropsychiatric • neuropsychiatry • *postcode for* Newport • New Providence (Bahamas) • *Firearms* nitro proof • Nobel Prize • *Maths.* nondeterministic polynomial (in **NP-complete**) • *Chem.* nonpolar • Notary Public • noun phrase • (USA) nurse practitioner • *British vehicle registration for* Worcester

**NPA** National Park Authority • National Pigeon Association • (Phillipines) New People's Army • Newspaper Publishers' Association

**NPACI** National Production Advisory Council on Industry

**NPB** *Physics* neutral particle beam

**NPBA** National Pig Breeders' Association

**NPC** (China) National People's Congress • (USA) National Petroleum Council • National Ports Council • (USA) National Press Club • no-player character (in the game Dungeons and Dragons) • (Nigeria) Northern People's Congress

**NPD** Nationaldemokratische Partei Deutschlands (German: National Democratic Party; neo-Nazis) • *Marketing* new product development • *Astronomy* north polar distance

**n.p.f.** not provided for

**NPF** (Syria) National Progressive Front • Newspaper Press Fund

**NPFA** National Playing Fields Association

**NPG** National Portrait Gallery • Nuclear Planning Group (in NATO)

**NPH** *Chem.* normal paraffin hydrocarbon

**NPK** nitrogen, phosphorus, and potassium (in fertilizers; from the chemical symbols of these elements)

**NPL** National Physical Laboratory (Teddington, Middlesex)

**npn** (*or* **n-p-n**) *Electronics* n-type p-type n-type semiconductor (as in **npn transistor**)

**NPN** *Med.* nonprotein nitrogen

**n.p.n.a.** *Commerce* no protest for nonacceptance

**NP/ND** not published, no date given

**n.p.o.** *Med.* ne per oris (Latin: not by mouth)

**NPO** New Philharmonia Orchestra

**n.p. or d.** no place or date

**n.p.p.** no passed proof

**NPP** nuclear power plant

**NPR** (USA) National Public Radio • noise power ratio

**NPRA** National Petroleum Refiners Association

**n.p.s.** nominal pipe size • no prior service

**NPS** nuclear power source • nuclear power station

**NPT** non-proliferation treaty

**n.p.u.** ne plus ultra (Latin: nothing beyond; i.e. extreme or perfect state)

**NPU** National Pharmaceutical Union • National Postal Union • *Med.* not passed urine

**NPV** *Finance* net present value • no par value (of shares)

**NPW** nuclear-powered warship

**n.q.a.** *Finance* net quick assets

**NQOC** *Colloquial* not quite our class

**NQR** *Physics* nuclear quadrupole resonance

**nr** near

**n.r.** net register • *Insurance* no risk

**Nr** Nummer (German: number)

**NR** *British vehicle registration for* Leicester • National Register • natural rubber • naval rating • Navy Regulations • *Insurance* no risk • (formerly) North Riding (Yorkshire) • *postcode for* Norwich

**n.r.a.** never refuse anything

**NRA** National Reclamation Association • (USA) National Recovery Administration (former agency) • National Recreation Area • National Rifle Association • National Rivers Authority • nuclear-reaction analysis

**NRAA** National Rifle Association of America

**NRAO** (USA) National Radio Astronomy Observatory

**NRC** (Ghana) National Redemption Council • National Research Council • (USA) Nuclear Regulatory Commission

**NRCA** National Retail Credit Association

**NRCC** National Research Council of Canada

**NRD** National Register of Designers (*or* Registered Designer)

**NRDC** National Research Development Corporation • (USA) Natural Resources Defense Council

**NRDS** *Med.* neonatal respiratory distress syndrome

**NREM** *Physiol.* non-rapid eye movement (as in **NREM sleep**)

**NRF** National Relief Fund

**NRFL** Northern Rugby Football League

**NRI** National Resources Institute

**NRK** (Norway) Norsk Rikskringkasting (state broadcasting company)

**NRL** National Reference Library • (USA) Naval Research Laboratory

**NRM** (Uganda) National Resistance Movement

**NRMA** (Australia) National Roads and Motorists Association

**nrml** normal

**NRN** *Physics* neutron-rich nucleus

**NROTC** Naval Reserve Officer Training Corps

**NRP** nuclear reprocessing plant

**NRPB** National Radiological Protection Board

**NRR** net reproduction rate (of populations) • Northern Rhodesia Regiment

**NRs** *symbol for* Nepalese rupee (monetary unit)

**NRS** National Readership Survey • National Rose Society

**NRT** (*or* **n.r.t.**) net registered tonnage

**NRTA** (USA) National Retired Teachers Association

**NRV** *Finance* net realizable value • nonreturn valve

**Nrw.** Norwegian

**NRZ** *Computing* nonreturn to zero (method of encoding binary signals)

**ns** *symbol for* nanosecond(s) • (Graduate of the Royal) Naval Staff (College, Greenwich)

**n.s.** near side • new series • nickel steel • not satisfactory • not specified • *Banking* not sufficient (funds)

**n/s** nonsmoker • *Banking* not sufficient (funds)

**Ns** (ital.) *Meteorol., symbol for* nimbostratus

**NS** *British vehicle registration for* Glasgow • Nachschrift (German: postscript; PS) • *Computing* Nassi–Schneidermann (as in **NS chart**) • National Service • National Society • natural science • naval service • *Irish fishing port registration for* New Ross • new series • Newspaper Society • New Style (method of reckoning dates) • *Meteorol.* nimbostratus • (*or* **N/S**) nonsmoker • not significant • Nova Scotia • nuclear science • nuclear ship • Numismatic Society

**N–S** Notre-Seigneur (French: Our Lord)

**NSA** (USA) National Security Agency • (USA) National Shipping Authority • National Skating Association • (USA) National Standards Association • (USA) National Student Association • New Society of Artists • nonsterling area

**NSACS** National Society for the Abolition of Cruel Sports

**NSAE** National Society of Art Education

**NSAFA** National Service Armed Forces Act

**NSAID** *Med.* nonsteroidal anti-inflammatory drug

**NSB** National Savings Bank • (USA) National Science Board

**NSBA** National Sheep Breeders' Association

**NSC** National Safety Council • (USA) National Security Council • National Sporting Club

**NSCR** National Society for Cancer Relief

**NSD** naval supply depot

**NSDAP** Nationalsozialistische Deutsche Arbeiterpartei (German: National Socialist German Workers' Party; Nazi party)

**NSERC** (USA) Natural Sciences and Engineering Research Council

**NSF** (USA) National Science Foundation • (*or* **N/S/F, n.s.f.**) *Banking* not sufficient funds • Nuclear Structure Facility (Daresbury, Cheshire)

**NSFGB** National Ski Federation of Great Britain

**NSG** *Education* nonstatutory guidelines (concerning the National Curriculum)

**NSGT** non-self-governing territory (*or* territories)

**NSHEB** North of Scotland Hydroelectric Board

**NSI** (USA) National Security Information

**NSL** National Sporting League

**NSLR** *Physics* nuclear spin-lattice relaxation

**NSM** new smoking material • non-stipendiary minister

**NSO** Naval Staff Officer

**NSPCC** National Society for the Prevention of Cruelty to Children

**NSPE** (USA) National Society of Professional Engineers

**n.s.p.f.** not specially provided for

**NSRA** National Small-bore Rifle Association

**NSS** national sample survey • New Shakespeare Society • *Med.* normal saline solution

**NSSA** National School Sailing Association

**NSSU** National Sunday School Union

**NST** Newfoundland Standard Time

**NSTC** Nova Scotia Technical College

**NSTP** Nuffield Science Teaching Project

**NSU** *Med.* nonspecific urethritis

**NSW** New South Wales

**NSY** New Scotland Yard

**n.t.** net terms • net tonnage

**NT** (Ireland) National Teacher • National Theatre • National Trust • neap tide(s) • *British fishing port registration for* Newport • New Testament • New Translation • Northern Territory (Australia) • *Bridge* no-trump(s) • not titled • Nurse Teacher • *British vehicle registration for* Shrewsbury

**NTA** (USA) National Technical Association • net tangible assets

**NTB** *Economics* nontariff barrier

**NTC** *Physics* negative temperature coefficient

**NTD** *Colloquial* not top drawer

**NTDA** National Trade Development Association

**NTEU** (USA) National Treasury Employees Union

**ntfy** notify

**NTG** North Thames Gas

**NTGB** North Thames Gas Board

**NTGk** New Testament Greek

**Nth** North

**nthn** northern

**NTI** noise transmission impairment

**NTIA** (USA) National Telecommunications and Information Administration

**n.t.l.** no time lost

**NTL** *Electronics* nonthreshold logic

**NTM** *Economics* nontariff measure

**n.t.o.** not taken out

**NTO** Naval Transport Officer

**n.t.p.** no title page

**NTP** *Physics* normal temperature and pressure • *Biochem.* nucleoside triphosphate

**NTS** National Trust for Scotland • Nevada Test Site • not to scale

**NTSB** (USA) National Transportation Safety Board

**NTSC** (USA) National Television System Committee

**NTUC** (Singapore) National Trades Union Congress

**NTV** Nippon Television

**NTVLRO** National Television Licence Records Office

**nt. wt.** (*or* **nt wt**) net weight

**n.u.** name unknown • number unobtainable

**Nu** *symbol for* ngultrum (monetary unit of Bhutan) • (ital.) *Physics, symbol for* Nusselt number

**NU** National Union • Nations Unies (French: United Nations; UN) • natural uranium • Northern Union • *British vehicle registration for* Nottingham • number unobtainable

**NUAAW** National Union of Agricultural and Allied Workers

**nuc.** (*or* **nucl.**) nuclear

**NUCPS** National Union of Civil and Public Servants

**NUCUA** National Union of Conservative and Unionists Associations

**nud.** nudism • nudist

**NUDETS** ('njuːdɛts) nuclear detection system

**NUFLAT** National Union of Footwear, Leather, and Allied Trades (now amalgamated with the NUHKW to form the National Union of Knitwear, Footwear, and Apparel Trades)

**NUHKW** National Union of Hosiery and Knitwear Workers (*see* NUFLAT)

**NUI** National University of Ireland

**NUIW** National Union of Insurance Workers

**NUJ** National Union of Journalists

**NUJMB** Northern Universities Joint Matriculation Board

**NUL** (USA) National Urban League

**num.** number • numeral(s) • numerical • numerology

**Num.** *Bible* Numbers

**NUM** National Union of Mineworkers • New Ulster Movement

**NUMAST** ('njuːmæst) National Union of Marine, Aviation, and Shipping Transport Officers

**numis.** (*or* **numism.**) numismatic(s)

**NUOS** naval underwater ordnance station

**NUPE** ('njuːpɪ) National Union of Public Employees

**NUR** National Union of Railwaymen (*see* RMT)

**NUS** National Union of Seamen (*see* RMT) • National Union of Students

**NUT** National Union of Teachers

**N-u-T** Newcastle-upon-Tyne

**NUTG** National Union of Towns-women's Guilds

**NUTGW** (*or* **NUT&GW**) National Union of Tailors and Garment Workers (now amalgamated with the GMB)

**NUTN** National Union of Trained Nurses

**nutr.** nutrition

**NUU** New University of Ulster

**NV** (Netherlands) Naamloze Vennootschap (after the name of a public limited company; equivalent to plc) • (*or* **n.v.**) needle valve • *US postcode for* Nevada • New Version • nonvintage (of wine, etc.) • (*or* **n.v.**) *Finance* nonvoting (shares) • *Shipping* (Norway) Norske Veritas (classification society) • *British vehicle registration for* Northampton

**N/V** nonvintage (of wine etc.) • *Banking* no value

**NVB** National Volunteer Brigade

**NVG** *Military* night-vision goggles

**NVGA** (USA) National Vocational Guidance Association

**NVI** nonvalue indicator (type of postage stamp)

**NVM** Nativity of the Virgin Mary • *Chem.* nonvolatile matter

**NVQ** National Vocational Qualification

**NVRS** National Vegetable Research Station

**n.w.** net weight • no wind

**NW** *British vehicle registration for* Leeds • net worth • North Wales • north-west(ern) • *airline flight code for* Northwest Airlines • *postcode for* northwest London

**NWC** (USA) National War College

**NWEB** North Western Electricity Board

**Nwfld** Newfoundland

**NWFP** North-West Frontier Province (Pakistan)

**NWGA** National Wool Growers' Association

**NWIDA** North West Industrial Development Association

**NWP** North-Western Province (India)

**NWS** (USA) National Weather Service • normal water surface

**n. wt.** net weight

**n.w.t.** nonwatertight

**NWT** Northwest Territories (Canada)

**NWTV** North West Television

**NX** *British vehicle registration for* Dudley

**NY** *British vehicle registration for* Cardiff • New Year • New York (abbrev. *or* state postcode)

**NYA** (USA) National Youth Administration

**NYC** New York City

**NYCSCE** New York Coffee, Sugar, and Cocoa Exchange

**NYD** *Med.* not yet diagnosed

**nyl.** nylon

**NYME** New York Mercantile Exchange

**NYMT** National Youth Music Theatre

**NYO** National Youth Orchestra

**NYOS** National Youth Orchestra of Scotland

**NYP** not yet published

**NYS** New York State

**NYSE** New York Stock Exchange

**NYT** National Youth Theatre • (ital.) New York Times

**NZ** *airline flight code for* Air New Zealand • *British vehicle registration for* Londonderry • neutral(ity) zone • New Zealand (abbrev. *or* IVR)

**NZAP** (formerly) New Zealand Associated Press

**NZBC** New Zealand Broadcasting Corporation

**NZDSIR** New Zealand Department of Scientific and Industrial Research

**N. Zeal.** New Zealand

**NZEF** New Zealand Employers' Federation • New Zealand Expeditionary Force (in World Wars I and II)

**NZEFIP** New Zealand Expeditionary Force in the Pacific (in World War II)

**NZEI** New Zealand Educational Institute

**NZFL** New Zealand Federation of Labor

**NZIA** New Zealand Institute of Architects

**NZLR** New Zealand Law Reports

**NZMA** New Zealand Medical Association

**NZPA** New Zealand Press Association

**NZRFU** New Zealand Rugby Football Union

**NZRN** New Zealand Registered Nurse

# O

**o** *Computing, Maths., symbol for* order (*see under* O) • (ital.) *Chem.* ortho (as in **o-cresol**)

**o.** occasional • *Printing* octavo • off • old • only • optimus (Latin: best) • order • organ • *Baseball* out(s) • over • *Meteorol.* overcast • overseer

**O** *Genetics, symbol for* operator • *Slang* opium • *Computing, Maths., symbol for* order (followed in brackets by limiting value of a function) • *Geology* Ordovician • *Chem., symbol for* oxygen • *Pharmacol.* pint (Latin *octarius*) • *Med.*, indicating a blood group (*see also under* ABO) • *Logic, indicating* a particular negative categorial proposition • (ital.) *Chem., indicating* substitution on an oxygen atom (in names of compounds)

**O.** (*or* **O**) observer • occupation • Ocean • *Printing* octavo • October • *Med.* oculus (Latin: eye) • Oddfellows • oeste (Spanish *or* Portuguese: west) • Office • officer • Ohio • old • operation • orange • order (of knighthood, etc.) • ordinary • Orient • Osten (German: east) • *Music* ottava (Italian: octave) • ouest (French: west) • *Cricket* over • ovest (Italian: west) • owner

**o/a** on account (of) • on or about

**OA** *British vehicle registration for* Birmingham • objective analysis • office address • (*or* **o.a.**) office automation • Officers' Association • Officier d'Académie (French: Officer of the Academy; award for services in education) • *Banking* old account • *Chem.* oleic acid • *airline flight code for* Olympic Airways • operational analysis • osteoarthritis • (*or* **o.a.**) overall

**OAA** Organisation pour l'alimentation et l'agriculture (French: Food and Agriculture Organization; FAO) • Outdoor Advertising Association of Great Britain

**OAC** *Chem.* organo-aluminium compound(s)

**OACI** Organisation de l'aviation civile internationale (French: International Civil Aviation Organization; ICAO)

**o.a.d.** overall depth

**OAG** (USA) Official Airline Guide

**o.a.h.** overall height

**o. alt. hor.** *Med.* omnibus alternis horis (Latin: every other hour)

**OAM** Medal of the Order of Australia

**OAMDV** omnia ad majorem Dei gloriam (Latin: all to the greater glory of God)

**OANA** Organization of Asian News Agencies

**O & A** October and April (on bills)

**O & C** Oxford and Cambridge (Schools Examination Board)

**O & E** (USA) Operations and Engineers

**O & M** organization and method(s)

**O & O** Oriental and Occidental Steamship Company • owned and operated

**o.a.o.** off and on

**OAO** one and only • Orbiting Astronomical Observatory

**OAP** old age pension(er)

**OAPC** (USA) Office of Alien Property Custodian

**OAPEC** (əu'eɪpek) Organization of Arab Petroleum-Exporting Countries

**OAr** Old Arabic

**OAR** *RC Church* (of the) Order of Augustinian Recollects

**OAS** *Military* offensive air support • on active service • *Physics* optical absorption spectroscopy • Organisation de l'armée secrète (French: Secret Army Organization; opposed Algerian independence) • Organization of American States

**OASIS** (əu'eɪsɪs) optimal aircraft sequencing using intelligent systems

**OAT** outside air temperature

**OATC** Oceanic Air Traffic Control

**OATUU** Organization of African Trade Union Unity

**OAU** Organization of African Unity

**ob.** obiit (Latin: (he *or* she) died) • obiter (Latin: incidentally) • obligation • oboe • observation • obsolete • obstetric(s)

**o.b.** ordinary building (grade; of timber)

**o/b** on or before (preceding a date)

**Ob.** *Bible* Obadiah

**OB** *British vehicle registration for* Birmingham • *British fishing port registration for* Oban • observed bearing • (USA)

obstetric(s) • (USA) obstetrician • off
Broadway • official board • Old Bailey •
old bonded (whisky) • old boy • Order
of Barbados • order of battle • ordinary
business (in life-assurance policies) •
ordnance board • outside broadcast •
*international civil aircraft marking for* Peru

**OBA** optical bleaching agent (in detergents)

**Obad.** *Bible* Obadiah

**obb.** (*or* **obbl.**) *Music* obbligato (Italian:
obligatory)

**ÖBB** Österreichische Bundesbahnen
(German: Federal Railways of Austria)

**OBC** old boys' club

**ob. dk** observation deck

**obdt** obedient

**OBE** Officer of the Order of the British
Empire • out-of-the-body experience

**OBEV** (ital.) Oxford Book of English
Verse

**ob-gyn** (*or* **ob-gyne**) obstetrics–
gynaecology

**OBI** Order of British India

**obit.** obituary

**obj.** *Grammar* object(ive) • (*or* **objn**)
objection

**obl.** obligation • oblige • oblique • oblong

**OBLI** Oxford and Buckinghamshire
Light Infantry

**OBM** *Surveying* Ordnance benchmark

**OBO** ore-bulk-oil (ship)

**Obogs** ('əʊbɒgz) *Military* on-board
oxygen-generating system

**ob. ph.** *Surveying* oblique photog-
raph(y)

**obre.** octobre (French: October)

**obs.** obscure • observation • observatory • observe(d) • observer • obsolete •
obstetric(s)

**Obs.** Observatory • (ital.) The Observer

**OBS** *Meteorol.* observe(d) • *Med.*
organic brain syndrome

**obsc.** obscure

**OBSC** *Meteorol.* obscure(d)

**obscd** obscured

**obsol.** obsolescent • obsolete

**o.b.s.p.** obiit sine prole (Latin: died
without issue)

**obst.** oboist

**obstet.** obstetric(s) • obstetrician

**obstn** obstruction

**obt** obedient

**obtd** obtained

**OBU** offshore banking unit • One Big
Union

**obv.** obverse

**OBV** ocean boarding vessel

**o.c.** office copy • official classification •
*Architect.* on centre • (*or* **oc**) only child •
*Shipping* open charter • open cover •
opere citato (*see* op. cit.)

**o/c** officer commanding • overcharge

**Oc.** Ocean

**OC** *British vehicle registration for* Birmingham • Observer Corps • Officer
Commanding • *Electrical engineering*
operating characteristic • operations
centre • oral contraceptive • (Officer of
the) Order of Canada • Orienteering
Club • *Philately* original cover • Oslo
Convention • Ottawa Convention •
overseas command • overseas country

**oca.** *Music* ocarina

**OCA** Old Comrades Association

**OCAM** (*or* **OCAMM**) Organisation
commune africaine et malgache (*or*
africaine, malgache, et mauritienne)
(French: African and Malagasy (*or* African, Malagasy, and Mauritian)
Common Organization)

**O.Carm.** (of the) Order of Carmelites

**O.Cart.** (of the) Order of Carthusians

**OCAS** Organization of Central American States

**OCAW** (USA) Oil, Chemical, and
Atomic Workers International Union

**Oc.B/L** *Shipping* ocean bill of lading

**occ.** (*or* **occn**) occasion • (*or* **occas.**)
occasional(ly) • occident(al) • occupa-
tion • occurrence

**OCD** *Med.* obsessive compulsive disorder • (USA) Office of Civil Defense •
*Computing* on-line communications
driver • Ordo (*or* Ordinis) Carmelit-
arum Discalceatorum (Latin: (of the)
Order of Discalced Carmelites;
Discalced Carmelite Fathers)

**OCDE** Organisation de coopération et
de développement economiques
(French: Organization for Economic
Cooperation and Development; OECD)

**OCDM** (USA) Office of Civil Defense
Mobilization (1958–61)

**OCDS** (*or* **ocds Can**) (Canada) Overseas College of Defence Studies

**O/Cdt** Officer-Cadet

**oceanog.** oceanography

**OCelt** Old Celtic

**OCF** Officiating Chaplain to the Forces

**och.** ochre

**OCNL** *Meteorol.* occasional(ly)

**OCorn** Old Cornish

**OCP** *Chem.* organic conducting polymer

**OCPSF** organic chemicals, plastics, and synthetic fibers

**OCR** *Computing* optical character recognition (*or* reader) • Ordo (*or* Ordinis) Cisterciensium Reformatorum (Latin: (of the) Order of Reformed Cistercians; Trappists)

**OCS** (USA) Officer Candidate School • Old Church Slavonic • outer continental shelf

**OCSO** (of the) Order of Cistercians of the Strict Observance (Trappists)

**ocst.** *Meteorol.* overcast

**oct.** *Music* octave • *Printing* octavo

**Oct** *Astronomy* Octans • (*or* **Oct.**) October

**OCTU** ('ɒktuː) Officer Cadet Training Unit

**OCTV** open-circuit television

**OCU** Operational Conversion Unit

**OCUC** Oxford and Cambridge University Club

**OCV** open-circuit voltage

**od.** oder (German: or)

**o.d.** *Med.* oculus dexter (Latin: right eye) • *Military* olive drab • outer (*or* outside) diameter

**OD** *Med.* oculus dexter (Latin: right eye) • Doctor of Optometry • *British vehicle registration for* Exeter • *international civil aircraft marking for* Lebanon • officer of the day • Old Dutch (language) • *Military* olive drab • operations division • (Jamaica) (Officer of the) Order of Distinction • ordinary seaman • Ordnance datum (standard sea level of the Ordnance Survey) • ordnance department • ordnance depot • organization development • other denominations • outer (*or* outside) diameter • (*or* **o/d**) overdose

**O/D** (*or* **O/d, o/d**) on deck • *Banking* on demand • *Banking* overdraft (*or* overdrawn)

**ODA** *Chem.* 4,4′-oxydianiline • *Computing* open (formerly office) document architecture • *Med.* Operating Department Assistant • Overseas Development Administration (formerly Ministry of Overseas Development, ODM)

**ODan** Old Danish

**ODAS** Ocean Data Station

**ODC** (of the) Order of Discalced Carmelites

**ODCh** Chaplain for Other Denominations

**ODE** *Maths.* ordinary differential equation

**ODECA** Organización de estados centroamericanos (Spanish: Organization of Central American States)

**ODESSA** (əʊ'dɛsə) Organisation der SS-Angehörigen (German: Organization of SS members)

**ODI** Overseas Development Institute

**ODM** Ministry of Overseas Development (*see under* ODA)

**ODO** outdoor officer (at customs)

**ODP** official (*or* overall) development planning • open-door policy

**ODS** *Metallurgy* oxide dispersion strengthening

**ODV** *Colloquial* eau de vie (French: cognac)

**o.e.** omissions excepted • open end

**Oe** *Physics, symbol for* oersted

**OE** *international civil aircraft marking for* Austria • *British vehicle registration for* Birmingham • (USA) Office of Education • Old English (language) • Old Etonian • *Med.* on examination • (Guyana) Order of Excellence • original error • outboard engine

**OEA** Overseas Education Association • oxygen-enriched air

**OEC** oxygen-enriched combustion

**OECD** Organization for Economic Cooperation and Development

**OECS** Organization of Eastern Caribbean States

**OED** (ital.) Oxford English Dictionary

**OEEC** Organization for European Economic Cooperation (superseded by OECD)

**OEF** Organization of Employers' Federations and Employers in Developing Countries

**OEL** occupational exposure limit (of radiation)

**OEM** *Computing* original equipment manufacturer

**OEO** (USA) Office of Economic Opportunity

**OEP** (USA) Office of Economic Preparedness

**OER** Officers' Emergency Reserve • Organization for European Research • *Chem.* oxygen enhancement ratio

**OES** ocean (wave and tidal) energy system(s) • (USA) Office of Economic Stabilization • *Physics* optical emission spectroscopy • Order of the Eastern Star • Organization of European States

**o.f.** optional form • outside face

**OF** *British vehicle registration for* Birmingham • Oddfellows • oil-filled • oil-fired • *Printing* old-face (type) • Old French (language) • operational (*or* operating) forces • Order of the Founder (of the Salvation Army) • oxidizing flame

**OFA** *Med.* oncofetal antigen

**O factor** *Psychol.* oscillation factor

**OFEMA** Office français d'exportation de matériel aéronautique (French: Office for the Export of Aeronautical Material)

**off.** offer(ed) • office • (*or* **offr**) officer • (*or* **offcl**) official • officinal

**OFFER** (*or* **Offer**) ('ɒfə) Office of Electricity Regulation

**OFGAS** (*or* **Ofgas**) ('ɒf,gæs) Office of Gas Supply

**OFHC** *Engineering* oxygen-free high-conductivity copper

**OFlem** Old Flemish

**OFM** (of the) Order of Friars Minor (Franciscans)

**OFMCap.** (of the) Order of Friars Minor Capuchin (Franciscan order)

**OFMConv.** (of the) Order of Friars Minor Conventual (Franciscan order)

**OFr** Old French

**OFR** Order of the Federal Republic of Nigeria

**OFris** Old Frisian

**OFS** Orange Free State

**OFSTED** (*or* **Ofsted**) ('ɒf,stɛd) Office for Standards in Education

**OFT** Office of Fair Trading

**OFTEL** (*or* **Oftel**) ('ɒf,tɛl) Office of Telecommunications

**OFWAT** (*or* **Ofwat**) ('ɒf,wɒt) Office of Water Services

**o.g.** *Philately* original gum • *Sport* own goal

**OG** *British vehicle registration for* Birmingham • Officer of the Guard • *Architect.* ogee • Olympic Games • (USA) original gangster (used in the criminal world for a respected elder) • *Brewing* original gravity • *Philately* original gum • outside guard

**OGael** Old Gaelic

**ÖGB** Österreichischer Gewerkschaftsbund (German: Austrian Federation of Trade Unions)

**OGCM** *Meteorol.* ocean general circulation model

**OGL** *Commerce* open general licence

**OGM** ordinary general meeting

**OGO** Orbiting Geophysical Observatory

**Ogpu** (*or* **OGPU**) ('ɒgpuː) Obyedinyonnoye Gosudarstvennoye Politicheskoye Upravleniye (Russian: United State Political Administration; Soviet state security system, 1923–34)

**OGS** Oratory of the Good Shepherd • *Electronics* oxide glassy (*or* glasslike) semiconductor

**o.h.** observation helicopter • office hours • *Med.* omni hora (Latin: hourly) • on hand

**OH** *British vehicle registration for* Birmingham • *international civil aircraft marking for* Finland • *US postcode for* Ohio • *Physics* ohmic heating • *Numismatics* old head (of Victoria)

**OHBMS** On Her (*or* His) Britannic Majesty's Service

**OHC** (*or* **o.h.c.**) overhead cam (*or* camshaft)

**OHDETS** ('əudɛtz) over-horizon detection system

**OHG** *Commerce* Offene Handelsgesellschaft (German: partnership) • Old High German

**OHMS** On Her (*or* His) Majesty's Service

**OHN** occupational health nurse

**OHNC** occupational health nursing certificate

**OHP** overhead projector

**OHS** occupational health service • *Metallurgy* open-hearth steel

**OHV** (*or* **o.h.v.**) overhead valve

**OI** *British vehicle registration for* Belfast • office instruction • Old Irish (language) • operating instructions • *Med.* osteogenesis imperfecta

**OIC** (*or* **O i/c**) officer in charge • Organisation internationale du commerce (French: International Trade Organization; ITO) • Organization of Islamic Conference

**OIcel** Old Icelandic

**OIG** organisation intergouvernementale (French: intergovernmental organization)

**OII** *Physics* optical imaging instrument

**OIPC** Organisation internationale de police criminelle (French: International Criminal Police Organization; Interpol)

**OIr** Old Irish

**OIS** organizer industrial safety

**OIt** Old Italian

**OIT** Organisation internationale du travail (French: International Labour Organization; ILO)

**o.j.** open joist (*or* joint)

**OJ** *British vehicle registration for* Birmingham • (USA) orange juice • Order of Jamaica

**OJAJ** October, January, April, July (months for quarterly payments)

**OJCS** Office of the Joint Chiefs of Staff

**OJR** old Jamaica rum

**OJT** on-the-job training

**OK** all correct (from *orl korrect*, phonetic spelling) • *British vehicle registration for* Birmingham • (*or* **o.l.**) *Med.* oculus laevus (Latin: left eye) • *international civil aircraft marking for* the Czech Republic and Slovakia • *US postcode for* Oklahoma • *Chem.* oxidation kinetics

**o.k.a.** otherwise known as

**OKE** *Physical chem.* optical Kerr effect

**OKH** Oberkommando der Heeres (German Army High Command, World War II)

**Okla.** Oklahoma

**Okt.** Oktober (German: October)

**OKTA** *Meteorol.*, *indicating* one-eighth of the sky area

**ol.** *Med.* oil (Latin *oleum*) • olive

**Ol.** Olympiad • Olympic

**OL** *British vehicle registration for* Birmingham • (*or* **o.l.**) *Med.* oculus laevus (Latin: left eye) • *postcode for* Oldham • Old Latin • *Computing* on-line • operating licence • (Officer of the) Order of Leopold • Ordnance Lieutenant • *Sport* outside left • overflow level • overhead line

**Old Test.** Old Testament

**O level** *Education* Ordinary level (replaced by GCSE)

**OLG** Old Low German

**Oli** *Geology* Oligocene

**OLQ** officer-like qualities

**OLRT** *Computing* on-line real time

**OLS** *Statistics* ordinary least squares

**o.m.** old measurement • *Med.* omni mane (Latin: every morning)

**Om.** Oman

**OM** *British vehicle registration for* Birmingham • old man • optical microscopy • Optimus Maximus (Latin: greatest and best; title given by Romans to Jupiter) • Order of Merit • ordnance map • organic matter

**OMA** *Physics* optical multichannel analyser • (ˈəumə) *Finance* (USA) orderly marketing agreement

**OMB** (USA) Office of Management and Budget

**OMC** operation and maintenance costs • *Chem.* organometallic compound

**OMC-1** *Astronomy* Orion molecular cloud

**OMCS** Office of the Minister for the Civil Service

**OMI** Oblate(s) of Mary Immaculate

**OMM** (Canada) Officer of the Order of Military Merit

**omn. hor.** *Med.* omni hora (Latin: every hour)

**omn. noct.** *Med.* omni nocte (Latin: every night)

**OMO** one-man operator *or* operation (of buses)

**OMPA** *Chem.* octamethyl pyrophosphoramide

**OMR** *Computing* optical mark reading

**o.m.s.** output per man shift

**OMS** *Astronautics* orbital manoeuvring system • Organisation mondiale de la santé (French: World Health Organization; WHO)

**o.n.** *Med.* omni nocte (Latin: every night)

**ON** *British vehicle registration for* Birmingham • octane number • Old Norse • Ontario • (Jamaica) Order of the Nation • orthopaedic nurse

**ONC** Ordinary National Certificate • Orthopaedic Nursing Certificate

**OND** Ophthalmic Nursing Diploma • Ordinary National Diploma

**ONERA** Office national d'études et de recherches aerospatiales (French: National Office of Aerospace Study and Research)

**ONF** Old Norman (*or* Northern) French

**ONG** organisation non-gouvernementale (French: nongovernmental organization)

**ONGC** (USA) Oil and Natural Gas Commission

**ONI** Office of Naval Intelligence

**o.n.o.** or near(est) offer

**onomat.** onomatopoeia • onomatopoeic

**ONorw** Old Norwegian

**ONR** (USA) Office of Naval Research

**Ont.** Ontario

**ONZ** Order of New Zealand

**o/o** (*or* **o.o.**) on order • order of

**O/o** offers over

**OO** *international civil aircraft marking for* Belgium • *British vehicle registration for* Chelmsford • Observation Officer • *Colloquial* once-over (i.e. a preliminary inspection) • operation order • Orderly Officer

**OOD** *Computing* object-oriented design • officer of the day • officer of the deck

**OOG** officer of the guard

**OOL** *Computing* object-oriented language

**OON** Officer of the Order of the Niger

**OOP** *Computing* object-oriented programming

**OOT** out of town

**OOW** officer of the watch

**op.** opaque • opera (Latin: works) • operation • operator • opinion • opposite • optical • optimus (Latin: excellent) • opus (Latin: a work; *see also* Op.)

**o.p.** *Theatre* opposite prompt side (i.e. actor's right) • out of print • overproof (of alcohol)

**Op.** *Music* Opus (preceding a number; indicating a piece by a particular composer)

**OP** *British vehicle registration for* Birmingham • *Military* observation post • Old Persian (language) • old prices • *Insurance* open policy • *Theatre* opposite prompt side (i.e. actor's right) • Ordo (*or* Ordinis) Praedictatorum (Latin: (of the) Order of Preachers; Dominicans) • osmotic pressure • *Colloquial* other people (*or* people's; *see also under* OPM; OP's) • out of print • outpatient • overproof (of alcohol) • *Chem.* oxide precipitate

**OPA** (USA) Office of Price Administration (during World War II) • *Meteorol.* opaque (rime ice)

**op-amp** *Electronics* operational amplifier

**op art** optical art

**OPAS** Occupational Pensions Advisory Service

**OPB** Occupational Pensions Board

**OPC** (*or* **opc**) ordinary Portland cement • outpatients' clinic • Overseas Press Club of America

**op. cit.** opere citato (Latin: in the work cited; used in textual annotations)

**OPCON** ('ɒp,kɒn) operational control

**OPCS** Office of Population Censuses and Surveys

**OPD** outpatients' department

**OPDAR** ('ɒp,dɑ:) optical detection and ranging

**OPE** *Chem.* organic phosphate ester

**OPEC** ('əʊ,pɛk) Organization of Petroleum-Exporting Countries

**Op-Ed** ('ɒp,ɛd) (USA) opposite editorial (page; of a newspaper)

**OPEIU** (USA) Office and Professional Employees International Union

**OPEP** Organisation des pays exportateurs de pétrole (French: Organization of Petroleum Exporting Countries; OPEC)

**OPers** Old Persian

**OPEX** ('əʊ,pɛks) operational, executive, and administrative personnel (in the UN)

**OPg** Old Portuguese

**OPG** *Dentistry* orthopantomogram

**Oph** *Astronomy* Ophiuchus

**ophthal.** (*or* **oph.**) ophthalmic • (*or* **ophthalmol.**) ophthalmologist • (*or* **ophthalmol.**) ophthalmology

**opl** operational

**OPM** (USA) Office of Personnel Management • operations per minute • *Colloquial* (USA) other people's money • output per man

**OPMA** Overseas Press and Media Association

**opn** operation • opinion • option

**o.p.n.** ora pro nobis (Latin: pray for us)

**OPO** one-person operator *or* operation (of buses)

**OPol** Old Polish

**opp.** (*or* **Opp.**) opuses (*or* opera; *see also under* Op.) • opportunity • opposed • opposite • opposition

**OPP** oriented polypropene (in **OPP film**, used for packaging) • out of print at present

**oppy** opportunity

**OPQ** occupational personality questionnaire

**opr.** operate • operator

**OPr** (*or* **OProv**) Old Provençal

**OPruss** Old Prussian

**ops.** operations

**OP's** *Colloquial* other people's (as in **OP's cigarettes**)

**opt.** *Grammar* optative • optical • optician • optics • optimal • optimum • optional

**OPT** *Chem.* orientation phase transition

**OptD** Doctor of Optometry

**OQ** Officer of the National Order of Quebec

**or.** orange • oratorio • orient(al) • original • other

**o.r.** operationally risky • operational (*or* operations) requirement • operations room • out of range • overhaul and repair • *Insurance* owner's risk

**Or** Oriel College, Oxford

**OR** *Statistics* odds ratio • official receiver • official referee • Old Roman • *Med.* (USA) operating room • operational (*or* operations) requirement • operational (*or* operations) research • *Electronics* or (from its sense in logic, as in **OR gate, OR operation**) • orderly room • *US postcode for* Oregon • *Military* other ranks • *Sport* outside right • *Insurance* owner's risk • *British vehicle registration for* Portsmouth

**ÖR** Österreichischer Rundfunk (Austrian broadcasting service)

**Oracle** ('ɒrək³l) optional reception of announcements by coded line electronics (teletext service of Independent Television)

**orat.** oration • orator • oratorical(ly) • oratorio • oratory

**o.r.b.** *Insurance* owner's risk of breakage

**ORB** oceanographic research buoy • omnidirectional radio beacon

**ORBIS** ('ɔːbɪs) orbiting radio beacon ionospheric satellite

**ORC** (USA) Officers' Reserve Corps • Overseas Research Council

**ORCA** Ocean Resources Conservation Association

**orch.** orchestra(l) • (*or* **orchd**) orchestrated by • orchestration

**ord.** ordain(ed) • order • ordinal • ordinance • ordinary • ordnance

**o.r.d.** *Insurance* owner's risk of damage

**ORD** *Chem.* once-run distillate • *Chem.* optical rotary dispersion

**ordn.** ordnance

**Ore.** Oregon

**ORE** occupational radiation exposure

**Oreg.** Oregon

**ORELA** (USA) Oak Ridge Electron Linear Accelerator

**ORESCO** (ɒ'rɛskəu) Overseas Research Council

**o.r.f.** *Insurance* owner's risk of fire

**ORF** *Genetics* open reading frame

**org.** organ • organic • organism • organist • organization • organized

**ORGALIME** Organisme de liaison des industries métalliques européennes (French: Liaison Group for the European Metal Industries)

**organ.** organic • (*or* **orgzn**) organization

**orgst.** organist

**Ori** *Astronomy* Orion

**orient.** oriental • orientalist

**orig.** origin • original(ly) • originate(d)

**ORIT** Organización regional interamericana de trabajadores (Spanish: Inter-American Regional Organization of Workers)

**Ork.** (*or* **Orkn**.) Orkney Islands

**o.r.l.** *Insurance* owner's risk of leakage

**ORL** *Med.* otorhinolaryngology (ear, nose, and throat specialty; ENT)

**orn.** ornament • ornithology

**ornithol.** (*or* **ornith**.) ornithological • ornithology

**ORNL** (USA) Oak Ridge National Laboratory

**OROM** *Computing* optical read-only memory

**orph.** orphan(age)

**o.r.r.** *Insurance* owner's risk rates

**ors.** others

**ORS** *Geology* Old Red Sandstone • Operational Research Society

**ORSL** Order of the Republic of Sierra Leone

**ORSORT** Oak Ridge School of Reactor Technology

**ORT** *Med.* oral rehydration therapy • (USA) Organization for Rehabilitation by Training

**ORTF** (France) Office de Radiodiffusion-Télévision Française (former state radio and television service)

**orth.** orthography • orthopaedic(s)

**Orth.** Orthodox (religion)

**ORuss** Old Russian

**ORV** (USA) off-road vehicle

**o.s.** ocean station • *Med.* oculus sinister (Latin: left eye) • oil switch • old series • (*or* **os**) only son • on station • outside (measurement)

**o/s** on sale • out of service • (*or* **O/s**) out of stock • outsize (of clothing) • (*or* **O/s**) *Banking* outstanding

**Os** *Chem., symbol for* osmium

**OS** *British vehicle registration for* Glasgow • *Med.* oculus sinister (Latin: left eye) • Old Saxon (language) • Old School • old series • Old Side • Old Style (method of reckoning dates) •

*Computing* operating system (*see also* OS/2) • Ordinary Seaman • Ordnance Survey • out of stock • outsize (of clothing)

**OS/2** *Computing* Operating System/2 (produced by IBM and Microsoft)

**OSA** (USA) Office of the Secretary of the Army • Official Secrets Act • *Typography* old style antique • (of the) Order of St Augustine (Augustinians) • Overseas Sterling Area

**OSAF** (USA) Office of the Secretary of the Air Force

**OS&W** *Building trades* oak, sunk and weathered

**OSax** Old Saxon

**OSB** (of the) Order of St Benedict (Benedictines)

**osc** *Military* (graduate of) overseas staff college

**osc.** oscillator

**OSC** (of the) Order of St Clare (Poor Clares) • *Chem.* organic sulphur compound

**OScan** (*or* **OScand**) Old Scandinavian

**OSCAR** ('ɒskə) Orbital Satellites Carrying Amateur Radio • Organization for Sickle Cell Anaemia Research

**OSD** (USA) Office of the Secretary of Defense • (of the) Order of St Dominic (Dominicans)

**OSE** operational support equipment

**OSerb** Old Serbian

**OSF** *Computing* Open Software Foundation • (of the) Order of St Francis (Franciscans)

**OSFC** (of the) Order of St Francis, Capuchin

**OSHA** ('əuʃə) (USA) Occupational Safety and Health Administration

**OSI** (USA) Office of Scientific Integrity • on-site inspection • *Computing* open systems interconnection

**O/Sig** Ordinary Signalman

**Osl.** Oslo

**OSl** (*or* **OSlav**) Old Slavonic

**OSL** Old Style Latin

**OSM** (of the) Order of the Servants of Mary (Servites)

**OSN** (USA) Office of the Secretary of the Navy

**OSNC** Orient Steam Navigation Company

**OSO** orbiting solar observatory

**o.s.p.** obiit sine prole (Latin: died without issue)

**OSp** Old Spanish

**OSR** (USA) Office of Science and Research

**OSRB** Overseas Service Resettlement Bureau

**OSRD** (USA) Office of Scientific Research and Development

**OSRO** Office for Special Relief Operations (in the FAO)

**OSS** (USA) Office of Space Sciences (in NASA) • (USA) Office of Strategic Services (during World War II)

**O.SS.S** Ordo (*or* Ordinis) Sanctissimi Salvatoris (Latin: (of the) Order of the Most Holy Saviour; Bridgettines)

**O.SS.T** Ordo (*or* Ordinis) Sanctissimae Trinitatis Redemptionis Captivorum (Latin: (of the) Order of the Most Holy Trinity for the Redemption of Captives; Trinitarians)

**OST** (USA) Office of Science and Technology

**osteo.** osteopath(ic) • osteopathy

**OSTI** (USA) Office of Scientific and Technical Information • (USA) Organization for Social and Technological Innovation

**OStJ** Officer of the Order of St John of Jerusalem

**OSU** (of the) Order of St Ursula (Ursulines)

**OSUK** Ophthalmological Society of the United Kingdom

**OSw** Old Swedish

**OT** occupational therapy (*or* therapist) • off time • Old Testament • *Med.* operating theatre • (Australia) Overland Telegraph (from Adelaide to Darwin) • overseas trade • overtime • *British vehicle registration for* Portsmouth

**OTA** (USA) Office of Technology Assessment • *Chem.* organic trace analysis

**OTAN** Organisation du traité de l'Atlantique nord (French: North Atlantic Treaty Organization; NATO)

**OTASE** Organisation du traité de défense collective pour l'Asie du sud-est (French: South-East Asia Treaty Organization; SEATO)

**OTB** (USA) off-track betting • oxide titanium bronze

**otbd** outboard

**OTC** (USA) officer in tactical command • Officers' Training Corps • Officers' Transit Camp • one-stop-inclusive tour charter • Organization for Trade Cooperation • over the counter (as in **OTC market** (in securities), **OTC medicines**) • oxytetracycline (an antibiotic)

**OTE** on-target earnings (for a salesman)

**OTEC** ('əʊtɛk) ocean thermal-energy conversion

**OTeut** Old Teutonic

**OTF** *Photog.* off the film

**OTH** *Telecom.* over the horizon (as in **OTH radar**)

**otol.** otological • otology

**OTP** *Meteorol.* on top

**OTR** *Physics* optical transition radiation

**OTS** Office of Technical Services • Officers' Training School • *Advertising* opportunities to see

**ott.** *Music* ottava (Italian: octave) • ottobre (Italian: October)

**Ott.** Ottawa

**OTT** *Med.* oesophageal transit test • *Colloquial* over the top (i.e. excessive)

**OTU** *Biology* operational taxonomic unit • operational training unit

**OTurk** Old Turkish

**OU** *British vehicle registration for* Bristol • official use • Open University • Oxford University

**OUAC** Oxford University Appointments Committee • Oxford University Athletic Club

**OUAFC** Oxford University Association Football Club

**OUBC** Oxford University Boat Club

**OUCC** Oxford University Cricket Club

**OUDS** ('əʊ 'juː 'diː 'ɛs *or* aʊdz) Oxford University Dramatic Society

**OUP** (Northern Ireland) Official Unionist Party • Oxford University Press

**OURC** Oxford University Rifle Club

**OURFC** Oxford University Rugby Football Club

**OURT** Order of the United Republic of Tanzania

**out.** outlet

**outbd** outboard

**ov.** ovary • over • overture

**Ov.** Ovid (43 BC–AD 17, Roman poet)

**OV** *British vehicle registration for* Birmingham

**ovbd** overboard

**ovc.** (*or* **OVC**) *Meteorol.* overcast

**o.v.c.** other valuable consideration (in contract law)

**ovfl.** overflow

**OVH** overhead projector

**ovhd** overhead

**ovld** overload

**o.v.n.o.** or very near offer

**ÖVP** (Austria) Österreichische Volkspartei (People's Party)

**ovpd** overpaid

**Ovra** Opera di vigilanza e di repressione dell'anti-fascismo (Italian secret police of the Fascist regime)

**ovrd.** override

**o.w.** one way • out of wedlock

**OW** Office of Works • Old Welsh (language) • *British vehicle registration for* Portsmouth

**O/W** oil in water (emulsion)

**OWC** Ordnance Weapons Command

**OWF** optimum working frequency

**OWI** (USA) Office of War Information (during World War II) • (USA) operating (a motor vehicle) while intoxicated

**OWRS** (USA) Office of Water Regulations and Standards

**OWS** ocean weather service • ocean weather ship (*or* station)

**ox** *Chem.* oxalate ion (used in formulae)

**Ox.** Oxford

**OX** *British vehicle registration for* Birmingham • *postcode for* Oxford

**Oxbridge** ('ɒks,brɪdʒ) Oxford and Cambridge (Universities; regarded collectively)

**Oxf.** Oxford(shire)

**OXFAM** (*or* **Oxfam**) ('ɒksfæm) Oxford Committee for Famine Relief

**Oxon** Oxfordshire (Latin *Oxonia*) • Oxoniensis (Latin: of Oxford)

**OY** *international civil aircraft marking for* Denmark • *British vehicle registration for* London NW

**oz** (*or* **oz.**) ounce(s) (Italian *onza*)

**OZ** *British vehicle registration for* Belfast

**oz ap** apothecaries' ounce

**oz av** (*or* **oz avdp**) avoirdupois ounce

**oz T** troy ounce

# P

**p** (bold ital.) *Physics, symbol for* electric dipole moment • (ital.) *Physics, symbol for* (in vector equations) • (ital.) *Chem.* para (as in **p-cresol**) • *symbol for* penny (*or* pence) • (bold ital.) *Chem., symbol for* permanent dipole moment of a molecule • *Biochem., symbol for* (terminal) phosphate (in a polynucleotide) • (ital.) *Music* piano (Italian; softly, quietly) • *symbol for* pico- (prefix indicating $10^{-9}$ as in **ps**, picosecond) • (ital.) *Physics, symbol for* pressure • *Physics, symbol for* proton • *Electronics* p-type (semiconductor) • (ital.) *Biochem., symbol for* pyranose • *Meteorol., symbol for* shower • *Physics, Chem., indicating* the electron state $l=1$ (where $l$ is orbital angular momentum quantum number)

**p.** page • pamphlet • paragraph • part • participle • particle • partim (Latin: in part) • pass(ed) • *Nautical* passing showers • past • peak • *Ichthyol.* pectoral • per (Latin: by, for) • perch (solid measure for stone) • *Music* percussion • *Grammar* person • *Currency* piastre • pied (French: foot) • pint • pipe • pius (Latin: holy) • polar • pole • pondere (Latin: by weight) • population • port • post (Latin: after) • pouce (French: inch) • pour (French: for *or* per) • primus (Latin: first) • pro (Latin: for, in favour of) • professional • *Knitting* purl

**P** (bold ital.) *Physics, symbol for* dielectric polarization • *medieval Roman numeral for* four hundred • *international aircraft marking for* North Korea • *Genetics, symbol for* parental generation • (ital.) *Physics, symbol for* parity • *symbol for* parking (on road signs) • *Education* (USA) passing (performance rating) • *Chess, symbol for* pawn • pedestrian crossing • *Botany* perianth (in a floral formula) • *Geology* Permian • *symbol for* peta- (prefix indicating $10^{-15}$ as in **PJ**, petajoule) • pharmacy (on medicines obtained without a prescription from a pharmacy) • *Biochem., symbol for* phosphate • *Chem., symbol for* phosphorus • *Botany, symbol for* phytochrome • *Physics, symbol for* poise • *Computing* polynomial (referring to a class of formal languages recognizable in polynomial time) • *British fishing port registration for* Portsmouth • *international vehicle registration for* Portugal • Post Office (on maps) • (ital.) *Physics, symbol for* power • (ital.) *Physics, symbol for* pressure • *Biochem., symbol for* proline • (ital.) *Genetics, symbol for* promoter • proprietary (product) • *symbol for* pula (monetary unit of Botswana)

**P.** (*or* **P**) *RC Church* Papa (Latin: Pope) • parson • Pastor • pater (Latin: father) • *Music* pedal • *Ecclesiast.* Père (French: Father) • *Horticulture* perennial • period • personnel • pitch • populus (Latin: people) • positive • post • postage • *Med.* posterior • Presbyterian • President • Priest • Prince • probate • pro-consul • Progressive (party, movement, etc.) • *Theatre* prompt side (i.e. the actor's left) • Protestant • public • pupil

**P2** *international civil aircraft marking for* Papua New Guinea • Propaganda due (Italian masonic lodge)

**P4** *international civil aircraft marking for* Aruba

**P45** *indicating* a form relating to unemployment benefit issued by the DSS

**pa.** past

**p.a.** participial adjective • per annum • permanent address • personal appearance • press agent

**p/a** *Book-keeping* personal account

**p.A.** per Adresse (German: care of)

**Pa** *Physics, symbol for* pascal • *Chem., symbol for* protactinium

**Pa.** Pennsylvania

**PA** *British vehicle registration for* Guildford • *postcode for* Paisley • Pakistan Army • *international vehicle registration for* Panama • *airline flight code for* Pan American World Airways • *Chem.* parent atom • (*or* **P/A**) *Insurance* particular average • *US postcode for* Pennsylvania • performance assessment • *Med.* pernicious anaemia • *Insurance* personal accident • *Accounting* personal account • *Taxation* personal allowance • personal appearance • personal assistant • *Chem.* phosphoric

acid • (USA) physician assistant • Pierre
Allain (climbing boot; named after its
inventor) • Piper Aircraft (as in **PA-
28**) • *Engineering* pitch angle • *Med.*
plasminogen activator • political agent •
por autorización (Spanish: by authority
of) • *Astronomy* position angle • *Military*
Post Adjutant • power amplifier • (*or*
**P/A**) power of attorney • *RC Church*
Prefect Apostolic • press agent • Press
Association • press attaché • (*or* **P/A**)
*Banking, Book-keeping* private account •
product analysis • programme assistant • *Med.* psoriatic arthritis • (USA)
public accountant • public address
(system) • publicity agent • Publishers
Association • *Engineering* pulsed annealing • purchasing agent • (USA) Prosecuting Attorney

**PAA** *Chem.* peracetic acid • *Physics*
photon activation analysis • *Chem.* poly-
acrylic acid • *Chem.* primary aromatic
amine

**PAADC** Principal Air Aide-de-camp

**PAB** *Chem.* *p*-aminobenzamidine

**PABA** ('pɑːbə) *Biochem., Pharmacol.*
*p*-aminobenzoic acid

**PABLA** ('pæblə) problem analysis by
logical approach

**PABP** *Biochem.* poly(A)-binding protein

**PABX** *Telephony* private automatic
branch exchange

**pac** passed (final examination of the)
advanced class (of the Military College
of Science)

**Pac.** Pacific

**PAC** *US Air Force* Pacific Air
Command • Pan-African(ist)
Congress • Pan-American Congress •
*Building trades* passive air cycle • (pæk)
(USA) political action committee •
*Chem.* polycyclic aromatic compound •
polymer–asphalt composite • *Chem.*
powdered activated carbon • Public
Accounts Committee • Public Assist-
ance Committee • *Stock exchange* put-
and-call (option)

**P-A-C** *Psychol.* parent, adult, child (in
transactional analysis)

**PACAF** *US Air Force* Pacific Air Forces

**PACE** (peɪs) performance and cost
evaluation • Police and Criminal
Evidence Act (1984) • precision
analogue computing equipment • Protestant and Catholic Encounter

**Pacif.** Pacific

**PACOM** ('pækɒm) (USA) Pacific
Command

**PACS** (pæks) Pacific area communications system

**PACT** (*or* **Pact**) (pækt) Producers' Alliance for Cinema and Television

**PaD** Pennsylvania Dutch

**PAD** (pæd) *Computing* packet assem-
bler/disassembler • (pæd) passive air
defence • payable after death

**PADAR** ('peɪdɑː) *Military* passive
detection and ranging

**PADLOC** ('pædlɒk) *Military* passive
detection and location of countermeasures

**p. Adr.** per Adresse (German: care of;
c/o)

**p. ae.** *Pharmacol.* partes aequales
(Latin: equal parts)

**p.a.f.** puissance au frein (French: brake
horsepower)

**PAF** *Computing* peripheral address
field • *Med.* platelet-activating factor

**PAFC** phosphoric acid fuel cell

**PaG** Pennsylvania German

**PAg** Professional Agronomist

**PAGB** Proprietary Association of Great
Britain

**PAGE** *Biochem.* polyacrylamide gel electrophoresis

**PAH** *Chem.* polycyclic aromatic hydrocarbon

**PAHO** Pan American Health Organization

**PAI** *Med.* platelet accumulation index

**PAICV** (Cape Verde) Partido Africano
da Independencia de Cabo Verde
(Portuguese: African Party for the Independence of Cape Verde)

**PAIS** (USA) Public Affairs Information
Service

**Pak.** Pakistan(i)

**Pak Re** Pakistan rupee (monetary unit)

**pal.** palaeography • palaeontology

**Pal** *Geology* Palaeocene

**Pal.** Palace • Palestine

**PAL** (pæl) (USA) Parcel Air Lift •
*Computing* peripheral availability list •
*Television* phase alternation line •
*Botany* phenylalanine ammonia lyase •
Philippine Airlines • (USA) Police
Athletic League • present atmospheric
level • *Computing, Electronics* program-
mable array logic

**palaeob.** (*or* **palaeobot.**) palaeo-
botanical • palaeobotany

**palaeog.** palaeographical • palaeography

**palaeontol.** palaeontology

**PALS** (pælz) *Computing* permissive action link systems

**pam.** (*or* **pamph.**) pamphlet

**PAM** (pæm) *Telecom.* pulse-amplitude modulation

**PAMA** Pan-American Medical Association • Press Advertisement Managers' Association

**pan.** panchromatic • panoramic • pantomime • pantry

**Pan.** Panama

**PAN** (Mexico) Partido Acción Nacional (Spanish: National Action Party) • peroxyacetyl nitrate (atmospheric pollutant) • polyacrylonitrile (polymer)

**PANAFTEL** (pæn'æftel) Pan-African Telecommunications Network

**Pan Am** Pan American World Airways

**Pan. Can.** Panama Canal

**P&E** plant and equipment

**P & F chart** point-and-figure chart

**P & G** Procter and Gamble (pharmaceutical company)

**P & L** profit and loss

**P & O** Peninsular and Oriental (Steamship Company)

**P&OSNCo** Peninsular and Oriental Steam Navigation Company

**p & p** postage and packing

**P&RT** physical and recreational training

**P&S** *Stock exchange* (USA) purchase and sales

**PANH** *Chem.* polycyclic aromatic nitrogen heterocyclic (compound)

**PANS** procedures for air navigation services

**PAO** *Med.* peak acid output • Prince Albert's Own (regiment) • public affairs officer

**Pap.** Papua(n)

**PAP** (Singapore) People's Action Party • Polska Agencja Prasowa (Polish Press Agency) • *Med.* pulmonary arterial pressure

**PAPS** (pæps) periodic armaments planning system

**par.** paragraph • parallax • parallel • paraphrase • parenthesis • parish • parochial

**p.a.r.** planed all round (in woodworking)

**Par.** Paraguay

**PAR** (pɑː) *Military* perimeter acquisition radar • phased-array radar • *Botany* photosynthetically active radiation • *Computing* positive acknowledgment and retransmission • *Aeronautics* precision approach radar • programme analysis review • *Electronics* pulse acquisition radar

**para.** paragraph

**parab.** parabola

**par. aff.** *Pharmacol.* pars affecta (Latin: (to the) part affected)

**parch.** parchment

**Par. Ch.** parish church

**paren.** parenthesis

**parens.** parentheses

**Parl.** Parliament • (*or* **parl.**) parliamentary

**parl. agt.** parliamentary agent

**parl. proc.** parliamentary procedure

**Parly Sec.** Parliamentary Secretary

**PARM** programme analysis for resource management

**part.** partial • participate • participial • participle • particle • particular • partition • partner(ship)

**part. aeq.** *Pharmacol.* partes aequales (Latin: in equal parts)

**pas.** *Grammar* passive

**p.a.s.** power-assisted steering

**PAS** *Med.* p-aminosalicylic acid (tuberculosis treatment) • *Chem.* periodic acid–Schiff (as in **PAS reaction**) • *Physics* plasma activated source • *Physics* positron annihilation spectroscopy • public-address system

**PASCAL** (*or* **Pascal**) ('pæs,kæl) *Computing, indicating* a programming language (named after Blaise Pascal (1623–62), French philosopher, mathematician, and physicist)

**PASH** (pæʃ) *Chem.* polynuclear aromatic sulphur heterocyclic (compound)

**Pasok** Panhellenic Socialist Movement

**pass.** passage • passenger • passim (Latin: here and there throughout) • *Grammar* passive

**Pass.** Passover

**PASSIM** ('pæsɪm) (USA) Presidential Advisory Staff on Scientific Management

**pat.** patent(ed) • pattern

**p.a.t.** *Chem.* poids atomique (French: atomic weight)

**PAT** *Football* (USA) point(s) after touchdown • (pæt) *Physics* positron annihilation technique • *Banking* preauthorized automatic transfer • Professional Association of Teachers

**Pata.** Patagonia

**patd** patented

**path.** (*or* **pathol.**) pathological • pathology

**Pat. Off.** Patent Office

**pat. pend.** patent pending

**PAU** Pan American Union • programmes analysis unit

**pav.** pavilion

**Pav** *Astronomy* Pavo

**PAW** plasma-arc welding • powered all the way

**PAWA** Pan American World Airways

**PAWR** (USA) Public Authority for Water Resources

**PAX** *Telephony* private automatic exchange

**PAYE** pay as you earn (income tax) • pay as you enter

**paymr** paymaster

**payt** payment

**PAYV** pay as you view

**p.b.** *Baseball* passed ball(s)

**Pb** *Chem., symbol for* lead (Latin *plumbum*)

**PB** Bachelor of Philosophy (Latin *Philosophiae Baccalaureus*) • *British vehicle registration for* Guildford • pass book • permanent base • *Athletics* personal best • Pharmacopoeia Britannica (Latin: British Pharmacopoeia) • *Pharmacol.* phenobarbitone • plastic-bonded • Plymouth Brethren • power brakes • Prayer Book • premium bond • Primitive Baptists • (USA) Publications Board • *Knitting* purl into back of stitch

**PBA** *Colloquial* poor bloody assistant • (USA) Professional Bowlers Association • (USA) Public Buildings Administration

**PBAB** please bring a bottle

**PBB** *Chem.* polybrominated biphenyl (toxic constituent of plastics, etc.)

**PBC** powerboat club

**PBI** *Colloquial* poor bloody infantry(man) • *Med.* protein-bound iodine

**pbk** paperback (book)

**PBM** *Surveying* permanent benchmark • play by mail (of games)

**PBR** payment by results

**PBS** *Med.* phosphate-buffered saline • Public Broadcasting Service

**p.b.t.** *Finance* profit before tax

**PBT** *Accounting* pay-back time

**PBX** *Telephony* private branch exchange

**pc** *Astronomy, symbol for* parsec

**pc.** percentage • *Printing* pica • piece • price

**p.c.** per cent • postcard • *Med.* post cibum (Latin: after meals; in prescriptions)

**PC** *British vehicle registration for* Guildford • Panama Canal • *Chem.* paper chromatography • *Chem.* paraffin concentration • Parish Council(lor) • Parliamentary Commissioner (ombudsman) • (France) Partie Communiste (Communist Party) • Past Commander • Paymaster Captain • (Ireland) Peace Commissioner • (USA) Peace Corps • perpetual curate • personal computer • *Physics* phase conjugation • *Military* pioneer corps • *Machinery* pitch circle • *Politics* Plaid Cymru • Police Constable • (USA) politically correct (*or* political correctness) • *Chem.* polycarbonate • polymer concrete • *Chem.* polypropylene (*or* polypropene) carbonate (plastic) • Portland cement • Post Commander • potentially correct • preparatory commission • Press Council • prestressed concrete • Prince Consort • *Electronics* printed circuit • Prison Commission • Privy Council(lor) • process control • (USA) professional corporation • (Canada) Progressive Conservative • propositional calculus • *Chem.* propylene (*or* propene) carbonate • public convenience (on maps) • pulverized coal • *Microbiol.* pure culture

**P/C** (*or* **p/c**) petty cash • price(s) current

**PCA** Parliamentary Commissioner for Administration (ombudsman) • *Med.* patient-controlled analgesia • Permanent Court of Arbitration • *Statistics* principal component analysis

**PCB** petty cash book • *Chem.* polychlorinated biphenyl (toxic constituent of plastics, etc.) • (*or* **pcb**) *Electronics* printed-circuit board • *Insurance* private car benefits

**pcc** *Chem.* precipitated calcium carbonate

**PCC** parochial church council • Partido Comunista de Cuba (Spanish: Communist Party of Cuba) • political consultative committee • Press Complaints Commission • Privy Council cases

**PCE** Partido Comunista de España (Communist Party of Spain) • Postgraduate Certificate of Education • *Engineering* pyrometric cone equivalent

**P-Celtic** *Linguistics, indicating* one of two main groups of languages that developed from Common Celtic. *See also* Q-Celtic

**pcf** pounds per cubic foot

**PCF** Parti Communiste Français (French Communist Party) • pistol, centre fire (calibre of pistol)

**PCFC** Polytechnics and Colleges Funding Council

**PCGC** pulverized coal gasification and combustion

**PCGN** Permanent Committee on Geographical Names

**P. Ch.** parish church

**pci** pounds per cubic inch

**PCI** Partito Comunista Italiano (Italian Communist Party; now renamed Partito Democratico della Sinistra, Democratic Party of the Left)

**pcl** parcel

**PCL** *Computing* printer control language

**pcm** per calendar month

**PCM** *Physics* phase-change material • phase-contrast microscope • photochemical machinery • (USA) plug-compatible manufacturer • polyatomic ceramic material • protein-calorie malnutrition • *Telecom.* pulse-code modulation

**PCMI** photochromic microimage

**PCMO** Principal Colonial Medical Officer

**PCN** (El Salvador) Partido de Conciliación Nacional (Spanish: National Conciliation Party) • *Computing* personal communications network

**PCNB** *Chem.* pentachloronitrobenzene

**PCOB** Permanent Central Opium Board (in the UN)

**PCOD** polycystic ovary disease

**p-code** *Computing, indicating* an intermediate language designed as the target language for UCSD Pascal

**PCP** Past Chief Patriarch • *Chem.* pentachlorophenol (wood preservative) • phencyclohexylpiperidine (the drug phencylidine; angel dust) • *Med. Pneumocystis carinii* pneumonia (complication of Aids) • polychloroprene (rubber) • prime commercial paper

**PCPA** *Pharmacol.* p-chlorophenylalinine

**PCR** Pedestrian Crossings Regulations • *Med.* plasma clearance rate • *Biochem.* polymerase chain reaction • *Physics* primary cosmic rays

**PCRS** Poor Clergy Relief Society

**pcs.** pieces • prices

**PCS** *Physics* photon-correlation spectroscopy • *Electronics* plasma-current switch • (Scotland) Principal Clerk of Session

**PCSP** Permanent Commission for the South Pacific

**pct** per cent

**PCT** *Med.* positron computed tomography • product consistency test

**PCTE** *Computing* portable common tool environment

**PCTFE** polychlorotrifluoroeth(yl)ene (plastic coating)

**p.c.u.** passenger car unit

**PCU** plant control unit • power-control (*or* -conversion) unit • pressurization-control unit

**PCV** *Med.* packed cell volume • passenger-controlled vehicle • (USA) Peace Corps Volunteers • positive crankcase ventilation (in a car) • pressure containment vessel

**PCZ** Panama Canal Zone

**PCZST** Panama Canal Zone Standard Time

**pd** paid • passed

**p.d.** per diem (Latin: daily) • *Engineering* pitch diameter • poop deck • postage due • (*or* **p/d**) post-dated • *Physics* potential difference • preliminary design • printer's devil

**Pd** *Chem., symbol for* palladium

**PD** Doctor of Pharmacy (Latin *Pharmaciae Doctor*) • *British vehicle registration for* Guildford • per diem (Latin: daily) • *British fishing port registration for* Peterhead • Pharmacopoeia Dublinensis (Latin: Dublin Pharmacopoeia) • polar distance • (USA) Police Department • port dues • posdata (Spanish: postscript; PS) • postal district • preventive detention (*or* detainee) • (Germany) Privatdozent (unsalaried university teacher) • probability of detection • production department • (Ireland) Progressive Democrat(s) • progressive disease • *Insurance* property damage • (USA) Public Defender • *Computing* public domain (software) • *Chem.* pyrimidine dimer

**P/D** price–dividend (in **P/D ratio**)

**PDA** *Med.* patent ductus arteriosus • pour dire adieu (French: to say goodbye) • *Navigation* predicted drift angle

**PDAD** Probate, Divorce, and Admiralty Division (former division of the High Court)

**PdB** (USA) Bachelor of Pedagogy

**PDC** (El Salvador) Partido Demócrata Cristiana (Spanish: Christian Democratic Party) • personnel dispatch (*or* dispersal) centre • *Engineering* pulse-discharge cleaning • *Chem.* pyridinium dichromate

**PDCI** Parti Démocratique de la Côte d'Ivoire (French: Democratic Party of Côte d'Ivoire)

**PdD** (USA) Doctor of Pedagogy

**PDD** precise delay detonator

**PDE** *Maths.* partial differential equation • Projectile Development Establishment

**P-de-C** Pas-de-Calais (department of France)

**P-de-D** Puy-de-Dôme (department of France)

**PDF** *Statistics* probability density function

**PDFLP** Popular Democratic Front for the Liberation of Palestine

**PDG** Parti Démocratique de Guinée (French: Democratic Party of Guinea) • Paymaster Director-General • président directeur général (French: chairman and managing director)

**PDGF** *Med., Biochem.* platelet-derived growth factor

**p.d.i.** predelivery inspection

**PDI** *Astronautics* powered descent initiation

**pdl** *Physics, symbol for* poundal

**PDL** *Computing* page description language • poverty datum line • *Computing* program design language

**PdM** (USA) Master of Pedagogy

**PDM** physical distribution management • *Telecom.* pulse-duration modulation

**pdn** production

**PDN** public data network

**PDOS** *Physics* partial density of states

**PDP** *Computing* parallel distributed processing • program development plan (in NASA) • programmed data processor

**PDPA** People's Democratic Party of Afghanistan

**pdq** (*or* **PDQ**) *Colloquial* pretty damn quick

**PDR** People's Democratic Republic • *Engineering* pitch-to-diameter ratio • price–dividend ratio

**PDRA** postdoctoral research assistant

**P/D ratio** price–dividend ratio

**PDS** Parkinson's Disease Society • (Germany) Party of Democratic Socialism (formerly the Communist Party) • *Physics* phase differential scattering • previously digested sludge • *Computing* programming documentation standards

**PDSA** People's Dispensary for Sick Animals

**PDSR** Principal Director of Scientific Research

**PDT** Pacific Daylight Time • personal development technology • *Med.* photodynamic therapy

**PDTC** Professional Dancer's Training Course Diploma

**PDU** process-development unit

**p.e.** *Law* personal estate • printer's error

**Pe** *RC Church* (Spain) Padre

**PE** *British vehicle registration for* Guildford • peat extract • *Meteorol.* (ice) pellets • permissible error • *Insurance* personal effects • *international vehicle registration for* Peru • *postcode for* Peterborough • (USA) Petroleum Engineer • Pharmacopoeia Edinburgensis (Latin: Edinburgh Pharmacopoeia) • *Computing* phase-encoded (of tape format) • physical education • plastic explosive • pocket edition • *British fishing port registration for* Poole • polyeth(yl)ene • Port Elizabeth (South Africa) • *Physics* potential energy • Presiding Elder • printer's error • *Statistics* probable error • *Computing* processing element • procurement executive • (USA) Professional Engineer • Protestant Episcopal • *Med.* pulmonary embolism

**P/E** port of embarkation • (*or* **p/e**) price–earnings (in **P/E ratio**)

**PEA** Physical Education Association of Great Britain and Northern Ireland

**PEC** (*or* **p.e.c.**) photoelectric cell • photoelectrochemical cell • Protestant Episcopal Church

**PECD** *Electronics* photoelectric conversion device

**ped.** pedal • pedestal • pedestrian

**PedD** (USA) Doctor of Pedagogy

**pediat.** pediatrics

**PEDir** Director of Physical Education

**Peeb.** Peebles (former Scottish county)

**PEEP** (piːp) pilot's electronic eye-level presentation

**PEF** *Insurance* (USA) personal effects floater • *Electronics* pulsed electric field

**Peg** *Astronomy* Pegasus

**PEG** *Chem.* polyethylene glycol

**PEI** (Canada) Prince Edward Island

**p.ej.** por ejemplo (Spanish: for example; e.g.)

**Pek.** Peking

**PEL** permissible exposure level (*or* limit)

**Pemb** Pembroke College (Oxford *or* Cambridge)

**Pembs** Pembrokeshire (former Welsh county)

**Pemex** ('pemɛks) Petróleos Mexicanos (Mexican oil company)

**pen.** penal • penetration • peninsula(r)

**Pen** *Geology* Pennsylvanian

**Pen.** Peninsula • Penitentiary

**PEN** (pen) International Association of Poets, Playwrights, Editors, Essayists, and Novelists

**PEng** Member of the Society of Professional Engineers • (Canada) Registered Professional Engineer

**Penn.** Pennsylvania

**penol.** penology

**pent.** pentagon

**Pent.** Pentateuch • Pentecost

**PEO** (USA) Philanthropic Educational Organization • *Chem.* polyeth(yl)ene oxide

**PEP** *Radio* peak envelope power • (*or* **Pep;** pɛp) personal equity plan • *Biochem.* phosphoenolpyruvate • political and economic planning

**PEPP** (USA) Professional Engineers in Private Practice

**per.** percentile • period • person

**Per** *Astronomy* Perseus

**Per.** Persia(n)

**PER** price–earnings ratio • Professional and Executive Recruitment • Professional Employment Register

**PERA** Production Engineering Research Association of Great Britain

**per an.** (*or* **per ann.**) per annum (Latin: yearly)

**P/E ratio** price–earnings ratio

**perc.** *Music* percussion

**per con** *Book-keeping* per contra (Latin: on the other side)

**perd.** *Music* perdendosi (Italian: dying away)

**perf.** perfect • perfection • perforated • perforation • performed (by) • performance

**peri.** (*or* **perig.**) perigee

**PERK** (pɜːk) perchloreth(yl)ene (solvent)

**PERME** Propellants, Explosives, and Rocket Motor Establishment

**perp.** perpendicular • perpetual

**per pro.** per procurationem (*see under* pp)

**pers.** person • personal(ly) • (*or* **persp.**) perspective

**Pers.** Persia(n)

**pert.** pertaining

**PERT** (pɜːt) *Computing, Management* project (*or* programme, performance) evaluation and review technique

**Peruv.** Peruvian

**PES** *Chem.* photoelectron spectroscopy • *Chem.* potential-energy surface • *Computing* programmable electronic system

**PESA** *Physics* particle elastic scattering analysis

**PESC** Public Expenditure Survey Committee

**Pesh.** Peshawar (Pakistan)

**PEST** (pɛst) Political, Environmental, Social, and Technological (framework for analysing these aspects of a business environment) • Pressure for Economic and Social Toryism (left-wing Conservative group)

**pet.** petroleum • petrological • petrologist • petrology

**Pet.** *Bible* Peter • Peterhouse (Cambridge college) • (Gaius) Petronius (1st-century Roman satirist)

**PET** *Chem.* polyeth(yl)ene terephthalate (plastic used in food packaging) • (pɛt) *Med.* positron-emission tomography (as in **PET scan**) • *Taxation* potentially exempt transfer

**PETA** *Chem.* pentaerythritol triacrylate

**Pet.E** (USA) Petroleum Engineer

**petn** petition

**PETN** pentaerythritol tetranitrate (explosive)

**PETP** polyethylene (*or* polyethene) terephthalate (polyester)

**petr.** petrification • petrify • petrology

**PETRAS** ('petras) Polytechnic Educational Technology Resources Advisory Service

**Petriburg.** Petriburgensis (Latin: (Bishop) of Peterborough)

**petro.** petrochemical

**petrog.** petrography

**petrol.** petrology

**PETS** *Computing* posting and enquiry terminal system

**p.ex.** par exemple (French: for example; e.g.)

**PEX** *indicating* a discounted airline fare (probably a back formation from APEX, advance-purchase excursion)

**pf** pfennig (German currency) · *Music* piano (instrument; from *pianoforte*)

**pf.** perfect · *Finance* preferred (stock) · proof

**p.f.** (ital.) *Music* piano e forte (Italian; soft and then loud) · (ital.) *Music* più forte (Italian; louder) · pneumatic float · pro forma (invoice)

**pF** *Physics, symbol for* picofarad(s)

**PF** *British vehicle registration for* Guildford · panchromatic film · Patriotic Front · phenol–formaldehyde (as in **PF resin**) · *Building trades* plain face · *Physics* poloidal field · *Physical chem.* polycrystalline film · power factor · Procurator-Fiscal · *Finance* public funding · pulverized fuel

**PFA** (USA) Private Fliers' Association · Professional Footballers' Association · pulverized fuel ash

**P factor** *Psychol.* preservation factor

**PFB** *Building trades* preformed beams · *Chemical engineering* pressurized fluidized bed

**PFBC** *Chemical engineering* pressurized fluidized-bed combustion (*or* combustor)

**PFBG** *Chemical engineering* pressurized fluidized-bed gasification (*or* gasifier)

**PFBR** *Nuclear engineering* prototype fast breeder reactor

**pfc** passed flying college (in the RAF)

**PFC** *Chem.* perfluorocarbon · polychlorinated fluorocarbon (synthetic resin) · *Colloquial* (USA) poor foolish (*or* forlorn) civilian · (*or* **Pfc**) *Military* (USA) Private first class

**pfce** performance

**pfd** *Finance* preferred

**Pfd** Pfund (German: pound)

**PFD** personal flotation device · position-fixing device

**pfd sp.** preferred spelling

**PFF** pathfinder force

**pfg** pfennig (German currency)

**PFGE** *Biochem.* pulsed-field gel electrophoresis

**PFLO** Popular Front for the Liberation of Oman

**PFLP** Popular Front for the Liberation of Palestine

**PFM** *Telecom.* pulse-frequency modulation

**PFP** personal financial planning · (South Africa) Progressive Federal Party

**PFR** *Nuclear engineering* prototype fast reactor

**PFRT** preliminary flight rating test

**PFSA** pour faire ses adieux (French: to say goodbye)

**PFT** *Med.* pulmonary function test

**pft acct** *Music* piano(forte) accompaniment

**PFV** pour faire visite (French: to make a call)

**pfx** prefix

**pg.** page

**p.g.** pay group · paying guest · persona grata (Latin: acceptable person) · proof gallon (of alcohol) · proving ground

**Pg** *Geology* Palaeogene

**Pg.** Portugal · Portuguese

**PG** *British vehicle registration for* Guildford · *Films* parental guidance (certification) · *Freemasonry* Past Grand · paying guest · postgraduate · Preacher General · *Colloquial* (USA) pregnant · prisonnier de guerre (French: prisoner of war) · Procurator-General · *Pharmacol.* prostaglandin (as in **PGE₁**, etc.) · *Chem.* pyrolytic graphite

**PGA** *Biochem., Botany* phosphoglyceric acid · *Electronics* pin grid array · Professional Golfers' Association · *Computing* programmable gate array · *Biochem.* pteroylglutamic acid (folic acid)

**PGAL** *Biochem.* phosphoglyceraldehyde

**p.g.c.** *Navigation* per gyrocompass

**PGCE** Postgraduate Certificate of Education

**PG Cert** Postgraduate Certificate

**PGD** *Freemasonry* Past Grand Deacon

**PG Dip** Postgraduate Diploma

**PgDn** page down (on a keyboard)

**PGDRS** psychogeriatric dependency rating scale

**PGF** *Med.* polypeptide growth factor

**PGJD** *Freemasonry* Past Grand Junior Deacon

**PGL** *Med.* persistent generalized lymphadenopathy (a stage of Aids) · *Freemasonry* Provincial Grand Lodge

**PGM** *Freemasonry* Past Grand Master · precision-guided munition

**PGR** *Films* (Australia) parental guidance recommended (certification) · population growth rate · *Psychol.* psychogalvanic response

**PGSD** *Freemasonry* Past Grand Senior Deacon

**p.g.t.** per gross ton

**PgUp** page up (on a keyboard)

**ph** *Optics, symbol for* phot(s)

**ph.** phase

**p.h.** *Engineering* precipitation hardening

**pH** *Chem.* potential of hydrogen ions (measure of acidity or alkalinity)

**Ph** *Geology* Phanerozoic · *Chem., symbol for* phenyl group (in formulae) · (*or* **Ph.**) Philosophy (in degrees)

**PH** *British vehicle registration for* Guildford · *international civil aircraft marking for* Netherlands · *postcode for* Perth · petroleum hydrocarbon · *British fishing port registration for* Plymouth · *airline flight code for* Polynesian Airlines · previous (medical) history · public health · public house (on maps) · *Med.* pulmonary hypertension · (USA) Purple Heart (military decoration)

**PHA** *Immunol.* phytohaemagglutinin · Public Health Act · (USA) Public Housing Administration · (USA) public housing authority · *Physics* pulse-height analyser (*or* analysis)

**PHAB** (fæb) Physically Handicapped and Able-Bodied (a charity)

**phal.** phalanx

**phar.** pharmaceutical · pharmacist · (*or* **Phar.**) pharmacopoeia · pharmacy

**PharB** (*or* **PharmB**) Bachelor of Pharmacy (Latin *Pharmaciae Baccalaureus*)

**PharD** (*or* **PharmD**) Doctor of Pharmacy (Latin *Pharmaciae Doctor*)

**pharm.** pharmaceutical · pharmacist · pharmacology · (*or* **Pharm.**) pharmacopoeia · pharmacy

**PharM** (*or* **PharmM**) Master of Pharmacy (Latin *Pharmaciae Magister*)

**pharmacol.** pharmacology

**pharm. chem.** pharmaceutical chemistry

**PhB** Bachelor of Philosophy (Latin *Philosophiae Baccalaureus*)

**ph. brz.** phosphor bronze

**PHC** Pharmaceutical Chemist · primary health care

**PhD** Doctor of Philosophy (Latin *Philosophiae Doctor*)

**PHD** Doctor of Public Health

**PhDEd** Doctor of Philosophy in Education

**Phe** (*or* **phe**) *Biochem.* phenylalanine · *Astronomy* Phoenix

**PHE** Public Health Engineer

**phen** *Chem.* 1,10-phenanthroline (used in formulae)

**PhG** (USA) Graduate in Pharmacy

**PHI** permanent health insurance · Public Health Inspector

**PHIBLANT** ('fiblænt) *US Navy* Amphibious Forces, Atlantic

**PHIBPAC** ('fib,pæk) *US Navy* Amphibious Forces, Pacific

**PHIGS** (figs) *Computing* programmers' hierarchical interactive graphics standard

**phil.** philological · philology · philosopher · philosophical · philosophy

**Phil.** (*or* **Phila.**) Philadelphia · Philharmonic · *Bible* Philippians · Philippines

**Philem.** *Bible* Philemon

**Phil. I.** (*or* **Phil. Is.**) Philippine Islands

**philol.** philological · philology

**philos.** philosopher · philosophical · philosophy

**Phil. Soc.** Philharmonic Society

**Phil. Trans.** (ital.) Philosophical Transactions of the Royal Society of London

**PhL** Licentiate in (*or* of) Philosophy

**PHLS** Public Health Laboratory Service

**PhM** Master of Philosophy (Latin *Philosophiae Magister*)

**PhmB** Bachelor of Pharmacy

**PHN** Public Health Nurse

**Phoen.** Phoenician

**phon.** (*or* **phonet.**) phonetics · (*or* **phonol.**) phonology

**phot.** (*or* **photog.**) photograph(ic) · photographer · photography

**photom.** photometrical · photometry

**p.h.p.** pounds per horsepower · pump horsepower

**phr.** phrase · phraseology

**PHR** *Engineering* power-to-heat ratio

**phren.** (*or* **phrenol.**) phrenological · phrenology

**PHS** (USA) Public Health Service

**PHTS** (USA) Psychiatric Home Treatment Service

**PHWR** *Nuclear engineering* pressurized heavy-water reactor

**phys.** physical(ly) · physician · physicist · physics · physiological · physiology

**phys. ed.** physical education

**physiog.** physiography

**physiol.** physiological · physiologist · physiology

**phys. sc.** physical science

285

**p.i.** *Insurance* professional indemnity (policy)

**PI** *Irish vehicle registration for* Cork • *Med.* parainfluenza virus • Pasteur Institute • *Maths.* path integral • *Law* (USA) personal injury • petrol-injected • Pharmacopoeia Internationalis (Latin: International Pharmacopoeia) • Philippine Islands • photographic interpretation (*or* interpreter) • *Colloquial* (USA) pimp • (USA) principal investigator • private investigator • *Computing* programmed instruction

**PIA** Pakistan International Airlines Corporation • *Computing* peripheral interface adaptor

**piang.** *Music* piangendo (Italian: plaintive)

**pianiss.** *Music* pianissimo (Italian: very soft)

**PIARC** Permanent International Association of Road Congresses

**PIAT** *Military* projector infantry anti-tank (portable weapon)

**PIB** Petroleum Information Bureau • *Chem.* polyisobutylene • Prices and Incomes Board (superseded by NBPI)

**PIBOR** ('piːbɔː) *Finance* Paris Inter-Bank Offered Rate

**pic.** *Music* piccolo • (*or* **pict.**) pictorial

**Pic** *Astronomy* Pictor

**PIC** product of incomplete combustion • *Computing* programmable interrupt controller

**PID** pelvic inflammatory disease • *Computing* personal identification device • prolapsed intervertebral disc (slipped disc)

**PIDE** (Portugal) Polícia Internacional e de Defesa do Estado (International Police for the Defence of the State; former state security system)

**PIDS** (pɪdz) *Med.* primary immune deficiency syndrome

**PIE** *Physics* positive-ion emission • Proto-Indo-European (language)

**PIGE** *Physics* proton-induced gamma-ray emission

**pigmt** pigment

**pigmtn** pigmentation

**PIH** pregnancy-induced hypertension

**PIK** payment in kind

**pil.** pilula (Latin: pill; in prescriptions)

**PIL** payment in lieu

**PILL** (pɪl) *Computing* programmed instruction language learning

**PILOT** ('paɪlət) *Computing* programmed inquiry, learning, or teaching

**PIM** *Computing* personal information manager • *Telecom.* pulse-interval modulation

**PIMS** profit impact of market strategy

**p-i-n** *Electronics* p-type, intrinsic, n-type (semiconductor)

**PIN** (pɪn) personal identification number (used, with cash or credit card, to access computer-based bank accounts, etc.)

**P-in-C** Priest-in-Charge

**Pind.** Pindar (518–438 BC, Greek lyric poet)

**PINS** (pɪnz) (USA) person in need of supervision

**pinx.** pinxit (Latin: (he *or* she) painted it)

**PIO** *Computing* parallel input/output • photographic interpretation officer • *Military* (USA) public information office (*or* officer)

**PIP** (Peru) Policía de Investigiones del Peru Federales (Spanish: Peruvian Federal Investigation Police; Peruvian equivalent of the FBI)

**PIPO** *Computing* parallel in, parallel out

**PIPPY** (*or* **Pippy**) ('pɪpɪ) *Colloquial* person inheriting parent's property

**PIRA** Paper Industries Research Association

**Pis.** *Astrology* Pisces

**PISO** *Computing* parallel in, serial out

**PITCOM** ('pɪtkɒm) Parliamentary Information Technology Committee

**PIXE** ('pɪksɪ) *Physics* particle-induced X-ray emission

**pixel** ('pɪksəl) *Computing* picture element

**pizz.** *Music* pizzicato (Italian: pinched *or* plucked)

**p.j.** physical jerks • (*or* **p-j**) *Colloquial* pyjama

**PJ** *British vehicle registration for* Guildford • *international civil aircraft marking for* Netherlands Antilles • *Physics, symbol for* petajoule(s) • Presiding Judge • Probate Judge • *Colloquial* pyjama

**pk** pack • package • park • peak • peck (unit)

**pK** *Chem.* potential of $K$ (symbol for the dissociation constant; a measure of the strength of acids)

**PK** *British vehicle registration for* Guildford • *international civil aircraft marking* *for* Indonesia and West Irian • *international vehicle registration for* Pakistan • *airline flight code for* Pakistan International Airlines • personal knowledge • *Immunol.* Prausnitz-Kustner (as in **PK test**) • psychokinesis

**PKD** polycystic kidney disease

**pkg.** (*or* **pkge**) package • packing

**PKI** Partai Komunis Indonésia (Indonesian Communist Party)

**PKP** Polskie Koleje Panstwowe (Polish State Railways)

**pkt** packet • pocket

**PKU** *Med.* phenylketonuria

**pkwy** (USA) parkway

**pl.** place • plate • platoon • plural • pole (measure)

**Pl.** Place (in street names) • Plate(s) (in books, etc.) • (Germany) Platz (in street names)

**PL** *British vehicle registration for* Guildford • (*or* **P/L**) *Marine insurance* partial loss • *Insurance* passenger liability • patrol leader (in the Scouting movement) • Paymaster Lieutenant • *British fishing port registration for* Peel • Pharmacopoeia Londiniensis (Latin: Pharmacopoeia of London) • Plimsoll line (on a ship) • *postcode for* Plymouth • Poet Laureate • *international vehicle registration for* Poland • position line • Primrose League • (*or* **P/L**) *Law* product liability • product licence (on labels of medicinal products) • programmed learning • *Computing* programming language (as in **PL/I**, **PL/M**, etc.) • public law • public library

**P-L** *Astronomy* period–luminosity (as in **P-L relation**)

**PL/I** (*or* **PL/1**) *Computing* Programming Language I

**p.l.a.** passengers' luggage in advance

**Pla.** Plaza

**PLA** (China) People's Liberation Army • Port of London Authority • *Computing, Electronics* programmed (*or* programmable) logic array

**plan.** planet • planetarium

**plas.** plaster • plastic

**plat.** plateau • (*or* **platf.**) platform • platinum • platonic • platoon

**PLATO** (*or* **Plato**) ('pleɪtəʊ) *Computing* programmed logic for automatic teaching operation

**Plaut.** (Titus Maccius) Plautus (*c.* 254–184 BC, Roman dramatist)

**plc** public limited company (following the name of a company)

**PLC** Poor Law Commissioners • *Marketing* product life cycle • *Computing* programmable logic controller • public limited company (following the name of a company)

**plcy** policy

**pld** payload

**PLD** potentially lethal damage • *Computing* programmable logic device

**Ple** *Geology* Pleistocene

**Plen.** Plenipotentiary

**plf** (*or* **plff**) plaintiff

**PLG** private/light goods (vehicle)

**Pli** *Geology* Pliocene

**PLI** Partito Liberale Italiano (Italian Liberal Party) • President of the Landscape Institute

**PLM** Paris–Lyons–Mediterranean (Railway) • *Telecom.* pulse-length modulation

**PL/M** *Computing* Programming Language for Microcomputers

**plmb.** plumber • plumbing

**plng** planning

**PLO** Palestine Liberation Organization

**PLP** Parliamentary Labour Party • (Bermuda) Progressive Labour Party • (Bahamas) Progressive Liberal Party

**PLR** public lending right

**Pls** Plates (in books, etc.)

**PLS** *Statistics* partial least-squares

**Pl Sgt** Platoon Sergeant

**PLSS** (plɪs) *Astronautics* personal (*or* portable) life-support system

**plstr** plasterer

**plt** pilot

**PLT** Princeton Large Torus (experimental fusion reactor)

**pltc.** political

**pltf** plaintiff

**plu.** plural

**PLU** *Colloquial* people like us

**Pluna** (*or* **PLUNA**) ('pluːnə) Primeras Líneas Uruguayas de Navegación Aérea (Uruguayan airline)

**plup.** (*or* **plupf.**) pluperfect

**plur.** plural • plurality

**Pluto** (*or* **PLUTO**) ('pluːtəʊ) pipe line under the ocean (conveying fuel to Allied forces, World War II)

**Ply.** Plymouth

**plywd** plywood

**PL/Z** *Computing* Programming Language Zilog

**pm.** premium

**p.m.** permanent magnet · post meridiem (Latin: after noon) · postmortem (examination) · (*or* **pm**) premolar (tooth)

**Pm** *Chem., symbol for* promethium

**PM** *British vehicle registration for* Guildford · Pacific mail · parachute mine · *Music* particular (*or* peculiar, proper) metre · Past Master (of a fraternity) · Paymaster · *Physics* perturbation method · *Telecom.* phase modulation · piae memoriae (Latin: of pious memory) · Pipe Major · Police Magistrate · polícia militar (Portuguese: military police) · polizia militare (Italian: military police) · Pope and Martyr · Postmaster · post meridiem (*see under* p.m.) · postmortem (examination) · powder metallurgy · preventive (*or* predictive) maintenance (esp. of computers) · Prime Minister · product manager · *Military* Provost Marshal

**PMA** Pakistan Medical Association · *Dentistry* papillary, marginal, attached (gingivitis; in **PMA index**) · paramethoxyamphetamine (hallucinogenic drug) · personal military assistant · *Chem.* phenylmercuric acetate · *Chem.* polymethyl acrylate (synthetic polymer) · (USA) Purchasing Management Association

**PMAF** (USA) Pharmaceutical Manufacturers' Association Foundation

**PM & ATA** Paint Manufacturers' and Allied Trades Association

**PM&R** physical medicine and rehabilitation

**PMB** Potato Marketing Board

**PMBX** *Telephony* private manual branch exchange

**PMC** Personnel Management Centre · *Building trades* plaster-moulded cornice

**PMD** (USA) Program for Management Development

**PME** *Electronics* protective multiple earthing

**PM-ECM** *Electrical engineering* permanent-magnet electronically commutated motor

**PMF** probable maximum flood · *Physics* pulsating magnetic field

**PMG** (ital.) Pall Mall Gazette · Paymaster General · *Electrical engineering* permanent-magnet generator · Postmaster General · *Military* Provost Marshal General

**p.m.h.** per man-hour

**PMH** previous medical history

**pmk** postmark

**PML** Prime Minister's list · *Insurance* probable maximum loss

**PMM** platinum-metal minerals · *Telecom.* pulse-mode multiplex

**PMMA** polymethylmethacrylate (synthetic resin)

**PMN** *Med.* polymorphonuclear (leucocyte *or* neutrophil)

**PMO** Principal Medical Officer

**pmr** paymaster

**PMR** Pacific missile range

**PMRAFNS** Princess Mary's Royal Air Force Nursing Service

**PMS** *Printing* Pantone Matching System · *Med.* pregnant mare's serum · *Med.* premenstrual syndrome · President of the Miniature Society · *Computing* processor-memory-switch (notation) · project management system

**PMSF** *Chem.* phenylmethylsulphonyl fluoride

**PMSG** *Med.* pregnant mare's serum gonadotrophin

**pmt** payment

**PMT** *Photog.* photomechanical transfer · *Med.* premenstrual tension · project management team

**PMV** predicted mean vote

**PMX** *Telephony* private manual exchange

**pn** *Chem.* propylenediamine (used in formulae) · (*or* **p-n**) *Electronics* p-type n-type semiconductor (as in **pn junction**)

**p.n.** percussion (*or* percussive) note · please note · *Commerce* promissory note · *Physics* proton number

**PN** *British vehicle registration for* Brighton · Pakistan Navy · *Med.* parenteral nutrition · *Engineering* performance number · *Astronomy* planetary nebula · *Med.* postnatal · *Physics* post-Newtonian · *British fishing port registration for* Preston · *Commerce* promissory note · *Computing* pseudonoise (as in **PN sequence**) · psychoneurotic

**P/N** part number · *Commerce* promissory note

**Pna** Panama

**PNA** Pakistan National Alliance · paranitroaniline (dye) · *Chem.* polynuclear aromatic (compound) · Psychiatric Nurses Association

**PNAA** *Physics* prompt-neutron activation analysis

**PNB** Philippine National Bank

**PNC** Palestinian National Council • *Physics* parity nonconserving • (Guyana) People's National Congress

**PND** *Med.* postnatal depression

**PNdB** *symbol for* perceived noise decibel(s)

**pndg** pending

**pneu.** (*or* **pneum.**) pneumatic

**PNEU** Parents' National Educational Union

**p.n.g.** persona non grata

**PNG** Papua New Guinea (abbrev. *or* IVR)

**PNI** *Med.* psychoneuroimmunology

**pnl** panel

**PNL** Pacific Northwest Laboratory • *Med.* polymorphonuclear leucocyte

**PNM** (Trinidad and Tobago) People's National Movement

**PNO** Principal Nursing Officer

**pnp** (*or* **p-n-p**) *Electronics* p-type n-type p-type semiconductor (as in **pnp transistor**)

**PNP** (Puerto Rico) Partido Nuevo Progresista (New Progressive Party) • (Jamaica) People's National Party

**pnr** pioneer

**p.n.r.** prior notice required

**PNR** *Physics* prompt nuclear reaction

**PNS** *Med.* parasympathetic nervous system

**PNSB** *Microbiol.* purple nonsulphur bacteria

**Pnt.** (USA) Pentagon

**PNTO** Principal Naval Transport Officer

**pntr** painter

**PNV** (Spain) Partido Nacional Vasco (Basque Nationalist Party)

**pnxt** pinxit (Latin: (he *or* she) painted it)

**PNYA** Port of New York Authority

**Pnz.** Penzance

**p.o.** part of • *Med.* per os (Latin: by mouth; in prescriptions) • postal order • power oscillator • previous order(s) • *Baseball* putout(s)

**Po** *Chem., symbol for* polonium

**PO** parcels office • parole officer • par ordre (French: by order) • Passport Office • Patent Office • personnel officer • petty officer • Philharmonic Orchestra • pilot officer • Portsmouth (postcode *or* British vehicle registration) • postal order • Post Office • power-operated • *Chem.* propylene oxide • Province of Ontario • public

office(r) • Pyrénées-Orientales (department of France)

**POA** *Engineering* post-oxidation annealing • primary optical area (in graphic design) • Prison Officers' Association (trade union)

**POAC** Post Office Advisory Council

**POB** Post Office Box

**POC** *Chem.* particulate organic carbon • (*or* **p.o.c.**) port of call • *Chem.* product of combustion

**POD** pay on death • pay(ment) on delivery • (ital.) Pocket Oxford Dictionary • port of debarkation • (USA) Post Office Department

**POE** port of embarkation • port of entry

**POED** Post Office Engineering Department

**poet.** poetic(al) • poetry

**POETS day** ('pəʊɪtz) *Colloquial, indicating* Friday (piss off early tomorrow's Saturday)

**POEU** Post Office Engineers Union

**P. of W.** Prince of Wales

**POGO** ('pəʊgəʊ) Polar Orbiting Geophysical Observatory

**poi.** poison(ous)

**pol.** polar • polarize • police • political • politician • politics

**Pol.** Poland • Polish

**POL** Patent Office Library • petroleum, oil, and lubricants • *Computing* problem-oriented language

**pol. ad.** political adviser

**pol. econ.** political economy

**pol. ind.** pollen index

**Polis** ('pɒlɪs) Parliamentary On-Line Information Service

**polit.** political • politics

**poll.** pollution

**pol. sci.** political science

**Poly.** (*or* **Polyn.**) Polynesia(n)

**Polyb.** Polybius (*c.* 200–c. 120 BC, Greek historian)

**POM** particulate organic matter • prescription-only medicine (*or* medication)

**POMEF** Political Office Middle East Force

**Ponsi** ('pɒnsɪ) *Military slang* person of no strategical importance

**pont. br.** pontoon bridge

**Ponti** ('pɒntɪ) *Military slang* person of no tactical importance

**POO** Post Office order

**POOF** *Computing* peripheral on-line oriented function

**PPH** (USA) paid personal holidays •
*Med.* post-partum haemorrhage

**p.p.i.** parcel post insured

**PP₁** *Biochem., symbol for* pyrophosphate

**PPI** (USA) patient package insert
(instructions included with a prescription) • *Radar* plan-position indicator •
*Insurance* policy proof of interest •
*Economics* producer price index

**PPInstHE** Past President of the Institute of Highway Engineers

**PPIStructE** Past President of the
Institution of Structural Engineers

**PPITB** Printing and Publishing Industry Training Board

**PPK** Polizei Pistole Kriminal (German:
police criminal pistol)

**PPL** Phonographic Performance
Limited • private pilot's licence

**pple** participle

**PPLO** *Microbiol.* pleuropneumonia-like
organism(s)

**ppm** pages per minute • parts per
million • pulse per minute

**PPM** *Electronics* peak programme
meter • *Telecom.* pulse-position modulation

**PPMA** Produce Packaging and Marketing Association

**PPN** *Computing* public packet network

**PPO** (USA) *Med.* preferred-provider
organization

**ppp** (ital.) *Music* pianississimo (Italian;
as quietly as possible)

**PPP** Pakistan's People's Party •
*Biochem.* pentose phosphate pathway •
(Gambia, Guyana) People's Progressive
Party • personal pension plan • private
patients plan • psychology, philosophy,
and physiology (course at Oxford
University) • *Economics* purchasing
power parity

**PPPS** (*or* **ppps**) post post postscriptum (Latin: third postscript)

**ppr** paper • (*or* **p.pr.**) present participle • proper

**PPR** printed paper rate (of postage)

**PPRA** Past President of the Royal
Academy

**PPRBA** Past President of the Royal
Society of British Artists

**PPRBS** Past President of the Royal
Society of British Sculptors

**PPRE** Past President of the Royal Society of Painter-Etchers and Engravers

**p.pro.** per procurationem (*see under* pp)

**PPROI** Past President of the Royal
Institute of Oil Painters

**PPRTPI** Past President of the Royal
Town Planning Institute

**PPS** Parliamentary Private Secretary •
*Med.* pelvic pain syndrome • *Biochem.*
pentose phosphate shunt • (*or* **pps**)
post postscriptum (Latin: further postscript) • (Australia) prescribed
payments system • Principal Private
Secretary • (ital.) Proceedings of the
Prehistoric Society

**PPSIAD** Past President of the Society
of Industrial Artists and Designers

**ppt.** *Chem.* precipitate

**PPT** Parti Progressiste Tchadien (Chad
Progressive Party) • *Electrical engineering*
peak power transfer

**PPTA** (New Zealand) Post-primary
Teachers Association

**pptd** *Chem.* precipitated

**pptg** *Chem.* precipitating

**pptn** *Chem.* precipitation

**ppty** property

**PPU** Peace Pledge Union • Primary
Producers' Union

**pq** previous (*or* preceding) question

**PQ** parliamentary question • *Politics*
(Canada) Parti Québecois (French:
Quebec Party) • personality quotient •
Province of Quebec

**pr** painter • pair • paper • per • power

**pr.** prayer • *Finance* (USA) preferred
(stock) • present • pressure • price •
print(ed) • printer • printing • pronoun •
proper • prove • provincial

**p.r.** parcel receipt • *Med.* per rectum
(Latin: by the rectum)

**Pr** (ital.) *Physics, symbol for* Prandtl
number • *Chem., symbol for* praseodym-
ium • *Chem., symbol for* propyl group (in
formulae)

**Pr.** Praça (Portuguese: square; in place
names) • *Finance* (USA) preferred
(stock) • Priest • Prince • Protestant •
Provençal

**PR** *British vehicle registration for*
Bournemouth • parliamentary report •
*Med.* partial remission • partial
response • (Chile) Partido Radical
(Radical Party) • (France) Parti
Républicain (Republican Party) •
*Computing* pattern recognition • (*or*
**P/R**) payroll • percentile rank • perfor-
mance ratio • *Law* personal representa-
tive • *airline flight code for* Philippine
Airlines • photographic reconnaissance •
Pipe Rolls (public records, 1130–

1832) • plotting and radar • Populus Romanus (Latin: the Roman people) • postal regulations • preliminary report • Pre-Raphaelite • press release • press representative • *postcode for* Preston • *Boxing* prize ring • production rate • profit rate • progress report • project report • proportional representation • public relations • Puerto Rican • Puerto Rico • purchase request

**PRA** *Med.* plasma renin activity • President of the Royal Academy • probabilistic risk analysis (*or* assessment) • (USA) Public Roads Administration

**prag.** pragmatic • pragmatism

**PRB** People's Republic of Bulgaria • Pre-Raphaelite Brotherhood

**PRBS** President of the Royal Society of British Sculptors

**PRC** People's Republic of China • *Med.* plasma renin concentration • (USA) Postal Rate Commission • post Romam conditam (Latin: after the foundation of Rome) • (USA) Price Regulation Committee

**PRCA** President of the Royal Cambrian Academy • Public Relations Consultants' Association

**prchst** parachutist

**prcht** parachute

**PRCP** President of the Royal College of Physicians

**prcs.** process

**PRCS** President of the Royal College of Surgeons

**PRE** Petroleum Refining Engineer • President of the Royal Society of Painter-Etchers and Engravers

**Preb.** Prebend(ary)

**prec.** preceding • precision

**Prec.** Precentor

**PRECIS** ('preɪsɪ) preserved context index system

**pred.** predicate • (*or* **predic.**) predicative

**pref.** preface • prefatory • preferably • preference • preferred • prefix

**Pref.** Prefect

**prehist.** prehistoric(al) • prehistory

**prej.** prejudice

**prelim.** preliminary

**prem.** premium

**pre-mRNA** *Biochem.* precursor messenger RNA

**PrEng.** (USA) Professional Engineer

**prep.** preparation • preparatory • preposition

**prepd** prepared

**prepg** preparing

**prepn** preparation

**PREPP** *Med.* Post-Registration Education and Practice Project (for establishing standards of nursing practice)

**pres.** present (time) • presentation • presidency • presidential • presumed • presumptive

**Pres.** (*or* **Presb.**) Presbyter(ian) • President

**press.** pressure

**PRESTO** ('prestəʊ) (USA) program reporting and evaluation system for total operation

**presv.** preservation • preserve

**pret.** *Grammar* preterite

**prev.** previous(ly)

**prf** proof

**PRF** Petroleum Research Fund • *Electronics* pulse repetition (*or* recurrence) frequency

**prfnl** professional

**prfr** proofreader

**PRHA** President of the Royal Hibernian Academy

**pri.** primate • primer • priority • private

**PRI** (Mexico) Partido Revolucionario Institucional (Institutional Revolutionary Party) • Partito Repubblicano Italiano (Italian Republican Party) • Plastics and Rubber Institute • President of the Royal Institute of Painters in Water Colours

**PRIA** President of the Royal Irish Academy

**PRIAS** President of the Royal Incorporation of Architects in Scotland

**PRIBA** President of the Royal Institute of British Architects

**PRII** Public Relations Institute of Ireland

**prim.** primary • primate • primer • primitive

**primip.** *Med.* primipara (woman who has borne one child)

**prin.** principal • principle

**Prin.** Principal • Principality

**print.** printing

**PRISA** Public Relations Institute of South Africa

**prism.** prismatic

**PRISM** ('prɪzəm) (USA) program reliability information system for management

**priv.** private • privative

**prm** premium

**PRM** personal radiation monitor

**p.r.n.** *Med.* pro re nata (Latin: as the situation demands; in prescriptions)

**pro.** procedure • proceed • procure • profession(al)

**Pro** (*or* **pro**) *Biochem.* proline

**Pro.** Provost

**Pr.O** Press Officer

**PRO** Public Record Office • public relations officer

**pro-am** ('prəu'æm) *Sport* professional–amateur

**prob.** probability • probable • probably • probate • problem

**prob. off.** probation officer

**proc.** procedure • proceedings • process

**Proc.** Proceedings • Proctor

**Proc. Roy. Soc.** (ital.) Proceedings of the Royal Society

**prod.** produce(d) • producer • product • production

**prof.** profession(al)

**Prof.** Professor

**Prof. Eng.** (USA) Professional Engineer

**prog.** prognosis • *Computing* program • programme • progress • progressive

**Prog.** Progressive (party, movement, etc.)

**PROI** President of the Royal Institute of Oil Painters

**proj.** project • projectile • projection • projector

**prol.** prologue

**PROLOG** (*or* **Prolog**) ('prəulɒg) *Computing* programming in logic (a programming language)

**prom.** promontory • promote(r) • promotion

**PROM** (prɒm) *Computing* programmable read-only memory

**pron.** pronominal • pronoun • pronounceable • pronounce(d) • pronouncement • pronouncing • pronunciation

**pron. a.** pronominal adjective

**PRONED** ('prəu,nɛd) Promotion of Non-Executive Directors

**pro. note** *Finance* promissory note

**pronunc.** pronunciation

**prop.** proper(ly) • property • proposition • proprietary • proprietor

**PROP** Preservation of the Rights of Prisoners

**propl** proportional

**propn** proportion

**propr** proprietor

**PRORM** Pay and Records Office, Royal Marines

**pros.** prosodical • prosody • *Advertising* prospectus rate

**PROS** preventive maintenance, repair, and operational services

**Pros. Atty** Prosecuting Attorney

**prost.** *Med.* prostate • prostitution

**Prot.** Protectorate • Protestant

**pro tem.** pro tempore (Latin: for the time being)

**prov.** proverb • (*or* **provb.**) proverbial(ly) • province • provincial • provisional

**Prov.** Provençal • Provence • *Bible* Proverbs • Province • Provost

**Prov. GM** *Freemasonry* Provincial Grand Master

**prox.** proximo (Latin: in (*or* of) the next (month))

**prox. acc.** proxime accessit (Latin: (he *or* she) came nearest; next in order of merit to the winner)

**prox. luc.** proxima luce (Latin: the day before)

**pr.p.** present participle

**PrP** *Biochem.* prion protein (constituent of scrapie agent)

**PRP** petrol refilling point • profit- (*or* performance-)related pay

**pr. pr.** praeter propter (Latin: about, nearly)

**PRR** *Electronics* pulse repetition rate

**prs** pairs

**PRs** *symbol for* Pakistan rupee (monetary unit)

**PRS** Performing Right Society Ltd • President of the Royal Society

**PRSA** President of the Royal Scottish Academy • Public Relations Society of America

**prsd** pressed

**PRSE** President of the Royal Society of Edinburgh

**PRSH** President of the Royal Society for the Promotion of Health

**Pr.ST** (USA) Prairie Standard Time

**PRSW** President of the Royal Scottish Water Colour Society

**PRT** (USA) personal rapid transit • petroleum revenue tax

**prtg** printing

**PRU** photographic reconnaissance unit(s) (in the RAF)

**PRUAA** President of the Royal Ulster Academy of Arts

**Prus.** Prussia(n)

**p.r.v.** pour rendre visite (French: to return a call)

**PRV** pressure-reducing valve

**PRWA** President of the Royal West of England Academy

**PRWS** President of the Royal Society of Painters in Water Colours

**ps** *Military* passed school of instruction (of officers) • *Physics, symbol for* picosecond(s) • postscript

**ps.** pieces • pseudonym

**p.s.** particle size • pull switch

**Ps** *Physics, symbol for* positronium

**Ps.** *Bible* (Book of) Psalms • Psalm

**PS** *British vehicle registration for* Aberdeen • paddle steamer • Parliamentary Secretary • (Portugal) Partido Socialista (Socialist Party) • (France) Parti Socialiste (Socialist Party) • passenger steamer • Pastel Society • penal servitude • Permanent Secretary • *Biochem.* phosphatidyl serine • *Botany* photosystem (in **PSI, PSII**) • *Linguistics* phrase structure • *Electronics* plasma switch • *Meteorol.* plus • Police Sergeant • *Chem.* polystyrene • postscript • power steering • press secretary • private secretary • Privy Seal • *Theatre* prompt side (i.e. the actor's left) • *Biochem.* protein synthesis • *Physics* proton synchrotron • Provost Sergeant • (Italy) Pubblica Sicurezza (police force) • (USA) public school • (Australia) public service (equivalent to the civil service)

**psa** *indicating* Graduate of RAF Staff College

**Psa.** *Bible* (Book of) Psalms • Psalm

**PsA** *Astronomy* Piscis Austrinus

**PSA** Passenger Shipping Association • Petty Sessions Area • *Physics* phase-shift analysis • Photographic Society of America • pleasant Sunday afternoon • Political Studies Association of the United Kingdom • President of the Society of Antiquaries • (Australia) Prices Surveillance Authority • probabilistic safety analysis (*or* assessment) • Property Services Agency • *Med.* prostatic specific antigen • (New Zealand) Public Service Association

**PSAB** Public Schools Appointments Bureau

**PSAC** (USA) President's Science Advisory Committee

**p's and q's** *Colloquial, indicating* manners (phonetic spelling of p(lea)se and (than)k you's)

**PSAT** (USA) Preliminary Scholastic Aptitude Test

**PSB** pistol, small-bore • (Japan) Postal Savings Bureau

**PSBA** Public School Bursars' Association

**PSBR** public sector borrowing requirement

**psc** *Military* passed staff college

**Psc** *Astronomy* Pisces

**PSC** (Belgium) Parti Social Chrétien (Francophone Christian Social Party) • *Meteorol.* polar stratospheric clouds • Professional Services Committee • (USA) Public Service Commission

**PSCD** patrol service central depot

**PSCM** *Meteorol.* progression, southerly, cyclonicity, and meridionality (in **PSCM index**)

**PSD** (Portugal) Partido Social Democrata (Social Democratic Party) • (Madagascar) Parti Social Démocrate (Social Democratic Party) • pay supply depot • *Law* Petty Sessional Divison • *Physics* position-sensitive detector • (USA) prevention of significant deterioration • *Physics* proportional scintillation detector

**PSDI** Partito Socialista Democratico Italiano (Italian Democratic Socialist Party)

**PSDR** public sector debt requirement

**PSE** Pacific Stock Exchange • pale soft exudate (in meat processing) • Pidgin Sign English • *Computing* programming (*or* project) support environment • psychological stress evaluator (lie detector)

**pseud.** pseudonym

**psf** (*or* **p.s.f.**) pounds per square foot

**PSF** *Image technol.* point spread function

**PSG** *Linguistics* phrase-structure grammar

**PSHFA** Public Servants Housing Finance Association

**psi** (*or* **p.s.i.**) pounds (*or* pound-force) per square inch

**PSI** Partito Socialista Italiano (Italian Socialist Party) • *Education* personalized system of instruction • Pharmaceutical Society of Ireland • Policy Studies Institute

**psia** pounds per square inch, absolute

**PSIAD** President of the Society of Industrial Artists and Designers

**psid** pounds per square inch, differential

**psig** pounds per square inch, gauge

**PSIS** Permanent Secretaries Committee on the Intelligence Services

**PSIUP** Partito Socialista Italiano di Unità Proletaria (Italian Socialist Party of Proletarian Unity)

**PSK** *Telecom.* phase shift keying

**PSL** Paymaster Sublieutenant • (USA) Primary Standards Laboratory • *Economics* private-sector liquidity • public-sector loan(s)

**PSL/PSA** *Computing* problem statement language/problem statement analyser

**psm** passed school of music (Certificate of the Royal Military School of Music)

**PSM** product sales manager

**PSMA** President of the Society of Marine Artists

**PSN** *Computing* packet-switching network • *Meteorol.* position • *Computing* public switched network

**PSNC** Pacific Steam Navigation Company

**PSO** personal staff officer • Principal Scientific Officer

**PSOE** (Spain) Partido Socialista Obrero Español (Spanish Workers Socialist Party)

**PSP** (Netherlands) Pacifistich Socialistische Partij (Pacifist Socialist Party) • *Med.* phenolsulphonphthalein (in **PSP test** for kidney function)

**PSR** *Physics* proton storage ring

**PSRO** (USA) Professional Standards Review Organization

**Pss** Psalms

**PSS** *Computing* Packet Switch Stream (PPN of British Telecom) • *Med.* physiological saline solution • (*or* **pss.**) postscripts • power-system stabilizer • Printing and Stationery Service • professional services section

**PSSC** Personal Social Services Council

**psso** *Knitting* pass slipped stitch over

**PST** (USA, Canada) Pacific Standard Time

**pstl** postal

**PSTN** public switched telephone network

**PSU** (Italy) Partito Socialista Unitario (Unitary Socialist Party) • police support unit • *Computing* power supply unit • process support unit

**p. surg.** plastic surgery

**PSV** public service vehicle

**PSW** *Computing* processor (*or* program) status word • psychiatric social worker

**psych.** psychic(al) • psychological • psychologist • psychology

**psychoanal.** psychoanalysis

**psychol.** psychological • psychologist • psychology

**pt** part • patient • payment • pint (abbrev. *or* symbol) • point (abbrev. *or* (in printing) symbol) • port

**pt.** *Grammar* preterite

**p.t.** part time • past tense • point of turn(ing) • primary target • pro tempore (Latin: for the time being)

**Pt** *Chem., symbol for* platinum • Point (in place names) • Port (in place names)

**PT** *international civil aircraft marking for* Brazil • *British vehicle registration for* Newcastle-upon-Tyne • (USA) Pacific Time • (USA) patrol torpedo (in **PT boat**) • *Insurance* perte totale (French: total loss) • *Physics* perturbation theory • *Physics* phase transition • physical therapy • physical training • physiotherapist • *British fishing port registration for* Port Talbot • postal telegraph • post town • preferential treatment • *Med.* previously treated • Public Trustee • pupil teacher • purchase tax

**Pta** *symbol for* peseta (Spanish monetary unit) • Pretoria

**PTA** Parent–Teacher Association • Passenger Transport Authority • *Med.* percutaneous transluminal angioplasty • Pet Traders' Association • *Med.* plasma thromboplastin antecedent • *Med.* post-traumatic amnesia • preferential trade area • Printing Trades Alliance • *Chem.* $p$-terephthalic acid

**ptbl.** portable • potable

**PT boat** (USA) patrol torpedo boat

**PTBT** partial test-ban treaty

**PTC** *Med.* percutaneous transhepatic cholangiography • *Diving* personnel transfer capsule • *Genetics* phenylthiocarbamide (referring to the inherited ability to taste it) • photographic type composition • *Med.* plasma thromboplastin component • primary training centre

**PTCA** *Med.* percutaneous transluminal coronary angioplasty

**ptd** painted • printed

**Pte** Plate (in books, etc.) • *Military* Private • (India, etc.) private limited company (after company name; equivalent to Ltd)

**PTE** Passenger Transport Executive • post-test examination

**pt ex.** (*or* **pt exch.**) part exchange

**PTFCE** *Chem.* polytrifluorochloroeth(yl)ene

**PTFE** polytetrafluoroeth(yl)ene

**ptg** printing

**Ptg** *Geology* Pleistogene

**Ptg.** Portugal • Portuguese

**PTH** *Biochem.* parathyroid hormone • (USA) public teaching hospital

**PTI** physical training instructor • Press Trust of India • *Computing* public tool interface

**PTM** *Telecom.* pulse-time modulation

**PTMA** phosphotungstomolybdic acid (used in manufacture of certain pigments)

**ptn** partition • portion

**PTN** *Colloquial* pay through the nose • public telephone network (of British Telecom) • public transportation network

**ptnr** partner

**PTO** (USA) Patent and Trademark Office • (*or* **pto**) please turn over • *Astronautics* power takeoff • public telecommunications operator • Public Trustee Office

**ptp** past participle

**pt/pt** point-to-point

**ptr** printer

**pts** parts • payments • pints • points • ports

**Pts.** Portsmouth

**PTS** Philatelic Traders' Society • pressurized thermal shock • printing technical school

**ptsc** *Military* passed technical staff college

**PTSD** *Med.* post-traumatic stress disorder

**pts/hr** parts per hour

**Ptsmth** Portsmouth

**PTT** *Med.* partial thromboplastin time • Postal, Telegraph, and Telephone Administration

**pt-tm.** part-time

**PTV** (USA) public television (noncommercial television)

**p.t.w.** per thousand words

**pty** party

**Pty** (Australia, South Africa, etc.) Proprietary (after a company name; equivalent to Ltd)

**p.u.** paid up

**Pu** *Chem., symbol for* plutonium

**PU** *British vehicle registration for* Chelmsford • *Med.* passed urine • pick-up • *airline flight code for* Pluna • *Chem.* polyurethane • *Computing* processing unit • public utility

**pub.** public • publican • publication • publish(ed) • publisher • publishing

**Pub.** *Advertising* publishers' announcement

**pubd** published

**pub. doc.** public document

**publ.** public • publican • publication • publicity • published • publisher • publishing

**pubn** publication

**pubr** publisher

**pub. wks** public works

**PUC** papers under consideration • pick-up car • (USA) Public Utilities Commission

**PUD** pick-up and delivery • (USA) planned unit development (a large condominium)

**pug.** pugilist

**PUHCA** (USA) Public Utility Holding Company Act

**pulv.** *Pharmacol.* pulvis (Latin: powder)

**p.u.m.s.** permanently unfit for military service

**pun.** punish(ment)

**punc.** punctuation

**Punj.** Punjab

**PUO** *Med.* pyrexia (fever) of unknown origin

**Pup** *Astronomy* Puppis

**PUP** People's United Party • (USA) Princeton University Press

**pur.** (*or* **purch.**) purchase(r) • purification • purify • (*or* **purp.**) purple • pursuit

**PURV** powered underwater research vehicle

**p.u.s.** permanently unfit for service

**PUS** Parliamentary Undersecretary • Permanent Undersecretary

**PUVA** ('puːvə) *Med.* psoralen ultraviolet A (treatment for psoriasis)

**PUWP** Polish United Workers' Party

**pv.** *Microbiol.* pathovar

**p.v.** *Med.* per vaginam (Latin: by the vagina)

**PV** *British vehicle registration for* Ipswich • *Physics* parity violation • patrol vessel • petite vitesse (French: goods *or* slow train) • *Sport* pole vault • positive vetting • power–voltage • pressure vessel • (*or* **P–V**) pressure–volume

**PVA** polyvinyl acetate (synthetic resin) • *Chem.* polyvinyl alcohol

**PVB** *Chem.* polyvinyl butyral

**p.v.c.** pigment volume concentration (in paint technology)

**PVC** polyvinyl chloride (synthetic resin)

**PVCH** *Chem.* polyvinylcyclohexane

**PVD** *Med.* peripheral vascular disease • physical vapour deposition

**PVDA** (*or* **PvdA**) (Netherlands) Partij van de Arbeid (Labour Party)

**PVDC** *Chem.* polyvinylidenechloride

**PVF** polyvinyl fluoride (synthetic resin)

**PVG** *Chem.* polyvinylene glycol

**PVO** Principal Veterinary Officer

**PVP** polyvinyl pyrrolidone (synthetic resin)

**PVS** *Med.* persistent vegetative state • post-Vietnam syndrome • *Med.* post-viral syndrome (myalgic encephalo-myelitis)

**PVSM** (India) Param Vishishc Seva Medal

**p.v.t.** par voie télégraphique (French: by telegraph)

**Pvt.** *Military* Private

**PVT** *Chem.* polyvinyltoluene • pressure, volume, temperature

**PVTCA** *Chem.* polyvinyltrichloro-acetate

**PVX** *Microbiol.* potato virus X

**PVY** *Microbiol.* potato virus Y

**p.w.** per week

**PW** *British vehicle registration for* Norwich • *British fishing port registration for* Padstow • *Physics* plane wave • policewoman • power windows (in vehicles) • prisoner of war • public works • *Electronics* pulse width

**PWA** *Med.* person with Aids • (USA) Public Works Administration (1933–43)

**PWC** post-war credits (after World War II)

**pwd** powered

**PWD** Public Works Department

**PWE** Political Welfare Executive

**PWLB** Public Works Loan Board

**PWM** *Telecom.* pulse-width modulation

**PWO** *Military* Prince of Wales's Own

**p.w.p.** price when perfect

**pwr** power

**PWR** *Nuclear engineering* pressurized-water reactor

**pwr sup.** power supply

**pwt** pennyweight

**px** Pedro Ximénez (grape; referring to sweet wines and sherries)

**PX** physical examination • please exchange • *British vehicle registration for* Portsmouth • (USA) Post Exchange (army or navy retail store) • *Telephony* private exchange

**pxt** pinxit (Latin: (he *or* she) painted it)

**py** *Chem.* pyridine (used in formulae)

**PY** *British vehicle registration for* Middles-brough • *international vehicle registration for* Paraguay

**pyo** (*or* **PYO**) pick your own (fruit, etc.)

**pyro.** (*or* **pyrotech.**) pyrotechnics

**Pyx** *Astronomy* Pyxis

**Pz** *Geology* Palaeozoic

**PZ** *British vehicle registration for* Belfast • *British fishing port registration for* Penzance • *international civil aircraft marking for* Surinam

**PZI** *Med.* protamine zinc insulin (diabetes treatment)

**PZS** President of the Zoological Society

**PZT** *Astronomy* photographic zenith tube

# Q

**q** (ital.) *Physics, symbol for* density of heat flow rate • (ital.) *Physics, symbol for* electric charge • (bold ital.; *or* $q_i$) *Maths., symbol for* a generalized coordinate • (ital.) *Chem., symbol for* partition function (individual entity) • *Physics, symbol for* quark • (ital.) *symbol for* quintal (100 kg) • (ital.) *Meteorol., symbol for* specific humidity • *Meteorol., symbol for* squall

**q.** quaere (Latin: inquire) • quaque (Latin: every) • quart • quarter • quarterly • quarto • quasi (Latin: almost) • quench • query • question • quick • quire

**Q** *Biochem.*, *symbol for* glutamine • (ital.) *Chem.*, *symbol for* partition function (whole system) • *Electronics* quality (in **Q factor**) • (ital.) *Electrical engineering*, *symbol for* quality factor • (ital.) *Physics*, *symbol for* quantity of electricity (i.e. electric charge) • (ital.) *Physics*, *symbol for* quantity of heat • (ital.) *Physics*, *symbol for* quantity of light • *Geology* Quaternary • *Chess*, *symbol for* queen • query (hence camouflaged or disguised, as in **Q-boat** (*or* **Q-ship**), **Q car**) • *symbol for* quetzal (Guatemalan monetary unit) • (ital.) *Electrical engineering*, *symbol for* reactive power • (ital.) *Chemical engineering*, *symbol for* throughput • *indicating* the highest level of security according to the Nuclear Regulatory Commission (as in **Q clearance**)

**Q.** (*or* **Q**) quantity • quarterly • Quartermaster • quarter-page (in advertisement placing) • Quarto (Shakespeare manuscript) • Quebec • Queen (*or* Queen's) • Queensland • question • *pseudonym of* (Sir Arthur Thomas) Quiller-Couch (1863–1944, British writer)

**q.a.** quick assembly

**QA** (*or* **Q/A**) qualification approval • quality assurance • quarters allowance

**QAB** *Church of England* Queen Anne's Bounty

**QADS** quality-assurance data system

**QAIMNS** Queen Alexandra's Imperial Military Nursing Service

**QAM** *Telecom.* quadrature amplitude modulation

**Q & A** question and answer

**Qantas** ('kwɒntəs) Queensland and Northern Territory Aerial Service (Australian national airline)

**QARANC** Queen Alexandra's Royal Army Nursing Corps

**QARNNS** Queen Alexandra's Royal Naval Nursing Service

**QAS** *Chem.* quaternary ammonium sulphanilamide

**QB** (*or* **q.b.**) *Football* (USA) quarterback • *Law* Queen's Bench • *Chess* queen's bishop

**Qbc** Quebec

**QBD** Queen's Bench Division

**QBI** *Slang* quite bloody impossible

**QBO** *Meteorol.* quasi-biennial oscillation

**QBP** *Chess* queen's bishop's pawn

**QC** *airline flight code for* Air Zaire • quality control • Quartermaster Corps • Queen's College • Queen's Counsel • *Law* quit claim

**QCD** *Physics* quantum chromodynamics

**QCE** quality-control engineering

**Q-Celtic** *Linguistics*, *indicating* one of two main groups of languages developed from Common Celtic. *See also* P-Celtic

**QC Is** Queen Charlotte Islands (Canada)

**QCM** *Physics* quark cluster (*or* confinement) model

**QCR** quality-control reliability

**QCT** quality-control technology • *Med.* quantitative computed tomography

**QCVSA** Queen's Commendation for Valuable Service in the Air

**q.d.** *Med.* quaque die (Latin: every day) • quasi dicat (Latin: as if one should say) • quasi dictum (Latin: as if said)

**QDE** *Physics* quantum detection efficiency

**QDRI** (USA) qualitative development requirement information

**q.d.s.** *Med.* quater in die sumendus (Latin: to be taken four times a day)

**q.e.** quod est (Latin: which is)

**QE** *Physics* quantum efficiency • quantum electronics

**QE2** (ital.) Queen Elizabeth II (passenger liner)

**QED** *Physics* quantum electrodynamics • quod erat demonstrandum (Latin: which was to be proved)

**QEF** quod erat faciendum (Latin: which was to be done)

**QEH** Queen Elizabeth Hall (London)

**QEI** quod erat inveniendum (Latin: which was to be discovered *or* found out)

**QEO** Queen Elizabeth's Own

**QER** (ital.) Quarterly Economic Review

**QF** *airline flight code for* Qantas Airways • *Electronics* quality factor • quick-firing

**QFD** *Physics* quantum flavourdynamics

**QFSM** Queen's Fire Service Medal for Distinguished Service

**QFT** *Physics* quantum field theory

**QG** Quartermaster-General • quartiere generale (Italian: headquarters) • quartier-général (French: headquarters)

**QGM** Queen's Gallantry Medal

**QGP** *Physics* quark-gluon plasma

**q.h.** *Med.* quaque hora (Latin: every hour)

**QHC** Queen's Honorary Chaplain

**QHDS** Queen's Honorary Dental Surgeon

**QHM** Queen's Harbour Master

**QHNS** Queen's Honorary Nursing Sister

**QHP** Queen's Honorary Physician

**QHS** Queen's Honorary Surgeon

**QI** quartz–iodine (in **QI lamp**)

**q.i.d.** *Med.* quater in die (Latin: four times a day)

**QIP** quiescat in pace (Latin: may (he *or* she) rest in peace)

**QISAM** *Computing* queued indexed sequential access method

**qk** quick

**QKt** *Chess* queen's knight

**QKtP** *Chess* queen's knight's pawn

**ql** quintal (100 kg)

**q.l.** *Med.* quantum libet (Latin: as much as you please; in prescriptions)

**QL** Queen's Lancers • *Computing* query language

**Qld** (*or* **QLD**) Queensland

**qlty** quality

**qly** quarterly

**qm.** quomodo (Latin: by what means)

**q.m.** *Med.* quaque mane (Latin: every morning; in prescriptions)

**QM** *Physics* quantum mechanics • *Physics* quark model • Quartermaster • Queen's Messenger

**QMAAC** Queen Mary's Army Auxiliary Corps

**QMC** Quartermaster Corps • Queen Mary College, London (now part of QMW)

**QMD** *Physical chem.* quantum molecular dynamics

**Q. Mess.** Queen's Messenger

**QMG** Quartermaster-General

**QMGF** Quartermaster-General to the Forces

**Qmr** Quartermaster

**QMR** qualitative material requirement

**QMS** *Physics* quadrupole mass spectrometry (*or* spectrometer) • Quartermaster Sergeant

**QMW** Queen Mary and Westfield College, London

**qn** question • quotation

**q.n.** quaque nocte (Latin: every night; in prescriptions)

**Qn** Queen

**QN** *Chess* queen's knight

**QNI** Queen's Nursing Institute

**QNP** *Chess* queen's knight's pawn

**QNS** quantity not sufficient

**qnt** quintet

**qnty** quantity

**QO** *Navy* qualified in ordnance • qualified officer

**QOCH** Queen's Own Cameron Highlanders

**QOOH** Queen's Own Oxfordshire Hussars

**Q(ops)** Quartering (operations)

**QOR** qualitative operational requirement

**q.p.** *Med.* quantum placet (*see* q.pl.)

**QP** qualification pay • *Chess* queen's pawn • *Computing* query processing

**QPC** Qatar Petroleum Company

**QPFC** Queen's Park Football Club (Scotland)

**q.pl.** *Med.* quantum placet (Latin: as much as seems good; in prescriptions)

**QPM** Queen's Police Medal

**QPR** Queen's Park Rangers (football club)

**qq.** questions

**Qq.** Quartos (Shakespeare manuscripts)

**qq. hor.** *Med.* quaque hora (Latin: every hour; in prescriptions)

**qq.v.** quae vide (Latin: which (words, items, etc.) see; textual cross reference)

**qr.** quarter • quarterly • quire

**QR** Quarterly Review • *Chess* queen's rook • *Marketing* quick response • *symbol for* riyal (monetary unit of Qatar)

**QRA** quick reaction alert (of military aircraft)

**QRIH** Queen's Royal Irish Hussars

**QRP** *Chess* queen's rook's pawn

**QRR** Queen's Royal Rifles

**qrs** quarters

**QRV** Qualified Valuer, Real Estate Institute of New South Wales

**q.s.** *Med.* quantum sufficit (Latin: as much as will suffice; in prescriptions) • quarter section (of land)

**QS** quadraphonic-stereophonic (of audio equipment) • quantity surveyor • quarantine station • quarter sessions • Queen's Scholar • *Building trades* quick sweep

**QSE** qualified scientist and engineer

**QSM** *Physics* quantum-statistical model • (New Zealand) Queen's Service Medal

**QSO** *Astronomy* quasistellar object (i.e. a quasar) • (New Zealand) Queen's Service Order

**QSS** *Astronomy* quasistellar source

**QSTOL** ('kjuː,stɒl) *Aeronautics* quiet short takeoff and landing

**QSTS** quadruple screw turbine ship

**qt** *symbol for* quart

**qt.** quantity • quartet

**q.t.** (*or* **QT**) *Colloquial* quiet (as in **on the q.t.**)

**qtly** quarterly

**qto** quarto

**QTOL** ('kjuː,tɒl) *Aeronautics* quiet takeoff and landing

**qtr** quarter

**qty** quantity

**qu.** quart • quarter • quarterly • queen • query • question

**QU** *airline flight code for* Uganda Airlines

**quad.** quadrant • quadraphonic • quadrilateral • quadruple • (*or* **quadr.**, **quadrupl.**) quadruplicate

**qual.** qualification • qualitative • quality

**qualgo** ('kwælgəʊ) quasi-autonomous local government organization

**qualn** qualification

**quango** ('kwæŋgəʊ) quasi-autonomous nongovernmental (*or* national government) organization

**quant.** quantitative • quantity

**quant. suff.** *Med.* quantum sufficit (*see under* q.s)

**quar.** (*or* **quart.**) quarter • quarterly

**quasar** ('kweɪzɑː) *Astronomy* quasistellar object

**quat.** *Med.* four (Latin *quattuor*, in prescriptions)

**QUB** Queen's University, Belfast

**Que.** Quebec

**ques.** question

**questn.** questionnaire

**quint.** quintuplicate

**QUIP** (kwɪp) *Computing* query interactive processor

**quor.** quorum

**quot.** quotation • quote

**quotid.** *Med.* quotidie (Latin: daily)

**q.v.** *Med.* quantum vis (Latin: as much as you wish) • quod vide (Latin: which (word, item, etc.) see; textual cross reference)

**QVR** Queen Victoria Rifles

**QWERTY** ('kwɜːtɪ) *indicating* a standard keyboard in English-speaking countries (from the first six of the upper row of keys on a typewriter)

**QWL** quality of work(ing) life

**qy** quay • query

**qz** quartz

**QZ** *airline flight code for* Zambia Airways

# R

**r** (ital.) *Electricity, symbol for* internal resistance • (ital.) *Maths., symbol for* a polar coordinate • (bold ital.) *Maths., Physics, symbol for* position vector • (ital.) *symbol for* radius • (bold ital.) *Maths., symbol for* radius vector • (ital.) *Ecology, symbol for* rate of increase (as in **r-strategist**) • *Music* ray (in tonic sol-fa) • *Biochem., symbol for* ribonucleoside (preceding the nucleoside symbol; as in **rA**, ribosyladenine)

**r.** radius • (USA) railroad • railway • rain • range • rare • ratio • *Commerce* received • recipe • *Printing* recto • red • replacing • reply • reserve • residence • resides • response • retired • right • rises • river • road • rod (unit of length) • rouble • *Cards* rubber • ruled • *Cricket, Baseball, etc.* run(s) • rupee

**R** *Biochem., symbol for* arginine • *Medieval Roman numeral for* eighty • (ital.) *Chem., symbol for* molar gas constant • *Chem., symbol for* a radical (in formulae, as in **ROH**) • *symbol for* radius • *British fishing port registration for* Ramsgate • *symbol for* rand (South African monetary unit) • *Maths., symbol for* ratio • *Physics, symbol for* Réaumur (temperature scale) • (ital.) *Chem.* rectus (as in **(R)-butan-2-ol**) • *Electrical engineering, symbol for* resistance • *Chem., symbol for* resonance effect • *Films* (Australia, USA) restricted (certification) • retarder (French: slow down; on a clock or watch regulator) • return (ticket *or* fare) • reverse (on selector mechanism of vehicle with automatic transmission) • *Physics, symbol for* roentgen • *Chess, symbol for* rook • *Microbiol.* rough (in **R-form** of a bacterial colony)

**R.** (*or* **R**) rabbi • *Politics* Radical • radius • (USA) railroad • railway • Rapido (Italian: express train) • Recht (German: law) • *Med.* recipe (Latin: take; in prescriptions) • recommendation • rector • red • redactor • Regiment • Regina (Latin: Queen) • registered • Regius • regular (clothing size) • *Navigation* relative • report • Republic • Republican • reserve • response (in Christian liturgy) • Respublica (Latin: Republic) • reward • Rex (Latin: King) • *Military* Rifles • right *or* (in the theatre) stage right • River • road • Roman • Romania(n) • Rome • rosary • rouble • route • Royal • Rue (French: street) • *Nautical* run (i.e. deserted)

**3** (*or* **three**) **Rs** reading, (w)riting, and (a)rithmetic

**ra.** radio

**Ra** *Chem., symbol for* radium • (ital.) *Physics, symbol for* Rayleigh number

**RA** *international vehicle registration for* Argentina • *British vehicle registration for* Nottingham • *Meteorol.* rain • Ramblers' Association • Rear-Admiral • reduction of area • *Soccer* Referees' Association • (USA) Regular Army • República Argentina (Spanish: Argentine Republic) • (USA) Resettlement Administration • *Med.* rheumatoid arthritis • *Astronomy* right ascension • Road Association • Royal Academy (*or* Academician) • Royal Artillery • *international civil aircraft marking for* Russia

**R/A** *Finance* refer to acceptor (on a bill of exchange) • return to author

**RAA** Rabbinical Alliance of America • Regional Arts Association • Royal Academy of Arts • Royal Artillery Association • Royal Australian Artillery

**RAAF** Royal Australian Air Force • Royal Auxiliary Air Force

**RAAFNS** Royal Australian Air Force Nursing Service

**RAAMC** Royal Australian Army Medical Corps

**RAANC** Royal Australian Army Nursing Corps

**Rab.** Rabat (Morocco)

**Rabb.** Rabbinate • Rabbinic(al)

**RABDF** Royal Association of British Dairy Farmers

**RABI** Royal Agricultural Benevolent Institution

**RAC** Railway Association of Canada • Regional Advisory Committee (of the TUC) • Regional Advisory Council • Royal Agricultural College • Royal Armoured Corps • Royal Automobile Club

**RACA** Royal Automobile Club of Australia

**RACE** (reɪs) rapid automatic checkout equipment • Research and Development in Advanced Communication Technologies for Europe

**RACGP** Royal Australian College of General Practitioners

**RAChD** Royal Army Chaplains' Department

**RACI** Royal Australian Chemical Institute

**RACO** Royal Australian College of Ophthalmologists

**RACOG** Royal Australian College of Obstetricians and Gynaecologists

**RACON** (*or* **racon**) ('reɪkɒn) radar beacon

**RACP** Royal Australasian College of Physicians

**RACS** Royal Arsenal Cooperative Society • Royal Australasian College of Surgeons

**rad** *Maths., symbol for* radian

**rad.** radar • radiator • radical • radio • radiologist • radiology • radiotherapist • radiotherapy • radius • *Maths., Anatomy* radix

**r.a.d.** radiation absorbed dose (of radiation) • rapid automatic drill

**Rad.** *Politics* Radical • Radnorshire (former Welsh county)

**RAD** *Med.* reflex anal dilation • Royal Academy of Dancing • Royal Albert Docks

**RADA** ('rɑːdə) Royal Academy of Dramatic Art

**radar** ('reɪdɑː) radio detection and ranging

**RADAR** Royal Association for Disability and Rehabilitation

**RADC** Royal Army Dental Corps

**raddol.** *Music* raddolcendo (Italian: becoming calmer)

**RADIUS** ('reɪdɪəs) Religious Drama Society of Great Britain

**RAdm** (*or* **RADM**) Rear-Admiral

**radmon** ('ræd,mɒn) radiological monitor(ing)

**radn** radiation

**RAE** Royal Aerospace (formerly Aircraft) Establishment • Royal Australian Engineers

**RAEC** Royal Army Educational Corps

**RAeroC** Royal Aero Club of the United Kingdom

**RAeS** Royal Aeronautical Society

**RAF** Rote Armee Faktion (German: Red Army Faction; terrorist group) • Royal Aircraft Factory • Royal Air Force

**RAFA** Royal Air Forces Association • Royal Australian Field Artillery

**RAFBF** Royal Air Force Benevolent Fund

**RAFES** Royal Air Force Educational Service

**RAFG** Royal Air Force Germany

**RAFMS** Royal Air Force Medical Services

**RAFR** Royal Air Force Regiment

**RAFRO** Royal Air Force Reserve of Officers

**RAFSAA** Royal Air Force Small Arms Association

**RAFSC** Royal Air Force Staff College

**RAFTC** Royal Air Force Transport Command

**RAFVR** Royal Air Force Volunteer Reserve

**RAGA** Royal Australian Garrison Artillery

**RAH** Royal Albert Hall

**RAHS** Royal Australian Historical Society

**RAI** Radiotelevisione Italiana (Italian broadcasting corporation; originally Radio Audizioni Italiane) • Royal Anthropological Institute

**RAIA** Royal Australian Institute of Architects

**RAIC** Royal Architectural Institute of Canada

**Raj.** Rajasthan (India)

**RAL** Rutherford Appleton Laboratory (Harwell, Oxfordshire)

**rall.** *Music* rallentando (Italian: becoming slow)

**RALS** *Aeronautics* remote augmented lift system

**r.a.m.** relative atomic mass

**RAM** *Aeronautics* radar absorbing material • (ræm) *Computing* random-access memory • (ræm) (USA) reverse annuity mortgage • rocket-assisted

motor • (Member of the) Royal Academy of Music • Royal Air Maroc (Moroccan airline) • *Freemasonry* Royal Arch Masons

**RAMAC** Radio Marine Associated Companies

**ramb.** rambler (rose)

**RAMC** Royal Army Medical Corps

**RAN** request for authority to negotiate • Royal Australian Navy

**RANC** Royal Australian Naval College

**R & A** Royal and Ancient (Golf Club, St Andrews)

**R & B** (*or* **r & b**) rhythm and blues • ring and ball (game)

**r. & c.c.** riot and civil commotion

**R & D** research and development

**R & E** research and engineering

**R & I** Regina et Imperatrix (Latin: Queen and Empress) • Rex et Imperator (Latin: King and Emperor)

**r & m** reports and memoranda

**R & M** reliability and marketing

**R & R** (*or* **R and R**) *Med.* rescue and resuscitation • rest and recreation • rock and roll

**R & T** research and technology

**R&VA** Rating and Valuation Association

**RANN** (USA) Research Applied to National Needs

**RANR** Royal Australian Naval Reserve

**RANVR** Royal Australian Naval Volunteer Reserve

**RAOB** Royal Antediluvian Order of Buffaloes

**RAOC** Royal Army Ordnance Corps

**RAOU** Royal Australian Ornithologists' Union

**rap.** rapid

**RAP** ready-assembled price • Regimental Aid Post • remedial action programme (*or* plan) • *Med.* right atrial pressure

**RAPC** Royal Army Pay Corps

**RAPID** ('ræpɪd) Register for the Ascertainment and Prevention of Inherited Diseases

**RAPRA** Rubber and Plastics Research Association of Great Britain

**RAR** Royal Australian Regiment

**RARDE** Royal Armament Research and Development Establishment

**RARE** *Computing* réseaux associés pour la recherche européenne (French: Associate Networks for European Research)

**RARO** Regular Army Reserve of Officers

**RAS** *Aeronautics* rectified air speed • Royal Agricultural Society • Royal Asiatic Society • Royal Astronomical Society

**RASC** Royal Army Service Corps (now called Royal Corps of Transport, RCT)

**RASE** Royal Agricultural Society of England

**raser** ('reɪzə) radio-frequency amplification by stimulated emission of radiation

**RASH** *Meteorol.* rain shower

**RASN** *Meteorol.* rain and snow

**RAST** *Immunol.* radio-allergosorbent test

**rat.** rateable • rating • ration

**RAT** (ræt) rocket-assisted torpedo

**RATAN** ('reɪtæn) radar and television aid to navigation

**RATO** ('reɪtəu) rocket-assisted takeoff

**RATP** (France) Régie autonome des transports parisiens (Paris transport authority)

**RAuxAF** Royal Auxiliary Air Force

**RAVC** Royal Army Veterinary Corps

**RAX** *Telephony* rural automatic exchange

**r.b.** *Sport* right back • rubber band

**Rb** *Chem., symbol for* rubidium

**RB** *British vehicle registration for* Nottingham • *Astronomy* radiation belt • radiation burn • reconnaissance bomber (aircraft; as in **RB-57**) • representative body • República Boliviana (Spanish: Republic of Bolivia) • *international vehicle registration for* Republic of Botswana • review body • Rifle Brigade • Royal Ballet

**RBA** (Member of the) Royal Society of British Artists

**RBAF** Royal Belgian Air Force

**RBC** *Med.* red blood cell • *Med.* red blood (cell) count • Royal British Colonial Society of Artists

**RBE** relative biological effectiveness (of radiation)

**RBerks** Royal Berkshire Regiment

**RBG** Royal Botanic Gardens (Kew)

**r.b.i.** require better information • *Baseball* run(s) batted in

**RBI** resource-based industry • *Skating* right back inside (of skate) • ('rɪbɪ) *Baseball* run(s) batted in

**RBK&C** Royal Borough of Kensington and Chelsea

**rbl.** rouble

**RBL** Royal British Legion

**RBNA** Royal British Nurses' Association

**RBO** *Skating* right back outside (of skate)

**RBP** *Biochem.* retinol-binding protein

**RBS** *Med.* radionuclide bone scintigraphy • Royal Society of British Sculptors • *Physics* Rutherford backscattering spectroscopy (*or* spectrometry)

**RBSA** (Member of the) Royal Birmingham Society of Artists

**rbt** roundabout

**RBT** random breath testing

**RBY** Royal Bucks Yeomanry

**r.c.** radio code (*or* coding) • reinforced concrete • release clause • reverse course • right centre • rotary combustion • rubber-cushioned

**RC** *British vehicle registration for* Nottingham • *Cycling* racing club • *Med.* red (blood) cell • Red Cross • Reformed Church • reinforced concrete • reproductive capacity • (USA) Republican Convention • research centre • Reserve Corps • *Photog.* resin-coated (as in **RC paper**) • *Electronics* resistor-capacitor (*or* resistance-capacitance) • rifle club • *Cycling* road club • Roman Catholic • *Building trades* rough cutting • Royal Commission • *international vehicle registration for* Taiwan (Republic of China)

**R/C** recredited

**RCA** *international vehicle registration for* Central African Republic • Rabbinical Council of America • Racecourse Association • Radio Corporation of America • *Med.* right coronary artery • (Member of the) Royal Cambrian Academy • (Member of the) Royal Canadian Academy of Arts • Royal College of Art • Royal Company of Archers • Rural Crafts' Association

**RCAC** Royal Canadian Armoured Corps

**RCAF** Royal Canadian Air Force

**RCamA** (Member of the) Royal Cambrian Academy

**RCAMC** Royal Canadian Army Medical Corps

**RCASC** Royal Canadian Army Service Corps

**RCB** *international vehicle registration for* Republic of the Congo • *Theatre* right centre back (of stage)

**RCC** recovery control centre • *Med.* renal cell carcinoma • rescue coordination centre • Roman Catholic Chaplain • (*or* **RCCh**) Roman Catholic Church • Rural Community Council

**rcd** received

**RCD** (Tunisia) Rassemblement Constitutionnel Démocratique (pro-government political party) • Regional Cooperation for Development (association of Asian countries) • *Electronics* residual current device

**RCDC** Royal Canadian Dental Corps

**RCDS** Royal College of Defence Studies

**RCE** *Engineering* rotary combustion engine

**RCFCA** Royal Canadian Flying Clubs' Association

**RCGA** Royal Canadian Golf Association

**RCGP** Royal College of General Practitioners

**RCGS** Royal Canadian Geographical Society

**RCH** railway clearing house • *international vehicle registration for* Republic of Chile

**RCHA** Royal Canadian Horse Artillery

**RCHM** Royal Commission on Historical Monuments

**r.c.i.** radar coverage indicator

**RCI** Royal Canadian Institute

**RCJ** Royal Courts of Justice

**RCL** Royal Canadian Legion • ruling case law

**RCM** radar (*or* radio) countermeasures • *Med.* radiological contrast medium • regimental court martial • Royal College of Midwives • (Member of the) Royal College of Music

**RCMP** Royal Canadian Mounted Police (formerly RNWMP)

**RCN** Royal Canadian Navy • (*or* **Rcn**) Royal College of Nursing

**RCNC** Royal Corps of Naval Constructors

**RCNR** Royal Canadian Naval Reserve

**RCNT** Registered Clinical Nurse Teacher

**RCNVR** Royal Canadian Naval Volunteer Reserve

**RCO** Royal College of Organists

**RCOG** Royal College of Obstetricians and Gynaecologists

**RCP** Royal College of Physicians

**RCPath** Royal College of Pathologists

**RCPE** (*or* **RCPEd**) Royal College of Physicians, Edinburgh

**RCPI** Royal College of Physicians of Ireland

**RCPSG** Royal College of Physicians and Surgeons of Glasgow

**RCPsych** Royal College of Psychiatrists

**rcpt** receipt

**RCR** Royal College of Radiologists

**RCS** reaction control system (in a spacecraft) • *Nuclear engineering* reactor coolant (*or* cooling) system • remote control system • Royal Choral Society • Royal College of Science • Royal College of Surgeons of England • Royal Commonwealth Society • Royal Corps of Signals • Royal Counties Show

**RCSB** Royal Commonwealth Society for the Blind

**RCSE** (*or* **RCSEd**) Royal College of Surgeons of Edinburgh

**RCSI** Royal College of Surgeons in Ireland

**RCSS** random communications-satellite system

**rct** receipt • recruit

**RCT** regimental combat team • remote control transmitter (for TV operation, etc.) • Royal Corps of Transport

**RCU** remote-control unit • road-construction unit • rocket-countermeasure unit

**rcvr** receiver

**RCVS** Royal College of Veterinary Surgeons

**rd** rendered • road • round • *Physics, symbol for* rutherford

**r.d.** *Physics* relative density • rive droite (French: right bank) • *Shipping* running days

**Rd** Road

**RD** radiation dose • *Metallurgy* radiation-induced defect • *British vehicle registration for* Reading • récemment dégorgé (French: recently disgorged; referring to wines having a longer ageing period on their first cork) • (*or* **R/D**) refer to drawer (on a cheque) • (USA) registered dietician • República Dominicana (Spanish: Dominican Republic) • research department • Royal Dragoons • Royal Naval and Royal Marine Forces Reserve Decoration • Rural Dean • (New Zealand) Rural Delivery

**RDA** Rassemblement Démocratique Africain (French: African Democratic Rally; political party) • recommended dietary (*or* daily) allowance (of nutrients) • Retail Distributors' Association •

Royal Defence Academy • Royal Docks
Association

**RD&D** research, development, and
demonstration

**RD&E** research, development, and
engineering

**RDAT** (*or* **R-DAT**) rotary-head digital
audio tape

**RDB** *Military* Research and Development Board • Royal Danish Ballet •
Rural Development Board

**RDBMS** *Computing* relational database
management system

**RDC** Royal Defence Corps • *Insurance*
running-down clause • Rural District
Council

**RDCA** Rural District Councils' Association

**r.d.d.** required delivery date

**RDD** *Marketing* (USA) random digital
dialing

**RDE** Research and Development Establishment • *Chem.* rotating-disc electrode

**RDF** radio direction finder (*or* finding) •
*Military* (USA) Rapid Deployment
Force • Royal Dublin Fusiliers

**RDI** Royal Designer for Industry (of the
Royal Society of Arts)

**rDNA** *Biochem.* ribosomal DNA

**RDP** *Botany* ribulose diphosphate (*see*
RuBP)

**RDPL** *international civil aircraft marking
for* Laos

**rdr** radar

**rds.** *Shipping* roadstead

**RDS** radio data system (for automatic
tuning of receivers) • *Med.* respiratory
distress syndrome • Royal Drawing Society • Royal Dublin Society

**RDT&E** research, development, testing, and engineering

**RDV** (*or* **rdv**) rendezvous

**RDX** Research Department Explosive
(cyclonite)

**rdy** ready

**RDy** (*or* **RDY**) Royal Dockyard

**RDZ** radiation danger zone

**r.e.** *Football* (USA) right end

**Re** (ital.) *Physics, symbol for* Reynolds
number • *Chem., symbol for* rhenium •
*symbol for* rupee (Indian monetary unit;
*see also* Rs)

**RE** *Chem.* rare earth • (*or* **R/E**) (USA)
real estate • Reformed Episcopal • religious education • renewable energy •
revised edition • Right Excellent • *Med.*
right eye • Royal Engineers • Royal

Exchange • Royal Society of Painter-
Etchers and Engravers • *British vehicle
registration for* Stoke-on-Trent

**REA** Radar and Electronics Association • request for engineer's authorization • Rubber Export Association •
(USA) Rural Electrification Administration

**reac.** reactor

**REAC** Regional Education Advisory
Committee (of the TUC)

**REACH** (riːtʃ) Retired Executives'
Action Clearing House

**react** (rɪˈækt) research education and
aid for children with potentially terminal illness

**Rear-Adm.** Rear-Admiral

**reasm.** reassemble

**REB** regional examining body • *Physics*
relativistic electron beam

**rec.** receipt • receive • *Med.* recens
(Latin: fresh; in prescriptions) • recent •
reception • recipe • record(ed) •
recorder • recording • recreation

**REC** Railway Executive Committee •
(rɛk) regional electricity company

**recd** received

**recep.** reception

**recip.** reciprocal • reciprocity

**recirc.** recirculate

**recit.** recitation • *Music* recitative

**reclam.** reclamation

**recm.** recommend

**RECMF** Radio and Electronic Component Manufacturers' Federation

**recog.** recognition • recognize

**recom.** recommend

**recon.** reconciliation • (*or* **recond.**)
recondition • reconnaissance • reconnoi-
tre • reconsign(ment) • (*or* **reconst.**)
reconstruct(ion)

**REconS** Royal Economic Society

**recpt** receipt

**recryst.** *Chem.* recrystallized

**rec. sec.** recording secretary

**rect.** receipt • rectangle • rectangular •
*Med.* rectificatus (Latin: rectified; in
prescriptions) • rectify

**Rect.** Rector(y)

**rec-v** (*or* **recvee**) (ˈrɛkˈviː) (USA)
recreational vehicle (e.g. a motorized
caravan)

**red.** *Finance* redeemable • reduce(d) •
reduction

**redisc.** rediscount

**redox** (ˈrɛdɒks) *Chem.* reduction–
oxidation

**Red R** Register of Engineers for Disaster Relief

**redupl.** reduplicate • reduplication

**REE** *Chem.* rare-earth element

**ref.** refer(red) • referee • reference • refining • reform(ed) • reformation • reformer • refrigerated ship • refund(ing) • refuse

**refash.** refashioned

**Ref. Ch.** Reformed Church

**refd** referred • refund

**refl.** reflect(ion) • reflective • reflex • reflexive

**Ref. Pres.** Reformed Presbyterian

**refrig.** refrigerate • refrigeration • refrigerator

**Ref. Sp.** Reformed Spelling

**reg.** regiment • region • register(ed) • registrar • registration • registry • regular(ly) • regulation • regulator

**Reg.** Regent • (*or* **Reg**) Regent's Park College, Oxford • Regina (Latin: Queen)

**REGAL** ('riːgˀl) *Aeronautics* range and elevation guidance for approach and landing

**regd** registered

**Reg-Gen.** Registrar-General

**Reg. Prof.** Regius Professor

**regr.** registrar

**Regt** Regent • Regiment

**regtl** regimental

**Reg. TM** Registered Trade Mark

**REHAB** ('riːhæb) *Med., Psychiatry* Rehabilitation Evaluation of Hall and Baker

**reinf.** reinforce

**reinfmt** reinforcement

**reit.** *Printing* reiteration

**REIT** (USA) real-estate investment trust

**rej.** reject

**rel.** relate • relating • relation • relative(ly) • release(d) • relic • *Bibliog.* relié (French: bound) • religion • religious • reliquiae (Latin: relics)

**REL** recommended exposure limit (for radiation)

**rel. pron.** relative pronoun

**rem** (rɛm) roentgen equivalent man (former unit of radioactivity)

**rem.** remark(s) • remit • remittance

**REM** (rɛm *or* 'ɑː 'iː 'ɛm) *Physiol.* rapid eye movement (as in **REM sleep**) • *Chem.* rare-earth metal

**REME** ('riːmiː) Royal Electrical and Mechanical Engineers

**remitt.** remittance

**Ren.** Renaissance

**Renf.** Renfrewshire (former Scottish county)

**Renfe** (*or* **RENFE**) Red Nacional de Ferrocarriles Españoles (Spanish state railways)

**REngDes** Registered Engineering Designer

**renv.** renovate • renovation

**REO** regional education officer

**rep.** repair • repeat • *Med.* repetatur (Latin: let it be repeated; in prescriptions) • report(ed) • reporter • represent(ing) • representative • reprint

**Rep.** (USA) Representative • Republic • (USA) Republican

**REPC** Regional Economic Planning Council

**repl.** replace(d) • replacement

**repo.** repossess

**repr.** (*or* **repres.**) represent(ative) • represented • representing • reprint(ed)

**repro.** reproduced • reproduction

**rept** receipt • report

**repub.** republish

**Repub.** Republic • (USA) Republican

**req.** request • require(d) • requisition

**reqd** required

**reqn** requisition

**reqs** requires

**RER** renewable energy resource(s) • *Cytology* rough endoplasmic reticulum

**RERO** Royal Engineers Reserve of Officers

**res.** rescue • research(er) • reservation • reserve(d) • residence • resident • reside(s) • resigned • resolution

**RES** renewable energy source (*or* system) • *Physiol.* reticuloendothelial system • Royal Entomological Society of London

**resgnd** resigned

**resig.** resignation

**resp.** respective(ly) • respiration • respondent • responsibility

**res. phys.** resident physician

**res. sec.** resident secretary

**rest.** (*or* **restr.**) restaurant • restoration • restrict(ion)

**Rest.** *History* Restoration

**ret.** retain • retire(d) • return(ed)

**Ret** *Astronomy* Reticulum

**retd** retained • retired • returned

**R. et I.** Regina et Imperatrix (Latin: Queen and Empress) • Rex et Imperator (Latin: King and Emperor)

**retnr** retainer

**RETRA** ('retrə) Radio, Electrical, and Television Retailers' Association

**RETRO** (*or* **Retro**) ('retrəu) *Astronautics* (USA) Retrofire Officer

**rev.** revenue • reverse(d) • review(ed) • revise(d) • revision • revolution • revolve • revolver • revolving

**Rev.** *Bible* Revelation • (*or* **Rev**) Reverend • Review

**REV** *Astronautics* re-entry vehicle

**rev. a/c** revenue account(s)

**Revd** Reverend

**Rev. Stat.** Revised Statutes

**Rev. Ver.** Revised Version (of the Bible)

**rew.** reward

**rf** reef

**rf.** *Music* rinforzando (Italian: reinforcing)

**r.f.** radio frequency • range finder • rapid fire • *Telecom.* reception fair • relative flow • *Baseball* right field(er) • rough finish (of paper)

**Rf** *symbol for* rufiyaa (monetary unit of Maldives) • *Chem., symbol for* rutherfordium

**RF** radio frequency • reconnaissance fighter (aircraft; as in **RF-4E**) • *Military* regular forces • *Genetics* release factor • *Cartography* representative fraction • République française (French Republic) • research foundation • *Military* Reserve Force • *Chem.* retention factor (in chromatography) • Rockefeller Foundation • Royal Fusiliers • rugby football • *symbol for* Rwanda franc (monetary unit) • *British vehicle registration for* Stoke-on-Trent

**RFA** Royal Field Artillery • Royal Fleet Auxiliary

**RFAC** Royal Fine Art Commission

**R factor** *Genetics* resistance factor (*see* R plasmid)

**r.f.b.** (*or* **RFB**) *Football* (USA) right fullback

**RFC** (USA) Reconstruction Finance Corporation • Royal Flying Corps • Rugby Football Club

**RFD** radio-frequency device • reporting for duty • (USA) rural free delivery (postal service)

**RFDS** (Australia) Royal Flying Doctor Service

**RFE** Radio Free Europe

**RFH** Royal Festival Hall (London)

**RFI** radio-frequency interference • request for information • *Skating* right forward inside (of skate)

**RFL** Rugby Football League

**RFLP** *Genetics* restriction fragment length polymorphism

**Rfn** Rifleman

**RFN** Registered Fever Nurse

**RFO** *Skating* right forward outside (of skate)

**r.f.p.** retired on full pay

**RFP** *Nuclear engineering* reversed-field pinch

**RFPC** *Electronics* radio-frequency pulse compression

**RFQ** *Physics* radio-frequency quadrupole • *Commerce* request for quotation

**RFR** Royal Fleet Reserve

**rfrd** referred

**RFS** Registry of Friendly Societies • Royal Forestry Society

**RFSU** Rugby Football Schools' Union

**RFT** *Astronomy* richest-field telescope

**RFU** Rugby Football Union

**rfz.** *Music* rinforzando (Italian: reinforcing)

**r.g.** *Football* (USA) right guard • rive gauche (French: left bank)

**RG** *British vehicle registration for* Newcastle upon Tyne • *postcode for* Reading • reserve guard • *airline flight code for* Varig Brazilian Airlines

**RGA** remote geological analysis • residual-gas analyser • Royal Garrison Artillery • Royal Guernsey Artillery

**RGB** *Electrical engineering, Image technol.* red green blue (as in **RGB signals**)

**rgd** registered • reigned

**rge** range

**R-Genl** Registrar-General

**RGG** Royal Grenadier Guards

**RGH** Royal Gloucestershire Hussars

**RGI** Royal Glasgow Institute of the Fine Arts

**RGJ** Royal Green Jackets

**rgn** region

**Rgn** Rangoon

**RGN** Registered General Nurse (formerly SRN)

**RGNP** *Economics* real gross national product

**RGO** Royal Greenwich Observatory (now in Cambridge)

**RGS** Royal Geographical Society

**RGSA** Royal Geographical Society of Australasia

**Rgt** Regiment

**RGT** *Physics* relativistic gravitational theory

**rgtl** regimental

**r.h.** right half • right hand(ed)

**Rh** *Med.* rhesus (factor) (as in **Rh positive**) • *Chem., symbol for* rhodium

**RH** *British vehicle registration for* Hull • *postcode for* Redhill • *Meteorol.* relative humidity • remote handling (*or* handled) • *international vehicle registration for* Republic of Haiti • right hand(ed) • *British fishing port registration for* Rochester • Royal Highness • Royal Hospital

**RHA** Regional Health Authority • Road Haulage Association • Royal Hibernian Academy • Royal Horse Artillery

**RHamps** Royal Hampshire Regiment

**rhap.** rhapsody

**RHAS** Royal Highland and Agricultural Society of Scotland

**RHB** Regional Hospital Board • (*or* **r.h.b.**) *Football* (USA) right halfback

**RHBNC** Royal Holloway and Bedford New College, London

**r.h.d.** right-hand drive (of a motor vehicle)

**RHEED** *Physics* reflection high-energy electron diffraction

**rheo.** rheostat

**rheol.** rheological • rheology

**rhet.** rhetoric(al)

**RHF** Royal Highland Fusiliers

**RHG** Royal Horse Guards

**RHHI** Royal Hospital and Home for Incurables (Putney)

**RHIC** *Physics* relativistic heavy-ion collider (*or* collisions)

**RHistS** Royal Historical Society

**RHM** Ranks Hovis McDougall

**RHMS** Royal Hibernian Military School

**rhom.** (*or* **rhomb.**) rhombic • rhomboid • rhombus

**r.h.p.** rated horsepower

**RHQ** regimental headquarters

**RHR** Royal Highland Regiment (Black Watch)

**r.h.s.** right-hand side • round-headed screw

**RHS** Royal Highland Show • Royal Historical Society • Royal Horticultural Society • Royal Humane Society

**RHSI** Royal Horticultural Society of Ireland

**RHV** Registered Health Visitor

**r.i.** reflective insulation • rubber insulation

**Ri** (ital.) *Meteorol., symbol for* Richardson number

**RI** *Irish vehicle registration for* Dublin • radio interference • radioisotope • Railway Inspectorate • refractive index • Regimental Institute • Regina et Imperatrix (Latin: Queen and Empress) • *Shipping* (Italy) Registro Italiano Navale (classification society) • (*or* **R/I**) reinsurance • religious instruction • report of investigation • *international vehicle registration for* Republic of Indonesia • Rex et Imperator (Latin: King and Emperor) • Rhode Island (abbrev. *or* postcode) • Rockwell International Corporation • Rotary International • (Member of the) Royal Institute of Painters in Water Colours • Royal Institution

**RIA** *Med.* radioimmunoassay • Royal Irish Academy

**RIAA** Recording Industry Association of America

**RIAC** Royal Irish Automobile Club

**RIAF** Royal Indian Air Force

**RIAI** Royal Institute of the Architects of Ireland

**RIAM** Royal Irish Academy of Music

**RIAS** Royal Incorporation of Architects in Scotland

**RIASC** Royal Indian Army Service Corps

**Rib** *Biochem.* ribose

**RIB** Racing Information Bureau • rigid-hull inflatable boat • Rural Industries Bureau

**RIBA** Member of the Royal Institute of British Architects • (*or* **Riba**) Royal Institute of British Architects

**RIBI** Rotary International in Great Britain and Ireland

**RIC** *Chem.* radiation-induced change • *Physics* radiation-induced conductivity • Radio Industry Council • Royal Institute of Chemistry (now called Royal Society of Chemistry, RSC) • Royal Irish Constabulary

**RICA** Research Institute for Consumer Affairs

**RICE** (rais) rest, ice, compression, elevation (for treating sports injuries)

**RICO** (USA) Racketeer Influenced and Corrupt Organizations Act

**RICS** Royal Institution of Chartered Surveyors

**RID** *Physics* radiation-induced defect • *Physics* radiation-induced diffusion

**RIE** *Commerce* recognized investment exchange • Royal Indian Engineering (College)

**RIF** *Military* reduction in force • Royal Inniskilling Fusiliers

**Rif. Brig.** Rifle Brigade

**RIIA** Royal Institute of International Affairs

**RIM** *international vehicle registration for* Islamic Republic of Mauritania • Royal Indian Marines

**RIMB** (South Africa) Research Institute for Medical Biophysics

**RIN** *Aeronautics* reference indicator number • Royal Indian Navy

**RINA** Royal Institution of Naval Architects

**rinf.** *Music* rinforzando (Italian: reinforcing)

**RINVR** Royal Indian Naval Volunteer Reserve

**RIO** reporting in and out

**RIOP** Royal Institute of Oil Painters

**rip.** *Music* ripieno (Italian; all instrumentalists)

**RIP** *Computing* raster input processor • requiescat (*or* requiescant) in pace (Latin: may (he, she, *or* they) rest in peace)

**RIPA** Royal Institute of Public Administration

**RIPH&H** (*or* **RIPHH**) Royal Institute of Public Health and Hygiene

**RIrF** Royal Irish Fusiliers

**RIS** Research Information Service

**RISC** (rɪsk) reduced-instruction-set computer

**rit.** *Music* ritardando (Italian: holding back) • *Music* ritenuto (Italian: held back)

**RIT** *Psychiatry* Rorschach inkblot test

**riten.** *Music* ritenuto (Italian: held back)

**riv.** (*or* **Riv.**) river

**RIY** *Physics* relative ion yield

**RJ** *British vehicle registration for* Manchester • ramjet • *Military* road junction • *airline flight code for* Royal Jordanian Airlines

**RJA** Royal Jersey Artillery

**RJE** *Computing* remote job entry

**RJLI** Royal Jersey Light Infantry

**RJM** Royal Jersey Militia

**RK** *airline flight code for* Air Afrique • *British vehicle registration for* London NW • *Med.* radical keratotomy (used in

treatment of shortsightedness) • religious knowledge

**RKO** (USA) Radio-Keith-Orpheum (film studio, now broadcasting company)

**rky** rocky

**RL** reference library • *international vehicle registration for* Republic of Lebanon • research laboratory • rocket launcher • Rugby League • *British vehicle registration for* Truro

**RLD** (USA) retail liquor dealer

**RLF** Royal Literary Fund

**R Lincolns** Royal Lincolnshire Regiment

**RLL** *Computing* run length limited

**RLO** railway liaison officer • returned letter office (formerly dead letter office, DLO)

**RLPO** Royal Liverpool Philharmonic Orchestra

**RLPS** Royal Liverpool Philharmonic Society

**Rls** *symbol for* rial (monetary unit of Iran)

**RLS** Robert Louis Stevenson (1850–94, Scottish writer)

**RLSS** Royal Life Saving Society

**rly** (*or* **Rly**) railway • relay

**rm** ream • room

**RM** *British vehicle registration for* Carlisle • *international vehicle registration for* Madagascar • radiation monitoring • radio monitoring • Registered Midwife • *symbol for* Reichsmark (former German currency) • remote monitoring • Resident Magistrate • riding master • *postcode for* Romford • Royal Mail • Royal Marines

**RMA** Royal Marine Artillery • Royal Marines Association • Royal Military Academy (Sandhurst; formerly Woolwich) • Royal Musical Association

**RMB** (*or* **Rmb**) (China) renminbi (Chinese: people's money (the currency used by the indigenous population); *compare* FEC, Foreign Exchange Certificate)

**RMC** regional meteorological centre • (formerly) Royal Military College (Sandhurst; *see under* RMA)

**RMCC** Royal Military College of Canada

**RMCM** (Member of the) Royal Manchester College of Music

**RMCS** Royal Military College of Science

**r.m.d.** ready money down
**RMedSoc** Royal Medical Society, Edinburgh
**RMetS** Royal Meteorological Society
**RMFVR** Royal Marine Forces Volunteer Reserves
**RMH** Royal Marsden Hospital (London)
**RMI** Resource Management Initiative (for the NHS)
**RMIT** Royal Melbourne Institute of Technology
**RMLI** Royal Marine Light Infantry
**r.m.m.** *Chem.* relative molecular mass
**RMM** *international vehicle registration for* Republic of Mali
**RMN** Registered Mental Nurse
**RMO** Regimental Medical Officer · Regional Medical Officer · resident medical officer · Royal Marine Office
**RMP** Royal Marine Police · Royal Military Police
**RMPA** Royal Medico-Psychological Association
**RMRA** Royal Marines Rifle Association
**rms** *Maths.* root mean square
**RMS** radiation-monitoring system · (USA) Railway Mail Service · remote monitoring system · *Maths.* root mean square · Royal Mail Service · Royal Mail Ship (*or* Steamer) · Royal Microscopical Society · Royal Society of Miniature Painters
**RMSchMus** Royal Marines School of Music
**RMSM** Royal Military School of Music
**RMT** National Union of Rail, Maritime, and Transport Workers (formed by amalgamation of the NUR with the NUS)
**r.n.** *Telecom.* reception nil
**Rn** *Chem., symbol for* radon
**RN** *British vehicle registration for* Preston · (USA) Registered Nurse · *international vehicle registration for* Republic of Niger · Royal Navy (*or* Naval) · *British fishing port registration for* Runcorn
**RNA** *Biochem.* ribonucleic acid · Royal Naval Association
**RNAS** Royal Naval Air Service · Royal Naval Air Station
**RNase** (*or* **RNAase**) *Biochem.* ribonuclease
**RNAW** Royal Naval Aircraft Workshop
**RNAY** Royal Naval Aircraft Yard
**R 'n' B** rhythm and blues
**RNB** Royal Naval Barracks

**RNBT** Royal Naval Benevolent Trust
**RNC** (USA) Republican National Committee · Royal Naval College
**RNCM** (Member of the) Royal Northern College of Music
**rnd** round
**RND** Royal Naval Division
**RNEC** Royal Naval Engineering College
**Rnf.** Renfrewshire (former Scottish county)
**RNF** Royal Northumberland Fusiliers
**RNIB** Royal National Institute for the Blind
**RNID** Royal National Institute for the Deaf
**RNLAF** Royal Netherlands Air Force
**RNLI** Royal National Lifeboat Institution
**RNLO** Royal Naval Liaison Officer
**RNMDSF** Royal National Mission to Deep Sea Fishermen
**RNMH** Registered Nurse for the Mentally Handicapped
**RNMS** Royal Naval Medical School
**RNoN** Royal Norwegian Navy
**RNP** *Biochem.* ribonucleoprotein
**RNPFN** Royal National Pension Fund for Nurses
**R 'n' R** rock and roll
**RNR** Royal Naval Reserve
**RNRA** Royal Naval Rifle Association
**rns** runs
**RNS** *Maths.* residue number system · Royal Numismatic Society
**RNSA** Royal Naval Sailing Association
**RNSC** Royal Naval Staff College
**RNSR** Royal Naval Special Reserve
**RNSS** Royal Naval Scientific Service
**RNT** Registered Nurse Tutor · Royal National Theatre
**RNTE** Royal Naval Training Establishment
**RNTNEH** Royal National Throat, Nose, and Ear Hospital
**RNTU** Royal Naval Training Unit
**RNVR** Royal Naval Volunteer Reserve
**RNVSR** Royal Naval Volunteer Supplementary Reserve
**RNWMP** (formerly, in Canada) Royal Northwest Mounted Police (*see* RCMP)
**rnwy** runway
**RNXS** Royal Naval Auxiliary Service
**RNZAC** Royal New Zealand Armoured Corps
**RNZAF** Royal New Zealand Air Force

**RNZIR** Royal New Zealand Infantry Regiment

**RNZN** Royal New Zealand Navy

**RNZNVR** Royal New Zealand Naval Volunteer Reserve

**ro.** (*or* **r°**) *Printing* recto • roan

**r.o.** *Rowing* rowed over • *Cricket* run out

**RO** *British vehicle registration for* Luton • radar operator (*or* observer) • radio operator • Radio Orchestra • *Psychol.* reality orientation • receiving office(r) • receiving order • record(s) office • recruiting officer • regimental order • registered office • relieving officer • reserved occupation • returning officer • *Chem.* reverse osmosis • *symbol for* rial Omani (monetary unit of Oman) • *international vehicle registration for* Romania • *British fishing port registration for* Rothesay

**ROA** (*or* **RoA**) *Education* record of achievement • Reserve Officers' Association • *Finance* return on assets

**ROAM** *Finance* return on assets managed

**ROAR** right of admission reserved

**ROB** remaining on board

**ROC** *Finance* return on capital • Royal Observer Corps

**ROCE** *Finance* return on capital employed

**ROE** *Finance* return on equity • Royal Observatory, Edinburgh

**ROF** Royal Ordnance Factory

**Roffen.** Roffensis (Latin: (Bishop) of Rochester)

**R of O** Reserve of Officers

**ROG** (*or* **r.o.g.**) receipt of goods

**ROI** region of interest • *Finance* return on investment • (Member of the) Royal Institute of Oil Painters

**ROK** *international vehicle registration for* Republic of Korea

**rom.** roman (type)

**Rom.** Roman • Romance *or* Romanic (languages) • Romania(n) • *Bible* Romans

**ROM** (rom) *Computing* read-only memory

**Rom. Cath.** Roman Catholic

**RONA** *Finance* return on net assets

**ROP** *Advertising* run of paper (as in **ROP printing**)

**RORC** Royal Ocean Racing Club

**ro-ro** (*or* **RORO**) ('rəʊrəʊ) roll-on/roll-off (ferry)

**Ros.** Roscommon

**ROSE** *Computing* Research Open Systems in Europe

**ROSLA** ('rɒzlə) raising of school-leaving age

**RoSPA** (*or* **Rospa**) ('rɒspə) Royal Society for the Prevention of Accidents

**rot** (rɒt) *Maths., symbol for* curl (of a function)

**rot.** rotary • rotating • rotation • rotor

**Rot.** Rotterdam

**ROT** remedial occupational therapy • rule of thumb

**ROTC** (USA) Reserve Officers' Training Corps

**ROU** *international vehicle registration for* Republic of Uruguay

**rout.** routine

**ROV** remotely operated vehicle

**ROW** right of way

**ROWPU** reverse osmosis water-purification unit

**Rox.** Roxburghshire (former Scottish county)

**Roy.** Royal

**r.p.** *Telecom.* reception poor • regimental policeman • reply paid

**Rp** *symbol for* rupiah (Indonesian monetary unit)

**RP** *British vehicle registration for* Northampton • radiation protection • *Chem.* reaction product • (*or* **rp**) Received Pronunciation • recommended practice • recommended price • recovery phase • *Chem.* redox potential • redundancy payment • Reformed Presbyterian • Regimental Police(man) • registered plumber • Regius Professor • reinforced plastic • reply paid • (*or* **R/P**) reprint(ing) • República Portuguesa (Republic of Portugal) • *international vehicle registration or international civil aircraft marking for* Republic of the Philippines • *Finance* (USA) repurchase agreement • research paper • *Med.* retinitis pigmentosa • *Insurance* return (of) premium • Révérend Père (French: Reverend Father) • rocket projectile • (Member of the) Royal Society of Portrait Painters • rules of procedure

**RPA** radiation protection adviser • *Education* record of personal achievement • Registered Plumbers' Association

**RPB** *Finance* recognized professional body

**RPC** rapid Portland cement • (USA) Republican Party Conference • request the pleasure of your company • Royal Pioneer Corps

**RPD** Doctor of Political Science (Latin *Rerum Politicarum Doctor*) • regional port director

**RPE** radio production executive • Reformed Protestant Episcopal

**RPF** *Med.* renal plasma flow • *Med.* retroperitoneal fibrosis

**r.p.g.** rounds per gun

**RPG** *Computing* report program generator • *Military* rocket-propelled grenade • role-playing game

**rph** revolutions per hour

**RPhilS** Royal Philharmonic Society

**RPI** retail price index

**R plasmid** *Genetics* resistance plasmid (formerly factor)

**RPLC** *Chem.* reverse-phase liquid chromatography

**rpm** revolutions per minute

**RPM** reliability performance measure • resale price maintenance

**RPMS** Royal Postgraduate Medical School

**RPN** Registered Psychiatric Nurse • *Computing, Maths.* reverse Polish notation

**RP/ND** reprinting, no date

**RPO** railway post office • regional personnel officer • Royal Philharmonic Orchestra

**RPQ** request for price quotation

**RPR** (France) Rassemblement pour la République (French: Rally for the Republic; Gaullists)

**r-protein** *Biochem.* ribosomal protein

**rps** revolutions per second

**RPS** radiological protection service • rapid processing system • Royal Philharmonic Society • Royal Photographic Society

**RPSGB** Royal Pharmaceutical Society of Great Britain

**rpt** repeat • report • reprint

**RPV** *Nuclear engineering* reactor pressure vessel • *Military* remotely piloted vehicle

**RQ** (*or* **r.q.**) regraded (*or* remoulded) quality (of tyres) • (*or* **R/Q**) *Commerce* request for quotation • *Med.* respiratory quotient

**RQL** reference quality level

**RQMS** regimental quartermaster sergeant

**rqmt** requirement

**rqr.** require(ment)

**rr.** rare

**r.r.** ready reckoner

**RR** *British vehicle registration for* Nottingham • radiation resistance • (USA) railroad • Remington Rand (US company) • research report • return rate • Right Reverend • *Cycling* road race • (*or* **R-R**) Rolls-Royce • (USA) rural route

**RRA** Royal Regiment of Artillery

**RRB** Race Relations Board

**RRC** *Cycling* Road Racing Club • (Lady of the) Royal Red Cross

**RRE** Royal Radar Establishment (*see* RSRE)

**RRF** Royal Regiment of Fusiliers

**RRI** Rowett Research Institute (Aberdeen)

**RRL** Registered Record Librarian • Road Research Laboratory

**RRM** (USA) renegotiable-rate mortgage

**rRNA** *Biochem.* ribosomal RNA

**RRP** recommended retail price

**RR. PP.** Révérends Pères (French: Reverend Fathers)

**RRR** (USA) return receipt requested (of registered mail)

**3** (*or* **three**) **Rs** reading, (w)riting, and (a)rithmetic

**RRS** Royal Research Ship

**RRT** rail rapid transit

**rs** *Meteorol., symbol for* sleet (rain and snow)

**r.s.** right side

**Rs** *symbol for* rupees (*see also under* Re)

**RS** *British vehicle registration for* Aberdeen • *Physics* Raman scattering • Received Standard (English) • reconnaissance squadron • reconnaissance strike • recording secretary • recruiting service • *Computing* Reed–Solomon (as in **RS code**) • Reformed Spelling • remote sensing • research station • *Med.* respiratory system • *Law* Revised Statutes • *Military* Royal Scots • Royal Society

**R/S** rejection slip

**RSA** Republic of South Africa • (New Zealand) Returned Services Association • *Computing* Rivest, Shamir, and Adelman (denoting a method of encryption, as in **RSA cipher, RSA system**) • Road Safety Act • Royal Scottish Academy (*or* Academician) • Royal Society for the Encouragement of Arts, Manufactures, and Commerce •

Royal Society of Arts • Royal Society of Australia

**RSAA** Royal Society for Asian Affairs

**RSAD** Royal Surgical Aid Society

**RSAF** Royal Small Arms Factory

**RSAI** Royal Society of Antiquaries of Ireland

**RSAMD** Royal Scottish Academy of Music and Drama

**RSAS** Royal Surgical Aid Society

**r.s.b.** range safety beacon

**RSC** Royal Shakespeare Company • Royal Society of Canada • Royal Society of Chemistry • Rules of the Supreme Court

**RSCDS** Royal Scottish Country Dance Society

**rsch** research

**RSCJ** Religiosae Sacratissimi Cordis Jesu (Latin: Nuns of the Most Sacred Heart of Jesus; Sacred Heart Society)

**RSCM** Royal School of Church Music

**RSCN** Registered Sick Children's Nurse (formerly SRCN)

**RSD** recovery, salvage, and disposal • Royal Society of Dublin

**RSE** Received Standard English • Royal Society of Edinburgh

**RSF** *Building trades* rough sunk face • Royal Scots Fusiliers

**RSFS** Royal Scottish Forestry Society

**RSFSR** (formerly) Russian Soviet Federative Socialist Republic

**RSG** rate-support grant • recirculating steam generator • regional seat of government (in civil defence) • *Military* Royal Scots Greys

**RSGB** Radio Society of Great Britain (amateur radio operators)

**RSGS** Royal Scottish Geographical Society

**RSH** Royal Society for the Promotion of Health

**RSHA** Reichssicherheitshauptamt (Reich Security Central Office; in Nazi Germany)

**RSI** *Med.* repetitive strain (*or* stress) injury

**R. Signals** Royal Corps of Signals

**RSJ** *Building trades* rolled-steel joist

**RSL** (Australia) Returned Services League • Royal Society of Literature

**RSLA** raising of school-leaving age

**RSM** regimental sergeant major • regional sales manager • *international vehicle registration for* Republic of San Marino • Royal School of Mines • Royal

Society of Medicine • Royal Society of Musicians of Great Britain

**RSMA** Royal Society of Marine Artists

**RSME** Royal School of Military Engineering

**rsn** reason

**RSNA** Radiological Society of North America

**RSNC** Royal Society for Nature Conservation

**RSNZ** Royal Society of New Zealand

**RSO** radiological safety officer • Radio Symphony Orchestra • railway sorting office • railway suboffice • *Military* range safety officer • recruiting staff officer • resident surgical officer • Royal Scottish Orchestra • rural suboffice

**RSocMed** Royal Society of Medicine

**r.s.p.** rain stopped play

**RSPB** Royal Society for the Protection of Birds

**RSPCA** Royal Society for the Prevention of Cruelty to Animals

**RSPP** Royal Society of Portrait Painters

**rsq.** rescue

**RSRE** Royal Signals and Radar Establishment (formerly RRE)

**RSS** Fellow of the Royal Society (Latin *Regiae Societatis Socius*) • Royal Statistical Society

**RSSA** Royal Scottish Society of Arts

**RSSPCC** Royal Scottish Society for the Prevention of Cruelty to Children

**RSTM&H** Royal Society of Tropical Medicine and Hygiene

**rstr.** restricted

**RSU** road safety unit

**RSUA** Royal Society of Ulster Architects

**RSV** *Med.* respiratory syncytial virus • Revised Standard Version (of the Bible) • *Microbiol.* Rous sarcoma virus

**RSVP** répondez s'il vous plaît (French: please reply)

**rsvr** reservoir

**RSW** (Member of the) Royal Scottish Society of Painters in Water Colours

**RSWC** right side up with care

**RSwN** Royal Swedish Navy

**rt** right

**r.t.** *Football* (USA) right tackle

**RT** *British vehicle registration for* Ipswich • radiation therapy • (*or* **R/T**) radio telegraph (*or* telegraphy) • radio telephone (*or* telephony) • reaction time • reading test • received text • return ticket • room temperature • round table • round trip

**RTA** reciprocal trade agreement(s) • *Med.* road traffic accident • Road Traffic Act

**RTB** *Military* return to base

**RTBA** rate to be agreed

**RTBF** (Belgium) Radio-Télévision Belge de la Communauté Française (French broadcasting company)

**rtc.** ratchet

**RTC** (India) Road Transport Corporation • Round Table Conference

**rtd** returned

**rtd ht** *Cricket* retired hurt

**RTDS** *Computing* real-time data system

**rte** route

**RTE** Radio Telefís Éireann (Gaelic: Irish Radio and Television) • *Computing* real-time execution

**RTECS** ('ɑːtɛks) Registry of Toxic Effects of Chemical Substances

**RTF** Radiodiffusion-Télévision Française (French television network) • *Genetics* resistance transfer factor

**rtg** rating

**RTG** *Physics* relativistic theory of gravitation

**Rt Hon.** Right Honourable

**RTI** Round Table International

**RTITB** Road Transport Industry Training Board

**RTK** right to know

**RTL** *Computing* real-time language • *Electronics* resistor-transistor logic

**rtn** retain • return

**rtng** returning

**RTO** (USA) railroad transportation officer • railway transport officer

**RTOL** ('ɑːˌtɒl) *Aeronautics* reduced take-off and landing

**RTP** *Engineering* rated thermal power • *Physics* room temperature and pressure

**RTPI** Royal Town Planning Institute

**RTR** Royal Tank Regiment

**RTRA** Road Traffic Regulation Act

**Rt Rev.** Right Reverend

**RTS** Religious Tract Society • reserve tug service • Royal Television Society • Royal Toxophilite Society

**RTSA** Retail Trading Standards Association

**RTT** (*or* **RTTY**) radioteletype

**RTTC** *Cycling* Road Time Trials Council

**RTU** *Military* returned to unit

**Rt W** Right Worshipful

**RTW** (*or* **rtw**) ready to wear

**RTYC** Royal Thames Yacht Club

**RTZ** Rio Tinto Zinc Corporation Limited

**Ru** *Chem., symbol for* ruthenium

**Ru.** Russia(n)

**RU** *British vehicle registration for* Bournemouth • Readers' Union • *Computing* registered user • reprocessed uranium • *international vehicle registration for* Republic of Burundi • *Med., Pharmacol.* Roussel-Uclaf (French pharmaceutical company; in **RU-486**, abortion pill) • Rugby Union

**RUA** Royal Ulster Academy of Painting, Sculpture, and Architecture

**RUAS** Royal Ulster Agricultural Society

**RUBISCO** (ruːˈbɪskəʊ) *Botany* RuBP carboxylase

**RuBP** (*or* **RUBP**) *Botany* ribulose 1,5-bisphosphate (formerly diphosphate, RuDP *or* RDP)

**RUC** Royal Ulster Constabulary

**RUCR** Royal Ulster Constabulary Reserve

**rud.** rudder

**RuDP** *Botany* ribulose diphosphate (*see* RuBP)

**RUF** *Banking* revolving underwriting facility

**RUG** *Computing* restricted users group

**RUI** Royal University of Ireland

**RUKBA** (*or* **Rukba**) Royal United Kingdom Beneficent Association

**rumpie** ('rʌmpɪ) *Colloquial* rural upwardly mobile professional

**RUPP** road used as public path

**RUR** Royal Ulster Regiment

**RURAL** ('rʊərəl) Society for the Responsible Use of Resources in Agriculture and on the Land

**Rus.** Russia(n)

**RUS** *international vehicle registration for* Russia

**RUSI** Royal United Services Institute for Defence Studies (formerly Royal United Service Institution)

**RUSM** Royal United Service Museum

**Russ.** Russia(n)

**Rut.** (*or* **Rutd**) Rutland (former county)

**r.v.** *Statistics* random variable • rendezvous

**RV** *British vehicle registration for* Portsmouth • rateable value • (USA) recreational vehicle (e.g. a motorized caravan) • *Astronautics* re-entry vehicle • rendezvous • research vessel • *Med.*

residual volume • Revised Version (of the Bible) • Rifle Volunteers • *Med.* right ventricle (*or* ventricular)

**RVB** *Chem.* resonating valence bond

**RVC** Rifle Volunteer Corps • Royal Veterinary College

**RVCI** Royal Veterinary College of Ireland

**RVLR** Road Vehicles Lighting Regulations

**RVO** Royal Victorian Order

**RVR** runway visual range

**RVSVP** répondez vite, s'il vous plaît (French: please reply quickly)

**RVU** research vessel unit

**Rw.** Rwanda

**RW** *British vehicle registration for* Coventry • rainwater • (*or* **R/W**) right of way • Right Worshipful • Right Worthy • Royal Warrant • runway

**RWA** Race Walking Association • (Member of the) Royal West of England Academy • *international vehicle registration for* Rwanda

**RWAFF** Royal West African Frontier Force

**R War. R** Royal Warwickshire Regiment

**RWAS** Royal Welsh Agricultural Society

**r.w.d.** rear-wheel drive

**RWD** radioactive-waste disposal

**RWEA** (Member of the) Royal West of England Academy

**RWF** Radio Wholesalers' Federation • Royal Welch Fusiliers

**RwFr** Rwanda franc

**RWGM** *Freemasonry* Right Worshipful Grand Master

**RWGR** *Freemasonry* Right Worthy Grand Representative

**RWGS** *Freemasonry* Right Worthy Grand Secretary

**RWGT** *Freemasonry* Right Worthy Grand Templar • *Freemasonry* Right Worthy Grand Treasurer

**RWGW** *Freemasonry* Right Worthy Grand Warden

**R Wilts Yeo.** Royal Wiltshire Yeomanry

**RWK** Queen's Own Royal West Kent Regiment

**RWM** radioactive waste management

**RWP** rainwater pipe

**RWS** (Member of the) Royal Society of Painters in Water Colours

**rwy** (*or* **Rwy**) railway

**RX** *British vehicle registration for* Reading • *British fishing port registration for* Rye

**ry** (*or* **Ry**) railway

**RY** *British vehicle registration for* Leicester • *British fishing port registration for* Ramsey

**RYA** Royal Yachting Association

**RYC** in reply to your cable

**RYS** Royal Yacht Squadron

**r.z.** return to zero

**RZ** *British vehicle registration for* Antrim

**RZSI** Royal Zoological Society of Ireland

**RZSScot** (*or* **RZSS**) Royal Zoological Society of Scotland

# S

**s** *Physics, symbol for* electron state *l*=0 (where *l* is orbital angular momentum quantum number) • (ital.) *Chem., Physics, symbol for* path length • *symbol for* second(s) • (ital.) *Chem.* secondary (isomer; as in **s-butyl alcohol**) • (ital.) *Chem., symbol for* sedimentation coefficient • *Spectroscopy, symbol for* singlet • *Music* soh (in tonic sol-fa) • *Chem.* solid (as in **NaCl(s)**) • (ital.) *Physics, symbol for* specific entropy •

(ital.) *Physics, symbol for* spin quantum number • *Physics* strange (a quark flavour) • *Spectroscopy, symbol for* strong absorption • (ital.) *Chem.* symmetric (as in **s-dichloroethane**)

**s.** school • sea • seaman • section • see • semi- • series • sermon • sets • shilling • siècle (French: century) • siehe (German: see) • sign(ed) • sine (Latin: without) • *Grammar* singular • sinister (Latin: left) • sinistra (Italian: left) •

sire • sister • small • snow • society • solidus (Latin: shilling) • solo • son • *Music* soprano (instrument) • spherical • steamer • steel • stem • stock • stratus (cloud) • *Grammar* substantive • succeeded • suit • sun(ny)

**s/** sur (French: on; in place names)

**S** (ital.) *Electrical engineering, symbol for* apparent power • (ital.) *Physics, symbol for* entropy • (bold ital.) *Physics, symbol for* Poynting vector • *symbol for* Schilling (Austrian monetary unit) • *Biochem., symbol for* serine • *Medieval Roman numeral for* seven(ty) • *postcode for* Sheffield • *Electrical engineering, symbol for* siemens • *Med.* signā (*see under* Sig.) • *Geology* Silurian • (ital.) *Chem.* sinister (as in **(S)-butan-2-ol**) • *Irish fishing port registration for* Skibbereen • slow (on a clock or watch regulator) • small (size) • *Microbiol.* smooth (in **S-form** of a bacterial colony) • *Astronomy, symbol for* solar mass • south(ern) • (ital.) *Physics, symbol for* spin quantum number (of a system) • *Astronomy, symbol for* spiral galaxy (followed by letter(s)) • (ital.) *Physics, symbol for* strangeness quantum number • *Chem., symbol for* substitution reaction • sucre (Ecuadorian monetary unit) • *Chem., symbol for* sulphur • *Shipping* summer loading (on load line) • *Biochem., symbol for* Svedberg unit (as in **S value, 70S ribosome**) • *international vehicle registration for* Sweden • (ital.) *Chem., indicating* substitution on a sulphur atom (in names of compounds)

**S.** (*or* **S**) Sabbath • *Heraldry* sable • *Anatomy* sacral (of vertebrae) • Saint • San (Italian: Saint) • Sankt (German: Saint) • Santo *or* Santa (Italian: Saint) • São (Portuguese: Saint) • satisfactory • Saturday • Saxon • School • Scotland • Scottish • Sea • secondary • secretary • (ital.) *Music* segno (Italian: sign) • Seite (German: page) • Senate • Señor (Spanish: Mr) • sentence • September • sepultus (Latin: buried) • series • ship • signaller • signature • Signor (Italian: Mr) • Signora (Italian: Mrs) • Socialist • Society • Socius (Latin: Fellow; in titles) • solar • *Music* soprano (voice) • south(ern) • *Cards* spades • staff • *Law* statute • *Microbiol.* strain (followed by a number) • submarine • summer • sun • Sunday • Sweden

**S2** *international civil aircraft marking for* Bangladesh

**S7** *international civil aircraft marking for* Seychelles

**S9** *international civil aircraft marking for* São Tomé

**sa.** *Heraldry* sable

**s.a.** safe arrival • *Med.* secundum artem (Latin: by skill) • see also • *Horticulture* semiannual • sex appeal • siehe auch (German: see also) • sine anno (Latin: without date; undated) • *Chem.* soluble in alkali • special agent • storage area • subject to approval • subsistence allowance

**Sa.** Saturday

**SA** *British vehicle registration for* Aberdeen • Salvation Army • *Meteorol.* sandstorm • Saudi Arabia(n) • seaman apprentice • (USA) Secretary of the Army • *Horticulture* semiannual • sex appeal • *Microbiol.* simian agent (as in **SA12**) • *Med.* sinoatrial (as in **SA node**) • small arms (Spain, Portugal) sociedad anónima *or* (in Portugal) sociedade anónima (public limited company; plc) • (France, Belgium, Luxembourg, Switzerland) société anonyme (public limited company; plc) • Society of Antiquaries • Society of Arts • Society of Authors • Soil Association • Son Altesse (French: His *or* Her Highness) • South Africa(n) • *airline flight code for* South African Airways • South America(n) • South Australia(n) • Sturmabteilung (German: storm troopers; Nazi terrorist militia) • surface area • *Military* surface-to-air (missile; as in **SA-9**) • Swansea (postcode *or* British fishing port registration)

**S/A** subject to acceptance • *Banking* (USA) survivorship agreement

**SAA** small arms ammunition • South African Airways • Speech Association of America • Standards Association of Australia • *Chem.* surface-active agent • *Computing* systems application architecture

**SAAA** Scottish Amateur Athletic Association

**SAAAU** South African Amateur Athletic Union

**SAAB** (*or* **Saab**) (sɑːb) Svensk Aeroplan Aktiebolag (Swedish aircraft and car company)

**SAAD** small-arms ammunition depot

**SAAF** South African Air Force

**SAAFA** Special Arab Assistance Fund for Africa

**SAAO** South African Astronomical Observatory

**SAAU** South African Agricultural Union

**sab.** sábado (Portuguese: Saturday) • sabato (Italian: Saturday)

**Sab.** Sabbath

**SAB** Science (or Scientific) Advisory Board • Society of American Bacteriologists • Music soprano, alto, bass • South Atlantic Bight

**SABA** Scottish Amateur Boxing Association

**Sabat.** Sabbatical

**SABC** Scottish Association of Boys' Clubs • South African Broadcasting Corporation

**Sabena** (or **SABENA**) (sə'bi:nə) Société anonyme belge d'exploitation de la navigation aérienne (Belgian World Airlines)

**SABMIS** ('sæb,mɪs) seaborne antiballistic missile intercept system

**sabo.** sabotage

**SABRA** ('sæbrə) South African Bureau of Racial Affairs

**SABS** South African Bureau of Standards

**sac** Military, indicating qualified at a small-arms technical long course

**SAC** Scientific Advisory Committee • Scottish Automobile Club • Senior Aircraftman • small-arms club • South Atlantic coast • (USA) State Athletic Commission • (USA) Strategic Air Command

**SACEUR** (or **Saceur**) ('sæk,jʊə) Supreme Allied Commander Europe

**SACL** South African Confederation of Labour

**SACLANT** ('sæk,lænt) Supreme Allied Commander Atlantic

**SACO** Sveriges Akademikers Central-organisation (Swedish Confederation of Professional Associations; trade union)

**SACP** South African Communist Party

**Sacr.** Sacramento (USA) • Sacrist

**SACSEA** ('sæk,si:) Supreme Allied Command, SE Asia

**SACSIR** South African Council for Scientific and Industrial Research

**SACU** Southern African Customs Union

**SACW** Senior Aircraftwoman

**SAD** Psychiatry seasonal affective disorder

**SADCC** Southern Africa Development Coordinating Conference (or Committee)

**SADF** South African Defence Force

**SADG** Société des architectes diplômés par le gouvernement (French: Society of Government-Certified Architects)

**SADT** Computing, trademark structured analysis and design technique

**SAE** (or **s.a.e.**) self-addressed envelope • (USA) Society of Automotive Engineers (designating a viscosity scale for motor oils) • (or **s.a.e.**) stamped addressed envelope

**SAEF** Stock Exchange Automatic Execution Facility

**SAF** (USA) Secretary of the Air Force • Society of American Foresters • (USA) Strategic Air Force

**SAFA** South Africa Freedom Association

**s.a.f.e.** stamped addressed foolscap envelope

**S. Afr.** South Africa(n)

**S.Afr.D.** South African Dutch

**SAFU** Scottish Amateur Fencing Union

**SAG** (USA) Screen Actors' Guild

**SAGA** Society of American Graphic Artists

**SAGB** Spiritualist Association of Great Britain

**SAGE** (seɪdʒ) Military (USA, Canada) semiautomatic ground environment

**SAH** Med. subarachnoid haemorrhage • Supreme Allied Headquarters

**Sai.** Saigon

**SAIDS** (seɪdz) simian acquired immune deficiency syndrome

**SAIF** South African Industrial Federation

**SAIMR** South African Institute of Medical Research

**SAIRR** South African Institute of Race Relations

**sal.** salary

**SAL** South Arabian League • surface airlifted mail

**SALA** South African Library Association

**SALP** South African Labour Party

**SALR** Meteorol. saturated adiabatic lapse rate • South African Law Reports

**SALT** (sɔ:lt) Strategic Arms Limitation Talks (or Treaty)

**salv.** salvage

**Salv.** Salvador

**sam.** samedi (French: Saturday)

**Sam.** Samaria · Samaritan · Samoa · Samstag (German: Saturday) · *Bible* Samuel

**S. Am.** South America(n)

**SAM** (sæm) *Physics* scanning Auger microprobe (*or* microscopy) · (USA) shared-appreciation mortgage · (USA) Space Available Mail · surface-to-air missile

**SAMA** Saudi Arabian Monetary Agency

**Samar.** Samaritan

**SAMC** South African Medical Corps

**S. Amer.** South America(n)

**SAMH** Scottish Association for Mental Health

**san.** sanitary

**SAN** *Chem.* styrene–acrylonitrile (polymer)

**sanat.** sanatorium

**SANCAD** ('sænkæd) Scottish Association for National Certificates and Diplomas

**s & d** song and dance

**sand.** sandwich

**S&F** *Insurance* stock and fixtures

**S&FA** shipping and forwarding agents

**S&H** (*or* **S and H**) shipping and handling (charges)

**S&L** (USA) savings and loan association

**s & m** sausages and mash

**S & M** sadism and masochism · *Insurance* stock and machinery

**s & s** *Colloquial* sex and shopping (type of popular fiction)

**SANDS** (*or* **Sands**) (sændz) Stillbirth and Neonatal Death Society

**s. & s.c.** sized and supercalendered (of paper)

**S & T** Salmon & Trout Association · supply and transport

**Sane** (seɪn) Schizophrenia – A National Emergency

**SANE** (seɪn) (USA) Committee for a Sane Nuclear Policy

**sanit.** sanitary · sanitation

**s.a.n.r.** subject to approval, no risk

**SANROC** ('sæn,rɒk) South African Non-Racial Olympics Committee

**sans.** *Printing* sanserif

**Sans.** (*or* **Sansk.**) Sanskrit

**SANS** *Physics* small-angle neutron scattering

**SANZ** Standards Association of New Zealand

**SAO** Scottish Association of Opticians

**SAOS** Scottish Agricultural Organization Society

**s.a.p.** soon as possible

**SAP** South African Police

**SAPA** (sæpə) South African Press Association · South African Publishers' Association

**sapfu** ('sæpfuː) *Slang* surpassing all previous foul-ups (*or* fuck-ups)

**s.a.p.l.** *Shipping* sailed as per list (i.e. Lloyd's List)

**sap. no.** *Chem.* saponification number

**Sar.** Sarawak · Sardinia(n)

**SAR** search and rescue · Son Altesse Royale (French: His (*or* Her) Royal Highness) · Sons of the American Revolution · South African Republic · *Physics* specific absorption rate · synthetic-aperture radar

**SARAH** ('sɛərə) search and rescue homing (radar system) · surgery assistant robot acting on the head (in brain surgery)

**SARBE** ('sɑːbɪ) search and rescue beacon equipment (of SARAH)

**Sarl.** (*or* **Sàrl.**) (France, Belgium, Luxembourg, Switzerland) société à responsabilité limitée (private limited company; Ltd)

**SARSAT** ('sɑːsæt) search and rescue satellite-aided tracking

**Sarum.** Sarumensis (Latin: (Bishop) of Salisbury)

**Sas.** (Italy) società in accomandita semplice (limited partnership)

**SAS** Fellow of the Society of Antiquaries (Latin *Societatis Antiquariorum Socius*) · Scandinavian Airline System · *Physics* small-angle scattering · Small Astronomical Satellite · Son Altesse Sérénissime (French: His (*or* Her) Most Serene Highness) · *Military* Special Air Service

**SASC** Small Arms School Corps

**SASE** (*or* **sase**) (USA) self-addressed stamped envelope

**Sask.** Saskatchewan

**SASO** Senior Air Staff Officer · South African Students' Organization

**SASR** Special Air Service Regiment

**sat.** satellite · saturate(d)

**Sat.** Saturday · *Astronomy* Saturn

**S. At.** South Atlantic

**SAT** (USA) scholastic aptitude test · Senior Member of the Association of Accounting Technicians · ship's apparent time · South Australian Time · (sæt) *Education* standard assessment task

**SATB** *Music* soprano, alto, tenor, bass

**SATCO** ('sætkəʊ) signal automatic air-traffic control system

**SATEX** ('seitɛks) semiautomatic telegraph exchange

**satn** saturation

**SATRO** Science and Technology Regional Organization

**SATS** South African Transport Services

**S. Aus.** (*or* **S. Austral.**) South Australia(n)

**s.a.v.** sale at valuation • stock at valuation

**SAV** *Microbiol.* simian adenovirus

**SAVAK** (*or* **Savak**) ('sævæk *or* 'sɑːvæk) (Iran) Sāzmān-i-Attalāt Va Amnīyat-i-Keshvar (National Security and Intelligence Organization, 1957–79)

**SAVS** Scottish Anti-Vivisection Society

**SAW** space at will (of advertisements) • submerged arc welding • *Telecom.* surface acoustic wave

**SAWS** synoptic automatic weather station

**sax.** saxophone

**Sax.** Saxon • Saxony

**SAXS** *Physics* small-angle X-ray scattering

**SAYE** save as you earn (savings scheme)

**sb** *Physics, symbol for* stilb

**sb.** *Grammar* substantive

**s.b.** single-breasted • small bore (rifle) • smooth bore • *Baseball* stolen base(s)

**Sb** *Chem., symbol for* antimony (Latin *stibium*)

**SB** (USA) Bachelor of Science (Latin *Scientiae Baccalaureus*) • *Astronomy, symbol for* barred spiral galaxy (as in **SBa**, **SBb**) • *British vehicle registration for* Glasgow • sales book • Sam Browne (military officer's belt and strap) • savings bank • selection board • Serving Brother (of an order) • *Commerce* short bill (of exchange) • sick bay • Signal Boatswain • signal book • simultaneous broadcast(ing) • *Chemical engineering* slurry bed • *Commerce* small business • *Chem.* sodium borate • South Britain (i.e. England and Wales) • Special Branch (of police) • Statute Book • *Med.* stillborn • stretcher bearer • sub-branch

**SBA** School of Business Administration • sick-bay (*or* -berth) attendant • (USA) Small Business Administration • *Aeronautics* standard beam approach

**SBAA** Sovereign Base Areas Administration

**SBAC** Society of British Aerospace Companies (formerly Aircraft Constructors)

**SBB** Schweizerische Bundesbahnen (Swiss Federal Railways)

**SBBNF** Ship and Boat Builders' National Federation

**SBC** School Broadcasting Council • single-board computer • *Electrical engineering* small bayonet cap

**SBD** Soviet Block Division (of the CIA) • *Electronics* surface-barrier (*or* Schottky-barrier) diode

**SbE** south by east

**SBE** Southern British English (dialect)

**SBGI** Society of British Gas Industries

**SBH** Scottish Board of Health

**SBIC** (USA) small business investment company

**SBL** *Electronics* surface boundary layer

**SBLI** (USA) savings bank life insurance

**SBM** single buoy mooring

**SBN** Standard Book Number (replaced by ISBN)

**SBNO** Senior British Naval Officer

**s'board** starboard

**SBOT** Sacred Books of the Old Testament

**SBP** *Med.* systolic blood pressure

**SBR** styrene–butadiene rubber

**sbre.** septiembre (Spanish: September)

**SBS** *Med.* sick-building syndrome • *Military* Special Boat Service

**SBStJ** Serving Brother of the Order of St John of Jerusalem

**SBT** *Shipping* segregated ballast tanks

**SBU** strategic business unit

**SBV** seabed vehicle

**SbW** south by west

**sc** *Printing* small capitals • *Military* (student at the) staff college

**sc.** scale • scene • science • scientific • scilicet (namely *or* that is; from Latin *scire licet*) • screw • scruple (unit of weight) • sculpsit (Latin: (he *or* she) carved (*or* engraved) this)

**s.c.** salvage charges • self-contained • *Printing* single column • *Printing* small capitals • steel casting • supercalendered (of paper)

**s/c** self-contained • *Commerce* son compte (French: (on) his account)

**Sc** *Chem., symbol for* scandium • (ital.) *Physics, symbol for* Schmidt number • (ital.) *Meteorol., symbol for* stratocumulus

**Sc.** Scandinavia(n) • Scotch • Scotland • Scots • Scottish

**SC** *British vehicle registration for* Edinburgh • safe custody • sailing club • Salvage Corps • *Law* same case • *Military* (USA) Sanitary Corps • (Australia, New Zealand) School Certificate • Schools Council • *British fishing port registration for* Scilly • Security Council (of the UN) • self-contained • Senatus Consultum (Latin: decree of the Senate) • Senior Counsel • service certificate • *Law* Sessions Cases • shooting club • short course • Signal Corps • *Printing* single column • *Chem.* single crystal • skating club • skiing club • small craft • social club • solar cell • South Carolina (abbrev. *or* postcode) • *Military* Southern Command • special case • Special Constable (*or* Constabulary) • sports club • Staff Captain • staff college • Staff Corps • standing committee • standing conference • (Canada) Star of Courage • statutory committee • *Meteorol.* stratocumulus • *Engineering* stress corrosion • structural change (in transformational grammar) • Suffolk and Cambridgeshire (regiment) • supercalendered (paper) • Supreme Court • surface contamination • swimming club

**SCA** sickle-cell anaemia

**SCAAA** Southern Counties Amateur Athletic Association

**SCAHT** Scottish Churches Architectural Heritage Trust

**Scand.** (*or* **Scan.**) Scandinavia(n)

**SCAO** Senior Civil Affairs Officer

**SCAP** (skæp) Supreme Command (*or* Commander) Allied Powers

**SCAPA** Society for Checking the Abuses of Public Advertising

**s. caps** *Printing* small capitals

**SCAR** (skɑː) Scientific (*or* Special) Committee on Antarctic Research

**SCARA** ('skɛərə) selective compliance assembly robot arm

**Scarab** ('skærəb) submerged craft assisting repair and burial

**SCAT** *Med.* sheep-cell agglutination test

**ScB** Bachelor of Science (Latin *Scientiae Baccalaureus*)

**SCB** Solicitors Complaints Bureau • Speedway Control Board (in motorcycling)

**ScBC** Bachelor of Science in Chemistry

**ScBE** Bachelor of Science in Engineering

**SCBU** *Med.* special-care baby unit

**s.c.c.** *Printing* single column centimetre • *Electrical engineering* single cotton-covered (wire)

**SCC** Sea Cadet Corps • Society of Church Craftsmen • *Engineering* stress-corrosion cracking

**SCCA** Sports Car Club of America

**SCCAPE** Scottish Council for Commercial, Administrative, and Professional Education

**SCCL** Scottish Council for Civil Liberties

**scd** scheduled

**ScD** Doctor of Science (Latin *Scientiae Doctor*)

**SCD** sickle-cell disease

**SCDA** Scottish Community Drama Association

**SCDC** Schools Curriculum Development Committee

**ScDHyg** Doctor of Science in Hygiene

**ScDMed** Doctor of Science in Medicine

**sce.** scenario

**SCE** schedule compliance evaluation • Scottish Certificate of Education • *Genetics* sister-chromatid exchange

**scf** standard cubic feet

**SCF** Save the Children Fund • *Physics* self-consistent field • Senior Chaplain to the Forces

**scfh** standard cubic feet per hour

**scfm** standard cubic feet per minute

**scg** scoring

**SCG** Sydney Cricket Ground

**Sc. Gael.** Scottish Gaelic

**SCGB** Ski Club of Great Britain

**sch.** scholar • scholarship • scholastic • scholium (Latin: note) • school • schooner

**Sch.** *Taxation* schedule (followed by a letter) • Schilling (Austrian monetary unit) • School

**sched.** schedule

**schem.** schematic

**scherz.** *Music* scherzando (Italian: playful, humorous)

**SchMusB** Bachelor of School Music

**schol.** scholar • scholarship • scholastic • scholium (Latin: note)

**schr** schooner

**sci.** science • scientific

**s.c.i.** *Printing* single-column inch

**SCI** Scottish Central Institutions • Society of the Chemical Industry

**SCID** (*or* **skid**) (skɪd) *Med.* severe combined immunodeficiency disease

**sci. fa.** scire facias (Latin: that you cause to know)

**sci-fi** ('saɪ'faɪ) *Colloquial* science fiction

**scil.** scilicet (*see under* sc.)

**SCIT** Special Commissioners of Income Tax

**SCK** Servants of Christ the King

**Scl** *Astronomy* Sculptor

**SCL** Scottish Central Library • Student in (*or* of) Civil Law

**SCLC** *Med.* small-cell lung cancer (*or* carcinoma) • (USA) Southern Christian Leadership Conference

**SCLI** Somerset and Cornwall Light Infantry

**ScM** Master of Science (Latin *Scientiae Magister*)

**SCM** State Certified Midwife (replaced by RM, Registered Midwife) • Student Christian Movement • summary court-martial

**SCMA** Society of Cinema Managers of Great Britain and Ireland (Amalgamated)

**SCMES** Society of Consulting Marine Engineers and Ship Surveyors

**ScMHyg** Master of Science in Hygiene

**SCNE** Select Committee on National Expenditure

**SCNO** Senior Canadian Naval Officer

**Sco** *Astronomy* Scorpius

**SCOBEC** ('skəubɛk) Scottish Business Education Council

**S. Con. Res.** (USA) Senate concurrent resolution

**SCONUL** Standing Conference of National and University Libraries

**SCOR** Scientific Committee on Oceanic Research • Standing Committee on Refugees

**Scot.** Scotch (whisky) • Scotland • Scottish

**ScotBIC** ('skɒt,bɪk) Scottish Business in the Community

**SCOTEC** ('skəutɛk) Scottish Technical Education Council

**SCOTUS** ('skəutəs) Supreme Court of the United States

**SCOTVEC** ('skɒt,vɛk) Scottish Vocational Education Council

**SCOUT** (skaut) *Commerce* Shared Currency Option Under Tender

**SCP** single-cell protein (in food technology) • (Canada) Social Credit Party

**SCPC** *Telecom.* single channel per carrier

**SCPR** Scottish Council of Physical Recreation

**SCPS** Society of Civil and Public Servants

**scr.** *Finance* scrip • scruple (unit of weight)

**SCR** *Chemical engineering* selective catalytic reactor (*or* reaction) • senior common room (in a university) • *Electronics* silicon-controlled rectifier • Society for Cultural Relations with the USSR

**SCRE** Scottish Council for Research in Education

**Script.** Scriptural • Scripture(s)

**scRNA** *Biochem.* small cytoplasmic RNA

**scRNP** *Biochem.* small cytoplasmic ribonucleoprotein

**SCS** (USA) Soil Conservation Service • space communications system

**SCSA** Soil Conservation Society of America

**SCSI** ('skuːzɪ) small computer systems interface

**SCSS** Scottish Council of Social Service

**Sct** *Astronomy* Scutum

**SCTR** Standing Conference on Tele-communications Research

**SCU** Scottish Cricket Union • Scottish Cycling (*or* Cyclists') Union

**SCUA** Suez Canal Users' Association

**scuba** ('skjuːbə) self-contained under-water breathing apparatus

**sculp.** (*or* **sculps., sculpt.**) sculpsit (*see under* sc.) • sculptor (*or* sculptress) • sculptural • sculpture

**SCV** Stato della Città del Vaticano (Italian: Vatican City State)

**SCWS** Scottish Co-operative Whole-sale Society

**SCY** *British vehicle registration for* Truro (Isles of Scilly)

**SCYA** Scottish Christian Youth Assembly

**sd** said • sailed • sewed (of books) • signed • sound

**s.d.** safe deposit • same date • sans date (French: no date) • semidetached • *Philosophy* sense datum • several dates • *Commerce* short delivery • siehe dies (German: see this) • sine die (Latin: without a day (being fixed)) • *Statistics* standard deviation

**SD** Diploma in Statistics • Doctor of Science (Latin *Scientiae Doctor*) • *British*

*vehicle registration for* Glasgow • salutem dicit (Latin: (he *or* she) sends greeting) • sea-damaged • (USA) Secretary of Defense • semi-detached • Senatus Decreto (Latin: by decree of the Senate) • send direct • *Med.* senile dementia • Senior Deacon • sequence date • *Military* service dress • *Commerce* short delivery • Sicherheitsdienst (German: Security Service; in Nazi Germany) • *Finance* sight draft • Signal Department • Signal Division • South Dakota (abbrev. *or* postcode) • special delivery • special duty • staff duties • stage door • *Statistics* standard deviation • (USA) State Department • structural description (in transformational grammar) • submarine detector • *airline flight code for* Sudan Airways • *British fishing port registration for* Sunderland • supply depot • *international vehicle registration for* Swaziland

**S/D** (USA) school district • *Finance* sight draft

**SDA** Scottish Development Agency • Scottish Dinghy Association • Scottish Diploma in Agriculture • Seventh Day Adventists • Social Democratic Alliance • spray-drying absorption (*or* absorber)

**S. Dak.** South Dakota

**SD&T** staff duties and training

**SDAT** *Med.* senile dementia of the Alzheimer type

**S-DAT** stationary digital audio tape

**SDC** Society of Dyers and Colourists • submersible decompression chamber

**SDD** Scottish Development Department • *Telephony* subscriber direct dialling

**SDECE** (France) Service de documentation étrangère et de contre-espionage (counterintelligence agency)

**SDF** Social Democratic Federation

**SDG** Soli Deo Gloria (Latin: Glory to God Alone)

**SDHE** spacecraft data-handling equipment

**SDI** selective dissemination of information • Strategic Defense Initiative (US Star Wars programme)

**SDIO** (USA) Strategic Defense Initiative Office

**sdl.** saddle

**SDL** special duties list

**SDLC** *Computing* synchronous data link control

**SDLP** (Northern Ireland) Social Democratic and Labour Party

**SDMJ** September, December, March, June (dates for quarterly payments)

**SDO** Senior Dental Officer • senior duty officer • station duty officer • subdivisional officer

**S. Doc.** (USA) Senate document

**SDP** Social Democratic Party • *Insurance* social, domestic, and pleasure

**SDR** special despatch rider • *Finance* special drawing right(s)

**SDS** scientific data system • Sisters of the Divine Saviour • sodium dodecyl sulphate (detergent) • (Germany) Sozialistischer Deutscher Studentenbund (Federation of Socialist Students) • (USA) strategic defense system • (USA) Students for a Democratic Society

**SDS-PAGE** *Biochem.* sodium dodecyl sulphate–polyacrylamide gel electrophoresis

**SDT** Society of Dairy Technology

**s.e.** single end(ed) • single engine • *Book-keeping* single entry • special equipment • *Statistics* standard error • straight edge

**Se** *Chem., symbol for* selenium

**SE** *British vehicle registration for* Aberdeen • *British fishing port registration for* Salcombe • sanitary engineering • Society of Engineers • *Computing* software engineering • Son Eminence (French: His Eminence) • Son Excellence (French: His (*or* Her) Excellency) • southeast(ern) • *postcode for* southeast London • Staff Engineer • Standard English • Stirling engine • (*or* **S/E**) stock exchange • *Building trades* stopped end • *international civil aircraft marking for* Sweden

**SEA** South-East Asia

**SEAAC** South-East Asia Air Command

**SEAC** ('siːæk) School Examination and Assessment Council • South-East Asia Command • Standard Eastern Automatic Computer

**SEAL** (siːl) *US Navy* sea-air-land

**SEALF** South-East Asia Land Forces

**SE & CR** South Eastern and Chatham Railway

**SEAQ** ('siːæk) Stock Exchange Automated Quotations

**SEATO** ('siːtəu) Southeast Asia Treaty Organization (1954–77)

**SEATS** Stock Exchange Alternative Trading Service

**SEB** Southern Electricity Board

**sec** (sɛk) *Maths.* secant

**sec.** second (of time or an angle) • secondary • seconded • (*or* **Sec.**) secretary • section • sector • secundum (Latin: according to) • security

**SEC** (USA) Securities and Exchange Commission • *Chem.* size-exclusion chromatography • *Military* Southeastern Command

**SECAM** ('siːˌkæm) séquentiel couleur à mémoire (colour-television broadcasting system developed in France)

**SECC** Scottish Exhibition and Conference Centre

**Sec. Gen.** (*or* **Sec-Gen**) Secretary General

**sech** (sɛtʃ) *Maths.* hyperbolic secant

**sec. leg.** secundum legem (Latin: according to law)

**Sec. Leg.** Secretary of the Legation

**sec. nat.** secundum naturam (Latin: according to nature, naturally)

**sec. reg.** secundum regulam (Latin: according to rule)

**sect.** section

**secy** (*or* **Secy**) secretary

**sed.** sedative • sediment

**SED** Scottish Education Department • shipper's export declaration • (formerly, in East Germany) Sozialistische Einheitspartei Deutschlands (Socialist Unity (i.e. Communist) Party)

**SEDAR** ('siːdɑː) *Navigation* submerged electrode detection and ranging

**sedt** sediment

**sedtn** sedimentation

**SEE** *Physics* secondary electron emission • Senior Electrical Engineer • Society of Environment Engineers

**SEEB** (*or* **Seeboard**) Southeastern Electricity Board

**SEF** Shipbuilding Employers' Federation

**seg.** segment • segregate • *Music* segue (Italian: follows, comes after)

**SEG** socioeconomic grade

**SEH** St Edmund Hall (Oxford University)

**SEIF** (Portugal) Secretaria de Estado da Informação e Turismo (State Information and Tourist Board)

**SEIS** submarine escape immersion suit

**seismol.** seismological • seismology

**SEIU** (USA) Service Employees International Union

**sel.** select(ed) • selection • selig (German: deceased)

**Sel** (*or* **Selw**) Selwyn College, Cambridge

**Selk.** Selkirk

**SELNEC** ('sɛlˌnɛk) South-East Lancashire, North-East Cheshire

**sem.** semester • semicolon • seminary

**Sem.** Seminary • Semitic

**s.e.(m.)** (*or* **SE(M)**) *Statistics* standard error (of the mean)

**SEM** scanning electron microscope (*or* microscopy)

**semp.** *Music* sempre (Italian: always)

**sen.** senior • *Music* senza (Italian: without)

**Sen.** Senate • Senator • (Marcus Annaeus) Seneca (*c.* 55 BC–AD 4l, Roman writer) • Senior

**SEN** special educational needs • (formerly) State Enrolled Nurse (*see* EN(G))

**S en C** (France) société en commandite (limited partnership)

**S en NC** (France) société en nom collectif (partnership)

**Senr** Senior

**sent.** sentence

**SEO** Senior Executive Officer • Senior Experimental Officer • Society of Education Officers

**s.e.o.o.** (*or* **s.e. ou o.**) sauf erreur ou omission (French: errors or omissions excepted)

**sep.** sepal • separable • separate(d) • separation

**Sep.** (*or* **Sep**) September • Septuagint

**SEP** (USA) simplified employee pension

**SEPM** Society of Economic Palaeontologists and Mineralogists

**sepn** separation

**SEPON** ('siːpɒn) Stock Exchange Pool Nominees Ltd

**sept.** septem (Latin: seven) • septembre (French: September) • (*or* **sept^e**) septiembre (Spanish: September)

**Sept.** (*or* **Sept**) September • Septuagint

**seq.** sequel • sequence • sequens (Latin: the following (one)) • sequente (Latin: and in what follows) • sequitur (Latin: it follows)

**seq. luce** *Med.* sequenti luce (Latin: the following day; in prescriptions)

**seqq.** sequentia (Latin: the following (ones)) • sequentibus (Latin: in the following places)

**ser.** serial • series • sermon • servant • service

**Ser** (or **ser**) Biochem. serine • Astronomy Serpens

**SER** Cytology smooth endoplasmic reticulum

**SERA** Socialist Environment and Resources Association

**Serb.** Serbia(n)

**SERC** (sɜːk) Science and Engineering Research Council (formerly SRC)

**Serg.** (or **Sergt**) Sergeant

**Serj.** (or **Serjt**) Serjeant

**SERL** Services Electronics Research Laboratory

**SERLANT** ('sɜːlænt) US Navy Service Forces, Atlantic

**SERPAC** ('sɜːpæk) US Navy Service Forces, Pacific

**SERPS** (or **Serps**) (sɜːps) State Earnings-Related Pension Scheme

**SERT** Society of Electronic and Radio Technicians

**serv.** servant • service

**SES** Singapore Stock Exchange • (USA) socioeconomic status

**SESCO** ('seskəu) secure submarine communications

**SESDAQ** ('sesdæk) Stock Exchange of Singapore Dealing and Automated Quotation System

**SESI** Stock Exchange of Singapore Index

**SESO** Senior Equipment Staff Officer

**sess.** session

**set.** setembro (Portuguese: September) • settlement

**SET** ('es 'iː 'tiː or set) Securities Exchange of Thailand • selective employment tax (1966–73)

**SETI** ('seti) Astronomy search for extra-terrestrial intelligence

**S-et-L** Saône-et-Loire (department of France)

**S-et-M** Seine-et-Marne (department of France)

**S-et-O** Seine-et-Oise (department of France)

**sett.** settembre (Italian: September)

**sev.** sever • several

**SEV** Meteorol. severe (icing, etc.)

**sevl** several

**sew.** sewage • sewer • sewerage

**SEW** safety-equipment worker

**sex.** sextet • sexual

**Sex** Astronomy Sextans

**Sexag.** Sexagesima

**sext.** sextant

**sf** (or **sf.**) Baseball sacrifice fly • Music sforzando (Italian; strongly accented)

**s.f.** Commerce sans frais (French: no expenses) • (or **s-f**) science fiction • Telecom. signal frequency • Finance sinking fund • sub finem (Latin: towards the end)

**Sf** symbol for Suriname guilder (monetary unit)

**SF** British vehicle registration for Edinburgh • San Francisco • science fiction • senior fellow • Military Sherwood Foresters • shipping federation • Telecom. signal frequency • Finance sinking fund • Sinn Fein • Society of Friends • special facilities • special forces • Electrical engineering standard frequency

**SFA** Scottish Football Association • sulphated fatty alcohol (detergents) • Colloquial sweet Fanny Adams (i.e. nothing)

**SFB** Sender Freies Berlin (German: Broadcasting Station of Free Berlin)

**SFBMS** Small Farm Business Management Scheme

**Sfc** (USA) Sergeant first class

**SFC** specific fuel consumption (of jet engines) • Meteorol. surface

**sfgd** safeguard

**SFInstE** Senior Fellow, Institute of Energy

**SFL** Scottish Football League • Aeronautics sequenced flashing lights

**sfm** surface feet per minute

**SFO** Senior Flag Officer • Serious Fraud Office • Superannuation Funds Office

**SFOF** spaceflight operations facility (in NASA)

**sfp** Music sforzato-piano (Italian; strong accent, followed immediately by soft)

**SFr** Swiss franc

**SFR** Finance sinking fund rate of return

**SFT** supercritical fluid technology

**SFTCD** Senior Fellow, Trinity College Dublin

**SFU** signals flying unit • suitable for upgrade (on airline tickets)

**sfz** (or **sfz.**) Music sforzando (see under sf)

**sg.** Grammar singular

**s.g.** specific gravity • steel girder

**Sg.** Surgeon

**SG** *British vehicle registration for* Edinburgh • Sa Grâce (French: His (*or* Her) Grace • Sa Grandeur (French: His (*or* Her) Highness • Scots Guards • Seaman Gunner • Secretary General • *Education* (USA) senior grade • *Astronomy* Seyfert galaxy • ship and goods • singular (in transformational grammar) • *Meteorol.* snow grains • Society of Genealogists • Solicitor General • spinglass (type of crystal) • *postcode for* Stevenage • Surgeon General

**SGA** *Med.* small for gestational age • (Member of the) Society of Graphic Art

**SGB** Schweizerischer Gewerkschaftsbund (German: Swiss Federation of Trade Unions)

**SGBI** Schoolmistresses' and Governesses' Benevolent Institution

**SgC** Surgeon Captain

**SgCr** Surgeon Commander

**sgd** signed

**SGD** *Freemasonry* Senior Grand Deacon

**s.g.d.g.** sans garantie du gouvernement (French: without government guarantee; of patents)

**Sge** *Astronomy* Sagitta

**SGF** Scottish Grocers' Federation

**SGHWR** steam-generating heavy-water reactor

**sgl.** single

**S. Glam** South Glamorgan

**SgLCr** Surgeon Lieutenant-Commander

**SGM** Sea Gallantry Medal

**SGML** *Computing* standard generalized markup language

**SGO** Squadron Gunnery Officer

**SGOT** *Med.* serum glutamic oxalo-acetic transaminase

**SGP** *international vehicle registration for* Singapore

**SGPT** *Med.* serum glutamic pyruvic transaminase

**Sgr** *Astronomy* Sagittarius

**SgRA** Surgeon Rear-Admiral

**Sgt** Sergeant

**SGT** Society of Glass Technology

**Sgt Maj.** Sergeant Major

**SGU** Scottish Gliding Union • Scottish Golf Union

**SgVA** Surgeon Vice-Admiral

**SGW** *Freemasonry* Senior Grand Warden

**sh** *Maths.* hyperbolic sine • *Baseball* sacrifice hit

**sh.** shall • *Stock exchange* share • sheep • *Bookbinding* sheet • shilling • shower

**s.h.** second-hand • slant (*or* slope) height

**Sh.** *Military* Shipwright

**SH** *British vehicle registration for* Edinburgh • *British fishing port registration for* Scarborough • Schleswig-Holstein • school house • *Rugby* scrum-half • *Meteorol.* showers • *Numismatics* small head • southern hemisphere

**SHA** Scottish Hockey Association • Secondary Heads Association • *Astronomy, Navigation* sidereal hour angle • Special Health Authority • *Maths.* spherical harmonic analysis

**SHAC** Shelter Housing Aid Centre

**SHAEF** (ʃeɪf) Supreme Headquarters Allied Expeditionary Forces

**Shak.** (*or* **Shaks.**) William Shakespeare (1564–1616, English dramatist and poet)

**SH&MA** Scottish Horse and Motormen's Association

**SHAPE** (ʃeɪp) Supreme Headquarters Allied Powers Europe (of NATO)

**SHC** *Physics* specific heat capacity

**SHCJ** Society of the Holy Child Jesus

**shd** should

**S/HE** *Shipping* Sundays and holidays excepted

**Shef.** (*or* **Sheff.**) Sheffield

**Shet.** (*or* **Shetl.**) Shetland Islands

**SHEX** *Shipping* Sundays and holidays excepted

**Sh.F.** shareholders' funds

**SHF** *Radio, etc.* superhigh frequency

**SHHD** Scottish Home and Health Department

**shipt** shipment

**SHM** *Physics* simple harmonic motion • Society of Housing Managers

**SHMO** Senior Hospital Medical Officer

**sho** *Baseball* shutout

**SHO** Senior House Officer

**shoran** (ˈʃɔːræn) short-range navigation

**shp** shaft horsepower (of an engine)

**SHP** *Chemical engineering* selective hydrogenation process • *Horticulture* single-flowered hardy perennial (*or* hybrid perpetual) (rose)

**shpg** shipping

**shpt** shipment

**SHQ** station headquarters • supreme headquarters

**shr.** share(s)

**shrap.** shrapnel

**Shrops** Shropshire

**SHS** Fellow of the Historical Society (Latin *Societatis Historicae Socius*) • Shire Horse Society

**sht** *Bookbinding* sheet

**SHT** single-flowered hybrid tea (rose)

**shtg.** shortage

**s.h.v.** sub hac voce (*or* hoc verbo) (Latin: under this word)

**SHW** safety, health, and welfare

**s.i.** sum insured

**Si** *Chem., symbol for* silicon

**SI** *Irish vehicle registration for* Dublin • Sandwich Islands (former name for Hawaii) • seriously ill • Shetland Isles • Smithsonian Institution (Washington, DC) • (USA) Society of Illustrators • South Island (New Zealand) • staff inspector • (Order of the) Star of India • Staten Island (New York) • *Government* statutory instrument • *Chem.* styrene–isoprene (polymer) • Système International (d'Unités; French: International System of Units; in **SI unit(s)**)

**SIA** Society of Investment Analysts • Spinal Injuries Association

**SIAC** (USA) Securities Industry Automation Corporation

**SIAD** Society of Industrial Artists and Designers (now called Chartered Society of Designers, CSD)

**SIAM** (USA) Society of Industrial and Applied Mathematics

**Sib.** Siberia(n)

**SIB** Securities and Investments Board • *Med.* self-injurious behaviour • Shipbuilding Industry Board • Special Investigation Branch (of the Police)

**SIBOR** ('siːbɔː) *Finance* Singapore Inter-Bank Offered Rate

**sic.** *Pharmacol.* siccus (Latin: dry)

**Sic.** Sicilian • Sicily

**SIC** (USA) Scientific Information Center • Standard Industrial Classification

**SICAV** (France) société d'investissement à capital variable (unit trust)

**SICOT** Société internationale de chirurgie orthopédique et de traumatologie (French: International Society of Orthopaedic Surgery and Traumatology)

**SID** Society for International Development • Spiritus in Deo (Latin: his (*or* her) spirit is with God) • (*or* **s.i.d.**) *Radio* sudden ionospheric disturbance

**SIDA** Swedish International Development Authority

**SIDS** (sɪdz) *Med.* sudden infant death syndrome (cot death)

**SIE** *Physics* secondary ion emission

**SIEC** Scottish Industrial Estates Corporation

**SIESO** Society of Industrial and Emergency Service Officers

**SIF** selective identification feature • *Engineering* stress-intensity factor

**SIFS** special instructors flying school

**sig.** signal • signature • signetur (Latin: let it be written *or* labelled) • signification • signifies

**Sig.** *Med.* signā (Latin: write; in prescriptions, preceding instructions to be written on the label for the patient's use) • Signor (Italian: Mr) • Signore (Italian: Sir)

**SIG** *Numismatics* signature of engraver present • special-interest group

**SIGAC** Scottish Industrial Groups Advisory Council

**sig. fig.** *Maths.* significant figures

**sigill.** sigillum (Latin: seal)

**SIGINT** (*or* **Sigint**) ('sɪgɪnt) signals intelligence (gathering network)

**SIGMA** ('sɪgmə) Science in General Management

**Sigmn** *Navy* Signalman

**sign.** signature

**sig. n. pro.** *Med.* signa nomine proprio (Latin: label with the proper name)

**Sig.O.** Signal Officer

**SIGWEX** *Meteorol.* significant weather

**SII** Société internationale de la lèpre (French: International Leprosy Association)

**Sil.** Silesia

**SIL** (sɪl) *Electronics* single in-line (as in **SIL device**)

**sim.** similar(ly) • simile

**SIM** *Physics* secondary-ion microscopy • self-inflicted mutilation • Société internationale de musicologie (French: International Musicological Society) • survey information on microfilm

**SIMA** Scientific Instrument Manufacturers' Association of Great Britain • Steel Industry Management Association • *Psychiatry* system for identifying motivated abilities

**SIMC** Société internationale pour la musique contemporaine (French: International Society for Contemporary Music)

**SIMCA** (*or* **Simca**) ('sɪmkə) Société industrielle de mécanique et carrosserie automobiles (French car manufacturers)

**SIMD** *Computing* single instruction (stream), multiple data (stream)

**SIME** Security Intelligence Middle East

**SIMG** International Society of General Medicine (Latin *Societas Internationalis Medicinae Generalis*)

**SIMM** *Computing, Electronics* single in-line memory module

**SIMPL** Scientific, Industrial, and Medical Photographic Laboratories

**SIMS** *Chem.* secondary-ion mass spectrometry (*or* spectroscopy)

**sin** (saɪn) *Maths.* sine

**sin.** sinecure

**SinDrs** Doctor of Chinese

**sing.** *Grammar* singular · *Med.* singulorum (Latin: of each; in prescriptions)

**Sing.** Singapore

**sinh** (saɪn) *Maths.* hyperbolic sine

**Sinh.** Sinhalese

**SINS** (sɪnz) ship's inertial navigation system

**SIO** Senior Intelligence Officer · *Computing* serial input/output

**SIOP** ('saɪɒp) (USA) single integrated operations plan (for nuclear war)

**SIP** (USA) supplemental income plan

**SIPC** (USA) Securities Investor Protection Corporation

**SIPO** *Computing* serial in, parallel out

**SIPRC** Society of Independent Public Relations Consultants

**SIPRI** Stockholm International Peace Research Institute

**SIR** *Taxation* small income relief

**SIRA** Scientific Instrument Research Association

**sis.** sister

**SIS** Secret Intelligence Service (MI6) · (New Zealand) Security Intelligence Service

**SISD** *Computing* single instruction (stream), single data (stream)

**SISO** *Electronics* serial in, serial out · *Electronics* single input, single output

**SISS** submarine integrated sonar system

**SISTER** ('sɪstə) Special Institutions for Scientific and Technological Education and Research

**sit.** sitting room · situation

**s.i.t.** stopping in transit · storing in transit

**SIT** Society of Industrial Technology · Society of Instrument Technology · *Engineering* spontaneous ignition temperature

**SITA** Société internationale de télécommunications aéronautiques (French: International Society of Aeronautical Telecommunications) · Students' International Travel Association

**SITC** Standard International Trade Classification

**SITC(R)** Standard International Trade Classification (Revised)

**SITPRO** ('sɪtprəʊ) Simpler Trade Procedures Board (formerly Simplification of International Trade Procedures)

**sitt.** sitting-room

**sit. vac.** (pl. **sits vac.**) situation vacant

**SIUNA** Seafarers International Union of North America

**SIV** *Microbiol.* simian immunodeficiency virus

**SIW** self-inflicted wound

**s.j.** *Law* sub judice

**SJ** *British vehicle registration for* Glasgow · Society of Jesus · supersonic jet

**SJA** St John Ambulance (Brigade *or* Association)

**SJAA** St John Ambulance Association

**SJAB** St John Ambulance Brigade

**SJC** Standing Joint Committee · (USA) Supreme Judicial Court

**SJD** Doctor of Juristic (*or* Juridical) Science (Latin *Scientiae Juridicae Doctor*)

**S. J. Res.** (USA) Senate joint resolution

**sk** sack · sick

**sk.** sketch

**SK** *British vehicle registration for* Inverness · Saskatchewan · *airline flight code for* Scandinavian Airline System · *postcode for* Stockport

**SKAMP** (skæmp) station keeping and mobile platform (unmanned self-navigating sailing boat)

**SKC** Scottish Kennel Club · *Meteorol.* sky clear

**S. Ken.** South Kensington (London)

**skid** (skɪd) *Med. see* SCID

**Skm** Stockholm

**s.k.p.o.** *Knitting* slip one, knit one, pass slipped stitch over

**SKr** *symbol for* Swedish krona (monetary unit)

**Skt** (*or* **Skr.**) Sanskrit

**sl.** sleet • slightly • slip

**s.l.** *Insurance* salvage loss • secundum legem (*see* sec. leg.) • seditious libel • *Bibliog.* sine loco (Latin: without place (of publication)) • support line

**Sl.** Slovak(ian)

**SL** *British vehicle registration for* Dundee • *Insurance* salvage loss • scout leader • sea level • Second Lieutenant • security list • Serjeant-at-Law • *Building trades* short lengths • *postcode for* Slough • *international civil aircraft marking for* Slovenia • Solicitor-at-Law • source language • southern league • south latitude • Squadron Leader

**SLA** Scottish Library Association • special landscape area (in conservation) • (USA) Special Libraries Association • Symbionese Liberation Army

**SLAC** Stanford Linear Accelerator Center

**SLADE** (sleɪd) Society of Lithographic Artists, Designers, Engravers, and Process Workers

**SLAET** Society of Licensed Aircraft Engineers and Technologists

**SLAM** (*or* **Slam**) (slæm) standoff land-attack missile

**s.l.a.n.** sine loco, anno, vel nomine (Latin: without place, year, name (of printer))

**SLAR** (*or* **Slar**) (slɑː) *Military* side-looking airborne radar

**SLAS** Society for Latin American Studies

**S. Lat.** south latitude

**Slav.** Slavonian • Slavonic (*or* Slavic)

**SLBM** submarine-launched ballistic missile

**SLC** Stanford Linear Collider (at SLAC) • Statute Law Committee • Surgeon Lieutenant-Commander

**SLCM** sea- (*or* ship-, submarine-) launched cruise missile

**sld** sailed • sealed • sold • solid

**SLD** self-locking device • Social and Liberal Democrats

**S. Ldr.** Squadron Leader

**SLE** *Med.* systemic lupus erythematosus

**s.l. et a.** sine loco et anno (Latin: without place and year (of publication))

**S level** *Education* Special (formerly Scholarship) level

**s.l.f.** *Telecom.* straight-line frequency

**SLF** Scottish Landowners' Federation

**SLFP** Sri Lanka Freedom Party

**SLIC** (USA) (Federal) Savings and Loan Insurance Corporation

**SLIM** South London Industrial Mission

**Slipar** ('slaɪpɑː) *Military* short light pulse alerting receiver (in an aircraft)

**SLLA** Scottish Ladies Lacrosse Association

**SLLW** solid low-level (radioactive) waste

**SLM** ship-launched missile

**SLMA** (USA) Student Loan Marketing Association

**SLMC** Scottish Ladies' Mountaineering Club

**s.l.n.d.** sine loco nec data (Latin: without indication of date or place (of printing))

**SLO** Senior Liaison Officer

**SLORC** (Burma) State Law and Order Restoration Council

**slp** slip

**s.l.p.** sine legitime prole (Latin: without lawful issue)

**SLP** Scottish Labour Party • (USA) Socialist Labor Party

**SLR** satellite laser ranging • self-loading rifle • single-lens reflex (camera)

**SL Rs** *symbol for* Sri Lanka rupee (monetary unit)

**SLS** sodium lauryl sulphate (detergent) • Stephenson Locomotive Society

**SLSC** surf life-saving club

**SLTA** Scottish Licensed Trade Association

**Slud** (slʌd) *Military slang* salivate, lachrymate, urinate, defecate (effects of chemical weapons)

**SLV** space (*or* standard) launch vehicle

**SLW** *Meteorol.* slow • solid low-level (radioactive) waste

**sly** slowly • southerly

**sm.** small

**s-m** (*or* **s/m**) sadomasochism (*or* sadomasochist)

**Sm** *Chem., symbol for* samarium

**SM** *airline flight code for* Aberdeen Airways • *British vehicle registration for* Glasgow • Master of Science (Latin *Scientiae Magister*) • (*or* **S-M**) sadomasochism (*or* sadomasochist) • sales manager • Sa Majesté (French: His (*or* Her) Majesty) • sanctae memoriae (Latin: of holy memory) • Seine Majestät (German: His (*or* Her) Majesty) • senior magistrate • Sergeant Major • (USA) service mark (registered proprietary name) • *Astronautics* service module • shipment memorandum • *British fishing port registration for* Shoreham • *Music* short metre • silver medal(list) • Sisters of Mercy • Society of Miniaturists • Sons of Malta • Staff Major • stage manager • *Astronomy* standard model • (USA) state militia • station master • stipendiary magistrate • strategic missile • Sua Maestà (Italian: His (*or* Her) Majesty) • (officer qualified for) Submarine Duties • Su Magestad (Spanish: His (*or* Her) Majesty) • Surgeon Major • *postcode for* Sutton (Surrey)

**SMA** (USA) Surplus Marketing Administration

**SMAC** Standing Medical Advisory Committee

**SMATV** satellite (formerly small) master antenna television

**SMAW** shielded metal-arc welding

**SMB** Bachelor of Sacred Music • Sa Majesté Britannique (French: Her (*or* His) Britannic Majesty)

**SMBA** Scottish Marine Biological Association

**SMBG** *Med.* self-monitoring of blood glucose (for diabetics)

**SMC** Sa Majesté Catholique (French: His (*or* Her) Catholic Majesty) • Scottish Mountaineering Club • *Astronomy* Small Magellanic Cloud • *Aeronautics* standard mean chord

**sm. caps.** *Printing* small capitals

**SMC(Disp)** Dispensing Certificate of the Worshipful Company of Spectacle Makers

**SMD** Doctor of Sacred Music • *Med.* senile macular degeneration • *Music* short metre double • submarine mine depot • *Electronics* surface mount device

**SME** Sancta Mater Ecclesia (Latin: Holy Mother Church) • seismic-margin earthquake • *international vehicle registration for* Suriname

**SMERSH** (*or* **Smersh**) Smert Shpionam (Russian: death to spies; section of KGB)

**S.Met.O.** Senior Meteorological Officer

**SMG** submachine gun

**SMHD** Higher Diploma in Ophthalmic Optics of the Worshipful Company of Spectacle Makers

**SMHI** Swedish Meteorological and Hydrological Institute

**SMHO** (Malta) Sovereign Military Hospitaller Order

**SMI** Sa Majesté Impériale (French: His (*or* Her) Imperial Majesty)

**SMIA** Sheet Metal Industries Association

**SMIEEE** (USA) Senior Member of the Institute of Electrical and Electronics Engineers

**SMIRE** (USA) Senior Member of the Institute of Radio Engineers

**Smith. Inst.** Smithsonian Institution (Washington, DC)

**SMJ** Sisters of Mary and Joseph

**smk.** smoke

**sml.** simulate • simulation • simulator • small

**SML** Science Museum Library

**SMLE** short magazine Lee-Enfield (rifle)

**SMM** Master of Sacred Music • Sancta Mater Maria (Latin: Holy Mother Mary)

**SMMB** Scottish Milk Marketing Board

**SMMT** Society of Motor Manufacturers and Traders Ltd

**SMO** Senior Medical Officer • Sovereign Military Order

**SMON** (smɒn) *Med.* subacute myelo-opticoneuropathy

**smorz.** *Music* smorzando (Italian; gradually slower and softer)

**s.m.p.** sine mascula prole (Latin: without male issue)

**SMP** Society of Mural Painters • statutory maternity pay

**SMPS** Society of Master Printers of Scotland

**SMPTE** (USA) Society of Motion Picture and Television Engineers

**SMR** Sa Majesté Royale (French: His (*or* Her) Royal Majesty) • standardized mortality ratio • standard Malaysian rubber • *Med.* standard metabolic rate

**SMRE** Safety in Mines Research Establishment

**SMRTB** Ship and Marine Requirements Technology Board

**SMS** synchronous meteorological satellite

**SMSA** (USA) Standard Metropolitan Statistical Area

**SMSO** Senior Maintenance Staff Officer

**SMT** ship's mean time • *Maths.* Steiner minimum tree

**SMTA** Scottish Motor Trade Association

**SMTF** Scottish Milk Trade Federation

**SMTO** Senior Mechanical Transport Officer

**SMV** *Med.* submentovertical (in radiology)

**SMW** standard metal window

**SMWIA** (USA) Sheet Metal Workers' International Association (trade union)

**sn.** snow

**s.n.** secundum naturam (Latin: according to nature, naturally) • serial number • series number • service number • sine nomine (Latin: without name) • sub nomine (Latin: under a specified name)

**Sn** *Chem. symbol for* tin (Latin *stannum*)

**SN** *British vehicle registration for* Dundee • *airline flight code for* Sabena Belgian World Airlines • (USA) Secretary of the Navy • *international vehicle registration for* Senegal • Sergeant Navigator • shipping note • *Meteorol.* snow • *Astronomy* supernova • *postcode for* Swindon

**S/N** shipping note • *Electronics* signal-to-noise (in **S/N ratio**) • *Engineering* stress-number (in **S/N curve**)

**SNA** *Computing* systems network architecture

**snafu** (snæ'fuː) *Slang* situation normal, all fouled (*or* fucked) up

**SNAME** (USA) Society of Naval Architects and Marine Engineers

**SNAP** (snæp) Shelter Neighbourhood Action Project • systems for nuclear auxiliary power

**SNB** *Stock exchange* sellers no buyers

**SNCB** Société nationale des chemins de fer belges (Belgian National Railways)

**SNCC** (snɪk) (USA) Student Nonviolent (later National) Coordinating Committee

**SNCF** (France) Société nationale des chemins de fer français (state railway authority or system)

**Snd** Sound (in place names)

**SND** Sisters of Notre Dame

**SNECMA** (*or* **Snecma**) ('snɛkmə) (France) Société nationale d'étude et de construction de moteurs d'aviation (state-owned aeroengine company)

**SNF** solids, nonfat (in nutrition) • spent nuclear fuel • (USA) strategic nuclear forces

**SNFA** Standing Naval Force, Atlantic

**SNFU** Scottish National Farmers' Union

**Sng.** Singapore

**SNG** substitute (*or* synthetic) natural gas

**SNH** Scottish National Heritage

**SNIF** *Finance* short-term note issuance facility

**SNIG** sustainable noninflationary growth

**SNL** Sandia National Laboratories (Albuquerque) • standard nomenclature list

**SNLR** services no longer required

**SNLV** strategic nuclear launch vehicle

**SNM** (USA) Society of Nuclear Medicine • Somali National Movement

**SNO** (formerly) Scottish National Orchestra (renamed Royal Scottish Orchestra, RSO) • Senior Naval Officer • Senior Navigation Officer • Senior Nursing Officer

**SNOBOL** ('snəu,bɒl) *Computing,* indicating a programming language designed for text manipulation

**snoRNP** *Biochem.* small nucleolar ribonucleoprotein

**SNP** Scottish National Party

**SNPA** Scottish Newspaper Proprietors' Association

**Snr** Senior

**SNR** *Electronics* signal-to-noise ratio • Society for Nautical Research • *Astronomy* supernova remnant

**snRNA** *Biochem.* small nuclear RNA

**snRNP** *Biochem.* small nuclear ribonucleoprotein

**s 'n' s** *Colloquial* sex and shopping (type of popular fiction)

**SNSC** Scottish National Ski Council

**SNSH** *Meteorol.* snow showers

**SNTPC** Scottish National Town Planning Council

**SNTS** Society for New Testament Studies

**SNU** (snjuː) *Astronomy* solar neutrino unit

**so.** sonata • south(ern)

**s.o.** seller's option • shipping order • siehe oben (German: see above) • strike out • substance of (specifying weight of paper)

**So.** south(ern)

**SO** *British vehicle registration for* Aberdeen • Scientific Officer • Scottish Office • section officer • Senior Officer • shale oil (residue) • Signal Officer • *Irish fishing port registration for* Sligo • sorting office • *postcode for* Southampton • *Meteorol.* southern oscillation • special order • Staff Officer • standing order • Stationery Office • statistical office • suboffice • Supply Officer • Symphony Orchestra

**S/O** Section Officer • shipowner

**SOA** state of the art

**SOAD** Staff Officer, Air Defence

**SOAP** (səup) *Med.* subjective, objective, analysis, plan (method of compiling patients' records)

**SOAS** School of Oriental and African Studies (University of London)

**SOB** (USA) Senate office building • *Colloquial* silly old bastard (*or* blighter) • (*or* **s.o.b.**) *Colloquial* son of a bitch • state office building

**soc.** social • socialist • society • sociology

**Soc.** Socialist • (Italy) società (company *or* partnership) • Society • Socrates (469–399 BC, Greek philosopher)

**SOC** Scottish Ornithologists' Club • *Colloquial* slightly off colour

**SocCE(France)** Société des ingénieurs civils de France (Society of Civil Engineers of France)

**Soc. Dem.** Social Democrat

**sociol.** sociological • sociologist • sociology

**SOCO** scene-of-crime officer (in the police)

**SOCS** Society of County Secretaries

**soc. sci.** social science (*or* scientist)

**socy** (*or* **Socy**) society

**sod.** sodium

**SODAC** Society of Dyers and Colourists

**SODEPAX** ('səudɪ,pæks) Committee on Society, Development, and Peace

**SOE** Special Operations Executive (in World War II) • state-owned enterprise

**SOED** (ital.) Shorter Oxford English Dictionary

**SOES** *Finance* (USA) Small Order Execution System (of NASDAQ)

**SOF** *Chem.* soluble organic fraction • *Films* sound on a film

**SOFAA** Society of Fine Art Auctioneers

**sofar** ('səufɑ:) sound fixing and ranging

**SOFCS** self-organizing flight-control system

**SOFFEX** ('sɒfɛks) Swiss Options and Financial Futures Exchange

**S. of S.** Secretary of State • *Bible* Song of Songs

**S. of Sol.** *Bible* Song of Solomon

**S. of T.** Sons of Temperance

**S. of TT** School of Technical Training

**SOGAT** ('səugæt) Society of Graphical and Allied Trades (*see* GPMU)

**SOHIO** (səu'haɪəu) Standard Oil of Ohio

**Sohyo** Nihon Rodo Kumiai So Hygikai (General Council of Japanese Trade Unions)

**SO(I)** Staff Officer (Intelligence)

**SO-in-C** Signal Officer-in-Chief

**sol.** solicitor • soluble • solution

**s.o.l.** *Insurance* shipowner's liability

**Sol.** Solicitor • *Bible* Song of Solomon

**SOL** *Slang* (USA) strictly (*or* shit) out of luck

**SOLACE** (*or* **Solace**) ('sɒlɪs) Society of Local Authority Chief Executives

**Sol. Gen.** Solicitor General

**soln** solution

**solr** (*or* **Solr**) solicitor

**solv.** solvent

**soly** solubility

**Som.** Somerset • (*or* **Som**) Somerville College, Oxford

**SOM** Society of Occupational Medicine

**SOMA** ('səumə) Society of Mental Awareness

**SOME** Senior Ordnance Mechanical Engineer

**SOMPA** ('sɒmpə) (USA) System of Multicultural Pluralistic Assessment (intelligence testing)

**Som.Sh.** Somali shilling (monetary unit)

**SON** Spear of the Nation (military arm of African National Congress)

**sonar** ('səunɑ:) sound navigation and ranging

**SO(O)** Staff Officer (Operations)

**sop.** soprano

**SOP** sleeping-out pass • standard operating procedure • *Computing* sum of products (in **SOP expression**)

**soph.** sophomore

**Soph.** Sophocles (496–406 BC, Greek dramatist and poet)

**SoR** (*or* **SOR**) sale or return

**SORD** submerged-object recovery device

**s.o.s.** *Med.* si opus sit (Latin: if necessary; in prescriptions)

**SOS** save our souls (also, the clearest letters to transmit and receive in Morse code) • (*or* **SoS**) Secretary of State • senior officers' school • services of supply

**SOSc** Society of Ordained Scientists

**SoSh** *symbol for* Somali shilling (monetary unit)

**sost.** *Music* sostenuto (Italian: sustained)

**SOTS** Society for Old Testament Study

**Sou.** (*or* **sou.**) south(ern) • (*or* **Soton**) Southampton

**sov.** sovereign

**s.o.v.** shut-off valve

**Sov.** Soviet

**SOV** *Linguistics* subject-object-verb (in **SOV language**)

**Sov. Un.** Soviet Union

**sowc** senior officers' war course

**Soweto** (sə'wetəu) Southwestern Townships (South Africa)

**sp.** space • special • specie • *Biology* species • specific • specimen • speed • spelling • spirit • sport

**s.p.** self-propelled • *Music* senza pedale (Italian: without pedal) • sine prole (Latin: without issue) • *Electricity* single phase • starting point • starting price • *Banking* stop payment

**Sp.** Spain • Spaniard • Spanish

**SP** *British vehicle registration for* Dundee • *international civil aircraft marking for* Poland • Saint-Père (French: Holy Father) • *postcode for* Salisbury • Sanctissimus Pater (Latin: Most Holy Father) • Self-Propelled (Antitank Regiment) • service pistol • *Military* service police • shore patrol • Sisters of Providence • Socialist Party • *Building trades* soil pipe • spark(ing) plug • Staff Paymaster • starting price (odds in a race) • stirrup pump • stop press • stretcher party • submarine patrol • Summus Pontifex (Latin: Supreme Pontiff; the pope) • supply point • *Finance* supra protest

**SpA** (Italy) società per azioni (public limited company; plc)

**SPA** (USA) Society for Personnel Administration

**SPAA** Scottish Passenger Agents' Association

**SPAB** Society for the Protection of Ancient Buildings

**Sp. Am.** Spanish American

**Span.** Spaniard • Spanish

**SPANA** Society for the Protection of Animals in North Africa

**SPANDAR** ('spændɑ:) space and range radar (in NASA)

**Sp. Ar.** Spanish Arabic

**SPAR** (spɑ:) superprecision-approach radar • *indicating* a member of the women's reserve of the US Coast Guard in World War II (from its motto, *Semper paratus* (Latin: always ready))

**SPARC** (spɑ:k) *Computing* scalable processor architecture

**SPAS** Fellow of the American Philosophical Society (Latin *Societatis Philosophicae Americanae Socius*)

**SPATC** South Pacific Air Transport Council

**SPC** Society for the Prevention of Crime • *Telecom.* stored-program control (as in **SPC exchange**)

**SPCA** (USA) Society for the Prevention of Cruelty to Animals

**SPCK** Society for Promoting Christian Knowledge

**s.p.d.** *Finance* subject to permission to deal

**SPD** Salisbury Plain District • *Astronomy* south polar distance • Sozialdemokratische Partei Deutschlands (Social Democratic Party of Germany)

**SPDA** single-premium deferred annuity

**SPDL** *Computing* standard page description language

**SPE** Society for Pure English • (USA) Society of Petroleum Engineers • *Electronics* solid-phase epitaxy

**spec.** special(ly) • specific(ally) • specification • specimen • spectrum • speculation

**SPEC** (Canada) Society for Pollution and Environmental Control • South Pacific Bureau for Economic Cooperation

**special.** specialized

**specif.** specifically • specification

**SPECT** *Med.* single photon emission computed tomography

**SPECTRE** ('spektə) Special Executive for Counter-Intelligence, Revenge, and Extortion (fictional terrorist organization in Ian Fleming's James Bond novels)

**Sp.Ed.** (USA) Specialist in Education

**SPF** South Pacific Forum • sun protection factor (of sunscreening preparations)

**SPF/DB** *Aeronautics* super-plastic forming/diffusion bonding (manufacturing method)

**s.p.g.** self-propelled gun

**SPG** Society for the Propagation of the Gospel (*see* USPG) • Special Patrol Group

**SPGA** Scottish Professional Golfers' Association

**SPGB** Socialist Party of Great Britain

**sp. gr.** specific gravity

**sp. ht** specific heat

**SPI** *Finance* selected period investment • (USA) Society of the Plastics Industry

**SPIRE** (spaɪə) *Navigation* spatial inertial reference equipment

**spirit.** *Music* spiritoso (Italian: in a spirited manner) • spiritualism • spiritualistic

**SPIW** special-purposes individual weapon

**s.p.l.** sine prole legitima (Latin: without legitimate issue)

**SPLA** Sudan People's Liberation Army

**s.p.m.** sine prole mascula (Latin: without male issue)

**SPM** scanning proton microscope • *Music* short particular metre

**SPMO** Senior Principal Medical Officer

**SPMU** Society of Professional Musicians in Ulster

**SPN** stop press news

**SPNM** Society for the Promotion of New Music

**SPNR** Society for the Promotion of Nature Reserves

**SPO** Senior Press Officer

**SPÖ** Sozialistische Partei Österreichs (Austrian Socialist Party)

**SPOD** Sexual Problems of the Disabled (department of the Royal Association for Disability and Rehabilitation)

**SPOE** Society of Post Office Engineers

**sport.** sporting

**spp.** *Biology* species (plural)

**SPQR** Senatus Populusque Romanus (Latin: the Senate and People of Rome) • small profits and quick returns

**spr.** spring • sprinkle

**Spr** *Military* Sapper

**SPR** Society for Psychical Research • strategic petroleum reserve

**SPRC** Society for the Prevention and Relief of Cancer

**SPREd** Society of Picture Researchers and Editors

**SPRI** Scott Polar Research Institute (Cambridge)

**SPRINT** (sprɪnt) *Military* solid-propellant rocket-intercept missile

**sprl** (France) société de personnes à responsabilité limitée (private limited company; Ltd)

**SPRL** Society for the Promotion of Religion and Learning

**s.p.s.** sine prole supersite (Latin: without surviving issue)

**SPS** Scottish Painters' Society • *Physics* Super Proton Synchrotron (at CERN) • syndiotactic polystyrene (a plastic)

**SPSL** Society for the Protection of Science and Learning

**SPSO** Senior Principal Scientific Officer

**SPSP** St Peter and St Paul

**sp. surf.** *Chem.* specific surface

**spt** seaport • support

**sptg** sporting

**SPTL** Society of Public Teachers of Law

**SPUC** (*or* **Spuc**) (spʌk) Society for the Protection of the Unborn Child

**SPURV** (spɜːv) self-propelled underwater research vehicle

**sq** *Military* staff qualified

**sq.** sequence • sequens (*see under* seq.) • squadron • square

**Sq.** Squadron • Square (in place names)

**SQ** sick quarters • *airline flight code for* Singapore Airlines • *Meteorol.* squall • *Building trades* squint quoin • stereophonic-quadraphonic (of audio equipment) • survival quotient

**SQA** *Computing* software quality assurance

**sq cm** square centimetre(s)

**sqd** squad

**sqdn** (*or* **Sqdn**) squadron

**Sqdn Ldr** Squadron Leader

**sq ft** square feet (*or* foot)

**sq in** square inch(es)

**sq km** square kilometre(s)

**SQL** *Computing* standard query language • *Computing* structured query language

**sq m** square metre(s)

**sq mi** square mile(s)

**sq mm** square millimetre(s)

**SQMS** Staff Quartermaster Sergeant

**sqn** (*or* **Sqn**) squadron

**Sqn Ldr** Squadron Leader

**SqnQMS** Squadron Quartermaster Sergeant

**SqnSM** Squadron Sergeant Major

**SqO** Squadron Officer

**sqq.** sequentia (*see under* seqq.)

**squid** (*or* **SQUID**) (skwɪd) *Electronics* superconducting quantum interference device

**sq yd** square yard

**sr** *Maths.*, *symbol for* steradian

**s.r.** self-raising • shipping receipt • short rate

**Sr** Senhor (Portuguese: Mr, Sir) • Senior (after a name) • Señor (Spanish: Mr, Sir) • Sir • Sister (religious) • *Chem.*, *symbol for* strontium

**SR** *British vehicle registration for* Dundee • *Cytology* sarcoplasmic reticulum • Saudi riyal (Saudi Arabian monetary unit) • Saunders Roe (aircraft) • (USA) Senate resolution • service rifle • *symbol for* Seychelles rupee (monetary unit) • (formerly, USSR) Socialist Revolutionary (Party) • Society of Radiographers • (USA) Sons of the Revolution • Southern Railway (now Region) • *Physics* special relativity • *Military* Special Reserve • *Taxation* standard rate • (*or* **S–R**) *Psychol.* stimulus–response (as in **SR theory**) • *Chem.* stoichiometric ratio • *British fishing port registration for* Stranraer • *postcode for* Sunderland • Sveriges Radio (Swedish broadcasting corporation) • *airline flight code for* Swissair • *Physics* synchrotron radiation • synthetic rubber

**S/R** sale or return

**Sra** Senhora (Portuguese: Mrs) • Señora (Spanish: Mrs)

**SRA** Squash Rackets Association

**SRAM** short-range attack missile • *Computing* static random access memory

**SR & CC** strikes, riot, and civil commotion

**SRB** solid rocket booster • *Microbiol.* sulphate-reducing bacteria

**SRBC** *Med.* sheep red blood cell(s)

**SRBM** short-range ballistic missile

**SRBP** synthetic resin-bonded paper

**SRC** sample return container • Science Research Council (*see* SERC) • (Spain) sociedad regular colectiva (partnership) • solvent-refined coal • *Chem.* standard reference compound • *Engineering* steam Rankine cycle • Students' Representative Council • Swiss Red Cross

**SRCh** State Registered Chiropodist

**SRCN** (formerly) State Registered Children's Nurse (*see* RSCN)

**SRD** service rum diluted

**SRDE** Signals Research and Development Establishment

**SRE** Sancta Romana Ecclesia (Latin: Holy Roman Church)

**S. Rept** (USA) Senate report

**S. Res.** (USA) Senate resolution

**SRG** standard reformed gas • Strategic Research Group (marketing research company)

**SRHE** Society for Research into Higher Education

**SRI** Sacrum Romanum Imperium (Latin: Holy Roman Empire)

**SRIS** Science Reference Information Service

**Srl.** (Italy) società a responsabilità limitata (private limited company; Ltd)

**SRIs** *symbol for* Saudi riyal (monetary unit of Saudi Arabia)

**SRM** short-range missile • speed of relative movement

**SRN** (formerly) State Registered Nurse (*see* RGN)

**sRNA** *Biochem.* soluble RNA

**SRNA** Shipbuilders and Repairers National Association

**SRO** *Finance* self-regulatory organization • *Microbiol.* sex-ratio organism • (USA) single-room occupancy (as in **SRO hotel**) • standing room only • Statutory Rules and Orders • Supplementary Reserve of Officers

**SRP** State Registered Physiotherapist • suggested retail price • supply refuelling point

**SRS** Fellow of the Royal Society (Latin *Societatis Regiae Sodalis*)

**SRSA** Scientific Research Society of America • *Immunol.* slow-reacting substance A (of anaphylaxis)

**SRSS** *Maths.* square-root sum of squares

**Srta** Senhorita (Portuguese: Miss) • Señorita (Spanish: Miss)

**SRU** Scottish Rugby Union

**SRY** Sherwood Rangers Yeomanry

**ss.** sections • *Med.* semis (Latin: half; in prescriptions) • *Baseball* shortstop • subsection

**s.s.** screw steamer • sensu stricto (Latin: in the strict sense) • *Music* senza sordini (Italian: without mutes) • steamship • supra scriptum (Latin: written above)

**SS** *British vehicle registration for* Aberdeen • Sacra Scriptura (Latin: Holy Scripture) • Saints • Santa Sede (Italian: Holy See) • Sa Sainteté (French: His

Holiness) • Schutzstaffel (German: protection squad; Nazi paramilitary organization) • secondary school • Secretary of State • secret service • security service • short sleeves • Sidney Sussex College, Cambridge • social security • *Chem.* sodium sulphate • *postcode for* Southend-on-Sea • Staff Surgeon • stainless steel • standard size • steamship • *British fishing port registration for* St Ives • (Italy) Strada Statale (National Highway) • Straits Settlements • *Chem.* styrylstilbene • Sunday school • surface to surface (missile)

**SS.** Saints • sanctissimus (Latin: most holy)

**S/S** same size (of illustrations) • *Printing* silk screen • steamship

**SSA** Scottish Schoolmasters' Association • (USA) Social Security Administration • Society of Scottish Artists • standard spending assessment (in local government)

**SSAC** Scottish Sub-Aqua Club • Social Security Advisory Committee

**SSADM** *Computing* structured systems analysis and design method

**SSAE** stamped self-addressed envelope

**SSAFA** (*or* **SS&AFA**) Soldiers', Sailors', and Airmen's Families Association

**SSAP** Statement of Standard Accounting Practice

**SSB** Bachelor of Sacred Scripture (Latin *Sacrae Scripturae Baccalaureus*) • *Telecom.* single-sideband (transmission) • *Genetics* single-strand binding (as in **SSB protein**) • (USA) Social Security Board • *Physics* spontaneous symmetry breaking

**SSBN** *US Navy* strategic submarine, ballistic nuclear

**SSC** Scottish Ski Club • Sculptors' Society of Canada • (India) Secondary School Certificate • Short Service Commission • (USA) small-saver certificate • Society of the Holy Cross (Latin *Societas Sanctae Crucis*) • (Scotland) Solicitor before the Supreme Court • Species Survival Commission • *Physics* Superconducting Super Collider

**SScD** Doctor of Social Science

**SSD** Doctor of Sacred Scripture (Latin *Sacrae Scripturae Doctor*) • Social Services Department

**SS.D** Sanctissimus Dominus (Latin: Most Holy Lord; the pope)

**ssDNA** *Biochem.* single-stranded DNA

**SSE** Society of St Edmund • southeast

**SSEB** South of Scotland Electricity Board

**SSEC** Secondary School Examinations Council

**S-SEED** *Optics* symmetric self-electro-optic-effect device

**SSEES** School of Slavonic and East European Studies (University of London)

**SSF** *Military* single-seater fighter (aircraft) • Society of St Francis

**SSFA** Scottish Schools' Football Association • Scottish Steel Founders' Association

**S/Sgt** (*or* **S.Sgt**) Staff Sergeant

**SSHA** Scottish Special Housing Association

**SSI** Scottish Symphony Orchestra • site of scientific interest • *Electronics* small-scale integration • Social Services Inspectorate • Society of Scribes and Illuminators • (USA) supplemental security income

**SSJE** Society of St John the Evangelist

**SSL** Licentiate in Sacred Scripture (Latin *Sacrae Scripturae Licentiatus*)

**SSM** *Telecom.* single-sideband modulation • Society of the Sacred Mission • Staff Sergeant Major • *Military* surface-to-surface missile

**SSMA** Stainless Steel Manufacturers' Association

**SSN** severely subnormal • Standard Serial Number

**SSO** Senior Scientific Officer • Senior Supply Officer • Staff Signal Officer • Station Staff Officer

**ssp.** *Biology* subspecies

**SSP** statutory sick pay

**SSPCA** Scottish Society for the Prevention of Cruelty to Animals

**SSPE** *Med.* subacute sclerosing panencephalitis

**sspp.** *Biology* subspecies (plural)

**SS.PP.** Sancti Patres (Latin: Holy Fathers)

**SSQ** *Military* station sick quarters

**SSR** secondary surveillance radar • Soviet Socialist Republic

**SSRA** Scottish Squash Rackets Association

**SSRC** Social Science Research Council (*see under* ESRC)

**SSRI** (USA) Social Science Research Institute

**SSS** Secretary of State for Scotland •
(USA) Selective Service System (for
mobilizing military forces) • *Med.* sick
sinus syndrome • single-screw ship •
*British fishing port registration for* South
Shields • *Golf* standard scratch score

**SSSI** site of special scientific interest

**SSSR** Soyuz Sovietskikh Sotsialisticheskikh Respublik (Russian: Union of
Soviet Socialist Republics)

**SSStJ** Serving Sister, Order of St John
of Jerusalem

**SST** *Telecom.* single-sideband transmission • Society of Surveying Technicians • supersonic transport

**SSTA** Scottish Secondary Teachers'
Association

**SSU** Sunday School Union

**SSV** *Med.* simian sarcoma virus

**SSW** Secretary of State for War •
south-southwest • special security wing
(of a prison)

**SSWA** Scottish Society of Women
Artists

**st.** stanza • state • statement • statute •
stem • *Printing* stet • *Knitting* stitch •
stone (weight) • strait • street • *Prosody*
strophe • *Cricket* stumped by

**s.t.** select time • short ton • static
thrust • steam trawler

**St** Saint • (ital.) *Physics, symbol for* Stan-
ton number • *Physics, symbol for* stokes •
(ital.) *Meteorol., symbol for* stratus

**St.** Statute • Strait • Street

**ST** *British vehicle registration for* Inverness • septic tank • shipping ticket •
(Hubble) Space Telescope • speech
therapist • spring tide • Standard Time •
*British fishing port registration for* Stock-
ton • *postcode for* Stoke-on-Trent •
*Meteorol.* stratus • *international civil
aircraft marking for* Sudan • Summer
Time • (ital.) Sunday Times • *Building
trades* surface trench • surtax

**sta.** (*or* **Sta.**) station • stationary

**Sta** Santa (Italian, Spanish, Portuguese:
Saint (female))

**STA** Sail Training Association • (USA)
Science and Technology Agency • Scottish Typographical Association • Society of Typographic Arts • Swimming
Teachers' Association

**stab.** stabilization • stabilizer • stable

**stacc.** *Music* staccato

**Staffs** Staffordshire

**STAGS** (stægz) Sterling Transferable
Accruing Government Securities

**STANAG** ('stænæg) Standard NATO
Agreement

**St And.** St Andrews (Scotland)

**stand.** standard

**START** (stɑːt) Strategic Arms Reduction Talks

**stat.** statics • *Med.* statim (Latin:
immediately; in prescriptions) • stationary • statistical • statistics • statuary •
statue • statute

**STATE** (steɪt) *Military* simplified tactical approach and terminal equipment

**Stat. Hall** Stationers' Hall (London)

**STAUK** Seed Trade Association of the
United Kingdom

**STB** Bachelor of Sacred Theology
(Latin *Sacrae Theologiae Baccalaureus*)

**stbd** starboard

**stbt** steamboat

**STC** Samuel Taylor Coleridge (1772–
1834, British poet) • Senior Training
Corps • Short-Title Catalogue • Standard Telephones and Cables Ltd •
(India) State Trading Corporation

**std** standard • started

**Std.** Stunde (German: hour)

**STD** Doctor of Sacred Theology (Latin
*Sacrae Theologiae Doctor*) • salinity-
temperature-depth (sensor system) •
*Med.* sexually transmitted disease • Society of Typographic Designers • (New
Zealand) subscriber toll dialling •
subscriber trunk dialling

**Ste** Sainte (French: Saint (female))

**Sté** (*or* **Sᵗᵉ**) société (French: company;
Co.)

**STE** Society of Telecom Executives
(trade union)

**STEL** short-term exposure level *or* limit
(of radiation)

**STEM** (stɛm) scanning transmission
electron microscope (*or* microscopy)

**sten.** stenographer • stenography

**Sten** Shepherd and Turpin (inventors),
Enfield (in **Sten gun**)

**steno.** (*or* **stenog.**) stenographer •
stenographic • stenography

**STEP** (stɛp) Special Temporary
Employment Programme

**ster.** (*or* **stereo.**) stereophonic • (*or*
**stereo.**) stereotype • sterling

**St. Ex.** Stock Exchange

**STF** *Meteorol.* stratiform

**stg** sterling

**StGB** Strafgesetzbuch (German: Penal
Code)

**stge** storage

**STGWU** Scottish Transport and General Workers' Union

**Sth** South

**STh** Scholar in Theology

**STH** *Biochem.* somatotrophic hormone

**sthn** southern

**STI** Straits Times Index (of the Singapore Stock Exchange)

**STIM** scanning transmission ion microscope

**STINGS** (stɪŋz) *Aeronautics* stellar inertial guidance system

**stip.** stipend • (*or* **Stip.**) stipendiary • stipulation

**s.t.i.r.** surplus to immediate requirements

**Stir.** Stirlingshire (former Scottish county)

**stk** stock

**STL** Licentiate in Sacred Theology (Latin *Sacrae Theologiae Licentiatus*) • Reader (*or* Professor) of Sacred Theology (Latin *Sacrae Theologiae Lector*) • Standard Telecommunications Laboratories • *Telecom.* studio-to-transmitter link

**stlg** sterling

**STLO** Scientific Technical Liaison Office(r)

**STLV** *Med.* simian T-lymphotropic virus

**STM** Master of Sacred Theology (Latin *Sacrae Theologiae Magister*) • scanning tunnelling microscope (*or* microscopy) • *Med., Psychiatry* short-term memory

**STMS** *Finance* short-term monetary support (within the EMS)

**stmt** statement

**stn** stain • (*or* **Stn**) station

**STNR** *Meteorol.* stationary

**Stº** Santo (Portuguese: Saint)

**STO** Sea Transport Officer • Senior Technical Officer • standing order

**STOL** (stɒl) *Aeronautics* short takeoff and landing

**STOLVCD** *Aeronautics* short takeoff and landing, vertical climb and descent

**S'ton** Southampton

**S to S** ship to shore • station to station

**stp** (*or* **s.t.p.**) *Physics* standard temperature and pressure

**STP** Professor of Sacred Theology (Latin *Sacrae Theologiae Professor*) • *Trademark* scientifically treated petroleum (an oil substitute; refers colloquially to a hallucinogenic drug) • sewage treatment plant • *Physics* standard temperature and pressure

**STPMA** Scottish Theatrical Proprietors' and Managers' Association

**str** seater • steamer

**str.** straight • (*or* **Str.**) strait • (*or* **Str.**) street • strength • *Journalism* stringer • *Music* strings (*or* stringed) • *Rowing* stroke (oar) • strong • structural • structure

**s.t.r.** surplus to requirements

**STRAC** (stræk) (USA) strategic air command • strategic army corps

**STRAD** (stræd) signal transmitting, receiving, and distribution

**stratig.** stratigraphy

**strd** stranded

**STRICOM** ('straɪˌkɒm) US Strike Command

**string.** *Music* stringendo (Italian; intensifying)

**STRIVE** (straɪv) Society for the Preservation of Rural Industries and Village Enterprises

**STROBE** (strəʊb) satellite tracking of balloons and emergencies

**Sts** Saints

**STS** Scottish Text Society • *Astronautics* space transportation system

**STSO** Senior Technical Staff Officer

**st. st.** *Knitting* stocking stitch

**STTA** Scottish Table Tennis Association

**STUC** Scottish Trades Union Congress

**stud.** student

**Stuka** ('stuːkə) Sturzkampfflugzeug (German: dive bomber)

**STV** Scottish Television • single transferable vote • standard test vehicle • (USA) subscription television

**stvdr.** stevedore

**stwy** stairway

**s.u.** set up • siehe unten (German: see below)

**Su.** Sudan(ese) • Sunday

**SU** *airline flight code for* Aeroflot • *international civil aircraft marking for* Egypt • *British vehicle registration for* Glasgow • Scripture Union • *British fishing port registration for* Southampton • Soviet Union • *Physics, Maths.* special unitary (group; as in **SU₃**) • *Physics* strontium unit (of radioactive strontium)

**SUA** (USA) State Universities Association

**sub.** subaltern · subeditor · *Music* subito (Italian: immediately, suddenly) · subject · subjunctive · submarine · subordinated · subscription · subsidiary · subsidy · subsistence · *Grammar* substantive · substitute · suburb(an) · subvention · subway

**SUB** (USA) supplemental unemployment benefits

**subd.** subdivision

**sub-ed.** subeditor

**subj.** subject · subjective(ly) · subjunctive

**SUBLANT** ('sʌblænt) *US Navy* Submarine Forces, Atlantic

**Sub-Lt** (*or* **Sub-Lieut.**) Sub-Lieutenant

**subord. cl.** subordinate clause

**SUBPAC** ('sʌb,pæk) *US Navy* Submarine Forces, Pacific

**SUBROC** ('sʌb,rɒk) submarine rocket

**subs.** subsidiary · subsistence

**subsc.** subscription

**subsec.** subsection

**subseq.** (*or* **subsq.**) subsequent(ly)

**subsp.** *Biology* (pl. **subspp.**) subspecies

**subst.** substantive(ly) · substitute

**substand.** substandard

**suc.** (*or* **succ.**) succeed · (*or* **succ.**) success · (*or* **succ.**) successor · suction

**suff.** sufficient · (*or* **suf.**) suffix

**Suff.** Suffolk · (*or* **Suffr.**) Suffragan

**sug.** suggest(ion)

**SUIT** Scottish and Universal Investment Trust

**suiv.** suivant (French: following)

**Sult.** Sultan

**sum.** *Med.* sumat *or* sumendum (Latin: let him (*or* her) take *or* let it be taken; in prescriptions) · summary · summer

**SUM** surface-to-underwater missile

**sums.** summons

**Sun.** (*or* **Sund.**) Sunday

**SUNS** (sʌnz) sonic underwater navigation system

**SUNY** State University of New York

**sup** *Maths.* supremum

**sup.** superficial · superfine · superior · superlative · *Grammar* supine (noun) · supplement(ary) · supply · supra (Latin: above) · supreme

**sup. ben.** supplementary benefit

**Sup. Ct** Superior Court · Supreme Court

**Supdt** Superintendent

**super.** superficial · superfine · superior · supernumerary

**superhet** ('suːpə,hɛt) *Telecom.* supersonic heterodyne

**superl.** superlative

**supp.** (*or* **suppl.**) supplement(ary)

**Supp. Res.** Supplementary Reserve (of officers)

**supr.** superior · (*or* **Supr.**) supreme

**Supt** Superintendent

**supvr** (*or* **supr**) supervisor

**sur.** surface · surplus

**Sur.** Surrey

**surg.** surgeon · surgery · surgical

**Surg. Cdr** (*or* **Surg. Comdr**) Surgeon Commander

**Surg. Gen.** Surgeon General

**Surg. Lt-Cdr** Surgeon Lieutenant-Commander

**Surg. Maj.** Surgeon Major

**surr.** surrender · (*or* **surro.**) surrogate

**Surr.** Surrey

**surv.** survey · (*or* **survey.**) surveying · surveyor · survive · surviving

**SURV** standard underwater research vessel

**Surv. Gen.** Surveyor General

**Sus.** Sussex · Susanna (in the Apocrypha)

**SUS** Scottish Union of Students

**susp.** suspend · suspension

**Suss.** Sussex

**SUSY** *Physics* supersymmetry

**SUT** Society for Underwater Technology

**Suth.** Sutherland (former Scottish county)

**sv** *Baseball* save

**sv.** *Microbiol.* serovar

**s.v.** sailing vessel · side valve · sub verbo (*or* voce) (Latin: under the word *or* heading) · *Insurance* surrender value

**Sv** *Physics, symbol for* sievert

**SV** safety valve · Sancta Virgo (Latin: Holy Virgin) · Sanctitas Vestra (Latin: Your Holiness) · *airline flight code for* Saudia-Saudi Arabian Airlines · *Microbiol.* simian virus (as in **SV40**) · stroke volume (of an engine)

**svc.** (*or* **svce**) service

**SVC** *Med.* superior vena cava

**SVD** swine vesicular disease

**svgs** savings

**S-VHS** super-VHS

**SVO** Scottish Variety Orchestra · *Linguistics* subject-verb-object (in **SVO**

**language**) • Superintending Veterinary Officer

**s.v.p.** s'il vous plaît (French: if you please)

**SVP** saturated vapour pressure

**s.v.r.** *Med.* spiritus vini rectificatus (Latin: rectified spirit of wine; in prescriptions)

**SVS** still-camera video system

**SVTP** sound velocity, temperature, pressure

**s.vv.** sub verbis (Latin: under the words or headings)

**svy** survey

**sw.** switch

**s.w.** salt water • sea water

**s/w** sea water • seaworthy

**Sw.** Sweden • Swedish • Swiss

**SW** *British vehicle registration for* Glasgow • senior warden • shipper's weight • shock wave • *Radio* short wave • small women (clothing size) • South Wales • southwest(ern) • *postcode for* southwest London • standard weight

**S/W** *Computing* software

**SWA** *international vehicle registration for* Namibia (formerly South West Africa)

**Swab.** Swabia(n)

**SWACS** space warning and control system

**SWA(L)K** (swɔːlk *or* swæk) sealed with a (loving) kiss (on envelopes)

**SWANU** ('swɑːuː) South West Africa National Union

**SWANUF** ('swɑːnʊf) South West Africa National United Front

**SWAPO** (*or* **Swapo**) ('swɑːpəʊ) South-West Africa People's Organization

**S/WARE** *Computing* software

**SWAT** (swɒt) (USA) Special Weapons and Tactics (police unit)

**SWB** short wheel base • *Military* South Wales Borderers

**swbd** switchboard

**SWCI** *Computing* software configuration item

**swd** *Bookbinding* sewed

**SWE** (USA) Society of Women Engineers

**SWEB** South Wales Electricity Board • Southwest Electricity Board

**Swed.** Sweden • Swedish

**SWET** Society of West End Theatre

**SwF** *symbol for* Swiss franc (monetary unit)

**SWG** standard wire gauge

**SWH** solar water heating

**SWIE** South Wales Institute of Engineers

**SWIFT** (swɪft) Society for Worldwide Interbank Financial Transmission

**Swing** (swɪŋ) *Finance* Sterling warrant into gilt-edged stock

**Switz.** (*or* **Swit.**) Switzerland

**SWL** safe working load

**SWLA** (*or* **SWIA**) Society of Wildlife Artists

**SWMF** South Wales Miners' Federation

**SWO** Station Warrant Officer

**SWOA** Scottish Woodland Owners' Association

**SWOPS** single-well oil-production system

**SWOT** (swɒt) *Marketing* strengths, weaknesses, opportunities, and threats (of a new product)

**SWP** safe working pressure • Socialist Workers' Party

**SWPA** South-West Pacific Area

**SWR** *Telecom.* standing-wave ratio

**SWRB** Sadler's Wells Royal Ballet (now the Royal Ballet)

**SWS** static water supply

**Swtz.** Switzerland

**SWWJ** Society of Women Writers and Journalists

**Sx** Sussex

**SX** *British vehicle registration for* Edinburgh • *international civil aircraft marking for* Greece • soft X-rays • *Shipping* Sundays excepted

**SXES** soft X-ray electron spectroscopy

**SXR** soft X-rays (*or* radiation)

**SXT** sextant

**Sy.** Seychelles • supply • Surrey • Syria

**SY** *international vehicle registration for* Seychelles • *postcode for* Shrewsbury • steam yacht • *British fishing port registration for* Stornoway

**SYB** (ital.) The Statesman's Year-Book

**Syd.** Sydney

**S. Yd** Scotland Yard

**SYHA** Scottish Youth Hostels Association

**syl.** (*or* **syll.**) syllable • syllabus

**sym.** symbol • symbolic • *Chem.* symmetrical • symmetry • symphonic • symphony • symptom

**symp.** symposium

**syn.** synchronize • synonym(ous) • synonymy • synthetic

**sync** *Image technol.* synchronization (*or* synchronize)

**Syncom** ('sɪnkɒm) (USA) synchronous communications satellite

**synd.** syndicate • syndicated

**synon.** synonymous

**synop.** synopsis

**synth.** *Music* synthesizer • synthetic

**Sy. PO** Supply Petty Officer

**syr.** *Pharmacol.* syrup

**Syr.** Syria(n) • Syriac

**SYR** *international vehicle registration for* Syria

**syst.** system • systematic

**sz.** size

**SZ** *British vehicle registration for* Down

---

# T

**t** (ital.) *symbol for* Celsius temperature • *Astronomy, symbol for* hour angle • (ital.) *Statistics, symbol for* Student's t distribution • *Music* te (in tonic sol-fa) • (ital.) *Chem.* tertiary (isomer; as in **t-butane**) • *symbol for* tonne(s) • *Physics* top (a quark flavour) • (ital.) *Chem., symbol for* transport number

**t.** table • tabulated • *Sport* tackle • taken (from) • *Commerce* tare • teaspoon(ful) • teeth • *Music* tempo • tempore (Latin: in the time of) • tenor • *Grammar* tense • terminal • territorial • territory • thunder • time • tome (French: volume) • tonneau (French: ton) • ton(s) *or* tonne(s) • town • township • transit • *Grammar* transitive • troy • tun • turn

**T** (ital.) *Physics, symbol for* kinetic energy • (ital.) *Physics, symbol for* period • *Biochem., symbol for* ribosylthymine • *Chem., symbol for* tautomeric effect • *Meteorol.* temperature • tera- (prefix indicating $10^{12}$ as in **TJ**, terajoule) • *Physics, symbol for* tesla(s) • *international vehicle registration for* Thailand • (ital.) *symbol for* thermodynamic temperature • *Biochem., symbol for* threonine • *Biochem., symbol for* thymine • *Immunol.* thymus (in **T cell** *or* **lymphocyte**) • *Physics* time reversal (as in **T invariance**) • (bold ital.) *Physics, Engineering, symbol for* torque • *Photog.* total light transmission (in **T-number**) • trainer (aircraft; as in **T-37**) • *Irish fishing port registration for* Tralee • *Chem., symbol for* tritium • *Shipping* tropical loading (on load line) • *Logic, Computing, symbol for* true • (ital.) *Biochem., symbol for* twisting number

**T.** (*or* **T**) tablespoon(ful) • *Music* tace (Italian: be silent) • tanker • target • tea (rose) • teacher • telegraph(ic) • telephone • *Music* tempo • temporary • *Music* tenor • Territorial • Territory • Testament • thermometer • *Advertising* third of a page (type area) • Thursday • time • torpedo • transaction(s) • translation • transport(ation) • *Obstetrics* transverse (presentation) • Treasury • Trinity • Tuesday • Turkish • *Knitting* twist

**2,4,5-T** 2,4,5-trichlorophenoxyacetic acid (herbicide)

**T2** *international civil aircraft marking for* Tuvalu

**T3** *international civil aircraft marking for* Kiribati

**T₃** *Biochem.* triiodothyronine

**T₄** *Biochem.* thyroxine (tetraiodothyronine)

**T7** *international civil aircraft marking for* San Marino

**ta.** tableau • tablet

**t.a.** target area • time and attendance • true altitude

**Ta** *Chem., symbol for* tantalum

**TA** *British vehicle registration for* Exeter • *Taxation* table of allowances • *postcode for* Taunton • (USA) teaching assistant • telegraphic address • temporary admission • Territorial Army • *Physics* thermal analysis • tithe annuity • training adviser • *Psychol.* transactional analysis • (USA) transit authority • travelling allowance

**T/A** temporary assistant

**TAA** Territorial Army Association • *Chem.* tertiary amyl alcohol • test of academic aptitude • Trans-Australia Airlines

**TA&VRA** Territorial Auxiliary and Volunteer Reserve Association

**tab.** table (list *or* chart) • tablet • tabulation • tabulator

**TAB** tabulator (on a typewriter) • Technical Assistance Board (of the UN) • (Australia, New Zealand) Totalizator Administration (*or* Agency) Board • *Med.* typhoid, paratyphoid A, paratyphoid B (vaccine)

**TABA** Timber Agents' and Brokers' Association of the United Kingdom

**Tac.** Publius Cornelius Tacitus (*c.* AD 55–*c.* 120, Roman historian)

**TAC** *US Air Force* Tactical Air Command • Technical Assistance Committee (of the UN) • Television Advisory Committee • The Athletics Congress • Tobacco Advisory Committee • Trades Advisory Council

**TACAN** ('tækæn) tactical air navigation

**TACL** Training for Action-Centred Leadership

**TACMAR** ('tækmɑː) tactical multifunction array radar

**TACS** tactical air-control system

**TACV** tracked air-cushion vehicle

**Tads** (tædz) *Military* target acquisition and designation sight

**TAF** Tactical Air Force

**TAFE** ('tæfi) technical and further education

**tafu** ('tæfuː) *Slang* things are fouled (*or* fucked) up

**tafubar** ('tæfuːˌbɑː) *Slang* things are fouled (*or* fucked) up beyond all recognition

**Tag.** Tagalog (language)

**TAG** (USA) The Adjutant-General

**T/Agt** (*or* **T Agt**) (USA) transfer agent

**Tai.** Taiwan

**TAI** temps atomique international (French: International Atomic Time; IAT)

**tal.** talis (Latin: such)

**Tal.** *Judaism* Talmud

**TAL** *Insurance* traffic and accident loss

**TALISMAN** (*or* **Talisman**) ('tælɪzmən) *Stock exchange* Transfer Accounting Lodgement for Investors and Stock Management

**tal. qual.** talis qualis (Latin: average quality)

**Tam.** Tamil (language)

**TAM** tactical air missile • (tæm) Television Audience Measurement (as in **TAM rating**)

**Tamba** ('tæmbə) Twins and Multiple Births Association

**tan** (tæn) *Maths.* tangent

**T & A** (*or* **T and A**) *Slang* (USA) tits and ass • *Med.* (USA) tonsils and adenoids (*or* tonsillectomy and adenoidectomy)

**T&AFA** Territorial and Auxiliary Forces Association

**T & AVR** Territorial and Army Volunteer Reserve

**t. & b.** top and bottom

**T & E** test and evaluation • *Colloquial* tired and emotional (i.e. drunk) • travel and entertainment • trial and error

**t. & g.** *Carpentry* tongued and grooved

**T & G** Transport and General Workers' Union

**t. & o.** *Bookmaking* taken and offered

**t. & p.** *Insurance* theft and pilferage

**t. & s.** toilet and shower

**T & S** transport and supply

**T&SG** Television and Screen Writers' Guild

**T & T** Trinidad and Tobago

**Tang.** Tangier

**tanh** *Maths.* hyperbolic tangent

**TANS** terminal-area navigation system • Territorial Army Nursing Service (now merged with QARANC)

**TANU** ('tænuː) Tanganyika African National Union

**TAO** Technical Assistance Operations (of the UN)

**TAOC** (USA) Tactical Air Operations Center

**TAP** (USA) Technical Assistance Program • Transportes Aéreos Portugueses (Portuguese Airlines)

**Tapline** ('tæp,laɪn) (Saudi Arabia) Trans-Arabian Pipeline Company

**TAPPI** (USA) Technical Association of the Pulp and Paper Industry

**TAPS** Trans-Alaska Pipeline System

**tar.** tariff • tarpaulin

**TAR** terrain-avoidance radar • Territorial Army Regulations • thrust-augmented rocket

**TARA** Technical Assistant, Royal Artillery • Territorial Army Rifle Association

**TARAN** test and replace as necessary

**tarfu** ('tɑːfuː) *Slang* things are really fouled (*or* fucked) up

**TARO** Territorial Army Reserve of Officers

**TARS** Technical Assistance Recruitment Service (of the UN)

**Tas.** Tasmania(n)

**TAS** torpedo antisubmarine (course) • *Aeronautics* true air speed

**TASI** *Telecom.* time-assignment speech interpolation

**Tasm.** Tasmania(n)

**TASMO** tactical air support of maritime operations

**TASR** terminal area surveillance radar

**Tass** (tæs) Telegrafnoye Agentstvo Sovetskovo Soyuza (Russian news agency)

**TASS** Transport Aircraft Servicing Specialist (in the RAF)

**TAT** *Psychol.* thematic apperception test • *Astronautics* thrust-augmented Thor • *Med.* tired all the time • transatlantic telephone cable

**TATSA** transportation aircraft test and support activity

**Tau** *Astronomy* Taurus

**TAUN** Technical Assistance of the United Nations

**TAURUS** ('tɔːrəs) *Stock exchange* Transfer and Automated Registration of Uncertified Stock

**taut.** tautology

**t.-à-v.** tout-à-vous (French: yours ever; in correspondence)

**tav.** tavern

**TAVR** Territorial and Army Volunteer Reserve (1967–79)

**TAVRA** Territorial Auxiliary and Volunteer Reserve Association

**t.a.w.** twice a week

**tax.** (*or* **taxn**) taxation

**tb** *Baseball* total bases

**t.b.** temporary buoy • *Book-keeping* trial balance • true bearing • tubercle bacillus • tuberculosis

**Tb** *Chem., symbol for* terbium

**TB** *British vehicle registration for* Liverpool • torpedo boat • torpedo bomber • training battalion • training board • Treasury bill • *Book-keeping* trial balance • tuberculosis

**t.b.a.** *Commerce* to be advised • to be agreed • to be announced

**TBA** tyres, batteries, and accessories

**t.b.&s.** top, bottom, and sides

**TBC** *Image technol.* time-based corrector

**TBCEP** *Chem.* tri-beta-chloroethyl phosphate (flame retardant)

**t.b.c.f.** to be called for

**t.b.d.** to be determined

**TBD** torpedo-boat destroyer

**TBF** Teachers Benevolent Fund

**TBG** *Immunol.* thyroxine-binding globulin

**TBI** *Engineering* throttle-body injection • *Med.* total body irradiation

**T-bill** Treasury bill

**t.b.l.** *Knitting* through back of loop

**TBL** *Commerce* through bill of lading

**TBM** *Military* tactical ballistic missile • *Surveying* temporary benchmark • *Computing* terabit memory • tunnel-boring machine

**TBO** *Aeronautics* time between overhauls • *Theatre* total blackout

**t-BOC** *Chem.* tertiary butoxycarbonyl

**T-bond** Treasury bond

**TBP** *Chem.* tertiary butyl peroxide • *Chem.* tributyl phosphate

**tbs.** (*or* **tbsp.**) tablespoon(ful)

**TBS** talk between ships (radio apparatus) • tight building syndrome • training battle simulation

**TBSV** *Microbiol.* tomato bushy stunt virus

**TBT** tributyl tin (used in marine paints)

**tc.** *Music* tierce (organ stop)

**t.c.** temperature control • till cancelled • time check • true course

**Tc** *Chem., symbol for* technetium

**TC** *British vehicle registration for* Bristol • *Military* Tank Corps • (USA) Tariff Commission • *Law* Tax Cases • technical college • temporary clerk • Temporary Constable • tennis club • touring club • town clerk • town council(lor) • training centre • training college • training corps • *Military* Transport Command • traveller's cheque • *Music* tre corde (Italian: three strings; i.e. release soft pedal) • Trinity College • (Trinidad and Tobago) (Order of the) Trinity Cross • *Meteorol.* tropical cyclone • Trusteeship Council (of the UN) • *Chem.* tungsten carbide • *international civil aircraft marking for* Turkey • twin carburettors (on motor vehicles)

**TCA** *Biochem.* tricarboxylic acid (in **TCA cycle**) • trichloroacetic acid (herbicide) • tricyclic antidepressant (drug)

**TCB** *Slang* (USA) take care of business • *Chem.* tetrachlorobiphenyl • Thames Conservancy Board

**TCBM** transcontinental ballistic missile

**TCC** *Telecom.* time compression coding • Transport and Communications Commission (of the UN) • Trinity College, Cambridge • (USA) Troop Carrier Command

**TCCB** Test and County Cricket Board

**TCD** Trinity College, Dublin

**TCDD** tetrachlorodibenzodioxin (dioxin; environmental pollutant)

**TCE** *Chem.* trichloroeth(yl)ene (solvent)

**tcf** trillion cubic feet (measure of natural gas)

**TCF** Temporary Chaplain to the Forces • time-correction factor • Touring Club de France

**TCFB** Transcontinental Freight Bureau

**TCGF** *Immunol.* T-cell growth factor

**tchg** teaching

**tchr** teacher

**TCI** Touring Club Italiano (Italian Touring Club)

**TCL** *Chem.* trichloroeth(yl)ene (solvent) • Trinity College (of Music) London

**TCM** Trinity College of Music (London)

**TCMA** Telephone Cable Makers' Association

**TCNE** *Chem.* tetracyanoeth(yl)ene

**TCNQ** *Chem.* tetracyanoquino-dimethane

**TCO** test control office • (Sweden) Tjänstemännens Centralorganisation (Central Organization of Salaried Employees; trade union) • Trinity College, Oxford

**TCP** *Computing* transmission control protocol • *Trademark* trichlorophenyl-methyliodisalicyl (an antiseptic) • *Chem.* tricresyl phosphate

**TCPA** Town and Country Planning Association

**TCR** *Immunol.* T-cell receptor • *Physics* temperature coefficient of resistance

**TCS** target cost system • (USA) traffic control station

**tctl** tactical

**TCU** *Meteorol.* towering cumulus • (USA) Transportation, Communications, International Union

**td.** touchdown

**t.d.** technical data • *Med.* ter in die (Latin: three times a day; in prescriptions) • test data • time delay • tractor-drawn

**TD** *postcode for* Galashiel's • *British vehicle registration for* Manchester • *Military*

Tactical Division • tank destroyer • *Med.* tardive dyskinesia • Teaching Diploma • (Ireland) Teachta Dála (Gaelic: Member of the Dáil) • technical development • technical drawing • Territorial (Efficiency) Decoration (in the Territorial Army) • Tilbury Docks • torpedo depot • *Football* (USA, Canada) touchdown(s) • (USA) traffic director • (USA) Treasury Department • trust deed • Tunisian dinar (monetary unit)

**TDA** 2,4-toluene diamine (possible carcinogen released by breast implants)

**TDAL** *Chem.* tetradecenal

**TDB** temps dynamique barycentrique (French: barycentric dynamical time) • total disability benefit

**TDC** Temporary Detective Constable • through-deck cruiser • (*or* **t.d.c.**) *Engineering* top dead centre

**TDD** telecommunications device for the deaf • Tubercular Diseases Diploma

**TDDA** *Chem.* tetradecadien-1-yl acetate

**TDDL** *Telecom.* time-division data link

**TDG** twist drill gauge

**TDI** *Chem.* toluene-2,4-diisocyanate

**TDL** tunable diode laser

**TDM** telemetric data monitor • *Telecom.* time-division multiplexing

**TDMA** *Telecom.* time-division multiple access

**TDN** total digestible nutrients

**T-DNA** *Genetics* transferred DNA

**TDO** *Meteorol.* tornado

**TDP** technical development plan

**t.d.r.** tous droits réservés (French: all rights reserved)

**TDR** *Finance* Treasury deposit receipt

**TDRSS** (*or* **TDRS**) tracking and data-relay satellite system

**t.d.s.** *Med.* ter die sumendum (Latin: to be taken three times a day; in prescriptions)

**TDS** *Computing* tabular data stream • *Physics* thermal desorption spectroscopy (*or* spectrum) • *Nuclear physics* thermal diffuse scattering

**TDT** *Astronomy* terrestrial dynamical time

**t.e.** thermal efficiency • tinted edge (of paper) • trailing edge • turbine engine

**t/e** twin-engined

**Te** *Chem., symbol for* tellurium

**TE** *British vehicle registration for* Manchester • telecommunications engineering · *Biochem.* trace element · trade expenses · *Telecom.* transverse electric (as in **TE wave**)

**TEAC** Technical Educational Advisory Council

**TEC** *Physics* thermal expansion coefficient · *Physics* thermionic energy conversion · (tɛk) Training and Enterprise Council

**tech.** (*or* **techn.**) technical(ly) · technician · technique · technology

**Tech(CEI)** Technician (Council of Engineering Institutions)

**technol.** technological · technology

**TED** *Chem.* trieth(yl)enediamine

**TEE** Telecommunications Engineering Establishment · Torpedo Experimental Establishment · Trans-Europe Express (train)

**TEF** toxicity equivalence factor

**TEFL** teaching (of) English as a foreign language

**t.e.g.** *Bookbinding* top edges gilt

**Teh.** Tehran

**tel.** telegram · telegraph(ic) · telephone

**Tel** *Astronomy* Telescopium

**TEL** tetraethyl lead (petrol additive) · *Astronautics* transporter-erector-launcher

**telecom.** telecommunication(s)

**teleg.** telegram · telegraph(ic) · telegraphy

**teleph.** telephone · telephony

**telex** ('tɛlɛks) teleprinter exchange

**TELNET** ('tɛlnɛt) *Computing* teletype network

**tel. no.** telephone number

**TEM** Territorial Efficiency Medal · transmission electron microscope (*or* microscopy) · *Telecom.* transverse electromagnetic

**TEMA** Telecommunications Engineering and Manufacturing Association

**temp.** temperance · temperate · temperature · *Music* tempo · temporal · temporary · tempore (Latin: in the time of)

**Templar** ('tɛmplə) tactical expert mission-planner (military computer)

**temp. prim.** *Music* tempo primo (Italian; at the original pace)

**ten.** tenant · tenement · tenor · *Music* tenuto (Italian: held, sustained)

**tency** tenancy

**Tenn.** Tennessee

**TENS** (tɛnz) *Med.* transcutaneous electrical nerve stimulation

**TeolD** Doctor of Theology

**TEPP** tetraethyl pyrophosphate (pesticide)

**ter.** (*or* **Ter.**) terrace · territorial · territory

**terat.** teratology

**TERCOM** ('tɜːkɒm) *Aeronautics* terrain contour matching (*or* mapping)

**term.** terminal · terminate · termination · terminology

**terr.** (*or* **Terr.**) terrace · territorial · territory

**tert.** tertiary

**TES** thermal-energy storage · (ital.) Times Educational Supplement

**TESL** teaching (of) English as a second language

**TESOL** ('tiːsɒl) teaching (*or* teacher) of English to speakers of other languages

**Tessa** ('tɛsə) Tax-Exempt Special Savings Account

**test.** testament · testator (*or* testatrix) · testimonial · testimony

**TET** Teacher of Electrotherapy

**T.-et-G.** Tarn-et-Garonne (department of France)

**TETOC** technical education and training for overseas countries

**tet. tox.** tetanus toxin

**TEU** *Shipping* twenty-foot equivalent unit

**Teut.** Teuton(ic)

**TeV** *Physics, symbol for* teraelectronvolt

**TEWT** (*or* **Tewt**) (tjuːt) *Military* tactical exercise without troops

**Tex.** Texan · Texas

**text.** textile

**text. rec.** textus receptus (Latin: the received text)

**t.f.** tabulating form · tax-free · travaux forcés (French: hard labour)

**TF** *British vehicle registration for* Reading · *postcode for* Telford · Territorial Force · *Electronics* thin film · *Biochem.* transcription factor · *Shipping* tropical freshwater (on load lines) · *international civil aircraft marking for* Iceland

**TFA** Tenant Farmers' Association · *Biochem.* total fatty acids · *Chem.* trifluoroacetic acid

**TFAA** *Chem.* trifluoroacetic anhydride

**TFAP** Tropical Forestry Action Plan

**tfc** traffic

**TFD** *Electronics* thin-film detector

**TFECG** Training and Further Education Consultative Group

**TFMS** *Physical chem.* time-of-flight mass spectrometer

**tfr** transfer

**TFR** Territorial Force Reserve

**TFSC** (or **TFSK**) Turkish Federated State of Cyprus (Turkish *Kibris*)

**TFT** *Electronics* thin-film transistor

**TFTR** *Nuclear engineering* Tokamak Fusion Test Reactor (Princetown, USA)

**TFU** telecommunications flying unit

**TFW** *Military* tactical fighter wing

**TFX** tactical fighter experimental (aircraft)

**tg** *Maths.* tangent

**t.g.** tail gear • *Biology* type genus

**TG** *British vehicle registration for* Cardiff • *international civil aircraft marking for* Guatemala • Tate Gallery (London) • temporary gentleman • *airline flight code for* Thai Airways International • *Colloquial* thank God • (USA) Theater Guild • *international vehicle registration for* Togo • training group • transformational-generative (grammar) • transformational grammar • Translators' Guild (London)

**TGA** *Chem.* thermal gravimetric analysis

**TGAT** ('tiːgæt) *Education* Task Group on Assessment and Testing

**T-gate** *Computing* ternary selector gate

**t.g.b.** *Carpentry* tongued, grooved, and beaded

**TGB** (France) Très Grande Bibliothèque (or Bibliothèque de France; proposed French national library)

**TGEW** Timber Growers England and Wales Ltd

**TGF** *Med.* transforming growth factor

**TGI** *Marketing* Target Group Index

**TGIF** *Colloquial* thank God it's Friday

**TGM** torpedo gunner's mate

**TGMV** *Microbiol.* tomato golden mosaic virus

**T-group** training group

**tgt** target

**TGT** *Physics* temperature gradient technique • *Aeronautics* turbine gas temperature

**TGV** (France) train à grande vitesse (high-speed passenger train)

**TGWU** Transport and General Workers' Union

**th** *Maths.* hyperbolic tangent

**th.** thermal

**Th** *Chem., symbol for* thorium

**Th.** Theatre • Thursday

**TH** *British vehicle registration for* Swansea • Technische Hochschule (German: technical university *or* college) • *British fishing port registration for* Teignmouth • Territory of Hawaii • *Numismatics* toothed border • town hall (on maps) • Toynbee Hall • Transport House • Trinity House

**THA** *Biochem.* tetrahydroaminoacridine

**Thai.** Thailand

**thanat.** thanatology

**ThB** Bachelor of Theology (Latin *Theologicae Baccalaureus*)

**THC** tetrahydrocannabinol (cannabis component) • (New Zealand) Tourist Hotel Corporation

**ThD** Doctor of Theology (Latin *Theologicae Doctor*)

**THD** total harmonic distortion (in sound recording)

**THE** Technical Help to Exporters (division of the British Standards Institute)

**theat.** theatre • theatrical

**THELEP** Therapy of Leprosy

**Theoc.** Theocritus (*c.* 310–250 BC, Greek poet)

**theol.** theologian • theological • theology

**Theoph.** Theophrastus (*c.* 370–*c.* 286 BC, Greek philosopher)

**theor.** theorem • (or **theoret.**) theoretical • theory

**theos.** theosophical • theosophist • theosophy

**therap.** (or **therapeut.**) therapeutic(s)

**therm.** thermometer • thermometry

**thermochem.** thermochemistry

**thermodyn.** thermodynamics

**thermom.** thermometer • thermometry

**thes.** thesis

**THES** (ital.) Times Higher Education Supplement

**thesp.** thespian

**Thess.** *Bible* Thessalonians • Thessaly

**THF** *Chem.* tetrahydrofuran • Trusthouse Forte plc

**THI** temperature–humidity index

**thk** thick

**ThL** Theological Licentiate

**ThM** Master of Theology (Latin *Theologiae Magister*)

**THN** *Chem.* tetrahydronaphthalene

**thor.** thorax

**thoro.** thoroughfare

**thou.** thousand

**thp** thrust horsepower

**thr.** their • through • thrust

**Thr** (or **thr**) *Biochem.* threonine

**THR** *Med.* total hip replacement

**3i** Investors in Industry

**3M** Minnesota Mining and Manufacturing Company

**three** (*or* **3**) **Rs** reading, (w)riting, and (a)rithmetic

**throt.** throttle

**ThSchol** Scholar in Theology

**Thuc.** Thucydides (*c.* 460–*c.* 400 BC, Greek historian)

**Thurs.** (*or* **Thur.**) Thursday

**THWM** Trinity (House) high-water mark

**THz** *Physics, symbol for* terahertz

**Ti** *Chem., symbol for* titanium • *Genetics* tumour-inducing (in **Ti plasmid**)

**Ti.** Tiberius (42 BC–AD 37, Roman emperor) • Tibet

**TI** *international civil aircraft marking for* Costa Rica • *Irish vehicle registration for* Limerick • technical inspection • technical institute • temperature indication (*or* indicator) • *Med.* thermal imaging • *Chem.* toluene-insoluble

**T/I** target identification • target indicator

**TIA** Tax Institute of America • *Med.* transient ischaemic attack

**Tib.** Tibet(an)

**TIBC** *Med.* total iron-binding capacity

**TIBOR** ('tiːbɔː) *Finance* Tokyo Inter-Bank Offered Rate

**TIC** (*or* **tic**) *Law* taken into consideration (of an offence) • total inorganic carbon (in chemical analysis) • tourist information centre

**t.i.d.** *Med.* ter in die (Latin: three times a day; in prescriptions)

**TIE** theatre in education

**tier.** *Music* tierce (organ stop)

**TIF** telephone interference (*or* influence) factor • *Biochem.* transcription initiation factor • Transports Internationaux par Chemin de Fer (French: International Rail Transport)

**TIG** tungsten inert gas (welding)

**TIGR** ('taɪgə) Treasury Investment Growth Receipts (type of bond)

**TIH** Their Imperial Highnesses

**TIL** *Med.* tumour-infiltrating lymphocyte

**TILS** Technical Information and Library Service

**t.i.m.** time is money

**Tim.** *Bible* Timothy

**TIM** transient intermodulation distortion (in sound recording)

**timp.** *Music* timpani

**TIMP** *Med.* tissue inhibitor of metalloproteinase

**TIMS** The Institute of Management Sciences • *Physical chem.* thermal ionization mass spectrometry

**TIN** (USA) taxpayer identification number

**TINA** ('tiːnə) *Politics, colloquial* there is no alternative (usually referring to Margaret Thatcher)

**tinct.** tincture

**TIO** Technical Information Officer

**Tip.** Tipperary

**TIP** *Computing* terminal interface processor

**TIR** *Optics* total internal reflection • Transport International Routier (French: International Road Transport; on continental lorries)

**TIRC** Tobacco Industry Research Committee

**TIROS** ('taɪrəs) television and infrared observation satellite

**tis.** tissue

**TIS** technical information service

**tit.** title • titular

**Tit.** *Bible* Titus

**TJ** *international civil aircraft marking for* Cameroon • *British vehicle registration for* Liverpool • (*or* **t.j.**) talk jockey • *Physics, symbol for* terajoule • *Athletics* triple jump

**tk** tank • truck

**Tk** *symbol for* taka (monetary unit of Bangladesh)

**TK** *British vehicle registration for* Exeter • *airline flight code for* Turkish Airlines

**TKO** (*or* **t.k.o.**) *Boxing* technical knock-out

**tkr** tanker

**tks** thanks

**tkt** ticket

**tl** *Meteorol., symbol for* thunderstorm

**t.l.** test link • *Engineering* thrust link • time length • total load • *Insurance* total loss • trade list

**Tl** *Chem., symbol for* thallium

**TL** *international civil aircraft marking for* Central African Republic • *British vehicle registration for* Lincoln • target language • *Physics* thermoluminescence • thermoluminescent (as in **TL-dating**) • Torpedo Lieutenant • *Insurance* total loss • *Colloquial* (USA) trade-last • transmission line • Turkish lira (monetary unit)

**T/L** *Banking* time loan • *Insurance* total loss

**TLA** three-letter abbreviation (*or* acronym)

**t.l.b.** temporary lighted buoy

**TLC** tender loving care • *Chem.* thin-layer chromatography • *Med.* total lung capacity • (Australia) Trades and Labour Council

**tld** tooled

**TLG** Theatrical Ladies' Guild

**t.l.o.** *Insurance* total loss only

**TLO** Technical Liaison Officer

**TLP** *Astronomy* transient lunar phenomena

**tlr** tailor • trailer

**TLR** Times Law Reports • *Photog.* twin-lens reflex

**TLS** (ital.) Times Literary Supplement • typed letter, signed

**tltr** translator

**TLU** *Computing* table look-up

**TLV** *Electronics* threshold-limit value

**TLWM** Trinity (House) low-water mark

**t.m.** temperature meter • true mean

**Tm** *Chem., symbol for* thulium

**TM** *British vehicle registration for* Luton • tactical missile • technical manual • technical memorandum • test manual • Their Majesties • *Telecom.* tone modulation • trademark • training manual • transcendental meditation • *Telecom.* transverse magnetic (as in **TM wave**) • trench mortar • tropical medicine • *Computing* Turing machine

**TMA** Theatrical Management Association • Trans-Mediterranean Airways (Lebanese national airline) • *Chem.* trimellitic acid

**TMB** *Chem.* tetramethylbenzidine • travelling medical board

**tmbr** timber

**TMC** Tanglewood Music Center (USA)

**TMCS** *Chem.* trimethylchlorosilane

**TMD** *Military* theatre missile defence

**tme** time

**TMEDA** *Chem.* tetramethylethylenediamine

**TMI** (USA) Three Mile Island

**TMJ** *Med.* temporomandibular joint (as in **TMJ syndrome**)

**tmkpr** timekeeper

**TML** *Chem.* tetramethyl lead • *Shipping* three-mile limit

**TMMG** Teacher of Massage and Medical Gymnastics

**TMO** telegraph(ic) money order

**TMP** thermomechanical pump

**tmpry** temporary

**tmr** timer

**TMS** *Chem.* tetramethylsilane

**TMSDEA** *Chem.* trimethylsilyldiethylamine

**TMT** turbine motor train

**TMV** *Microbiol.* tobacco mosaic virus • true mean value

**tn** ton (*or* tonne) • town • train • transportation

**t.n.** technical note • telephone number

**Tn** *Genetics* transposon (followed by a number or letter)

**TN** *airline flight code for* Australian Airlines • *British vehicle registration for* Newcastle upon Tyne • *international civil aircraft marking for* Republic of the Congo • *US postcode for* Tennessee • *postcode for* Tonbridge • *British fishing port registration for* Troon • true north • *international vehicle registration for* Tunisia

**TNBT** *Chem.* titanium(IV) butoxide

**TNC** Theatres National Committee • total numerical control • transnational corporation

**TNF** *Military* theatre nuclear forces • *Med.* tumour necrosis factor

**tng** training • turning

**TNG** (USA) The Newspaper Guild

**TNIP** (South Africa) Transkei National Independence Party

**TNM** tactical nuclear missile • *Med.* tumour (size), (lymph) node (involvement), metastasis (in **TNM classification**)

**T-note** *Finance* Treasury note

**TNP** (France) Théâtre National Populaire (national theatre)

**TNPG** The Nuclear Power Group

**tnpk.** turnpike

**TNT** 2,4,6-trinitrotoluene (explosive)

**TNW** *Military* theatre nuclear weapon

**TNX** *Chem.* trinitroxylene

**t.o.** takeoff • turnover

**To.** Togo

**TO** *British vehicle registration for* Nottingham • *Management* table of organization • Technical Officer • telegraphic order • telegraph office • telephone office • telephone order • Torpedo Officer • trained operator • Transport Officer • *British fishing port registration for* Truro • turn over (page)

**T/O** turnover

**tob.** tobacco(nist)

**Tob.** *Old Testament* Tobit

**ToB** *Cycling* Tour of Britain

**TOB** temporary office building

**TobRV** *Microbiol.* tobacco ringspot virus

**TOC** total organic carbon (in chemical analysis)

**Toc H** Talbot House (obsolete telegraphic code for its initials; original headquarters of the movement)

**TOD** time of delivery

**t.o.e.** ton oil equivalent

**TOE** *Physics* theory of everything

**TOEFL** test(ing) of English as a foreign language

**TOET** test of elementary training

**TOF** *Physics* time of flight

**TOFC** trailer on flat car (type of freight container)

**TOFMS** *Chem.* time-of-flight mass spectroscopy

**TOFPET** ('tɒf,pɛt) *Med.* time-of-flight positron-emission tomography

**tog.** (*or* **togr**) together

**Tok.** Tokyo

**TOL** Tower of London

**tom.** (*or* **tomat.**) tomato • tomus (Latin: volume)

**TOM** territoire d'outre mer (French: overseas territory) • total organic matter (in chemical analysis)

**TOMCAT** ('tɒm,kæt) *Military* theatre of operations missile continuous-wave antitank weapon

**TOMS** Total Ozone Mapping Spectrometer

**TON** total organic nitrogen (in chemical analysis)

**tonn.** tonnage

**TOO** (*or* **t.o.o.**) time of origin • *Commerce* to order only

**TOP** (tɒp) *Computing* technical office protocol • temporarily out of print

**TOPIC** ('tɒpɪk) *Stock exchange* Teletext Output Price Information Computer

**topog.** topographer • topographical • topography

**topol.** togological • topology

**TOPS** (tɒps) Training Opportunities Scheme

**t.o.r.** time of receipt (*or* reception)

**Tor.** Toronto

**TOR** Tertiary Order Regular of St Francis

**torn.** tornado

**torp.** torpedo

**t.o.s.** temporarily out of stock • terms of service

**TOSD** Tertiary Order of St Dominic

**TOSF** Tertiary Order of St Francis

**Toshiba** (tɒ'ʃiːbə) Tokyo Shibaura Denki KK (Japanese corporation)

**tot.** total

**t.o.t.** time on (*or* over) target

**TOTC** time-on-target computation (military computer)

**TOTP** Top of the Pops (television programme)

**Tou.** Toulon (France)

**tour.** tourism • tourist

**tourn.** tournament

**TOW** (təʊ) tube-launched optically tracked wire-guided (antitank missile) • tug-of-war

**toxicol.** toxicological • toxicologist • (*or* **tox.**) toxicology

**tp** township • troop

**t.p.** target practice • teaching practice • title page • to pay • *Commerce* tout payé (French: all expenses paid)

**TP** *British vehicle registration for* Portsmouth • *airline flight code for* TAP Air Portugal • taxpayer • technical paper (*or* publication) • teleprinter • *Computing* teleprocessing • *Music* tempo primo (Italian; at the original tempo) • tempore Paschale (Latin: at Easter) • test panel • *Insurance* third party • town planner (*or* planning) • *Computing* transaction processing • Transvaal Province • treaty port • *Surveying* trigonometric point • true position • *Surveying* turning point

**TPA** *Chem.* tetradecanoylphorbol-13-acetate • (*or* **tPA**) *Med.* tissue plasminogen activator

**TPC** (USA) The Peace Corps • (Australia) Trade Practices Commission

**tpd** (*or* **TPD**) tons per day

**tph** (*or* **TPH**) tons per hour

**tpi** *Engineering* teeth per inch • *Computing* tracks per inch • *Engineering* turns per inch

**TPI** tax and price index • *Computing* terminal phase initiation • *Engineering* threads per inch • *Shipping* tons per inch (immersion) • (Australia) totally and permanently incapacitated • transpolyisoprene (synthetic gutta percha) • Tropical Products Institute

**tpk.** turnpike

**TPLF** Tigrean People's Liberation Front

**TPM** *Computing, etc.* third-party maintenance • (*or* **tpm**) tons per minute • *Chem.* triphenylmethane

**TPN** *Med.* total parenteral nutrition • *Biochem.* triphosphopyridine nucleotide (now called NADP)

**TPO** travelling post office • Tree Preservation Order

**TPP** *Chem.* thiamine pyrophosphate

**Tpr** *Military* Trooper

**TPR** *Med.* temperature, pulse, respiration

**TPS** toughened polystyrene

**tpt** transport • *Music* trumpet

**tptr** *Music* trumpeter

**TQ** (*or* **t.q.**) *Banking* tel quel (exchange rate) • *postcode for* Torquay • total quality (quality control)

**TQM** total quality management

**tr.** *Med.* tinctura (Latin: tincture) • trace • track • tragedy • train • transaction • transfer • transitive • translate(d) • translation • translator • transport(ation) • *Printing* transpose • transposition • treasurer • *Music* treble • *Music* trill • troop • truck • *Music* trumpet(er) • trust • trustee

**Tr** *Chem., former symbol for* terbium • *Geology* Triassic • *Chem., symbol for* trityl (triphenylmethyl) group (in formulae)

**TR** *international civil aircraft marking for* Gabon • *British vehicle registration for* Portsmouth • target rifle • tariff reform • Telephone Rentals plc • tempore regis *or* reginae (Latin: in the time of the king *or* queen) • Territorial Reserve • test run • Theodore Roosevelt (1858–1919, US president 1901–09) • tons registered • tracking radar • *Telecom.* transmit–receive (as in **TR switch**) • *postcode for* Truro • trust receipt • *international vehicle registration for* Turkey

**T/R** transmitter-receiver

**TrA** *Astronomy* Triangulum Australe

**TRA** (USA) Thoroughbred Racing Association

**trac.** tracer • tractor

**TRACALS** ('trækælz) *Aeronautics* traffic control and landing system

**TRACE** (treɪs) task reporting and current evaluation • *Aeronautics* test equipment for rapid automatic check-out evaluation

**trad.** tradition(al) • traduttore (Italian: translator) • traduzione (Italian: translation)

**TRADA** Timber Research and Development Association

**trag.** tragedy • tragic

**TRAMPS** (træmps) temperature regulator and missile power supply

**trans.** transaction • transfer(red) • transit • transitive • transitory • translate(d) • translation • translator • transparent • transport(ation) • *Printing* transpose • transposition • transverse

**Trans.** Transvaal

**transcr.** transcribed (by *or* for) • transcription

**transf.** transferred

**transl.** translate(d) • translation • translator

**translit.** transliterate • transliteration

**transp.** transport(ation)

**trany** transparency

**trav.** traveller • travels

**trbn.** *Music* trombone

**TRC** Thames Rowing Club • Tobacco Research Council

**tr. co.** trust company

**tr. coll.** training college

**Trd** Trinidad

**TRDA** Timber Research and Development Association

**treas.** treasurer • (*or* **Treas.**) treasury

**tree.** trustee

**trem** (trɛm) transport emergency (in **trem card**; carried by chemical tank vehicles)

**trem.** *Music* tremolando (Italian: trembling) • *Music* tremulant (device in an organ)

**tren** *Chem.* triaminotriethylamine (used in formulae)

**trf.** tariff • transfer

**TRF** *Biochem.* thyrotrophin-releasing factor • tuned radio frequency

**trg** training

**trg.** (*or* **trge**) *Music* triangle

**TRG** Tory Reform Group

**TRH** Their Royal Highnesses • *Biochem.* thyrotrophin-releasing hormone

**Tri** *Astronomy* Triangulum

**TRI** Television Reporters International • (USA) Textile Research Institute

**trib.** tribal • tributary

**TRIC** Television and Radio Industries Club • *Med.* trachoma inclusion conjunctivitis

**trid.** *Med.* triduum (Latin: three days; in prescriptions)

**trien** *Chem.* trimethylenetetramine (used in formulae)

**trig.** trigger • trigonometric(al) • trigonometry

**TRIGA** ('trɪgə) *Engineering* training, research, and isotope-production reactors – General Atomic (in **TRIGA reactor**)

**trike** (traɪk) *Chem.* trichloroeth(yl)ene (solvent)

**trim.** trimester

**Trin.** Trinidad • Trinity • Trinity College (Oxford) • Trinity Hall (Cambridge)

**Trip.** Tripos

**tripl.** triplicate

**triple A** (*or* **AAA**) anti-aircraft artillery

**trit.** triturate

**TRITC** *Immunol.* tetramethylrhodamine isothiocyanate (fluorescent dye)

**TRJ** turboramjet (engine)

**TRLFSW** tactical range landing-force support weapon

**trlr** trawler

**TRM** trademark

**trml** terminal

**t.r.n.** technical research note

**tRNA** *Biochem.* transfer RNA

**TRNC** Turkish Republic of Northern Cyprus

**trng** training

**TRO** *Law* temporary restraining order

**trom.** (*or* **tromb.**) trombone

**trombst** trombonist

**trop.** tropic(al)

**Trop. Can.** Tropic of Cancer

**Trop. Cap.** Tropic of Capricorn

**trop. med.** tropical medicine

**Trp** (*or* **trp**) *Military* troop • *Biochem.* tryptophan

**TRPGDA** *Chem.* tripropylene glycol diacrylate

**TRRL** Transport and Road Research Laboratory

**trs.** transfer • *Printing* transpose • trustees

**TRS** Torry Research Station (Scotland)

**TRSB** time reference scanning beam

**trsd** transferred • transposed

**trsp.** transport

**TRSR** taxi and runway surveillance radar

**TRSSGM** tactical range surface-to-surface guided missile

**TRSSM** tactical range surface-to-surface missile

**trt** turret

**Truron.** Truronensis (Latin: (Bishop) of Truro)

**try.** truly

**t.s.** temperature switch • tensile strength • test summary • till sale •

turbine ship • twin screw • type specification

**Ts** *Chem., symbol for* tosyl group (in formulae)

**TS** *postcode for* Cleveland • *British vehicle registration for* Dundee • *Music* tasto solo (Italian: one key alone; in figured-bass playing) • Television Society • Theosophical Society (in England) • tool steel • *Slang* tough shit • *Med.* Tourette's syndrome • training ship • *Chem.* transition state • Treasury Solicitor • *Med.* tuberous sclerosis • tub-sized (paper) • *international civil aircraft marking for* Tunisia • typescript

**T/S** trans-shipment

**TSA** The Securities Association Ltd • *Statistics* time-series analysis • total surface area • Training Services Agency (now called Training Agency)

**TSB** Trustee Savings Bank

**tsc** *indicating* passed a Territorial Army course in staff duties

**TSD** Tertiary of St Dominic

**TSDS** two-speed destroyer sweeper

**TSE** Tokyo Stock Exchange • Toronto Stock Exchange • *Med.* transmissible spongiform encephalopathy

**TSF** two-seater fighter

**tsfr** transfer

**T.Sgt** Technical Sergeant

**TSh** *symbol for* Tanzanian shilling (monetary unit)

**TSH** Their Serene Highnesses • *Biochem.* thyroid-stimulating hormone

**TSH-RH** *Biochem.* thyroid-stimulating-hormone-releasing hormone

**tsi** tons per square inch

**TSO** Trading Standards Officer

**tsp.** teaspoon(ful)

**TSR** tactical strike reconnaissance • *Computing* terminate and stay resident (program) • torpedo-spotter reconnaissance • Trans-Siberian Railway

**TSRB** Top Salaries Review Body

**TSS** time-sharing system • *Med.* toxic shock syndrome • turbine steamship • twin-screw steamer (*or* steamship, ship) • typescripts

**TSSA** Transport Salaried Staffs' Association

**tstr** tester

**t.s.u.** this side up

**TSV** *Microbiol.* tobacco streak virus

**t.s.v.p.** tournez s'il vous plaît (French: please turn over; PTO)

**TSW** Television South West

**TT** *international civil aircraft marking for* Chad · *British vehicle registration for* Exeter · *British fishing port registration for* Tarbert · technical training · teetotal-(ler) · *Banking* telegraphic transfer · *Geology* Tertiary · tetanus toxoid · *Cycling* time trial · torpedo tube · *Motorcycling* Tourist Trophy (races) · *international vehicle registration for* Trinidad and Tobago · Trust Territories (abbrev. *or* postcode) · tuberculin-tested (as in **TT milk**)

**TTA** Travel Trade Association

**TTAPS** Turco, Toon, Ackerman, Pollack, and Sagan (in **TTAPS study** on effects of nuclear winter; from authors' names)

**TTB** tetragonal tungsten bronze

**TTBT** Threshold Test Ban Treaty

**TTC** teachers' training course · technical training centre · *Military* Technical Training Command · *Med.* transcutaneous transhepatic cholangiography

**TTF** Timber Trade Federation

**TTFN** *Colloquial* ta-ta for now

**TTL** *Photog.* through the lens · (*or* **t.t.l.**) to take leave · *Electronics* transistor-transistor logic · (Zimbabwe) tribal trust land

**Tto** Toronto

**TTS** teletypesetter (*or* teletypesetting) · *Acoustics* temporary threshold shift

**TTT** *Cycling* team time trial · Tyne Tees Television Limited

**TTY** (USA) teletypewriter

**Tu.** Tudor · Tuesday

**TU** *British vehicle registration for* Chester · *international civil aircraft marking for* Côte d'Ivoire (Ivory Coast) · thermal unit · toxic unit · trade union · *Telecom.* traffic unit · training unit · *Acoustics, Telecom.* transmission unit · *airline flight code for* Tunis Air · Tupolev (aircraft; as in **TU-104**)

**TUAC** Trade Union Advisory Committee

**tub.** *Cycling* tubular (tyre)

**tuberc.** tuberculosis

**Tuc** *Astronomy* Tucana

**TUC** Trades Union Congress

**TUCC** Transport Users' Consultative Committee (*or* Council)

**TUCGC** Trades Union Congress General Council

**Tues.** Tuesday

**TUG** Telephone Users' Group

**TULRA** Trade Union and Labour Relations Act (1974)

**TUR** *Med.* transurethral resection

**turb.** turbine

**TURB** *Meteorol.* turbulence

**Turk.** Turkey · Turkish

**t.v.** terminal velocity · test vehicle

**TV** *British vehicle registration for* Nottingham · television · (USA) *Colloquial* transvestite

**TVA** taxe à (*or* sur) la valeur ajoutée (French: value-added tax; VAT) · (USA) Tennessee Valley Authority

**TVEI** Technical and Vocational Educational Initiative

**tvl** travel

**Tvl** Transvaal

**TVO** tractor vaporizing oil

**TVP** textured vegetable protein (a meat substitute)

**TVR** television rating · *Physics* temperature variation of resistance

**TVRO** television receive only (type of antenna)

**t.w.** tail wind

**TW** *British vehicle registration for* Chelmsford · *airline flight code for* Trans World Airways · *Telecom.* travelling wave (in **TW antenna**) · *postcode for* Twickenham

**T-W** (USA) three-wheeler (motorcycle)

**TWA** Thames Water Authority · time-weighted average · Trans-World Airlines

**TWh** (*or* **TW h**) *Electricity, symbol for* terawatt hour(s)

**TWIMC** to whom it may concern

**TWN** teleprinter weather network

**twocing** ('twɒkɪŋ) *Colloquial* taking without owner's consent (car theft)

**TWT** transonic wind tunnel · *Electronics* travelling-wave tube

**TWU** Transport Workers' Union of America

**TWX** (USA) teletypewriter exchange service

**twy** twenty

**tx** tax(ation)

**TX** *British vehicle registration for* Cardiff · *US postcode for* Texas

**Ty** Territory · truly (in correspondence)

**TY** *international civil aircraft marking for* Benin · *British vehicle registration for* Newcastle upon Tyne

**TYC** *Horse racing* two-year-old course

**TYMV** *Microbiol.* turnip yellow mosaic virus

**t.y.o.** *Horse racing* two-year-old

**typ.** typical • typing • typist • typographer • typographic(al) • typography

**typh.** typhoon

**typo.** (*or* **typog.**) typographer • typographic(al) • typography

**typw.** typewriter • typewriting • typewritten

**Tyr** (*or* **tyr**) *Biochem.* tyrosine

**Tyr.** Tyrone

**Tyrol.** Tyrolean • Tyrolese

**TZ** *British vehicle registration for* Belfast • *international civil aircraft marking for* Mali

# U

**u** (ital.) *Electricity, symbol for* instantaneous potential difference • (ital.) *Optics, symbol for* object distance • (ital.) *Thermodynamics* specific internal energy • *Meteorol., symbol for* ugly threatening sky • *Physics* ungerade (German: odd; in spectroscopy) • *Chem., symbol for* unified atomic mass unit • *Physics* up (a quark flavour) • (ital.) *Physics, symbol for* a velocity component or speed

**u.** uncle • und (German: and) • unit • unsatisfactory • unter (German: under *or* among) • upper • utility

**U** (ital.) *Thermodynamics, symbol for* internal energy • (ital.) *Electricity, symbol for* potential difference • *symbol for* rate of heat loss (measured in British thermal units; in **U value**, a measure of insulating power) • *Films* universal (certification) • *Colloquial* upper class (of characteristics, language habits, etc.; also in **non-U**) • *Biochem., symbol for* uracil • *Chem., symbol for* uranium • *Biochem., symbol for* uridine • you (from phonetic spelling, as in **IOU, while U wait**)

**U.** (*or* **U**) Union • Unionist • unit • United • University • unsatisfactory • upper

**u.a.** under age • unter anderem (German: among other things) • usque ad (Latin: as far as)

**U/a** *Insurance* underwriting account

**UA** *British vehicle registration for* Leeds • Ulster Association • *airline flight code for* United Airlines • United Artists Corporation • University of Alabama

**UAB** Unemployment Assistance Board • Universities Appointments Board • University of Alabama in Birmingham

**UABS** Union of American Biological Societies

**UAC** Ulster Automobile Club

**UADW** Universal Alliance of Diamond Workers

**UAE** United Arab Emirates

**UAI** Union des associations internationales (French: Union of International Associations)

**UAL** United Airlines

**UAM** underwater-to-air missile

**u. & l.c.** *Printing* upper and lower case

**u. & o.** use and occupancy

**UAOD** United Ancient Order of Druids

**UAOS** Ulster Agricultural Organization Society

**UAP** United Australia Party

**UAPT** Union africaine des postes et télécommunications (French: African Postal and Telecommunications Union)

**UAR** United Arab Republic (1958–71)

**UARS** upper-atmosphere research satellite

**UART** ('ju:,ɑːt) *Electronics, Computing* universal asynchronous receiver/transmitter

**u.a.s.** upper airspace

**UAS** University Air Squadron

**UAU** Universities Athletic Union

**UAW** (USA) United Automobile Workers (United International Union of Automobile, Aerospace, and Agricultural Implement Workers of America; trade union)

**u.A.w.g.** um Antwort wird gebeten (German: an answer is requested)

**UB** *British vehicle registration for* Leeds • *postcode for* Southall • United Brethren

**UB40** *indicating* the index card used for unemployment benefit

**UBA** *Med.* ultrasonic bone analysis

**UBC** University of British Columbia (Vancouver)

**UBF** Union of British Fascists

**UBI** Understanding British Industry (organization)

**U-boat** *indicating* a German submarine during the World Wars (German *Unterseeboot*)

**UBR** *Taxation* Uniform Business Rate · University Boat Race

**UBS** United Bible Societies

**UBV** *Astronomy* ultraviolet, blue, visual (green-yellow)

**u.c.** *Music* una chorda (*see under* UC) · *Printing* upper case

**u/c** *Commerce* undercharge

**UC** *British vehicle registration for* London (central) · *Music* una corda (Italian: on one string; i.e. use soft pedal) · under construction · undercover · University College · *Civil engineering* upcast shaft · *Theatre* up centre (of stage) · Upper Canada · urban council · urbe condita (Latin: the city being built) · *Obstetrics* uterine contraction

**U$_c$** *Films* universal, particularly suitable for children (certification)

**UCA** United Chemists' Association

**UCAE** Universities' Council for Adult Education

**UCATT** (*or* **Ucatt**) ('juːkət) Union of Construction, Allied Trades, and Technicians

**u.c.b.** unless caused by

**UCBSA** United Cricket Board of South Africa

**UCC** Union Carbide Corporation · Universal Copyright Convention · University Computing Company

**UCCA** (*or* **Ucca**) ('ʌkə) Universities Central Council on Admissions

**UCCD** United Christian Council for Democracy

**UCD** University College, Dublin · *Oceanog.* upper critical depth

**UCET** Universities Council for Education of Teachers

**UCG** underground coal gasification

**UCH** University College Hospital (London)

**UCI** Union cycliste internationale (French: International Cyclists' Union) · University of California, Irvine

**UCITS** *Finance* Undertakings for Collective Investment in Transferable Securities

**UCJG** Alliance universelle des unions chrétiennes de jeunes gens (French: World Alliance of Young Men's Christian Associations)

**u.c.l.** *Engineering* upper cylinder lubricant

**UCL** University College London · upper control limit

**UCLA** University of California at Los Angeles

**UCM** University Christian Movement

**UCMJ** (USA) uniform code of military justice

**UCMSM** University College and Middlesex School of Medicine

**UCNS** Universities' Council for Non-academic Staff

**UCNW** University College of North Wales

**UCR** *Physiol., Psychol.* unconditioned reflex (*or* response) · (USA) Uniform Crime Report

**UCS** *Physiol., Psychol.* unconditioned stimulus · Union of Concerned Scientists · University College School (London) · Upper Clyde Shipbuilders

**UCSB** University of California, Santa Barbara

**UCSD** University of California, San Diego

**UCSW** University College of South Wales

**UCTA** United Commercial Travellers' Association (now part of the MSF union)

**UCV** (USA) United Confederate Veterans

**UCW** Union of Communication Workers · University College of Wales

**UCWRE** Underwater Countermeasures and Weapons Research Establishment

**u.d.** unfair dismissal · *Med.* ut dictum (Latin: as directed; in prescriptions)

**UD** *British vehicle registration for* Oxford · United Dairies

**U/D** (USA) under deed

**UDA** Ulster Defence Association

**UDAG** ('juːdæg) (USA) Urban Development Action Grant

**u.d.c.** upper dead centre

**UDC** (USA) United Daughters of the Confederacy · universal decimal classification · Urban Development Corporation · Urban District Council

**UDCA** Urban District Councils' Association

**UDE** Underwater Development Establishment

**UDEAC** Union douanière et économique de l'Afrique centrale (French: Central African Customs and Economic Union)

**UDEAO** Union douanière des états d'Afrique d'Ouest (French: Customs Union of West African States)

**UDF** Ulster Defence Force • (South Africa) Union Defence Force • (Bulgaria) Union of Democratic Forces • (France) Union pour la démocratie française (French Democratic Union; political party) • (South Africa) United Democratic Front

**u. dgl.** und dergleichen (German: and the like)

**UDI** unilateral declaration of independence

**UDM** Union of Democratic Mineworkers

**UDMH** *Chem.* unsymmetrical dimethyl hydrazine

**UDN** ulcerative dermal necrosis (fish disease)

**UDP** United Democratic Party • *Biochem.* uridine 5′-diphosphate

**UDR** Ulster Defence Regiment • (France) Union des démocrates pour la république (French: Union of Democrats for the Republic; former name of the RPR)

**UDSR** (France) Union démocratique et socialiste de la résistance (Democratic and Socialist Union of the Resistance; 1946–58)

**UE** *British vehicle registration for* Dudley • (New Zealand) university entrance (examination)

**UEA** Universal Esperanto Association • University of East Anglia

**UED** University Education Diploma

**u.e.f.** universal extra fine (screw)

**UEF** Union européenne des fédéralistes (French: European Union of Federalists) • Union européenne féminine (French: European Union of Women)

**UEFA** (juːˈeɪfə) Union of European Football Associations

**UEI** Union of Educational Institutions

**UEIC** United East India Company

**UEL** United Empire Loyalists

**UEO** Union de l'Europe occidentale (French: Western European Union; WEU) • Unit Education(al) Officer

**UEP** Union européenne de paiements (French: European Payments Union) • *Genetics* unit evolutionary period

**UEPS** Union européenne de la presse sportive (French: European Sports Press Union)

**UER** Union européenne de radiodiffusion (French: European Broadcasting Union; EBU) • university entrance requirements

**UETA** (USA) universal engineer tractor, armoured

**UETRT** (USA) universal engineer tractor, rubber-tyred

**UF** *British vehicle registration for* Brighton • United Free (Church, of Scotland) • urea–formaldehyde (as in **UF resin**) • utilization factor (of an electric lamp)

**UFA** (formerly, in Germany) Universum Film-Aktiengesellschaft (German: Universal Film Company) • *Biochem.* unsaturated fatty acid

**UFAW** Universities Federation for Animal Welfare

**UFC** United Free Church (of Scotland) • University Funding Council

**UFCW** (USA) United Food and Commercial Workers International Union (trade union)

**UFF** Ulster Freedom Fighters

**UFFI** urea–formaldehyde foam insulation

**UFO** (ˈjuː ˈɛf ˈəʊ *or* ˈjuːfəʊ) unidentified flying object

**UFT** *Physics* unified field theory • (USA) United Federation of Teachers

**UFTAA** Universal Federation of Travel Agents' Association

**UFTU** (Romania) Union of Free Trades Union

**UFU** Ulster Farmers' Union

**UFW** United Farm Workers of America (trade union)

**u/g** underground

**Ug.** (*or* **Ugan.**) Uganda(n)

**UG** *British vehicle registration for* Leeds

**UGC** underground gasification of coal • University Grants Committee (now Funding Council, UFC)

**UGLE** *Freemasonry* United Grand Lodge of England

**UGT** (Spain) Unión General de Trabajadores (General Union of Workers)

**UGWA** United Garment Workers of America (trade union)

**UH** *British vehicle registration for* Cardiff

# UHA · UKCSBS

354

**UHA** (South Africa) Union House of Assembly

**UHB** *Colloquial* urban haute bourgeoisie

**UHCC** Upper House of the Convocation of Canterbury

**UHCY** Upper House of the Convocation of York

**UHF** ultrahigh frequency

**UHT** ultra-heat-treated (as in **UHT milk**) • ultrahigh temperature

**UHV** ultrahigh vacuum

**u.i.** ut infra (Latin: as below)

**u/i** under instruction

**UI** *British vehicle registration for* Londonderry • (USA) unemployment insurance • *Computing* user interface

**UIA** Union of International Associations

**UIAA** Union internationale des associations d'alpinisme (French: International Union of Alpine Associations)

**UIC** Union internationale des chemins de fer (French: International Union of Railways)

**UICC** Union internationale contre le cancer (French: International Union against Cancer)

**UICN** Union internationale pour la conservation de la nature et de ses resources (French: International Union for Conservation of Nature and Natural Resources; IUCNN)

**UICPA** Union internationale de chimie pure et appliquée (French: International Union of Pure and Applied Chemistry; IUPAC)

**UIE** Union internationale des étudiants (French: International Union of Students)

**UIEO** Union of International Engineering Organizations

**UIHPS** Union internationale d'histoire et de philosophie des sciences (French: International Union of the History and Philosophy of Science)

**UIJS** Union internationale de la jeunesse socialiste (French: International Union of Socialist Youth)

**UIL** Unione Italiana del Lavoro (Italian Federation of Trade Unions) • United Irish League

**UIP** Union internationale de patinage (French: International Skating Union) • Union internationale de physique pure et appliquée (French: International Union of Pure and Applied Physics; IUPAP) • Union interparlementaire (French: Inter-Parliamentary Union)

**UIPC** Union internationale de la presse catholique (French: International Catholic Press Union)

**UIPM** Union internationale de pentathlon moderne (French: International Modern Pentathlon Union)

**UISB** Union internationale des sciences biologiques (French: International Union of Biological Sciences)

**UISM** Union internationale des syndicats des mineurs (French: Miners' Trade Unions International)

**UISPP** Union internationale des sciences préhistoriques et prohistoriques (French: International Union of Prehistoric and Prohistoric Sciences)

**UIT** Union internationale des télécommunications (French: International Telecommunications Union; ITU) • unit investment trust

**UITP** Union internationale des transports publics (French: International Union of Public Transport)

**UIU** Upholsterers' International Union of North America

**UJ** *British vehicle registration for* Shrewsbury • Union Jack • *Engineering* universal joint

**UJC** Union Jack Club (London)

**UJD** Utriusque Juris Doctor (Latin: Doctor of Civil and Canon Law)

**UK** *airline flight code for* Air UK • *British vehicle registration for* Birmingham • United Kingdom

**UK(A)** *Athletics* United Kingdom Allcomers

**UKA** Ulster King of Arms • United Kingdom Alliance

**UKAC** United Kingdom Automation Council

**UKADGE** United Kingdom Air Defence Ground Environment

**UKAEA** United Kingdom Atomic Energy Authority

**UKAPE** United Kingdom Association of Professional Engineers

**UKBG** United Kingdom Bartenders' Guild

**UKCC** United Kingdom Central Council for Nursing, Midwifery, and Health Visiting

**UKCIS** United Kingdom Chemical Information Service

**UKCOSA** (juːˈkəʊzə) United Kingdom Council for Overseas Students' Affairs

**UKCSBS** United Kingdom Civil Service Benefit Society

**UKCTA** United Kingdom Commercial Travellers' Association

**UKDA** United Kingdom Dairy Association

**UKFBPW** United Kingdom Federation of Business and Professional Women

**UKgal** *symbol for* UK gallon

**UKIAS** (*or* **Ukias**) (juːˈkaɪəs) United Kingdom Immigrants' Advisory Service

**UKIRT** UK Infrared Telescope (Mauna Kea, Hawaii)

**UKISC** United Kingdom Industrial Space Committee

**UKLF** United Kingdom Land Forces

**UKMF(L)** United Kingdom Military Forces (Land)

**UKMIS** United Kingdom Mission

**UK(N)** *Athletics* United Kingdom National

**UKOOA** United Kingdom Offshore Operators Association

**UKOP** United Kingdom Oil Pipelines

**UKPA** United Kingdom Pilots' Association

**UKPIA** United Kingdom Petroleum Industry Association Ltd

**Ukr.** Ukraine • Ukrainian

**UKSATA** United Kingdom South Africa Trade Association

**UKSLS** United Kingdom Services Liaison Staff

**UKSMA** United Kingdom Sugar Merchant Association Ltd

**UKST** UK Schmidt Telescope (Siding Spring, Australia)

**UKW** Ultrakurzwelle (German: ultrashort wave, i.e. VHF)

**u.l.** upper limit

**UL** *airline flight code for* Air Lanka • *British vehicle registration for* London (central) • *British fishing port registration for* Ullapool • (USA) Underwriters' Laboratories (on labels for electrical appliances) • university library • *Biochem.* unsaturated lipid • *Theatre* up left (of stage) • *Med.* upper limb

**ULA** *Computing* uncommitted logic array

**ULC** *Theatre* up left centre (of stage)

**ULCC** ultralarge crude carrier (oil tanker) • University of London Computer Centre

**ULCI** Union of Lancashire and Cheshire Institutes

**ULF** *Radio, etc.* ultralow frequency • upper limiting frequency

**ULICS** University of London Institute of Computer Science

**ULM** ultrasonic light modulator • universal logic module

**ULMS** underwater long-range missile system

**ULS** *Finance* unsecured loan stock

**ULSEB** University of London School Examinations Board

**ult.** ultimate(ly) • (*or* **ulto.**) ultimo (Latin: in (*or* of) the last (month); in correspondence)

**ULT** United Lodge of Theosophists

**ult. praes.** *Med.* ultimum praescriptum (Latin: last prescribed)

**ULV** ultralow volume (as in **ULV sprayer**)

**um.** unmarried

**u/m** undermentioned

**UM** *British vehicle registration for* Leeds • *symbol for* Mauritanian ouguiya (monetary unit) • University of Minnesota

**UMa** *Astronomy* Ursa Major

**UMA** Union du Maghreb Arabe (French: Arab Maghreb Union; customs union)

**UMB** Union mondiale de billard (French: World Billiards Union) • *Computing* upper memory block

**umbl.** umbilical

**UMC** University of Missouri, Columbia

**UMCP** University of Maryland, College Park

**UMDS** United Medical and Dental Schools

**UMEJ** Union mondiale des étudiants juifs (French: World Union of Jewish Students)

**UMF** Umbrella Makers' Federation

**UMFC** United Methodist Free Churches

**UMi** *Astronomy* Ursa Minor

**UMIST** (*or* **Umist**) (ˈjuːˌmɪst) University of Manchester Institute of Science and Technology

**UMNO** United Malays (later Malaysia) National Organization

**ump.** umpire

**UMP** *Biochem.* uridine monophosphate

**UMT** universal military training

**UMTS** universal military training service (*or* system)

**UMW** (*or* **UMWA**) United Mine Workers (of America; trade union)

**un.** unified • union • united • unsatisfactory

**UN** *British vehicle registration for* Exeter • United Nations

**UNA** United Nations Association

**UNAA** United Nations Association of Australia

**unab.** unabridged

**unacc.** (*or* **unaccomp.**) unaccompanied

**UNACC** United Nations Administrative Committee and Coordination

**UNACOM** universal army communication system

**unan.** unanimous

**UNARCO** United Nations Narcotics Commission

**unasgd** unassigned

**unatt.** unattached

**unattrib.** unattributed

**UNAUS** United Nations Association of the United States

**unauthd** unauthorized

**unb.** (*or* **unbd**) unbound

**UNB** universal navigation beacon • University of New Brunswick

**UNBRO** (*or* **Unbro**) (ˈʌnbrəʊ) United Nations Border Relief Operation

**unc.** uncertain • uncle

**UNC** *Numismatics* uncirculated • Union Nationale Camerounaise (French: Cameroon National Union *or* Cameroon People's Democratic Movement) • United Nations Command • University of North Carolina

**UNCAST** United Nations Conference on the Applications of Science and Technology

**UNCC** United Nations Cartographic Commission

**UNCCP** United Nations Conciliation Commission for Palestine

**UNCDF** United Nations Capital Development Fund

**UNCED** United Nations Conference on Environment and Development

**UNCIO** United Nations Conference on International Organization

**UNCITRAL** United Nations Commission on International Trade Law

**unclas.** (*or* **unclass.**) unclassified

**UNCLE** (ˈʌŋkᵊl) United Network Command for Law Enforcement (fictional organization in TV series 'The Man from UNCLE')

**UNCLOS** United Nations Conference on the Law of the Sea

**UNCOK** United Nations Commission on Korea

**uncond.** unconditional

**uncor.** uncorrected

**UNCSTD** United Nations Conference on Science and Technology for Development

**UNCTAD** (*or* **Unctad**) (ˈʌŋkˌtæd) United Nations Conference on Trade and Development

**UNCURK** United Nations Commission for Unification and Rehabilitation of Korea

**UND** University of North Dakota

**UNDP** United Nations Development Programme

**UNDRO** (*or* **Undro**) (ˈʌnˌdrəʊ) United Nations Disaster Relief Organization

**undsgd** undersigned

**undtkr** undertaker

**UNE** underground nuclear explosion

**UNEC** United Nations Education Conference

**UNECA** United Nations Economic Commission for Asia

**UNEDA** United Nations Economic Development Administration

**UNEF** (ˈjuːˌnɛf) United Nations Emergency Force

**UNEP** (ˈjuːˌnɛp) United Nations Environment Programme

**UNESCO** (*or* **Unesco**) (juːˈnɛskəʊ) United Nations Educational, Scientific, and Cultural Organization

**UNETAS** United Nations Emergency Technical Aid Service

**unexpl.** unexplained • unexploded • unexplored

**UNFAO** United Nations Food and Agriculture Organization

**UNFB** United Nations Film Board

**UNFC** United Nations Food Conference

**UNFICYP** United Nations (Peace-Keeping) Force in Cyprus

**UNFPA** United Nations Fund for Population Activities

**ung.** *Med.* unguentum (Latin: ointment)

**UNGA** United Nations General Assembly

**Unh** *Chem., symbol for* unnilhexium (element 106)

**UNH** *Chem.* uranyl nitrate hexahydrate

**UNHCR** United Nations High Commissioner for Refugees

**UNHQ** United Nations Headquarters

**Uni.** University College, Oxford

**UNI** Ente Nazionale Italiano di Unificazione (Italian Standards Association)

**UNIA** (USA) Universal Negro Improvement Association

**UNIC** United National Information Centre

**UNICA** Union internationale du cinéma d'amateurs (French: International Union of Amateur Cinema)

**UNICE** Union des industries de la communauté européenne (French: Union of Industries of the European Community)

**UNICEF** (*or* **Unicef**) ('juːnɪˌsef) United Nations Children's Fund (formerly United Nations International Children's Emergency Fund)

**UNICOM** (*or* **Unicom**) ('juːnɪˌkɒm) universal integrated communication system

**UNIDO** (*or* **Unido**) (juːˈniːdəʊ) United Nations Industrial Development Organization

**UNIDROIT** Institut international pour l'unification du droit privé (French: International Institute for the Unification of Private Law)

**unif.** uniform

**UNIFIL** (*or* **Unifil**) ('juːnɪˌfɪl) United Nations Interim Force in Lebanon

**UNIMA** Union internationale des marionnettes (French: International Union of Puppeteers)

**UNIO** United Nations Information Organization

**UNIP** (*or* **Unip**) ('juːnɪp) (Zambia) United National Independence Party

**UNIPEDE** Union internationale des producteurs et distributeurs d'énergie électrique (French: International Union of Producers and Distributors of Electrical Energy)

**unis.** *Music* unison

**UNIS** United Nations International School

**UNISCAT** (*or* **Uniscat**) ('juːnɪˌskæt) United Nations Expert Committee on the Application of Science and Technology

**UNISIST** (*or* **Unisist**) ('juːnɪˌsɪst) Universal System for Information in Science and Technology

**Unit.** Unitarian(ism)

**UNITA** (*or* **Unita**) (juːˈniːtə) União Nacional para a Independência Total de Angola (Portuguese: National Union for the Total Independence of Angola)

**UNITAR** United Nations Institute for Training and Research

**univ.** universal(ly) • university

**Univ.** Universalist • University • University College, Oxford

**UNIVAC** ('juːnɪˌvæk) universal automatic computer

**UNIX** ('juːnɪks) *Trademark, indicating* a type of computer operating system

**UNJSPB** United Nations Joint Staff Pension Board

**unkn.** unknown

**UNKRA** (*or* **Unkra**) United Nations Korean Reconstruction Agency

**UNLC** United Nations Liaison Committee

**unm.** unmarried

**UNM** University of New Mexico

**UNMC** United Nations Mediterranean Commission

**UNO** United Nations Organization • (Nicaragua) *indicating* National Opposition Union (Spanish; political party)

**unop.** unopposed

**unp.** unpaged • unpaid

**Unp** *Chem., symbol for* unnilpentium (element 105)

**UNP** (Sri Lanka) United National Party

**UNPA** United Nations Postal Administration

**UNPC** United Nations Palestine Commission

**UNPCC** United Nations Conciliation Commission for Palestine

**unpd** unpaid

**UNPROFOR** (ˈʌnprəʊˌfɔː) United Nations Protection Force in Yugoslavia

**unpub.** (*or* **unpubd**) unpublished

**Unq** *Chem., symbol for* unnilquadium (element 104)

**UNREF** (*or* **Unref**) ('ʌnref) United Nations Refugee Emergency Fund

**UNRISD** United Nations Research Institute for Social Development

**UNRPR** United Nations Relief for Palestine Refugees

**UNRRA** (*or* **Unrra**) ('ʌnrə) United Nations Relief and Rehabilitation Administration

**UNRWA** (*or* **Unrwa**) ('ʌnrə) United Nations Relief and Works Agency

**unsat.** unsatisfactory • unsaturated

**UNSC** United Nations Security Council • United Nations Social Commission

**UNSCC** United Nations Standards Coordinating Committee

**UNSCCUR** United Nations Scientific Conference on the Conservation and Utilization of Resources

**UNSCOB** United Nations Special Committee on the Balkans

**UNSCOP** United Nations Special Committee on Palestine

**UNSF** United Nations Special Fund for Economic Development

**UNSG** United Nations Secretary-General

**UNSR** United Nations Space Registry

**UNSW** University of New South Wales

**UNTAA** United Nations Technical Assistance Administration

**UNTAB** United Nations Technical Assistance Board

**UNTAC** (*or* **Untac**) ('ʌntæk) United Nations Transitional Authority for Cambodia

**UNTAG** United Nations Transition Assistance Group (in Namibia)

**UNTAM** United Nations Technical Assistance Mission

**UNTC** United Nations Trusteeship Council

**UNTT** United Nations Trust Territory

**UNWCC** United Nations War Crimes Commission

**UO** *British vehicle registration for* Exeter

**u.o.c.** ultimate operating capability

**UOD** ultimate oxygen demand (in water conservation)

**U of A** University of Alaska

**U of NC** University of North Carolina

**U of S** University of Saskatchewan

**U of T** University of Toronto

**up.** (*or* **u.p.**) underproof (of alcohol) • upper

**UP** *British vehicle registration for* Newcastle upon Tyne • Ulster Parliament • Union Pacific • United Party (esp. in South Africa) • United Presbyterian • United Press (news agency) • University of Paris • University of Pennsylvania • University of Pittsburgh • University Press • unsaturated polyester (polymer) • (USA) Upper Peninsula • Uttar Pradesh (formerly United Provinces)

**UPA** Union postale arabe (French: Arab Postal Union) • United Productions of America (cartoon film producer)

**UPC** Uganda People's Congress • Union des Populations Camerounaises (French: Union of the Populations of Cameroon) • United Presbyterian

Church • Universal Postal Convention • universal product code (bar code)

**upd** unpaid

**UPD** united port district • Urban Planning Directorate

**UPF** untreated polyurethane foam

**UPGC** University and Polytechnic Grants Committee

**UPGWA** United Plant Guard Workers of America (trade union)

**uphd** uphold

**uphol.** upholsterer • upholstery

**UPI** United Press International

**UPIU** (USA) United Paperworkers International Union

**UPIGO** Union professionnelle internationale des gynécologues et obstétriciens (French: International Union of Professional Gynaecologists and Obstetricians)

**UPNI** Unionist Party of Northern Ireland

**UPOA** Ulster Public Officers' Association

**UPOW** Union of Post Office Workers (now merged with UCW)

**UPP** (Poland) United Peasant Party

**UPR** *Insurance* unearned premiums reserve • Union Pacific Railroad

**UPS** *Chem.* ultraviolet photoelectron spectroscopy • uninterruptible power supply (to computers, etc.) • *Trademark* (USA) United Parcel Service • United Publishers' Services

**UPU** Universal Postal Union (UN agency; formerly General Postal Union, GPU)

**UPUP** Ulster Popular Unionist Party

**uPVC** unplasticized polyvinyl chloride

**UPW** Union of Post Office Workers (now merged with UCW)

**UPWA** United Packinghouse Workers of America (former trade union)

**ur.** *Med.* urine

**Ur.** Urdu • Uruguay(an)

**UR** *British vehicle registration for* Luton • *international civil aircraft marking for* Ukraine • *Physiol., Psychol.* unconditioned reflex (*or* response) • uniform regulations • *Theatre* up right (of stage)

**URA** (USA) Urban Renewal Administration

**Uran.** *Astronomy* Uranus

**urb.** urban

**URBM** ultimate-range ballistic missile

**URC** United Reformed Church • *Theatre* up right centre (of stage)

**Urd.** Urdu

**URF** Union des services routiers des chemins de fer européens (French: Union of European Railways Road Services)

**urg.** urgent

**URI** *Med.* upper respiratory infection

**URL** Unilever Research Laboratory

**UR-NAP** *Med.* urea-resistant neutrophil alkaline phosphatase (enzyme)

**urol.** urology

**URSI** Union radio scientifique internationale (French: International Scientific Radio Union)

**URTI** *Med.* upper respiratory tract infection

**URTU** United Road Transport Union

**Uru.** Uruguay(an)

**Urupabol** Uruguay, Paraguay, and Bolivia (commission for cooperation, trade, and integration)

**URW** United Rubber, Cork, Linoleum, and Plastic Workers of America (trade union)

**u.s.** ubi supra (Latin: where (mentioned *or* cited) above) • ut supra (Latin: as above)

**u/s** unserviceable • useless

**US** *British vehicle registration for* Glasgow • (Italy) ufficio stampa (press office) • *Med.* ultrasound (*or* ultrasonic) scanning • (USA) Uncle Sam • *Physiol., Psychol.* unconditioned stimulus • (USA) United Service • United States • United States highway (as in **US66**) • *airline flight code for* US Air

**U/S** unserviceable • useless

**USA** United States Army • United States of America (abbrev. *or* IVR) • United Synagogue of America

**USA/ABF** United States of America Amateur Boxing Federation

**USAAC** United States Army Air Corps (forerunner of USAF)

**USAAF** United States Army Air Force (forerunner of USAF)

**USAC** United States Air Corps • United States Auto Club

**USAEC** United States Atomic Energy Commission

**USAF** United States Air Force

**USAFA** United States Air Force Academy

**USAFC** United States Army Forces Command

**USAFE** United States Air Forces in Europe

**USAFI** United States Armed Forces Institute

**USAFR** United States Air Force Reserve

**USAID** United States Agency for International Development

**USAMC** United States Army Materiel Command

**USAMedS** United States Army Medical Service

**USAR** United States Army Reserve

**USAREUR** United States Army, Europe

**USASA** United States Army Security Agency

**USAT** United States Army Transport

**USATDC** United States Army Training and Doctrine Command

**USBC** United States Bureau of the Census

**USBM** United States Bureau of Mines

**USC** Ulster Special Constabulary • United Services Club • United Somali Congress • United States Code • United States Congress • United States of Colombia • University of South Carolina • University of Southern California

**USCA** United States Code Annotated

**USCC** United States Circuit Court

**USCCA** United States Circuit Court of Appeals

**USCG** United States Coast Guard

**USCGA** United States Coast Guard Academy

**USCGR** United States Coast Guard Reserve

**USCGS** (*or* **USC&GS**) United States Coast and Geodetic Survey

**USCL** United Society for Christian Literature

**USCRC** United States Citizens Radio Council

**USCSC** United States Civil Service Commission

**USC Supp.** United States Code Supplement

**USDA** United States Department of Agriculture

**USDAW** (*or* **Usdaw**) ('ʌz,dɔ:) Union of Shop, Distributive, and Allied Workers

**USDOE** United States Department of Energy

**USEA** United States Energy Association

**U/sec.** Undersecretary

**USECC** United States Employees' Compensation Commission

**USES** United States Employment Service

**usf.** und so fort (German: and so on; etc.)

**USF** United States Forces

**USFL** United States Football League

**USG** United States Government • *Railways* United States Standard Gauge

**USGA** United States Golf Association

**USgal** *symbol for* US gallon

**USGPO** United States Government Printing Office

**USGS** United States Geological Survey

**USh** *symbol for* Uganda shilling (monetary unit)

**USHA** United States Housing Authority

**USI** United Schools International • United Service Institution • United States Industries

**USIA** United States Information Agency

**USIS** United States Information Service

**USITC** United States International Trade Commission

**USL** United States Legation

**USLTA** United States Lawn Tennis Association

**USM** ultrasonic machining • underwater-to-surface missile • United States Mail • United States Marines • United States Mint • *Stock exchange* unlisted securities market

**USMA** United States Military Academy

**USMC** United States Marine Corps • United States Maritime Commission

**USMH** United States Marine Hospital

**USMS** United States Maritime Service

**USN** United States Navy

**USNA** United States National Army • United States Naval Academy

**USNC** United States National Committee

**USNG** United States National Guard

**USNI** United States Naval Institute

**USNO** United States Naval Observatory

**USNR** United States Naval Reserve

**USNRC** United States Nuclear Regulatory Commission

**USNS** United States Navy Ship

**USO** (USA) United Service Organization

**US of A** *Colloquial* United States of America

**USP** *Papermaking* unbleached sulphite pulp • *Advertising* unique selling proposition (of a product) • (*or* **USPat.**) United States Patent • United States Pharmacopeia

**USPC** Ulster Society for the Preservation of the Countryside

**USPG** United Society for the Propagation of the Gospel (formerly SPG)

**USPHS** United States Public Health Service

**USPO** United States Post Office

**USPS** United States Postal Service

**USR** United States Reserves • Universities' Statistical Record

**USRC** United States Reserve Corps

**USS** Undersecretary of State • Union Syndicale Suisse (French: Swiss Federation of Trade Unions) • United States Senate • United States Service • United States Ship • United States Steamer (*or* Steamship) • Universities Superannuation Scheme

**USSB** United States Shipping Board

**USSC** (*or* **USSCt**) United States Supreme Court

**USSR** Union of Soviet Socialist Republics

**USSS** United States Steamship

**UST** undersea technology

**USTA** United States Tennis Association • United States Trademark Association

**USTC** United States Tariff Commission

**USTS** United States Travel Service

**usu.** usual(ly)

**USV** United States Volunteers

**USVA** United States Volleyball Association

**USVB** United States Veterans' Bureau

**USVI** United States Virgin Islands

**usw.** und so weiter (German: and so forth; etc.)

**USW** *Radio, etc.* ultrashort wave • underwater sea warfare

**USWA** United Steelworkers of America (trade union)

**USWB** United States Weather Bureau

**USWI** United States West Indies • urban solid-waste incinerator

**ut.** utility

**u.t.** universal trainer • user test

**Ut.** Utah

**UT** *British vehicle registration for* Leicester • ultrasonic testing • ultrasonic transducer • (India) Union Territory • unit trust • *Astronomy* universal time • University of Texas at Austin • *Med.*

urinary tract • *airline flight code for* UTA French Airlines • *US postcode for* Utah

**U/T** under trust

**UTA** Ulster Transport Authority • Union de Transports Aériens (French airline) • Unit Trust Association

**UTC** Coordinated Universal Time (French *universel temps coordonné*) • University Training Corps

**Utd** United

**UTDA** Ulster Tourist Development Association

**ut dict.** *Med.* ut dictum (Latin: as directed; in prescriptions)

**utend.** *Med.* utendus (Latin: to be used)

**U3A** University of the Third Age

**UTI** *Med.* urinary-tract infection

**ut inf.** ut infra (Latin: as below)

**UTK** University of Tennessee, Knoxville

**UTP** *Biochem.* uridine 5'-triphosphate

**UTS** ultimate tensile strength

**ut sup.** ut supra (Latin: as above)

**UTU** (USA) United Transportation Union

**UTWA** United Textile Workers of America (trade union)

**u.U.** unter Umständen (German: circumstances permitting)

**UU** *British vehicle registration for* London (central) • Ulster Unionist

**UUA** (USA) Unitarian Universalist Association

**UUCP** *Computing* UNIX to UNIX copy

**UUM** underwater-to-underwater missile

**UUUC** United Ulster Unionist Coalition (*or* Council)

**UUUP** United Ulster Unionist Party

**u.u.V.** unter üblichem Vorbehalt (German: errors and omissions excepted)

**UV** *British vehicle registration for* London (central) • ultraviolet

**UV-A** (*or* **UVA**) *indicating* ultraviolet radiation of wavelength 320–380 m

**UVAS** ultraviolet astronomical satellite

**uvaser** (juːˈveɪzə) ultraviolet amplification by stimulated emission of radiation

**UV-B** (*or* **UVB**) *indicating* ultraviolet radiation of wavelength 280–320 m

**UVF** Ulster Volunteer Force

**UVL** ultraviolet light

**UW** *British vehicle registration for* London (central) • underwater • University of Washington • unladen weight

**U/W** *Law* under will • (*or* **U/w**) underwriter

**UWA** University of Western Australia

**UWC** Ulster Workers' Council

**UWCE** Underwater Weapons and Countermeasures Establishment

**UWIST** (*or* **Uwist**) (ˈjuːˌwɪst) University of Wales Institute of Science and Technology

**UWT** Union of Women Teachers (now merged with NAS/UWT)

**UWUA** Utility Workers Union of America

**UWUSA** United Workers' Union of South Africa

**ux.** uxor (Latin: wife)

**UX** *British vehicle registration for* Shrewsbury

**UXB** unexploded bomb

**UY** Universal Youth • *British vehicle registration for* Worcester

**Uz.** Uzbek(istan)

**UZ** *British vehicle registration for* Belfast

# V

**v** (ital.) *Optics, symbol for* image distance • (ital.) *Physics, symbol for* instantaneous potential difference • *Physics, symbol for* instantaneous voltage • (ital.) *Chem., symbol for* specific volume • *Spectroscopy, symbol for* variable absorption • (bold ital.) *Physics, symbol for* velocity • (ital.) *Physics, symbol for* a velocity component *or* speed • (ital.) *Chem., symbol for* vibrational quantum number • *Meteorol., symbol for* (abnormally good) visibility

**v.** vacuum • vagrant • vale • valley • valve • vein • vel (Latin: or) • ventilator • ventral • verb(al) • verse • version • *Printing* verso • versus • vertical • very •

**via** • **vicarage** • **vice** (Latin: in place of) • **vide** (Latin: see) • **village** • **violin** • **virus** • **visibility** • *Med.* vision • *Grammar* vocative • *Music* voice • volcano • volume • **von** (German: of; in names) • **votre** (French: your) • vowel

**V** (ital.) *Electricity, symbol for* electric potential • *Roman numeral for* five • (ital.) *Physics, symbol for* luminous efficiency • (ital.) *Electricity, symbol for* potential difference • (ital.) *Physics, symbol for* potential energy • *Biochem. symbol for* valine • *Chem., symbol for* vanadium • *Immunol.* variable region (of an immunoglobulin chain) • *international vehicle registration for* Vatican City • verb (in transformational grammar) • Vergeltungswaffe (German: reprisal weapon, as in **V-1** and **V-2**, World War II missiles) • victory (as in **V-Day**, **V-sign**) • *symbol for* volt • (ital.) *symbol for* volume (capacity) • *indicating* types of aircraft (*see* V bomber)

**V.** (*or* **V**) Venerable • version • Very (in titles) • vespers • Via (Italian: Street) • Vicar • Vice (in titles) • Viscount (*or* Viscountess) • *Music* volti (Italian: turn over) • voltmeter • Volunteer(s)

**V1** (*or* **V-1**) Vergeltungswaffe 1 (*see under* V)

**V¹** *Music* violino primo (Italian: first violin)

**V2** *international civil aircraft marking for* Antigua • (*or* **V-2**) Vergeltungswaffe 2 (*see under* V)

**V²** *Music* violino secondo (Italian: second violin)

**V3** *international civil aircraft marking for* Belize

**V5** *international civil aircraft marking for* Namibia

**V8** *international civil aircraft marking for* Brunei

**va** *Music* viola

**v.a.** value analysis • verb active • verbal adjective

**Va.** Virginia (USA)

**VA** *British vehicle registration for* Peterborough • value-added • *Commerce* value analysis • *Med.* ventricular arrhythmia • (USA) Veterans' Administration • *airline flight code for* VIASA Venezuelan International Airways • Vicar Apostolic • Vice-Admiral • (Order of) Victoria and Albert • *US postcode for* Virginia • *Med.* visual acuity • *Radio* Voice of America • Volunteer Artillery • Volunteers of America • Vostra Altezza

(Italian: Your Highness) • Votre Altesse (French: Your Highness) • Vuestra Alteza (Spanish: Your Highness)

**V/A** voucher attached

**v.a. & i.** verb active and intransitive

**VAB** *Astronautics* vehicle assembly building (of NASA)

**VABF** Variety Artists' Benevolent Fund

**VABM** *Surveying* vertical angle benchmark

**vac.** vacancy • vacant • vacation • vacuum

**vacc.** vaccination • vaccine

**vac. dist.** vacuum distilled (*or* distillation)

**vac. pmp** vacuum pump

**VAD** (member of the) Voluntary Aid Detachment

**VADAS** *Med.* voice-activated domestic appliance system

**V-Adm** Vice-Admiral

**VAF** Variety Artists' Federation

**vag.** vagabond • vagina • vagrancy • vagrant

**VAH** (USA) Veterans' Administration Hospital

**val.** valley • valuation • value(d)

**Val** (*or* **val**) *Biochem.* valine

**valid.** validate • validation

**valn** valuation

**Valpo** Valparaiso

**VAM** *Botany* vesicular-arbuscular mycorrhiza

**vamp.** vampire

**van** (væn) *Tennis* advantage

**van.** vanguard • vanilla

**VAN** (væn) *Computing* value-added network

**Vanc.** Vancouver

**V&A** Victoria and Albert Museum

**V & M** Virgin and Martyr

**V & V** *Computing* verification and validation

**VAPI** *Aeronautics* visual approach path indicator

**vapor.** vaporization

**vap. prf** vapour proof

**var.** variable • variant • variation • *Botany* variety • variometer • various

**VAR** *Computing* value-added reseller • visual aural range • volunteer air reserve • Votre Altesse Royale (French: Your Royal Highness)

**varactor** ('veə,ræktə) *Electronics* variable reactor

**Varig** (or **VARIG**) ('værɪg) (Empresa de) Viação Aérea Rio Grandense (Brazilian airline)

**varistor** (və'rɪstə) *Electronics* variable resistor

**var. lect.** varia lectio (Latin: a variant reading)

**varn.** varnish

**vas.** vasectomy

**VAS** *Med.* ventricular-atrial shunt

**vasc.** vascular

**Vascar** (or **VASCAR**) ('væskɑ:) visual average speed computer and recorder

**VASI** *Aeronautics* visual approach slope indicator

**VASP** Viação Aérea São Paulo (Brazilian airline)

**Vat.** Vatican

**VAT** ('vi: 'eɪ: 'ti: or væt) value-added tax

**VATE** versatile automatic test equipment

**Vat. Lib.** Vatican Library

**vaud.** vaudeville

**v. aux.** auxiliary verb

**VAV** variable air volume (in **VAV** (air-conditioning) **system**)

**VAWT** vertical-axis wind turbine

**VAX** *Computing, trademark* virtual address extension (range of computers manufactured by DEC)

**VAX/VMS** *Trademark, indicating* the standard operating system for VAX processors (*see under* VAX; VMS)

**vb** (or **vb.**) verb(al)

**v.b.** vehicle borne • vertical bomb

**VB** *airline flight code for* Birmingham European Airways • *British vehicle registration for* Maidstone • *Chem.* valence bond • verbal constituent (in transformational grammar) • volunteer battalion

**VBI** *Med.* vertebrobasilar insufficiency

**vbl** verbal

**V bomber** *indicating* various types of aircraft (named after the types Victor, Vulcan, and Valiant)

**vc.** *Music* cello (from *violoncello*)

**v.c.** valuation clause • vehicular communication • visual communication

**VC** *British vehicle registration for* Coventry • *Engineering* vapour compression • Vatican City • *Cycling* velo club • *Finance* venture capital • (USA) Veterinary Corps • Vice-Chairman • Vice-Chamberlain • Vice-Chancellor • Vice-Consul • Vickers Commercial (aircraft, as in **VC10**) • Victoria Cross • Viet Cong • *Chem.* vinyl chloride •

*Med., Physiol.* vital capacity • *indicating* acuity of colour vision

**VCA** *Chem.* vinyl carbonate • *Microbiol., Med.* viral capsid antigen • (USA) Volunteer Civic Association

**VCAS** Vice-Chief of the Air Staff

**VCC** Veteran Car Club of Great Britain • Vice-Chancellors' Committee

**VCCS** *Electronics* voltage-controlled current source

**VCDS** Vice-Chief of the Defence Staff

**Vce** Venice

**VCE** variable-cycle engine

**VCG** vertical centre of gravity • Vice-Consul-General

**VCGS** Vice-Chief of the General Staff

**VCH** Victoria County History (reference book) • *Chem.* vinyl cyclohexene

**v.Chr.** vor Christus (German: before Christ; BC)

**VCI** volatile corrosion inhibitor

**vcl.** *Music* cello (from *violoncello*) • vehicle

**VCM** vinyl chloride monomer (a plastic)

**VCNS** Vice-Chief of the Naval Staff

**vcnty** vicinity

**VCO** (India) Viceroy's Commissioned Officer • *Electronics* voltage-controlled oscillator • voluntary county organizer (in the Women's Institute)

**VCPI** *Computing* virtual control program interface

**Vcr** Vancouver

**VCR** video-cassette recorder • visual control room (at an airfield)

**vcs** voices

**V. Cz.** Vera Cruz (Mexico)

**vd** void

**v.d.** vapour density • various dates

**VD** *Med.* vascular dementia • venereal disease • Victorian Decoration • Volunteer Decoration (formerly awarded in the Territorial Army or the Royal Naval Volunteer Reserve)

**V-Day** Victory Day

**Vdc** volts direct current

**VDC** Volunteer Defence Corps

**v. def.** verb defective

**v. dep.** verb deponent

**VDH** valvular disease of the heart

**VDI** *Computing* virtual device interface

**VDJ** video disc jockey

**VDM** Verbi Dei Minister (Latin: Minister of the Word of God) • *Computing* Vienna Development Method (notation)

**VDQS** vin délimité de qualité supérieure (French; superior-quality wine; wine classification)

**VDR** variable-diameter rotor • video-disc recording

**VDRL** venereal disease research laboratory (in **VDRL test**, for syphilis)

**VDS** variable-depth sonar

**VDT** *Computing* visual display terminal

**VDU** *Computing* visual display unit

**VDW** *Chem.* van der Waals (as in **VDW force**)

**ve.** (*or* **v⁰**) veuve (French: widow)

**VE** *British vehicle registration for* Peterborough • *Chem.* valence electron • Victory in Europe (in **VE Day**, 8 May 1945) • vocational education • Vostra Eccellenza (Italian: Your Excellency) • Votre Éminence (French: Your Eminence) • Vuestra Excelencia (Spanish: Your Excellency)

**VEB** (formerly, in East Germany) Volkseigener Betrieb (German: People's Concern; state-owned company)

**vec.** vector

**ved.** vedova (Italian: widow)

**veg.** vegetable • vegetarian • vegetation

**veh.** vehicle • vehicular

**vel.** vellum • velocity • velvet

**Vel** *Astronomy* Vela

**ven.** vendredi (French: Friday) • veneer • venerdì (Italian: Friday) • venereal • venery • venison • venom(ous) • ventral • ventricle

**Ven.** Venerable • (*or* **Venet.**) Venetian • (*or* **Venez.**) Venezuela(n) • Venice • *Astronomy* Venus

**vent.** ventilate • ventilation • ventriloquist

**ver.** verification • verify • vermilion • verse • version

**Ver.** Verein (German: association *or* company)

**VER** *Meteorol.* vertical

**VERA** ('vɪərə) versatile reactor assembly • vision electronic recording apparatus

**verb.** verbessert (German: improved *or* revised)

**verb. et lit.** *Law* verbatim et literatim (Latin: word for word and letter for letter)

**verb. sap.** (*or* **sat.**) verbum sapienti satis (Latin: a word is enough to the wise)

**verdt** verdict

**Verf.** Verfasser (German: author)

**Verl.** Verlag (German: publisher)

**verm.** vermiculite • vermilion

**vern.** vernacular

**vers** *Maths.* versed sine (*or* versine)

**vers.** version

**vert.** vertebra(l) • vertical • vertigo

**Very Rev.** (*or* **Very Revd**) Very Reverend

**ves.** (*or* **vesp.**) *Med.* vespere (Latin: in the evening; in prescriptions) • vessel • vestry

**VESPER** ('vɛspə) Voluntary Enterprises and Services and Part-time Employment for the Retired

**vet.** veteran • (*or* **veter.**) veterinarian • (*or* **veter.**) veterinary

**Vet. Admin.** (USA) Veterans' Administration

**VetMB** Bachelor of Veterinary Medicine

**vet. sci.** veterinary science

**vet. surg.** veterinary surgeon

**v.f.** very fair • very fine

**VF** *British vehicle registration for* Norwich • *Med.* ventricular fibrillation • *RC Church* Vicar Forane • video frequency • *Telecom.* voice frequency

**VFA** (Australia) Victorian Football Association • *Chem.* volatile fatty acid

**VFD** verified free distribution • (USA) volunteer fire department

**VFL** (Australia) Victorian Football League

**VFM** *Accounting* value for money (audit)

**VFO** *Electronics* variable-frequency oscillator

**VFOAR** *US Air Force* Vandenberg Field Office of Aerospace Research

**VFR** *Aeronautics* visual flight rules

**VFT** (Australia) very fast train

**VFU** *Computing* vertical format unit

**VFW** (USA) Veterans of Foreign Wars

**vfy** verify

**v.g.** verbigracia (Spanish: for example) • verbi gratia (Latin: for example) • very good

**Vg.** *Ecclesiast.* Virgin

**VG** *British vehicle registration for* Norwich • vaisseau de guerre (French: warship) • very good • Vicar General • *Freemasonry* Vice Grand • Votre Grâce (French: Your Grace) • Votre Grandeur (French: Your Highness)

**VGA** *Computing* video graphics array

**v.g.c.** very good condition

**vgl.** vergleiche (German: compare)

**VGPI** *Aeronautics* visual glide path indicator (in World War II)

**v.h.** vertical height • very high

**VH** *international civil aircraft marking for* Australia • *British vehicle registration for* Huddersfield • Votre Hautesse (French: Your Highness)

**v.h.b.** very heavy bombardment

**VHC** (*or* **v.h.c.**) very highly commended • *Chem.* volatile halocarbon compound

**VHD** video high density (system)

**VHE** very high energy

**VHF** very high fidelity (in sound recording) • *Radio, etc.* very high frequency

**VHLW** vitrified high-level (radioactive) waste

**VHN** *Engineering* Vickers hardness number

**VHO** very high output

**VHP** (India) Vishwa Hindu Parishad (militant Hindu group)

**VHS** *Trademark* Video Home System

**VHT** very high temperature

**VHV** very high vacuum

**v.i.** verb intransitive • vide infra (Latin: see below)

**VI** Vancouver Island • *Cartography* vertical interval • Virgin Islands • viscosity index • volume indicator

**VIA** Visually Impaired Association

**viad.** viaduct

**VIASA** Venezolana Internacional de Aviácion, SA (Venezuelan International Airways)

**vib.** *Music* vibraphone • vibrate • vibration

**VIB** vertical integration building

**vic.** vicar • vicarage • vicinity • victory

**Vic.** Victoria (Australia)

**VIC** Victoria Institute of Colleges

**Vic. Ap.** (*or* **Vic. Apos.**) Vicar Apostolic

**Vice-Adm.** Vice-Admiral

**Vic. Gen.** Vicar General

**vid.** vide (Latin: see) • *Law* vidua (Latin: widow)

**VID** *Computing* virtual image display

**Vien.** Vienna

**VIF** variable import fee

**vig.** (*or* **vign.**) vignette

**vil.** village

**v. imp.** verb impersonal

**v. imper.** verb imperative

**vin.** vinegar

**VIN** (USA) vehicle identification number

**vind.** vindicate • vindication

**vini.** viniculture

**VIO** Veterinary Investigation Officer

**VIP** *Med.* vasoactive intestinal peptide • very important person

**vir.** viridis (Latin: green)

**Vir** *Astronomy* Virgo

**Vir.** (*or* **Virg.**) Virgil (70–19 BC, Roman poet)

**VIR** Victoria Imperatrix Regina (Latin: Victoria, Empress and Queen)

**Virg.** Virginia (USA)

**v. irr.** verb irregular

**vis.** viscosity • visibility • visible • visual

**Vis.** Viscount (*or* Viscountess)

**VIS** Veterinary Investigation Service • *Meteorol.* visibility

**visc.** viscosity

**Visc.** (*or* **Visct.**) Viscount (*or* Viscountess)

**VISS** *Computing* VHS index search system

**VISTA** ('vɪstə) Volunteers in Service to America

**vit.** vitreous

**VITA** Volunteers for International Technical Assistance

**viti.** viticulture

**vitr.** vitreum (Latin: glass)

**vit. stat.** vital statistics

**viv.** *Music* vivace (Italian: lively, animated)

**vivi.** vivisection

**vix.** vixit (Latin: (he *or* she) lived)

**viz** videlicet (Latin: namely; *z* is medieval Latin symbol of contraction)

**v.J.** vorigen Jahres (German: of last year)

**VJ** *British vehicle registration for* Gloucester • (Australia) Vaucluse Junior (yacht) • Victory over Japan (in **VJ Day**, 15 Aug. or 2 Sept. 1945) • video jockey

**v.k.** vertical keel

**VK** *British vehicle registration for* Newcastle upon Tyne

**vl.** violin

**v.l.** varia lectio (Latin: a variant reading)

**VL** *British vehicle registration for* Lincoln • Vulgar Latin

**vla** *Music* viola

**VLA** *Astronomy* Very Large Array (system of radio telescopes, New Mexico)

**Vlad.** Vladivostok

**VLB** vertical-lift bridge

**VLBC** very large bulk carrier (ship)

**VLBI** *Astronomy* very long-baseline interferometry

**VLBW** *Med.* very low birth weight

**VLCC** very large crude carrier (oil tanker)

**VLCFA** *Biochem.* very long-chain fatty acid

**VLDL** *Biochem.* very low-density lipoprotein

**vle** *Music* violone (double-bass viol)

**VLE** *Chem.* vapour–liquid equilibrium

**VLF** *Radio, etc.* very low frequency

**VLIW** *Computing* very long instruction word

**VLLW** very low-level (radioactive) waste

**vln** violin

**VLR** very long range (aircraft) • Victoria Law Reports

**VLS** *Physics* vapour–liquid–solid (as in **VLS system**)

**VLSI** *Electronics* very large-scale integration

**vltg.** voltage

**vlv.** valve • valvular

**v.M.** vorigen Monats (German: last month)

**VM** *British vehicle registration for* Manchester • *Physics* velocity modulation • Victory Medal • Viet Minh • Virgin Mary • *Computing* virtual machine • *Chem.* volatile matter • Votre Majesté (French: Your Majesty)

**V-Mail** *Military* (USA) victory mail

**VMC** *Aeronautics* visual meteorological conditions

**VMCCA** Veteran Motor Car Club of America

**VM/CMS** *Computing, trademark* virtual machine, conversational monitor system

**VMD** Doctor of Veterinary Medicine (Latin *Veterinariae Medicinae Doctor*)

**VMH** Victoria Medal of Honour (awarded by the Royal Horticultural Society)

**VMS** *Computing* virtual machine system (*see also* VAX/VMS) • Voluntary Medical Services

**v.m.t.** very many thanks

**vn** violin

**v.n.** verb neuter

**VN** *British vehicle registration for* Middlesbrough • Vietnam (abbrev., IVR, *or* international civil aircraft marking) • Vietnamese

**Vna** Vienna

**VNM** (Canada) Victoria National Museum

**VNTR** *Genetics* variable number tandem repeat

**vo.** verso

**VO** *British vehicle registration for* Nottingham • valuation officer • verbal order • very old (of brandy, whisky, etc.) • Veterinary Officer • (Royal) Victorian Order • voice-over (commentary)

**VOA** *Radio* Voice of America • Volunteers of America

**voc.** vocal(ist) • vocation • *Grammar* vocative

**VOC** Vehicle Observer Corps • volatile organic compound (*or* chemical)

**vocab.** vocabulary

**VOCAL** ('vəukªl) Voluntary Organizations Communication and Language

**vocat.** *Grammar* vocative

**voc-ed** (ˌvɒk'ɛd) vocational education

**voctl** vocational

**VOD** velocity of detonation

**VODAT** voice-operated device for automatic transmission

**vol.** volatile • volcanic • volcano • (*or* **Vol.**) volume • voluntary • (*or* **Vol.**) volunteer

**Vol** *Astronomy* Volans

**volc.** volcanic • volcano

**vols** (*or* **Vols**) volumes

**volum.** *Chem.* volumetric

**voly** voluntary

**VONA** vehicle of the new age (rapid transport shuttle)

**VOP** very oldest procurable (of brandy, port, etc.)

**VOR** very-high-frequency omnirange *or* omnidirectional radio range (navigation aid)

**vorm.** vormals (German: formerly) • vormittags (German: in the morning; a.m.)

**Vors.** Vorsitzender (German: chairman)

**vou.** voucher

**vox pop** (vɒks pɒp) vox populi (Latin: voice of the people)

**v.p.** *Photog.* vanishing point • vapour pressure • variable pitch • verb passive

**VP** *British vehicle registration for* Birmingham • *Chem., Physics* vapour phase • *Building trades* vent pipe • verb phrase (in transformational grammar) • Vice-President • Vice-Principal • victory points • vita patris (Latin: during the life of his (*or* her) father)

**VPC** *Chem.* vapour-phase chromatography • vente par correspondence (French: mail order)

**v.p.d.** vehicles per day

**VPE** *Electronics* vapour-phase epitaxy

**VP-F** *international civil aircraft marking for* Falklands Islands

**v.ph.** vertical photography

**v.p.h.** vehicles per hour

**VPI** *Chem.* vapour-phase inhibitor

**VP-LA** *international civil aircraft marking for* Anguilla

**VP-LMA** *international civil aircraft marking for* Montserrat

**VP-LV** *international civil aircraft marking for* Virgin Islands

**v.p.m.** vehicles per mile

**Vpo** Valparaiso

**VPO** Vienna Philharmonic Orchestra

**VPP** (India) value payable post • *Vet. science* virus pneumonia of pigs • Volunteer Political Party

**V.Pres.** Vice-President

**VPRGS** Vice-President of the Royal Geographical Society

**VPRP** Vice-President of the Royal Society of Portrait Painters

**VPRS** Vice-President of the Royal Society

**v.p.s.** vibrations per second

**VPZS** Vice-President of the Zoological Society

**VQMG** Vice-Quartermaster-General

**VQ-T** *international civil aircraft marking for* Turks and Caicos Islands

**v.r.** variant reading • vedi retro (Italian: please turn over; PTO) • verb reflexive

**VR** *British vehicle registration for* Manchester • variant reading • *Physics* velocity ratio • *Med.* ventricular reflux • Vicar Rural • Victoria Regina (Latin: Queen Victoria) • *Computing* virtual reality • voltage regulator • Volunteer Reserve • vulcanized rubber

**VRA** (USA) Vocational Rehabilitation Administration

**VRAM** *Computing* video random access memory

**VRB** *Meteorol.* variable

**VR-B** *international civil aircraft marking for* Bermuda

**VRC** Vehicle Research Corporation • Volunteer Rifle Corps

**VR-C** *international civil aircraft marking for* Cayman Islands

**VRD** Royal Naval Volunteer Reserve Officers' Decoration

**v. refl.** verb reflexive

**V. Rev.** Very Reverend

**VRG** *Biochem.* vaccinia rabies glycoprotein

**VR-G** *international civil aircraft marking for* Gibraltar

**VR-H** *international civil aircraft marking for* Hong Kong

**VRI** Victoria Regina et Imperatrix (Latin: Victoria, Queen and Empress) • *Aeronautics* visual rule instrument (landing)

**VRM** (USA) variable rate mortgage

**VRO** vehicle registration office

**Vry** Viceroy

**vs.** versus

**v.s.** variable speed • vide supra (Latin: see above) • *Music* volti subito (Italian: turn over quickly)

**VS** *British vehicle registration for* Luton • *Freemasonry* Venerable Sage • Veterinary Surgeon • vieux style (French: Old Style; method of reckoning dates) • *airline flight code for* Virgin Atlantic Airways • *Chem.* volatile solid • *Music* volti subito (Italian: turn over quickly) • *Chem.* volumetric solution • Vostra Santità (Italian: Your Holiness) • Votre Sainteté (French: Your Holiness)

**VSAM** *Computing* virtual storage access method

**VSB** *Telecom.* vestigial sideband

**vsby** visibility

**VSC** Volunteer Staff Corps

**VSCC** Vintage Sports Car Club

**VSD** vendor's shipping document • *Med.* ventricular septal defect

**VSG** *Immunol.* variable (cell-)surface glycoprotein

**VSI** *Navigation* vertical speed indicator

**V-sign** victory sign

**VSL** venture scout leader

**VSM** *Telecom.* vestigial sideband modulation

**VSO** *Linguistics* verb-subject-object (as in **VSO language**) • very superior old (of brandy, port, etc.) • Vienna State Opera • Voluntary Service Overseas

**VSOP** very special (*or* superior) old pale (of brandy, port, etc.)

**VSP** *Meteorol.* vertical speed

**VSR** very short range • very special reserve (of wine)

**vst** violinist

**V/STOL** (*or* **V-STOL, VSTOL**) ('viːˌstɒl) vertical and short takeoff and landing (aircraft)

**VSV** *Med.* vesicular stomatitis virus

**VSW** vitrified stoneware

**VSWR** *Telecom.* voltage standing-wave ratio

**v.t.** vacuum technology • variable transmission • verb transitive

**Vt** Vermont

**VT** *international civil aircraft marking for* India • *British vehicle registration for* Stoke-on-Trent • variable time (as in **VT fuse**) • *symbol for* vatu (monetary unit of Vanuatu) • *Med.* ventricular tachycardia • *US postcode for* Vermont

**VTC** Volunteer Training Corps • voting trust certificate

**Vte** Vicomte (French: Viscount)

**VTE** *Psychol.* vicarious trial and error

**Vtesse** Vicomtesse (French: Viscountess)

**vtg** voting

**VTL** *Computing* variable threshold logic

**VTMoV** *Microbiol.* velvet tobacco mottle virus

**VTO** vertical takeoff (aircraft)

**VTOHL** vertical takeoff, horizontal landing (aircraft)

**VTOL** ('viːˌtɒl) vertical takeoff and landing (aircraft)

**VTOVL** vertical takeoff, vertical landing (aircraft)

**VTR** videotape recorder

**VU** *British vehicle registration for* Manchester • *Acoustics* volume unit (as in **VU meter**)

**Vul** *Astronomy* Vulpecula

**Vul.** (*or* **Vulg.**) Vulgate

**vulg.** vulgar(ly)

**vv.** verbs • verses • *Music* (first and second) violins • *Music* voices • volumes

**v.v.** vice versa • viva voce

**v/v** *Chem.* volume in volume

**VV** *British vehicle registration for* Northampton

**VVD** (Netherlands) Volkspartij voor Vrijheid en Democratie (People's Party for Freedom and Democracy)

**vve** veuve (French: widow)

**vv.ll.** variae lectiones (Latin: variant readings)

**VV.MM.** Vos Majestés (French: Your Majesties)

**VVO** very very old (of brandy, port, etc.)

**VW** Very Worshipful • Volkswagen

**VWH** Vale of the White Horse

**vx** vertex

**VX** *British vehicle registration for* Chelmsford

**vy** very

**v.y.** *Bibliog.* various years

**VY** *British vehicle registration for* Leeds

**VZ** *British vehicle registration for* Tyrone

**VZIG** *Immunol.* varicella zoster hyperimmune globulin

# W

**w** *Meteorol., symbol for* dew • (*ital.*) *Chem., symbol for* mass fraction • (*ital.*) *Physics, symbol for* a velocity component • *Spectroscopy, symbol for* weak absorption

**w.** war • warm • water • weather • week • weight • wet • white • *Cricket* wicket • *Cricket* wide • width • wife • win • wind • wire • with • won • word • work

**W** (*ital.*) *Engineering, symbol for* load • *Biochem., symbol for* tryptophan • *Chem., symbol for* tungsten (formerly wolfram) • *Colloquial* water closet; WC • *Irish fishing port registration for* Waterford • *symbol for* watt • (*ital.*) *Physics, symbol for* weight • *Genetics* Weigle (in **W reacti-**

vation) • west(ern) • *postcode for* west London • *Shipping* winter loading (on load line) • women's (clothing size) • *symbol for* won (South Korean monetary unit) • (*ital.*) *Physics, symbol for* work • (*ital.*) *Biochem., symbol for* writhing number • *Genetics, indicating* a sex chromosome in birds and some insects • *Physics, indicating* a type of fundamental particle

**W.** (*or* **W**) Wales • Warden • Wednesday • Welsh • Wesleyan • west(ern) • white • wide • widow(er) • widowed

**w.a.** with answers

**WA** *British vehicle registration for* Sheffield • *postcode for* Warrington • *US* *postcode for* Washington (state) • (USA) Welfare Administration • West Africa(n) • Western Australia • Westminster Abbey • *Banking* (USA) withholding agent • *British fishing port registration for* Whitehaven • *Netball* wing attack • *Insurance* with average • Woodworkers of America (trade union)

**WAA** Women's Auxiliary Association

**WAAA** Women's Amateur Athletic Association

**WAAAF** (wæf) Women's Auxiliary Australian Air Force

**WAAC** (wæk) Women's Army Auxiliary Corps

**WAAE** World Association for Adult Education

**WAAF** (wæf) Women's Auxiliary Air Force • Women's Auxiliary Australian Air Force

**WAAS** Women's Auxiliary Army Service • World Academy of Art and Science

**WAC** (wæk) (USA) Women's Army Corps (in World War II) • World Aeronautical Chart

**WACC** World Association for Christian Communications

**WACCC** Worldwide Air Cargo Commodity Classification

**WACSM** (USA) Women's Army Corps Service Medal

**Wad** (*or* **Wadh**) Wadham College, Oxford

**WADEX** (*or* **Wadex**) ('wɒdɛks) word and author index

**WADF** (USA) Western Air Defense

**WADS** wide-area data service

**w.a.e.** when actually employed

**WAF** West African Forces • (*or* **w.a.f.**) with all faults • (USA) Women in the Air Force

**WAFC** West African Fisheries Commission (of the FAO)

**W. Afr.** West Africa(n)

**WAFS** (USA) Women's Auxiliary Ferrying Squadron

**WAG** *international vehicle registration for* (West Africa) Gambia • Writers' Action Group

**WAGBI** Wildfowl Association of Great Britain and Ireland

**WAGGGS** World Association of Girl Guides and Girl Scouts

**WAIF** World Adoption International Fund

**WAIS** *Psychol.* Wechsler Adult Intelligence Scale

**WAIS-R** *Psychol.* Wechsler Adult Intelligence Scale – Revised

**Wal.** Walloon

**WAL** *international vehicle registration for* (West Africa) Sierra Leone

**WAM** work analysis and measurement • (USA) wrap around mortgage

**WAN** *international vehicle registration for* (West Africa) Nigeria • (wæn) *Computing* wide-area network

**Wand.** *Football* Wanderers

**w & i** weighing and inspection

**W & L** (USA) Washington and Lee University

**W & M** William and Mary (English joint sovereigns 1689–1702 and 1689–94, respectively)

**W & S** whisky and soda

**W & T** *Taxation* wear and tear

**WANS** Women's Australian National Service

**WAOS** Welsh Agricultural Organization Society

**WAP** work assignment plan (*or* procedure)

**WAPC** Women's Auxiliary Police Corps

**WAPOR** World Association for Public Opinion Research

**war.** warrant

**War.** Warsaw • Warwickshire

**WAR** West Africa Regiment

**WARC** (USA) Western Air Rescue Center • World Administrative Radio Conference • World Alliance of Reformed Churches

**WARI** (Australia) Waite Agricultural Research Institute

**Warks** Warwickshire

**warn.** warning

**warr.** (*or* **warrty**) warranty

**WASA** Welsh Amateur Swimming Association

**Wash.** Washington

**WASP** (wɒsp) (*or* **Wasp**) (USA) white Anglo-Saxon Protestant • (USA) Women Airforce Service Pilots

**WAST** Western Australia Standard Time

**Wat.** Waterford

**WAT** *Aeronautics* weight, altitude, temperature (as in **WAT curves**) • *Psychol.* word association test

**WATA** World Association of Travel Agencies

**WATFOR** ('wɒtfɔː) *Computing* University of Waterloo Fortran (Fortran compiler)

**WATS** (USA) Wide Area Telephone Service

**W. Aus.** (*or* **W. Aust.**) Western Australia

**WAVES** (*or* **Waves**) (weɪvz) *US Navy* Women Accepted for Volunteer Emergency Service

**WAWF** World Association of World Federalists

**WAY** World Assembly of Youth

**WAYC** Welsh Association of Youth Clubs

**w.b.** wage board • waste ballast • water ballast • waybill • westbound • wheel base • *Knitting* wool back

**Wb** *Magnetism, symbol for* weber

**WB** *British vehicle registration for* Sheffield • (*or* **W/B**) warehouse book • Warner Brothers (Pictures, Incorporated) • water board • (*or* **W/B**) *Telecom.* waveband • (*or* **W/B**) *Commerce* waybill • weather bureau • *Psychol.* Wechsler–Bellevue (Intelligence Scale) • *Insurance* weekly benefits • World Bank

**WBA** West Bromwich Albion (Football Club) • World Boxing Association

**WBAFC** (USA) Weather Bureau Area Forecast Center

**WBAN** (USA) Weather Bureau, Air Force and Navy

**WBC** *Med.* white blood cell • *Med.* white blood (cell) count • World Boxing Council

**WBF** World Bridge Federation

**WBGT** *Meteorol.* wet-bulb globe temperature (*or* thermometer)

**w.b.i.** will be issued

**WBI** *Med.* whole-body irradiation

**WbN** west by north

**w.b.s.** *Engineering* walking-beam suspension • *Insurance* without benefit of salvage

**WbS** west by south

**WBS** *Med.* whole-body scan • *Physics* wide-band spectrometer (*or* spectrum)

**WBT** *Meteorol.* wet-bulb temperature

**w.c.** watch committee • water closet • water cock • without charge

**WC** *British vehicle registration for* Chelmsford • war cabinet • war council • water closet • Wesleyan chapel • *postcode for* west central London • *Military* Western Command • Whitley Council • working capital

**W/C** Wing Commander

**WCA** Wholesale Confectioners' Alliance • Wildlife and Countryside Act • Women's Christian Association

**WCAT** Welsh College of Advanced Technology

**WCC** War Crimes Commission • World Council of Churches

**W/Cdr** (*or* **W. Cdr**) Wing Commander

**WCEU** World Christian Endeavour Union

**WCF** World Congress of Faiths

**WCL** World Confederation of Labour

**WCP** World Climate Programme • World Council of Peace

**WCRA** (USA) Weather Control Research Association • Women's Cycle Racing Association

**WCT** World Championship Tennis

**WCTU** (USA, Canada) Women's Christian Temperance Union

**WCWB** World Council for the Welfare of the Blind

**wd** ward • warranted • weed • wood • word • would • wound

**w/d** warranted • well developed

**WD** *international vehicle registration for* (Windward Islands) Dominica • *British vehicle registration for* Dudley • War Department • *postcode for* Watford • *Irish fishing port registration for* Wexford • *Astronomy* white dwarf • *Netball* wing defence • Works Department

**W/D** *Banking* withdrawal

**WDA** Welsh Development Agency • *Taxation* writing-down allowance

**WDC** War Damage Commission • (USA) War Damage Corporation • Woman Detective Constable • Women's Diocesan Association • World Data Centre

**w.d.f.** wood door and frame

**wdg** winding

**WDM** *Telecom.* wavelength division multiplex

**Wdr** *Navy* Wardmaster

**WDS** Woman Detective Sergeant

**wd sc.** wood screw

**WDSPR** *Meteorol.* widespread

**wdth** width

**WDV** *Taxation* written-down value

**w/e** weekend • week ending

**WE** *British vehicle registration for* Sheffield

**wea.** weapon • weather

**WEA** Royal West of England Academy • Workers' Educational Association

**WE&FA** Welsh Engineers' and Founders' Association

**WEARCON** ('wɛə,kɒn) weather observation and forecasting control system

**WEC** wave (or wind) energy converter • World Energy Conference

**WECOM** ('wɛkɒm) (USA) Weapons Command

**Wed.** Wednesday

**WEDA** Wholesale Engineering Distributors' Association

**Weds.** Wednesday

**w.e.f.** with effect from

**WEFC** West European Fisheries Conference

**WEFT** (wɛft) *Aeronautics* wings, engine, fuselage, tail

**Wel.** Welsh

**weld.** welding

**Well.** Wellington (New Zealand)

**WEN** (or **Wen**) (wɛn) Women's Environmental Network

**Wes.** Wesleyan

**WES** Women's Engineering Society • World Economic Survey

**WES/PNEU** Worldwide Education Service of Parents' National Educational Union

**west.** western

**Westm.** Westmeath • Westminster • Westmorland (former English county)

**WET** West(ern) European Time

**WETUC** Workers' Educational Trade Union Committee

**WEU** Western European Union (for defence policy)

**Wex.** (or **Wexf.**) Wexford

**wf** (or **w.f.**) *Printing* wrong fount

**WF** *British vehicle registration for* Sheffield • *postcode for* Wakefield • *Physics* wave function • (USA) Wells Fargo and Company • (USA) white female • *Sport* wing forward

**WFA** White Fish Authority • Women's Football Association • World Friendship Association

**w factor** *Psychol.* will factor

**WFB** World Fellowship of Buddhists

**WFC** World Food Council

**w.fd** *Knitting* wool forward

**WFD** World Federation of the Deaf

**WFDY** World Federation of Democratic Youth

**WFEO** World Federation of Engineering Organizations

**wff** *Logic* well-formed formula

**WFF** World Friendship Federation

**WFGA** Women's Farm and Garden Association

**Wfl** Worshipful

**WFL** Women's Freedom League

**WFMH** World Federation for Mental Health

**WFMW** World Federation of Methodist Women

**WFN** World Federation of Neurology

**WFP** World Food Programme (of the FAO)

**WFPA** World Federation for the Protection of Animals

**WFSW** World Federation of Scientific Workers

**WFTU** World Federation of Trade Unions

**WFUNA** World Federation of United Nations Associations

**w.fwd** *Knitting* wool forward

**wg** weighing • wing

**WG** *international vehicle registration for* (Windward Islands) Grenada • *British vehicle registration for* Sheffield • (or **w.g.**) water gauge • (or **w.g.**) weight guaranteed • Welsh Guards • West German(y) • West Germanic (language group) • *Colloquial* W(illiam) G(ilbert) Grace (1848–1915, English cricketer) • (or **w.g.**) wire gauge • Working Group

**WGA** Writers' Guild of America

**WGC** Welwyn Garden City • *Freemasonry* Worthy Grand Chaplain

**Wg/Cdr** (or **Wg Comdr**) Wing Commander

**W. Ger.** West German(y) • West Germanic (language group)

**WGG** *Freemasonry* Worthy Grand Guardian (or Guide)

**WGI** world geophysical interval

**w. gl.** wired glass

**W. Glam.** West Glamorgan

**WGM** *Freemasonry* Worthy Grand Master

**WGmc** West Germanic (language group)

**WGPMS** warehouse gross performance measurement system

**WGS** *Chem.* water-gas shift (reaction) • *Freemasonry* Worthy Grand Sentinel

**WGU** Welsh Golfing Union

**wh.** wharf • which • whispered • white

**W h** *Electricity, symbol for* watt hour(s)

**WH** *British vehicle registration for* Manchester • water heater • *British*

*fishing port registration for* Weymouth •
*Cycling* wheelers • (USA) White
House • *Sport* wing half • (*or* **w/h**)
*Banking* withholding

**WHA** World Health Assembly (of
WHO) • World Hockey Association

**W'hampton** Wolverhampton

**w.h.b.** wash-hand basin

**whd** warhead

**whf.** wharf

**WhF** Whitworth Fellow

**whfg.** wharfage

**whfr** wharfinger

**Whi.** Whitehall (London)

**whis.** whistle

**whmstr** weighmaster

**WHO** (USA) White House Office •
World Health Organization

**WHOA!** (wəʊ) (USA) Wild Horse
Organized Assistance

**WHOI** (USA) Woods Hole Oceanographic Institution

**whr** whether

**WHRA** World Health Research Centre

**whs.** (*or* **whse**) warehouse

**WhSch** Whitworth Scholar

**whsle** wholesale

**whsng** warehousing

**whs. rec.** warehouse receipt

**whs. stk** warehouse stock

**WHT** William Herschel Telescope (La
Palma)

**WHTSO** Welsh Health Technical
Services Organization

**w.i.** *Finance* when issued

**WI** *Irish vehicle registration for* Waterford • West Indian • West Indies •
Windward Islands • *British fishing port
registration for* Wisbech • *US postcode for*
Wisconsin • Women's Institute •
wrought iron

**WIA** wounded in action

**WIBC** (USA) Women's International
Bowling Congress

**WICA** Warsaw International Consumer
Association

**Wich.** *Horticulture* Wichuraiana (rose)

**Wick.** Wicklow

**wid.** widow(er)

**WID** West India Docks (London)

**WIDF** Women's International Democratic Federation

**WIF** West Indies Federation

**Wig.** Wigtown (Scotland) • Wigtown-
shire (former Scottish county)

**Wigorn.** Wigorniensis (Latin: (Bishop)
of Worcester)

**wilco** ('wɪl,kəʊ) will comply (in radio
communications, etc.)

**WILPF** Women's International League
for Peace and Freedom

**Wilts** Wiltshire

**WIMP** (wɪmp) *Physics* weakly interacting massive particle • (*or* **wimp**)
*Computing* windows icons menus
pointers

**WIN** (wɪn) (USA) Work Incentive

**Winch.** Winchester

**W. Ind.** West Indian • West Indies

**Wind. I.** Windward Islands

**Wing Cdr** Wing Commander

**Wings** (wɪŋz) *Finance* warrants in negotiable government securities

**Winn.** Winnipeg

**wint.** winter

**Winton.** Wintoniensis (Latin: (Bishop)
of Winchester)

**WIP** waste incineration plant • work in
progress

**WIPO** (*or* **Wipo**) ('waɪpəʊ) World
Intellectual Property Organization

**WIRA** (*or* **Wira**) Wool Industries
Research Association

**WIRDS** weather information reporting
and display system

**Wis.** Wisconsin

**WISC** *Psychol.* Wechsler Intelligence
Scale for Children

**WISC-R** *Psychol.* Wechsler Intelligence Scale for Children – Revised

**Wisd.** *Old Testament* Wisdom of Solomon

**WISP** (wɪsp) wide-range imaging spectrometer

**wit.** witness

**WITA** Women's International Tennis
Association

**withdrl** withdrawal

**witht** without

**Wits.** Witwatersrand

**WIZO** (*or* **Wizo**) ('waɪtzəʊ) Women's
International Zionist Organization

**WJ** *British vehicle registration for* Sheffield

**WJC** World Jewish Congress

**WJEC** Welsh Joint Education Committee

**wk** weak • week • work • wreck

**w.k.** warehouse keeper • well-known

**Wk** Walk (in place names)

**WK** *British vehicle registration for* Coventry • *British fishing port registration for*
Wick

WKB**

**WKB** *Physics* Wentzel–Kramers–Brillouin (as in **WKB solution** of the Schrödinger equation)

**wkds** weekdays

**wkg** working

**wkly** weekly

**WKN** *Meteorol.* weaken(ing)

**wkr** worker • wrecker

**wks** weeks • works

**wks.** workshop

**wkt** *Cricket* wicket

**wl** wool

**WL** *British vehicle registration for* Oxford • *international vehicle registration for* (Windward Islands) St Lucia • wagon-lit (French: sleeping car) • waiting list • (*or* **w.l.**) water line • (*or* **W/L**) wavelength • West Lothian (former Scottish county) • Women's Liberation

**WLA** Women's Land Army

**WLB** (USA) War Labor Board

**wld** would

**Wld Ch.** World Championship

**wldr** welder

**WLF** Women's Liberal Federation

**wl fwd** *Knitting* wool forward

**WLGS** Women's Local Government Society

**WLHB** Women's League of Health and Beauty

**WLI** workload index

**WLM** Women's Liberation Movement

**Wln** Wellington (New Zealand)

**W. long.** west longitude

**W. Loth.** West Lothian (former Scottish county)

**WLPSA** Wild Life Preservation Society of Australia

**WLR** Weekly Law Reports

**WLRI** World Life Research Institute

**WLS** *Statistics* weighted least squares

**WLTBU** Watermen, Lightermen, Tugmen, and Bargemen's Union

**WLU** World Liberal Union

**WLUS** World Land Use Survey

**wly** westerly

**wlz** waltz

**WM** *British vehicle registration for* Liverpool • war memorial • wattmeter • (USA) white male • wire mesh • *Freemasonry* Worshipful Master

**W/M** (*or* **w/m**) *Shipping* weight or measurement

**WMA** Working Mothers' Association • World Medical Association

**WMAA** Whitney Museum of American Art

**WMC** (USA) War Manpower Commission (in World War II) • Ways and Means Committee • working men's club • Working Men's College • World Meteorological Centre • World Methodist Council

**WMCIU** Working Men's Club and Institute Union Ltd

**wmk** watermark

**WMM** World Movement of Mothers

**WMO** World Meteorological Organization

**WMP** with much pleasure

**WMS** Wesleyan Missionary Society • World Magnetic Survey

**WMTC** Women's Mechanized Transport Corps

**WN** *British vehicle registration for* Swansea • *postcode for* Wigan

**WNA** *Shipping* winter North Atlantic loading (on load line)

**w.n.d.p.** with no down payment

**WNE** Welsh National Eisteddfod

**WNL** within normal limits

**WNLF** Women's National Liberal Federation

**WNO** Welsh National Opera

**WNP** Welsh Nationalist Party

**WNW** west-northwest

**w.o.** walkover • wie oben (German: as mentioned above) • *Commerce* written order

**w/o** without • *Accounting* written off

**WO** *British vehicle registration for* Cardiff • walkover • War Office • Warrant Officer • welfare officer • wireless operator • *British fishing port registration for* Workington • written order

**w.o.a.** without answers

**WOA** Wharf Owners' Association

**WOAR** Women Organized Against Rape

**w.o.b.** washed overboard

**w.o.c.** without compensation

**WOCA** ('wəukə) world outside centrally planned economic areas

**WOC(S)** *Building trades* waiting on cement (to set)

**w.o.e.** without equipment

**WOF** (New Zealand) Warrant of Fitness (for vehicles)

**W/offr** welfare officer

**w.o.g.** water, oil, or gas • with other goods

**w.o.l.** wharf-owner's liability

**Wolfs.** Wolfson College, Oxford

**WOMAN** ('wʊmən) World Organization for Mothers of All Nations

**w.o.n.** *Knitting* wool on needle

**WOO** *Navy* Warrant Ordnance Officer • World Oceanographic Organization

**w.o.p.** with other property • without personnel

**w.o.p.e.** without personnel or equipment

**Wor.** Worshipful

**WOR** without our responsibility

**Worc.** Worcester College, Oxford

**WORC** (USA) Washington Operations Research Council

**Worcs** Worcestershire

**WORM** (*or* **worm**) (wɜːm) *Computing* write once read many (times)

**WOSAC** ('wəʊsæk) worldwide synchronization of atomic clocks

**WOSB** ('wɒzbɪ) War Office Selection Board

**WOW** waiting on weather • Women Against the Ordination of Women

**wp.** *Baseball* wild pitch(es)

**w.p.** waste paper • waste pipe • weather permitting • will proceed • *Law* without prejudice • word processing (*or* processor)

**Wp.** Worship • Worshipful

**WP** weather permitting • Western Province (South Africa) • (USA) West Point (military academy) • *Government* White Paper • (USA) wire payment • *Law* without prejudice • *British vehicle registration for* Worcester • word processing (*or* processor) • working paper • working party • working pressure • *Freemasonry* Worthy Patriarch • *Freemasonry* Worthy President

**WPA** Water Polo Association • Western Provident Association • *Insurance* with particular average • (USA) Work Projects (originally Progress) Administration (1935–43) • World Parliament Association • World Pool-Billiard Association • World Presbyterian Alliance

**WPB** (USA) War Production Board (in World War II) • (*or* **w.p.b.**) wastepaper basket

**WPBL** (USA) Women's Professional Basketball League

**WPBSA** World Professional Billiards and Snooker Association

**WPC** War Pension(s) Committee • Woman Police Constable • wood–

plastic (*or* –polymer) composite • World Petroleum Congress

**WPCA** (USA) Water Pollution Control Administration

**WPCF** (USA) Water Pollution Control Federation

**WPE** white porcelain enamel

**WPESS** within pulse electronic sector scanning (in **WPESS sonar**)

**WPFC** West Pacific Fisheries Commission

**Wpfl** Worshipful

**wpg** waterproofing

**WPGA** Women's Professional Golfers' Association

**WPHC** Western Pacific High Commission

**WPI** wholesale price index • World Press Institute

**WPL** warning-point level

**w.p.m.** words per minute

**WPMSF** World Professional Marathon Swimming Federation

**wpn** weapon

**WPPSI** *Psychol.* Wechsler Preschool and Primary Scale of Intelligence

**WPRL** Water Pollution Research Laboratory

**w.p.s.** with prior service

**WPT** Women's Playhouse Trust

**w.r.** warehouse receipt • *Insurance* war risk • water repellent

**WR** *British vehicle registration for* Leeds • ward room • warehouse receipt • war reserve • *Med.* Wassermann reaction • *Railways* Western Region • (formerly) West Riding (Yorkshire) • Willelmus Rex (Latin: King William) • (*or* **W–R**) *Astronomy* Wolf–Rayet (in **WR stars**) • *postcode for* Worcester

**WRA** (USA) War Relocation Authority • Water Research Association • *Horticulture* Wisley Rose Award

**WRAAC** (ræk) Women's Royal Australian Army Corps

**WRAAF** (ræf) Women's Royal Australian Air Force

**WRAC** (ræk) Women's Royal Army Corps

**WRAF** (ræf) Women's Royal Air Force

**WRANS** (rænz) Women's Royal Australian Naval Service

**WRC** Water Research Centre • (USA) Welding Research Council

**WRE** (Australia) Weapons Research Establishment

**w. ref.** with reference (to)

**WRI** war risks insurance • Women's Rural Institute

**w.r.n.** *Knitting* wool round needle

**WRNG** *Meteorol.* warning

**WRNR** Women's Royal Naval Reserve

**WRNS** Women's Royal Naval Service

**wrnt** warrant

**w.r.o.** *Insurance* war risks only

**WRO** Weed Research Organization (of the AFRC)

**WRP** Worker's Revolutionary Party

**WRRA** *Cycling* Women's Road Records Association

**wrt** wrought (of iron)

**w.r.t.** with respect to

**WRU** Welsh Rugby Union • Wesleyan Reform Union

**WRVS** Women's Royal Voluntary Service (formerly WVS)

**WS** *British vehicle registration for* Bristol • *postcode for* Walsall • water-soluble • weapon system • *international vehicle registration for* Western Samoa • West Saxon • wind speed • *Law* (Scotland) Writer to the Signet

**WSA** (USA) War Shipping Administration

**W. Sam.** Western Samoa

**WSC** World Series Cricket

**WSCF** World Student Christian Federation

**WSF** *Chem.* water-soluble fraction

**WSI** Writers and Scholars International

**WSJ** (ital.) (USA) Wall Street Journal

**WSL** Warren Spring Laboratory (Stevenage, Herts)

**WSM** Women's Suffrage Movement

**WSP** water supply point

**WSPU** Women's Social and Political Union

**WSSA** Welsh Secondary Schools Association

**WSTN** World Service Television News

**WSTV** World Service Television

**WSU** Wichita State University

**WSW** west-southwest

**wt** warrant • watertight • weight • without

**WT** *British vehicle registration for* Leeds • *airline flight code for* Nigeria Airlines • *Navy* warrant telegraphist • war transport • *Irish fishing port registration for* Westport • (*or* **W/T**) wireless telegraphy (*or* telephony) • withholding tax

**WTA** winner takes all • Women's Tennis Association • World Transport Agency

**WTAA** World Trade Alliance Association

**WTAU** Women's Total Abstinence Union

**WTC** Wheat Trade Convention

**wtd** warranted

**Wtf.** Waterford

**WTG** wind turbine generator

**WTH** whole-tree harvesting

**wthr** weather

**WTIS** World Trade Information Service

**WTMH** watertight manhole

**WTN** Worldwide Television News

**WTO** Warsaw Treaty Organization • World Tourism Organization

**WTP** willing(ness) to pay

**wtr** winter • writer

**WTRC** Wool Textile Research Council

**WTS** Women's Transport Service (now amalgamated with FANY)

**WTT** World Team Tennis

**WTTA** Wholesale Tobacco Trade Association of Great Britain and Northern Ireland

**WTUC** World Trade Union Conference

**WTUL** Women's Trade Union League

**WU** *British vehicle registration for* Leeds • Western Union

**WUCT** World Union of Catholic Teachers

**WUF** World Underwater Federation

**WUJS** World Union of Jewish Students

**WUPJ** World Union for Progressive Judaism

**WUR** World University Round Table

**WUS** World University Service

**WUSL** Women's United Service League

**w/v** *Chem.* weight in volume (of solution)

**WV** *British vehicle registration for* Brighton • *international vehicle registration for* (Windward Islands) St Vincent and the Grenadines • water valve • *US postcode for* West Virginia • *postcode for* Wolverhampton

**W. Va.** West Virginia

**WVA** World Veterinary Association

**wvd** waived

**WVD** Wereldverbond van Diamant Bewerkers (Dutch: Universal Alliance of Diamond Workers)

**WVF** World Veterans' Federation

**WVS** Women's Voluntary Service (*see* WRVS)

**WVT** water vapour transfer (*or* transmission)

**WVU** West Virginia University

**w/w** weight for weight • *Chem.* weight in weight

**WW** *British vehicle registration for* Leeds • (*or* **W/W**) wall-to-wall (in estate agency) • (*or* **W/W**) warehouse warrant • warrant writer • (ital.) Who's Who • World War (*see* WW1, WW2) • worldwide

**WW1** (*or* **WWI**) World War One (1914–18)

**WW2** (*or* **WWII**) World War Two (1939–45)

**WWDC** World War Debt Commission

**WWDSHEX** *Shipping* weather working days, Sundays, and holidays excluded

**Wwe** Witwe (German: widow)

**WWF** Worldwide Fund for Nature (formerly World Wildlife Fund)

**WWMCCS** World Wide Military Command and Control System

**WWO** Wing Warrant Officer

**WWSSN** worldwide standard seismograph network

**WWSU** World Water Ski Union

**WWW** (ital.) Who Was Who • World Weather Watch (of the WMO)

**WWY** Queen's Own Warwickshire and Worcestershire Yeomanry

**WX** *British vehicle registration for* Leeds • *Meteorol.* weather • women's extra-large (clothing size)

**Wy.** Wycliffe (*see* Wycl.) • Wyoming

**WY** *British vehicle registration for* Leeds • *British fishing port registration for* Whitby • *US postcode for* Wyoming

**Wycl.** John Wycliffe (*c.* 1330–84, English religious reformer)

**Wyo.** Wyoming

**WYR** West Yorkshire Regiment

**wysiwyg** (*or* **WYSIWYG**) ('wizi,wig) *Computing* what you see (on the screen) is what you get (from the printer)

**Wz.** Warenzeichen (German: trademark)

**WZ** *British vehicle registration for* Belfast

**WZO** World Zionist Organization

# X

**x** *Genetics, symbol for* the basic number of chromosomes in a genome • (ital.) *Maths., symbol for* a Cartesian coordinate (usually horizontal, as in **x-axis**) • *Bridge, symbol for* any card other than an honour • *symbol for* cross (as in **x-cut**, **x'd out**) • *Commerce, Finance, etc.* ex • extra • *Meteorol., symbol for* hoar-frost • (ital.) *Chem., symbol for* mole fraction • (ital.) *Maths., symbol for* an algebraic variable

**X** *Films, symbol for* adults only (former certification, still used in **X-rated**, **X-rating**) • *symbol for* beer strength (in **XX**, **XXX**, etc.) • *symbol for* choice (on a ballot paper) • Christ (from Greek letter X (chi), representing *ch*) • *symbol for* Cross (as in **King's X**) • *symbol for* error • experiment(al) • explosive • (ital.) *Physics, symbol for* exposure dose • extension • extra • extraordinary • *Chem., symbol for* a halogen (as in **MgX**) • *symbol for* a kiss • *symbol for* the location of a place or point on a map, diagram, etc • *symbol for* his (*or* her) mark • (ital.) *Electricity, symbol for* reactance • *Roman numeral for* ten • *symbol for* any unknown, unspecified, or variable thing, factor, number, or person. *See also* X-ray • *Biochem., symbol for* xanthosine • X-ray • *symbol for* xylonite (a plastic) • *Genetics, indicating* a sex chromosome in humans and most animals (as in **X chromosome**, **X-linked**, **XYY syndrome**)

**xa** *Finance* ex all (without any benefits)

**XA** *international civil aircraft marking for* Mexico

**Xaa** *Biochem., symbol for* an unknown amino acid (in a sequence)

**xan.** *Chem.* xanthene • *Chem.* xanthic

**XAS** *Chem.* X-ray absorption spectroscopy

**xb** *Finance* ex bonus (i.e. without bonus shares)

**XB** *international civil aircraft marking for* Mexico

**Xber** December

**X^bre** (*or* **xbre**) décembre (French: December)

**xbt** exhibit

**XBT** expendable bathythermograph

**xc** *Finance* ex capitalization (without capitalization) • *Finance* ex coupon (without the interest on the coupon)

**XC** (*or* **X-C**) (USA, Canada) cross-country (in **XC skiing**) • *international civil aircraft marking for* Mexico

**x.c.l.** *Insurance* excess current liabilities

**xcp** (*or* **x.cp.**) *Finance* ex coupon (*see under* xc)

**xcpt** except

**XCT** *Med.* X-ray computed tomography

**xd** *Finance* ex dividend (without dividend)

**x'd** executed

**XD** *Physics* X-ray diffraction

**xdiv** *Finance* ex dividend (without dividend)

**XDP** *Biochem.* xanthosine 5′-diphosphate

**Xdr** crusader

**XDR** extended dynamic range (of cassettes)

**Xe** *Chem., symbol for* xenon

**Xen.** Xenophon (*c.* 430–*c.* 356 BC, Greek historian)

**Xer.** Xerox

**XES** *Chem.* X-ray emission spectroscopy (*or* spectrum)

**XFA** *Chem.* X-ray fluorescence analysis

**xfer** transfer

**xfmr** (*or* **xformer**) transformer

**xg** crossing

**x-height** *Printing, indicating* typesize of lower-case letters excluding ascenders and descenders (from the height of the lower-case x)

**xhst** exhaust

**xi** (*or* **x in**) *Finance* ex interest (without interest)

**XI** *British vehicle registration for* Belfast • *Med.* X-ray imaging

**XL** extra large (clothing size)

**xlnt** excellent

**xlwb** extra-long wheelbase

**XM** experimental missile

**Xmas** ('ɛksməs) Christmas

**xmit** transmit

**XMP** *Biochem.* xanthosine monophosphate

**XMS** *Computing* extended memory specification

**xmsn** transmission

**xmtr** transmitter

**xn** *Finance* ex new (without right to new shares)

**Xn** Christian

**x/nt** excellent

**Xnty** Christianity

**XO** executive officer • *Chem.* xylenol orange (indicator) • *indicating* a cognac of superior quality

**XOR** (*or* **xor**) ('ɛksɔː) *Electronics, Computing* exclusive-OR (as in **XOR gate**)

**XP** *symbol or monogram for* Christ *or* Christianity (from X (chi) and P (rho), the first two letters of the Greek word for Christ) • (*or* **x.p.**) express paid • *Med.* xeroderma pigmentosum

**XPES** *Chem.* X-ray photoelectron (*or* photoemission) spectroscopy (*or* spectrum)

**xpl.** explosive

**xplt** exploit

**xpn** expansion

**XPS** X-ray photoelectron spectroscopy

**xq** (*or* **XQ**) cross-question

**xr** *Finance* ex rights (without rights)

**Xr** examiner

**XR** X-ray(s)

**X-ray** *indicating* electromagnetic radiation of very short wavelength (*X* refers to its unknown nature at the time of its discovery)

**XRD** X-ray diffraction

**Xrds** crossroads

**XRE** X-ray emission

**x ref.** (*or* **X ref.**) cross reference

**XRF** X-ray fluorescence

**XRFA** *Chem.* X-ray fluorescence analysis

**XRFS** *Chem.* X-ray fluorescence spectrometry

**XRM** *Med.* X-ray mammography

**XRMA** X-ray microprobe analysis

**XRT** *Med.* X-ray topography

**x.rts** *Finance* ex rights (without rights)

**xs** expenses

**Xt** Christ

**XT** *international civil aircraft marking for* Burkina Faso

**xtal** crystal

**X-tgd** *Building trades* cross-tongued

**Xtian** Christian

**XTP** *Biochem.* xanthosine 5′-triphosphate

**xtra** extra
**xtry** extraordinary
**Xty** Christianity
**XU** *international civil aircraft marking for* Cambodia
**XUV** *Astronomy* extreme ultraviolet
**xw** *Finance* ex warrants (without warrants)
**x/wb** extra-long wheelbase
**X-Windows** *Computing, trademark*

*indicating* a precisely defined form of windowing mechanism developed by MIT
**XX** *Meteorol.* heavy
**XY** *international civil aircraft marking for* Burma
**xyl.** xylophone
**Xyl** *Biochem.* xylose
**XZ** *British vehicle registration for* Armagh

# Y

**y** (*ital.*) *symbol for* altitude • (*ital.*) *Maths., symbol for* a Cartesian coordinate (usually vertical, as in **y-axis**) • *Meteorol., symbol for* dry air • (*ital.*) *Aeronautics, symbol for* lateral axis • (*ital.*) *Maths., symbol for* an algebraic variable
**y.** yacht • yard • year • yellow • young • youngest
**Y** (*ital.*) *Electricity, symbol for* admittance • (*ital.*) *Physics, symbol for* hypercharge • *Biochem., symbol for* tyrosine • *symbol for* yen (Japanese monetary unit) • (*or* **Y.**) Yeomanry • *Colloquial* YMCA, YWCA, YMHA, *or* YWHA • *Irish fishing port registration for* Youghal • *Chem., symbol for* yttrium • *symbol for* yuan (Chinese monetary unit; *see also* RMB) • (*or* **Y.**) Yugoslavia • *Genetics, indicating* a sex chromosome of humans and most animals (as in **Y chromosome, Y-linked, XYY syndrome**)
**YA** *international civil aircraft marking for* Afghanistan • *British vehicle registration for* Taunton • (*or* **Y/A**) *Marine insurance* York–Antwerp (Rules) • (USA) young adult
**YABA** Young American Bowling Alliance
**YAC** *Genetics* yeast artificial chromosome(s)
**YACC** (jæk) *Computing* yet another compiler-compiler
**YAG** (*or* **yag**) (jæg) *Electronics* yttrium–aluminium garnet
**YAL** Young Australia League
**Y & D** *US Navy* yards and docks
**Y & LR** York and Lancaster Regiment

**YAR** *Marine insurance* York–Antwerp Rules
**Y-ARD** Yarrow-Admiralty research department
**YAS** Yorkshire Agricultural Society
**YASSR** (formerly) Yakut Autonomous Soviet Socialist Republic
**YAVIS** ('jɑːvɪs) *Colloquial* (USA) young, attractive, verbal, intelligent, and successful
**Yb** *Chem., symbol for* ytterbium
**YB** *British vehicle registration for* Taunton • yearbook
**YC** *British vehicle registration for* Taunton • yacht club • Yale College (USA) • Young Conservative • youth club
**YCA** Youth Camping Association
**YC&UO** Young Conservative and Unionist Organization
**YCL** (USA) Young Communist League
**YCNAC** Young Conservative National Advisory Committee
**YCS** (International) Young Catholic Students
**yct** yacht
**YCW** (*or* **y.c.w.**) *Colloquial* you can't win • (International) Young Christian Workers
**yd** yard
**YD** *British vehicle registration for* Taunton • *symbol for* Yemeni dinar (monetary unit)
**y'day** (*or* **yday**) yesterday
**ydg** yarding
**yds** yards

**YE** *British vehicle registration for* London (central) • Your Excellency

**YEA** (USA) Yale Engineering Association

**yearb.** yearbook

**yel.** yellow

**Yel. NP** Yellowstone National Park (USA)

**Yem.** Yemen(i)

**yeo.** (*or* **Yeo.**) yeoman • yeomanry

**YEO** Youth Employment Officer

**YER** (*or* **y.e.r.**) *Finance* yearly effective rate (of interest)

**YES** Youth Employment Service • Youth Enterprise Scheme

**yesty** yesterday

**YF** *British vehicle registration for* London (central)

**YFC** Young Farmers' Club

**YFCU** Young Farmers' Clubs of Ulster

**YFG** *Electronics* yttrium–ferrite garnet

**YG** *British vehicle registration for* Leeds

**YH** *British vehicle registration for* London (central) • *British fishing port registration for* Yarmouth • *Numismatics* young head (of Queen Victoria) • youth hostel

**YHA** Youth Hostels Association

**YHANI** Youth Hostels Association of Northern Ireland

**YHWH** (*or* **YHVH**) *indicating* the Hebrew name for God (Yahweh *or* Jehovah; as revealed to Moses)

**Yi.** (*or* **Yid.**) Yiddish

**YI** *Irish vehicle registration for* Dublin • *international civil aircraft marking for* Iraq

**YIG** (jɪg) *Electronics* yttrium–iron garnet

**YIP** (*or* **Yippie**) (jɪp *or* ˈjɪpɪ) *Colloquial* (USA) (a member of the) Youth International Party

**YJ** *British vehicle registration for* Brighton • *international civil aircraft marking for* Vanuatu

**YK** *airline flight code for* Cyprus Turkish Airlines • *British vehicle registration for* London (central) • *international civil aircraft marking for* Syria

**YL** *international civil aircraft marking for* Latvia • *British vehicle registration for* London (central) • yield limit

**YLI** Yorkshire Light Infantry

**YM** *British vehicle registration for* London (central) • (*or* **Y-M**) *Physics* Yang–Mills (as in **YM theory**) • *Colloquial* YMCA (*or* a YMCA hostel)

**YMBA** Yacht and Motor Boat Association

**YMCA** Young Men's Christian Association

**YMCath.A** (USA) Young Men's Catholic Association

**YMCU** Young Men's Christian Union

**YMFS** Young Men's Friendly Society

**YMHA** Young Men's Hebrew Association

**YMV** *Microbiol.* yellow mosaic virus

**YN** *British vehicle registration for* London (central) • *international civil aircraft marking for* Nicaragua

**YNP** Yellowstone National Park (USA)

**y.o.** *Knitting* yarn over • year(s) old (following a number)

**YO** *British vehicle registration for* London (central) • *postcode for* York

**YOB** (*or* **y.o.b.**) year of birth

**YOC** Young Ornithologists' Club (of the RSPB)

**YOD** (*or* **y.o.d.**) year of death

**YOM** (*or* **y.o.m.**) year of marriage

**YOP** (jɒp) Youth Opportunities Programme

**Yorks** Yorkshire

**y.p.** *Finance* year's purchase

**YP** *British vehicle registration for* London (central) • *Mechanics* yield point • young person (*or* people) • young prisoner

**YPA** Young Pioneers of America

**YPFB** (Bolivia) Yacimientos Petroliferos Fiscales Bolivianos (state petroleum organization)

**YPSCE** (USA) Young People's Society of Christian Endeavour

**YPSL** (USA) Young People's Socialist League

**YPTES** Young People's Trust for Endangered Species

**yr** year • younger • your

**YR** *British vehicle registration for* London (central) • *international civil aircraft marking for* Romania

**yrbk** yearbook

**YRls** *symbol for* Yemen riyal (monetary unit)

**yrly** yearly

**yrs** years • (*or* **Yrs**) yours (in correspondence)

**Ys.** Yugoslavia(n)

**YS** *international civil aircraft marking for* El Salvador • *British vehicle registration for* Glasgow • *Mechanics* yield strength • Young Socialists

**YSA** (USA) Young Socialist Alliance

**YSAG** *Electronics* yttrium–scandium–aluminium garnet

**YSO** *Astronomy* young stellar object

**yst** youngest

**yt** yacht

**YT** *British vehicle registration for* London (central) • Yukon Territory

**y.t.b.** *Knitting* yarn to back

**YTD** *Accounting* year to date

**y.t.f.** *Knitting* yarn to front

**YTS** Youth Training Scheme

**YU** *British vehicle registration for* London (central) • Yale University (USA) • *international vehicle registration or international civil aircraft marking for* Yugoslavia

**Yugo.** Yugoslavia

**Yuk.** Yukon

**YUP** Yale University Press

**yuppie** (*or* **yuppy**) ('jʌpɪ) *Colloquial* young urban (*or* upwardly mobile) professional

**YV** *British vehicle registration for* London (central) • *international vehicle registration or international civil aircraft marking for* Venezuela

**YVF** Young Volunteer Force

**YVFF** Young Volunteer Force Foundation

**YW** *British vehicle registration for* London (central) • *Colloquial* YWCA (*or* a YWCA hostel)

**YWCA** Young Women's Christian Association

**YWCTU** Young Women's Christian Temperance Union

**YWF** Young World Federalists

**YWHA** Young Women's Hebrew Association

**YWS** Young Wales Society • Young Workers' Scheme

**YX** *British vehicle registration for* London (central)

**YY** *British vehicle registration for* London (central)

**YZ** *British vehicle registration for* Londonderry

# Z

**z** (ital.) *Maths.*, *symbol for* a Cartesian coordinate (as in **z-axis**) • (ital.) *Chem.*, *symbol for* charge number • *Meteorol.*, *symbol for* haze • (ital.) *Maths.*, *symbol for* an algebraic variable

**z.** zero • zone

**Z** *Irish vehicle registration for* Dublin • (ital.) *Electricity*, *symbol for* impedance • (ital.) *Physics*, *symbol for* proton number • *symbol for* zaïre (monetary unit of Zaïre) • *international vehicle registration for* Zambia • *international civil aircraft marking for* Zimbabwe • *Genetics*, indicating a sex chromosome in birds and some insects • *Physics*, indicating a type of fundamental particle

**Z.** (*or* **Z**) zero (as in **Z-day**) • Zion(ist) • Zoll (German: customs) • zone

**ZA** *international civil aircraft marking for* Albania • *Irish vehicle registration for* Dublin • *international vehicle registration for* South Africa

**Zag.** Zagreb

**Zam.** Zambia

**Zan.** (*or* **Zanz.**) Zanzibar

**ZANU** (*or* **Zanu**) ('zænuː) Zimbabwe African National Union

**ZANU (PF)** (*or* **Zanu (PF)**) ('zænuː 'piː 'ɛf) Zimbabwe African National Union (Patriotic Front)

**ZAP** *Military* zero anti-aircraft potential

**ZAPU** (*or* **Zapu**) ('zæpuː) Zimbabwe African People's Union

**z.B.** zum Beispiel (German: for example; e.g.)

**ZB** *Irish vehicle registration for* Cork • *airline flight code for* Monarch Airlines • Zen Buddhist

**ZBB** *Finance* (USA) zero-base(d) budgeting

**ZC** *Irish vehicle registration for* Dublin • Zionist Congress

**Z-car** indicating a police patrol car (from *zulu*, radio call sign)

**ZCY** *Electronics* zirconia–ceria–yttria

**ZD** *Irish vehicle registration for* Dublin • *Electronics* Zener diode • *Astronomy* zenith distance

**Z-day** *Military* zero day

**Z-DNA** *Biochem.* zigzagged DNA

**ZE** *Irish vehicle registration for* Dublin • *postcode for* Lerwick

**ZEBRA** ('ziːbrə) *Nuclear engineering* zero-energy breeder-reactor assembly

**Zech.** *Bible* Zechariah

**Zeep** (ziːp) *Nuclear engineering* zero-energy experimental pile

**ZEG** zero economic growth

**zen.** zenith

**ZENITH** ('zɛnɪθ) *Nuclear engineering* zero-energy nitrogen-heated thermal reactor

**Zeph.** *Bible* Zephaniah

**zero-g** zero gravity (weightlessness)

**ZETA** ('ziːtə) *Nuclear engineering* zero-energy thermonuclear apparatus (*or* assembly)

**ZETR** ('ziːtə) *Nuclear engineering* zero-energy thermal reactor

**ZF** *Irish vehicle registration for* Cork • (*or* **z.f.**) zero frequency

**ZFGBI** Zionist Federation of Great Britain and Ireland

**ZG** *Irish vehicle registration for* Dublin • Zoological Gardens

**z.H.** (*or* **z.Hd.**) zu Händen (German: for the attention of, f.a.o.; *or* care of, c/o)

**ZH** *Irish vehicle registration for* Dublin • zero hour

**ZHR** *Astronomy* zenithal hourly rate

**ZI** *Irish vehicle registration for* Dublin • *Military* zone of interior

**ZIF** (zɪf) *Electronics* zero insertion force (in **ZIF socket**)

**ZIFT** (zɪft) *Med.* zygote intrafallopian transfer (treatment for infertility)

**zip** (*or* **Zip**) (zɪp) (USA) zone improvement plan (in **zip code**, US postcode)

**ZJ** *Irish vehicle registration for* Dublin

**ZK** *Irish vehicle registration for* Cork • *international civil aircraft marking for* New Zealand

**Zl** *symbol for* zloty (Polish monetary unit)

**ZL** *Irish vehicle registration for* Dublin

**ZM** *Irish vehicle registration for* Galway

**Zn** *Chem., symbol for* zinc

**ZN** *Irish vehicle registration for* Meath

**ZO** *Irish vehicle registration for* Dublin • Zionist Organization

**ZOA** Zionist Organization of America

**zod.** zodiac

**zoogeog.** zoogeography

**zool.** zoological • zoologist • zoology

**ZP** *Irish vehicle registration for* Donegal • *international civil aircraft marking for* Paraguay

**ZPG** zero population growth

**ZQ** *airline flight code for* Ansett New Zealand

**Zr** *Chem., symbol for* zirconium

**ZR** *Irish vehicle registration for* Wexford

**ZRE** *international vehicle registration for* Zaïre

**Zs.** Zeitschrift (German: periodical *or* journal)

**ZS** *Irish vehicle registration for* Dublin • *international civil aircraft marking for* South Africa • Zoological Society

**ZSI** Zoological Society of Ireland

**ZST** zone standard time

**z.T.** zum Teil (German: partly)

**ZT** *Irish vehicle registration for* Cork • zone time

**Ztg** Zeitung (German: newspaper)

**ZU** *Irish vehicle registration for* Dublin

**Zulu.** Zululand

**ZUM** Zimbabwe Unity Movement

**Zur.** Zürich

**ZV** *Irish vehicle registration for* Dublin

**zw.** zwischen (German: between *or* among)

**ZW** *Irish vehicle registration for* Kildare • *international vehicle registration for* Zimbabwe

**ZX** *Irish vehicle registration for* Kerry

**ZY** *Irish vehicle registration for* Louth

**zz** zigzag

**Zz.** *Med., Pharmacol.* ginger (Latin zingiber)

**ZZ** *British vehicle registration for* vehicles temporarily imported by visitors from abroad

# Alphabets

| Arabic | | Hebrew | | Greek | | Russian | |
|--------|--|--------|--|-------|--|---------|--|
| ا ا ا أ 'alif ' | | א aleph ' | | $A\ \alpha$ alpha a | | А а a | |
| ب ب ب ب bā' b | | ב beth b,bh | | $B\ \beta$ beta b | | Б б b | |
| ت ت ت ت tā' t | | ג gimel g,gh | | $\Gamma\ \gamma$ gamma g | | В в v | |
| ث ث ث ث thā' th | | ד daleth d,dh | | $\Delta\ \delta$ delta d | | Г г g | |
| ج ج ج ج jīm j | | ה he h | | $E\ \epsilon$ epsilon e | | Д д d | |
| ح ح ح ح ḥā' ḥ | | ו waw w | | $Z\ \zeta$ zeta z | | Е е e | |
| خ خ خ خ khā' kh | | ז zayin z | | $H\ \eta$ eta ē | | Ё ё ё | |
| د د د د dāl d | | ח ḥeth ḥ | | $\Theta\ \theta$ theta th | | Ж ж zh | |
| ذ ذ ذ ذ dhāl dh | | ט ṭeth ṭ | | $I\ \iota$ iota i | | З з z | |
| ر ر ر ر rā' r | | י yodh y | | $K\ \kappa$ kappa k | | И и i | |
| ز ز ز ز zay z | | כ ך kaph k,kh | | $\Lambda\ \lambda$ lambda l | | Й й ĭ | |
| س س س س sīn s | | ל lamedh l | | $M\ \mu$ mu m | | К к k | |
| ش ش ش ش shīn sh | | מ ם mem m | | $N\ \nu$ nu n | | Л л l | |
| ص ص ص ص ṣād ṣ | | נ ן nun n | | $\Xi\ \xi$ xi x | | М м m | |
| ض ض ض ض ḍād ḍ | | ס samekh s | | $O\ o$ omicron o | | Н н n | |
| ط ط ط ط ṭā' ṭ | | ע 'ayin ' | | $\Pi\ \pi$ pi p | | О о o | |
| ظ ظ ظ ظ ẓā' ẓ | | פ ף pe p,ph | | $P\ \varrho$ rho r,rh | | П п p | |
| ع ع ع ع 'ayn ' | | צ ץ ṣadhe ṣ | | $\Sigma\ \sigma\varsigma$ sigma s | | Р р r | |
| غ غ غ غ ghayn gh | | ק qoph q | | $T\ \tau$ tau t | | С с s | |
| ف ف ف ف fā' f | | ר resh r | | $Y\ \upsilon$ upsilon u | | Т т t | |
| ق ق ق ق qāf q | | שׂ śin ś | | $\Phi\ \phi$ phi ph | | У у u | |
| ك ك ك ك kāf k | | שׁ shin sh | | $X\ \chi$ chi kh | | Ф ф f | |
| ل ل ل ل lām l | | ת taw t,th | | $\Psi\ \psi$ psi ps | | Х х kh | |
| م م م م mīm m | | | | $\Omega\ \omega$ omega ō | | Ц ц ts | |
| ن ن ن ن nūn n | | | | | | Ч ч ch | |
| ه ه ه ه hā' h | | | | | | Ш ш sh | |
| و و و و wāw w | | | | | | Щ щ shch | |
| ي ي ي ي yā' y | | | | | | Ъ ъ " | |
| | | | | | | ('hard sign') | |
| | | | | | | Ы ы y | |
| | | | | | | Ь ь ' | |
| | | | | | | ('soft sign') | |
| | | | | | | Э э é | |
| | | | | | | Ю ю yu | |
| | | | | | | Я я ya | |

# Musical Notation

## Values of notes and rests

| | notes | rests |
|---|---|---|
| 1 semibreve | | |
| equals | | |
| 2 minims | | |
| or | | |
| 4 crotchets | | |
| or | | |
| 8 quavers | | |
| or | | |
| 16 semiquavers | | |
| or | | |
| 32 demisemiquavers | | |

## Some common symbols

treble or G clef    bass or F clef    C (alto) clef    C (tenor) clef    key signature    time signature    } staff

(position for middle C is shown for each clef)

sharp    flat
(single &  (single &                                          dotted note
double)   double)   natural   staccato   legato   tie    (value increased
                                                          by half)        pause   repeat

## The circle of fifths

The circle of fifths, showing key signatures in treble and bass clefs for all major and minor keys. Major keys are indicated by capital letters; minor keys by lower-case letters. At the bottom of the circle the keys overlap, so that, for example, D♭ major is enharmonically equivalent to C♯ major.

# Monetary symbols

Note: Roman letters that are used as monetary symbols will be found in their alphabetic place in the text.

| Symbol | Name | Country |
|---|---|---|
| $A | Australian dollar | Australia; Kiribati |
| B$ | Bahamian dollar | Bahamas |
| | Brunei dollar | Brunei |
| Bd$ | Bermuda dollar | Bermuda |
| BD$ | Barbados dollar | Barbados |
| BZ$ | Belize dollar | Belize |
| ₵ | cedi | Ghana |
| | colón | El Salvador |
| | Costa Rican colón | Costa Rica |
| £C | Cyprus pound | Cyprus |
| C$ | Nicaraguan new córdoba | Nicaragua |
| Can$ | Canadian dollar | Canada |
| Ch$ | peso | Chile |
| CI$ | Cayman Islands dollar | Cayman Islands |
| Col$ | peso | Colombia |
| Cr$ | cruzeiro | Brazil |
| EC$ | East Caribbean dollar | Antigua & Barbuda; Dominica; Grenada; St Kitts and Nevis; St Lucia; St Vincent and the Grenadines |
| F$ | Fiji dollar | Fiji |
| ₲ | Paraguayan guaraní | Paraguay |
| G$ | Guyana dollar | Guyana |
| HK$ | Hong Kong dollar | Hong Kong |
| Ir£ | Irish pound | Ireland |
| J$ | Jamaica dollar | Jamaica |
| £ | pound sterling | UK |
| L$ | Liberian dollar | Liberia |
| M$ | Malaysian dollar (ringgit) | Malaysia |
| Mex$ | peso | Mexico |
| ₦ | Nigerian naira | Nigeria |
| NUr$ | Uruguayan new peso | Uruguay |
| $NZ | New Zealand dollar | New Zealand |
| NT$ | new Taiwan dollar | Taiwan |
| ₱ | Philippine peso | Philippines |
| RD$ | Dominican peso | Dominican Republic |
| S/. | sucre | Ecuador |
| S$ | Singapore dollar | Singapore |
| SI$ | Solomon Islands dollar | Solomon Islands |
| T$ | pa'anga | Tonga |
| TT$ | Trinidad and Tobago dollar | Trinidad and Tobago |
| US$ | United States dollar | USA; Guam; Federated States of Micronesia; Puerto Rico; Virgin Islands (US) |
| WS$ | tala | Western Samoa |
| ¥ | yen | Japan |
| Z$ | Zimbabwe dollar | Zimbabwe |

# Proof-correction symbols

(Where appropriate, the marks should also be used by copy-editors in marking up copy)

| Instruction to printer | Textual mark | Marginal mark |
|---|---|---|
| Correction made in error. Leave unchanged. | - - - - under character(s) to remain | ⊘ |
| Remove extraneous marks or replace damaged character(s) | Encircle marks to be removed or character(s) to be changed | × |
| (Wrong fount) Replace by character(s) of correct fount | Encircle character(s) to be changed | ⊗ |
| Insert in text the matter indicated in the margin | ⅄ | New matter followed by ⅄ |
| Delete | Stroke through character(s) to be deleted | ♂ |
| Substitute character or substitute part of one or more word(s) | / through character or ⊢———⊣ through word(s) | New character or New word(s) |
| Set in or change to italic type | ——— under character(s) to be set or changed | ⊔⊔⊔ |
| Change italic to roman type | Encircle character(s) to be changed | ⊔⊔ |
| Set in or change to capital letter(s) | ≡≡≡ under character(s) to be set or changed | ≡ |
| Change capital letter(s) to lower-case letter(s) | Encircle character(s) to be changed | ⧣ |
| Set in or change to small capital letter(s) | ══ under character(s) to be set or changed | ══ |
| Change small capital letter(s) to lower-case letter(s) | Encircle character(s) to be changed | ⧣ |
| Set in or change to bold type | ∿∿∿ under character(s) to be changed | ∿∿ |
| Set in or change to italic type | ∿∿∿ under character(s) to be changed | ⊔⊔∿∿ |
| Invert type | Encircle character to be inverted | ∩ |
| Substitute or insert character in 'superior' position | / through character or ⅄ where required | ⅂ under character (e.g. ) |
| Substitute or insert character in 'inferior' position | / through character or ⅄ where required | ⌐ over character (e.g. ) |
| Insert full or decimal point | ⅄ where required | ⊙ |
| Insert colon, semicolon, comma, etc. | ⅄ where required | ⊙ /;/,/(/)//[/]/ ?????? |
| Rearrange to make a new paragraph here | ⌐ before first word of new paragraph | ⊐ |
| Run on (no new paragraph) | ⌐⌐ between paragraphs | ⌐⌐ |
| Transpose characters or words | ⊔⊓ between characters or words to be transposed, numbered where necessary | ⊔⊓ |
| Insert hyphen | ⅄ where required | ⊢═⊣ |
| Insert rule | ⅄ where required | 1 em 4 mm (i.e. give the size of the rule in the marginal mark) |
| Insert oblique | ⅄ where required | ⊘ |
| Insert space between characters | ∣ between characters | Y |
| Insert space between words | Y between words | Y |
| Reduce space between characters | ∣ between characters | ⊤ |
| Reduce space between words | ⊤ between words | ⊤ |
| Equalize space between characters or words | ∣ between characters or words | ⋎ |

# Hallmarks

All marks shown relate to silver except where otherwise indicated

**A hallmark**

maker's mark   standard mark   Assay Office mark   date letter

## Maker's mark (from 1363)
originally symbols, now initials

 symbol

 symbol and initials

 initials

## Assay Office mark (from 1300)
now only London, Birmingham, Sheffield, and Edinburgh

### London

 gold and silver (leopard's head uncrowned from 1821; mark includes platinum from 1975)

 Britannia silver (prior to 1975)

### Edinburgh

 gold and silver (also platinum from 1975)

### Birmingham

 gold (also platinum from 1975)

 silver

### Sheffield

 silver (prior to 1975)

 gold (also silver and platinum from 1975)

## Some earlier Assay Office marks
(with dates of closure)

Norwich (1702)   York (1856)   Exeter (1883)   Newcastle (1884)   Chester (1962)   Glasgow (1964)

## Standard mark (from 1544)
Marks guaranteeing pure metal content of the percentage shown

sterling silver 92.5%

 marked in England

 marked in Scotland (from 1975)

marked in Scotland (prior to 1975)

Britannia standard silver (1697-1720, also occasional use since) 95.8%

gold (crown followed by millesimal figure of the standard)

 i.e. 18 carat 75%

 22 carat 91.6%

585 14 carat 58.5%

375 9 carat 37.5%

(prior to 1975 marks incorporated the carat figure, and Scottish 18 and 22 carat gold bore a thistle mark instead of the crown)

## Date letter (from 1478)
one letter per year before changing to next style of letter and/or shield
cycles vary between Assay Offices
London date letters (A-U used, excluding J) showing style of first letter and years of cycle

| | | | | | | | | | |
|---|---|---|---|---|---|---|---|---|---|
| | 1498-1518 | | 1598-1618 | | 1697-1716 | | 1796-1816 | | 1896-1916 |
| | 1518-1538 | | 1618-1638 | | 1716-1736 | | 1816-1836 | | 1916-1936 |
| | 1538-1558 | | 1638-1658 | | 1736-1756 | | 1836-1856 | | 1936-1956 |
| | 1558-1578 | | 1658-1678 | | 1756-1776 | | 1856-1876 | | 1956-1974 |
| | 1578-1598 | | 1678-1697 | | 1776-1796 | | 1876-1896 | | 1975[1]- |

Note 1. Year letter changed with each calendar year; from 1975 all UK Offices use the same date letters and shield shape

# Meteorological symbols

## Weather conditions

- • rain
- ❟ drizzle
- ▽ showers
- ∞ haze

- ✳ snow
- ▲ hail
- △ ice pellets
- ⌐ smoke

- ⌒ dew
- ≡ fog
- ℞ thunderstorm
- ‹ lightning

## Cloud cover

- ◯ clear
- ◑ 1 okta
- ◕ 2
- ◑ 3
- ◐ 4
- ◐ 5
- ◕ 6
- ◑ 7
- ● 8
- ⊗ sky obscured (1 okta = ⅛ of the sky)

**Wind** The arrow points in the direction from which the wind is blowing.

knots

- ◎ calm
- ◯— 1-2
- ◯— 3-7
- ◯— 8-12
- ◯— 13-17
- ◯— 18-22
- ◯— 23-27
- ◯— 28-32
- ◯— 33-37
- ◯— 38-42
- ◯— 43-47
- ◯—▲ 48-52

## Fronts

▼▼▼ **cold front** boundary between overtaking cold air mass and warm air mass.

⌒⌒ **warm front** boundary between overtaking warm air mass and cold air mass.

⌒▼⌒ **stationary** boundary between air masses of similar temperature.

▲⌒▲ **occluded** line where a cold front overtakes a warm front.

# Mathematical symbols

## General symbols

| | |
|---|---|
| ratio of circumference of circle to its diameter | $\pi$ |
| base of natural logarithms | $e$ |
| imaginary unit: $i^2 = -1$ | $i, j$ |
| infinity | $\infty$ |
| equal to | $=$ |
| not equal to | $\neq$ |
| identically equal to | $\equiv$ |
| corresponds to | $\hat{=}$ |
| approximately equal to | $\approx$ |
| asymptotically equal to | $\simeq$ |
| proportional to | $\propto$ |
| approaches | $\rightarrow$ |
| greater than | $>$ |
| smaller than | $<$ |
| much greater than | $\gg$ |
| much less than | $\ll$ |
| greater than or equal to | $\geq$ |
| less than or equal to | $\leq$ |
| plus | $+$ |
| minus | $-$ |
| plus or minus | $\pm$ |
| $a$ multiplied by $b$ | $ab, a \cdot b, a \times b$ |
| $a$ divided by $b$ | $a/b, \dfrac{a}{b}, ab^{-1}$ |
| $a$ raised to the power $n$ | $a^n$ |
| magnitude of $a$ | $|a|$ |
| square root of $a$ | $\sqrt{a}, \sqrt{a}, a^{1/2}$ |
| mean value of $a$ | $\bar{a}, \langle a \rangle$ |
| factorial $p$ | $p!$ |
| binomial coefficient: $n!/[p!(n-p)!]$ | $\binom{n}{p}$ |

## Symbols for functions

| | |
|---|---|
| exponential of $x$ | $\exp x, e^x$ |
| logarithm to base $a$ of $x$ | $\log_a x$ |
| natural logarithm of $x$ | $\ln x, \log_e x$ |
| common logarithm of $x$ | $\lg x, \log_{10} x$ |
| binary logarithm of $x$ | $\text{lb}\, x, \log_2 x$ |
| sine of $x$ | $\sin x$ |
| cosine of $x$ | $\cos x$ |
| tangent of $x$ | $\tan x, \text{tg}\, x$ |
| contangent of $x$ | $\cot x, \text{ctg}\, x$ |
| secant of $x$ | $\sec x$ |
| cosecant of $x$ | $\text{cosec}\, x, \csc x$ |
| inverse sine $x$ | $\sin^{-1} x, \arcsin x$ |
| inverse cosine $x$ | $\cos^{-1} x, \arccos x$ |
| inverse tangent $x$ | $\tan^{-1} x, \arctan x$ |
| integral | $\int$ |
| summation | $\Sigma$ |
| product | $\Pi$ |
| finite increase of $x$ | $\Delta x$ |
| variation of $x$ | $\delta x$ |
| total differential of $x$ | $\mathrm{d}x$ |
| function of $x$ | $f(x)$ |
| composite function of $f$ and $g$ | $f \cdot g$ |
| convolution of $f$ and $g$ | $f * g$ |
| limit of $f(x)$ | $\lim_{x \to a} f(x), \lim\limits_{x \to a} f(x)$ |
| derivative of $f$ | $\dfrac{\mathrm{d}f}{\mathrm{d}x}, \mathrm{d}f/\mathrm{d}x, f'$ |
| time derivative of $f$ | $\dot{f}$ |
| partial derivative of $f$ | $\dfrac{\partial f}{\partial x}, \partial f/\partial x, \partial_x f, f_x$ |
| total differential of $f$ | $\mathrm{d}f$ |
| variation of $f$ | $\delta f$ |

## Symbols in set theory

| | |
|---|---|
| is an element of: $x \in A$ | $\in$ |
| is not an element of: $x \notin A$ | $\notin$ |
| contains as element: $A \ni x$ | $\ni$ |
| set of elements | $\{a_1, a_2, \cdots\}$ |
| empty set | $\varnothing$ |
| the set of positive integers and zero | $\mathbb{N}, N$ |
| the set of all integers, $\{\ldots, -2, -1, 0, 1, 2, \ldots\}$ | $\mathbb{Z}, Z$ |
| the set of rational numbers | $\mathbb{Q}, Q$ |
| the set of real numbers | $\mathbb{R}, R$ |
| the set of complex numbers | $\mathbb{C}, C$ |

| | |
|---|---|
| set of elements of $A$ for which $p(x)$ is true | $\{x \in A \mid p(x)\}$ |
| is included in, subset of: $B \subseteq A$ | $\subseteq, (\subset)$ |
| contains: $A \supseteq B$ | $\supseteq, (\supset)$ |
| is properly contained in | $\subset$ |
| contains properly | $\supset$ |
| union: $A \cup B$ $= \{x \mid (x \in A) \vee (x \in B)\}$ | $\cup$ |
| intersection: $A \cap B$ $= \{x \mid (x \in A) \wedge (x \in B)\}$ | $\cap$ |
| difference: $A \backslash B$ $= \{x \mid (x \in A) \wedge (x \notin B)\}$ | $\backslash$ |
| complement of: $\complement A$ $= \{x \mid x \notin A\}$ | $\complement$ |

## Logic symbols

| | |
|---|---|
| conjunction | $\wedge$ |
| disjunction | $\vee$ |
| negation | $\neg$ |
| implication | $\Rightarrow$ |
| equivalence | $\Leftrightarrow$ |
| universal quantifier | $\forall$ |
| existential quantifier | $\exists$ |

| | | |
|---|---|---|
| AND | $\wedge$ | |
| OR | $\vee$ | |
| NOT | $\neg$ | |
| NAND | $\Delta$ | $\mid$ |
| NOR | $\nabla$ | $\downarrow$ |
| XOR | xor | |

# Graphical symbols used in electronics

## Qualifying graphical symbols

alternating current

variability (noninherent)

variability in steps

thermal effect

electromagnetic effect

radiation, electromagnetic nonionizing

coherent radiation

ionizing radiation

positive-going pulse

negative-going pulse

pulse of a.c.

positive-going step function

negative-going step function

fault

## Graphical symbols

connection of conductors

terminal (circle may be filled in)

junction of conductors

plug & socket (male & female)

earth

primary cell or accumulator (longer line represents +ve pole)

battery of accumulators or primary cells

switch, general symbol; make contact

resistor, general symbol (first form preferred)

variable resistor

resistor with sliding contact

capacitor, general symbol (first form preferred)

IGFET, enhancement type, single gate, p-type channel without substrate connection

amplifier, general symbol

AND gate, general symbol

OR gate, general symbol

inverter (NOT gate)

NAND gate (negated AND)

inductor, coil, winding, choke, general symbol

inductor with magnetic core

transformer, 2 windings

piezoelectric crystal, 2 electrodes

semiconductor diode, general symbol

light-emitting diode, general symbol

photodiode

pnp transistor

npn transistor

JFET, n-type channel

JFET, p-type channel

NOR gate (negated OR)

exclusive-OR gate

indicating instrument (first form) & recording instrument; asterisk is replaced by symbol of unit of quantity being measured (e.g. V for voltmeter, A for ammeter, or by some other appropriate symbol)

antenna, general symbol

# Greek letters used as symbols for physical quantities

Note: Roman letters that are used as symbols for physical quantities will be found in their alphabetic place in the text.

| Symbol | Name | Physical quantity |
|---|---|---|
| $\alpha$ | alpha | absorptance; linear expansion coefficient |
| $\gamma$ | gamma | surface tension; cubic expansion coefficient |
| $\delta$ | delta | inclination |
| $\varepsilon$ | epsilon | emissivity; permittivity |
| $\eta$ | eta | efficiency; viscosity |
| $\theta$ | theta | angular displacement; Bragg angle; characteristic temperature |
| $\theta_N$ | theta | Néel temperature |
| $\lambda$ | lambda | thermal conductivity; decay constant; mean free path; wavelength |
| $\mu$ | mu | coefficient of friction; permeability |
| $\nu$ | nu | kinematic viscosity; frequency |
| $\Pi$ | pi (cap.) | osmotic pressure |
| $\varrho$ | rho | charge density; density; reflectance; resistivity |
| $\sigma$ | sigma | electrical conductivity; wave number |
| $\tau$ | tau | mean life |
| $\phi$ | phi | luminous flux |
| $\Phi$ | phi (cap.) | magnetic flux; work function |
| $\Phi_e$ | phi (cap.) | radiant flux |
| $\chi$ | chi | magnetic susceptibility |
| $\psi$ | psi | electric flux |
| $\omega$ | omega | angular frequency; angular velocity |
| $\Omega$ | omega (cap.) | solid angle |

# Miscellaneous symbols

@ at (in commerce)
& and (ampersand)
© copyright
° degree (angle, temperature, proof of alcohol)
® registered trademark
♂ male
♀ female

# Accents, diacritical marks, and special letters

| ç | cedilla | ñ | tilde |
|---|---|---|---|
| ü | umlaut | a̱ | bar-under |
| ā | macron | ȧ | dot |
| å | hacek | ạ | dot-under |
| Å | Swedish boll | ł Ł | Polish barred 'l' |
| é | acute | ø Ø | Scandinavian barred 'O' |
| è | grave | æ Æ | a, e ligature |
| ô | circumflex | œ Œ | o, e ligature |
| ă | breve | ß | German double 'S' |

## International vehicle registration marks

| Country | Mark | Country | Mark |
|---------|------|---------|------|
| Afghanistan | AFG | Guyana | GUY |
| Albania | AL | Haiti | RH |
| Alderney | GBA | Hong Kong | HK |
| Algeria | DZ | Hungary | H |
| Andorra | AND | Iceland | IS |
| Argentina | RA | India | IND |
| Australia | AUS | Indonesia | RI |
| Austria | A | Iran | IR |
| Bahamas | BS | Iraq | IRQ |
| Bahrain | BRN | Ireland | IRL |
| Bangladesh | BD | Isle of Man | GBM |
| Barbados | BDS | Israel | IL |
| Belgium | B | Italy | I |
| Belize | BH | Jamaica | JA |
| Benin | DY | Japan | J |
| Botswana | RB | Jersey | GBJ |
| Brazil | BR | Jordan | HKJ |
| Brunei | BRU | Kenya | EAK |
| Bulgaria | BG | Korea (Republic of) | ROK |
| Burma | BUR | Kuwait | KWT |
| Burundi | RU | Laos | LAO |
| Cambodia | K | Latvia | LV |
| Canada | CDN | Lebanon | RL |
| Central African Republic | RCA | Lesotho | LS |
| Chile | RCH | Liberia | LB |
| Colombia | CO | Libya | LAR |
| Congo | RCB | Liechtenstein | FL |
| Costa Rica | CR | Lithuania | LT |
| Côte d'Ivoire (Ivory Coast) | CI | Luxembourg | L |
| Cuba | C | Madagascar | RM |
| Cyprus | CY | Mali | RMM |
| Czech Republic | CS | Malta | M |
| Denmark | DK | Malawi | MW |
| Dominica | WD | Malaysia | MAL |
| Dominican Republic | DOM | Mauritania | RIM |
| Ecuador | EC | Mauritius | MS |
| Egypt | ET | Mexico | MEX |
| El Salvador | ES | Monaco | MC |
| Estonia | EW | Morocco | MA |
| Ethiopia | ETH | Namibia | SWA |
| Faroe Islands | FR | Netherlands Antilles | NA |
| Fiji | FJI | Netherlands | NL |
| Finland | FIN | New Zealand | NZ |
| France | F | Nicaragua | NIC |
| Gambia | WAG | Niger | RN |
| Germany | D | Nigeria | WAN |
| Ghana | GH | Norway | N |
| Gibraltar | GBZ | Pakistan | PK |
| Great Britain | GB | Panama | PA |
| Greece | GR | Papua New Guinea | PNG |
| Grenada | WG | Paraguay | PY |
| Guatemala | GCA | Peru | PE |
| Guernsey | GBG | Philippines | RP |

| Country | Mark | Country | Mark |
|---|---|---|---|
| Poland | PL | Syria | SYR |
| Portugal | P | Taiwan | RC |
| Romania | RO | Tanzania | EAT |
| Russia | RUS | Tanzania (Zanzibar) | EAZ |
| Rwanda | RWA | Thailand | T |
| San Marino | RSM | Togo | TG |
| Senegal | SN | Trinidad and Tobago | TT |
| Seychelles | SY | Tunisia | TN |
| Sierra Leone | WAL | Turkey | TR |
| Singapore | SGP | Uganda | EAU |
| Slovakia | CS | United States of America | USA |
| South Africa | ZA | Uruguay | ROU |
| Spain | E | Vatican City | V |
| Sri Lanka | CL | Venezuela | YV |
| St Lucia | WL | Vietnam | VN |
| St Vincent and the Grenadines | WV | Western Samoa | WS |
|  |  | Yemen | ADN |
| Suriname | SME | Yugoslavia | YU |
| Swaziland | SD | Zaïre | ZRE |
| Sweden | S | Zambia | Z |
| Switzerland | CH | Zimbabwe | ZW |

# British vehicle registration marks

| Registration office | Marks |
|---|---|
| Aberdeen | PS, RS, SA, SE, SO, SS |
| Antrim | DZ, IA, KZ, RZ |
| Armagh | IB, LZ, XZ |
| Bangor | CC, EY, FF, JC |
| Belfast | AZ, EZ, FZ, GZ, MZ, OI, OZ, PZ, TZ, UZ, WZ, XI |
| Birmingham | DA, JW, OA, OB, OC, OE, OF, OG, OH, OJ, OK, OL, OM, ON, OP, OV, OX, UK, VP |
| Bournemouth | AA, CG, EL, FX, HO, JT, LJ, PR, RU |
| Brighton | AP, CD, DY, FG, HC, JK, NJ, PN, UF, WV, YJ |
| Bristol | AE, EU, FB, HT, HU, HW, HY, OU, TC, WS |
| Cardiff | AX, BO, DW, HB, KG, NY, TG, TX, UH, WO |
| Carlisle | AO, HH, RM |
| Chelmsford | AR, EV, HJ, HK, JN, NO, OO, PU, TW, VX, WC |
| Chester | DM, FM, LG, MA, MB, TU |
| Coventry | AC, DU, HP, KV, RW, VC, WK |
| Down | IJ, JZ, SZ, BZ |
| Dudley | DH, EA, FD, FK, HA, NX, UE, WD, ES |
| Dundee | SL, SN, SP, SR, TS |
| Durham | J |
| Edinburgh | FS, RRC, LS, MS, SC, SF, SG, SH, SX |
| Exeter | CO, DR, DV, FJ, JY, OD, TA, TK, TT, UN, UO |
| Fermanagh | IL |
| Glasgow | CS, DS, GA, GB, GD, GE, GG, HS, NS, OS, SB, SD, SJ, SM, SU, SW, US, YS |

| Registration office | Marks |
|---|---|
| Gloucester | AD, CJ, DD, DF, DG, FH, FO, VJ |
| Guildford | PA, PB, PC, PD, PE, PF, PG, PH, PJ, PK, PL, PM |
| Haverfordwest | BX, DE, EJ |
| Huddersfield | HD, CP, CX, JX, VH |
| Hull | AG, AT, KH, RH |
| Inverness | AS, BS, JS, SK, ST |
| Ipswich | BJ, DX, GV, PV, RT |
| Leeds | BT, DN, NW, UA, UB, UG, UM, VY, WR, WT, WU, WW, WX, WY, YG |
| Leicester | AY, BC, FP, JF, JU, NR, RY, UT, BE |
| Lincoln | CT, DO, EE, FE, FU, FW, JL, JV, TL, VL |
| Liverpool | BG, CM, DJ, ED, EK, EM, FY, HF, JP, K, KA, KB, KC, KD, KF, LV, TB, TJ, WM |
| London (central) | JD, HM, HV, HX, UC, UL, UU, UV, UW, YE, YF, YH, YK, YL, YM, YN, YO, YP, YR, YT, YU, YV, YW, YX, YY |
| London (NE) | MC, MD, ME, MF, MG, MH, MK, ML, MM, MP, MT, MU |
| London (NW) | BY, LA, LB, LC, LD, LE, LF, LH, LK, LL, LM, LN, LO, LP, LR, LT, LU, LW, LX, LY, OY, RK |
| London (SE) | GU, GW, GX, GY, MV, MX, MY |
| London (SW) | GC, GF, GH, GJ, GK, GN, GO, GP, GT |
| Londonderry | IW, NZ, UI, YZ |
| Luton | BH, BM, GS, KX, MJ, NK, NM, PP, RO, TM, UR, VS |
| Maidstone | FN, JG, JJ, KE, KJ, KK, KL, KM, KN, KO, KP, KR, KT, VB |

| Registration office | Marks | Registration office | Marks |
|---|---|---|---|
| Manchester | BA, BN, BU, CB, DB, DK, EN, JA, NA, NB, NC, ND, NE, NF, RJ, TD, TE, VM, VR, VU, WH, AJ | Preston | BV, CK, CW, EC, EO, FR, FV, HG, RN |
| Middlesbrough | DC, EF, HN, PY, VN | Reading | AN, BL, CF, DP, GM, JB, JH, JM, MO, RD, RX, TF |
| Newcastle upon Tyne | BB, BR, CN, CU, FT, GR, JR, RG, TN, TY, UP, VK, NL, PT | Sheffield | AK, DT, ET, HE, HL, KU, KW, KY, WA, WB, WE, WF, WG, WJ |
| Northampton | BD, NH, NV, RP, VV | Shrewsbury | AW, NT, UJ, UX |
| Norwich | AH, CL, EX, NG, PW, VF, VG | Stoke-on-Trent | BF, EH, FA, RE, RF, VT |
| Nottingham | AL, AU, CH, NN, NU, RA, RB, RC, RR, TO, TV, VO | Swansea | CY, EP, TH, WN |
| | | Swindon | AM, HR, MR, MW |
| Oxford | BW, FC, JO, UD, WL | Taunton | YA, YB, YC, YD |
| Peterborough | AV, CE, EB, EG, ER, EWA, FL, JE, VA, VE | Truro | AF, CV, GL, RL |
| | | Truro (Isles of Scilly) | SCY |
| Portsmouth | PO, BK, BP, CR, DL, OR, OT, OW, PX, RV, TP, TR | Tyrone | HZ, JI, VZ |
| | | Worcester | AB, NP, UY, WP |

# British postcodes

| Area | Postcode | Area | Postcode |
|---|---|---|---|
| Aberdeen | AB | Kirkwall | KW |
| Bath | BA | Lancaster | LA |
| Belfast | BT | Leeds | LS |
| Birmingham | B | Leicester | LE |
| Blackburn | BB | Lerwick | ZE |
| Blackpool | FY | Lincoln | LN |
| Bolton | BL | Liverpool | L |
| Bournemouth | BH | Llandrindod Wells | LD |
| Bradford | BD | Llandudno | LL |
| Brighton | BN | London (east) | E |
| Bristol | BS | London (east central) | EC |
| Bromley | BR | London (north) | N |
| Canterbury | CT | London (northwest) | NW |
| Cardiff | CF | London (southeast) | SE |
| Carlisle | CA | London (southwest) | SW |
| Cambridge | CB | London (west) | W |
| Chelmsford | CM | London (west central) | WC |
| Chester | CH | Luton | LU |
| Cleveland | TS | Manchester | M |
| Colchester | CO | Medway | ME |
| Coventry | CV | Milton Keynes | MK |
| Crewe | CW | Motherwell | ML |
| Croydon | CR | Newcastle upon Tyne | NE |
| Darlington | DL | Newport (Gwent) | NP |
| Dartford | DA | Northampton | NN |
| Derby | DE | Nottingham | NG |
| Doncaster | DN | Norwich | NR |
| Dorchester | DT | Oldham | OL |
| Dudley | DY | Oxford | OX |
| Dumfries | DG | Paisley | PA |
| Dundee | DD | Perth | PH |
| Durham | DH | Peterborough | PE |
| Edinburgh | EH | Plymouth | PL |
| Enfield | EN | Portsmouth | PO |
| Exeter | EX | Preston | PR |
| Falkirk | FK | Reading | RG |
| Galashiel's | TD | Redhill | RH |
| Glasgow | G | Romford | RM |
| Gloucester | GL | Sheffield | S |
| Guildford | GU | Salisbury | SP |
| Halifax | HX | Shrewsbury | SY |
| Harrogate | HG | Slough | SL |
| Harrow | HA | Southall | UB |
| Hemel Hempstead | HP | Southampton | SO |
| Hereford | HR | Southend-on-Sea | SS |
| Huddersfield | HD | St Albans | AL |
| Hull | HU | Stevenage | SG |
| Ilford | IG | Stoke-on-Trent | ST |
| Inverness | IV | Stockport | SK |
| Ipswich | IP | Sunderland | SR |
| Kilmarnock | KA | Sutton | SM |
| Kingston-upon-Thames | KT | Swansea | SA |
| Kirkcaldy | KY | Swindon | SN |

| Area | Postcode | Area | Postcode |
|------|----------|------|----------|
| Taunton | TA | Walsall | WS |
| Telford | TF | Warrington | WA |
| Tonbridge | TN | Watford | WD |
| Torquay | TQ | Wigan | WN |
| Truro | TR | Wolverhampton | WV |
| Twickenham | TW | Worcester | WR |
| Wakefield | WF | York | YO |

OXFORD

# MORE OXFORD PAPERBACKS

This book is just one of nearly 1000 Oxford Paperbacks currently in print. If you would like details of other Oxford Paperbacks, including titles in the World's Classics, Oxford Reference, Oxford Books, OPUS, Past Masters, Oxford Authors, and Oxford Shakespeare series, please write to:

**UK and Europe:** Oxford Paperbacks Publicity Manager, Arts and Reference Publicity Department, Oxford University Press, Walton Street, Oxford OX2 6DP.

Customers in UK and Europe will find Oxford Paperbacks available in all good bookshops. But in case of difficulty please send orders to the Cash-with-Order Department, Oxford University Press Distribution Services, Saxon Way West, Corby, Northants NN18 9ES. Tel: 0536 741519; Fax: 0536 746337. Please send a cheque for the total cost of the books, plus £1.75 postage and packing for orders under £20; £2.75 for orders over £20. Customers outside the UK should add 10% of the cost of the books for postage and packing.

**USA:** Oxford Paperbacks Marketing Manager, Oxford University Press, Inc., 200 Madison Avenue, New York, N.Y. 10016.

**Canada:** Trade Department, Oxford University Press, 70 Wynford Drive, Don Mills, Ontario M3C 1J9.

**Australia:** Trade Marketing Manager, Oxford University Press, G.P.O. Box 2784Y, Melbourne 3001, Victoria.

**South Africa:** Oxford University Press, P.O. Box 1141, Cape Town 8000.

# THE WORLD'S CLASSICS

The World's Classics series makes available annotated editions of the major works of such important women writers as Jane Austen, the Brontë sisters, Fanny Burney, Maria Edgeworth, George Eliot, and Elizabeth Gaskell.

## VIRGINIA WOOLF

Edited with notes and introductions by leading scholars, Virginia Woolf's most popular works are now available in ten World's Classics.

# THE WORLD'S CLASSICS

Oxford Paperbacks offers the best new translations of the classic works of world literature, from the epic poetry and political and literary theory of the ancient world to the drama and fiction of the nineteenth and twentieth centuries.

## THE KALEVALA

*Translated and Edited by Keith Bosley*
*Foreword by Albert B. Lord*

Words shall not be hid
nor spells buried;
might shall not sink underground
though the mighty go.

*The Kalevala* is the great Finnish epic which, like the *Iliad* and *Odyssey*, grew out of a rich oral tradition with prehistoric roots. During the first millenium of our era, speakers of Uralic languages (outside the Indo-European group) who had settled in the Baltic region developed an oral poetry that was to last into the nineteenth century. This poetry provided the basis of the *Kalevala*, assembled by a Finnish scholar Elias Lönnrot and published in its final form in 1849. It played a central role in the process towards Finnish independence and inspired some of the greatest music of Sibelius.

The poet Keith Bosley is the prize-winning translator of the anthology *Finnish Folk Poetry: Epic*. This translation of the *Kalevala* is the first truly to combine liveliness with accuracy in a way that reflects the richness of the original.

Also available in the World's Classics:

# OXFORD BOOKS

Oxford Books began in 1900 with Sir Arthur Quiller-Couch ('Q')'s *Oxford Book of English Verse*. Since then over 60 superb anthologies of poetry, prose, and songs have appeared in a series that has a very special place in British publishing.

## THE OXFORD BOOK OF ENGLISH GHOST STORIES

### Chosen by Michael Cox and R. A. Gilbert

This anthology includes some of the best and most frightening ghost stories ever written, including M. R. James's 'Oh Whistle, and I'll Come to You, My Lad', 'The Monkey's Paw' by W. W. Jacobs, and H. G. Wells's 'The Red Room'. The important contribution of women writers to the genre is represented by stories such as Amelia Edwards's 'The Phantom Coach', Edith Wharton's 'Mr Jones', and Elizabeth Bowen's 'Hand in Glove'.

As the editors stress in their informative introduction, a good ghost story, though it may raise many profound questions about life and death, entertains as much as it unsettles us, and the best writers are careful to satisfy what Virginia Woolf called 'the strange human craving for the pleasure of feeling afraid'. This anthology, the first to present the full range of classic English ghost fiction, similarly combines a serious literary purpose with the plain intention of arousing pleasing fear at the doings of the dead.

'an excellent cross-section of familiar and unfamiliar stories and guaranteed to delight' *New Statesman*

Also in Oxford Paperbacks:

*The Oxford Book of Short Stories* edited by V. S. Pritchett
*The Oxford Book of Political Anecdotes*
edited by Paul Johnson
*The Oxford Book of Ages*
edited by Anthony and Sally Sampson
*The Oxford Book of Dreams* edited by Stephen Brock

## OXFORD POETS

Oxford Paperbacks has one of the finest lists of contemporary poetry. It includes well-established and highly regarded names, as well as exciting newcomers from Britain, America, Europe, and the Commonwealth.

Winner of the 1989 Whitbread Prize for Poetry

### SHIBBOLETH
#### *Michael Donaghy*

This is Michael Donaghy's first full-length collection. His work has a wit and grace reminiscent of the metaphysical poets, and his subjects range widely, responding in unexpected ways to his curiosity and inventiveness. Among the varied pieces collected here are a number of love poems remarkable for their blend of tenderness and irony; a terse 'news item'; playful 'translations' of a mythical Welsh poet; and an 'interview' with Marcel Duchamp.

As the American critic Alfred Corn says:
'Michael Donaghy's poems have the fine-tuned precision of a ten-speed bike, the wit of a streetwise don, a polyphonic inventiveness . . . Poems so original, wry, and philosophical as these are hard to come by. Don't think of passing them up.'

Also in Oxford Poets:

*Blood and Family*   Thomas Kinsella
*Selected Poems*   Fleur Adcock
*Adventures with My Horse*   Penelope Shuttle

# PAST MASTERS

*General Editor: Keith Thomas*

*Past Masters* is a series of concise and authoritative introductions to the life and works of men and women whose ideas still influence the way we think today.

'Put end to end, this series will constitute a noble encyclopaedia of the history of ideas.' Mary Warnock

# SHAKESPEARE

## *Germaine Greer*

'At the core of a coherent social structure as he viewed it lay marriage, which for Shakespeare is no mere comic convention but a crucial and complex ideal. He rejected the stereotype of the passive, sexless, unresponsive female and its inevitable concommitant, the misogynist conviction that all women were whores at heart. Instead he created a series of female characters who were both passionate and pure, who gave their hearts spontaneously into the keeping of the men they loved and remained true to the bargain in the face of tremendous odds.'

Germaine Greer's short book on Shakespeare brings a completely new eye to a subject about whom more has been written than on any other English figure. She is especially concerned with discovering why Shakespeare 'was and is a popular artist', who remains a central figure in English cultural life four centuries after his death.

'eminently trenchant and sensible . . . a genuine exploration in its own right' John Bayley, *Listener*

'the clearest and simplest explanation of Shakespeare's thought I have yet read' Auberon Waugh, *Daily Mail*

Also available in Past Masters:

# LITERARY BIOGRAPHY AND
# CRITICISM IN OXFORD PAPERBACKS

Oxford Paperbacks's impressive list of literary biography and criticism includes works ranging from specialist studies of the prominent figures of the world literature to D. J. Enright on television soap opera.

## BRITISH WRITERS OF THE THIRTIES
### Valentine Cunningham

'He has steeped himself in the period ... *British Writers of the Thirties* is by far the best history of its kind published in recent years ... and it will become required reading for those who wish to look back at a society and a culture in which writers, for all their faults, were taken seriously.' Peter Ackroyd, *The Times*

'a serious and often brilliant book, provoking one to argument, forcing one back to known texts and forward to unread ones ... it is simply so packed with information that it will speak as much to readers with an interest in social history as to the students of literature for whom it was first intended.' Claire Tomalin, *Independent*

'this should henceforth be the standard treatment ... a minor classic of literary history' Frank Kermode, *Guardian*

'brilliant survey and analysis ... Mr Cunningham's narrative is cleverly constructed, wonderfully detailed, and he deploys his findings to great effect.' Charles Causley, *Times Educational Supplement*

Also in Oxford Paperbacks:

*Fields of Vision*   D. J. Enright
*Modern English Literature*   W. W. Robson
*The Oxford Illustrated History of English Literature*
edited by Pat Rogers
*The Pursuit of Happiness*   Peter Quennell

# ILLUSTRATED HISTORIES IN
# OXFORD PAPERBACKS

Lavishly illustrated with over 200 full colour and black and white photographs, and written by leading academics, Oxford Paperbacks' illuminating histories provide superb introductions to a wide range of political, cultural, and social topics.

## THE OXFORD ILLUSTRATED HISTORY
## OF ENGLISH LITERATURE

### *Edited by Pat Rogers*

Britain possesses a literary heritage which is almost unrivalled in the Western world. In this volume, the richness, diversity, and continuity of that tradition are explored by a group of Britain's foremost literary scholars.

Chapter by chapter the authors trace the history of English literature, from its first stirrings in Anglo-Saxon poetry to the present day. At its heart towers the figure of Shakespeare, who is accorded a special chapter to himself. Other major figures such as Chaucer, Milton, Donne, Wordsworth, Dickens, Eliot, and Auden are treated in depth, and the story is brought up to date with discussion of living authors such as Seamus Heaney and Edward Bond.

'[a] lovely volume . . . put in your thumb and pull out plums' Michael Foot

'scholarly and enthusiastic people have written inspiring essays that induce an eagerness in their readers to return to the writers they admire' *Economist*

Other illustrated histories in Oxford Paperbacks:

The Oxford Illustrated History of Britain
The Oxford Illustrated History of Medieval Europe